Education and Mind in the Knowledge Age

Education and Mind in the Knowledge Age

Carl Bereiter
*Ontario Institute for Studies in Education
of the University of Toronto*

LAWRENCE ERLBAUM ASSOCIATES, PUBLISHERS
2002   Mahwah, New Jersey   London

Lawrence Erlbaum Associates, Inc., Publishers
10 Industrial Avenue
Mahwah, NJ 07430

Cover design by Kathryn Houghtaling Lacey

Library of Congress Cataloging-in-Publication Data

Bereiter, Carl.
Education and mind in the knowledge age / Carl Bereiter.
    p. cm.
Includes bibliographical references and index.
ISBN 0-8058-3942-9 (cloth : alk. paper)
ISBN 0-8058-3943-7 (pbk. : alk. paper)
1. Learning, Psychology of. 2. Knowledge, Theory of.
    3. Cognition. 4. Educational change.   I. Title.
LB1057 .B47   2002
370.15′23—dc21   2001033887
                                                                    CIP

Books published by Lawrence Erlbaum Associates are printed on acid-free paper, and their bindings are chosen for strength and durability.

Printed in the United States of America
10 9 8 7 6 5 4 3 2 1

For Marlene

Contents

Part II. Education and Knowledge Work

Preface

Here we are in the Information Age, relying on a theory of mind that is older than the wheel. Every other folk theory—folk physics, folk biology, folk economics—has had to yield to more powerful theories, better equipped to address the problems of an adventurous civilization. According to one story, this has also happened with theory of mind. Something called "cognitive science" arose in the 1950s and developed rapidly. Its most conspicuous manifestations have been in artificial intelligence and robotics, but it has had a significant and sometimes revolutionary effect on all the behavioral sciences. Although it may be true that most of the world's business is still conducted according to folk theories of mind, this may be only a matter of cultural lag, which will be overcome as cognitive science takes hold.

The trouble with this story is that for most purposes the effect of cognitive science has not been to replace folk theory but to reinstate it, after its exile by behaviorism. I do not mean to discount the accomplishments of cognitive scientists in expert systems, language comprehension, and the like. But the cognitive science that produced these accomplishments has been rooted in the same basic conception of the mind that has been with us at least since Plato's time, and that children in the Western world pick up spontaneously by the age of 6. It is this folk conception, along with its formalizations in cognitive theories, that has recently started to be challenged.

What is being challenged is the basic conception of the mind as a container of objects—beliefs, desires, conjectures, remembered events, and the like—that the mind works on in cognition. The challenges have been on various theoretical grounds. The plausibility, coherence, and explanatory adequacy of folk theory and its derivatives have been called into question. Critics typically concede that in practical applications folk theory does just fine. For most uses, that is true and for good reason. Our social institutions all embody the folk theory. We could hardly make it through a day—indeed, could hardly make it across a busy street—without decisions based on beliefs and intentions that we attribute to others.

Folk theories of all kinds characteristically work well for everyday purposes, however. Medieval physics lives on in the baseball park, where fly balls have "legs" that may or may not be sufficient to carry them over the outfield wall. Expert gardeners get along believing they are providing food to the plants. But if the task is launching a missile into orbit rather than over the left-field fence or doubling the yield of rice paddies, folk theories are not up to the task. Folk theory of mind lives on, I believe, because it has never been put to severe tests.

Until now. How might a nation or an organization double its rate of knowledge production? How do we educate a populace to be knowledge workers? How does an organization become a learning organization? These questions pose novel challenges, which our ancient theory of mind has never had to wrestle with. Also, they involve queer juxtapositions of terms—knowledge production, knowledge work, learning organization—resulting in expressions whose meaning is unclear. These expressions don't, in fact, make much sense under a theory that has knowledge consisting of objects in people's minds. Yet there is a widespread conviction that they refer to very important things. This is not a happy state of affairs. To correct it, I believe, we need a new theory of mind.

Better to say we need a new way of thinking about knowledge and the mind. What I have been calling, following a common usage, "folk theory of mind" is not actually a theory. It is just a way that we commonly think about knowledge and mentation. Correspondingly, what I try to develop in this book is not a theory, either. It is a different way of thinking about the mind. New ways of thinking about knowledge and mind are much in evidence these days. A recent issue of *Educational Psychologist* was devoted to six of them, identified as information processing, cognitive psychology, situated cognition, constructivism, social constructivism, and connectionism. I draw to some extent on all of these, plus the thinking of philosophers like Daniel Dennett, who do not belong to any particular camp. Above all, however, I am concerned with developing a way of thinking about the mind that works for the new challenges faced by education.

One need not be a thorough-going pragmatist to adopt a pragmatic attitude toward theory of mind. Brains are material things, and if someone says the average human brain weighs 10 pounds, you can check and see if this is right. But mind is pretty much whatever we decide to make it out to be. If you say the mind contains propositional representations of beliefs and I say it doesn't, that the mind only has dispositions to agree with certain propositions, neither of us can prove the other wrong. All we can do is see how well these competing notions work out in practice. For most everyday purposes, your notion will work better than mine. But my notion will work better for designing an education system or a knowledge-creating organization. That, at any rate, is what I hope to be able to show.

In taking this pragmatic stance, I open myself to questions of the "So what?" variety, which can be avoided by those who stick to the theoretical high ground. In compensation, I am spared having to deal with questions along the lines of "What's your evidence?" "What is it really?" and "How do you explain ...?" Or ought to be spared. Such questions tend to arise regardless. They are the basic tools of critical thinking and people look for occasions to use them, just like the proverbial child with a new hammer. So I do try to deal with these questions, but only to the extent necessary to keep people from shaking their heads and walking away. It is not my main purpose.

Dealing with the "So what?" question is challenge enough. In studying scientific revolutions, Paul Thagard observed that the people who most stoutly resist a new theory are not the fuddy-duddies but are the scientists most accomplished in getting results with the old theory. His example was Joseph Priestley, artfully demonstrating the virtues of phlogiston theory long after other chemists had given it up. B. F. Skinner defending behaviorism may serve as a modern example. If you peruse his published notebooks you find him time and again responding to some finding from cognitive research by showing how it can be explained without bringing in mental events. He was amazingly good at it. The meager principles of operant behavior worked well for him as explanatory tools, and he went to his grave still clutching them, while many of his less skillful followers had given them up in favor of the high-tech tools of cognitive science. When it comes to theory of mind, we are all Priestleys and Skinners. Having practiced assiduously since early childhood, we are consummate artists in using folk psychology to predict and explain human behavior. It takes a lot to convince us that we need a new tool, especially because the new tool will at first be unwieldy, unreliable, and just won't feel right.

Important advances are taking place in pedagogy. For the most part they are being conceived and articulated within the framework of folk theory of mind. I believe, however, they are headed toward a limit that cannot be passed without a better theory of mind and knowledge. In recent years I have had the unusual opportunity of being part of a project in which three different innovative research groups tried to get together in designing an educational program that would synthesize their three approaches. The groups were the Fostering Communities of Learners project at Berkeley, the Cognition and Technology Group at Vanderbilt, and the CSILE/Knowledge Building team at Toronto (which I belong to). Although a very worthwhile model program emerged from this effort, I think all the participants would agree that the looked-for grand synthesis never occurred, indeed never even got on the table. We had a good vocabulary for discussing our similarities, and that was enough to get things going at a practical level. It was, roughly speaking, the vocabulary of social constructivism. But we had no vocabulary for discussing our differences. These have come to seem profound, but there has been no mutually comprehensible way of articulating them. I do not think such a way can be found within a conception that treats knowledge as stuff in people's minds and learning as a process that produces it there.

Knowledge is the pivotal idea in this book. The main faults I find in folk theory of mind are in its treatment of knowledge. How important the issues raised here seem to readers will, accordingly, depend on the importance they attach to knowledge. But here is a Catch 22 that is, I believe, one of the most serious barriers to progress in educational thought. Folk theory of mind affords such a limited and incoherent conception of knowledge that people in the grip of folk theory cannot be expected to appreciate the importance of knowledge from an educational standpoint. It will be difficult for them to think of it as anything more than the rapidly obsolescent contents of a mental filing cabinet. So, although they may concede there is some value in having such a filing cabinet and updating its contents periodically, they will not find this a very exciting prospect and they will likely recoil from any proposal that seems to them to suggest that education's main mission should be stuffing students' filing cabinets—as well they should. But the alternative should be to develop a richer conception of what it means to be knowledgeable, not to rush off in pursuit of chimerical "higher order thinking skills" or the fostering of "multiple intelligences." Developing a richer conception of knowledgeability, however, depends on adopting a view of mind that can support such a conception. The new conception of mind that has been taking shape in cognitive science in the past decade, and that I hope to advance here, is not easily adopted as a way of thinking. It takes work, and the motivation to do such work is hard to drum up if you cannot appreciate the point of it until you have done it. That is the Catch 22.

All I can hope to offer as a way out of this bind is enough in the way of secondary insights to keep readers engaged long enough that the major insights may start to take hold. Although its focus is education, particularly as it is carried out in schools, I have written this book with a larger audience in mind. It includes not only educators and people with a keen lay interest in education but also those who are caught up in and not entirely at ease with ideas such as "knowledge society," "learning organization," and "knowledge management." To accommodate such a diverse audience, I must at times belabor points that will strike some as obvious and oversimplified. What I am about, however, is not so much offering the latest ideas or a novel program as offering a way of thinking that is new to everyone, including this author. It takes work, but I hope readers will come away from the effort feeling that they have a better grounding for the ideas they care most about, that they have shed some moribund ideas that it had not occurred to them they could do without, and that they see new ways to move forward.

This book has been a long time in the making, and so I cannot begin to credit all the sources of benefit I have drawn on along the way. I will settle for acknowledging just two: The first is Marlene Scardamalia, my wife and closest colleague. There is scarcely an idea in this book that has not been affected by her imaginative and inventive mind and her endless drive to go beyond the prevailing catchwords to powerful and, in her word, "improvable" ideas. I should mention that our discussions on conceptual issues do not always end in complete agreement, and so she should not be held accountable for the construals I put on some of the terms that we jointly use, such as "knowledge building" and "understanding." The other acknowledgment is to the Telelearning Network of Centres of Excellence, which for several years supported a project on "Cognitive/Epistemological Models for Knowledge Building," of which this book was the principal product. That a federally supported program to advance the development and use of learning technologies should have devoted a part of its funds to research on the most fundamental issues of what such an enterprise is about is a rarity; I hope the result in this case will show it was not a mistake.

Part I

Mind in a Knowledge-Based Society

1

Our Oldest Unchallenged Folk Theory at Last Faces Its Day of Reckoning

Something is going on in elementary schools across North America that might strike the detached observer as insane. Millions of dollars are being poured into high-tech equipment that is used mainly to produce the kinds of "projects" that in an earlier day were produced using scissors, old magazines, and library paste. At the same time, and in the same schools, a back-to-basics movement has teachers obsessively concerned with covering traditional content and preparing students for tests.

One very naive response to this situation discerns no inconsistency. The computerized cut-and-paste work is believed to be teaching students computer skills that will insure their futures in the 21st century. It is therefore just another kind of skill practice to take its place with the more traditional drill in arithmetic, reading, and spelling. Adults are predictably overimpressed when children can do something they cannot. For instance, the things that can be done with photo image processing software these days look like magic, and when adults who have never encountered it before walk into a classroom and find

11-year-olds morphing images, changing coloration, and taking a figure from one image and planting it in another, they are likely to echo
the words of a superintendent who exclaimed, "I think I have just seen
the 21st century!" What they have seen, impressive as it may be, is,
however, something that can be learned in 2 or 3 hours.

More sophisticated educators recognize there is a conflict and try
to resolve it. But conceptual limitations put creative solutions beyond reach, leaving grudging compromise as the only choice. Computer activities are categorized as "constructivist". The other kind
are labeled "traditional," "transmission model," "teacher centered,"
or perhaps even "rote learning." Such a categorization brings with it
a baggage of false and stultifying beliefs that, however, remain hidden from view within the categorization and are therefore unlikely
to be questioned. Constructivism is taken to mean independent
hands-on activities, ignoring the outstanding examples of
constructivist education that depend on teacher-led, highly focused
inquiry (e.g., Hunt & Minstrell, 1994; Lampert, 1988). The possibility of finding a "constructivist" way of meeting back-to-basics demands for accountability is therefore virtually eliminated.
Categorizing instruction of the "nonconstructivist" kind as if it were
something old and familiar wrongly implies that teachers already
know how to do it and that it is an effective way to meet the demands
for mastery of basic skills. That is usually far from the truth.
Teachers are likely to have little knowledge of how to improve reading comprehension or how to overcome errors students make with
fractions and decimals, two of the key requirements for improving
achievement test scores.

Many different things are happening in education, some demonstrably good, some demonstrably bad, and many others of uncertain
value. Yet in very fundamental ways, education is stuck. It doesn't
know where to move and it doesn't have tools to move with. The dialogue, both within and outside the education profession, does not
advance. The same blunt statements (including this one) are made
over and over. The tools education needs are, of course, conceptual
tools. In this so-called Knowledge Age, that is the first requirement
for any human enterprise to advance. The argument I develop
throughout this book is that education's conceptual tools are woe-
fully inadequate. They are not even up to old tasks, such as the tasks
of understanding a textbook or solving an algebra problem, let alone
the new order of tasks that education must face in this era of global
competition. Better tools are coming available, but it takes conceptual tools to understand and use them. The most basic of tools are
our conceptions of knowledge and mind. That, I argue, is where
change has to start if education is to become unstuck.

KNOWLEDGE IS EVERYBODY'S BUSINESS

Knowledge used to be the sole province of philosophers; that is, philosophers were the only ones who studied and talked about knowledge as such. The rest of us might acquire, use, and perhaps even create knowledge, but we did not have to think about what any of that meant. In time, social scientists began studying knowledge from the standpoint of the people who create and use it. The real territorial shift began, however, with the advent of cognitive science and it became decisive once the business world discovered knowledge and acquired a fascination with intellectual property, or "IP" as it is familiarly called.[1] The barbarians are now within the gates. Perhaps philosophy's final loss of proprietorship over knowledge will be dated from 1997, when the Xerox Distinguished Professorship in Knowledge was established at the University of California, Berkeley—in the school of management, with the first occupant being a sociologist who made his name studying what he called "knowledge-creating companies" (Nonaka, 1991).

In Western philosophy, knowledge has typically meant something like true or warranted belief, usually in the form of propositions. When cognitive scientists began constructing computer models of human intelligence, knowledge in the form of propositions and rules played a central role. That is what made the models cognitive as opposed to behaviorist. But whether the propositions were true or not was irrelevant as far as understanding cognition was concerned. No one would imagine that the mind functions differently depending on whether it is operating on true propositions or false ones. Knowledge, accordingly, became whatever functions as knowledge in mental processes. Knowledge came to include beliefs of any sort and to include rules that constitute know-how or skill (Anderson, 1983).

Cognitive science spawned practical applications in artificial intelligence and expert systems, and with the latter came a new occupation: knowledge engineering. In designing an artificial system to provide expert guidance in medical diagnosis, for instance, the best model will often be a human expert. But human experts, it was soon found, had limited ability to articulate the knowledge that seemed to be guiding their actions, and so it became the job of knowledge engineers to observe experts at work and, using a combination of detailed observation and probing questions, dig out the expert's covert

---

[1]The emergence of a sociology of knowledge has also been important, but not in quite the same way. Sociological ideas have directly influenced some philosophers, especially through the influence of Thomas Kuhn (1970), and thus have become assimilated into philosophy, whereas cognitive science and the commercialization of knowledge have appropriated knowledge and bent its meaning to their purposes.

knowledge and formulate it as rules and propositions that a machine could process. For business managers eager to capitalize on the new information technologies, this development had a dual effect: It dramatized the importance and the vastness of knowledge that figures in expert performance. At the same time, it entrenched and gave an apparent scientific license for a simplistic conception of knowledge as items in individual minds.

Growing recognition of the economic importance of knowledge has brought all kinds of players into the knowledge arena who have no particular theoretical perspective on knowledge. Unhampered by philosophical or psychological strictures, they can shift indiscriminately between treating knowledge as stuff in people's heads and treating knowledge as stuff out in the world, to be found in books, patent applications, and the like. They do not distinguish between companies that strive to become better at what they are doing and companies whose work is to produce knowledge. Both are called learning organizations. They do not distinguish between knowledge that inheres in competence and knowledge that becomes negotiable property. Both are called intellectual capital (Stewart, 1997). As a result, there is no incisive way to talk about what is the main challenge for many organizations: how to get progressively more competent at producing advances in knowledge.

Despite these conceptual weaknesses, modern businesses are far in advance of the schools in understanding and appreciating the importance of knowledge. The Knowledge Age has not yet come to the schoolhouse. To many school people, knowledge is old fashioned, the stuff of pedants and test makers. Knowledge is what reactionary parents keep trying to force schools to go back to. Ever since the publication of Bloom's *Taxonomy of Educational Objectives* in 1956, educators in North America have been wedded to a hierarchical view of learning outcomes, with knowledge occupying the bottom rung (more about this in chap. 4). The upper rungs are occupied by "higher order thinking skills" or other elevated mental traits such as creativity. Business pundits, unhampered by requirements of consistency, buy all of this "higher order" talk as well. But they also value knowledge in a way that is foreign to the school world. They recognize knowledge as stuff to be produced and worked with.

I should make it clear from the beginning that I am to be counted among the barbarians. My interest in knowledge is practical, concerned especially with the improvement of education. But I have seen enough of the world outside education to be convinced that the muddles educators get into about knowledge are only a more acute form of the muddles people in the society at large are getting into. They all have their source in conceptions of mind and knowledge that we acquire as children and never think to examine—because they seem to be given directly by experience and because no alternatives have been presented.

To put my present effort in perspective, it is at one remove from books on how to reform education or to reinvent businesses for the Knowledge Age. Instead, it develops a way to *think about* knowledge and mind when going about these innovative efforts. I do not believe managers and educators can get along indefinitely with a theory of knowledge acquired at their mother's knee. It is not that the theory is wrong. Better to say it is obsolete. It is obsolete in much the same way as a 5-year-old personal computer. It is still serviceable and for many ordinary uses it is perfectly adequate. It may even offer advantages over later models in simplicity and freedom from glitches. But there are new tasks—in multimedia and in communication, for instance—that the old machine either cannot handle or can handle only with considerable effort and ingenuity on the part of the user.

FOLK PSYCHOLOGY AND EPISTEMOLOGY

There is a commonsense psychology that we all develop in early childhood and that we use in making our way in a world whose most significant objects (for us) are other human beings. The central tenet of this psychology, as it develops among children in the Western world, is that people's behavior is determined by their beliefs and desires. It is well understood by 6-year-olds, although not by 3-year-olds, that other people's beliefs may differ from their own, but they also understand they can, albeit imperfectly, infer other people's beliefs from their words and actions and from the facts of a situation (Astington, 1993).

Along with commonsense psychology comes a commonsense epistemology. Commonsense psychology posits a *mind*, which contains immaterial objects such as ideas, memories, facts, plans, goals, and principles. Commonsense epistemology posits a relationship between these things in the mind and an external world of observable things and actions. When this relationship is correct, the mental objects constitute *knowledge*. When the relationship is incorrect, the mental objects constitute false beliefs.

Together, the commonsense psychology and the commonsense epistemology make up what contemporary scholars refer to as "folk theory of mind." There is some dispute about calling it a theory, and I do so only because it is a common and handy usage. But regardless of what scholars may decide to call it, it seems clear that to ordinary people what I described in the preceding two paragraphs is not a theory—not, that is, a set of propositions vulnerable to counterevidence. It is just the way things are.

Folk theories, however, generally have this aura of certainty rooted in direct experience. That the sun rises in the east and moves across the sky once seemed to be given directly by experience, to involve no conjecture or interpretation whatever, whereas what happens to the sun between the time it disappears in the west and reappears in the east is conjectural (and folk theories accordingly differ widely in what they say about it). To the modern mind, however, it is evident that the daytime cycle is also a matter of interpretation, even if not in quite the same way as what happens to the sun at night, and that interpreting it the way folk astronomy does gets one off on a wrong path for understanding the cosmos. Similarly, folk mechanics is based on the unquestioned observation that objects set in motion gradually lose their initial impetus and come to rest. From the standpoint of Newtonian mechanics, we can now recognize that loss of impetus, far from being an uncontaminated observation, is an inference that must be questioned for physics to progress.

The mind is popularly regarded as mysterious. There are all kinds of questions for which folk theory of mind provides no answers: why we remember some things and forget others, how ideas come about, what the nature of dreaming is, and so on. What seems to be given directly by experience is the existence of the mind itself and its contents: beliefs, desires, memories, ideas, dreams—the whole carload of mental luggage. This is what, to the folk way of thinking, seems to be beyond question, the solid rock on which conjectures and theories must rest. There is this about folk theory of mind, however, that sets it apart from other folk theories and may explain why it has survived while other folk theories have fallen before the march of science: Although it may be difficult, we can begin to conjure up doubts about almost anything we perceive in the external world. In fact, playing with the idea that there is no world out there, that it is all a dream, is a favorite amusement of young people just awakening to the possibilities of philosophy. But to doubt our experience of the mind seems self-contradictory; for isn't the doubt itself an experience of the very kind we are supposing might be denied? That is the line of reasoning Descartes pursued, in trying to find a foothold of certainty, something on which a sure understanding of the world could be based. But might it not be that what we think we experience so directly as mental events is already heavily interpreted in ways we fail to imagine?

WHEN FOLK THEORIES GIVE WAY TO SCIENCE

The term "folk theory" is used in several ways. According to one usage, folk theories are what people believe in the absence of scientific theories. In ancient times folk theories were all there were. Then along came science, and by now most educated people have adopted scientific theories. According to this usage, folk theories are to be found mainly among primitive peoples and among children who have not yet been instructed in science.

According to the usage I adopt here, however, folk theories are whatever theories or conceptual frameworks people pick up from popular culture and use in their daily efforts to make sense of events and plan their actions. We all acquire folk theories and are apt to go on using them until we get far enough into some endeavor that we need specialized knowledge. Folk theories, thus conceived, are not necessarily rigid things, insensitive to evidence and closed to novelty. They change as new facts and ideas are absorbed into popular culture. The kind of folk theory of disease that children grow up with in modern nations is radically different from the folk theory of a few hundred years ago. Germs now play a central role. Although folk theory offers little explanation of how germs cause disease, the notion of evil, fast-breeding little creatures invisibly pervading the environment provides a basis for hygienic practices that would have been meaningless to people of an earlier age.

Shouldn't we say, then, that modern people hold a scientific theory of disease—even if it is a limited and distorted one—rather than a folk theory? This is a definitional issue that could be decided either way, but I think we will get farther in our inquiry into the educational implications of theories of mind if we follow the definitional course I have proposed: Ordinary people in the modern world hold and generally function according to folk theories of disease, but these are theories that have been significantly influenced by medical science. One reason for treating the matter this way is that it allows us to consider reverse influences: how medical science might be influenced by folk theory—not the folk theories of remote times and places but the folk theories today's doctors acquired as children, growing up in middle-class suburbs, watching the Saturday morning television cartoons, being lectured to by their parents about what they should and shouldn't put into their mouths. Folk notions, being largely unarticulated and unexamined, can influence the way people interpret and apply scientific information. Although these influences might be subtle in the case of medicine, the influence of folk theory of mind on scientific psychology and philosophy turns out, as will become evident later, to be obvious and profound.

Although higher learning may turn some of us into behaviorists who reject the notion of mind, idealists who deny there is a reality to which beliefs correspond, or antifoundationalists who deny there is a basis for comparing one belief with another, in our daily lives we function according to the psychology and epistemology we acquired in early childhood. There seems to be no practical alternative. That is probably true, as far as everyday life is concerned. Folk theory of mind is so intricately woven into the social fabric that there is no telling what would be left if we tried to remove it. Consider such socially important concepts as lying, pretending, promising, knowing, and joking. Everything from a criminal court decision to the fate of a friendship can turn on whether one of these concepts is thought to apply. But each of these concepts distinguishes a relation between something overt and something in a person's mind. Joking is saying something untrue but without the intent that others will believe it; lying is the same thing but with the intent to be believed. The capacity to hold a theory of mind seems to be an evolved capacity, with evidences of it in other primates (Premack & Premack, 1996). As humans evolved talents for cheating, lying, pretending, promising, making truth claims, and joking, the ability to detect and distinguish among these became important survival skills (Barkow, Cosmides, & Tooby, 1992). A complementary notion, however, is that only having a theory of mind enables us to do such things. Chimpanzees, according to this reasoning, are not by nature less deceitful than we are, they are simply not as good at imagining themselves into one another's minds.

That folk theory of mind serves us well in daily life does not mean, however, that it also serves well in all the more specialized activities of a modern society. There are other bodies of commonsense knowledge that serve us well in ordinary circumstances but that fail more severe challenges. I have already referred to commonsense astronomy, according to which the sun rises each day and moves across the sky, and commonsense physics, according to which objects in motion slow down as they lose impetus. There is also a commonsense botany, according to which plants draw food from the earth. These commonsense bodies of knowledge have proved sufficient not only for the unspecialized needs of daily life but also for practical arts, such as ocean navigation and farming. But they are inadequate for establishing a colony on the moon, for instance. For that we need sciences that do not merely extend commonsense knowledge but replace it with principles that hold more generally.

Teaching is a practical art, and it is safe to say that throughout its history it has relied on folk theory of mind.[2] It has served us up till

---

[2]American education is commonly said to have been dominated by behaviorism during a substantial portion of the 20th century, which would imply that education during this period eschewed folk theory of mind in favor of a theory that recognized only overt behavior and regarded education as the shaping of a behavioral repertoire. There is no question that behaviorism had an influence. It was, and in many places still is, manifested in practices such as the following

Breaking instruction down into small steps.

Formulating "behavioral objectives," which indicators used to assess them.

Using frequent small rewards rather than punishment and reprimand.

Paying less attention to issues of understanding and more to issues of performance and conduct. *(continued on next page)*

now, but I do not want to concede that it has served us well. Such a judgment depends on what education might be if yoked to a different theory of mind. While I do not want to concede that folk theory of mind has served education well, I also do not want to attribute all of education's present ills to bad theory. Everything that goes on in education is bitterly contested by people who claim to have a better theory. In fact, that is about all theories are used for in education: to buttress arguments for or against some already existing position. Piaget produced a novel psychological theory, first taken up in education by Susan and Nathan Isaacs in the forerunner of the British infant school, but its main use was to support "activity" methods that had already been instituted (N. Isaacs, 1965).

It is legitimate, of course, to use theories as backing in policy discussions; for theories in some of the social sciences, that may be all the practical value we should ever expect of them. But that is not what theories are mostly good for in applied fields. They should help us create new possibilities and solve problems. In this regard, commonsense beliefs generally prove inadequate as soon as a field of practice begins to advance beyond a traditional craft.

Every craft develops specialized knowledge, but in a traditional craft this specialized knowledge rests on a base of commonsense knowledge that is taken for granted and remains largely unquestioned as one learns the craft. The peasant farmer acquires abundant knowledge of local plants and their ways, but it rests on a botany that has no notion of photosynthesis. One result is that, through trial and error over generations, practices evolve that work, but for which there is no explanation. The limitations of traditional crafts show up when there is need to change. If the slash-and-burn practice, which returns necessary minerals to the soil, must be abandoned for economic or ecological reasons, commonsense botany offers no basis for discovering an alternative. If, because of population pressure, the land must be made to yield many times more food than before, traditional methods will fail. Without a better botany, there will be no Green Revolution.

---

[2] *(continued from previous page)*   These could add up to significant changes in the conduct of schooling, but they are all easily accommodated by folk theory of mind. Furthermore, behaviorists in education have continued to rely on the traditional epistemology for much of what they do. Questions of what to teach and in what order, all the details and strategies of conveying content to the learner, are left to the wisdom and traditions of teaching. Often the creation of a behaviorist program of instruction starts by taking a conventional textbook or curriculum guide and breaking it down into separately teachable bits. Thus, the epistemological assumptions frozen into textbooks and teaching practice are preserved. The same is true of assessment. Often the so-called "behavioral objective" merely specifies test items the student must pass, the items themselves being grounded in folk theory that treats learning as the accumulation of items of mental content. The reason for behaviorism's limited effect on education is not subversiveness or cultural lag on the part of educators; the reason is that behaviorism was never able to provide an alternative conceptual framework for teaching subject matter—facts, concepts, and the like.

The same story can be told in almost every field—in medicine and dentistry, navigation, engineering, metal work. Crafts based on commonsense understanding can often produce wondrous achievements, but when there is a need to adapt or innovate, commonsense knowledge falls short. We tend to think of science as having a life of its own, but in earlier times it was driven to a great extent by practical problems that were beyond the reach of commonsense knowledge. Even into the 19th century, most of physics was produced, not by university scholars, but by servants of industry. Then, as Alfred North Whitehead has explained, the production of knowledge itself began to be professionalized (Whitehead, 1925/1948).

Now we are seeing commonsense knowledge being supplanted everywhere, not because it has proved inadequate to some task, but because a scientific discipline has made it its business to advance beyond it. Folk knowledge of practical value may even get lost in the process, as it has in medicine and agriculture. The offsetting advantage is that we have knowledge available for innovation; we do not always have to wait for the inadequacies of present knowledge to be revealed by practical difficulties. That is what seems to be happening with theory of mind as it relates to education.

The manifest difficulties that education is running into do not forthrightly suggest that anything is wrong with our commonsense theory of mind. I am referring to the difficulties that typically make news—dropouts, violence, poor test performance, great inequalities of achievement, and so on. They may suggest that much is wrong with the culture, with our values, with the way schools are run, but it seems all the relevant issues can be discussed fully and from all sides without straining against the limits of folk theory of mind. The inadequacies of folk theory of mind are showing up elsewhere, in philosophy and in artificial intelligence especially. That is also where an alternative theory of mind is starting to take shape. It does not look as if the new theory is going to lead straightaway to solving any of education's problems. Rather, what it promises to do is free our thinking from some of the restrictions of the folk theory and give us a way to deploy knowledge of the mind in more powerfully innovative ways.

Teaching is a traditional craft, or at least it aspires to be. It is learned through experience and example. Depending on how you conceive of a theoretical basis, teaching either has none or it has one but teachers don't know about it and it would have little relevance to practice if they did. Modern efforts to improve teaching focus on master teachers mentoring less accomplished ones, and on teachers joining together to upgrade their craft. Consequently, you cannot expect what goes on in classrooms or in teacher development workshops to reveal inadequacies of the underlying folk theory. To see that, you would have to look at efforts to get outside the orbit of existing practices—outside the numerous variations on didactic instruction and child-centered or activity-centered methods.

Such efforts are going on, and I believe they are already stretching the limits of what folk theory of mind can handle. Interestingly, it is not the more spectacular sorts of high technology that are having this effect in education. Intelligent tutoring systems and virtual reality, whatever their value, fit comfortably within the folk theory. Intelligent tutoring systems develop hypotheses about what is in the student's mind and try to alter it. Virtual reality may allow students to walk around inside a molecule, but the reason for thinking this might be a good thing for them to do comes right out of the folk psychological belief in the primacy of direct experience.

MIND AS CONTAINER

Most of the time, when we explain or predict behavior on the basis of peoples beliefs, desires, plans, knowledge, and the like, we give no thought to how the mind works. If we have a theory of mind, it is dormant much of the time. A better way to put this was suggested by Ludwig Wittgenstein. He suggested certain ideas do not enter actively into our deliberations, but instead provide the *scaffolding* for our thoughts (Wittgenstein, 1969). Thus, there is a certain structure to the way we typically think about mental attributes, and this may be as close as people who are not cognitive scientists come to having an actual theory of mind.

This structure or scaffolding is what I believe we must struggle to replace, if education is to make headway in the Knowledge Age. As is often the case with everyday thinking, the scaffolding is provided by a metaphor (Lakoff, 1987; Lakoff & Johnson, 1980). In this case it is the metaphor of mind-as-container. Metaphors, as Lakoff argued, are basic to human thought, extremely productive, but also dangerous. The danger arises from the fact that, unlike explicit beliefs, they go unnoticed and uncriticized. Thus, they can limit or bias our thought, often in fundamental ways, without our awareness.

In everyday use, the mind-as-container metaphor is handy and probably harmless. It is well suited to social interactions in which we are dealing with other people as individuals. In these cases it is important to keep beliefs, desires, and so on connected with the people who hold them. It is not the general proposition that hospitals are dangerous places that concerns us, it is Uncle Roscoe's belief that hospitals are dangerous places, with all the quirks, colorations, prior associations, and implications that his particular belief may have.

Roscoe's children, who are trying to get him to enter hospital for an operation, hold other beliefs, which are also not to be considered in isolation but in relation to their other personal beliefs, goals, strategies, and so on. Such situations can become quite complicated, but the container metaphor helps us sort things out. Each of the people involved is credited with a mind, and all of the relevant cognitive and emotional stuff is thought of as residing in one or another of these minds. There are other ways of sorting things out, as I suggest later, but this way unquestionably serves its purpose very well.

The mind-as-container metaphor gives rise to a number of vexing philosophical problems, although these are usually of little concern in everyday applications. There is, for instance, the problem of how to ascertain that two people hold the same belief, or, indeed, how to compare their beliefs at all. In everyday life this is addressed as a problem of communication. Presumably, if people could be perfectly clear in expressing their beliefs, it could always be determined whether their beliefs were the same. Such a presumption will not stand up under critical analysis, but its practical import is all to the good: When in doubt, talk things out. Another vexing problem of long standing is known as the mind–body problem. How can mental objects, located in an immaterial mind, cause material things to happen? For our present purpose, the thing to note about these and other philosophical conundrums is that they arise from regarding the mind literally as a container. If mind-as-container is just a metaphor, we have to expect it will fail on certain points. "All the world is a stage" is a nice metaphor, but you cannot stretch it very far before it becomes ridiculous. We all recognize that the world is only metaphorically a stage, but by not recognizing that the mind is only metaphorically a container, by perhaps not even being aware that we are thinking of it as a container, we are susceptible to false dilemmas and often much worse.

THE CONTAINER METAPHOR IN EDUCATIONAL THOUGHT AND PRACTICE

Education necessarily goes beyond the face-to-face negotiations for which the mind-as-container metaphor has proved so helpful. It is true that school teachers deal with individual students and that for this purpose the container metaphor serves them well. The textbook may contain a rule for adding fractions, but teachers cannot be concerned only with this rule. Here is Alfred, who in adding 1/2 and 1/3 gets 2/5; Francine, who gets 1/5; and Blair, who gets 2/6. The insightful teacher will infer that Alfred is following a rule that calls for adding numerators to numerators and adding denominators to denominators. Other idiosyncratic rules may be inferred to account for the behavior of Francine and Blair. These rules will be thought of as residing in the respective minds of these students, and the teacher will deal with them accordingly, perhaps by encouraging the students to formulate their rules explicitly, so they can be examined, or perhaps simply by reiterating the textbook rule, with examples, and hoping it displaces the faulty rules in the students' minds.

That is one level of educational enterprise, and at that level the container metaphor can go without challenge. But there are other levels to the enterprise. Staying with our example, there is a level at which teachers, curriculum writers, and others must try to figure out what is wrong with mathematics education, such that a substantial proportion of children, after having undergone weeks of instruction in adding fractions, respond with a number that is less than 1/2 when they are asked to add 1/2 and 1/3. One of the concepts likely to be brought in at this level is *number sense*. The children in question will be said to lack number sense, and the educational program will be faulted for failing to develop it. But what is number sense, and how might it be promoted? Here the container metaphor fails, but if no one notices this, the discussion is likely to lose its way.

Number sense is clearly something attributable to individual minds. But it is not any specifiable set of facts or rules or skills. It is an attribute of the whole system, not a lot of items in a mental container. All the mathematics curriculum guides I have seen demonstrate that educators do not know what to make of something like number sense. They either leave it completely unspecified, relegating it to the status of an item of wishful thinking (along with love of learning and respect for cultural differences), or they reduce it to specifics and make it indistinguishable from teaching standard mathematics content. One of the most influential guidelines avoided defining number sense, but confidently stated that it must be taught through practical experiences. A few years later, after some crushing test results, the state's policymakers decided that, on the contrary, the way to teach number sense was through lots of exercises on carefully designed worksheets. But they still had not come clean about what number sense is and how either method was supposed to produce it. From what is known about number sense, I conclude that both approaches are wrong (Greeno, 1991; Griffin, Case, & Siegler, 1994), but the point I want to make here is that folk theory of mind makes the issue virtually undiscussable. The container metaphor fails miserably when we try to deal with sorts of knowledge and skill that cannot be defined as items in the container but that instead characterize the whole container.

There are still higher levels to which the adding fractions example may take us and where other weaknesses of folk theory of mind are revealed. A mathematics educator may suggest that the student who offers 2/5 as the sum of 1/2 and 1/3 probably doesn't recognize 2/5 as a number but only as a quotient or, worse, simply as two whole numbers with a line in between. This sounds plausible and enlightening, but what are we to make of it? What does it mean to "recognize 2/5 as a number"? Surely it means more than having a statement to that effect stored away in memory. Educators will say that it implies *understanding* that fractions are numbers. But what kind of object or set of objects in the mind constitutes understanding?

It turns out that understanding, one of the main objectives of education, is very hard to reconcile with the mind-as-container metaphor. To do so, cognitive scientists have had to posit some very large objects in the mental container. The most popular have been schemas (Rumelhart, 1980) and concept nets (Novak & Gowin, 1984). A student's *fraction* schema would include in one organized whole everything the student knows about fractions, and it would control all the student's behavior related to fractions, ranging from recognizing something as a fraction to performing arithmetic involving fractions and responding to questions such as, "Is a fraction a number?" *Understanding* may then be regarded as a characteristic of the whole schema. It could be thought of as a matter of how closely the schema in the mind of the student resembles the schema in the mind of a mathematician.

These megaobjects constitute a neat solution to the problem of how to deal with understanding and other large cognitive issues while preserving the metaphor of mind as container.[3] They make room for the intuition that understanding is a property of a whole system and not an item of mental content in itself. For the educator, however, schemas and concept nets raise more problems than they solve. How do such things get into the mind? You can't *teach* them in any straightforward sense, so what do you do to ensure that they get created and that they are good schemas or concept nets and not bad ones? How do you change a faulty schema into a more adequate

---

[3]Essentially the same commentary applies to concept nets. A schema may be thought of as a form, like the lost luggage forms air travelers must occasionally fill out. It contains blanks to fill in or alternatives to select in accordance with the present instance. However, unlike the lost luggage form, which may oblige you to choose from among drawings, none of which very much resembles your own luggage or indeed any other luggage manufactured in the last 25 years, the luggage schema in your own mind will nicely encapsulate descriptions of the luggage that has actually figured in your experience. A concept net looks entirely different but captures much the same information. It is usually depicted as a lot of circles connected by lines. Each circle represents a concept (in the case of fractions, things like *fraction, numerator, denominator, ratio, least common denominator, addition,* and *multiplication.* The connecting lines are labeled to indicate relationships, and these relationships, together with the concepts they link, constitute propositions: *fraction* has *numerator, addition* needs *least common denominator, fraction* is a *number,* and so on.

one? (This is an important question, because one of the premises of schema theory is that students already have fraction schemas, physics of motion schemas, and the like, which it is the formidable job of education to alter.) When we ponder these questions, two things become apparent: (a) These problems apply to a very large part of what formal education is concerned with, and (b) folk theory of mind has little to offer toward their solution.

There is a final level to which our fractions example may take us. What are numbers, anyway? What are we teaching when we teach that 2/5 is a number? In the ordinary business of the world, these are questions of mathematics. They have nothing to do with the mind. But, under the influence of postpositivism and other "post-isms," educators are likely to bring the mind in as a party to such issues. Having learned that there are no objective truths, they will conclude that number systems and propositions about numbers are ideas and beliefs in the minds of mathematicians. Accordingly, they will have qualms about ordaining that these mere opinions are to be forced on students. Shouldn't the students' own opinions be given equal weight? There are important issues here, but folk theory tends to muddy them. Folk theory of mind tends to recognize only two sorts of things: real, palpable things that exist out there in the material world, and immaterial things that exist as objects in people's minds. Thus, 2/5 of a quart of whisky is something real, to be found in abundance on the shelves of cheap liquor stores, whereas 2/5, the pure number, is found only in people's minds. Under the influence of such a theory, it is not surprising that many educators should decide to avoid dealing with pure numbers and concentrate mathematics instruction only on quantities of material things. From this it follows naturally that, when testers come out of the blue with a question about the sum of 1/2 and 1/3, students will be liable to produce answers that make no sense either mathematically or in relation to quantities they might encounter in the physical world.

It is perhaps unfair to blame this last anomaly on folk epistemology. To young children, numbers are perfectly real things (Cobb, Gravmeijer, Yackel, McClain, & Whitenack, 1997). Educators who honor (and often share) this intuition find that mathematics can be made quite a meaningful field of inquiry for students (Lampert, Rittenhouse, & Crumbaugh, 1996). The insistence on treating numbers as objects in people's minds comes about from trying to promote the mind-as-container metaphor into a genuine theory, with defensible premises and empirical implications. It therefore behooves us to look, as we do in the next chapter, at the efforts of cognitivists to build scientific theories embodying the container metaphor.

DO WE REALLY NEED A THEORY OF MIND?

Developmental psychologists are always posing problems to young children: Which side of the balance will go down? Are there more candies in that row or this row? How much is 1 less than 5? A dog undergoes cosmetic surgery so that it looks just like a cat: Is it now a cat? Frequently such questions are followed up by asking the child, "How do you know?" A not uncommon answer is, "My brain told me." What the children seem to be saying is something an adult would express as "It's obvious" or "I figured it out." But the children have already begun positing an agent that does this perceiving of the obvious and figuring things out. That agent will later come to be called the mind.

I don't think there is much to be gained by starting out with positing a mind and then trying to define what it is and how it relates to the brain. A more promising starting point is with the idea of a mentalistic level of description. A great deal of people's talk about themselves and each other takes place at this level. It is talk referring to what people know, believe, feel, experience, remember or forget, desire, like or dislike. Such mentalistic talk is what behaviorists have tried to eliminate from scientific discourse. Once that is done, the question of whether there is a mind distinct from the brain becomes moot. Except for the uncommonly clever Dr. Skinner, however, most behaviorists have found it necessary to use mental terms in their everyday speech. That a mentalistic level of description is necessary for education seems to me so obvious that I am not going to waste words arguing the point. I will simply leave it as a challenge to the doubter to figure out a way to deal with an issue such as *teaching for deeper understanding* without using mental terms.

A mentalistic level of description does not necessarily imply a mind as the agent, however. Much of the time in our mentalistic talk the implied agent is the whole person—*I* remember, *you* believe; *Gustav* wants, and so on—with no mention of a mind at all. The notion of mind comes in at a more systemic level. A person's beliefs, feelings, desires, and so on are not just so many bits and pieces. They hang together in some way, or, if they do not, that is a matter of concern. When we talk about the mind we are talking about this whole interconnected system of mental attributes. Thus, the concept of *mind* is rather like the concept of *economy*. There is an economic level of description, at which terms such as production, consumption, accumulation, and exchange are applied to people's activities. The notion of an economy enters in at a systemic level, when we consider all these activities as they interrelate and have joint effects. An economy as a whole may be characterized as healthy or sick, stagnant or expanding, complex or simple—terms that are also sometimes applied to minds.

A major difference between *economy* and *mind* is that no one ever gets the economy confused with a physical object (it may get confused with objective indicators, such as gross domestic product, but that is a different problem). There is endless dithering, however, about distinguishing the mind from the brain (Popper & Eccles, 1977; cf Taylor, 1999).[4] I suppose if a nation's economy were based on a single machine that was the source of all the goods produced in that country, a similar confusion might arise. Conversely, if cognition were fully distributed throughout the body, the mind–body problem might vanish. As it is, however, cognition is largely concentrated in the brain. But that does not localize cognition very much. The brain contains more neurons than there are people in the world and is about as complex in its functioning as the functioning of the world economy. From this viewpoint, to say, as some cognitivists are prone to do, that the mind and the brain are one is about as illuminating as saying that the economy and the human population are one and the same.

We—and by this I mean practically everyone, not just behavioral scientists and philosophers—need a concept of mind because we continually deal with mental phenomena at a systemic level. We do not simply record in list fashion what we take to be one another's beliefs and dispositions, but we try to make sense of them. This is important for practical as well as intellectual purposes. To succeed at it, we need some notion of an organized whole. It seems natural to treat that organized whole as a thing and to assign processes and attributes to it. Hence, the mind. Although objections can be raised against such reification, I do not think we should fight it. At least, we should not abandon the mind until a better alternative is offered, and as I try to show in the next three chapters the alternatives do not quite make the grade.

WHY EDUCATION, ESPECIALLY, NEEDS A NEW THEORY OF MIND

The main motivation for the present inquiry is my belief that education must advance beyond the state of a traditional craft if it is to do the job required of it in the post-Industrial Age. Folk theory of mind stands in the way of such advancement. The fault is not with the idea of mind itself, as behaviorists and some contemporary cognitivists

---

[4]The Cartesian dualism seems to keep coming back to life after repeated total destruction, like Chucky, the evil doll in the movie *Child's Play* and its sequels. See, for instance, Popper and Eccles (1977) and the commentaries following Dennett and Kinsbourne (1992).

claim, but with the root metaphor on which folk theory of mind is based. It is the *mind-as-container* metaphor. This metaphor leads to the positing of an array of mental objects contained in the mind—such old-fashioned objects as beliefs, desires, goals, and plans, or such new-fangled objects as schemata, production systems, and conceptual networks. Education is viewed as a matter of introducing new objects into the mind or modifying objects already there. According to an older view, learning consists of taking objects in from outside. According to the more fashionable constructivist view, the mind constructs the objects it contains. The container metaphor remains, however, and that is where the trouble starts.

Generally, folk theory of mind has great trouble dealing with any sort of knowledge that cannot be understood as an object in an individual mind. Thus, for many people, contemporary talk about a "learning society," "knowledge-based industries, "corporate memory," "team expertise," and the like has an unreal air about it, and for others it is degraded into more comfortable notions of mental or physical objects. Those of a sociocultural turn of mind may have no difficulty with the idea of knowledge existing at a supra personal level, but they have trouble linking this up to children's learning their times tables. A viable theory of mind for 21st century education, it seems to me, must be able to negotiate effectively between individual learning on one hand and knowledge conceived of as a product or as a cultural good on the other. Folk theory of mind, constrained by its container metaphor, simply can't do the job.

The most promising new developments in education involve restructuring school activities and discourse so that they resemble the workings of research groups, where real questions are being investigated and students are trying to contribute to progress on those questions. Within the conceptual framework of folk theory of mind, however, this kind of collaborative knowledge-building activity degenerates into "cooperative learning." It becomes students helping each other learn. There is nothing wrong with that, but it is not the same as collaborative knowledge-building. Folk theory of mind cannot support the distinction.

Even at the individual level there is an important distinction that folk theory of mind obscures. The individual scientist occasionally takes time out from research to learn something—to master a new piece of computer software, for instance. But to folk theory of mind, research *is* learning. It is obtaining knowledge, adding to the contents of the mental container. Folk theory of mind is unable to make anything significant of the fact that research and theorizing are meant to advance the world's knowledge (or that of some group, at any rate), whereas learning is only meant to advance one's own knowledge.

This inability to distinguish between knowledge building and learning produces a dilemma over which several generations of educators have agonized. On one hand is the official wisdom promoted by virtually all the education journals and professional associations and embodied in virtually all the publicized innovations. This is a wisdom identified with such phrases as "inquiry," "meaning making," "sciencing," and "constructivism." On the other hand is the unofficial wisdom of the workplace and of the teacher's lounge, which holds that there are a great many important things that people tend not to learn, or at least not to learn very thoroughly or efficiently, unless they are taught. Typically the dilemma is handled by compromise, but it is an uneasy, sometimes guilt-ridden compromise. I have heard education professors express dismay when they find that a teacher who was doing a marvelous job of following their precepts for inquiry-based mathematics teaching also devoted time to mental arithmetic drill. That this should be perceived as an inconsistency testifies to the conceptual impoverishment of present-day educational thought. As I try to show in chapter 8, there is reason to believe that this conceptual impoverishment is leading to an impoverishment of practice as well.

The mind-as-container metaphor is handy for talking about the acquisition of knowledge, but not for talking about what the knowledge is good for once it is in the container. A perennial educational concern is what Alfred North Whitehead called "inert knowledge." This is knowledge that just sits in the container until its name is called and does not participate actively in the conduct of life. But what else could we expect of immaterial lumps of mental content? If one ignores the mind for the time being, it is legitimate and illuminating to discuss such questions as, "What is the value of the concept of gravity?" Having obtained some positive answers ("It helps to explain such and such," "It makes it possible to predict thus and so"), one can then go on to plan ways of enabling students to avail themselves of these uses of the concept. Turn the concept of gravity into an object in the mind, however, and this straightforward pragmatic approach to knowledge suddenly becomes difficult to manage. To get these static objects in the mind to doing anything, one has to conjure up a process. Educators will speak of a process called "transfer"—a term properly applied to skills, where it means something quite unmysterious, whereas transfer becomes a *deus ex machina* when applied to conceptual knowledge.

On all of the counts I have mentioned, educational thinkers have managed to make progress despite holding to a folk theory of mind. Human thinkers, when in good form, can be quite agile and get past all sorts of impediments, including not only those created by an archaic theory of mind but also those that come from having to use a language that may be said to embody that theory. But as the demands on educational thought become more exacting, the impediments become increasingly detrimental. When you are not expecting to do anything about it, when you are just trying to provide a succinct description, it is perfectly all right to talk about students having models in their minds of biological systems, number lines, and so on. But when practice gets serious, to the point that educators are talking about changing the student's mental model of plant nutrition so that it more nearly resembles the botanist's mental model, then it is time to stop and ask, "Do we really mean what we're saying? Are we really prepared to assert that there are describable things in students' minds that can be compared to things in the minds of scientists and that we can get hold of the first kind of thing and make it over into something like the second kind of thing, or is this all just a manner of speaking?"

A more familiar line of questioning has to do with whether it is possible to base a successful science on folk theory of mind. Behaviorists have been vehemently negative on this point, although for reasons that no longer seem very compelling. More recently, a number of people within cognitive science have begun to offer negative answers as well, based on computational possibilities and what is known about the brain. Although I draw, in the next chapter, on the objections raised by these people, their arguments are not central to the case I try to make. My interest is in education. It is quite possible that cognitive science could be reconstructed on a new basis—on a neurological basis, for instance—without its making any difference to educational thought and practice. Most of the contemporary critics of folk theory of mind would probably agree. They think the folk theory is fine for conducting the practical affairs of the world; they just want it driven out of laboratories and philosophers' seminar rooms. They are called "eliminativists," because what they are pursuing is not a new theory of mind but rather a behavioral and brain science that gets along without a mental level of description.

BACK TO AQUINAS?

When I said in the preface that our folk theory of mind is older than the wheel, that was more an attention grabber than a calculated estimate of antiquity. In some respects—the respects in which theory of mind is innate—it is probably much older than the wheel (Barkow et al., 1992). But Julian Jaynes (1986) has argued, mainly on the basis of the way human action was portrayed in ancient myths, that early human beings did not have the subjective experience of thought, that what we perceive as mental events were perceived by them as voices from the beyond. However that may be, it is clear that by the time of Plato something very like contemporary folk theory had taken shape (Dreyfus, 1988). But there may yet have been an important difference. In an essay titled "How Old Is the Mind?" Hilary Putnam (1986) offered evidence that suggests the mind-as-container metaphor may not have taken hold among European philosophers until the Renaissance. In ancient and medieval thought the closest thing to the present-day concept of mind, the *nous*, was more like what we would call consciousness or active attention. Mental content was just what we are aware of or, in contemporary jargon, "processing" at the moment. The idea of the mind as a repository of unattended beliefs and memories was absent. Instead, these were conceived of as a sort of bodily material out of which the active mind formed, in Aquinas' words, "intellectual species." Putnam (1986) commented,

> The contemporary "common-sense" view is that it is obvious that memories are in the mind; what is still regarded as a difficult question is whether they are *identical* with brain traces or only *correlated* with brain traces. The view I have been attributing to Aquinas is that it is obvious that memories are in the body (the brain); when they are not actively being recalled, they are not "mental" at all. The *nous*/body distinction that Aquinas would have drawn is not at all the same as the modern mind/body distinction. Yet, when I think about it, it doesn't sound worse than the modern one. *Is it* obvious that there is something called the mind whose contents include all of my memories, whether I am actively recalling them or not, but whose functions do not include digestion or reproduction? Or are we in the grip of a picture, a picture whose origins are somewhat accidental and whose logic, once examined, is not compelling? (p. 34)

Like Putnam, I find this antique view of the mind intuitively appealing. Unlike behaviorism, it fully accepts the introspective evidence of mind—the experiences of thinking, remembering, understanding, and intending. What it excludes is the part we never experience directly but only infer: the vast archive of beliefs and memories that are not part of our immediate consciousness but that we assume to be stored away somewhere to be retrieved on occasion. That exclusion, of course, would pose what I can only think to call a "mind-boggling" question for education. What could education be if it is not in large part concerned with the contents of students' mental archives? But that is a question educators have been wrestling with in various ill-defined ways throughout the past century, and it is just possible that the antique view might render the question more tractable.

Curiously, the pre-Renaissance view, when translated into current language as Putnam has done, has a more modern ring to it than the contemporary folk theory with which it competes. At about the same time Putnam's essay was published, a monumental two-volume work also appeared, which has had a profound influence on cognitive science in all its many branches. I refer to *Parallel Distributed Processing* (McClelland, Rumelhart, & the PDP Research Group, 1986; Rumelhart, McClelland, and the PDP Group, 1986). Connectionism, as it is now generally called, demonstrates how a brain could be knowledgeable—that is, could retain and take advantage of the results of experience—without anything that might properly be called mental content. *Parallel Distributed Processing* did not offer a theory of mind, but it cleared a workspace for developing one.

CONCLUSION

The idea of knowledge as the contents of a mental filing cabinet is, I believe, the most stultifying conception in educational thought. But it has been shared by all the major combatants in the educational debates of this century. There are traditionalists who want to make sure the filing cabinet is filled and with the right things, there are child-centered and "constructivist" educators who insist the contents of the filing cabinet should be the result of the child's own inquiries, and there are the thinking skills enthusiasts who want to ignore the mental filing cabinet (whose contents they believe to be rapidly obsolescent) and to focus on developing skills in accessing various external filing cabinets and applying their contents. There is merit in all these positions, but they appear unreconcilable. Moreover, they all *undervalue* knowledge as it figures in a knowledge-based economy and in the careers of experts.

It is too much to expect that a reconstituted theory of mind would lead to consensus where we now have people at loggerheads over educational policies, although there might be a bit less talking past one another. I should hope, rather, that a new theory of mind would result in constructive disagreements where there is now superficial consensus. There is at this time widespread agreement on a number of educational ideas. These include higher order skills, teaching for understanding, constructivism (understood as the opposite of passive reception of information), authentic problem solving, and lifelong learning. The consensus, though far from complete, includes not only a broad spectrum of professional educators but also business people and politicians. There is seldom, however, any investigation of the possibility that people understand these terms quite differently; for if it turned out that they did, there would be no place for the discussion to go. It would be as if pirates met only to discover they held pieces of different treasure maps. We lack concepts for advancing beyond the stage educational enlightenment has currently reached. My hope in this book is to show that by adopting a new way of thinking about knowledge and mind, educational thought can be freed to do the job it must do if education is to earn its place in the Knowledge Age.

2

Keeping the Brain in Mind*

On its own, a neuron firing has no meaning, no symbolic quality whatsoever .... It is a level shift as drastic as that between molecules and gases that takes place when thought emerges from billions of in-themselves-meaningless neural firings.

—Hofstadter, (1985, p. 649)

Virtual reality experiences are making people physically ill. Recently there have been reports of people having flashback experiences, similar to those associated with LSD. One explanation that has been offered is that when people are harnessed to a virtual reality device, the brain receives visual and auditory signals indicating the body is in motion but it is not receiving the kinesthetic signals that normally go with them. Accordingly, the brain starts adapting to a new environment by establishing new neural pathways, which can then be activated by other signals, thus producing the flashback phenomenon. I have no idea how this conjecture will fare, but the way it is formed is most instructive for thinking about the mind in relation to the brain.

---

*Portions of chapter 2 appeared previously in the *Australian Journal of Education*, 2000, 44(3), 226–238.

Note that it is the *brain*, not the mind, that "expects" kinesthetic sensations of motion and that starts creating new structures when they do not appear. The *mind*, in one way, is not fooled. We know we are sitting in a room and not behind the wheel of a racing car roaring around a speedway. In another way, the mind is fooled whereas the brain is not. We experience the bodily sensations of movement along with the visual and auditory ones, and so we are unaware of the inconsistencies or error signals that our brains are busy trying to rectify. To describe and make sense of such phenomena, therefore, we need a concept of mind as well as a concept of brain. But the two conceptions ought to be in some accord.

This chapter is about two different models of mind, which have different implications for how the brain relates to mind and knowledge. According to one model, knowledge is encoded in the brain in something like the way data are encoded in a computer's memory. This model is fully consistent with folk theory and so it feels comfortable and seems intuitively compelling, but it starts to become less plausible when we begin to trace out its implications at the brain level. According to the other model, the brain does not actually contain knowledge in any sense that which readily conceive of. Thus, this model is radically at variance with folk theory and not even comprehensible until we get a handle on how a brain thus constituted could sustain knowledgeable, intelligent behavior. However, it is this second model that I believe we need to develop in order to have a theory of mind that will carry education into the Knowledge Age.

COMPUTATIONAL MODELS OF MIND-AS-CONTAINER

I wonder whether the pioneers of artificial intelligence ever asked themselves whether they should adopt the mind–as–container metaphor. I doubt it. Simulating human cognition on a computer means writing a program. A program consists of instructions, and these instructions apply to the contents of locations in the computer's memory. Thus, right from the start, we have something that closely resembles the folk conception of mind. There is a container (computer memory) with specified objects in it. These objects are of two kinds: beliefs (data) and rules (instructions). To simulate human cognition, all you have to do is load data that represent human beliefs, along with instructions that represent the rules human beings follow in operating on those beliefs.

Beliefs can be represented as propositions (e.g., "All birds are bipeds," "Some evangelists are lechers," "All evangelists are bipeds"). Rules can take the form of logical operators—if–then statements, which have come to be known as "productions." Of course, what must be represented are not ideal beliefs and rules, but rather beliefs and rules that actually appear in human cognition. Thus, to simulate human reasoning, you do not want a flawless logic machine, but you also do not want one that will infer from the preceding propositions that some birds are lechers or that some evangelists are birds. That would be a poor simulation, inasmuch as hardly any human being would arrive at such conclusions.

Such simulation failures can be avoided in two ways: either by building in more elaborate inferential rules or by building in more extensive knowledge. The first alternative leads to trouble. People do, on occasion, make the kind of logical error represented in "some evangelists are birds," so a valid simulation of human intelligence cannot build in rules that altogether eliminate such errors. The second alternative is more realistic: People avoid error in the present case because they already know that no birds are evangelists. Thus, to simulate human intelligence, it is not enough to build a system that reasons the way we do. The system must also possess what typically turns out to be vast amounts of knowledge that we human beings seem to rely on in dealing with even the most mundane of real world problems.

Work on artificial intelligence has made some notable contributions to our understanding of the mind. If it has not disposed of the mind–body problem, it has at least put its more simplistic versions to rest: Computers, acting as minds, now control all kinds of "bodies"—from traffic lights to unmanned space vehicles. It has also demonstrated ways to overcome the "homunculus" problem. In folk theory, the mind is like a homunculus, or little person, who sits in the head, interpreting incoming information and issuing commands to the body. Artificial intelligence programs are homunculi of this sort. The problem arises with the question, "What controls the homunculus?" The homunculus would seem to require a homunculus in its own head, and so on in an infinite regression. A solution that has produced impressive results amounts to endowing the first homunculus with a system of if–then rules that are executed automatically whenever conditions match the "if" portion of the rule, plus a few simple rules for deciding which of several matching rules gets to go first (Anderson, 1993). This solution may require a proliferation of rules, but it eliminates the need for a higher level agent to decide which rules to apply when.

From an educational standpoint, however, by far the most important contribution of work on artificial intelligence has been its demonstration of the magnitude of the role of knowledge in cognition (Bereiter & Scardamalia, 1992; Glaser, 1984). It is difficult to convey the revolutionary significance of this result, because it is a matter of degree. Everyone already recognizes that knowledge is essential. Students who have never heard of Abraham Lincoln and the American Civil War cannot be expected to understand the Gettysburg address, no matter how clever and skillful readers they may be. What people do not generally realize is the sheer amount of knowledge involved in mundane intelligent behavior. We notice the special, problematic items of knowledge, but not the ordinary, taken-for-granted ones. We recognize that to understand "four score and seven years ago" you have to know that a score is 20. We do not consider that you must also know what a year is and that "ago" indicates years in the past—so that you must also understand time and what it means for something to be in the past, and that 87 years is longer than most people live, so that something that took place 87 years in the past will be outside the experience of the listeners.

In later chapters I pursue some of the educational implications of this expanded realization of the role of knowledge—not only for ordinary intelligent behavior but more especially for expertise, which, again, depends on previously unrecognized amounts of knowledge, but uncommon rather than common knowledge. For education appropriate to the Knowledge Age, such realization ought to play a much larger role in educational thought and practice than it does now.

At this point, however, my concern is what this expansive view of the role of knowledge implies for folk theory of mind. Obviously, it implies the mental container has much more in it—orders of magnitude more—than common sense had suggested. But there are deeper problems. When I said earlier that everyone knows that no birds are evangelists, I cannot have meant that people have that particular fact firmly in mind. If they did, they would also need items specifying every other thing that birds are not, and similarly for everything else of which they have knowledge. That would imply not just a very large number of items in the mental container but a virtually infinite number. So knowledge in the mind cannot be that specific. It must consist of more general propositions or knowledge structures from which, whenever the need arises, we infer things like there being no feathered evangelists.

But do we, in fact, have to infer that no birds are evangelists? Is not this something we simply know, even though we have never thought of it before? Here is where the container metaphor, when carried to the point of an explicit theory or model, becomes implausible. Artificial intelligence models based on the container metaphor offer only two ways for a mind to "know" something. Either that something is explicitly represented in the mind, in something like a sentence, or it is logically inferable from things that are explicitly represented. Yet a great deal of what we seem to know does not plausibly belong in either category. We see a china plate hanging over the edge of a table and we push it back. If challenged for a reason, we would respond immediately and confidently that (a) the plate was in danger of falling off and (b) if it fell it would break. The first could be deduced from laws of physics, but that is not something we could do in a flash. The second is not deducible from physical laws, at least not from ones the ordinary person would know. If required to justify the second belief, we might appeal to premises such as "china plates are fragile," "a wood floor is a fairly hard surface," "the table is over 2 feet high," and "fragile objects falling from a height of 2 feet or more onto a hard surface are likely to break." But would we actually claim to have called up such propositions and performed the necessary logical operations on them? Furthermore, do those propositions represent explicit items of knowledge in our minds or are they also facts that have to be inferred?

Something just isn't right about this way of accounting for human knowledge. To provide a more plausible account, the philosopher Michael Polanyi (1964) invoked the concept of tacit knowledge. The most obvious examples are knowledge embedded in skills—for instance, the knowledge of ballistics implicit in throwing a paper wad into a wastebasket. But, as the preceding example shows, there is also tacit knowledge involved in purely cognitive acts, such as predicting and explaining.

The mere tacitness of knowledge presents no particular problem for folk theory or for theories based on the container metaphor. One simply allows that the mind contains many rules and propositions the owner is unaware of. No, the problem comes from the intuition that we have knowledge that does not take the form of rules or propositions at all and that this knowledge constitutes a large part—perhaps an overwhelmingly large part—of what we personally know.

That, as I read him, was the intuition Polanyi was trying to win a place for in epistemology. Until about a decade ago, however, that intuition was too insubstantial to make headway against the centuries-long development of formal logic and the dramatic rise of thinking machines, all based on treating knowledge as composed of explicit symbolic representations and thought as the application of definite rules to these representations. As a result, tacit knowledge was regarded as shadowy stuff in the background of the mind, possibly important but not anything you could do much with, compared with the propositions that present themselves in the foreground of the mind, sharp and ready to do work.

All this has begun to change with the rise of connectionism (McClelland et al., 1986; Rumelhart, McClelland et al., 1986). Connectionism is a different approach to designing artificial intelligence. If the rule-based kind of artificial intelligence I have been discussing up to this point is based on a metaphor of the mind, connectionism may be said to be based on a metaphor of the brain. It is the brain conceived of as a lot of interconnected units, activating or inhibiting each other by energy transmitted over their connections. Connectionism is not a theory. Indeed, from the distant vantage point of education, it serves more as an antitheory. It serves as a source of concrete demonstrations that you can have something like a mind that has something like knowledge, but that does not contain any identifiable rules, propositions, or other symbolic representations of that knowledge.

HOW DO BRAINS KNOW?

When philosophers talk about knowledge, they usually take as examples simple factual propositions (often called "*p*" for short): Kuala Lumpur is the capital of Malaysia. The sun rises in the east. And so on. These are just the kinds of knowledge items that folk theory of mind is best equipped to handle. Imagining these items are represented as sentences in the mind is not much of a stretch. In fact, it is hard to imagine them not being represented in some sentence-like form. After all, that is often the form in which they were first made known to us. However, just because knowledge of this itemized type seems so unproblematic, it is a poor source of examples for critical examination of folk theory and alternatives to it.

Let us, therefore, take a different starting point. Consider the following proposition: The world is composed of discrete objects that persist under movement in three-dimensional space. The interesting thing about this item of knowledge is that people show evidence of possessing it in early infancy, and may even be born knowing it (Spelke, 1982). Here there is no question of their having heard it somewhere. If you presented the idea in verbal form to 6-year-olds they would have trouble grasping what you were talking about. Yet babies who have not yet uttered their first words will evidence surprise and sometimes alarm if a trickster shows them something that violates the principle: for instance, an object that disappears behind one screen and reappears from behind another, without having been seen to cross the gap between the screens.

An upholder of folk theory could object that what we have here is not a matter of knowledge but a matter of how our perceptual system is built. We are built to see the world in three dimensions and to pick out objects in it and to track those objects as they move about. This tracking of objects presupposes that they persist, but that is not something we know or believe (at least, not as infants); it is, as it were, something our neurons have evolved or been conditioned to expect.

I agree with all of this except for the first statement, that it is not a matter of knowledge. Although it may have been acquired through evolution rather than through learning, it is knowledge very similar to the number sense we discussed earlier or to the acquired knowledge that enables us to find our way about in a familiar environment. To be sure, it is not the same as the knowledge represented by the proposition that the world consists of objects distributed in three-dimensional space. That is a debatable proposition, whereas the knowledge built into our perceptual system is not (although it may profoundly limit our ability to entertain alternatives to the theoretical proposition). But number sense and geographical place knowledge are not debatable either. Propositions based on them may be, but the knowledge guiding our actions is not.

A definitional issue begins to arise here that needs to be cleared up before proceeding to issues of substance. What counts as knowledge? Gilbert Ryle (1949) is credited with having clarified this question by distinguishing "knowing-how" from "knowing-that." In traditional discussions of epistemology, only the second is counted as knowledge. Knowing-that consists of holding a true or warranted belief. Knowing-how is a matter of skill and is therefore of no interest to epistemology, whose traditional concerns have been with the bases for belief. Cognitive scientists have used the term knowledge much more broadly, however. Knowledge includes false beliefs that the person acts upon as true. But it also includes skills or what has come to be called "procedural knowledge." One reason for lumping all these together as knowledge is that, on close inspection of cognitive behavior, the separation between knowing-how and knowing-that is not very firm. Today you may recall and therefore be said to "know that" the square of 16 is 256. Another day you may not recall it, or may recall it but not be sure it is right, and so will rely on your "knowing how" to multiply and thereby arrive at an answer. When we turn to more complex sorts of competence, the distinction becomes even less tenable. Few people know explicit rules for transforming English declarative sentences into questions and even linguists find some contingencies hard to account for, but native speakers can all make such transformations. Thus, they could be credited with knowing-how but not knowing-that. Native speakers can do more than this, however. They can also immediately detect nonstandard transformations of the kinds foreigners may make, such as "What you are doing?" or "How much it does cost?" In other words, they "know that" such sentences are not standard English but they do not "know how" to explain what is wrong with them.

Thus, knowi   w and knowing-that seem to be aspects of the same knowle   vhere knowledge of language is concerned.

Once we al   1at knowledge consists of more than statable beliefs, it is not clear where to draw the line. This uncertainty of delineation is evident in ordinary speech. People talk about their body's knowing when it needs a rest or about what their muscles know. It is never clear where literal meaning stops and figurative begins.

I propose that this is not merely a definitional matter but is a matter of what knowledge really amounts to at the level of the brain. "Really," I suppose, should be in scare quotes, because I do not want to have to defend use of the term. I merely use it as a reminder that, although we may be free to define knowledge and the mind any way we like, there is also a brain involved, and we do not enjoy nearly so much freedom in what we may attribute to it. You may or may not choose to attribute knowledge to the brain, but something or other characterizes the brain and is the counterpart of our "knowing that *p*" or knowing Spanish or whatever. To avoid prejudging issues, let us say that *the brain supports knowledgeable action*. How it does this is my concern in this chapter.

There are two major contenders as answers to how the brain supports knowledgeable action. This is a big step up from the state of things before 1986, when there was only one major contender—as Jerry Fodor (1985) put it, "the only game in town" (p. 90). The older of the contending answers comes from folk theory, as systematized by cognitive scientists. It is that the brain contains encoded versions of propositions and rules. How the brain does this is a problem for a different science. Suffice it to say that with billions of neurons, countless synapses connecting them, and new synapses being created all the time, there are plenty of degrees of freedom available for encoding all the knowledge that could accumulate in the course of an individual lifetime.

The nature of this code is a problem for cognitive science, however, and ultimately for education and other applied fields that must deal with mental states and personal knowledge. The brain's code cannot be like the Morse code and other such codes or like a scrambling device. These merely encode the sounds or spellings of linguistic utterances. That would leave the prelinguistic infant without a mind and would mean that "some dogs bark" and "there exist dogs that bark" are separate items in the mental storehouse. No, for this theory to work, the brain must encode concepts, meanings. Thus, it must have a grammar and a vocabulary. In short, the brain must have a language (Fodor, 1975).

This is just what philosophers and others who have thought about the matter under the influence of the container metaphor have assumed all along. Fodor's distinctive contribution has been to pursue this assumption far enough to reveal its more profound implications for a theory of mind—or, some would say, far enough to reveal its utter implausibility. This "language of thought" as Fodor called it in his 1975 book, has to be innate. Otherwise, the infant would have nothing to get started with in learning. Thus, the brain has to come already furnished with a grammar—as Chomsky (1975), on other grounds, had been arguing that it must—and with at least some initial vocabulary. Fodor went on to argue, however, that this initial endowment of language cannot be merely some neural version of baby talk. It has to embody the highest level concepts and structures the mature mind will exhibit. In effect, the learning of more complex cognitive structures is impossible, because it would involve using the existing language of thought to create a language capable of representing knowledge beyond what can be conceived of in terms of the existing language:

> There literally isn't such a thing as the notion of learning a conceptual system richer than the one that one already has; we simply have no idea of what it would be like to get from a conceptually impoverished to a conceptually richer system by anything like a process of learning. (Fodor, 1980, p. 149)

Such a paradoxical view of learning could not go unchallenged, and there have been challenges ranging from metatheoretical appeals to self-organizing systems (Molenaar, 1986) to arguments for developmental processes distinct from learning (Boom, 1991). But all of these bypass the problem of showing how a rule-based system can generate rules of a higher order than those that do the generating (Bereiter, 1985, 1991a). This is the challenge taken up by the second contender, connectionism.

CONNECTIONISM:
MIND WITHOUT MENTAL CONTENT

The question, as I put it earlier, is how does the brain support knowledgeable action? The reason for phrasing the question in this quaint way is to leave open the possibility that the brain can support knowledgeable action without actually containing the rules, propositions, images, recorded events, and so on that are conventionally reckoned to constitute knowledge. That is the kind of situation that connectionist and neural net models simulate.[1]

---

[1]The usual disclaimers apply, the likening of the brain to a connectionist network running on a computer being only a crude analogy (Smolensky, 1988). The point I am trying to make can survive the crudity, I believe, provided the reader is willing to put up with a style of exposition that treats brains as if they really are connectionist networks.

Before proceeding, I need to try to clarify this notion of containing or not containing rules. Anything that works can be said to embody rules. A mechanical clock embodies a rule, enforced by the pendulum or balance wheel, that the minute hand shall go around once and only once per hour. A doorbell circuit embodies the rule that the doorbell sounds only when the button is pushed. As simple a device as a pair of pliers embodies the rather formidable rule that the force exerted by the jaws is equal to the force of the grip, multiplied by the ratio of two relevant distances from the pivot. Naturally the brain embodies rules of this sort, but they are electrochemical rules and the like. Whether, in addition to that and in quite a different sense, the brain contains rules for making butter tarts and for pleading cases in court is the question before us and one not to be confused by characteristics that the brain shares with every other mechanism under the sun.[2]

The computer programs that implement connectionist models, being things that work, naturally also embody rules. These, however, are mathematical rules governing how the program runs, and they bear no relation to rules of the domain being modeled. A connectionist network consists of a (sometimes large) number of units with connections between them. Some are input units, which receive quantitative values from outside. Some are output units, which output quantitative values that are interpreted and sometimes fed back to the input units. The rest are "hidden" units whose inputs come from other units in the network and whose outputs similarly go only to other units in the network. Although in principle the whole system is active at once, connectionist programs that run on conventional computers simulate parallel processing by going through cycles. In each cycle, quantitative outputs pass from unit to unit, via the connections, changing them so that they may output different values on the next cycle. The rules, such as they are, determine these quantitative values and the effects they will have. The rules include parameters the operator can adjust to "tune" the network. When properly tuned, the network will, after going through enough cycles, "settle" into a state such that the inputs that units receive on each cycle leave them in approximately the same state they were in before, so that the outputs no longer change.

As described, this is as mindless a system as we could ask for. Thus, it models, at least abstractly, the paradoxical condition Hofstadter (1985) referred to in saying, "On its own, a neuron firing

---

[2]I feel I am belaboring the obvious here. The reason for doing so is that I have encountered several sophisticated colleagues who miss the point, being stuck on insisting that connectionist networks contain rules, just different kinds of rules, from more traditional artificial intelligence programs.

has no meaning, no symbolic quality whatsoever" (p. 649). If a system composed of such meaningless elements, and processes can begin to do meaningful, knowledgeable things, that is at least interesting and possibly illuminating as to our question, "How does the brain support knowledgeable action?"

Connectionist networks have learned to do meaningful, knowledgeable things. Many of them are not very impressive by human standards, because they are things people do easily: recognizing letters of the alphabet, guiding a car on a real road, learning grammatical conventions, recognizing faces. These are impressive by artificial intelligence standards, however, because they are accomplishments that have proved inordinately difficult for rule-based systems. Others, such as learning the evasive maneuvers of a fighter pilot and making insightful investment decisions, are impressive even by human standards. In all cases, one would look in vain in the program code or in its output for the rules that the network is following in accomplishing these things. That is because there are no rules in that sense. Connectionist networks can act knowledgeably without containing knowledge; they can behave lawfully without containing rules.

Educators who have gathered this much about connectionist models recognize, quite properly, that they do not have much of practical value to contribute to pedagogy. (I ignore here the value connectionist technology may have in educational software applications [cf. Schank, Ranney, & Hoadley, 1995] or in understanding neurological factors in learning difficulties [Manis, Seidenberg, Doi, McBride-Chang, & Petersen, 1996]. These are potentially important, but not germane to present issues.) That is, there is not much to be learned from a system that can do something intelligent but cannot reveal how it did it. Rule-based systems win easily on this account. A rule-based system that can read and solve mathematical word problems, for instance, contains a set of rules that are potentially teachable to students. This kind of potential was in fact exploited by Clancey (1987), who took an expert system for medical diagnosis and used it as the basis for a tutoring system that taught medical students the propositional knowledge and the reasoning procedures the system used in making its diagnoses. Nothing like that can be expected from connectionist research. Instead, the whole reason I have been trying to disseminate connectionist ideas among educators has been to provide a handle on a new way of thinking about knowledge and the mind.

To gain such a handle, one needs to acquire at least some experiential feel for how connectionist networks work. By far the best way is to get hold of some simple programs and fool around with them on a computer. Some of the pioneers of connectionism have made this easy by producing a handbook that comes with software in DOS or Macintosh versions (McClelland & Rumelhart, 1988). Most writings on the subject are at too abstract a level to give much feel. I have tried to provide something more down to earth using a network of frisbees as an analogy (Bereiter, 1991b). Here, I take a different down-to-earth approach, building on an example that will be familiar to people who use word processors.

THE MIND OF THE SPELLING CHECKER

The kinds of spelling checkers now found in most word processors are just barely complex enough to serve as examples for comparing the two models of mind we have been discussing. As far as I know, the spelling checkers in actual use are all built according to the rule-based model. That is, their source code contains explicit rules for checking spelling. Let us pretend, however, that we do not know this and that we are free to speculate about the mind of the spelling checker, constrained only by what we are able to observe of its behavior.

Starting at the behavioral level, this is what we observe: The spelling checker proceeds through a text sequentially. From time to time it highlights a word and presents a box giving us the option of changing the word or going on, with or without adding the highlighted word to the dictionary. It may also present a list of alternatives, words similar in spelling to the one highlighted, among which we may find correctly spelled the word we intended. In that case we may select the alternative and it will replace the highlighted word.

A mentalistic description captures more of the point of what goes on. The spelling checker *searches* through the text. When it *finds* a word it does not *recognize*, it opens a *dialog* with us. It *suggests* alternative spellings—we might even say it *tries to guess* what word we had in mind. And so on. The description raises further questions of a psychological sort. An interesting one is how the spelling checker *decides* which alternatives to suggest. We could begin to investigate this question by experimentation. The spelling checker I am using does puzzling things with variations on "psychology." Here are examples:

Word in Text	Spelling Checker's Suggestions
pyschology	psychology, psychologies, psychologic, psychological
pyschilogy, pyschalogy	psychology, psychologic
pyschiology	no suggestion
dsychology	no suggestion

sychology	psychology, psychologies, psychologic, psychological
cychology	cytology

It seems that first letters carry quite a bit of weight—yet the spelling checker is not thrown off by "sychology." Perhaps the number of letters in common determines a suggestion, but then why does it give up on "pyschiology?" I expected it might bring up both "psychology" and "physiology" as suggestions.[3]

What am I doing in these speculations? I am doing folk psychology, applied to an inanimate piece of software. I am trying to figure out what is in the spelling checker's mind, what rules it follows in arriving at judgments and decisions. Besides noticing what suggestions it gives in response to various misspellings, I also noticed it seems to "think" longer about some misspellings than others. For instance, it takes longer to respond to "sychology" than to "cychology." That, too, is information I might be able to use in forming a theory of its behavior. All this is not much different from what a teacher might do in trying to make sense of a child's idiosyncratic spelling habits.

The spelling checker can also be described at lower levels, which correspond to the neurological level in humans. It can be described at the level of subroutines, of source code, and of binary code. But even the programmers who understand the spelling checker at that level will still have reason to think about it at a mentalistic level. If they want to improve the spelling checker so that it does not give up on so many words and so that it recognizes "cychology" as a plausible misspelling of "psychology," they will not start by messing around with the code. They will have to start by, in effect, thinking like a teacher: What could I teach this spelling checker so that it would do a better job? Only after they have worked matters out at this level can they do what is denied to the teacher of living organisms: get inside and directly alter things in the mind.

The mental level of description does not, however, require a commitment to folk theory of mind. It does not, in other words, require us to believe that those rules we have been inferring are actually inside there somehow and determining what the spelling checker does. It could be that the spelling checker merely behaves in ways that correspond approximately to the rules we have thought of. The fact that our made-up rules do not fully account for the spelling

---

[3]Since performing this little experiment, I have acquired a new version of the word processor with, evidently, an improved spelling checker. It suggested "psychology" in all cases except for "cychology," which it still suggested was "cytology." Further experimentation might lead to plausible guesses about the content of the new or revised rules that accounted for the improvement.

checker's behavior may not be a fault of those rules. It may be that *no* rules could fully account for its behavior. In the case of a normal spelling checker, we know, of course, that there is a right set of rules; these are the rules the software developer built into the program and, barring bugs, they will fully account for its behavior. But if we did not have this outside information, we could not be sure. If all we had was observed behavior, we could not rule out the possibility that we were dealing with a connectionist system that contained no explicit rules.

A connectionist version of a spelling checker might be built as follows: Initially, some simple method is used to compute similarities between words in the dictionary. These are stored as connection weights between units that represent dictionary words.[4] There are also a number of other units that have connection weights to each other and to word units. Some of these are feature units. One feature might be "starts with the letter 'p'." This unit would have positive connection weights to every word that starts with "p" and negative weights to every other word. A number of other units would have no assigned identify at all, although there would be arbitrary connection weights to the other units. When the spelling checker is asked to suggest alternatives to a text word, feature units corresponding to the text word would be activated. These would send activation to other units, according to the connection weights, these units would send activation to others, and so on. Activation, positive or negative, would be sent back to the feature units, thus leading to another cycle of activation, and so on. The network of connections is designed so that with repeated cycles the activation levels tend to stabilize. When a point of stability is reached, the word units having the highest activation levels are chosen as suggested alternatives.

At first, such a system would probably not perform as well as the rule-based systems now in use. But it can be designed to learn. Every time a suggested word is selected as an alternative, the connection weights leading to it are increased a little, as are the weights leading to the units that sent positive activation to the units that activated the word. Although it might seem this would produce nothing more than a tendency to repeat past successes, experience with learning systems of this kind indicates that the learning can be much richer than that. A well-designed and well-trained system might be expected to match words on the basis of pronunciation as well as on the basis of letter sequences and, indeed, to work out useful correspondences the designers had never thought of. The spelling checker would seem to be working according to rules—sometimes obvious

---

[4]The number of connections this would mean with a dictionary of, say, 30,000 words suggests why this approach to spell checking has not caught on yet.

rules, other times rules too subtle for an observer to formulate. But this would be an illusion.

The same possibilities apply to the human mind. When we explain behavior using the conceptual framework of folk theory of mind—that is, when we explain behavior in terms of beliefs, plans, desires, and the like—we speak as if these things were actually in the mind of the behaver. We assume they are encoded in the brain somehow and if we had access to the code and could understand it, we could interpret the molecular structures or the patterns of synapses, we could know what a person's real beliefs and plans are. But the alternative is that the mind does not actually contain the entities folk theory of mind posits, that the brain is like a connectionist machine, producing rule-like behavior without actually containing such rules in any representation whatever. The fact that the theories we construct on the basis of folk theory of mind work in predicting behavior is no proof of the first alternative. But the fact that the brain consists of billions of neurons with billions of interconnections is no proof of the second alternative, either. Those billions of synaptic connections might or might not encode what folk theory of mind assumes they do, and it is not obvious how studying the brain itself could tell us which is true.

"This whole argument ignores consciousness," you might object. "We can't be sure what goes on in the so-called mind of the spelling checker, because the spelling checker has no way of telling us. But I am conscious of at least some of what goes on in my mind, and I know that my mind contains beliefs and rules and so on, that it is not just a lot of meaningless connections." But let's test this claim. What does your consciousness tell you about rules versus connection weights when it comes to checking visually for spelling errors? Ignore "*i* before *e* except after *c*" and a few other explicit rules that you may know, for they obviously account for only a tiny part of what goes on when you are checking for spelling errors. What I am mainly conscious of in proofreading a manuscript is running my eyes over the words and having nothing happen. I am certainly not conscious of applying rules to the words or of comparing each word with models stored in my mind. From time to time I spot an error and immediately correct it. For instance, I notice and delete the superfluous "t" in "intutition." Here, again, I am not aware of any rule application or indeed of any thinking at all. I simply notice and act. But then there are times when I look at a word and think, "This just doesn't look right." If I do not have an authoritative source at hand, I may try several different spellings of the word and hope that one of them clicks as looking right. All of this sounds to me much more like a connectionist system than a rule-based system. I could be wrong.

Maybe my brain contains 200 or more spelling rules[5] and runs through them at lightning speed, but my conscious awareness is no help in deciding if this is the case.

THE MIND AND THE WORLD

The connectionist mind is much more directly in contact with the world than is the symbol-processing mind conferred upon us by folk psychology. Being "more directly in contact with the world" does not, of course, mean bypassing sense organs and neural pathways. Remember, it is the mind, not the brain, I am talking about, and so the directness of contact is psychological. I like to think of psychological directness along the lines Joseph Church (1961), a phenomenologist, talked about in discussing the experience of writing with a pencil on rough paper. The sensation comes to us through vibrations of the pencil moving over the paper, but we do not experience the vibrations of the pencil. Instead, we feel the texture of the paper directly. Similarly, according to the connectionist view, we do not receive a pattern of visual stimuli that we interpret or recognize as a bear. Our visual system sees things, because that is what it is built to do. Given certain inputs, we see a bear. There is similar directness with respect to action. In the symbol-processing mind, the belief that a bear is approaching activates fear and a variety of escape schemata, whereas the connectionist mind has us clambering up the nearest tree.

Putting it more generally, the connectionist view of mind is at its best in making sense of people interacting in real time with things in the external world. The symbol-processing view interposes too many unlikely mental events. The symbol-processing view is best suited to rationalizing such behavior after the fact—to explaining, for instance, how one might reason one's way into climbing a tree to escape from a bear. In this case, the rationalized version probably has little resemblance to the actual mental events, which are likely to have been a jumble of thoughts and impressions accompanying rather than causing the physical actions. How do we explain someone's climbing a tree to escape a bear when they know bears can climb trees? For those who adopt the symbol-processing view, such behavior raises questions about human rationality. But from a connectionist view, there is nothing paradoxical about it. Given the real-world situation, there are only a few alternatives on which the cognitive system would have

---

[5]That is the number that Hanna, Hanna, Hodges, and Rudorf (1966) arrived at in an early attempt to work out rules for English spellings. However, even with that many rules a computer simulation was still able to spell correctly only about half of the 17,000 most common words (Simon & Simon, 1973).

much likelihood of settling: confront the bear, cower, turn tail and run (with the prospect of being seized from behind), step aside in hopes the bear will go past, and climb the tree.[6] Assuming there was no strong bias from prior experience, which option prevailed would likely depend on particularities of the situation. The sight of a reachable branch could well tip the balance in favor of tree climbing, whereas a slightly higher branch or a slightly less menacing bear might tip it in the direction of one of the other possibilities. Similarly, having previously seen a bear climb a tree (as opposed to having only heard that bears can do so) would no doubt greatly lower the attractiveness of the tree-climbing alternative.

There are cases, however, in which the rationalized version corresponds more closely to the experienced stream of thought. These are cases in which we are trying to work our way deliberately, step by step through a problem or a procedure. On such occasions we consciously invoke rules, recall facts, draw conclusions, and question beliefs. Indeed, when we are conscious of thinking, those are the kinds of things we are conscious of. No one is questioning that we have such abilities or that the experiences are genuine. There are times when we do act like logic machines, applying mental operations to symbolic representations.

Some cognitive scientists opt for a division of labor, awarding to a connectionist part of the mind the job of fleeing from bears and to a symbol-processing part of the mind the job of figuring out why going up a tree is not such a good idea. Keil and Silberstein (1996) argued very persuasively for what amount to two worlds inside the head, one part being occupied with theorizing and reasoning on the basis of causal relationships and the other part (the connectionist part) building up competence based on covariances (events and conditions that statistically go together in the environment, whether causally related or not). Others, such as John Anderson (1993) and Walter Kintsch (1998), treated it as a matter of levels. There is a cognitive level that works with rules or propositional representations and a subcognitive or subsymbolic level that functions in a connectionist manner. But a number of the world's cleverest people are busy trying to build connectionist systems that do the logical things that skeptics maintain they cannot do. To the extent that they succeed, we shall have support for a conception of the mind that is connectionist all the way to the top. According to this view, there are

---

[6]These options do not include what I have heard is the smart thing to do on meeting a bear, squat down so that the bear does not perceive you as challenging it. The behaviors I listed are all ones we are likely to have acquired in our encounters with menacing human beings. They may be thought of as templates for the rapid construction of a response in the bear situation. Our squatting template, however, is attuned to entirely different kinds of situations and so is unlikely to come into play unless we have been instructed.

no statements or rules for manipulating them in the head; it is just that, under favorable conditions, human beings are capable of doing a pretty good job of simulating the kind of logic machine that does manipulate stored symbols according to rules.

No matter how the theoretical differences are eventually worked out, there is one important departure from folk psychology that seems already too well established to fail any time soon. Because we are most conscious of mental activity at those times when we are deliberately applying rules to propositions, folk psychology assumes that the same kind of activity is going on the rest of the time, even though we are not aware of it or are not paying attention. The alternative view, urged by both connectionists and situativity theorists (e.g., Suchman, 1987), is that conscious thought is not simply being conscious of something that otherwise goes on unconsciously, it is a special kind of activity. We are not bystanders observing the flow of thought. Paying attention is a crucial part of thought itself. It produces a kind of thinking that does not occur otherwise, thinking that is systematic and deductive. This kind of thinking does not come easily to us. It is severely limited by the number of things we can pay attention to at the same time (Case, 1985b; Miller, 1956), and it is difficult to sustain over a long series of steps unless we have external aids. It has obvious strengths, as perhaps best exemplified by applied mathematics. Faced with a real-world problem, we can sometimes create a mathematical representation of it and then, by puzzling our way through the mathematical problem, arrive at a solution that, lo and behold, translates into a solution to the real-world problem. But most people go through 10 years or more of school mathematics without ever acquiring much facility in performing such a feat. Their normal ways of dealing with quantitative problems rely much more on affordances of the situation and on number sense (Lave, 1988), exhibiting behavior that is better modeled by connectionist than by rule-based systems.

MIND AND EMOTION

When asked about the role of emotions in cognition, an eminent cognitive scientist dismissed the question, saying, "That's just a hardware problem." In effect, he was saying that emotions may affect how well the cognitive computer runs its programs, but they have nothing to do with the programs themselves. Of course, there is some truth to that. Emotions can make the mind go haywire. But both common sense and decades of research on emotions and motivation argue for emotions having a much more extensive and complex role in our mental lives than that. These sources of wisdom argue, furthermore, that emotions can be beneficial as well as detrimental. From an evolutionary standpoint it can be argued that emotions must be good for something, otherwise we wouldn't have them. The unemotional would long ago have inherited the earth. However, it can also be argued that emotional volatility is a price we pay for having such a powerful and finely tuned cognitive engine.[7]

The problem for folk psychology and its symbol-processing derivatives is how to give emotions a role *in* cognition as contrasted with a relationship in which emotions and thoughts have effects *on* each another but are otherwise as distinct as the brain and the stomach, which also influence each other in sometimes quite pronounced ways. If the mind consists of mental content and rules for operating on it, emotions have no obvious place. They are not rules and they are not content in the usual sense. Emotions are states. That is how common sense puts it, in saying that an emotionally upset person is "in a state," and neuroscience offers us no reason to characterize emotions differently. How, then, can these states—which are physical as well as mental—affect cognition? They cannot function as rules, and they function as content only to the limited extent that we can have knowledge of our emotional states and use that knowledge in reaching decisions ("I'm too angry to talk calmly with him now; let's put off the meeting till tomorrow").

The prevailing view among cognitive psychologists who study emotion seems to be that emotions influence cognition by affecting attention and priorities (Oatley, 1992). Fear is not only a response to danger, it attunes us to look for danger. Anger sensitizes us to affronts. When we feel depressed we notice all the things that are wrong with ourselves and our lives. The result can be harmful buildups of emotion—acute or chronic anxiety, rage, or depression—but it can also lead to appropriate mobilization of our resources to meet problems and opportunities. Some clinical psychologists have proposed that depression, when it is brought on by things going badly, has adaptive value because it causes us to suspend action and think about what is wrong. Similarly, positive emotions of affection and happiness direct our attention to positive things that offer prospect of enhancing our well-being (and, in turn, that of the people we feel positively toward).

---

[7]Hebb and Thompson (1954) argued thus, offering evidence that the smarter the species, the more emotionally unstable it is, the apparent pinnacle having been reached by the chimpanzees. Anyone who has worked around these genetic neighbors of ours knows that their portrayal in movies as fun-loving free spirits is achieved only by editing out all their insane rages and panics. Hebb and Thompson went on to suggest that the trend toward emotional instability may not have reversed when it got to Homo sapiens, that we may be the most unstable species of all, except for the fact that we are able to arrange our physical and social environment in ways that keep us sane most of the time.

One of the problems for rule-based models of cognition is that at any given time there are likely to be a number of rules ready to be activated. (Rules have the form of if–then or condition–action pairings, and so whenever the "if" conditions are met, the rule is ready to fire.) Thus, there has to be an auxiliary process or set of rules that resolves issues of precedence (Anderson, 1983). Emotions could play this role, boosting the priority of certain rules and reducing that of others. They would not likely impinge on individual rules but could affect the priority of combinations of rules, such as plans. According to Oatley and Johnson-Laird (1987), emotions play a monitoring function with respect to people's goals. When something happens to alter the probability of achieving some goal, an emotional response

> draws the attention of the rest of the cognitive system, and sometimes of other individuals, to the kind of goal-relevant event that has occurred, a subgoal achievement, a goal loss, a goal conflict, or the like. The control signal tends to set the cognitive system into a distinctive mode appropriate to this kind of event. It makes ready a certain reportoire of actions, and it creates a preoccupation with what has occurred that assists further planning. (Oatley, 1992, p. 174)

These are important functions of emotions, but they still leave emotions on the outside of cognition, acting as a sort of Greek chorus, calling attention to discrepancies, cheering and encouraging one kind of action, discouraging another, but not contributing substance of their own to cognitive processes. In connectionist models, however, emotions enjoy a much more natural fit. Emotions are mental states, but so are thoughts and knowledge. In principle they need not be separated. Instead of thoughts arousing emotions and emotions triggering thoughts, we may simply think of feelings and cognitive content as attributes of any state of knowing. Often the content is vivid but the feelings are negligible, as when we learn that the square of 15 is 225. Sometimes both the content and the feelings are prominent, as when we receive alarming or cheering news. But of special interest are feelings about objects of knowledge accompanied by little or no content. These are instances when we say about an idea or a situation that it "feels good" or "doesn't feel right" but can say nothing much beyond that. Yet such feelings function as knowledge. They serve as guides to action and they play a central role in creative thinking (Bereiter & Scardamalia, 1993, chap. 5). In ordinary language they are referred to as intuitions and are mysterious. For symbol-processing conceptions of mind they are bound to remain mysterious, because they cannot be explained in terms of mental operations performed on mental objects. But for connectionist conceptions of mind there is nothing mysterious about them at all. Feeling good about an idea is a knowledge state as much as any other. It is what I discuss in chapter 5 as "impressionistic knowledge", but it is not categorically different from other knowledge. It lies at one end of a continuum, with things like knowing the square of 15 at the other end, and infinite gradations in between.

THE REDISCOVERY OF HUMAN NATURE

Let us return to the matter of babies apparently being born knowing that the world is composed of objects distributed in three-dimensional space. Research on young children has given reason to believe that babies are born either already endowed with a considerable amount of knowledge or at least biologically prepared so that they will readily acquire knowledge that takes certain predetermined forms (Hirschfeld & Gelman, 1994). Instead of the "booming, buzzing confusion" that William James said babies are born into, it seems they are born into a world their brains have already organized for them. Besides the general spatial organization just referred to, which enables them quickly to pick out and learn to identify objects, they are especially attuned to pick out one particular kind of object: the human face. Besides being disposed to associate sounds with their sources, they are especially attentive to linguistic sounds. The speed with which they master the awesome complexity of language suggests their brains automatically organize speech input in ways that conform to linguistic structures. Children also appear to grasp number quickly and in ways that go beyond what they could have gained from direct experience or instruction. For instance, at a time when they can only count up to 10, they seem already to have grasped the idea of infinity—that numbers go on increasing indefinitely, that there is always a next number. The infant's mental world seems to be organized causally: Young children spontaneously seek out causes for events and predict and watch for consequences. Along with this causal orientation comes a distinction between animate and inanimate things and a disposition to assign "essences" to things—inner characteristics that remain constant despite outward changes and that determine how things will behave.[8]

From studies of identical twins come indications that the innate mental endowment may include many more specific dispositions as well. By now most people have heard the amazing tales of twins separated as infants who are brought together in middle age and find that they have the same breed of dog as a pet and have given it the

---

[8]Evidence of these innate dispositions and capacities is gathered in Hirschfeld and Gelman (1994).

same name and that they have the same preferences in food, music, politics, sexual partners, and practically everything else. One need take only a small part of this seriously to appreciate that theories of mind face a significant challenge in accounting for what our brains already have in them at birth.

Ideas that link genetics and psychology inevitably encounter heated opposition. Ever since the Hitler era there has been the fear that accepting such links will open the door to eugenics and racial cleansing. But there is an additional obstacle to accepting the ideas summarized here, and that is that folk theory of mind makes them seem utterly mysterious. If the genes contain instructions that determine our fingerprints, such that identical twins have identical fingerprints, they could certainly contain an instruction to buy an Oldsmobile or a set of rules for parsing sentences. That is not the problem. The problem is how knowledge, attitudes, and the like that people acquire through experience could get translated into genetic material that gets passed to their offspring. That sounds like inheritance of acquired characteristics, which we have all been taught is wrong. Invoking natural selection does not solve the problem, however. Being able to recognize human faces no doubt has survival value for the infant, but how does the *knowledge* that distinguishes a human face from the same set of features arranged differently get from the mind into the genes? And how does it then get from the genes into the inheritor's mind? As far as I can see, these are unanswerable questions as long as we hold to a theory that posits the brain as one thing and mental content as another.

From a connectionist standpoint, there is nothing much more puzzling about the inheritance of knowledge than about the inheritance of any other complex characteristic. We are born with a connectionist network of sorts in our heads that is already running. As we learn, the network undergoes modifications. But what we learn and how we learn are heavily influenced by the initial state and structure of the network, which in turn are largely determined by the genes. At different points in its history, a connectionist network may be settled in its behavior, responding to inputs in stable and highly differentiated ways, or it may be quite unsettled, responding to inputs in variable and only grossly differentiated ways. It is still the same network. It is not a matter of there being different content or different amounts of content at different times.

Throughout most of its brief history, educational psychology has been absorbed with individual differences, and nature–nurture issues have been considered only from that standpoint. Attention to the genetic side yielded little of pedagogical interest, being an aspect of individual differences that education could not be expected to do anything about. As Benjamin Bloom (1969, p. 419) put it, "The educator must be an environmentalist .... If heredity imposes a limit—so be it. The educator must work with what is left, whether it be 20 percent of the variance or 50 percent." At the same time, however, pedagogical wisdom put great stress on "starting where the child is at"—that is, building on students' existing knowledge and skills instead of starting from zero or some arbitrary point, as prescribed curricula are wont to do. It is now becoming evident that applying this wisdom is a much more complex business than our default environmentalism had led us to imagine.

"Where the child is at" and what the child is best disposed to learn are turning out to have a great deal to do with "nature." But it is not nature conceived of as inherited individual differences. It is nature conceived of as the whole complex of cognitive attunements, dispositions, and prestructurings of knowledge that characterize our species. For instance, there is some reason to believe that we are born with a network well attuned to additive numerical structures, such as the structure represented by the whole number line, but that we have no prior attunement to multiplicative structures, such as we encounter with ratios and proportions, and that this goes some way toward explaining why ratios and proportions are so hard to learn (Resnick, 1987).

Connectionism is sometimes referred to as "the new connectionism" to distinguish it from an obsolete theory of the same name advanced by E. L. Thorndike (1949) and traceable to John Locke and British "associationism."[9] Now we have a "new innatism," different in focus and intent from the older kind. In combination, these provide a novel perspective on what a new theory of mind for the Knowledge Age should be like. Rather than its being some kind of high-tech theory that conceives of the mind at a very abstract level of logic or knowledge processing, it must be a theory rooted in the fact that we are biological organisms—in short, animals. Like all chordates, we come into the world with nervous systems designed to perceive the world, relate to it, and act toward it in certain ways. We are animals with an amazing range of capacities, which include a capacity to create and share bodies of abstract knowledge. But we do this using a brain whose design evolved under conditions radically different from those of a 21st-century knowledge worker. As Cosmides and Tooby (199) noted:

---

[9]The older connectionism did not entail rejecting the mind-as-container metaphor. Its distinctiveness lay in proposing that the items in the mental container were little bits of ideas, which acquired structure and force through connections to one another that were formed through experience. Thus, the older connectionism is really more similar to some symbolic artificial intelligence models (e.g., Anderson, 1983) than it is to the new connectionism.

The key to understanding how the modern mind works is to real- ize that its circuits were not designed to solve the day-to-day prob- lems of a modern American—they were designed to solve the day-to-day problems of our hunter-gatherer ancestors. These stone age priorities produced a brain far better at solving some problems than others. For example, it is easier for us to deal with small, hunter-gatherer-band sized groups of people than with crowds of thousands; it is easier for us to learn to fear snakes than electric sockets, even though electric sockets pose a larger threat than snakes do in most American communities. In many cases, our brains are better at solving the kinds of problems our ancestors faced on the African savannahs than they are at solving the more familiar tasks we face in a college classroom or a modern city. In saying that our modern skulls house a stone age mind, we do not mean to imply that our minds are unsophisticated. Quite the con- trary: they are very sophisticated computers, whose circuits are elegantly designed to solve the kinds of problems our ancestors routinely faced. (p. 56)

How that Stone Age brain biases and constrains the knowledge we create—including the knowledge we create about ourselves—is something developmental psychologists are only beginning to reckon with. At this time it is impossible to be definite about what the educational implications of rediscovering human nature will be. Some general expectations are the following:

- Curricula may be strengthened by building on innate knowl- edge or knowledge-constructing tendencies. This is already happening in elementary mathematics instruction.
- As knowledge advances in all the disciplines, it seems likely that more and more of what is to be learned will be counterintuitive in the way that theories in physics tend to be. Accordingly, it will become increasingly important to recog- nize obstacles imposed by built-in ways of thinking and con- ceptualizing.
- The kinds of behavior and dispositions required in educational institutions may run contrary to innate dispositions. For in- stance, distractability—now more ominously labeled "atten- tional deficit"—has come to be recognized as a trait, found in a substantial minority of children, that interferes with school learning. Yet if we consider a group of our ancestors engaged in hunting or gathering in a dangerous environment, a good ar- rangement would be to have most individuals in the group steadily focused on their tasks, while a significant minority are highly sensitive to extraneous stimuli that may signal danger

or an unanticipated opportunity. Thus, what we see in class-rooms may represent a generally beneficial species characteristic that happens to be ill-adapted to a particular recently created environment. This is only a speculation, but it illustrates the relevance of an evolutionary perspective on contemporary behavioral problems.

These are all in the nature of promissory notes. We do not know that recognizing built-in resistances to advanced learning will lead to our being able to do anything about those resistances. An evolutionary perspective on behavioral and attitudinal problems may have explanatory value yet not turn out to have practical value. But that is always how it is with advances in theoretical sciences. Practical people have to bet on futures. For those who sense that the burgeoning research on human nature will have future payoffs, there is good reason to start looking for a theory of mind that can make sense of this research.

A COMMONSENSE WAY OF GOING BEYOND COMMON SENSE

What I have been calling the "connectionist" mind could as well have been called the "self-organizing" mind. Connectionism is part of a much larger movement, affecting all the sciences, toward trying to provide rigorous explanations of emergent phenomena. Self-organization is one of the key ideas. Considering the rate at which the field is developing, connectionist models as they are presently known are sure to become old hat very soon, and the name itself is likely to be abandoned when its associations become bothersome. I am going to keep using the terms "connectionist" and "connectionism," because of their currency;[10] however, what really matters is not the particular scientific models that go by that name, but the way of thinking they represent.

Wherever biological or behavioral scientists look these days, they see marvelously complex systems that represent an assembly of much simpler components that have somehow gotten themselves organized without benefit of a higher, guiding intelligence. This is the case with evolution (Dennett, 1995; Kauffman, 1993), termite colonies (Wilson, 1996), business organizations (Svyantek & Brown,

---

[10]This may prove to be a tactical error. Tribalism and its accompaniment, tribal warfare, are stil lto be found in the social sciences and are especially common in education. So, to the extent that using the term "connectionism" identifies me with a tribe, I can expect hostility from that tribe's enemies.

2000), and child development (Thelen & Smith, 1994). Human learning itself must have this character, otherwise it is impossible to explain how we can ever learn anything more complex than what we already know (Quartz, 1993). In the popular and educational media there is overheated talk about fractals, chaos, and how the fluttering of a butterfly's wing can affect the climate on the other side of the world, but these effusions should not obscure the fact that a lot of serious work is under way.

A new level of explanation seems to be emerging. We all know the shortcomings of explanations that take the form A causes B, B causes C, and so on in a chain. A second level of explanation takes the form A, B, C, and so on, *in combination* produce X. You can find everything from creative genius to heart disease explained this way. The weakness of this kind of explanation is that it offers no explanation of how the various factors act to produce a result. It is just empirical. The new level of explanation depends heavily on computer simulation (which is partly why it is new). Simulate A, B, and C by creating computational objects that behave like A, B, and C. Also simulate the environment in which they act. Then set A, B, and C and their confederates in motion within the virtual environment and demonstrate that X emerges. With success, you have not only improved the prediction of X but have demystified it. You have shown how it comes about through the interaction of processes (the behavior of A, B, and C) that were already understood. Connectionist simulations have this character. Feed in data about the frequency with which various objects are found in the same room and you witness the emergence of concepts like *kitchen* and *bedroom*, such that the system can now make reasonable inferences about what room it is, given information about objects in it, or about what a room contains, given its type (Rumelhart, Smolensky, McClelland, & Hinton, 1986). Yet no definitions or rules have been introduced and none are to be found in the system. The concepts of *kitchen* and so on are the result of self-organization among the simpler elements.

Common sense is not well equipped in general to think along the lines of self-organizing systems, but it is especially handicapped in thinking this way about learning. Some version of A causes B or A, in conjunction with B, causes C tends to dominate the thinking of even postmodern educators. Too much is lost when new ideas are translated into those commonsense formulas, and so the practitioner-oriented literature keeps getting farther out of contact with what is going on in the underlying behavioral sciences.

A more immediate reason for learning to think in connectionist terms is to make progress in dealing with what is now vaguely referred to as tacit knowledge. Business people have suddenly become intensely aware of it and it is much discussed in the knowledge management literature (e.g., Nonaka & Takeuchi, 1995; Stewart, 1997). It is knowledge that isn't written down anywhere. It tends to vanish when people leave or when working groups dissolve. It isn't private facts. It is the skills and what I discuss in chapter 5 as "implicit understanding" that make people and organizations smart. For folk theory of mind it will remain forever mysterious, because it cannot be pinned down to objects in the mind. And so it also tends to be ignored in education. I have mentioned number sense as an example, but there is more: historical sense, geographical sense, moral sense, tact, taste and appreciation, background knowledge (what you need, for instance, to understand a Jane Austen novel in the context of the time and place and social world of its characters and of Austen herself as a part of that world), and acquired instincts—"a nose for news," the ability to recognize promising leads, problems, or ideas in a domain (Bereiter & Scardamalia, 1993, chap. 5). Educators readily acknowledge these as things that really count, that may be of more enduring value than any particular skill or item of knowledge, but they are addressed only through hand waving and wishful thinking.

Educators and knowledge managers alike need a way of thinking that brings these kinds of knowledge into the natural order. Folk theory and the psychologies grounded in it are out of their depth here. Recognizing that an alternative theory is only starting to take shape, however, what should those of us concerned with education and other knowledge arts do in the meantime? The following are suggestions:

- *Minimize cognitive speculation.* We need mentalistic description but we should not go farther with it than necessary. In chapter 4 I try to show how far we can get in dealing with problems of understanding without having to speculate on what is in the mind of the understander.
- *Recognize that talk about mental content and mental operations may be only a manner of speaking, useful for some purposes and not for others.* It may turn out to be more than a manner of speaking, but it is never going to turn out to be less. And as far as I can see, there is no practical loss and considerable practical gain from treating mental content and mental operations as useful fictions.
- *Instead of hypothesizing what does or does not come naturally, look at the evidence on what does or does not profit from instruction and on kinds of attainments that are particularly easy or difficult.* We know that many students who master whole-

number arithmetic get lost in ratios and proportions. Maybe this has something to do with how our brains are built, and it would be interesting to know, but in the meantime it stands as a brute fact that responsible mathematics educators must contend with. We also know that about 85% of children master reading relatively easily, regardless of how they are taught, and that the other 15% have difficulties, sometimes very serious ones. None of the arguments about whether reading is a natural outgrowth of innate language competence or a kind of unnatural act alters the proportions one bit. The problem is exacerbated, however, by ideologically committed reading specialists, some of whom ignore the 85% and some of whom ignore the 15%.

- *Don't worry about distinguishing knowledge from other kinds of competence. If it is mental and useful, call it knowledge.* Jane has studied weather maps and the location of the jet stream and has compared the predictions from several weather stations, from which she concludes it is going to be sunny tomorrow. Joe believes it is going to rain because it always rains on their picnic. Lana has a good feeling about tomorrow and is sure it will be a nice day. Hugh feels in his bones that rainy weather is coming. Do some of these have knowledge and others not? Does the answer depend on who turns out to be right? Or would you say that no one *knows* what tomorrow's weather will be? For practical purposes, we are better off avoiding such questions than trying to answer them. As I try to show in chapter 5, there is value in distinguishing among the different *kinds* of knowledge represented in these examples, but in practical terms they all represent knowledge that is relevant to action. Lana's feelings may not be good for predicting the weather but in other situations they may be a more reliable guide than Jane's bookish analyses and Joe's experience-based cautiousness. They are all kinds of knowledge worth cultivating, worth learning how to use.

These suggestions add up to a restrained kind of mentalism. We should not, like behaviorists, avoid mentalistic descriptions. We cannot function in the knowledge arts without talking about what people think, feel, know, and understand. Indeed, we want to widen not narrow the range of what counts as part of human knowing. But to do this sensibly we need to avoid premature commitments as to the nature of what goes on between the ears. That does not mean being theoretically unmindful. It means trying to adopt a course that will not prove gravely wrong however the theoretical cognitive issues are eventually worked out.

CONCLUSION

I am always dubious about educational discussions having to do with the brain. Too often they consist of excited reports of advances in neuroscience, accompanied by hints that any educator who fails to keep up with them will soon be out to pasture, but with no clear indication of why educators in general should be more than casually interested. Is this chapter further ado about matters that can safely be put on the "read later" pile? Of course I think the answer is no, but the reasons I can advance at this point cannot be very compelling. I must trust that conviction will grow as ideas are developed further and in more educationally targeted ways in later chapters.

No law requires that a theory of mind be biologically plausible. The endurance of the existing theory of mind is proof of that. To recapitulate an earlier argument, we need a mentalistic level of description, a way of talking about behavior in terms of intentions, beliefs, and the like. But we could employ mentalistic description without a concept of mind. That would seem to be what people do when they use mentalistic terms to explain the behavior of a computer or a fish. The concept of mind enters when we try to give more complete and integrated explanations of behavior. But mind could still be a hypothetical construct with no necessary correspondence to biological reality. It could be like the *market*, as referred to by financial reporters: "The market responded quickly to news of the assassination," "The market took a wait-and-see attitude toward the offering," and so on. Although "the market" is endowed with humanlike qualities, it has no necessary correspondence to anything in the material world. It is a way of expressing general trends and tendencies. Perhaps that is all "the mind" is required to be.

I have introduced two reasons, however, why a theory of mind for education needs to be more realistic. One is to deal with the vast areas of learning that do not lend themselves to formulation as mental content but that can better be understood as mental adaptations to things in the world. The other is to deal with what the newborn's brain brings into the world with it—human nature, instinct, innate knowledge, and dispositions—however we may choose to formulate it. I will not be pursuing this second reason in this book. I expect that the rediscovery of human nature is going to have much significance for education, but I am in no position to argue that case at present or to contribute to its furtherance. But I will be pursuing the first reason throughout the remaining chapters. I think I can show that a biologically more realistic theory of mind is better able to handle most of the major goals of education, especially teaching for understanding.

Perhaps the main reason we need a more realistic theory of mind for the Knowledge Age, however, is to get the mind disentangled from knowledge. Obviously mind and knowledge are related. But if, as some economists say, the main wealth-generating activity of the future is going to be knowledge production, it seems two things are required: (a) to conceive of knowledge as something other than stuff inside individual people's minds and (b) to understand the role of individual minds in societal knowledge production. Folk theory is not up to either of these requirements. A connectionist view of mind makes the first conceivable and provides at least a starting point for the second. In the next chapters I try to move beyond this starting point.

3

Knowledge Outside the Mind

The history of philosophy shows us very clearly that the full deter-
mination of a concept is very rarely the work of that thinker who
first introduced that concept. For a philosophical concept is, generally speaking, rather a problem than the solution of a problem—
and the full significance of this problem cannot be understood so
long as it is still in its first implicit state. It must become explicit in
order to be comprehended in its true meaning, and this transition
from an implicit to an explicit state is the work of the future.

—Cassirer (1944, p. 180)

One sign that we are ill-prepared for the Knowledge Age is that
we do not have enough words. Modern languages have a vast number of words for describing human traits and feelings, for instance,
far more words than most people can find a use for. And our vocabulary of technical terms expands as science and technology require.
But we find words like "learning," "information," "teaching," and
"knowledge" each holding down two or more jobs, not doing any of
them very well, and getting in each other's way to boot.

There is an obvious reason for this discrepancy. People have probably been discussing each other's traits and feelings since the dawn of civilization, whereas the need to talk about things like learning, information, and knowledge is a recent development, coinciding roughly with the institutionalization of these concerns. Within their own groups, educators, philosophers, information technologists, cognitive psychologists, and others may use such words with fair confidence that they know what their fellows are talking about. But now there is a need for these groups to talk to one another, and for this the old implicit meanings cannot be trusted.

The problem is not one that can be solved by getting people to agree on what each term means, however. That would leave some concepts with no words to represent them. Furthermore, it is not simply a matter of people being clear about what they mean; it is a matter of meaning the right things. That is, we need concepts, suitably labeled, that help rather than hinder the formulating and solving of problems and (I can't help using one of the terms already) the advancement of knowledge.

When people are speaking casually about knowledge, they make fairly good sense. It is only when they are trying to be careful or systematic that they get into tangles. In casual talk, people blithely treat knowledge as having a dual character. On one hand, they treat it as something real in itself. They talk about knowledge being contained in books, about the state of knowledge in a field, about the advance of knowledge, about the sharing and dissemination of knowledge, and so on. On the other hand, they treat it in the way that was discussed in the preceding chapter, as content in individual minds. That is how people talk about acquiring knowledge, about people having much or little knowledge of a subject, and so on. When they are writing articles for prestigious journals, however, people seem to become uncomfortable with this dualism and so they avoid talking about knowledge as having a life of its own and stick to the things-in-the-mind conception of knowledge, believing that to be the more defensible one.

If forced to choose, people dealing with social or economic issues would probably be better off making the opposite choice, treating knowledge as stuff out there in cyberspace and ignoring the psychological aspect. That is what epistemologists and historians of knowledge have generally done. But ignoring the human element is always dangerous, especially when the point of deliberations is to reform human institutions such as industries, governments, public media, and schools. Thus, we need either to face up to the dualism or to find a satisfactory way of resolving it.

In this chapter I discuss two approaches to resolving the dualism. One way comes from what is variously known as sociocultural theory, situated cognition, or situativity theory. This approach avoids both sides of the dualism: Knowledge does not exist either in a world of its own or as stuff in individual minds but is an aspect of cultural practice. Knowledge is not either produced or acquired but is *constituted* in communities of practice and *embodied* in the tools of such practice. This approach has proved illuminating in many respects, but in my view it is most applicable to traditional, slowly evolving communities of practice and is not an approach that will carry us very far into the Knowledge Age.

The alternative approach that I develop centers around the idea of *conceptual artifacts*, which are human constructions like other artifacts, except they are immaterial and, instead of serving purposes such as cutting, lifting, and inscribing, they serve purposes such as explaining and predicting. These conceptual artifacts, in turn, become part of the vast array of things we can become knowledgeable about. Thus, both of the commonsense ways of conceiving of knowledge are maintained but in a more coherent and—I hope to show—usable way.

KNOWLEDGE EMBEDDED IN CULTURAL PRACTICE

"Sociocultural" describes a variety of theoretical positions that attribute an inherently social character to knowledge and learning. Some versions remain implicitly based on folk theory of mind, extending it to the social plane with concepts such as *intersubjectivity* (Bruner, 1990; Olson & Bruner, 1996). Others, however—those going by the names of "activity theory" and "situated cognition" (Davydov & Radzikhovskii, 1985; Suchman, 1987)—explicitly reject the mind-as-container metaphor.

Where is knowledge if it isn't contained in individual minds? The kind of answer coming from activity and situated cognition theorists runs along the following lines: Knowledge is not lodged in any physical or metaphorical organ. Rather, knowledge inheres in social practices and in the tools and artifacts used in those practices. Learning, as it pertains to individuals, is a process of moving from peripheral to full participation in cultural practices (Lave & Wenger, 1991). At another level, learning is the evolution of those practices.

This "situated" view of cognition is very similar in form to the connectionist view of mind, although on a different plane. In both, knowledge is regarded as *distributed*. This does not mean merely that it is spread around, a bit here and a bit there, like the pieces of a treasure map. Knowledge does not consist of little bits. It has been said of connectionist models that "all the knowledge is in the connections" (Rumelhart, 1989, p. 135). Similarly, we may say of situated cognition that all the knowledge is in the relationships—relationships among the people engaged in an activity, the tools they use, and the material conditions of the environment in which the activity takes place. This does not mean that connectionism and situated cognition are essentially the same theory or even that they are compatible. It means they employ the same abstract model (Ohlsson, 1993), so that if you can understand one you can probably understand the other, and if you cannot understand one you probably cannot understand the other.

Some of the most compelling arguments against the mind-as-container metaphor have come from the situated cognition literature (e.g., Agre, 1997; Lave & Wenger, 1991; Suchman, 1987). An important body of research motivated by the situated view of cognition has examined how learning goes on in nonformal settings, such as workplaces (Rogoff & Lave, 1984; Suchman, 1987). This research has revealed an important irony. Learning, as it goes on among "just plain folks," as Jean Lave calls them, is not at all congruent with folk theory. People do not acquire items of mental content, which they then take out on occasion and use. Instead, they learn how to take part in what is going on and how to function intelligently in the work environment. Folk theory of mind much better fits what is supposed to go on in schools, as far as the official curriculum is concerned, than what goes on in ordinary life. This is understandable, however, inasmuch as schools are contrived institutions designed according to what people believe about knowledge and learning (Olson & Bruner, 1996).

For understanding the nature of knowledge and its uses, one of the most instructive studies is by Sylvia Scribner (1984) on dairy workers who load trucks or deliver dairy products to stores. The workers have to deal continually with quantitative relationships—assembling cases according to the number of pints of this and quarts of that in an order, computing costs, and so on, but little use of school mathematics was evident. Instead, the workers had clever ways of using the fixed row-by-column layouts of packing cases to minimize mental calculation (and to minimize bending and lifting). An observer could abstract the mathematical knowledge implicit in such activity and give it a formal description (which the workers might very likely have been unable to understand). But such formalized knowledge would have little value, because it would only apply to packing cases and items of certain dimensions. In effect, it would apply only to the observed situation and others much like it, and workers in those situations would not need such formalizations.

There is no question that a great deal of what we know is of this highly situated kind. One of my most routinized tasks is fixing two cups of café latte each morning to get my wife and me started on our day. General instructions for accomplishing this task—the kind that come with the espresso machine—cover only a small part of what actually goes on. Yet a more detailed description would for the most part be useless to people in other situations. The order in which things are done is adapted to the physical layout of the kitchen. That is why I discard the old coffee grounds on the way to picking up cups for the new batch. My coffee-making behavior is not rigidly fixed, however. There are all sorts of minor variations, some adapting to irregularities such as there being no clean coffee cups or the compost pail not being there to receive the coffee grounds, some having no apparent rationale at all, but they are all variations within the set of relationships connecting myself, the various tools of the task, and features of the kitchen environment. How long I run the espresso machine is not determined by time (which varies, depending on how tightly the coffee powder is packed) or by the measured volume of liquid that comes out. I just know what the right amount of coffee looks like when I peer into the cup, and this of course varies with the cup. One of the more eccentric features of my coffee-making practice is that I do push-ups while the espresso machine is running. This has nothing to do with making the coffee, but it nicely illustrates a point situativity researchers often make: that to understand situated action, we must not limit attention to discrete tasks and goals but must keep in mind that what people are mainly doing is living their lives, and this commonly means having multiple goals simultaneously operative. Coffee making provides the right place and the right amount of otherwise uncommitted time for doing the kind of modified push-ups I do, and making them part of the coffee routine makes it much less likely that I neglect to do them.

The distributed nature of situated knowledge becomes even more evident when we look at mass behavior, such as that of people walking along a crowded sidewalk. How everyone manages to keep moving at a fairly brisk pace without collisions, usually without even brushing up against one another, is quite amazing—although it is worth noting that fish are even better at getting about in dense traffic than we are. This is not just a matter of individual skills. There are evolved social practices, such as veering to the right, which make it possible. This becomes evident when the crowd contains people from different cultures with different right–left biases and no doubt different signals, different body language. Then one sees people zigging when they should be zagging and the smooth flow of traffic being disrupted.

Such homespun examples are not far off from the kinds of activity situated cognition researchers have studied most closely. Situated cognition research has dealt mainly with traditional crafts, everyday activities, and low-status occupations (reviewed in Lave & Wenger, 1991). This raises what is for me the most serious question about situated cognition: How relevant is it to the modern world—to nontraditional occupations, to formal education, to rapidly advancing technologies that draw on abstract knowledge, in short, to the Knowledge Age?

On one hand, there is no doubt that the activities of workers in a software development shop or a biomedical research laboratory or an investment firm show the same kinds of situatedness as my coffee-making behavior or the behavior of shoppers in the holiday season rush. To make short work of it, let us simply acknowledge that all our behavior is situated, in the same way that all fish behavior and all squirrel behavior is situated (Bereiter, 1997). Should not this be the starting point rather than the ending point of our effort to understand human knowledge?

Scribner's (1984) account of dairy work included an interesting subplot. During the summer, high school students were hired to work along with the regular truck loaders. These novices, it was observed, did use school mathematics in figuring out how many containers of one product and another were required to fulfill an order. The point Scribner made was that the students' procedures were slower and more prone to error than those of the experienced workers. But looked at another way, school mathematics enabled the students to start right in doing the job without having to go through an apprenticeship or a long period of bumbling around.

School arithmetic has the advantage that it works in an unlimited range of situations, perhaps never as well as knowledge evolved in and adapted to each particular situation, but usually much better than quantity-manipulating knowledge evolved in one situation being transferred to another (Saxe, 1991). School mathematics seems to represent a different kind of knowledge, a kind that is in some sense less situated. That is, it is not knowledge embedded in some community of practice but rather it is knowledge there for the taking, by anyone who has access to it and who can make something of it. This, I believe, is the knowledge we are talking about when we talk about the Knowledge Age and knowledge-creating companies. Without denying the importance of situated knowledge, we need to work out a clearer understanding of this other kind of knowledge.

KNOWLEDGE AS PRODUCT

The most fundamental confusion I see standing in the way of understanding what the Knowledge Age is about is a confusion between the knowledge used in productive work and the knowledge that is the object of such work. In traditional manufacturing and service industries the distinction is not important, because only the first kind of knowledge is involved. If a company is in the business of making ice cream or cleaning furnaces, then, as situated cognition theorists would put it, the company comprises a community of practice in which is constituted a knowledge of ice cream making or furnace cleaning. In the course of productive work, new knowledge is generated, but it is further knowledge of making ice cream or cleaning furnaces. Thus, the new knowledge remains constituted within the community of practice. The knowledge that comes out of the work remains part of the work. The product of the work is something entirely different.

But let us now consider a company whose business is producing knowledge. An opinion research organization will serve as an example. Such an organization carries out polls or interviews to find out what the public or some segment of it thinks about one thing or another. Its clientele may include political parties, manufacturers of consumer goods, or anyone who is prepared to put up money to gain some particular knowledge of current public opinion. The knowledge that goes into opinion research is quite various. It includes formal knowledge of sampling statistics but also a great deal of informal knowledge having to do with how questions are phrased and posed and with the interpretation of results. Much of this is situated knowledge along the lines discussed in the preceding section. However, this is not the knowledge delivered to customers. The knowledge delivered to them is knowledge about the public, its opinions, attitudes, and beliefs relative to some object or issue of interest. The work of the opinion research organization thus, generates knowledge of two kinds. One kind is knowledge that is inseparable from the work itself, because it is constituted by the evolving skills and practices of the people who compose the organization. The other kind is knowledge that is of no value unless it can be separated from the community that produced it. It is knowledge that the company produces and sells, much as a bootmaker produces and sells boots.

"Intellectual property" is a legal term applied to this merchantable kind of knowledge. The concept of intellectual property has limited value in characterizing knowledge, but it gives us a foothold. For intellectual property implies something that has existence in its own right. Otherwise, how could there be a dispute about who owns it?

But intellectual property is not something material. It is not the bound report that the opinion research company delivers to the client; it is the knowledge contained in that report.

By expanding the concept of intellectual property beyond its legal boundaries, we can identify more broadly a type of knowledge whose distinguishing features are the following:

1. it consists of immaterial things, not physical objects; and
2. these things have an objective, out-in-the-world existence—they are not the contents of people's minds.

This broader category of intellectual property is already widely recognized in science and scholarship. Professional ethics typically dictate acknowledging the source of ideas, even when they have not been published, and of recognizing priority when several people have independently proposed the same idea. But professional ethics stop short of giving credit for mental content. Your claim to have thought of a proof for Fermat's last theorem years ago, although you never publicized it or even wrote it down, will not get you much sympathy, let alone honor. As some writer I can no longer identify remarked, every good idea has already been thought of by somebody else, who did not appreciate its significance.

But it is not just making the private public or making the implicit explicit that is at issue here. Folk theory and situated cognition theory can handle those aspects of knowledge (cf. Nonaka & Takeuchi, 1995). What folk theory does not handle well is the status of knowledge once it is pried loose from the mind of the individual knower. Correspondingly, situated cognition theory falls short when it comes to handling the status of knowledge once it is pried loose from practice. What happens with such prying loose, I believe, is a level shift that is as radical as the shift from a barter to a money economy. Indeed, the shift is very similar to that from barter to money and it is what makes a knowledge-based economy a realistic possibility rather than merely a figure of speech.

Money, in fact, provides an instructive analogy for understanding this idea of knowledge as immaterial but real. We grow up thinking of money as material stuff—coins and bills. But as the movement advances toward a cashless economy, money becomes increasingly abstract. Getting paid for your work once meant being handed an envelope with cash in it; then it became receiving a check; now it is likely to mean a transfer between your employer's bank account and yours, with no material object of any kind changing hands. But money is no less real for being abstract, a fact that people with wallets full of credit cards reportedly sometimes fail to appreciate. And in a deeper sense money has always been abstract. That is what makes a dime a dime—a tenth of a dollar—and not just a small metal disk. An argument sometimes brought against treating knowledge as real is that it would cease to exist if all the people who know of it were to die. But the same is true of money. Roman coins are not money any longer; they are just coins. The money vanished with the people among whom those coins were accepted as legal tender.

Ideas, facts, theories, algorithms, designs, problem formulations and problem solutions—these are all abstract. Commonly they are represented in some material form, such as a book, just as money is commonly represented in the material form of coins and banknotes. But the representation or concrete embodiment is not the knowledge. When we argue about a theory or design we are not arguing about a piece of paper or about the particular words or lines on the piece of paper. We are arguing about the abstract knowledge object of which those words or lines are but one possible representation.

I refer to these abstract objects as *conceptual artifacts*. The idea, although not the name, comes from the work of Karl Popper. In the appendix to this book I discuss the idea and various controversies surrounding it, but here I simply try to show that the idea makes sense and is useful.

THE IDEA OF CONCEPTUAL ARTIFACTS

Popper (1972) distinguished between three worlds—the physical world, the subjective or mental world, and the world of ideas. To sharpen the distinction, he assigned them numbers: World 1, World 2, and World 3. Popper stressed three points about his third world that seem to me crucial for getting straight about the role of knowledge in the Knowledge Age. First, the contents of World 3 are entirely human creations. Second, these human creations, like other human creations, are fallible but improvable. Thus, knowledge becomes, in Popper's view, something you can work with. Finally, and most controversially, these human creations take on a life of their own, independent of their creators. They can be found to have characteristics, virtues and faults, implications and applications, that their creators could not have foreseen.

I elaborate on the meaning of conceptual artifacts later, and for those who are interested a much fuller discussion is given in the appendix. For a first pass, *conceptual* may be understood to refer to discussible ideas, ranging from theories, designs, and plans down to concepts, like unemployment and gravity. *Artifact* conveys that these are human creations and that they are created to some purpose. However, being conceptual, they are not concrete artifacts, either, as are books, statues, and fire hydrants.

Conceptual artifacts share many of the characteristics of material artifacts. Consider the concept of natural selection and how it compares with a material artifact like an automobile:

They both have origins and histories.
They can be described.
They can be compared with other artifacts of their type.
They may be valued or judged worthless.
They have varied uses.
They may be modified and improved upon.
They may be a subject of discussion.
New attributes, uses, or defects may be discovered that were not foreseen when they were created.
People differ in how well they understand them and in how skillful they are in using them.

Especially in practical affairs, conceptual artifacts often have a close relationship to material things, but the distinction remains important. Consider the relationship between the automobile, a material artifact, and the design for the automobile, a conceptual artifact. Suppose your car begins making alarming noises whenever you turn a sharp corner. Your mechanic will regard this as a problem with the physical artifact and will treat it accordingly. But suppose it becomes known that the same problem is occurring regularly with cars of the same model as yours. Engineers trying to determine the cause will consider the possibility of defective materials or manufacturing procedures, which are still material problems, but they will also consider the possibility of a design defect, and this is something wrong with the conceptual object.

Much of what is meant by the shift from an industrial to a knowledge society is that increasing amounts of work are being done on conceptual objects rather than on the physical objects to which they are related. A widely reported story is that of the Boeing 767 aircraft, for which no physical models were built. Instead all the testing of the design was done computationally. Thomas Stewart's book, *Intellectual Capital* (1997), provides many more examples of knowledge taking over the role of physical artifacts.

Like most writers of futuristic business literature, Stewart was quite loose about what he treated as knowledge. It is almost anything of value that is intangible, ranging from customer relations and worker morale to trade secrets. This looseness is probably justified at present. With people just starting to appreciate the full significance of knowledge in practical affairs, we should not be in a hurry to put limits on it. The traditional philosophers' definition of knowledge as true or warranted belief is obviously much too restrictive to cover what figures as knowledge in a knowledge-based economy, but once you abandon that definition it is not clear anymore what the limits should be. My purpose here is not to pin down what knowledge is but to argue for distinguishing knowledge in the form of identifiable conceptual artifacts from knowledge implicit or embedded in individual minds, in social practices, or in physical tools. Those other kinds of knowledge are important, too, and I expand on some of them in chapter 5. But they do not have the distinctive properties that conceptual artifacts have, properties that make them amenable to deliberate programs of knowledge creation and improvement.

Some intangibles are less intangible than others, we might say. Surely theories and plans are less intangible than intuitions and hopes. There might be no theories without intuitions or plans without hopes, but theories and plans represent a step forward that is more than a gain in clarity. Whereas intuitions and hopes are mental states that always remain to some extent private—belonging to World 2, in Popper's terms—theories and plans have the thing-like characteristics of artifacts. This makes it possible to treat them as objects of study and discussion. We can criticize them and propose improvements, experiment with applications—in short, make them part of the collective human enterprise in ways mental states never can be.

Folk theory typically recognizes only two of Popper's three worlds. We can have knowledge of the physical world and we can have knowledge of our own (and to some extent other people's) subjective states. If we accept the idea of conceptual artifacts, however, we should recognize it is also possible to have knowledge of them. In the folk or two-worlds view, understanding acceleration due to gravity means understanding something about the physical world—understanding that the speed of a falling object increases in proportion to the time it has been falling. But then one must also understand this is true only under ideal conditions, and so it is only approximately true of the world we inhabit. In the three-worlds view, understanding acceleration due to gravity means understanding both the theoretical idea and how it applies to actual phenomena. Understanding the theoretical idea might include understanding that gravity is a force and knowing how force and time are related to acceleration. It could include understanding the difference between the concept of gravity and the older notion that things have an inherent tendency to fall downward, and it could include understanding the universality of gravity, its relation to tides, planetary orbits, and so on. Of course, it could include a great deal more, or understanding of the conceptual artifact could be spotty and inconsistent. For instance, one could think gravity is universal and at the same time believe, as is sometimes stated in news reports, there is no gravity in outer space.

Understanding acceleration due to gravity as a physical phenomenon might include knowing the gravitational constant on earth and being familiar with the factors that influence how closely falling bodies conform to theoretical values. Clearly, understanding the conceptual artifact and understanding the physical phenomena it applies to can be closely related, but they are not the same. You could understand Newton's laws well enough and yet have very naive ideas about how things work in the physical world. That, according to research on naive conceptions in physics, seems to characterize the typical university student (Clement, 1982). Or, you could have quite a good qualitative[1] understanding of forces and motion as they appear in everyday phenomena and yet have little grasp of Newton's laws at a mathematical level.

In many situations, it will be impossible to make a clear distinction between knowing or thinking about the conceptual artifact and knowing or thinking about the material world the conceptual artifact applies to. For that reason, purists may believe the distinction should be abolished. If so, they ought also to argue against making a distinction between cars and trucks, now that manufacturers are producing a variety of vehicles that are not clearly one or the other. Motor vehicle offices still make the distinction and issue different license plates based on use; that is how we ought to be treating the distinction at issue here.

Finally, however, it does not matter much whether we can cleanly separate knowledge of conceptual artifacts from knowledge of the world they pertain to. What matters is that we recognize conceptual artifacts as real things, recognize creating and improving them as real work, and recognize understanding them as real understanding. Failure to do so, I am trying to argue, means playing the game of life in the Knowledge Age with a short hand.

Without the idea of conceptual artifacts, knowledge creation becomes merely a glorifying figure of speech. Suppose that, through varied experience as a bombardier, a basketball player, and a hurler

---

[1]Qualitative physics (deKleer & Brown, 1985) refers to physics that can be expressed in terms such as "the more this the more that," "this causes that," and functions whose shape can be described but not their mathematical form. According to deKleer and Brown, the expert has not only a grasp of formal laws but a very large amount of qualitative knowledge, which is particularized to concrete objects and phenomena. Thus, in Popper's terms, knowing formal laws would be knowledge of World 3; qualitative physics would be knowledge of World 1.

of stones off cliffs, I develop an excellent sense of trajectory. I have acquired knowledge but it is pointless to say I have created knowledge. I have not produced a conceptual artifact. Suppose that, to impart my knowledge to others, I produce a training videotape that reveals in slow motion the trajectories of objects propelled under various conditions, or suppose that I am clever enough to construct a simulation device, a sort of Link trainer, that will enable people to acquire in short order the skill and intuitive knowledge I possess. I have produced an artifact, all right, but not a conceptual one. To do that, I would have to produce something like a theory of ballistics. People might then continue to admire my ability to predict where propelled objects will fall but they might say that my theory was wrong or too simple or too complicated or impossible to understand—or that it was brilliant and bound to put Newton's laws out of business. In producing the theory I have created knowledge, whereas in the other cases I may be said to have *acquired* knowledge (possibly through some internal constructive process) and created ways of instilling similar knowledge in others. Thus, creating a knowledge object is one thing whereas knowing and helping others to know is another. The first I call *knowledge building*; the second, *learning*. Everyone learns and in some fashion everyone teaches. But not everyone produces or works with or is even aware of conceptual artifacts.

WORKING IN THREE WORLDS

One virtue of the idea of conceptual artifacts is that it offers us a straightforward way of defining knowledge work. If knowledge work does not seem to need defining, consider how you would distinguish it from white-collar work in general. You may find that the only way you can distinguish it is that it is somehow of a higher level than some white-collar work and accordingly more highly paid. But that only raises the question of what is higher level about it and why it is more highly paid. If you try to define knowledge work as work that requires or uses a great deal of knowledge, you surely have to include brain surgeons and jewel thieves as knowledge workers, and the term quickly loses its point. Some people try to avail themselves of a distinction between information and knowledge. If you work with information you are a white-collar flunky and if you work with knowledge you belong to the elite class of knowledge workers. But what is the difference between information and knowledge? About all you can say is that information is at a lower level than knowledge, which puts us back in the same loop as before. Once we have established a notion of conceptual artifacts, however, we can say quite simply that knowledge work is work with conceptual artifacts.

More specifically, knowledge work is work that creates or adds value to conceptual artifacts, in much the way that metalcrafting creates or adds value to metal artifacts. Many people may use a conceptual artifact, but that does not make them knowledge workers, anymore than driving a taxicab makes one an auto worker. Knowledge work seldom goes on in isolation from other kinds of work, however. Even scholars in the most rarified disciplines also do concrete things like writing papers and giving lectures, not to mention sharpening pencils and trekking to the library—all of which have something to do with knowledge work but are not themselves operations carried out on conceptual artifacts.

I think it helps in grasping the nature of work with conceptual artifacts to put it in a historical context, even though some of the history is rather speculative. World 1, we may suppose, exists for all animals whose nervous systems have some requisite degree of complexity. It is the world of practical action. To say it exists for us and our nonhuman relatives is to say our nervous systems have some way of representing the physical world so that our actions exhibit a degree of intelligence. World 2, however, if not strictly confined to the human species, is surely not so widely distributed. There is evidence that apes have capacities to deceive one another on purpose and perform actions such as deliberate teaching, which seem to require a representation of one another's beliefs and intentions (Premack & Premack, 1996). But that does not mean they have any concept of an inner world of experience. Julian Jaynes (1976), using evidence from mythology, has argued in effect that World 2 did not come into existence for human beings until after the time of Homer. In the ancient myths there is nothing to suggest inner experience. Everything is overt. What we would interpret as thoughts and feelings appear there as voices of the gods or of the dead. Jaynes' radical idea is that was not a mere literary convention but was how the ancients actually experienced cognitive events. Be that as it may, it is clear that the "inside view" in literature developed very gradually over a span of centuries. Only with the Romantic Movement, which straddled the 18th and 19th centuries, did people's inner lives come to be represented in the ways we now regard as natural (see Oatley, 1992, especially chap. 5). And even today the experiencing of an inner life appears to vary considerably as between introverts and extraverts, women and men, the educated and the uneducated. Talk therapies, which rely on exploration of World 2, are widely recognized as having little promise with people far out on the extraverted, masculine, uneducated dimensions. They are more like Achilles than they are like Anna Karenina. In practical terms, access to World 2 equips us to take initiative in improving our own knowledge and competence—to become "active learners" in the current educational jargon—and in recognizing our prejudices, resistances, and susceptibilities. Less obvious, but very important, it enables us to cultivate and make use of our feelings as a form of knowledge—what typically goes by the name of "intuition" and what I discuss in chapter 5 as "impressionistic knowledge."

World 3 also shows evidence of gradual emergence, although it may appear at first glance that Plato and Aristotle had it all. They certainly operated consciously in a realm of conjectures, explanations, proofs, and arguments. The world of ideas was probably more immediate to them than it is to 90% of the world's present population. Still, there are differences. The most obvious is they did not have the constructivist view that is essential to distinguishing World 3 from Worlds 1 and 2. Knowledge creation and the idea of conceptual artifacts would have made little sense to them. Truth existed and was to be discovered and apprehended, not constructed by human enterprise. Of course, that view persists today, but throughout most of recorded history it seems to have been universal. There is a famous quotation attributed to Newton. Whether apocryphal or not, it nicely conveys this premodern conception of knowledge:

> I do not know what I may appear to the world, but to myself I seem to have been only a boy playing on the seashore, diverting myself in now and then finding a smoother pebble or a prettier shell than ordinary, whilst the great ocean of truth lay all undiscovered before me.

What I see here is not a conception of World 3 but rather belief in a mysterious and superior World 1 lying beyond the World 1 available to our senses. This is the essence of mysticism. It is evident in Plato's image of the cave, and it is there in the "great ocean of truth." In a fascinating essay, John Maynard Keynes (1956), drawing on Newton's personal papers, placed him squarely among the mystics:

> Newton was not the first of the age of reason. He was the last of the magicians, the last of the Babylonians and Sumerians, the last great mind which looked out on the visible and intellectual world with the same eyes as those who began to build our intellectual inheritance rather less than 10,000 years ago. (p. 277)

Keynes inferred that for Newton the universe was a gigantic riddle set by God, with clues distributed (among the pebbles and shells, as it might be said) for the benefit of the solver. On this view, which certainly did not disappear with the Age of Reason, there is no World 3 of conceptual artifacts. There is World 1, there is World 2, and there is this ultra-World 1, the world of truth, which it is the thinker's job to puzzle out, using clues from the physical world.[2]

My hunch, supported by Alfred North Whitehead's (1925/1948) sketch of the history of knowledge, is that this mystical view did not really give way until the Industrial Revolution began to join science with invention. Inventions are obviously human creations (except to some die-hards who insist on construing inventions as gifts from God or the work of the devil). But if the steam engine is a human creation, why not the differential calculus?[3] And if the differential calculus, why not the kinetic theory of gases, and so on through all of theoretical knowledge? Where this leads is to what Whitehead called the greatest invention of the 19th century, the "method of invention":

> the full self-conscious realization of the power of professionalism in knowledge in all its departments, and of the way to produce professionals, and of the methods by which abstract knowledge can be connected with technology, and of the boundless possibilities of technological advance. (p. 92)

This made possible what Whitehead called "disciplined progress," progress achieved through the deliberate and orderly pursuit of solutions to theoretical and technical problems. It also, I suggest, marked the emergence of World 3 as a part of the real and knowable world and as a world in which productive work could be done.

Popper, to the best of my knowledge, never went so far as to characterize World 3 as a workspace, as a sphere of activity, and so I am stretching the concept to give it that character. He did, however, come fairly close to it in saying, "I suggest that one day we will have to revolutionize psychology by looking at the human mind as an organ for interacting with the objects of the third world; for understanding them, contributing to them, participating in them;

---

[2]There are other historical interpretations of Newton according to which he was the first of the moderns and a true Baconian (e.g., Bronowski & Mazlish, 1960). The important point for the present discussion, however, is the distinction between World 3 and ultra-World 1. Plato clearly believed in the latter and not the former. Whether Platonic mysticism carried as far as Newton and beyond is an interesting question, but what is more important is the failure of most philosophers and other thinkers to appreciate that there is nothing Platonic about World 3. It is a thoroughly modern and, I would say, post-positivist concept.

[3]Whether mathematical reality is constructed or discovered remains a disputed issue (Tait, 1986). Belief that mathematical truths were revelations of the mind of God persisted into the 19th century (White, 1956). All I wish to argue is that with the rise of technology it became more plausible and natural to treat mathematics as a product of invention.

and for bringing them to bear on the first world." (Popper, 1972, p. 156). Popper, thus, was describing what we would now call knowledge work.

Although World 3 is usually exemplified by such high-status cultural objects as theories and histories, a humbler example will serve better to illustrate basic ideas (mainly because it is less likely to stir up strong feelings about the nature of science or about cultural canons). Such a conceptual artifact is the kitchen recipe. Recipes have a life outside the minds of people who know them and outside their particular embodiments in printed form. We speak of recipes being handed down from generation to generation, undergoing modifications, splitting into various versions. A recipe may be tested, criticized, compared with others, kept secret or publicized, awarded prizes. It may become obsolete, or impossible to implement because of the unavailability of necessary ingredients; it may be adapted to new conditions, such as microwave cookery. New knowledge may reveal nutritional virtues or liabilities of the recipe that could not have been known to its originators.

What I have to say about recipes as conceptual artifacts is obvious and commonsensical, and so the conceptual distinctions I draw are likely to seem unnecessary and pedantic. The reason for making them is that when we move to higher status conceptual artifacts, the kinds that make up the subject matter of formal education, the same points apply but they are no longer part of conventional wisdom. A recipe might be regarded as a representation of something in a person's mind, but this is an inaccurate and unnecessary supposition. My mother-in-law, Bianca Contrucci, was noted for various succulent Italian dishes, which her offspring tried to induce her to prepare whenever they visited her or she them. From time to time one or another of the offspring got her to write out or dictate the recipe for one of these dishes. A comparison of different versions of the recipe for supposedly the same dish showed them to vary markedly on significant points. One explanation would be that she did not prepare the dish the same way every time. Another is that she did not measure ingredients or time things precisely, instead going by impression and various subtle clues that she herself was probably not aware of, so that the recipe represented only a guess about these variables. Folk theory, or its modern equivalents in cognitive psychology, would try to explain these phenomena as discrepancies between the recipe in the mind and the recipe as expressed in words. The gnocchi recipe in Bianca's mind, such theorizing might say, was complex and variable and, furthermore, not fully available to consciousness. So when it came to producing a verbal recipe, she had to improvise and fill in with inferences, possibly with remembered bits from other recipes.

Suppose we accept this last sentence as approximately right. The question I then ask is, what is the relevance of the preceding conjectures? What do we gain by dragging in the notion of a recipe (or a production system) in the mind? It is not that these conjectures are wrong or implausible (which is something we have already discussed); it is that they are on the wrong track. Making gnocchi and producing a recipe for gnocchi are two different tasks. Some of the same knowledge and skills are involved, but succeeding at one does not ensure success at the other. Producing a recipe for gnocchi means creating a conceptual artifact that can serve as a guide to people in making the dish so it will turn out a certain way. It also involves producing a representation of that recipe—normally a text of a certain conventional form (although it could be something more esoteric, such as a flow chart). To maintain clarity with regard to conceptual artifacts, we need to keep several things in mind at this point:

1. The written text is not, strictly speaking, the recipe. It is a representation of the recipe. If the written instructions are ambiguous, this does not make it a bad recipe; it means we cannot be sure what the recipe is.
2. The recipe, thus, is an abstract object of which there may be various representations. When people criticize, argue about, or try to improve upon the recipe, it is this abstract object they are attempting to deal with, not its representation.
3. This is not to imply the recipe is first conceived as an abstract conceptual artifact and then translated into language or some other representational form. Everything we know about written composition implies the mind does not work that way (Bereiter & Scardamalia, 1987b). But in the case of recipes, theories, and other conceptual artifacts, we try to think about the content separately from its vehicle.

Suppose the publishers of a well-established recipe book decide it is time for a thorough-going revision. In addition to setting editors to work revising the text and illustrations, they also set a team of chefs to work trying out and making improvements in the recipes. The editors and the chefs would have to work in close communication, of course, but their jobs would be distinguishable. Both are functioning as knowledge workers, but they are working with different conceptual artifacts. The editors are working with texts. These are immaterial objects, we should note; the same text might appear in different editions in different typography and might also appear in electronic forms that readers could configure in any fonts and sizes they wished. In their normal work, chefs are not knowledge workers; they are food workers. They *use* knowledge, as all workers do, and they *learn* or develop new knowledge in the course of their work. But their normal work is not producing or adding value to knowledge; it is producing and adding value to food. In the present instance, however, they have been seconded as knowledge workers. They are not getting paid for the food they produce but for the recipe evaluations and improvements they produce. If they take artistic license with the recipes and do various subtle things that cannot be translated into recipes, they may produce wonderful dishes but they will not be doing their job as knowledge workers.

Obvious as all this is, I believe it is something that neither folk theory of mind nor situated cognition theory can handle well. A folk psychological account of revising the recipe book would have knowledge in the minds of the chefs getting communicated to readers, with help from the editors. A situated cognition account would have knowledge constituted in the practice of the chefs getting externalized in the form of written recipes as tools. Both kinds of accounts capture something of significance but both seem to miss the central point, which is that what these chefs are working with are not the contents of their minds or of their practice but are things that already existed before they came onto the scene and that they are charged to do something with—namely, the abstract objects known as recipes.

Common sense wants to reduce everything to Worlds 1 and 2. Baking a cake is activity in World 1, the material world. A recipe may therefore be thought of as a representation of that activity—like a movie or a scenario, but stripped down to essentials. Alternatively it may, as already suggested, be thought of as a representation of something in the mind of the chef—accordingly, a part of World 2. Common sense, not being greatly concerned with conceptual precision, may well regard a recipe as being both at the same time. This may be inelegant, but it does not actually lead to bad results in the kitchen. Cooking is a well-established, traditional craft, and recipes play a limited but valuable role in contemporary versions of it. But what if, somehow, creating new and improved recipes became a national priority, with a premium on innovation, usability, and quality? What if the need exceeded the supply of top-level talent and the enterprise faced stiff competition from abroad? We might then find that commonsense muddling through was no longer sufficient. We might even find that we need a "theory of recipes," realizing that theories of nutrition, of cookery, and of food science, though all relevant, are not the same thing and do not quite fill the bill. A theory of recipes would be a theory of knowledge, albeit of a rather specific type of knowledge. It seems almost inevitable that a useful theory of recipes would have to make something like Popper's distinction between three worlds: World 1, the world of actual cookery, where actual people do actual things with actual utensils and materials in actual kitchens; World 3, the world of recipes that are being created, tested, discussed, and modified; and World 2, the world of mental activity that mediates between the other two worlds.

KNOWLEDGE IN RELATION TO OTHER CULTURAL ARTIFACTS

Once we agree to recognize the existence of conceptual artifacts as distinct from the content of people's minds, there remains the problem of distinguishing them from other kinds of artifacts such as totem poles, symphonies, and electric toasters. My efforts to do so have continually been defeated by sharp critics, and so I am prepared to concede that rigorous distinctions are impossible. But it is still useful to have a perspective on the issue, and so I offer a set of nested definitions, based on Fig. 3.1.

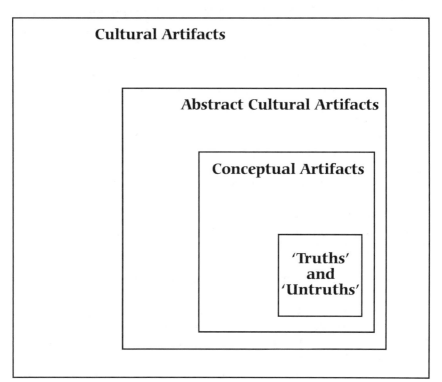

FIG. 3.1.

Starting with the broadest category, we may say that *cultural artifacts* include everything that is judged worth preserving because of its meaning. This doesn't include everything in the world, but anything in the world, concrete or abstract, could potentially become a cultural artifact. The electric toaster in your kitchen is not a cultural artifact. When it ceases to toast bread you throw it away. But if someone retrieved it from your trash can and it now appears in an art museum or a historical museum, it has become a cultural artifact. It is now being preserved because of its esthetic or historical significance. The tree in your back yard is not a cultural artifact or even an artifact at all. But if it should happen that the agreement that finally establishes world peace is signed under that tree, it will probably be preserved, having become a monument.

Some cultural artifacts are *abstract*. These include myths, folk tales and literary works, folk songs, and musical compositions, as well as the various kinds of conceptual artifacts we have been discussing. Whereas concrete cultural artifacts such as paintings and monuments are preserved as such, and secondarily in the form of reproductions and representations, abstract cultural artifacts can only be preserved in such secondary ways. So we have books, tape recordings, and other objects that are preserved not because of their singular value but because of their content, which is abstract.

Among abstract cultural artifacts, some can be treated as knowledge and some cannot. Here, drawing a sharp distinction is difficult and perhaps impossible, because there are always intermediate instances. In the appendix I suggest that *conceptual artifacts* can be distinguished by the logical relations that can exist between them, but this is more a rule of thumb than a definition. We can surely agree it is possible to argue about a theory in a way we cannot argue about a sonata, but it is not so obvious how to regard a poem, and poems vary in the extent to which they contain discussible ideas. As I read Popper, I find him wavering between including all abstract cultural artifacts in World 3 and limiting it to those that constitute knowledge. Trying to be practical about it, I maintain that for purposes of discussing issues of education, knowledge work, and knowledge creation, we need to distinguish as best we can those cultural objects that we want to treat as knowledge, hence, the category of *conceptual artifacts*.

Finally, there is an important subclass of conceptual artifacts I discuss in the next section as "assertive" artifacts. These are conceptual artifacts that can be argued about as to whether they are true or not. Theories, hypotheses, and factual claims fall into this class. This doesn't mean that it is fruitful to argue about their truth, only that it is something people find it possible to do, whereas they would not find it possible to argue about the truth of an icon or a business plan. (They might, however, argue about the beliefs about the meaning or power of an icon or about the truth of some of the statements in a business plan.) Epistemology's traditional concern has been confined to this little box. Education is necessarily concerned with it too, but not to the obsessive degree that many science educators are concerned with it. Education is really concerned with the whole range of cultural artifacts. That is what liberal education has been about, and contemporary arguments about multiculturalism, Eurocentrism, and the like reflect this broad concern. What I am trying to do in this chapter is pick out the subcategory of *conceptual artifacts* as one that deserves special attention as knowledge assumes a more salient role in society.

THEORIES: ASSERTIVE ARTIFACTS

By far the most troublesome conceptual artifacts have been those that assert something about World 1. Included in this category are the theories of empirical sciences, conjectures, facts, histories, and observational reports ("I saw the defendant leaving the building at 9 o'clock"). These objects have been almost the sole concern of epistemology. Traditionally, the term "knowledge" is reserved for objects of this sort, or, more precisely, for that subset of such objects that happen to be true—in this last qualification lies the constitutive problem of epistemology.

The last half of the 20th century has seen a great deal of ferment in epistemology and the closely related field of philosophy of science. It is no longer quite so obvious or easy to treat knowledge of the truth-asserting kind as consisting of autonomous objects. Antifoundationalism, postpositivism, and lately postmodernism, along with many less massive assaults on the ivory tower, must at the least be credited with making convincing cases for viewing knowledge within an extended network of relations. The following points, distilled and simplified from a variety of contemporary utterances, seem, on the surface at least, to argue against the Popperian approach:

- There are no isolated facts. All supposed facts have theoretical presuppositions and thus, are not fundamentally different from theoretical propositions.
- Theories do not exist in isolation either, but are embedded in paradigms. And paradigms are generally not fully articulated. They are more like traditions than they are like supertheories.

- What we call knowledge is merely belief that has gained acceptance in some group. Thus, knowledge cannot be separated from the people who uphold it.
- There is no value-free knowledge. The beliefs that a group upholds as knowledge or truth are ones that subserve its interests.

Without presuming to judge the merit of these assertions, I think it can be safely concluded that they do not constitute an argument or even part of an argument against treating knowledge as objects. They are statements about *how* we should treat these truth-assertive objects: We should treat them as theoretical, interconnected, and historically and socially situated. We should be attentive to the motives—in ourselves as well as in others—that lie behind the endorsement of certain conceptual artifacts and the rejection of others. Stated in these general terms, the postpositivist position is far from radical and is in fact plain common sense. In our daily lives we have to take enormous numbers of assertions on authority, having neither the time nor the resources to investigate them. Therefore, the credibility of the source is always important and open to question. How far one should go in this questioning—where reasonable skepticism leaves off and delusional suspiciousness begins—is an important matter, but I do not see that its consideration is in any way compromised by treating knowledge as consisting of real objects.

KNOWLEDGE IMPROVEMENT

"Modes of social knowledge such as theology, science, and magic are different, not inferior or superior" (Stanfield, 1985, p. 392). This statement sums up an extreme but increasingly popular outcome of what has been one of the most vigorously disputed issues in contemporary thought. Does science have a privileged claim on our belief or is it only one among a number of ways that different peoples have tried to make sense of the world? Cautious university students these days will not use the word "science" by itself. They will preface it with "Eurocentric," thus, making clear their awareness that there is not just one kind of science and that the belief there is such a privileged route to knowledge is ethnocentric and due for its comeuppance.

There are issues of lasting human concern here: What should we believe? Can we be certain of anything? What do we do about the fact that so much has to be taken on authority? Except for some minor attention to the last, I am not going to deal with those issues. Instead, I want to call attention to one obvious and important distinction between science and myth. People are constantly at work trying to improve the content of science. No such efforts at improvement are to be found amongst the priests, shamans, elders, divines, and the like who have custodial responsibility for the myths, religions, or magic of a people.

Does this mean science is more deserving of our credence? That is part of the issue I am trying to avoid. It surely depends on the criteria one applies, and problems multiply as soon as one tries to apply criteria of believability. What seems to me to be the important point for a new theory of mind and knowledge is that deliberate effort to improve a body of knowledge is something quite rare in the world. Relatively few of the world's many societies have undertaken it, and in those societies that have done so, it has been the occupation of a small minority.

Myths, rituals, magic, folk medicine, and the like undergo change over time, of course, and some of these changes, especially in practical arts, may be counted as improvements. But such change is an evolutionary process. Some cultural anthropologists treat it literally as such. Dawkins (1976) defined *memes* as cultural units comparable to genes. New ones arise as mutations; they proliferate and spread about through cultural processes and they are subject to selection pressures of various kinds. A culture as a whole may thus be characterized as a "meme pool," whose composition changes over time through the entry of new memes and through changes in the frequencies of existing ones. Like biological evolution, cultural evolution may appear in retrospect to have been rationally guided. The evolution of the English language, for instance, appears in retrospect to have been directed toward eliminating unnecessary inflections and toward minimizing effort in vocalization, but it is doubtful if either of these was ever a consciously entertained purpose. Had it been, we should probably have a record of groups of scholars commissioned to design improved versions of the language.

There have probably always been individuals who, in solving a particular problem, came up with something of general significance, thus, contributing a mutant meme that might survive and spread. But knowledge improvement as a social enterprise has been much more limited. Earlier I offered a speculative sketch of the evolution of knowledge work from a sort of mystical quest for truth, thought to reside in a world beyond the visible world, to the constructive, inventive activity that yields the "disciplined progress" Whitehead (1925/1948) talked about. Cultural evolution was not replaced, but it was greatly accelerated by the introduction of designer memes (cf. Dennett, 1995).

It is often said that science, for the modern masses, serves as religion or myth, and that technology is for them equivalent to magic. If so, however, part of the religion is belief in progress, and this sets it apart from older systems of belief. People expect our modern myths and magic to keep getting better—better in the sense that more and more will become explainable, curable, achievable. This belief that progress just happens and is inevitable has the irresponsible character of all sorts of fatalism and is in no way to be advocated (cf. Lasch, 1991). But we should recognize that it is an altogether different kind of fatalism from that of ancients and mystics.

Let us be clear that in talking about the improvement of knowledge we are not assuming it leads to improvement in the human condition. We are not even assuming the effort to improve knowledge is successful in any respect. The only point that bears on our overall purpose in this discussion is that knowledge improvement is a distinctive kind of effort, absent—often intentionally absent—from many spheres of human activity. Improvement of personal knowledge, acquiring a fuller grasp of the truths and skills already accessible and valued in the culture, is almost universally honored and of course figures prominently in all kinds of educational philosophies. But trying to improve knowledge itself, to extend the limits of the learnable, appears to be a relatively recent innovation and one that is far from firmly established in education, even in the most modern nations. It is what I have referred to as *knowledge building* and will later advocate as a proper activity for educational institutions at all levels.

SOCIO-POLITICAL OBJECTIONS

> The standpoint of women, which locates us in the particularities of our experience, is profoundly contradictory to objectified forms of knowledge.
>
> —Smith (1990, p. 61)

We need to be clear about where the sociocultural and the Popperian views of knowledge part company. It is not on the issue of abstractness. Sociocultural theorists commonly recognize knowledge that becomes abstracted from particular situations and available for more general use. (Arguments to the contrary would be self-refuting.) Where they draw the line is at detaching knowledge from the web of practices, motives, and power relations within which it has come to be treated as knowledge. As Dorothy Smith's remark at the opening of this section illustrates, the reason for drawing the line is often political rather than theoretical. Once knowledge is objectified, those who control the agencies through which it was created, propagandized, and bureaucratized—woven into the established social structure—are no longer accountable for it. It becomes a *fait accompli*, a part of the way things are, something to which people must now adjust. The authoritative status of textbook knowledge is just one, and by no means the most important, manifestation of how objectified knowledge can create subserviance and alienation for those whose standpoint on reality is different.

I need hardly acknowledge that the issues here are vast and that they do not lend themselves to cursory treatment. Yet I must say that my own view is the opposite of Smith's. I do not see objectified knowledge as the problem or as underlying the problems she addresses—mainly problems having to do with power and exclusion. It is the *un*objectified knowledge of the powerful that the weak are helpless against—the unwritten laws, the unofficial practices, the unconscious ways of thinking and acting that are from childhood bred into them. These frustrate both revolutionaries and people who are trying to gain membership in the elite. Objectified knowledge, by contrast, can be argued against, sometimes with success; it can be accepted with reservations or used for alternative purposes—even turned against the people who uphold it.

Basil Bernstein (1996) has criticized objectified knowledge on somewhat different grounds:

> Once knowledge is separated from inwardness, from commitments, from personal dedication, from the deep structure of the self, then people may be moved about, substituted for one another and excluded from the market .... Now we have two independent markets, one of knowledge and one of potential creators and users of knowledge. (p. 87)

Bernstein's fundamental concern here seems to be that objectification of knowledge licenses a kind of amoral detachment: No one takes responsibility for the knowledge or its uses. Again, it seems to me that the concern should be directed as much if not more to *un*objectified knowledge. No one takes responsibility for the unwritten laws and beliefs, the tacit knowledge of their group, because no individual is in fact responsible. The ethos is what it is, whereas individuals can be called to account for the explicit beliefs by which they justify their actions.

Bernstein is certainly correct to this extent, however: People are valued for what cannot be detached from them, which includes their tacit knowledge and skills. If everything you know that is of value to your employer can be put on paper, your employer can keep the paper and get rid of you. This has become an explicit concern in universities, where professors fear that if they put their courses online and the university claims ownership of the courses thus produced, the next step will be for the university to get rid of the professor. But this is not a problem of epistemology; it is a problem of property rights. Defending those rights depends, however, on a level of conceptual clarity that folk theory of knowledge and mind cannot achieve. The professors must be clear about what is they claim to own. Is it the knowledge their course materials are supposed to convey? Not likely. If there is any ownership of that knowledge at all, it belongs to the discipline, and part of the ethos of any respectable academic discipline is to make its knowledge freely available. Is it the particular videos, web pages, course outlines, and so on that constitute the course material? That seems a more defensible claim, but what if the media giant that wants to market the stuff redoes everything, including rewriting the lectures to make them more zingy and having them delivered by a professional actor? "Well, they can't use my name without my consent,"says the professor. "We're not interested in your name," say the media merchants (an exception being made for Nobel Laureates). "We're only interested in the name of your university, and we've already acquired the rights to it." "But this course wouldn't exist if it weren't for me," wails the professor. "I created it. I fought to get it on the calendar, against the objections of my more hide-bound colleagues. I perfected it over the years until it became a course that really works. Some students have even said it changed their lives. Now you think you can take it away, jazz it up, dumb it down, and sell it with nothing more than a credit line that says 'based on …'." Here we have it. *The course itself is a conceptual artifact.* It was created and improved by someone to a purpose. Like other conceptual artifacts, it can retain its identity, or at least a vestige of it, under changes in representation. That conceptual artifact is what the professor must claim to own, because all other claims to ownership can either be denied or circumvented. But how can you make and defend such a claim unless people recognize conceptual artifacts as real things? That is not the main argument for endorsing objectification, for recognizing Popper's World 3, but it is an argument that may turn out to cut close to the bone.

How has it gotten about that objectified knowledge is a tool of oppression? The rising economic value of work with objectified knowledge and the declining value of other kinds of work is producing grave inequities, but it is ridiculous to place the blame on objectification itself. Instead of trying to win a place for myth and emotion in science class, those concerned with social justice ought to be trying to win a place for alternative talents in the market place.

What we are seeing instead is a kind of epistemological Luddism. To battle against objectification is as futile as it was for the Luddites to battle against industrialization. The legitimate concerns of the Luddites eventually found effective expression in labor unionism, which, instead of battling against machines, battled for workers' rights and welfare. Those concerned with equity ought to be battling for alternative conceptions of human worth, not getting sidetracked onto feckless battles for alternative conceptions of truth.

PROGRESSIVE DISCOURSE

Where Popper and contemporary socioculturalists are in solid agreement is on the importance of dialogue in the practice of science and other disciplines. This applies to empirical sciences as well as to more speculative disciplines. Empirical observations by themselves do not constitute scientific knowledge. They influence the development of scientific knowledge by being brought into the discourse through which knowledge is constituted. One of the tenets of this discursive view of science is that science does not start with facts. Rather, statements become facts through a lengthy discursive practice, at the end of which people no longer see any virtue in contesting them (Latour, 1987). On that basis, we could say it is a fact that scientific knowledge is constituted through discourse. There is no longer any lively interest in disputing that statement. What this means about the epistemological status of scientific claims—whether they amount to anything more than consensus—is still a controversial matter. But regardless of your beliefs about truth and the nature of knowledge, you are likely to find little to gain by questioning the centrality of discourse.

To Popper, discourse was a sort of Darwinian process by which weaker theories are eliminated and the stronger survive—until replaced by yet hardier ones. That is not much different from the view of some contemporary sociologists of knowledge, who see scientific dialogue mainly as competitive and the whole business a struggle for dominance (Latour, 1987; Latour & Woolgar, 1979). Popper saw the process as rather more high-minded than the sociologists do, but that could be the difference between idealization and description. In either case, their focus seems to be on knowledge claims that have already been formed—that already constitute World 3 objects, in Popper's terms—rather than on how such knowledge comes about in the first place. Kevin Dunbar (1995), by contrast, has studied the discourse that goes on in research laboratories as interdisciplinary teams try to work their way to the solution of scientific problems. Dunbar found predominantly cooperative effort, with a great deal of explaining as opposed to argument. Woodruff and Meyer (1997) have suggested that both descriptions are valid but that they apply to different discourse communities. There is, on one hand, intragroup discourse in which the main work of knowledge construction is carried out and in which cooperation is the norm. On the other hand there is intergroup discourse in which the products of different research groups are brought under consideration and in which criticism and controversy are normal. Both kinds of discourse have valuable roles to play in the development of knowledge.

Discourse plays an important part in all human communities, but its role is obviously going to be different in a community of historians from what it is in a community of body builders, for instance. Our particular concern here is with communities whose job is creating and improving knowledge. With the possible exception of philosophers, this job is never carried out through discourse alone. To understand a community of practice such as a scientific discipline, we need to understand the social and material circumstances in which it functions, the tools at its disposal, the division of labor within the community, and the norms regulating behavior in the community (Engestrom, 1987). Accordingly, there is some danger in focusing too much on discourse, as if it were the community's preoccupation and reason for being. What I would say, rather, is that discourse is a screen onto which everything else is projected and from which the success of the community may be read.

What it means to create and advance knowledge is going to be understood differently in different communities, but whatever it means must be mirrored by a conception of progressive discourse. It would not make sense to claim that knowledge is advancing but that the discourse within a discipline is getting nowhere. When we talk about the centrality of discourse we are claiming more than that, however. We are saying that knowledge advancement and progress in knowledge-building discourse are not two things that mirror one another but are one and the same thing.

In psychology, which is the discipline I know best, the colloquium is a time-honored form of discourse. In the prototypic colloquium, a speaker presents a series of 4 to 10 experiments. The first tests some theoretical notion. Each succeeding experiment overcomes a limitation or eliminates an alternative explanation of the results of its predecessor until, with the final experiment, every cloud of doubt has been removed, including clouds hardly anyone else would have thought of. There follows a question period during which the more clever and informed members of the audience try to show that in fact unnoticed limitations or alternative explanations still exist. It is difficult not to be impressed by such performances, even when one is not much interested in the point at issue. This colloquium form clearly embodies the Popperian notion that science advances through the elimination of hypotheses. Also, it is clearly not just talk. No amount of discursive skill will take the place of having planned and conducted a series of experiments that interlock in the particular way required to support the kind of story that a successful colloquium speaker aims to deliver. But, just as clearly, the design of the experiments is guided by the kind of story the psychologist aspires to tell. The criticisms that arise during the question period may determine the next experiment the psychologist carries out, and hence the next chapter in the lengthening story to be told in subsequent colloquia, or they may mark the beginning of someone else's research program that extends or runs counter to that of the speaker.

The colloquium form I have described is most characteristic of experimental psychology, which has been the dominant branch of North American psychology throughout most of its history. A somewhat different form has evolved in developmental psychology. It is still based on a series of experiments, but the experiments are more likely to consist of various ingenious demonstrations of the same point. Although this might seem like a minor stylistic difference, it entails a different way of going about experimental research and it implies a different sort of progression in knowledge: The fitness of a theory is not so much determined by survival of criticism and counterexplanations as by its success in generating captivating experimental demonstrations. Knowledge advances not so much through progressive refinements and paring down of alternatives as through periodic innovations, not unlike progress in the automobile industry. A developmental psychologist I know, whose work is highly successful by this standard, applied for a position in a department dominated by the experimentalist paradigm. She was told her research was brilliant but it wasn't the way they did things there.

Traditionally, scientific method has meant empirical methods, and so-called "methods" courses perpetuate this view. On this view, one would look for differences between experimental and developmental psychology in the ways data are obtained and analyzed. No very profound differences would appear. The same principles of experimental design and control would be honored and the same kinds of statistical reasoning applied.[4] It would appear the same basic methodology is followed, except that the experimental psychologists follow it more rigorously. I suspect that that is in fact how some

---

[4]Many psychologists these days adopt what are called "qualitative" methods, which do deviate from the experimental psychology norm in how data are gathered and analyzed, but I have purposely chosen examples where the main differences do not take this form.

experimental psychologists see the difference. I have tried to suggest that the differences run deeper than this, that they might even be thought to represent divergent paradigms, but, if so, where do the differences reside? They do not reside in any particular rules or procedures but rather in the whole systems of practice to be found in the two subdisciplines. However, these differences show up in, are indeed vividly projected onto, the discourse of colloquia.

Just as discourse practices distinguish one discipline from another, they also show what disciplines have in common and what distinguishes knowledge-building communities in general from other kinds of discourse communities. Experimental psychologists and developmental psychologists can, after all, converse, criticize one another's ideas, suggest questions for further research, and—not least—argue constructively about their differences. On the other hand, there are adherents of cults whose principal tenets are psychological but with whom it is impossible to carry on a discussion of psychological issues. Many intellectuals these days question whether there is any fundamental difference between science and other ways of making sense of the world (e.g., Rorty, 1991). Any attempt to carry on a knowledge-building discussion with a cultist should make it evident, however, that important differences do exist, even if it is debatable whether the line of demarcation runs between science and nonscience or between some larger class of rational inquiry and sense-making activities that lie outside it.

The psychological cultist may tell you, for instance, that his leader has determined there are six types of personality. Having heard what these are, you may engage with him in an entertaining hour of classifying mutual acquaintances and public figures. But the cultist has no interest in comparing his typology with other typologies, such as Jung's, that have gained some scientific standing, much less any interest in examining the value of type theories in general. The six types are among the fundamental truths his cult has established beyond doubt. Only their application to particular cases is open to discussion. But how is this different from the scientist's acceptance of certain propositions as facts and no longer worth questioning?

I don't think the difference can be pinned down by examining what people take as disputable and indisputable. One must look instead at the dynamics of sense-making discourse, as carried out over sizeable stretches of time, and at the motives that drive and guide it. What becomes immediately apparent from this viewpoint is the scientists' commitment to knowledge improvement. This entails both a belief that all knowledge is potentially improvable and a moral conviction that one should keep trying to improve it. From this commitment to knowledge improvement flow a number of distinctive characteristics of what I have called progressive discourse (Bereiter, 1994):

1. *Focus on conceptual artifacts.* All serious discussions involve ideas, but it is not so common for the ideas themselves to become objects of discussion. Our psychological cultist is happy to apply the ideas represented in his six personality types, but he is not interested in discussing the typology itself or the ideas behind it. Without doing so, knowledge improvement cannot even get under way.

2. *Improvability as a positive attribute of conceptual artifacts.* I owe to Marlene Scardamalia the realization that not all conceptual artifacts are improvable. The clichés of education tend not to be: "Every child is different." "Children's minds are not empty vessels waiting to be filled." It is not just that such statements are irrefutable. They act as thought stoppers. Having assented to them, one has no place to go. There is no forward direction. An improvable conceptual artifact, by contrast, is likely to strike us as interesting, at least somewhat unsettling to our existing beliefs, and as raising questions and having implications beyond those that are immediately apparent. An example is the idea that children first develop an awareness of other minds and from this become aware of their own (Gopnik, 1993). Encountering this idea for the first time, you may realize that you have unquestioningly assumed the opposite, that the idea nevertheless has some immediate plausibility, and that the whole question of how theories of mind are acquired may involve quite perplexing chicken-and-egg issues. A commitment to knowledge advancement accordingly entails a commitment to formulate conceptual artifacts that are improvable—hence, vulnerable to criticism and disconfirmation.

3. *Common understanding given priority over agreement.* In politics and other practical affairs, it is often advantageous to have vague principles that you can get people to agree to even though they understand them differently. In knowledge-building discourse, however, agreement without common understanding is pointless, and one of the more discouraging things that can happen is to find that people who endorsed your ideas turn out not to have understood them. On the other hand, when there is mutual understanding of the ideas under discussion, there is a basis for productive discourse even if there are major differences of opinion.

4. *Commitment to expand the factual base.* Even though people may disagree seriously, there are bound to be some facts on which they do agree, and these form a necessary basis for progressive discourse. Facts constrain ideas. Opposing theories may be com-

pared to the extent that they attempt to explain the same facts (Thagard, 1989). Accordingly, people committed to knowledge advancement have a stake in expanding the set of accepted facts, while recognizing that any factual statement is itself a conceptual artifact open to criticism and improvement. This is quite a different commitment from that which prevails in formal debates and in court trials, where part of the strategy for success is to undermine as many as possible of the opponent's factual claims.

5. *Selective criticism based on knowledge-advancement goals.* Sophomoric criticism is criticism disconnected from purposes of advancing knowledge. In the behavioral sciences, students quickly learn how to criticize studies for not measuring certain variables, for not including this variation or that, for small sample sizes, for not meeting all the requirements of certain statistical tests, and so on down a list, but they are often dumfounded if asked why their criticism matters—what conclusion of the study is challenged, what of importance would be learned by elaborating the study in the ways they propose. A commitment to *constructive* criticism is not a commitment to being gentle or to making only positive suggestions. It is a commitment to using criticism in the service of knowledge advancement.

6. *Nonsectarianism.* No one expects complete impartiality, even in high court judges and Nobel Laureate scientists. What can be expected of those seeking to advance knowledge, however, is that they will not adhere to sects that actively limit the scope of ideas to be entertained or tested. Much of 19th century medicine consisted of a battle between sects, each adhering to a restrictive set of beliefs and practices. But as scientific medicine began to take shape, that changed. "Scientific medicine," said William Rothstein (1985, p. 325), "was not a triumph of any sect; it was the death of all sects." Of course, sects live on, in medicine as elsewhere, but a commitment to progressive discourse entails a commitment to their elimination.

These six commitments constitute virtues and imply a rather saintly standard of conduct. It is not for me to say how much the actual behavior of scientists and scholars conforms to them. What I am saying is that these commitments represent what it means to engage in knowledge-building discourse. Any group interested in advancing knowledge would want to do what it could to encourage these commitments. They also serve to distinguish knowledge-building discourse from other serious kinds of discourse. For instance, argumentation is a form of discourse often advocated in education (e.g., Kuhn, 1993). Raise an issue, get students to commit to a position on it, and then let those with opposing positions argue it out. Yet argumentation can proceed in quite a rational and civilized way without honoring any of these commitments[5] (which, to my mind, raises serious questions about its value as an educational activity). Knowledge-building discourse may take various forms and serve various specific purposes, but there is always an expectation that knowledge-building discourse will be progressive. Unlike social small talk, for instance, the discourse is supposed to *get* somewhere. Participants need to feel that something has been accomplished, that the state of knowledge in their community—however small or grand they may conceive their community to be—is in better shape than it was before.

CONCLUSION:
WHY TWO WORLDS ARE NOT ENOUGH

Every way of dividing up reality has its problems, and so a pragmatic choice has to weigh gains against losses. In the Western world, what has come to be the commonsense or intuitively obvious way is to divide the world into two parts: the external world of physical reality and the internal world of our thoughts and perceptions—what Popper called World 1 and World 2. Descartes declared such a dualistic view of the world back in the 17th century, and it has been the object of much philosophical controversy ever since. There have been repeated attempts to eliminate one or the other of these two worlds. Arguments for eliminating World 1 often turn on the claim that we can have no knowledge of it apart from our thoughts and perceptions, and so—like it or not—World 2 is all we have. Arguments for eliminating World 2, which I touched on in the preceding chapter, turn on the claim that we, along with our thoughts and perceptions, are part of the natural order and therefore ought to yield to the same explanatory efforts as other parts. But the dualism persists in ordinary thought, and for good reason. It is terribly important whether the gun is in fact loaded, irrespective of what we or anyone else happens to believe, and, in the event that the gun was loaded and discharged a bullet into an unfortunate visitor, the courts must do their best to determine whether the person who pulled the trigger believed the gun to be loaded. So, while the struggle against dualism continues in scholarly journals, everyday affairs—including those conducted by philosophers in their off hours—are bound to continue in the old dualistic mode.

---

[5]There are, however, approaches to argumentation that do place cooperative knowledge advancement above controversy, for instance, *Coalescent Argumentation* (Gilbert, 1997).

An important departure from the continuing controversies has been the idea elaborated by Popper that two worlds are not enough. The reasons Popper (and several major philosophers before him) thought two worlds were not enough are not, however, the reasons they are not enough for education. Or, at any rate, the educational reasons only partially reflect the underlying epistemological reasons. We might say simply that two worlds do not allow enough degrees of freedom for education to proceed in a sufficiently flexible and adaptive way. Or to put it in more visualizable terms, they do not provide enough dimensionality. They force educational thought into a two-dimensional space when it needs at least three dimensions.

The typical teaching situation involves three main elements. Let us consider them as they appear in science teaching. There is World 1, which may be thought of as how the physical world really is, how it really works. (Ignore for now any objections you may have to acknowledging such a reality; all I am claiming is that the typical science teaching situation presupposes a physical reality which it is the object of the course to teach students about.) Then there is World 2, which for the teacher is the content of students' minds. The third element is scientific knowledge, the stuff represented in textbooks. If everything is either World 1 or World 2, this third element must somehow be relegated to one of those. (There is another possibility— to ignore authoritative knowledge altogether and limit science education to what students can find out for themselves through experimentation—but for obvious reasons this cannot be considered a serious alternative.) The old-fashioned way is to treat the textbook as a stand-in for World 1, that is, as a record of "how it really is." Although this approach leans toward treating textbook information as infallible and immutable, it is possible to fudge a bit and allow skepticism to enter the picture. But the more uncertainty that is introduced, the more students are bound to question why they should be required to learn the stuff. The postmodern or "postpositivist" way is to treat the textbook as a record of what scientists believe, thus, relegating it to another World 2, the minds of those fellows in white coats. The question thus, naturally arises of why those people's beliefs should be taken more seriously than anyone else's. There are sophisticated answers available to that question, as well as various compromises (reviewed in Loving, 1997), but in practice answers will either tend back toward the old-fashioned position—what the scientists say is the best representation we have of "how it really is"; after all, they got us to the moon, didn't they?—or toward the conclusion that indeed scientists' beliefs should not receive preferential treatment in comparison with the students' own beliefs or those of folklore, religion, and supermarket tabloids. No matter whether you relegate textbook knowledge to World 1 or World 2, you run into serious problems of motivation and credibility. Leaf through issues of the journal, *Science Education*, and you will see these problems occupy an inordinate amount of science educators' attention, attention that might better be directed toward remedying the failures of science education to get across an understanding of fundamental scientific ideas.

Something else that seems to get lost in these two-dimensional approaches to science education is any realistic experience of what it is like to do science. Doing science may be reduced to activity in World 1—hands-on work with physical and biological things—or to mucking around with personal beliefs in World 2. Both of these go on in science, of course, but even in combination they miss the main point, which is creating scientific progress. There is no good way to represent this in the two-dimensional world of folk epistemology. There are ways to work around the limitations, especially if one is not concerned with logical consistency, but overall the impression is that of three dimensions having been squashed down to two. Many important relationships are no longer represented.

When we move to three worlds, the first two remain as before. There is the real physical world, which remains important because, inaccessible as it may be to direct knowledge, it is what science is trying to understand. And of course there are the mental states of students and others, also not directly accessible but unavoidably important to people in their roles as learners and teachers. But scientific knowledge need no longer be reduced to these two categories. It consists of conceptual artifacts that stand as a third element in their own right. There are now three dimensions, and these provide space for a number of relationships that are lost in the two-dimensional world of folk epistemology. There is the relation between theory and observation, between personal belief and observation, and between personal belief and theory. And there are the relations between different theories, different phenomena, and different people's readings of the same phenomenon. None of these relations are easy. They are all inferential and highly problematic. But they are what people work on when they are building scientific knowledge.

In other disciplines the conceptual artifacts are different. There are historical accounts and explanations, interpretations and criticisms of literary and artistic works, and so on. But in all cases these add an important third dimension, without which there is no way to give an adequate representation of the learner's relation to the content of the discipline.

The idea of World 3 has a strangeness to it, but I think that is one of its virtues. It is not actually a very radical notion at all. As noted earlier, treating knowledge as something real in itself is one of the ways commonsense deals with it, the other being treating it as mental content. All Popper has done is to sharpen the distinction and confront us with its implications. To do that with concepts that have characteristically gone unexamined and been muddled together, it is often a good idea to articulate them in some unusual, often metaphorical way—to make the familiar strange, so as to help people think about it in less habit-bound ways.

The Knowing Mind

Natural selection built the brain to survive in the world and only incidentally to understand it at a depth greater than is necessary to survive.

—E. O. Wilson, 1998 (p. 61)

W hat does it mean to know something, if it does not mean having something like a sentence or a picture in the mind that constitutes that knowledge? It seems to me that the prospects for a new theory of mind turn on this question. If it cannot be answered, or if the answer is some kind of conceptual monstrosity, then we are probably better off sticking with the theory acquired at our mother's knee.

As I remarked in chapter 2, it is misleading to use the trivial examples of knowledge that so often appear in philosophical treatments—knowing the capital of Malaysia, the chemical composition of water, and so on. Any account of such knowledge that does not posit sentences in the mind will surely appear to be awkward and a lot of work for little return. But education does not rise or fall on its ability to deal with such knowledge, and neither do most other human enterprises. Education does rise or fall on its ability to deal with problems of understanding, so let us turn to those as a fitting challenge for a modern theory of mind.

UNDERSTANDING: THE GHOST IN THE TAXONOMY

"Specifically, what does a student do who "really understands" which he does not do when he does not understand?" —Bloom (1956, p. 1). That is the question as put in the introduction to the mightily influential work known among educationists as Bloom's *Taxonomy* (1956).[1] One will look in vain through that work for an answer, however. There was hardly any way the authors could have produced an answer out of the mixture of behaviorist and folk theory that prevailed at that time.

Instead, *Taxonomy* set out a series of levels of cognitive attainment, with Knowledge (which means, roughly, literal knowledge) as the lowest level, followed by Comprehension, Application, Analysis, Synthesis, and Evaluation. Putting Comprehension next to the bottom of the hierarchy gives the unfortunate impression that the taxonomists considered understanding to be a rather low level of attainment. But a close reading of the monograph suggests the authors viewed the whole taxonomy as addressing the issue of understanding.[2] The ordering of the levels was based on logical dependency: To comprehend a text, you must be able to process it at a verbatim level, to apply information you must comprehend it, and so on. Most of the monograph consists of sample items for testing the various cognitive levels. Although they undoubtedly get at worthwhile educational attainments, they leave understanding as the ghost in the taxonomy. Success on each item may require understanding of some kind, but the emphasis on skills obscures any picture that might emerge of the examinee's understanding. For example, one item intended to test application of knowledge in phys-

---

[1]The *Taxonomy* was actually the work of a blue-ribbon committee sponsored by the American Educational Research Association (AERA) and chaired by Benjamin Bloom. Officially titled the *Taxonomy of Educational Objectives (Handbook I: Cognitive Domain)*, it was one of three taxonomies commissioned by the AERA, the others covering the affective and motor domains. These others never achieved the eminence of the taxonomy for the cognitive domain, however, probably because achievement testing in these areas never got much backing.

[2]The *Taxonomy* draws on material from *The Measurement of Understanding* (Brownell, 1946), in which items spanning all the *Taxonomy*'s levels are related to measuring understanding. The fact that the *Taxonomy* authors refer to the Comprehension level as representing "the lowest level of understanding" (Bloom, 1956, p. 204) more explicitly indicates that they saw the higher levels as also representing understanding.

ics asks what would happen to a ball if it were thrown into the air by a passenger in an elevator that was in free fall. This obviously demands a substantial understanding of Newtonian mechanics, but a student might understand the relevant principles perfectly well and yet be unable to put them together to solve such a complicated problem. One could give an array of such test items, at all of the levels, all bearing on the physics of falling bodies, and yet not end up with any clear idea of students' understanding of the topic. That possibility is not just hypothetical. Years of testing, using the commonsense approach, failed to reveal the deep and pervasive misconceptions[3] that students are now being found to hold in practically every area of science (Wandersee, Mintzes, & Novak, 1994).

The strong point of this commonsense approach is the elaboration of a whole range of performances that are relevant to judging understanding. Its weakness is in its reliance on the mind-as-container metaphor of folk theory of mind. Knowledge really figures in the *Taxonomy* only at the Knowledge level, the lowest level in the hierarchy. The higher levels are taken to represent "intellectual abilities and skills" (p. 204). The *Taxonomy* authors are quite explicit in their adoption of the container metaphor:

> It may be helpful in this case to think of knowledge as something filed or stored in the mind. The task for the individual in each knowledge test situation is to find the appropriate signals and cues in the problem which will most effectively bring out whatever knowledge is filed or stored. (Bloom, 1996, p. 29)

---

[3]Considerable opposition to use of the word "misconception" has arisen among educators. Preferred terms include "alternative conceptions" and 'experience-based conceptions.' Partly this reflects the same euphemistic etiquette that rejects "blind" and "visually handicapped" in favor of "differently sighted." But there is also a philosophical basis that I believe to represent a misconception in itself. Calling something a misconception is thought to imply a positivist epistemology; to call something a misconception, this reasoning goes, you have to believe there exists a true conception and perhaps even that you know what it is. That is nonsense. You can be perfectly confident that a certain key will not fit the lock without persuming to know what key will fit the lock or even whether such a key exists. If you want to be cautious, you should say "I *think* such and such is a misconception," just as you might hedge any other factual assertion you make. There is nothing *especially* risky or presumptuous about declaring something a misconception—compared, say, with declaring that it is time for lunch. Not only is the epistemology askew but so is the tender mindedness. There is nothing shameful about having misconceptions. The best minds in history not only had them but articulated them brilliantly—and, of course, some of what brilliant people are articulating today will someday be judged to be misconceptions. One of the most helpful kinds of criticism you can ever receive is to have it pointed out that you are harboring a misconception. That can make a big difference to your understanding, compared with the little differences that accrue from the ordinary uptake of facts and ideas. I think misconceptions should be openly discussed with students. Presented in the right spirit, they are fascinating. We spoil the fun and misdirect learning when we call them things like "alternative conceptions."

Comprehension, Application, Analysis, Synthesis, and Evaluation—the higher levels in the taxonomy—accordingly represent intellectual skills that operate on the contents of the mental filing cabinet (pp. 38–43). This view dominates much of the discourse of educational practice to this day. Such a view not only fails to account for understanding, it does not even make a place for it. Knowledge is reduced to stored reference material; intelligence and understanding are all in the skills that make use of this material.

A conspicuous failing of the *Taxonomy* is in providing no grounding for the notion of *depth* of understanding. Without that, we really have no handle on understanding at all. For knowledge is almost always characterized by understanding in some degree, however slight. Another item from Bloom's *Taxonomy*, this one intended to test skills of "Analysis," illustrates this point:

> Galileo investigated the problem of the acceleration of falling bodies by rolling balls down very smooth planes inclined at increasing angles, since he had no means of determining very short intervals of time. From the data obtained he extrapolated for the case of free fall. (p. 151)

Examinees are asked to identify an assumption implicit in Galileo's extrapolation. To do so requires understanding the concepts of acceleration due to gravity, rolling friction, and extrapolation. High school students who have taken physics and algebra may have encountered all three of these concepts, but I would expect most of them to fail the item nevertheless. Indeed, I expect that most high school students would not even be able to understand what was being asked of them. Is this because they lack analytic skill? It is not clear what that means or how it could be inferred from performance on such test items. What is obvious, however, is that this problem requires a *deeper* understanding of acceleration due to gravity, rolling friction, and extrapolation than high school students are likely to have acquired. If you only understand acceleration due to gravity as it applies to free fall, if you do not understand how rolling friction relates to incline, and if you think of extrapolation only as the extension of a straight line, then you have no hope of understanding the logic of Galileo's experiment. The *Taxonomy*, however, offers no help in determining how deeply a concept or principle is understood. An unfortunate consequence is that it has served to encourage spending time on hidden assumption problems and the like (practicing what are called "higher order thinking skills") while neglecting deeper understanding of subject matter. This glorification of high-sounding skills and contempt for knowledge is a large part of the reason why I say the Knowledge

Age has not yet come to the schools. I am not sure whether Bloom's *Taxonomy* deserves blame for this or whether its continued prominence merely reflects education's backwardness. At any rate, it is clearly part of the problem rather than part of the solution.

UNDERSTANDING AS AN ATTRIBUTE OF COGNITIVE STRUCTURES

With the so-called "cognitive revolution," knowledge assumed a much larger and more complex role in human cognition (Bereiter & Scardamalia, 1992). A science educator of the 1950s, encountering a student who knew the textbook facts about gravity and acceleration but who failed problems like the two discussed above, would conclude that the student lacked necessary cognitive skills (cf. Bloom, 1956, p. 126). A cognitively sophisticated science educator of today would take, as a first hypothesis, that the student did not really understand gravity and acceleration well enough to draw the appropriate implications. This hypothesis would be grounded in research indicating that such failures of understanding are common even among college students of physics (Kaiser, Proffitt, & McCloskey, 1985). But what does it mean to understand something well enough to draw the appropriate implications? How is this mental state different from having the facts stored away in memory and relying on general cognitive skills to apply them?

In what I take to be the prevalent cognitive view, knowledge is still thought to consist of things in the mind, but the things are considered to be large and to have complex internal structures. A student's knowledge of gravitation may be in the form of a schema, which may be visualized as a hierarchical outline with some lines filled in and others containing blanks waiting to be filled in. My relativity theory schema, for instance, would be mostly empty and would lack even the major headings and the right blanks to constitute what a physicist would credit as understanding. Alternatively, a student's knowledge of a topic may be in the form of a network of concepts and meaningful connections among them. According to either model, the answer to the preceding questions is much the same: The student with a good understanding of gravitation has the relevant concepts embedded in a complex cognitive structure with many connections and implications already filled in.

Understanding, thus, is a characteristic of the schema or network as a whole. To evaluate a student's understanding, we may compare the student's schema or concept net with that of an expert or with some ideal or minimally adequate schema or network. As Nickerson (1985) put it:

One understands a concept (principle, process, or whatever) to the degree that what is in one's head regarding that concept corresponds to what is in the head of an expert in the relevant field. (p. 222)

We may call this the "correspondence" view of understanding.[4] Such a view, of course, presumes that mind as container is not merely a handy metaphor but is how things really are. If the mind is not actually a container of mental objects, if it is only a system of capacities and tendencies as the connectionist view of mind suggests, Nickerson's idea evaporates. There is nothing on which to base a correspondence. You can, of course, get people to draw network diagrams representing what they understand and you can compare one diagram with another (Novak & Gowin, 1984), but only the most naive believe these are pictures of what is in the head. They are documents, in a class with essays and movies, not "mind maps" as some enthusiasts say. Like other documents, they may provide useful information, but comparing one with another is difficult and a far cry from comparing one mind with another. Presented with a document—whether it is an essay, a concept map, or something even more exotic—we cannot say we are looking at its author's understanding. We are looking at words or lines or icons. To make inferences from them about the author's understanding, we need a concept of understanding that will guide us in what to look for. The correspondence view fails to do that.

A RELATIONAL VIEW OF UNDERSTANDING

For a start on a more illuminating view of understanding as it relates to educational purposes, we need to go back a decade before Bloom's *Taxonomy*, to a time before understanding had been decomposed into cognitive behaviors and later reconstituted as mental structures. In 1946, the National Society for the Study of Education devoted a yearbook to the measurement of understanding. In a chapter titled "The Nature of Understanding," Brownell and Sims (1946) noted that "a technically exact definition of 'understand' or 'understanding' is not easily found or formulated" (p. 27). Observing, however, that most people seemed to be able to use the terms with "considerable agreement as to meaning," they proposed to take a practical and nontechnical approach to the topic, beginning with "a broad state-

---

[4]The correspondence view of understanding parallels the correspondence view of truth, which is a version of positivism—the notion that truth is a correspondence between theoretical propositions and an external reality.

ment (not a definition) about the nature of 'understanding'." Brownell and Sims' (1946) broad statement was the following:

> As a start, we may say that a pupil understands when he is able to act, feel, or think intelligently with respect to a situation. (p. 28)

Thus, understanding was seen not as some entity in the head but as an aspect of how we deal with the world. That is a valuable intuition, very much in tune with situated cognitive theory as it is developing today. What the statement gains on this account, however, it loses on another. It directs attention not toward understanding itself, as some distinctive form of human competence, but toward the ways people give evidence of understanding. Carried to the extreme, this can lead to the sort of empiricist reductionism represented in statements like, "Intelligence is what intelligence tests measure." In less extreme forms it leads toward what we have seen in the *Taxonomy* or in present-day performance assessment.

A recent and sophisticated version of this reduction of understanding to performance comes from David Perkins. He called it a "performance perspective":

> Our "performance perspective," in brief, says that understanding is a matter of being able to do a variety of thought-demanding things with a topic—like explaining, finding evidence and examples, generalizing, applying, analogizing, and representing the topic in a new way. (Perkins & Blythe, 1994, pp. 5–6)

When itemized, these "understanding performances" (Perkins, 1992, p. 77) cover the same ground as Bloom's taxonomy—explaining, applying, and so on. Also in keeping with Bloom, these performances are thought to represent not only ways of demonstrating or testing understanding but ways of teaching it as well.

> This performance perspective on understanding illuminates what a pedagogy of understanding should attempt: to enable students to display a variety of relevant understanding performances surrounding the content they are learning ....
>
> If we want students to understand, we should make the choice of teaching them understanding performances about Newton's first law or anything we want them to understand. (Perkins, 1992, p. 78)

Was Perkins saying that understanding just is these performance capabilities or was he saying that understanding is a mental state that makes these performances possible? Perkins was not entirely clear on this point, and it may seem to be one of little consequence. But if understanding is nothing more than a set of desirable performances, why do we bother talking about understanding at all? Why not just focus on the performances? Consider driver education. We could identify a set of performances and habits that constitute good driving and teach them, without giving any thought to understanding—unless we conceive of understanding as an objective that deserves attention in its own right, either as something beyond the performance objectives or as a prerequisite to mastering them. To get serious about teaching for understanding, as I see it, means treating understanding as something that warrants attention in its own right, over and above the attention we give to performance. It means giving attention to *what* it is that needs understanding, to the problems of understanding it, and only further down the line to *how* we will assess it. But this implies that understanding is a state that enables performance, that it is not the performance itself. How can we characterize this state, without falling back on the folk–cognitivist notion that it is a characteristic of objects in the mind? The answer, I believe, lies in considering understanding to be neither something in the mind nor a set of overt performances but rather a relation between the knower and an object of understanding.

This is not an easy conception to grasp, because it depends on both of the departures from folk theory previously discussed; it depends on a connectionist view of mind and a Popperian view of conceptual artifacts. Let us start with an analogy. Gravity is like understanding, in that we only know it through its effects. The childish belief that gravity must be a substance may be likened to the folk belief that understanding is something in the mind. With considerable difficulty, science educators try to get across the idea that gravity is a relation between objects. Suppose we apply the same idea to understanding—*that understanding is a relation between the knower and an object of knowledge.* You are not going to dig into the brain and find it, anymore than you are going to find gravity by digging into the earth. But we can learn a lot about the relationship. And, as is not the case with gravity, we can influence the relationship through our actions.

Adopting this relational perspective, we may restate the question that introduced Bloom's (1956) *Taxonomy*:

> What distinguishes the relationship we call "understanding" from the many other ways that a person may relate to an object of knowledge?

What, for instance, distinguishes understanding genetic engineering from being good at, having an opinion about, being interested in, knowing some things about, being worried about, maintaining an open mind about, or being in the business of genetic engineering? To relate to something is to have a certain disposition toward it, supported by the necessary abilities. The relation of "being good at" implies ability to carry out the work of genetic engineering along with a disposition to do so. The relation of "being worried about" implies a disposition to think dark thoughts about genetic engineering, which in turn implies some ability to infer consequences of it. "Understanding," by comparison, is broader and less definite in its implications. *Understanding implies abilities and dispositions with respect to an object of knowledge sufficient to support intelligent behavior.*

The difference between what I am proposing and what Perkins has proposed may seem too subtle a semantic distinction to be worth the extra trouble that my version entails. The difference takes on clearer significance, however, when we think about teaching for understanding. Perkins's version points inevitably toward teaching for the test—defining a set of performances that will be accepted as evidence of understanding and then schooling learners in those performances. According to the view I am advancing, teaching for understanding is a matter of cultivating the learner's relationship to objects of knowledge, developing it into a relationship capable of supporting intelligent action. Later 1 expand on what this entails, but first I need to show how this relational view fits with what we already understand about understanding in everyday life.

EVERYDAY UNDERSTANDING

Almost all discussion of understanding deals with understanding abstract entities such as concepts, principles, or theories. Because folk theory locates these things in the individual mind, it is natural to locate understanding there as well. But in our day-to-day lives we are often much more concerned with understanding objects and events in the external environment than we are with understanding ideational entities.

High on the list of things we try to understand in our daily lives are other people—not people in general, but the particular people who matter to us, each one of whom presents a distinctive problem of understanding. Although understanding other people is widely recognized as hard to do, we seem to have little difficulty understanding what it means to understand other people. No one is waiting for the experts to provide us a rigorous definition. Let us, therefore, see whether we can draw any generalizations from the understanding of people that may be usefully extended to other kinds of understanding. The following are commonplace observations that apply to understanding any particular person:

1. What constitutes understanding depends on your relationship to the person. Your understanding ought to be quite different depending on whether you are the person's child, spouse, assistant, client, or psychotherapist. Thus there are many different 'right' ways to understand a person.
2. Understanding is intimately bound up with ability to act intelligently in relation to the person. Each advances the other. Although, conceptually, understanding and intelligent action are not the same, it would be virtually impossible in any actual case to disentangle one from the other.
3. Understanding is also intimately bound up with interest. It is not just that interest motivates you to try to understand the person. Indifference toward another person implies lack of understanding.[5]
4. Understanding individual people may depend on understanding their relationships and the people, institutions, occupations, and so on, with which they have these relationships. In this sense, understanding does involve a network—but it is a network out in the world, not inside your head.
5. Understanding of a person is not necessarily accompanied by ability to explain. Explanation is an indication of understanding, but, more important, it is a *means* by which understanding is developed and shared.
6. Although there is no single correct, complete, or ideal understanding of a person, there are recognizably wrong understandings, and these are potentially correctable.
7. Many absorbing discussions in everyday life consist of two or more people trying to achieve a mutual understanding of somebody else. Although there may be considerable speculation about things in the mind of that third person, the discussants make little reference to objects in their own minds. Instead, they talk about the other person or about the conjectures and explanations that have been put forth for discussion.
8. A major way in which understanding of others is manifested, developed, and shared is through narratives in which the other person figures importantly. If the stories you tell about Smith strike others as implausible or incoherent or as failing to ring true, this will count as evidence that you do not understand Smith. Su-

---

[5]*Pace* Homer Simpson, who said, "Just because I'm not interested doesn't mean I don't understand."

perior understanding will be demonstrated by telling stories that other people who know Smith find revealing and enlightening.

9. Having a *deep* understanding of another person means understanding deep things about the person: underlying motives; basic values, dispositions, strengths, weaknesses; recurrent patterns in thought and behavior; and so on.

10. Deep understanding of a person is most readily demonstrated by insightful solution of problems involving the person and by telling stories that have depth of characterization.

11. Depth of understanding normally implies deep and complex involvement with the other person. "No understanding at a distance" is a sound enough rule that those who claim exemption from it are claiming mystical powers.

Without much adjustment, these same observations may be applied to understanding other things in our environments: devices, such as a computer or an automobile; institutions, such as a university or a bank; games, occupations, and rituals—in short, pretty much the full range of things we have some practical reason to understand. In all such cases, understanding inheres in the relation between us and the thing to be understood. The nature of our understanding will depend on the nature of that relationship and will be intimately tied to our goals, interests, and skills. Everything that needs to be said about our understanding can be said without referring to objects in our minds. It will in all cases be sufficient to refer to the object out there or to various conjectures, explanations, and narratives that enter into discussions of the object.[6]

In all these practical cases, deep understanding means understanding deep things about the object in question, which in turn implies deep and extensive involvement with the object. A complex device like a computer can be understood at a number of different levels—ranging roughly from outside to farther and farther into the components of the system. Different levels relate to different kinds of action requiring understanding at that level. Understanding that is limited to the front view of the computer may be sufficient for normal operation, but understanding what is on the back of the computer becomes necessary for installing peripherals, understanding something about the computer's memory and about memory allocations becomes useful for dealing with system crashes, and so on down to levels of understanding required to write system software.

---

[6]An exception would occur if, for example, a discussion concerned with understanding some commonplace occurrence took a bizarre turn that led us to question the mental state of the speaker. But in such a case, our task would have shifted from understanding the subject of discussion to understanding the discussant.

Practically everything dealt with in the practical world admits deeper levels of understanding relevant to certain purposes. An eggbeater is much simpler than a computer, but still there is a level of understanding required for designing an eggbeater that is notably deeper than the understanding required to use one.

The term "deep" is not meant to have a precise meaning in these contexts. It is often useful, especially for purposes of education and training, to think of a progression of levels of understanding that a learner may go through, with one level perhaps being necessary before the next can be achieved. But this does not mean all kinds of understanding can be ordered as to depth. There are things to be understood about a stone that are relevant to the work of a stonecutter and others that are relevant to mineral collecting. They are different enough that little would be gained by disputing which is deeper, although both are obviously deeper than the things one needs to understand about a stone to use it to hold down a picnic blanket.

The important point for our discussion is that these various kinds and levels of understanding can all be fully described and analyzed without ever talking about a mental object—some internal representation of the computer, the eggbeater, or the stone—that embodies the understanding. Understanding is an attribute of the person's relation to the thing that is understood. To behave with understanding is to act in ways attuned to relevant properties of the thing. To have deep understanding means one is attuned to nonobvious structural or causal properties of the thing and to that thing's relations to other things. Of course, there are problems in characterizing understanding in this way, but it does not seem they are alleviated by introducing the idea of mental content.

As far as understanding in the practical affairs of life goes, I have been preaching to the choir. What I have been proposing as a way of treating understanding is the way people already treat it in most walks of life. It is only when we talk about understanding for its own sake, the kind of understanding that is propagated in the schools and the learned disciplines, that we start positing schemas, mental models, or concept nets, and treat understanding as a property of those mental objects. I argue that that shift is unnecessary, that the way we treat practical understanding is a good way to treat theoretical understanding as well. As a stepping stone to that radical notion, however, I next consider what it means to understand a tool.

UNDERSTANDING A TOOL

Concepts, theories, explanatory principles, and the like may be thought of as tools. And so understanding the Newtonian concept of force, for instance, ought to be something like understanding a pipe wrench. Of course, there is a level of understanding a pipe wrench that requires understanding the Newtonian concept of force, but among people who use pipe wrenches, few would have reason to understand them in that scientific a way. Yet clearly there are differences between untutored people whose understanding of pipe wrenches is superficial and inadequate and people who can be credited with deep understanding.

There is a truly wonderful study of depth of understanding as it appears among those who live in the world of pipe wrenches and the like. It is *Working Knowledge* by Douglas Harper (1987). Harper devoted the study to Willie, who ran a repair shop in a rural area and was a genius at fixing everything that came his way. In our book on expertise (Bereiter & Scardamalia, 1993), we used Willie as the prototype of the expert, partly to overcome the stereotype of experts as people who wear white coats and have doctor's degrees. The following is our summary of Harper's findings about the nature of Willie's genius:

> It becomes immediately clear that Willie's skill is primarily mental. But it is not merely a matter of raw mental power, although something like that may also be involved. Willie knows a tremendous amount. He has a deep knowledge of materials, what can be done with them, how they will respond to various treatments. He understands his tools in the same way. His ability to fix things depends on understanding how they were made and why they were designed the way they were, and this often includes understanding shortcomings in manufacture or design that were responsible for the eventual breakdown. With this understanding, Willie is often able to modify the object in the process of repairing it, so that it is better than it was originally. His repair of a broken car door handle, for instance, does not involve simply fixing or reproducing the broken lever. It involves inventing a new lever that fits into the same handle but is less vulnerable to stress. Even Willie's manual skills have a basis in understanding. He understands why filing the teeth on a chain saw often results in rounding the edges, and this enables him to handle the file in such a way that it cuts straight.[7] This is not to say that Willie's knowledge is all conceptual, explainable. He knows how things sound or look or feel under different circumstances, and often there is no way to convey this knowledge except by demonstration. But it is knowledge nonetheless. A brilliant general problem solver, if there is such a

---

[7]Willie's analysis is that, in trying to keep the file level, people press down with equal force on both ends. But as the file moves across the blade, the leverage changes, so that the effect of equal force is that the front end goes down. To keep the file level, one must hold the file lightly and change the balance of pressure between the two hands as the file moves, so as to compensate for the change in leverage.

thing (it is what Sherlock Holmes purported to be), would be helpless trying to solve Willie's problems without Willie's knowledge. (pp. 12–13)

Let us try mapping this kind of understanding onto the set of characteristics developed earlier for understanding a person:

1. What constitutes understanding depends on your relationship to pipe wrenches—whether you are an ordinary user, a plumber, a hardware dealer, a tool designer, a physics teacher, and so on.
2. Understanding is intimately bound up with, but not the same as, ability to use and treat the tool intelligently.
3. Understanding is also intimately bound up with interest. Failure to appreciate the ingenious design of a pipe wrench suggests lack of understanding.
4. Understanding a pipe wrench may depend on understanding its relation to other things—for instance, how it is different from a monkey wrench and from a vice grip, what it is about pipes that makes a pipe wrench suited to gripping them.
5. Understanding of a pipe wrench is not necessarily accompanied by ability to explain. Explanation is an indication of understanding, but, more important, it is a *means* by which understanding is developed and shared.
6. Although there is no single correct, complete, or ideal understanding of a pipe wrench, there are recognizably wrong understandings, and these are potentially correctable.
7. Discussions aimed at advancing understanding of pipe wrenches will seldom make reference to mental states or mental contents of the discussants. Instead, discussion will focus on pipe wrenches themselves, their uses, and their relations to other things in the world.
8. A major way in which understanding of pipe wrenches is developed, manifested, and shared is through deliberating on and sharing insights into *problems* involving them.
9. Having a *deep* understanding of pipe wrenches means understanding deep things about them: why they are designed the way they are, the functions of various parts and design features, causes of faulty performance, underlying physical principles (this is where understanding force comes in), and so on.
10. Deep understanding of pipe wrenches is most clearly demonstrated by insightful solution of problems concerning them.
11. Deep understanding normally implies deep and complex involvement.

Although people are vastly more complex than pipe wrenches, it seems we can apply all the same principles in elaborating what it means to understanding them. Will the same principles, then, suffice to characterize the kinds of understanding that school curricula are supposed to promote?

SITUATIONAL UNDERSTANDING

Often the thing to be understood is not a single object or kind of object or event but is a whole situation or complex. We talk about people "knowing the ropes" or "knowing their way around." To say that you understand baseball or banking or human relations or, for that matter, that you understand numbers or Latin American history is to say not only that you understand a lot of individual things but that you understand the whole complex of which they are a part. What we may call "situational understanding" fits all 11 of the characteristics previously discussed with reference to persons and tools. The connection to intelligent action is particularly strong, however. Knowing the ropes or knowing ones way around implies an ability to act intelligently and resourcefully in the situation or domain but it also clearly implies this ability is rooted in thorough knowledge. It is not at all the same as native wit. A none-too-bright person who knows the ropes will often outsmart the ignorant genius.

What does it mean, however, to understand a whole situation or domain, other than understanding its parts? The geographical metaphor is helpful here. Knowing your way around in a city or a wilderness means, at the minimum, knowing how to get from one place to another by efficient routes. It is something more than knowing a lot of individual landmarks and routes, but is it understanding? In a modest way it fits the description. It is having a relationship to the place that is sufficient to support intelligent action of a certain kind. There are, moreover, deeper levels of understanding that also go by the name of "knowing ones way around," and that support more wide-ranging intelligent action. They amount to knowing deeper things about the place. We once vacationed on a small island in the Caribbean, staying in a house owned by a Toronto friend. The friend advised us to put ourselves into the hands of one of the taxi cab drivers who would meet the boat and let him "look after us" for the week. His looking after us turned out to include not only taking us places but finding us tuna and lobster on an island where these were thought to be unavailable, taking us to the right beach for the weather, fetching the police detective when our house was robbed, and generally solving any problems that arose. He knew his island, obviously, knew it better than most of the others who lived there, because he got around more and solved more various problems.

You learn your way around geographically by solving navigation problems. You learn your way around the shops and markets by solving supply problems. In general, you learn your way around in a domain by solving problems in it. Yet the textbook problems that are the mainstay of school mathematics and science seem not to have that result. It is not that the problems are not challenging enough. The problems you solve in finding your way around in a city may all be relatively easy (especially if you are not averse to asking directions), but they do the job. They engage you in putting information together in different ways to achieve different destinations or itineraries. Eventually everything fits together into what is often called a mental map, although that is not an apt metaphor. When you really know your way around you know where everything is in relation to yourself, wherever you happen to be, not in relation to points on a map. Textbook problems ought to have you putting information together in many different ways to achieve many different purposes. They ought to engage you in the equivalent of criss-crossing terrain in many different directions.[8] In the end, you ought to have something that might be called a mental map or a mental model except that, again, you are not aware of consulting a model; you simply feel confident that you know how to deal with problems in that domain.

What we know about textbook physics problems, which have been the most studied, is that they can often be solved without reference to the physics principles they are supposed to be teaching (Sweller, 1988) and that students tend to classify problems according to the concrete situations they are about (inclined planes, pulleys and weights, etc.) rather than according to the principles involved (Chi, Feltovich, & Glaser, 1981). This sounds like students are learning their way around in a domain, all right, but it is the domain of textbook physics problems, not the domain of physics, of which those problems occupy a small and isolated part. They may acquire understanding, which supports intelligent behavior in the context of doing textbook problem assignments, but it is not an understanding of the physical world, and even less is it an understanding of the theoretical world from which textbook problems are drawn.

THEORETICAL UNDERSTANDING

Perhaps the most thoroughly researched problems in theoretical understanding are those associated with Newtonian mechanics. Al-

---

[8]This is an idea elaborated in Spiro, Feltovich, Jacobson, & Coulson (1991), with the objective being what they call "cognitive flexibility."

though such principles as universal gravitation, inertia, and the relationship between force and acceleration are common parts of the school curriculum and are usually taught systematically in beginning physics, there is evidence that most students, including many who have studied physics, understand motion in a pre-Newtonian way. They believe continual force must be applied to keep a body in motion and that bodies propelled along a curved path will continue along the curved path (McCloskey, Caramazza, & Green, 1980).[9] Although they may be able to solve problems that explicitly deal with acceleration, they seldom make spontaneous use of this most fundamental concept of Newtonian mechanics in solving other problems or in explaining phenomena.

Let us, accordingly, use Newtonian mechanics as an example for investigating the extent to which theoretical understanding may be treated in the same way as practical understanding. The 11 observations made earlier about understanding people are here applied to what we shall for simplicity call "Newton's theory":

1. What constitutes understanding Newton's theory depends on your relationship to it. Different kinds of understanding (not just different levels of understanding) are appropriate to an elementary science teacher, a historian of science, a mechanical engineer, a theoretical physicist, and a croquet player.
2. Understanding is intimately bound up with ability to act intelligently in relation to the theory. Acting intelligently with regard to Newton's theory might mean using it intelligently as a tool or it might mean using it to make sense of physical phenomena. A person who has thoroughly "internalized" Newton's theory will perceive and act in ways consistent with the theory, without having to recall or deliberately apply its principles.[10]
3. Understanding is also intimately bound up with interest. Although exceptions are conceivable (as they are in the case of understanding persons), it seems a reasonable supposition that the person who has no interest in Newton's theory does not understand it.
4. Understanding Newton's theory depends on understanding its relationships to cosmology, vectorial representations of forces, and so on (Reif & Heller, 1982).

[9]Note that although the first belief is a reasonable inference based on experience, the second is not. Naive beliefs generally show this mixture of commonsense generalization and fanciful idealization.

[10]See "Translating Formal Knowledge Into Informal Knowledge and Skill" in Bereiter and Scardamalia (1993, pp. 65–72).

5. Understanding of Newton's theory is not necessarily accompanied by ability to explain. Explanation may, however, play a crucial role in acquiring and furthering its understanding.
6. Although there is no single correct, complete, or ideal understanding of Newton's theory, there are recognizably wrong understandings, and these are potentially correctable.
7. Discussions of Newton's theory will seldom make reference to mental states or mental contents of the discussants. Instead, discussion will focus on the theory itself, its implications, applications, limitations, and so on.
8. A major way in which understanding of Newton's theory will be manifested is through narratives in which ideas such as gravity, acceleration, and inertia figure. An account of placing a communications satellite in orbit, for instance, could be expected to reveal quite a bit about the extent and accuracy of the speaker's understanding of Newtonian physics. Inadequate understanding would be manifested in narratives that are incomplete, implausible, and incoherent.
9. Having a *deep* understanding of Newton's theory means understanding the deeper things about it—derivations, proofs, nonobvious implications and applications.
10. Deep understanding of Newton's theory is most clearly demonstrated by insightful solution of problems involving it.
11. A deep understanding of Newton's theory can only arise from deep involvement with the theory—from thinking about it a lot and from various angles, from using it in various contexts and for various purposes.

In short, we can rather satisfactorily characterize understanding of Newton's theory in the same way we can characterize understanding of a person or a pipe wrench. There are differences, but the differences tend to place Newton's theory between the other two rather than off on a different dimension. That is, there are more varied ways to understand a person than there are ways to understand Newton's theory, but more ways to understand Newton's theory than there are ways to understand a pipewrench. A similar ordering obtains with respect to potential for intelligent action, for interest and feelings, for complexity of relationships, for the value of explanation, and for levels of depth of understanding.

If we are to treat understanding a theory in the same way that we treat understanding material objects, we run into an ontological problem that continues to arouse a good deal of opinionated dissent among philosophers. A glance back over the preceding points reveals each of them implies that Newton's theory is a real thing enjoying an existence of its own independent of our cognition. For, otherwise, how could we stand in relation to it, have an interest in it, know things about it, and so on? Accordingly, this view of understanding requires accepting the idea of *conceptual artifacts*, as put forth in the preceding chapter. With the help of this notion, the point I have been trying to make can be stated in a more general form as follows: *We should treat the understanding of conceptual artifacts in the same commonsense way we treat the understanding of material objects—as inhering in the relationship between the person and the object rather than as a characteristic of a different kind of object located in the person's mind.*

UNDERSTANDING AND INTELLIGENT ACTION

"Understand" is a transitive verb. When we speak of understanding, we always speak of understanding something. The thing that is understood—the object of understanding—may be, as in previous examples, a person, a mechanical device, or a theory. Or it could be something less easily specified, such as a situation or a whole field of study or an aspect of life, such as love. Regardless, understanding implies something about the relation between a person and an object. The point of the preceding discussion is that instead of speculating about a mental state that constitutes understanding we should be looking at the nature of the relationship between the person and the object of understanding. What is it about such a relationship that makes it a relationship of understanding as distinct from a relationship of liking or disliking, owning, depending upon, admiring, having doubts about, being in control of, or any of the myriad other ways a person may relate to something else?

Many dog owners will insist and can marshal evidence to show that their dogs understand them. According to the 11 points by which we characterized understanding of a person, it is conceivable that a dog could qualify to some extent on all of them except those that involve explanation and narrative. But, still, how are we justified in calling it understanding when there is no verbal evidence? Migratory birds may act in accordance with principles of celestial navigation, and this implies something in their nervous systems is designed to carry out computations according to those principles, but, no matter how impressed we may be by this feat, we are not tempted to credit birds with even the most limited understanding of the subject. We do not imagine that if the birds could talk they would be able to expound on the principles of celestial navigation, but it is only fanciful and not blatantly silly to imagine that if the family dog could talk it would have some wise things to say about us. Why the difference?

When we attribute understanding to our dog it is on the basis of its whole relationship to us, which we take to be complex, sensitive, flexible—in a word, intelligent. We have no reason to suppose that such a relationship exists between a migratory bird and the stars (although we expect it to exist between an astronomer and the stars). The conventional, folk theoretic way of construing understanding is that it is a property of the dog's mental makeup, which is the *cause* of the intelligent characteristics of the relationship or which is *manifested* in various aspects of its relationship to us. Picking up on the intuition of Brownell and Sims (1946), however, we can eliminate an unnecessary intermediary and simply declare that understanding is an *aspect* of the relationship. The relationship may also have many other aspects. Our dog's relationship to us may be characterized as affectionate, dependent, playful—characteristics that carry no implication of understanding. *Understanding refers to that aspect of a relationship that has to do with its potential to support intelligent action.*

Notice that I am not saying that understanding *is* intelligent action or the ability to act intelligently. Intelligent action, as I pointed out before, may depend on a number of factors in addition to understanding: opportunity, motivation, enabling skills, general mental abilities, and so on. What I am proposing is a relational conception of understanding. Understanding, accordingly, is not a thing—an object in the mind—nor an attribute of a mind. Understanding refers just to the relation between an actor and an object. It is the relationship viewed from the standpoint of its ability to support intelligent action.

In practical terms, this means understanding is a precondition of intelligent action. No understanding means no intelligent action. You might immediately object that you do not need to understand how a microwave oven works, for instance, to use it intelligently. But of course you do need some understanding. If you had grown up in a remote village and had no acquaintance with either electrical appliances or ovens, a few how-to-do-it lessons would not be enough to enable you to use a microwave oven intelligently. The woman ahead of me at a take-out lunch counter, who recoiled in horror when the counterman proposed to warm her soup in a microwave, also lacked sufficient understanding to behave intelligently. And from my own experience as a heavy user of the microwave in cooking, I feel sure I could get better results if I understood its physics in greater depth. That is true of most complex artifacts, whether material or conceptual. But do you need to understand how a multidigit multiplication algorithm works to use multiplication intelligently? That is a live issue in mathematics education. I think the answer in this case is clearly no. You have to understand multiplication, but that is something different. The justification for trying to get children to understand the arithmetic algorithms they use is of a different order; it is to build up the conviction that mathematics in general makes sense, that it is not beyond understanding.

Understanding, or its opposite, is often accompanied by feelings. There is the exciting "Aha!" sensation of sudden illumination and the delightful feeling of "getting it" when understanding develops smoothly. There are feelings of bewilderment, confusion, and frustration, or sometimes instead feelings of wonderment and anticipation when we are confronted with something we do not understand. These feelings no doubt have much to do with our commonsense assumption that understanding is something in the mind.

Wittgenstein (1980) examined at length the feeling of understanding and concluded there is no particular feeling such as there is with grief or joy or pain or warmth. "Understand," he said, "just is not used like a word for sensation" (par. 311). Contemporary psychologists speak of "the illusion of understanding." Wittgenstein would probably have regarded this as a misuse of terms. True, we sometimes feel that we have understood something and it is later revealed that we did not, but our mistaken feeling is nothing like an optical illusion.

What is it, then, to *feel* that we understand? Taking a cue from Karl Popper (Popper & Eccles, 1977, p. 44), I would say it is a feeling of confidence. It is confidence that we know how to proceed, how to deal as appropriate with the object of understanding. If someone has given us directions, we feel that we understand them when we feel confident that we know how to get to the destination, how to assemble the cabinet, or whatever. Feeling that we understand a theory or a proof, Popper said, means feeling confident that we can reconstruct it at will. In studying for an examination, we feel that we understand when we are confident we will be able to answer the kinds of questions likely to be asked.

Like other kinds of confidence, confidence in our understanding may turn out to be ill-founded. The same is true of feelings of unconfidence. The directions we receive may seem unclear, but as we proceed they may prove to be perfectly adequate. But feelings of confidence and unconfidence are essential guides to our cognitive efforts. They constitute a form of what I discuss in the next chapter as "impressionistic knowledge." It is feeling-based knowledge that plays a part along with other kinds of knowledge and is especially important in making judgments. Like other kinds of knowledge, it is improvable. Young children often claim they understand a text as soon as they are able to say all the words. One thing traditional classroom recitation does is build up a better anticipation of the challenges that text understanding may face. This is bound to have an effect on confidence, requiring more thorough study of a text before students feel sure of their understanding. An important part of becoming sophisticated in any scholarly discipline amounts to educating your feelings so that your confidence in understanding becomes an increasingly reliable guide.

This "education of feelings of confidence" is an essential part of developing a close relationship with another person. Traditional courtship was carried out under such constraints that it hardly served much purpose in acquiring a deep and detailed understanding of the prospective mate. What it did enable a couple to do, however, was develop confidence in their feelings toward each other. If the marriage went well, their confidence would become elaborated as new information emerged and would evolve into feelings of understanding—confidence in their ability to predict and interpret the actions of each other and repair and improve their relationship. We may liken this to the early stages of learning a discipline. You cannot know enough at an early stage to have a warranted feeling of understanding, but you should begin to acquire confidence that the discipline is understandable and that you have the capacity to understand it. As learning proceeds, this feeling is not supplanted but evolves into confidence that you can explain, apply, find out what is needed, and correct errors—thus, improve and repair your relation to the objects of understanding.

Only occasionally would confidence in understanding be a result of conscious analysis. More often it appears as a spontaneous feeling, which is why we experience it as a direct feeling of understanding and why, accordingly, we locate understanding as something in our minds. But most feelings of confidence are spontaneous. If you have to jump over a ditch you may feel confident you can do it or you may be in some doubt; only in the latter case will you consciously gauge the distance against an estimate of your jumping ability. Otherwise you just feel confident and jump. The same is true of more complex psychological matters. For instance, your confidence that you will be able to handle yourself in an anticipated difficult social situation is likely to include confidence in understanding the situation but also confidence in your social skills, resourcefulness, emotional equilibrium, or even strength of character. In short, there is nothing very special about a feeling of understanding. It is similar to and often part of many other feelings of confidence or lack of confidence that are common in experience. All that is distinctive is what the confidence is about. It is confidence about knowledge. Specifically, it is confidence about the adequacy of our knowledge to support intelligent behavior in foreseeable situations—confidence that we will know how to proceed, that we will be able to treat the object of understanding in a suitable way.

Although feelings of understanding are important, as a kind of knowledge that guides action, we should not overrate them and above all should not make the mistake of equating understanding with feeling. Most of our understanding is not accompanied by any feeling. If the ditch is only a foot wide, we do not feel confident that we can get over it; we simply step over it and think nothing of it. Similarly, when reading easy material we have no feeling of understanding it, we simply pick up the information. Our thoughts are on what the text is about, not on our understanding of it. Understanding, as I have argued, is a relation between the knower and the object of understanding. As with other relationships that shape our lives, we may only occasionally be conscious of it and have feelings associated with it. Most of the time we just go about our business and our feelings are about the things and events we encounter, not about our relations to them. But there are times when our relations are problematic or when they undergo a sudden change. At those times feelings arise that importantly affect our actions (Oatley, 1992, chap. 4). It is no different with feelings of understanding.

NATURALIZING ABSTRACT KNOWLEDGE OBJECTS

Discourses about understanding commonly start off with an admission that understanding itself is not well understood (cf. Brownell & Sims, 1946; Nickerson, 1985). I have been arguing, on the contrary, that we already understand a great deal about understanding as it applies to the ordinary affairs of life; it is just that this knowledge tends to get left outside the school door. We know how to acquire an understanding of the various living and nonliving material things that we deal with in everyday life—our dogs, cars, neighbors, television sets and VCRs, espresso machines, African violets, pomegranates, income tax forms, cold tablets, martial arts academies, and so on. There is no single recipe for achieving an understanding of all these things. Each is distinctive, and yet we would seldom find ourselves at a loss in pursuing understanding or in guiding someone else in the pursuit of it. Not that we would care to pursue understanding of all of them: Understanding takes time and effort, and so we have to allocate our resources. But if we did decide to pursue understanding of any of these, we would tackle it as a problem. What is it about the object in question that we trying to understand and to what purpose? Having framed the problem—perhaps initially in rather vague terms—we would set about solving it. In the process we would likely reframe the problem (as understanding grows, so does our recognition of what needs understanding). We would never ask, "Have I finally achieved understanding?" No such end is in view. But we would ask whether we had achieved understanding sufficient for our purposes.

At the center of our attention always would be the object itself, what we are trying to understand. Its context would be the spheres of activity in which the object matters to us. This could be a very limited sphere of practical activity, thus calling for a very limited understanding (such might be the case with television sets, for most people), or it could be a very general effort to make sense of the world. Together, the object and the situation or situations in which it figures for us are all we need when it comes to framing problems of understanding. We do not need to occupy ourselves with structures in our minds. It would not even occur to us. We may have subjective impressions of understanding or bewilderment and will pay attention to those, but we would treat them as no different from the feelings of confidence or uncertainty, satisfaction or discomfort, that we feel in any kind of problematic endeavor. They would not be definitive of the problem we are trying to solve or direct indicators of our progress in solving it.

We are accomplished in pursuing understanding of things in the material world because we have been working at it since infancy and in many different situations. But when it comes to understanding abstract objects such as theories and scientific, mathematical, or literary concepts, our experience is of later origin and much more limited. Even if we are fortunate enough to encounter schooling that emphasizes understanding, it is likely throughout elementary school, and perhaps through high school as well, that the focus will be on understanding the natural world directly and not on understanding theories that purport to explain the natural world.

For most people, accordingly, the world of abstract knowledge objects—of conceptual artifacts—is an unreal world. In contrast, mental content does exist, or seems to; we seem to experience it and it seems to have a location, in our heads. Feelings of understanding and not understanding are undeniably real. And so, instead of attending to abstract objects we attend to mental states. This is satisfactory for many purposes, but it means the whole complex of skills we acquired for dealing with problems of understanding no longer applies because there is no longer a *thing* to apply those skills to.

My proposal is simply that we naturalize abstract objects, treat them as real things that we can nudge about and look at from different sides, take apart, try out, become fascinated with, discuss with our friends, and try to reinvent. We already do this with very familiar abstract objects, such as numbers. Unless we stop to worry about their ontological status, we will almost surely treat the whole numbers as enjoying an existence of their own, apart from the various ways of representing them concretely and symbolically. The number 25 has properties of its own, such as being odd and the square of 5 and the square root of 625, which are not properties of the Arabic or Roman numerals or of a collection of 25 bananas or of a 25-cent piece. Understanding numbers means understanding and being able to make intelligent use of these properties. Children brought up in a numerate environment have already acquired a considerable understanding of these abstract objects well before their first encounters with school arithmetic (Griffin et al., 1994). Numbers can be fun to play with, and playing-with is a child's way of developing a relationship. Ironically, however, when children enter school they are liable to fall into the hands of an adult who believes they must be shielded from abstraction and so they will spend their time working out puzzles with blocks and tokens, and later with numerals, without any discussion of what these exercises reveal about numbers in their own right. In the more reflective approaches to primary mathematics, however (e.g., Cobb, et al., 1997), even though concrete representations may be used, children are encouraged to think about numbers as such—to establish meaningful relationships with these abstract objects in the same way they establish meaningful relationships with the people, animals, and implements in their environment.

Other abstract objects that have managed to secure a place in the natural order include stories, poems, jokes, and songs. With respect to these, understanding also has a natural meaning that does not involve suppositions about mental representations. To "get" a joke is to *see* what is funny about it. You may *see* it and yet not *like* it. *See* and *like* are relational terms. They do not refer to something in your head but to something that obtains between you and something else. Extending that relational view of understanding to the objects dealt with in formal education is the nut of what I am arguing for in this chapter.

EDUCATION FOR UNDERSTANDING

"Teaching for understanding" has emerged as one of the banner principles of educational reform (Cohen, McLaughlin, & Talbert, 1993). Probably few teachers at any time would have declared they were not teaching for understanding, but its salience as a regulatory principle rises and falls, and tends to fall when people get overconcerned with test scores. Its rise is helped along by mounting evidence of students' lack of understanding in academic areas, especially science. I have already alluded to the research on misconceptions, but ordinary factual knowledge testing also points to deficient understanding. For instance, in a recent survey of Canadians aged 16 and over, almost a quarter indicated they believed the sun goes around the earth and half the respondents failed to choose 1 year as the time it takes the earth to go around the sun. These cannot be written off as isolated bits of missing or wrong information, like not being able to name the 10 provinces (another task Canadians often fail). They bespeak profound lack of understanding of the solar system.

A great deal of instructional research has dealt in one way or other with promoting understanding. This has been one of the main concerns of the enterprise known as "Instructional Design Theory" (Reigeluth, 1983). Despite many variations, there seem to be three basic approaches to teaching for understanding. The time-honored, commonsense way is by direct explanation. It is the approach we spontaneously adopt in everyday life when we are trying to get someone to understand something. We try to explain it as clearly as possible and in terms the listener will be able to understand. We may use diagrams or analogies, anything that will get the idea across. Instructional Design Theory has mainly dealt with refinements of direct explanation. There is clearly much of value in the direct approach (Hirsch, 1996). In fact, it is a pretty sure bet that civilization would collapse without it.

The second approach to teaching for understanding may be broadly characterized as a "process" approach. It is reflected in Bloom's *Taxonomy* and in Perkins' "performance perspective." It relegates knowledge to the status of reference material in a mental filing cabinet. All the intellectual richness resides in the cognitive skills that operate on this material. Such a standpoint offers no clear prescription for teaching for understanding, but it suggests that, besides mastering items of declarative knowledge, students ought to be engaged in a lot of interpreting, applying, analyzing, synthesizing, and evaluating. *Science: A Process Approach* (American Association for the Advancement of Science, 1967) exemplifies this approach; there is little direct focus on conceptual content but instead a focus on carrying out the various processes thought to constitute the "doing" of science.

The third approach, associated with contemporary cognitive science, is focused on students' mental models. "Conceptual change teaching" (Anderson & Roth, 1989) is perhaps the most straightforward exemplification. It involves trying to determine the student's present understanding and to devise some kind of experience that will change the student's mental model. There is no commitment to any particular kind of educational experience. It could involve direct explanation, problem solving, experiments or demonstrations, or discussions or debates among students upholding different ideas. The approach is essentially constructivist, however. Accordingly, it is presumed that conceptual change must take place through cognitive activity of the learner, that it cannot be merely conveyed.

The mental models approach is in the ascendancy, and it has the virtue of being able to incorporate advantages of the other two approaches as well. Still, something important is lacking, which is implicit in the direct explanation approach. It is close attention to the things to be understood. By casting everything in terms of mental content, the mental models approach focuses attention on the shortcomings of students' mental models rather than on the richness of what there is to be learned. Major theories have great depth and wide implications. Coming to understand a living theory means establishing a many-faceted relationship and one that will keep developing as one's experience grows and as the theory itself evolves. This grand sense of *what is there to be understood*—a sense that has guided traditionalists of the classic variety for centuries—tends to get lost in what amounts to a mental remodeling operation.

Yet a constructivist view of learning is in no way inconsistent with a regard for the abstract objects of understanding. This is most clearly shown in the writings of Karl Popper. On the one hand, Popper advanced the idea of a world of abstract objects existing independent of human cognition—World 3, as discussed in the preceding chapter. On the other hand, he regarded coming to understand such objects as a highly constructive mental process:

> According to my view, we may understand the grasping of a World 3 object as an active process. We have to explain it as the making, the re-creation, of that object. In order to understand a difficult Latin sentence, we have to construe it: to see how it is made, and to re-construct it, to re-make it. In order to understand a problem, we have to try at least some of the more obvious solutions, and to discover that they fail; thus we rediscover that there is a difficulty—a problem. In order to understand a theory, we have first to understand the problem which the theory was designed to solve, and to see whether the theory does better than do any of the more obvious solutions. In order to understand a somewhat difficult argument like Euclid's proof of the theorem of Pythagoras (there are simpler proofs of this theorem), we have to do the work ourselves, taking full note of what is assumed without proof. In all these cases the understanding becomes "intuitive" when we have acquired the feeling that we can do the work of reconstruction at will, at any time. (Popper & Eccles, 1977, p. 44)

According to the view I am trying to advance, educators ought to be less occupied with what is in students' minds and more concerned with what kinds of relationships are developing between the students and those conceptual artifacts that find their way into the curriculum. Formal education is inevitably much involved with conceptual artifacts. They might be and often are kept at bay in the elementary school, but it would make a travesty of education to keep them out of the picture indefinitely. They are what the sciences and learned disciplines produce, and formal education, regardless of the philosophy it ostensibly follows, must bring about some kind of relationship between students and such abstract objects. I do not see how anything less than that can be regarded as "teaching for understanding."

Teaching for understanding entails more than that, however. Students are not likely to find most abstract knowledge objects very engaging in their own right. As Popper said, the first step in understanding a theory is to understand the problem it is intended to solve. Understanding the problem may require understanding other abstract objects, but it also requires some engagement with the real-world phenomena that give rise to the theoretical problem. It is the same as with understanding a tool or a machine. Students cannot be expected to understand a clock until they understand the problem of metering time and why it matters. The problem has to be a problem to the students, in other words. And so teaching for understanding, in all its creditable versions, occurs within the context of students' efforts to understand their world.

The several approaches to teaching for understanding that I have touched on in this section represent a descending scale of definiteness about the nature of the teacher's job. In the didactic approach, the job is clear-cut. There are certain concepts and principles to be taught and the teacher's job is to present these in a lucid enough way that they will be understood. In the "process" approach this clarity of purpose is lost, but in its place are activities and skills that lend themselves to definite plans and to concrete action on the teacher's part. The conceptual change approach, however, asks teachers to get inside students' heads and to adjust their actions according to what is found there. As Roth (1992) observed, this task is so elusive that many teachers who declare in favor of a conceptual change approach are found actually to be pursuing one of the preceding two. But what, then, is a teacher to do on being told that understanding is a relation between the knower and the object of understanding and that the educational task is to make this relationship a rich and functional one? Shake one's head and walk away sounds like a reasonable response.

All I can do in defense of this seemingly outlandish fourth approach is to hark back to what was said earlier about everyday understanding. If your task as a teacher was to develop deep understanding of a radial arm saw, for instance, you might use elements of the first three approaches. There would be some stating of facts and explaining, but it would be limited to what seemed to need stating and explaining. Needed in what sense? Well, needed to proceed or needed because it is something that puzzles the learner or is likely to be overlooked. You might, for instance, feel it necessary to explain why, in doing a rip cut, you position the saw so that the teeth are coming up instead of down against the wood. Or you might even need to teach some trigonometry to get the student to understand the making of angle cuts. You might prescribe some experiments and skill practice, but these would be directly relevant to using the saw as a tool. You would not fancy that you were developing spatial reasoning skills or a woodworking schema by this means. And you would be on the watch for misconceptions, such as might arise from faulty generalization from other kinds of saws. But all of these would be subordinated to the purpose of helping the learner become an intelligent and versatile user of the saw, aware of its capabilities, limitations, and dangers, and familiar enough with its mechanisms to make necessary adjustments, recognize when something was out of whack, and improvise when novel problems were encountered. Theories are tools, too. Their main use is in explaining. Why should we take a more simplistic approach to understanding a scientific theory, something that represents a culminating achievement of civilization, than we do to understanding a piece of shop equipment?

FORMS OF UNDERSTANDING

Through a series of brilliantly reasoned and erudite books, Kieran Egan (e.g., 1979, 1988, 1997) has developed an educational theory that centers on understanding but that seems at first sight to stand on an island of its own apart from all of the educational thought that has swirled around this topic and that I have advanced or criticized here. It is indeed original but I think it can be brought onto the same continent as the ideas I have been discussing, where it can be shown that on one hand it shares some of the same weaknesses as other theories grounded in folk psychology and epistemology, whereas on the other hand it is compatible with and adds significant dimensionality to the view of understanding I am advocating.

The central idea, which Egan has derived mainly from cultural history, is that there are different kinds or forms of understanding, each one growing out of its predecessor. There is at bottom Somatic Understanding, which comes with the equipment, so to speak, and is not unique to human beings. Then there is Mythic Understanding, the characteristic way that preliterate societies make sense of the world. Literacy makes possible Romantic Understanding, which has the manifold characteristics commonly associated with the Romantic Age. It is a richly textured understanding that always has human beings and their feelings as integral to the understanding, unlike Philosophic Understanding, which has the detached character of science, mathematics, and the more rigorous forms of philosophizing. Finally there is Ironic Understanding, which might also be called wisdom; it recognizes the limitations of all forms of understanding.

To the extent that it is concerned with understanding at all, formal education may be seen to focus almost exclusively on Philosophic Understanding. According to Egan this is poor practice on two counts: First, it doesn't work. Children cannot go straightaway to Philosophic Understanding. Egan argues that they need to, in effect, recapitulate cultural history by developing first Mythic and then Romantic Understanding. In fact, Egan argues, this is what children normally do in their own efforts to make sense of the world, and so schooling would do well to take advantage of this naturally occurring evolution rather trying to override it. Second (and this is a much deeper argument), Philosophic Understanding by itself is sterile, bloodless, and overweening—as Romantic critics have often alleged. It needs to incorporate or preserve elements of Somantic, Mythic, and Romantic Understanding to be fully human (and, furthermore, to provide the groundwork for later development of Ironic Understanding).

With some reservations about the recapitulation notion, I find all the rest of this to be good medicine. From Egan's vantage point, my treatment of understanding will be seen to focus too narrowly on Philosophic Understanding—particularly its subtype, Theoretical Understanding. The reason for this emphasis, however, has to do with the purpose of this book, which is not to deal with everything that matters in education but instead to deal with the shortcomings of folk theory of mind for addressing the needs of a knowledge society. Those shortcomings are most pronounced in matters having to do with conceptual artifacts, which in turn are assuming more widespread importance in the emerging knowledge society. Although folk theory has weaknesses for dealing with all forms of understanding, it is, as I have already tried to show, at its worst when it comes to theoretical understanding. If someone tells you that understanding Keats' *Ode on a Grecian Urn* means having something in your mind that matches what is in the mind of an expert, you will immediately recognize that such a criterion is at least narrow and perhaps rather screwy. You do not need an enhanced theory of mind to realize there is something personal and contingent about understanding a poem or a work of art. It is not much of a stretch to think of understanding in these cases as involving the whole relationship between the knower and the object of understanding. But if someone tells you that understanding plate tectonics means having something in your mind that matches what is in the mind of a geologist, you may well accept that as reasonable. Many cognitive psychologists apparently do. I expect Egan would agree with me that such a conception of understanding is also narrow and rather screwy. Philosophic Understanding should involve the whole person as well. You should have feelings about ideas, intuitions that guide your thought. You should be excited by discoveries and insights; offended by distortion, oversimplification, and sloppy thinking; responsive to beauty in ideas; courageous in the face of difficulties and disapproval. (These are notions I develop more fully in the next chapter.)

For Egan, the job of acquiring the various kinds of understanding consists of learning to use the intellectual tools that make such understanding possible. Mythic Understanding depends on the tools of oral language, especially storytelling. Romantic Understanding depends on the expanded representational capabilities of written language. Philosophic Understanding uses the tools of logic, mathematics, the hypothetico-deductive method, and so on. Ironic Understanding involves the imaginative use of all of the tools "for putting into language meanings that the literal forms of language cannot contain" (Egan, 1997, p. 171). Although this treatment of intellectual tools may seem to resonate with what I have been saying about conceptual artifacts as tools, I see it as closer to Bloom's *Taxonomy* than to what I have been arguing for. Although it grows out of a different tradition, Egan's approach to teaching for understanding is, like that of Bloom and his committee, a process approach. Understanding, for Egan, consists of being able to use the appropriate "intellectual tools"; for Bloom, it consists of being able to apply the appropriate "intellectual skills." Egan's "tools" may be superior to Bloom's "skills," but they are alike in relegating content, the stuff to be understood, to the bottom of the ladder. Mind you, I don't think Egan wants knowledge to be down there. He has shown far too much fondness for it himself for that to be a plausible surmise. But he was stuck with a folk theoretic framework, as were the authors of the *Taxonomy*, that almost forces knowledge to be put there. To bring knowledge out of the cellar and into the light, you need to be able to recognize that concepts, theories, aphorisms, and the like can also be tools. They are constructed with tools of the kind Egan recognized, but they can function in turn as tools in their own right, as things we can use in making sense of the world.

It is important to realize, however, that conceptual artifacts are not *only* tools. What Mario Bunge (1977–1979) said of theories can be extended to many other kinds of conceptual artifacts: The same conceptual artifacts may be variously regarded as "ideal objects, systems of changeable meaning and truth value, growing bodies of knowledge, or prescriptions for doing things." Thus the relationship between a student and an idea has possibilities of great complexity and manifold values. To nurture such a relationship, educators need an epistemology that allows them to give full due both to the potentialities that inhere in the learner and to the potentialities that inhere in the idea, the thing to be understood. If they see the idea as only an opinion, then they will see the student's relationship to the idea as only some degree of belief or disbelief. If they see the idea as only an item of information, to be stored in the mind and acted on with intellectual skills as the occasion arises, they will see the student's relationship to the idea as similar to the relation of file clerk to the items stored in files: Has the item in question been retained and can it be retrieved when needed? If they see the idea as only a tool, they will be far in advance of most other educators, but they will tend to see the student's relationship to the idea in purely utilitarian terms, overlooking its more personal and emotional aspects and the possibility that the idea may change the way the student experiences the world.

CONCLUSION: WHAT DOES IT MEAN IN PRACTICE?

When I have tried out on educators the relational view of understanding developed in this chapter, they are generally sympathetic but then they ask, in a not too hopeful way, "What is a teacher supposed to do to produce this kind of understanding?" I think I have already offered the only answer that can be given for the general case: We all have a pretty good idea of how to teach for understanding when the thing to be understood is a material living or nonliving thing or an observable phenomenon. Just apply the same strategies when the thing to be understood is abstract, some kind of conceptual artifact.

Beyond that, we have to get down to particular cases. Do you want students to understand acceleration due to gravity? Then let's start with what this thing is that is to be understood. It is an idea for which Galileo gets first credit. People long before Galileo knew that things fall to earth at a fast clip, but they probably never thought much about the velocity. The implicit assumption was probably that things fall at a constant rate. Visualize a coconut falling from a tall tree. Now visualize this happening in slow motion. I'll bet that if you don't think much about it your mental image will be that of something falling at a constant rate. I suspect we are not wired to perceive or visualize accelerating motion. If that is true, the educational job set out for us is harder than we would have imagined from just examining the formula, $g = 32.174$ ft/sec^2. We have got to establish a good working relation between the students and a scientific notion that is quite foreign to the way they naturally make sense of the world.

A good starting point—the point from which much of scientific inquiry starts—is things that people recognize they can't explain. Most of the questions students come up with spontaneously will have to do with outer space, so you may have to step in with questions of your own to get them to realize there are things much closer to home they don't understand. Why is a glass more likely to break if you drop it from 3 feet than if you drop it from 1 foot? There may be a variety of answers, but the most cogent one is likely to be that it takes a while for a falling object to get up to full speed. What do we mean full speed? Why is a glass dropped from 100 feet onto a hard surface dead certain to break? Could it be that there isn't a "full speed," that things keep traveling faster and faster the farther they fall? Although acceleration is hard to measure with free fall, students can get measurable results with balls rolling down a long incline or things sinking in a tall container of water. Can something falling from a greater height ever overtake something falling from a lesser height? That is an interesting experiment that clearly demonstrates acceleration in falling objects.[11]

Up to this point, what I have described falls well within the range of things that inquiry-oriented elementary school teachers already do. Such teachers could adopt, criticize, or elaborate on these ideas without having to take on an esoteric new conception of understanding. Does this mean, then, that in practice the relational concept of understanding reduces to just another label for what several generations of educators have known by the name of "learning by discovery"?

My first response to this question is to point out that what I have described so far does not involve the understanding of a conceptual artifact—the concept of g, for instance. Teacher and students are dealing entirely with World 1, the physical, observable world. World 3 is not in the picture. A teacher could do a reasonably effective job of shepherding children through the learning experience without even mentioning theory. The understanding in question is understanding the phenomenon of things falling. As I have suggested, common sense is pretty good at handling this kind of understanding, as long as it doesn't get befuddled by abstract ideas. As long as teachers steer clear of Newton and concentrate on enriching students' understand-

---

[11]If they are dropped at the same moment, then of course the one dropped from higher up will never overtake the other. But if there is a delay, so that the lower one is released when the upper one is partway to it, you may see the upper one zoom past the lower one.

ing of concrete things and phenomena, common sense can guide them. But life since Newton is not that simple. The exploratory approach I have suggested will take substantial time and effort. To understand why it is worth the investment, why they should not dispense with the topic in 10 minutes and move onto something else, teachers need to appreciate the significance of acceleration due to gravity. Understanding it is not important for daily life. Students already know enough not to jump off cliffs, even though they may not understand the concept. Its main value is as a start on understanding acceleration in its general, Newtonian sense—one of the most powerful concepts in physics yet one that eludes many students even after they have taken university-level physics.

Inevitably, however, the word "gravity" will find its way into discussions of falling objects: What makes it happen? Gravity. But gravity is neither explained nor is it an explanation; it is more in the nature of a lexical filler. At the elementary school level that is all right. There are lots of things that children do not understand but that they still need words to talk about. However, especially if the word appears in curriculum standards, teachers are liable to feel that they have to teach it. It may even appear on a test. And so what might have been a meaningful inquiry into how things in the world behave when they fall risks degenerating into pseudoscientific verbalism. To avoid that, teachers need a clearer idea of what they are about. It needs to start with having a clear idea of what the *it* is that students are supposed to understand. A relational approach to understanding centers on building a sound and fruitful relation between the students and *it*. Pedagogy grounded in folk theory vacillates. Sometimes it goes all out for activities, which may include experiments of the kind I have suggested, except that there is no *it* there, no object of understanding that is the focus of all those activities. Other times it goes mental and concentrates on getting things into the students' heads or correcting what is already there. Again, the thing to be understood is lost sight of. In the first case it is replaced by activities. In the second case it is replaced by words. But in both cases understanding gets left behind.

No intellectually alive group of children or adults is going to remain satisfied with just describing the behavior of falling bodies. They are going to ask "why?" Note that in the example we are working through, teaching for understanding does not start with that question. It begins with getting students on sufficiently intimate terms with the object to be understood that they can ask *why* questions of some meat. "Why do things fall down?" or "What is gravity?"—which are the naive questions people will ask—are not promising questions to pursue. However, "Why do things keep falling faster the longer they fall?" is a question that can lead right into the heart of Newtonian physics. The purpose of the preliminary exploration was to make that a meaningful question. If it is not, if the students do not find themselves wondering about it, the exploration has failed.

The question "Why do things keep falling faster the longer they fall?" poses a theoretical problem and it wants a theoretical solution. So this is the point at which instruction enters World 3 and where, accordingly, it is liable to lose hold of common sense. We are still interested in World 1, the world of real physical things falling from real places, but our interest also includes conceptual artifacts created to explain observations of such World 1 phenomena. The obvious target, the *it* with which to establish an understanding relationship, is Newton's laws. If we simply give students the formula for acceleration due to gravity and teach them to make calculations with it, however, we will have given them a tool to be used without understanding. They will not understand where the number 32 comes from, and if we point out that the formula is an idealization and only applies in a vacuum, they will be justified in asking why we have not given them a more useful formula, one that applies to the world they happen to live in. What can we say to that?

A little reflection will make several things clear. First, students are not going to be able to understand acceleration due to gravity in isolation. They are going to have to get into force and motion and something about friction. So we are really talking about understanding a domain, not understanding a single object. Second, students' "Why?" questions are not really going to be answered. The kind of "here's how it works" answer they are looking for does not exist, and the latest scientific thinking on the matter is too far beyond them. Understanding gravitation, therefore, is rather like understanding another person. You cannot hope to understand everything.

My own inclination, drawn from some years of experimentation with students' efforts to construct their own conceptual artifacts (Bereiter, Scardamalia, Cassells, & Hewitt, 1997; Scardamalia & Bereiter, 1996a; Scardamalia, Bereiter, & Lamon, 1994) is not to introduce Newton's laws directly. Instead, have students construct their own theories, their own conceptual artifacts, and work to refine them. In the process they will encounter Newton, see his laws are vital to their enterprise, and start coming to terms with them in some way. Then, depending on the maturity of the students and the resources available, we can lead them into a thorough study of force and motion or we can allow them to make do with a partial theory that leaves unanswered questions. For instance, students might conclude that gravity keeps pulling on falling objects and the longer it pulls the faster they go. That is not a bad explanation for 10-year-olds to produce, although it leaves unexplained why the same rule does not apply to towing a wagon.

Understanding Newton's laws, according to the argument of this chapter, means having a relationship to them that supports intelligent action. Leaving aside astronauts and engineers, the kind of intelligent action that an understanding of Newton's laws might support is not likely to be of a practical nature. The action it can support is the pursuit of further understanding. This might range over understanding newspaper stories about space travel, understanding what your physics textbook means when it says there is no such thing as centrifugal force, and understanding how the gadget on your desk works—the one that has six steel balls hanging by strings and when you swing the first one the last one moves but the ones in between do not. Accordingly, instead of the usual textbook problems, which present a particular case and call for arriving at a numerical answer, instruction ought to focus on solving problems of understanding: What keeps a communications satellite in a stationary orbit? Why does an object thrown horizontally off a cliff follow the path it does? Would its path be any different in a vacuum? Why do light objects fall at the same speed as heavy ones? Can air resistance actually slow an object's fall or only slow its acceleration? If gravity affects air, why don't all the air molecules end up flat on the earth? These may not be the most fruitful problems of understanding to pursue. Once they get into it, the students are likely to come up with better ones themselves. The purpose, however, is not to get answers to any particular questions and it is certainly not to exercise "explaining" skills. Then what else could it be? Folk theory offers no significant third possibility.

The third possibility I am trying to illustrate here is developing a relationship between the learners and the object of understanding that is relevant to the kind of intelligent action that understanding is expected to support. Newton's laws are in one respect typical of the conceptual artifacts encountered in every school subject—historical concepts, literary concepts, social and economic concepts, and biology concepts. The intelligent action that understanding them supports is primarily the pursuit of further understanding. This is not always the case. When we teach health concepts, for instance, the kind of action that understanding should support is intelligent eating, drinking, recreation, and so on. Accordingly—and this is not easy to do in school—the students' relationship to these concepts ought to develop within the context of lifestyle decisions and not be mainly theoretical. Learning your way around in the domain of health knowledge means learning to make lifestyle decisions that are appropriately constrained by this knowledge. The obvious way to do this—by analogy with learning your way around in a large corporate headquarters, for instance—is by pursuing varied goals that bring you into contact with the resources and constraints.

With health knowledge, as with every other domain of practical knowledge, however, there is always a secondary purpose in acquiring understanding, and that is to support further understanding. New health-related information comes with the daily news and poses new challenges to understanding. But even without new information, there is need for understanding to go on developing. A healthy relationship is a growing relationship, and this applies as much to our relationships with bodies of knowledge as to our relationships with other people. For students in a technical college, Newton's laws may be tools for the practical execution of their work, and so it makes sense that understanding should develop around applications rather than mainly around explanation, as I am proposing it should do at school. But it will be a poor education if the students' understanding of Newton's laws is so narrowly technical that it does not help them understand the world better and master new tools.

Thus, solving problems of understanding is not just one among a number of approaches to teaching for understanding. It ought to be part of every approach, and for most school subjects it ought to be central. That does not necessarily mean an inquiry approach such as I have sketched here. Socratic questioning is another way to pursue problems of understanding (Collins & Stevens, 1982). There are also inquiry approaches to understanding that are more structured and that give the teacher a more leading role (Brown & Campione, 1994; Lampert, 1990; Minstrell, 1989). Finally, a capable teacher who cares about understanding can engage students in thinking through problems of understanding using the old-fashioned methods of lecture, demonstration, and teacher-led discussion. My high school physics teacher did that. There was no lab, the textbook was dreary, and he was not an eloquent or inspiring lecturer. But he knew his physics, invited questions and took them seriously, and had an obvious regard for the worth of his subject matter. The result was that every day I left his class feeling that I understood the world a little better than when I walked in. Most of the problems of understanding, the things that didn't quite make sense and that led to deeper understanding, only occurred to me years later, but at least I had some understanding to build on, not just an assortment of half-remembered facts, formulas, and experiments.

In a better designed educational program, those problems would have had a better chance to arise during the course. But teachers back then didn't understand understanding in a way that would have suggested a different approach. To them, teaching for understanding meant making things as clear as possible, going slowly, and encouraging students to ask questions whenever something was not clear. To many teachers that is what it still means. To others it means letting students experiment and helping them arrive at scientific principles themselves. That, too, misses the point.

5

Aspects of Knowledgeability

When I say what I know, how is what I say *what* I know?
—Wittgenstein, (1980, par. 88)

How many kinds of knowledge are there? When it refers to knowledge objects in World 3, the question obviously has no definite answer. It is like asking how many kinds of books there are in a catalogued library. The answer depends on the cataloguing system in use. When the question refers to World 2, however, to knowledge as a property of human minds, the possibility arises that nature may have imposed its own cataloguing system, that there may be natural categories based on ways the brain holds information. In cognitive psychology a number of distinctions have been made on evidence, for instance, that brain injuries may affect one kind of memory while leaving another intact. Such evidence has been used to support a distinction between "declarative" and "procedural" knowledge (Anderson, 1983) and between "explicit" and "implicit" memory (Schacter, 1989) and it played a part in Howard Gardner's (1983) identification of seven different "intelligences."

For a practical theory of mind, however, brain-related considerations are only indirectly relevant. The issue is what kinds of knowledge it is useful to distinguish. Useful distinctions would affect how we teach or how we work with knowledge. Tests to qualify for a driver's license typically contain two parts, a "knowing-that" part and a "knowing-how" part. The first might include knowing when it is legal to make a U-turn; the second might include being able to execute a U-turn. Very likely different brain systems are involved, but you should study differently whether this is the case or not. The reason has more to do with how the Ministry of Transport works than with how your brain works. To pass the first test, you must be prepared to deal with the unpredictable wording and focus of test questions. If you simply memorize the words of the driver's manual without understanding them, you are liable to be tripped up. Therefore, you will do well to work at *understanding* the U-turn regulations well enough that you can think through whatever question is posed. Not everyone knows how to do this, with the result that many people fail the written part of their driver's test, despite having worked hard at memorizing the rules. To pass the second test, you must be prepared to deal with unpredictable features of the situation in which the examiner asks you to execute a U-turn. Accordingly, you should not do all your practicing in one spot, but should practice U-turns in various settings. In the course of such practice, however, you should acquire knowledge that goes beyond mere skill in getting the car to reverse directions. You should acquire knowledge that links up with the first kind. The rule book likely says that U-turns are permissible in certain situations "provided oncoming traffic permits," or words to that effect. There is only so far you can get by analyzing such statements. Only through practice on real streets will you come to know whether an oncoming car is distant enough and proceeding slowly enough that you can execute a U-turn and be on your way before it gets to you. Eventually, rule book knowledge and skill should fuse in such a way that the instant the thought of making a U-turn enters your head you see the situation as one in which it is or is not okay to do so. In educational terms, therefore, we need to be able to distinguish two kinds of knowledge at one stage of learning but also to hold as an objective that these two kinds of knowledge will come together and form a third.

Practically speaking, then, how many kinds of knowledge are worth distinguishing? Under the influence of cognitive science, the currently favored number is two. These are our old friends, knowing-that and knowing-how, better known in cognitive science circles as declarative and procedural knowledge. These two types can be stretched to cover pretty much everything. In the U-turn example, what I have referred to as a third kind of knowledge can instead be treated as a more advanced level of procedural knowledge in which previous declarative knowledge (about when it is permissible to make a U-turn) becomes "proceduralized" and incorporated into the skill (Anderson, 1987). The possibility of covering all knowledge by two types does not, however, mean we should do so. We can have as many kinds of knowledge as we like. By an argument analogous to the one that explains why Inuit hunters need to distinguish many kinds of snow, it can be maintained that educators and others who work extensively with knowledge need to distinguish many kinds of knowledge.[1] We are still talking about knowledge in the World 2 sense, however, as a property of people's minds. The desirable set of categories will not necessarily resemble the set we would use for cataloguing books or for designing an information system. Rather, the categories ought to divide things up in ways that help us deal with problems of learning and intelligent action.

The Declarative–Procedural Dichotomy

The declarative–procedural dichotomy enjoys a natural fit with conventional educational thought, as embodied in curriculum guidelines, scope-and-sequence charts, and the like. In these, the dichotomy is more likely to be expressed as one of content and process, and process is likely to be described in terms of activities to be carried out rather than things to be learned, but underlying it all is still the Bloom's (1956) *Taxonomy* view criticized in the preceding chapter. "Content" is the itemizable content of memory, roughly equivalent to textbook content reproduced in the mind of the student. "Process" is all the cognitive skills that the curriculum activities are intended to develop and that are supposed to enable the student to do something with the content. I have already criticized this view for its inability to make sense of problems of understanding. In a later chapter I will discuss its limitations when it comes to identifying subject matter worth learning. In this chapter, however, my concern is with the dichotomy itself and what it leaves out.

There is such a thing as declarative knowledge, and "declarative" is a good name for it. It is knowledge that you can state or declare, thus exposing it to correction by verbal means. According to the

---

[1] I am aware of reports that Inuktatuk does not in fact contain a multiplicity of snow words, but the reason the myth will not die is that there are such compelling reasons why the Inuit *should* have a rich snow-related lexicon, and it is a *should* type argument that I am making here about the need for us knowledge workers to have a richer lexicon for the stuff we work with.

view of knowledge and mind that I have been advancing, declarative knowledge of some subject just is the ability to state its content in your own words, diagrams, or whatever. It is not some set of propositions in your mind that is the source of your utterances, but that issue has been belabored enough already. There is also procedural knowledge, which conforms to the ordinary sense of the word "procedure"; that is, a routine that can be represented by a set of rules, steps, or clearly demonstrable actions. Procedural knowledge is ability to carry out such a routine, with or without an accompanying ability to "declare" the procedures that make up the routine. In actual use these terms have gotten stretched over much wider territory than I have just indicated, but the stretching has been at a price. The categories become too broad to be useful.

No matter how far we stretch them, the categories of declarative and procedural knowledge still form a dichotomy. There is no gradual blending of one into the other. Consequently, they leave out—or at least make it easy for us to ignore—a vast range of knowledge that does not clearly belong in either category. The following is a suggestive, by no means exhaustive, list of kinds of knowledge that are given short shrift in the declarative–procedural dichotomy. Some items I have discussed before, others are thrown in to extend the range of possibilities:

Number sense.

Place knowledge—knowing your way about in a city, a harbor, a forest.

Connoisseurship—refined tastes in food, wine, literature, music, romance.

Tact.

Moral sense.

Acquired instincts—"a nose for news," "an eye for the main chance," ability to recognize promising leads, problems, or ideas in one's area of expertise (Bereiter & Scardamalia, 1993, chap. 5).

Human relations skills, very broadly conceived—ability to read body language and other clues to people's unstated thoughts and dispositions, ability to judge character, to make friends, to gain trust, to persuade or to influence feelings.

Style—in speech, dress, art, management, and so on.

Background knowledge—what you need, for instance, to understand a Jane Austen novel in the context of the time and place and social world of its characters and of Austen herself as a part of that world.

It may be objected that some of these items are not knowledge, that they are abilities, dispositions, perhaps personality traits. To object that way, however, is to backslide into folk theory of mind, which requires that knowledge be something statable, or at least amenable to demonstration of the "here's how you do it" kind. The items listed all involve learning (however much they might also depend on native traits). They are things that people at least try to convey to others through explanations, demonstration, and guidance. That it seems a bit strange to think of them as varieties of knowledge should be taken as a signal that our conception of knowledge needs expanding.

Functional Classifications

Distinguishing types of knowledge on practical grounds is not new to education. Indeed, knowledge typologies abound. In a literature review, Alexander, Schallert, and Hare (1991) found 26 different kinds of knowledge being addressed. Of course there is redundancy in such a list, as the reviewers recognized, but because researchers tend to generate new typologies without considering existing ones, there is not much to go on in reducing the redundancy.

Perhaps the most empirically grounded and functional of functional classifications in the educational literature is one worked out by Robert M. Gagné (1977). Gagné's classification is based on evidence that different conditions apply to different kinds of learning. There are different kinds of prerequisites, different appropriate methods of instruction, and different ways that learning is manifested. Repetition, for instance, is important for learning some things, not for others.

Whereas Gagné's criterion for distinguishing a knowledge type was *needs to be treated differently*, the one I apply is a bit looser and accordingly more inclusive: *deserves special attention*. The reason a type of knowledge might deserve special attention could be that, like Gagné's types, it needs to be treated differently for optimal learning to occur, or it could be simply that it needs special attention lest it be neglected, lest it get lost among more conspicuous and high-status kinds of knowledge. Accordingly, the types I identify here include ones not found in Gagné's typology.

ON "HAVING" KNOWLEDGE

In the folk conception of mind, *having knowledge* means having the knowledge in your head. In the conception of mind that I have been arguing for—a mind that is knowledgeable but that does not contain knowledge—things are not so simple. Knowledgeability is a property of the cognitive system. To talk about what people know is to talk about and try to describe that aspect of their minds. But what terms are we to use? "Knowledgeability" itself is an ugly term and the language cannot be expected to get any better if we start trying to tease apart different varieties or aspects of knowledgeability.

Rather than introduce a cadre of awkward neologisms, I have decided to accept the risk that goes with treating knowledge as something people can have. This means using the same vocabulary to talk about World 2 knowledgeability as is used to talk about World 3 knowledge. The risk, of course, is that this will contribute to conflating the two—the very thing I have been inveighing against and blaming on folk theory of mind. If someone wants to start a movement to establish different vocabularies for talking about World 2 and World 3, I shall be happy to join, but my personal opinion is that we need a few more believers first.

Michael Polanyi (1964) used the term "personal knowledge" to distinguish what characterizes individual minds from knowledge in the objective or public sense. Still, the term "personal knowledge" has unfortunate correlations with terms like "personal computer" (the now largely forgotten words that "PC" stands for) and "personal pizza" (a little empty box so labeled happened to clutter my desk at the moment of drafting this paragraph)—in other words, a diminutive version of the larger thing after which it is modeled. Of course, Polanyi meant no such thing by it. "Personal knowledge" remains the best term I can find to use when it is necessary to draw distinctions and one does not want to drag in Popper's three worlds for the purpose.

There is no harm in talking about "having" knowledge so long as we do not slide from there into assuming this means having particular symbolic objects, such as propositions or rules, in our heads. We should think of "having" knowledge in the same way we think of "having" abilities, attitudes, tastes, and traits of character. That is, we "have" them as attributes or properties. There is, of course, something in our neural organization that corresponds to "having" these attributes, but we would not expect to probe the brain and find them. We do not expect them to represent or correspond to anything in the outside world, although they commonly relate to the outside world—in fact, characterize the way we relate to the outside world. We do not expect to be able to enumerate them, although we may speak of someone as having an unusual diversity of abilities or tastes. We may note similar traits in two people, but this does not imply there is some *thing* their minds hold in common. So let it be with knowledge, when we are treating it as what individual people have. The complication to keep in mind is that, as people's knowledge relates to the outside world, some of what is out there for it to relate to is also known as knowledge, in a different sense.

With this extended caveat, we are now ready to examine the kinds of knowledge people have that deserve special attention from an educational point of view.

SIX KINDS OF PERSONAL KNOWLEDGE

What follows is a further development of a typology introduced in *Surpassing Ourselves* (Bereiter & Scardamalia, 1993). There we identified five kinds of expert knowledge, two of which were the familiar "declarative" and "procedural." The remaining three were kinds of knowledge that tend to be neglected by that dichotomy. The same general intent persists here, but I have dropped the two standard terms. They have become stretched to cover too much, thus losing the neat meanings that a narrower sense of the two terms conveys. The narrower sense of "declarative" is now captured in what I call "statable" knowledge. "Skills" now take the place of procedural knowledge, so that "procedural" can be recognized as a particular class of skills characterized by explicit steps. The newcomer to the list is "episodic knowledge." The neglect of this important kind of knowledge in the earlier work probably indicates our conception of knowledge was still too constrained by the prevailing declarative–procedural dichotomy. Perhaps it still is, but progress is being made.

Statable Knowledge

This is knowledge the knower can actually put into some explicit form—usually sentences, but possibly diagrams, formulas, stories, or enactments—such that it can be conveyed, argued about, compared with alternatives, and evaluated by others. It is part of what cognitive scientists refer to as "declarative" knowledge. It is the explicit part. It does not include the vast stretches of unarticulated, largely unconscious knowledge that cognitive theorists such as John Anderson (1983) have also put under the "declarative" umbrella. I will erect some other umbrellas to take care of that sort of thing. Admittedly, it is a very fuzzy line that separates what is statable from what is not, and the line may shift depending on the time of day or on how much effort one puts into formulating an idea. But it is still well worth trying to distinguish statable knowledge because of its unique cultural significance.

Statable knowledge has been the overriding and often the only concern of epistemologists through the ages. It is also, of course, what formal education is most obviously about, and certainly what the testing of subject matter knowledge is about. All overt actions and products can be discussed, evaluated and reflected on, but statable knowledge is distinctive in that it can be discussed, evaluated, and reflected on *as knowledge*. It can be contradicted. It can be argued with. By the same token, it can be defended as true, supported by other assertions, organized into larger wholes. If I pick up a violin and play it, my performance can be discussed as music or as demonstration of skill. But if I say, "This is how the violin was played when it was first invented," and then proceed to play, I have made the playing part of an assertion. It may now be treated as knowledge. People can agree or disagree with it. You cannot agree or disagree with a portrait, regarded as a work of art, but you can agree or disagree with it when it is being considered as a representation of how someone really looked.

Statable knowledge is thus the World 2 counterpart of World 3, the world of abstract knowledge objects. It is the personal knowledge that we can objectify and thus bring into the social processes of knowledge building (Nonaka, 1991). However, as we see later, its role is broader than that, influencing all the other aspects of knowledge that we consider.

Implicit Understanding

Work on expert systems, knowledge engineering, and expertise has led to a heightened appreciation of the role of knowledge people apparently have and use but cannot state. Unstated, tacit, or implicit knowledge covers a very wide range, however. In fact, it covers most of the aspects of knowledge I am discussing here. Accordingly, the qualifier "understanding" is meant to separate one kind of implicit knowledge from several others. One could say migratory birds have an implicit knowledge of celestial navigation, but few would say that they have an implicit understanding. "Understanding," as discussed in the preceding chapter, carries the implication of an intelligent relationship to what is known. Thus, implicit understanding refers to those aspects of our knowledge that characterize intelligent relationships to things or situations in the world.

Implicit understanding need not have a very exalted character, however. An example I like to use is that of predicting whether crockery of various kinds, dropped from various heights on to various surfaces, will shatter, chip, or remain whole. Most people would be able to make intelligent, though imperfect, predictions. But except in the rare case where they could recall a very similar instance, they would be quite unable to articulate the knowledge on which their predictions were based. It is knowledge *about* crockery, gravity, and so on. It is not skill. But it is not knowledge you would find in a physics textbook or a book about ceramics. It is knowledge gained from experience and it probably owes little or nothing to formal education.

Daily life is full of occasions when intelligent action depends on predicting what will occur. Indeed, that may be about all intelligent action requires in familiar circumstances: If you can predict results, the appropriate action is obvious. But in almost all cases, whether it is predicting the behavior of another person or predicting the effect of adding a touch of vinegar to a sauce, the knowledge on which the prediction is based is largely unspecifiable. It is just a sort of residue of past experience.

Cognitive theories based on the mind–as–container metaphor nevertheless require that this implicit knowledge exist as propositions or some other kinds of symbolic representations in the mind. Much of the argument in preceding chapters was devoted to making a case against this implausible notion and replacing it with a connectionist view of mind. In saying we make predictions based on knowledge, I am slipping back into the folk idiom, and it is well to be reminded that this is just a manner of speaking. When the teacup tumbles from the saucer, we do not experience any calling up of our knowledge of gravitation or ceramics or any forming of a prediction, on the basis of which we select an action. We just respond in a manner appropriate to the perceived situation. We make a grab for the cup or put out a foot to break its fall, steel ourselves for the inevitable crash or find ourselves anticipating the stain on the plush carpet rather than the unlikely breaking of the cup—all in a flash, as if by reflex. And yet the reflex-like response is conditioned by our past experience in ways that make it reasonable to think of there being a residue of knowledge that makes the response an "intelligent" one.

Implicit understanding is more like perception than like having propositions in the head (Clancey, 1991). In Wittgenstein's (1980) terms, implicit understanding is not knowing *that* the world is round but seeing the world *as* round—which may not be how we see it much of the time but is how we are likely to visualize it when thinking about a flight from New York to Moscow or about a lunar eclipse. If we do not see it that way, if we have to recall and interpret information about the earth's shape, we are liable to find the fact that the New York–Moscow flight passes over the North Pole very strange. Experimental evidence suggests that most people, even though they know about acceleration due to gravity, do not see falling bodies as accelerating. From a literally perceptual standpoint this is to be expected. Acceleration is not easy to gauge visually, especially over short distances. But by not seeing falling bodies *as* accelerating, people tend to ignore this factor in their predictions and explanations. For instance, many adults I have questioned can offer no sensible explanation of why one suffers worse injury falling out of a second floor window than out of a first floor window—this despite the fact that on further questioning they demonstrate the knowledge that acceleration due to gravity means that bodies gain speed as they fall.

Episodic Knowledge

Research on human memory has yielded considerable evidence that memory for events is basically different from memory for meaningful content or "semantic memory," as it is called (Schacter, 1989). Different kinds of brain damage can affect one and not the other. Thus, it is one thing to remember that moth larvae eat woolens and another to remember when moths chewed up a whole corner of an oriental rug. Remembering one can help you recall the other, but they are distinct.

From a functional standpoint, which is what I am trying to sustain here, episodic and semantic memory have different roles as knowledge. Semantic memory covers everything discussed under the previous labels of statable knowledge and implicit understanding. Episodic knowledge much more closely fits the filing cabinet model. Remembered episodes can be retrieved and considered in new contexts. The fact that moths destroy woolens is a useful but limited bit of knowledge. The remembered oriental rug episode, however, may yield many suggestions and questions. The ravaged part of the carpet was under a sofa. Do moths prefer dark enclosed places? Did several generations of moth larvae do the work or would they all have come from one generation? Other relevant episodes might come to mind, contributing to a more elaborate understanding of the clothes moth way of life. At another time the episode might be recalled and contribute to practical considerations about the purchase or arrangement of furnishings.

The functions of episodic knowledge have been extensively pursued by Roger Schank and his coworkers (e.g., Schank, Collins, & Hunter, 1986), who have developed artificial intelligence (AI) programs based on stored and indexed episodes. "Case-based reasoning" is the name for this lively and expanding area of AI work. Schank noted that much of conversation involves recounting, comparing, and drawing inferences from episodes, and that informal teaching does as well (Schank & Cleary, 1995). Much of the value of business consultants resides in their repertoires of cases relevant to their clients' problems. Reasoning based on cases is distinct from reasoning based on principles. It is reasoning by analogy rather than by deductive inference. But effective thinking and problem solving make flexible use of both.

Schank's work particularly highlights the "reminding" problem. We cannot search our episodic knowledge systematically. One thing reminds us of another, and most of the time the connections are superficial. Not very often does the falling of an apple remind someone of the planets in their orbits. Episodic knowledge seems to represent a great intellectual resource that is largely wasted.

It could be questioned whether memory for episodes in itself constitutes knowledge. Many memories seem to have no function. I remember all kinds of scenes from childhood—a bluebird on a fencepost; the crawlspace under the front porch, frequented by cats; a scary ride in the rumble seat of a car. Psychoanalysis might make something of these, but in their unanalyzed state they do not seem to constitute knowledge. They have no role. Is not episodic knowledge, therefore, just raw material out of which knowledge may at times be constructed? We may also, however, remember many facts to no evident purpose—names of casual acquaintances long gone, the combination of a high school locker, and so on. Should such trivia count as knowledge whereas miscellaneous episodes do not? The definitional issue evaporates if we remind ourselves we are not really talking about episodes and facts stored in the mind but about a mind with the ability to recall past experiences and previously encountered facts, coupled with a disposition to do so spontaneously as well as under conscious direction. What is recalled may amount to significant knowledge at some times and not at others, but there can be little doubt that the recall of past experiences is an important part of knowledgeability.

Impressionistic Knowledge

Beyond statable knowledge and beyond our more confidently held implicit understandings lies a realm of feelings and impressions that also influence our actions, that function like knowledge even though we tend not to think of them as such. Something about a situation or a decision doesn't feel right, or some prospect inspires confidence although we cannot say why. "I woke up that morning with a good feeling about American Motors," says the young stockbroker in Walker Percy's *The Movie Goer*. We trust or mistrust others, find actions morally okay or reprehensible, often with nothing specific we can point to as a reason.

All personal knowledge has an emotional aspect (although it may be quite attenuated, as in the case of knowledge of number facts for those free of mathematics phobias). What distinguishes impressionistic knowledge is that the feelings *are* the knowledge. This becomes most evident when our feelings appear to run contrary to reason or the weight of evidence. We have to decide which to trust. If we decide to go with our feelings, it means that in that circumstance we believe them to constitute more reliable knowledge. But feelings and impressions also constitute important knowledge in circumstances where reason and evidence offer no guidance. This is generally the case with creative efforts (Bereiter & Scardamalia, 1993, chap. 5), almost by definition. If you can reason your way to a result or get there by systematic empirical methods, the result does not count as creative (although, as in the case of mathematical inventions, you may be able to construct a logical path to the result after the fact). To achieve a creative goal you have to make decisions of uncertain result. The reason creativity isn't mere chance is that creative people become very adept, within their particular fields, at making risky choices that turn out to be good ones. They go by feeling, impression, or what in this context is often called intuition. Creativity remains clouded in mystery, however, unless we accept impressionistic knowledge as knowledge that grows and improves with experience like any other.

Impressionistic knowledge might be regarded as just extremely vague implicit understanding. If I were trying to create a rigorous taxonomy of knowledge I would have to treat it that way. But I am distinguishing types of knowledge on the basis of their deserving special attention, and on this basis impressionistic knowledge clearly warrants a category of its own. Because it is practically unmeasurable, it is almost totally ignored in education. Although growth in impressionistic knowledge may not be very obvious over the span of a school term, it becomes very obvious over long time spans, however—time spans long enough to be the stuff of biography. It may be reckoned as growth in wisdom, acumen, or moral sensibility, or as becoming a good judge of character or a connoisseur. In all cases it manifests itself in judgment, but in judgment based on knowledge acquired slowly, distilled from long experience. Without it, one grows older but not wiser.

Impressionistic knowledge is what we are left with after we have forgotten all the explicit content of a great literary or artistic work. When we speak of connoisseurship or of a person's having "standards" in language, literature, art, musical performance, cinema, professionalism, or personal integrity, we are talking about impressionistic knowledge. Efforts to formulate such standards as rules generally fail, or provide only crude approximations to the underlying impressionistic knowledge without which the rules are useless. Impressionistic knowledge is also the stuff of prejudices, phobias, and crazes, however. Pointing this out is only to recognize that any kind of personal knowledge can be dysfunctional, can lead us to act in ways that may seem intelligent to us at the time but that may be judged quite differently by others or by ourselves from a different vantage point.

Skill

Skill learning is ubiquitous. No matter what you do, if you do it repeatedly you will become more skillful at it. You may, however, become skillful at doing something wrong, such as grinding your teeth or slicing a golf ball or reading a textbook without grasping its content. Skills have both a cognitive and a subcognitive component, and it is worth distinguishing them, even though they are closely intertwined. The cognitive part is the knowing-how. When we say that someone *knows how* to read, to solve quadratic equations, or to swim we mean they can voluntarily call forth actions sufficient to achieve a certain result. No matter how learnedly I may expound on the art of swimming, I will not be credited with knowing how unless I can provide evidence of having got into the water and actually done something that would count as swimming. I might now be physically incapacitated and no longer able to swim, but if I could marshal witnesses who had seen me swim in years past, I would probably still be credited with having the knowledge. That is the sense in which the knowing-how is cognitive.

The subcognitive part is the inevitable change in any skill that takes place with practice. The performance becomes smoother, more automatic, and more economical of effort. This is learning, and so the result could perhaps be called knowledge, but I cannot think of any purpose in doing so. When you do push-ups daily, the increased endurance that enables you to do more push-ups is not mainly a result of increased muscle mass. It is a result of your nervous system's learning to distribute the work more efficiently to the muscle fibres you already have, so that, in relay team fashion, they can keep going longer. It is, thus, skill but of a definitely subcognitive kind. If, in addition, you learned a technique for controlling your breathing so as to increase your endurance, that would be a different matter. That would be a gain in knowledge.

In so-called cognitive skills, the cognitive and subcognitive components are harder to distinguish, but still evident. If you have to do a lot of adding columns of figures, part of your gain in performance will come from discovering shortcuts and memorizing combinations. These will constitute gains in knowledge. But your performance will also get faster, easier, and more automatic just through repetition. The difference between the two kinds of learning becomes evident in cases where the cognitive part, the knowing-how, is faulty. If your way of adding figures is wrong in the first place, and no knowledge advance takes place, you will just get increasingly proficient at doing it wrong. This can often be observed with school children if they are in the hands of a teacher who believes the way to remedy deficiencies in arithmetic is to assign more pages of exercises.

The cognitive and the subcognitive parts of skill learning can cooperate or they can get in each other's way, which is what makes skill learning an interesting challenge. Cooperation occurs when the automaticity gained through practice frees up mental resources that enable you to think about what you are doing while you are doing it and thereby, perhaps, discover ways to improve your procedures (Karmiloff-Smith, 1992). Cognition can interfere with subcognitive performance, however, as suggested by the old centipede aphorism. Interference can take several forms. "Inner tennis," "inner skiing," and the like are based on the premise that knowledge and reasoning have got to somehow be held in abeyance so that the body can do its subcognitive learning (e.g., Galway, 1974). On the other hand, automaticity renders your actions less accessible to examination and deliberate change. Thus, a well-practiced bad golf swing becomes hard to correct, not only because of ingrained habit but because you literally don't know what you're doing. The same goes for your accent in speaking a foreign language. You can't hear it and the articulatory actions that are responsible for it are controlled at levels of your neuromusculature too far down to be cognitively accessible.

Folk psychology rather arbitrarily separates knowledge, skill, and emotion. There is some sense to this, even at the level of brain anatomy, but functionally there are no sharp boundaries. Statable knowledge trails off into implicit understanding, which then trails off into the feeling states I call impressionistic knowledge, which in turn trails off into feelings that have no knowledge function ("I'm feeling low"). On another side, statable knowledge and implicit understanding trail off into skill, which trails off into subcognitive bodily adaptations. It is therefore important, when dealing with a psychomotor skill, to be aware that your body may be learning in ways over which you have little control and that may or may not cooperate with the cognitive part of your skill learning.

A striking example of this appeared in a study by Pam'la Ghent (1989) on expertise in piano performance. A concert pianist was working on a novel score, a transcription for piano of Indonesian wayan music, normally played on a variety of drums. The pianist was working through conceptually how he would have to adopt a more percussive style of playing to produce the desired effect. Then he stopped himself and said he had better start practicing, explaining he did not want his mind to get too far ahead of his body, because his body would then start taking shortcuts that would defeat the intention. Here was someone who seems to have understood clearly that skill is a form of knowledge, but that it depends on a body that also learns in its own unknowing way. That understanding of himself as a pianist and as a learner, however, exemplifies the sixth kind of personal knowledge, to which we now turn.

Regulative Knowledge

Originally this section was going to be titled "Self-Regulatory Knowledge," which is what the corresponding section was called in an earlier pass at this topic (Bereiter & Scardamalia, 1993). As such, it would cover rather familiar and noncontroversial ground, much of which has been studied under the rubric of "metacognition."[2] The general idea is that in any realm of activity there is knowledge that pertains to yourself as a factor in that activity. If it is history, it is knowledge of yourself as a student of history, not only of how you function in that role but of how to get yourself to function in it: how to stay awake while sifting through official documents, to take a lowly example. A higher level example would be knowledge of your own biases and shortcomings and how to take proper account of and deal with these as you go about the study of history.

But there is also regulative knowledge that pertains to collective activity, and here we get into a controversial zone, in which prejudices run rampant. There are what some philosophers refer to as *regulative ideas*. Prominent among these are *truth*, *objectivity*, and *perfection*. Let us throw in *equity* for good measure. In ordinary language these are referred to as ideals. They are goals no one can reasonably expect to attain, yet they are thought to have value in directing and sustaining desirable kinds of action. Or at least they used to be so judged. Artists and artisans who pursue the perfect tone, the perfect risotto, or the perfect welded joint continue to be honored, but those who pursue truth or objectivity are nowadays frequently condemned as deluded, arrogant, and self-serving. Those who do the condemning are frequently pursuers of the ideal of equity, a goal that is no more attainable or explicable than truth and objectivity, but that does not come under the same kinds of attack.

---

[2]"Metacognition," according to Swanson (1990) "is defined as the knowledge and control one has over one's thinking and learning activities" (p. 306).

To pursue in any depth the question of why *truth* and *objectivity* have become so tainted whereas *perfection* and *equity* remain pure would take us far afield. Instead, I only deal with one factor, which has to do with distinguishing among types of knowledge. Ordinarily, truth and objectivity are thought of as attributes of statable knowledge. If I am defending a scientific proposition, I am likely to be seen as implying it is both true and objective, whether I say so or not. If, as is widely believed these days, no empirically based proposition has or ever could have those two attributes, I must be deluded, arrogant, and so on. What I propose instead, however, is that truth and objectivity are not attributes of scientific knowledge; they are *components of the knowledge that regulates the conduct of inquiry.* In short, they are part of regulative knowledge.

⎯ As components of regulative knowledge, truth and objectivity are still open to criticism, but of a quite different kind from the popular postmodernist sort. We can examine them within the context of the whole body of regulative knowledge in a discipline and consider whether they are necessary, what their positive and negative effects are, and whether some other regulative ideas might be better. I have argued elsewhere (Bereiter, 1994) that truth and objectivity are not necessary regulative ideas and that scientific enterprises (including, especially, the teaching of science) would be on firmer ground if the pursuit of theory improvement were substituted for the pursuit of truth and if progressive discourse were substituted for objectivity. It remains, however, that most science has been carried out and still is being carried out by people who conceive of science as the pursuit of truth and objectivity, and it would be arrogant in the extreme to deny that this has proved to be a very productive and generative conception.

The issue before us here, however, is not judging one kind of regulative knowledge against another but rather appreciating the role of regulative knowledge in general. I see regulative knowledge as covering a very wide range, from explicit principles that may be debated and codified as codes of ethics or by-laws down to idiosyncratic personal knowledge, such as how you as a social worker deal with your aversion to assertive people. It may include knowledge of all the kinds discussed so far, but it is always knowledge pertaining more directly to the actors than to what is acted on.

Writing provides a nice illustration of this distinction, because it is an activity in which self-regulative knowledge plays a crucial part, over and above the part played by other kinds of knowledge. Even skilled writers often find writing difficult and stressful. Procrastination is the rule (Wason, 1980). Competence in writing of course involves many kinds of knowledge besides self-regulative. There is the kind of knowledge represented in rhetoric texts, plus a vast amount of implicit knowledge of conventions, principles, and strategies. Impressionistic knowledge plays an enormous role, especially in stylistic decisions. Epidsodic knowledge, in the form of knowledge of relevant examples, undoubtedly also plays a very large role. And then there is all the knowledge that goes to form the content of what is being written. Statable, implicit, episodic, and impressionistic knowledge figure in varying proportions, depending on the genre. But the more of these kinds of knowledge you have and the more you try to bring them all to bear in a coordinated way, the greater the mental burden becomes (Bereiter & Scardamalia, 1987b). That, I believe, is why experts generally find writing to be harder work than do nonexperts (Scardamalia & Bereiter, 1991). Their greater knowledge enables them to formulate more complex problems. Solving these problems advances their knowledge still further, thus leading to more complex problem formulations, and so on in a feedforward loop that generates better but increasingly effortful writing.

Managing themselves, shepherding their mental, emotional, and physical resources, thus becomes a major concern of writers. It is one of the few aspects of their craft that professional writers seem to show much inclination to talk about (cf. Plimpton, 1992). Most serious writers, it seems, have carefully nurtured habits as to where they write, when they write, with what kinds of instruments and materials they write, and in what sequence of stages they write. Deviating from these rituals tends to disrupt the process for them. Of course, one writer's successful self-regulatory strategies may be the opposite of another's. Nevertheless, writers often make bold to recommend their strategies to others. For instance, Peter Wason (1980) argued for the universal desirability of his own novel approach to writing, which involves among other things scrapping everything at a certain point and starting over.

In the last decade, there has been a trend toward assigning regulative knowledge a larger share of responsibility for what were previously counted as abilities or skills. Critical thinking is still being treated in schools as something to be taught and exercised, but as McPeck (1984) has pointed out, people are generally pretty good at criticizing propositions they are opposed to and need no further training in that. It is thinking critically about one's favored ideas that is difficult, and that is largely a matter of getting oneself to do it. I have made a similar argument about transfer of learned intelligent behavior more generally (Bereiter, 1995). It tends to be bound to the situations in which it was learned, and breaking free of such bondage is on one hand a matter of understanding what has been learned at an abstract enough level that it can transfer and on the other hand a matter of assimilating the learning into the way one responds to new situations, which is therefore a matter of regulative knowledge.

WELL-ROUNDED KNOWLEDGEABILITY

Of the six aspects of knowledgeability I have been discussing, only two—statable knowledge and skill—offer much to the external view, and so it is not surprising they should have received almost all the attention of educators and others who trade in knowledge. Episodic knowledge plays a lively role in people's private mental lives—people commonly devote considerable time to mulling over past experiences—and it is the stuff of small talk, but it is too idiosyncractic to be judged by a standard. It would be difficult to compare one person's episodic knowledge with another's or to judge whether a person's episodic knowledge in some area was adequate. Consequently, it has tended to be neglected and undervalued. Intuitive understanding, being mostly invisible even to the person who has it, continues to receive little more than a nod, except when it is judged to be erroneous, as in the case of scientific misconceptions. Impressionistic and regulative knowledge are usually not recognized as knowledge at all, or at least not as part of a person's knowledge of a domain.

Competence in any domain will likely involve all six kinds of knowledge. The prominence of the different kinds will of course vary from field to field, but it is hard to imagine a field in which any of them would be absent. When we look at a highly competent person, however, we cannot help but note that (a) the whole of the person's competence appears to be greater than the sum of identifiable parts and (b) the parts themselves are not easily distinguished. Everything seems to blend together. Statable knowledge trails off gracefully into intuitive understanding, significant parts of which could be rendered explicit if the need arose. Intuitive understanding in turn blends imperceptibly into impressionistic knowledge. Similarly, episodic knowledge blends into both implicit understanding and impressionistic knowledge. On occasion a specific episode may be recalled and explicitly applied to a current situation, but more often past experiences influence actions and choices without any recall and analysis. Regulative knowledge becomes integrated into habit and character.

This merging of aspects of knowledge takes place even at levels of competence well below those of the expert, however. If, for instance, you are painting a room, and this is something you do infrequently enough that you do not have well-practiced routines for the task, you may do some recalling of principles or past instances if a problem arises, but for the most part the residue of past wall painting episodes is experienced simply as confidence that you will know what to do as the need arises and that things are going all right. It would be impossible to mark off a place where this kind of tacit knowledge leaves off and skill in painting begins.

Put somewhat differently, the more fully developed and well-rounded a person's knowledge is, the more artificial seem the distinctions among its components or aspects. This is a universal characteristic of competence and has nothing to do with the particular set of distinctions I have drawn. AI theorists have had to deal with this phenomenon. "Chunking" (Rosenbloom & Newell, 1987) is one way. Items of information or procedure that are repeatedly used together are consolidated into larger units that are retrieved as a whole. In "proceduralization" (Anderson, 1987), statable knowledge used in solving problems is converted to procedures that are simply executed. Opposite to this is the process whereby the results of frequently used procedures are stored as factual knowledge and simply recalled. If you frequently have to convert between miles and kilometers, for instance, as in driving between the United States and Canada, you will soon learn equivalents corresponding to typical speed limits (e.g., 30 m.p.h. is approximately 50 km/hr) and no longer have to compute them. In all of these hypothesized processes, according to the mind-as-container metaphor, one kind of object in the mind is converted into another. This still leaves cognition with a kind of "chunkiness," which does not accord with the impression of everything blending together. In connectionist approaches to modeling learning, however, the chunkiness disappears. Instead, there is a whole system becoming increasingly differentiated in its response to environmental inputs. Parts of the connectionist network may come to be distinguishable. For instance, in a network that is learning to read, certain nodes may come to be consistently associated with certain letters of the alphabet. But it is still the system as a whole that responds to each new event and is modified by it.

This part–whole issue, which at one level seems academic and fussy, has nevertheless been close to the heart of the main educational debate that has raged through most of the past century and will no doubt continue well into the 21st. On one side are advocates of teaching the "whole" child and "whole" language, strenuously opposed to any approach that decomposes learning into separate skills or objectives. On the other side are people who advocate systematic teaching of subject matter and skills, and this typically involves identifying and sequencing elements to be learned. As so often happens in education, what could be treated as a fairly straightforward and practical pedagogical issue comes, without much justification, to be treated as a theoretical and finally as a moral and political issue.

At a theoretical level, the part–whole issue is a false issue. No one, I believe, denies that mature acquired abilities have the seamless, holistic character that we have already discussed. At the same time, no thoughtful person will deny what Paul Attewell (1990) has aptly stressed, that

> *all* human activity, even the most mundane, is quite complex. Things that everyone does—such as walking, crossing the road, and carrying on a conversation—are amazing accomplishments requiring a complex coordination of perception, movement, and decision, a myriad of choices, and a multitude of skills. (pp. 429–430)

The reason for educators to pay attention to the parts is so as not to neglect something that needs work. This is well understood in sports, where the part–whole issue tends to be handled on a purely pragmatic basis. Some trainers put more emphasis on the whole—on playing whole games, running whole races—whereas others put more emphasis on special exercises to strengthen particular skills, but they all recognize the importance of both. Only in academic areas do we find the kind of extremism that insists on one to the virtual exclusion of the other.

The teaching of reading provides the clearest example of the need to pay attention to the whole as well as to different kinds of knowledge that must come together for successful action to occur. On one hand, reading dramatically exhibits the holistic character of mature competence. For the skilled reader engaged in light reading, the meaning seems to come right off the page, with no intervening steps or subprocesses. Partly because of this, however—because introspection does not yield much sense of what actually goes into the reading process—reading education over the years has tended to neglect or undervalue every one of the six kinds of knowledge previously discussed, although usually not all of them at the same time. Thus, one of the effects of research and scholarship in reading has been to call attention to various facets of reading competence, which seem obvious once they are pointed out but which nevertheless become the objects of reform or resistance. The following are noteworthy facets of recent decades, classified here according to the type of knowledge brought into attention:

- *Implicit understanding in reading.* Cognitive research of the 1970s, particularly that carried out by Richard Anderson and others at the Center for the Study of Reading, brought to light the vast amount of informal knowledge required to understand the simplest texts. The same was being discovered by AI researchers trying to build text-understanding systems. *Becoming a Nation of Readers* (Anderson, Hiebert, Scott, & Wilkinson, 1985), a monograph that featured the role of background knowledge, became the basis for a wave of reform in curriculum and textbook adoption guidelines.

Another kind of implicit understanding more specific to reading has been brought out by more recent research. This is "phonemic awareness." Although variously treated as theory or as skill, it most clearly fits the category of implicit understanding as I have sketched it: It is understanding that manifests itself in a perceptual way—not merely knowing *that* spoken words are composed of identifiable sounds but hearing them *as* composites of such sounds (known as phonemes). As with other kinds of perception-like understanding, this does not mean hearing words that way all the time, but hearing them that way when appropriate. It is appropriate, for instance, in producing rhyme and alliteration. It is also appropriate, and by some accounts essential, in learning to read an alphabetic language.

Infants' babbling and much of the spontaneous vocal play of toddlers involves phonemes and their recombination. So do many of the songs and stories that appeal to young children, the Dr. Seuss books being outstanding examples. As a result, many children start school well equipped with phonemic awareness, and as they begin to attend to the spellings of words the connections between letters and sounds become obvious. But there are other children who show hardly any such awareness, and the prognosis for their success in reading is poor. However, experiments indicate phonemic awareness can be taught and with beneficial effects on beginning reading (Murray, 1998).

• *Statable knowledge in reading.* Statable knowledge as an outcome of reading is, of course, well recognized. It is what "book learning" is all about. But its role in the process of reading has been much less appreciated, so much so that a book arguing for its importance was one of the more maligned books of the 1980s in educational circles. In *Cultural Literacy*, E. D. Hirsch, Jr. (1987) pointed out the extent to which even popular media presuppose extensive, though low-level, knowledge of historical, scientific, and literary facts. The reader of an American news magazine, for instance, needs some familiarity with names such as Eisenhower, Castro, and Edison, and with concepts such as the speed of light, natural selection, and computer virus. Such terms are not explained and yet are essential to understanding texts. His argument for the importance of such knowledge, although set

out in plain language and with vivid examples, proved sufficiently novel that to this day most educational commentators
seem to miss his point.

• *Impressionistic knowledge in reading.* In "What Lesson Does This
Poem Teach You?" Louise Rosenblatt (1980) criticized school people for treating literature as a cryptic form of expository writing—that is, as if its purpose was to convey statable knowledge.
Rosenblatt argued for focusing literature teaching instead on
what matters most to people who actually know and understand
literature, the personal experience that comes when one is absorbed in a good poem or story. Rosenblatt's writings have made
"reader response" a new slogan in school literature curricula. Now
even the most pedestrian basal reading program will include
among the questions accompanying the reading selections a few
that ask children to report how the selection made them feel or
how they liked it or what personal experience it reminded them of.
Such trivialization of literary experience, which in the worst case
eliminates concern with actually understanding the text, comes
from placing reader response in contrast to knowledge. What
ought to be the concern is treating literature in the classroom in
ways that advance impressionistic knowledge of the kinds implied
by the broad meaning of the term "literate."

• *Episodic knowledge in reading.* Reading allows the accumulation of episodes, both factual and fictional, that can serve as episodic knowledge. A classically educated politician,
contemplating a return to private life, might recall the return of
Odysseus as well as the experiences of recently retired colleagues. On a less literate plane, discussions of sexual harassment in the workplace at the time of this writing are more likely
to draw on examples from a series of sensational movies on this
theme than on real-life cases. They are widely known, the facts
are clear, and they are safer to talk about. Roger Schank and colleagues at the Institute for the Learning Sciences have built instructional programs around real and fictitious narratives. Their
value at the school level has yet to be exploited, however. A
strong "don't look back" policy guides the reading curriculum
like all others, so that, except for testing memory, there is seldom
any recall of old stories for new purposes.

The importance of narrative as a form of knowledge has been emphasized in a number of critical examinations of school practice
(Bettelheim & Zelan, 1982; Bruner, 1986; Egan, 1989). Remembered
narratives are episodic knowledge. Yet, even though the basal read-

ers used in elementary schools consist largely of stories, there is little regard for their potential as knowledge, except for the moral lessons that may occasionally be extracted from them.[3] Although watchdog groups pay close attention to the impressionistic knowledge a story might convey, their influence has been deadening as far as episodic knowledge is concerned. In order not to give offense, stories are rendered trite and unmemorable, mythic lovability being perhaps the most common theme. Narratives are also much used as attention grabbers in expository text material, but Hidi, Baird, and Hildyard (1982) found them to deal with trivial or irrelevant points, and thus to draw attention away from main ideas.

• *Skills in reading.* In some educational circles it is impolitic to refer to reading as a skill and even worse to refer to it as a composite of skills. To these whole language advocates, "skill" is inseparably linked to "drill" and therefore is antithetical to their view of reading as a naturally developing sense-making process. Many of them reject phonemic awareness, mistaking it for a skill. Yet there is mounting evidence that word recognition is a skill quite separate from the kinds of knowledge involved in comprehension (Stanovich & Cunningham, 1991). An indication of this separability comes from the fact that for less than 100 dollars you can buy text-to-speech software that does a better job of oral reading than the bottom quartile of American high school students. Of course, it does not understand the text, but poor readers listening to it can do so, which dramatizes just how separable the decoding part of reading ability is. It is probably more separable than the skill of catching fly balls is from the other skills of a baseball outfielder. This is because in a baseball game the outfielder has to pay attention to base runners and several other things at the same time as trying to catch the ball, whereas for the skilled reader word recognition is so swift that it is completed before other processes arise to compete with it (Perfetti & Roth, 1981). Yet baseball training normally includes practice in chasing fly balls, with little worry that this may destroy the holistic character of fielding ability.

A reason skills have aroused so much opposition among reading specialists is, however, that they have often been dissociated from reading altogether. It is as if baseball players, instead of practicing catching flyballs, sat doing workbook exercises on ballistics.

---

[3]One exception, I make bold to point out, is the reading series I have helped author, *SRA/Open Court Reading*, which groups together selections that relate to a common "explorable concept" and engages students in work aimed at advancing their understanding of the concept, using story content along with other knowledge sources.

The most abused skill, and also the most controversial, has been phonics. Instead of being taught as a way to identify unrecognized words, it has been taught as a subject in its own right (largely through workbook exercises) and never applied to its intended task. Skill-oriented reading programs have also been full of exercises of so-called skills that are merely the inventions of workbook and test authors: "classification" skills, "seriation" skills (supposed to help children to get story events in the right order, as if that were a problem), and "inference" skills. As is well recognized in more successful areas of skill development, such as sports and music, there is a place for specific skill training, but it needs to be carefully designed so as to strengthen what actually needs strengthening and so as to insure that what is learned is incorporated into the global competence that is the ultimate objective of the training.

• *Regulative knowledge in reading.* Perhaps the strongest impact of cognitive research on reading instruction has been in the identifying and teaching of strategies for self-regulation of reading processes. Under the rubric of "study skills," there had already developed a body of practices aimed at improving learning from texts—summarizing, raising questions, reviewing, and so on. However, these were generally things to do after or between cycles of actual reading. Through use of thinking-aloud procedures, cognitive researchers were able to gain insight into what skilled readers do "on-line," during the actual reading of texts (Bereiter & Bird, 1985; Scardamalia & Bereiter, 1984).

CHANGING THE UNSCHOOLED MIND

In *The Unschooled Mind*, Howard Gardner (1991) described the vast body of implicit understanding of the world that children have already developed by the time they first encounter formal education. Much of what we know or infer about children's implicit understanding comes from research on misconceptions, research that reveals the many ways naive understanding is inconsistent with expert knowledge. Here we encounter a nice irony, however. Students' naive understandings of physics, biology, economics, and so on are interpreted by educators according to their own naive understanding of knowledge and mind.

To folk epistemology, ideas in the head and ideas in the textbook are the same kind of thing, except that ideas in the head may be unconscious. What are controversially called misconceptions, then, are simply cases of a mismatch between the ideas in students' heads and the ideas endorsed by experts. Resolving the mismatch ought to be a straightforward instructional problem. When it turns out not to be, when misconceptions are found to persist even after university-level instruction, this is taken as evidence that naive beliefs are very deeply held.

There are instances in which a new idea encounters a deeply held belief and the result is stubborn and sometimes violent opposition. This can happen, for instance, when science teaching contradicts religious beliefs. It can also happen when science teaching flies in the face of what appear to be indisputable facts. A recent book, *The Nurturance Assumption* (Harris, 1998), marshaled evidence against the belief that parenting makes much difference in the intellectual and personality development of children. The common response of friends of mine, including psychologists who might be expected to show an interest in the evidence, is instant denial, followed by declarations about how important they have been in making their own children the exemplary human beings that they are. This is a classic reaction to heresy. But students' reactions to new knowledge are not usually like that at all. More commonly, students fail to notice any inconsistency between their prior knowledge and what is being taught.

Treating the problem as one of belief change makes it unsolvable. Making it solvable requires abandoning the folk way of thinking about it and seeing it in terms of different kinds of knowledgeability related to conceptual artifacts. The problem is that you can acquire considerable knowledge of a conceptual artifact without undergoing any change in your implicit understanding of the world. This is so obviously true that it almost goes without saying. And yet if you don't say it, you are liable to fall into misconstruing the problem as one of new beliefs colliding or failing to collide with old ones. There is no collision because the phenomena in question occupy different worlds. Here is an object in World 3: Newton's first law of motion, which states that a body in motion will continue in motion unless acted on by a force. Here is our World 2 implicit understanding, which makes sense of a world in which everything is in the process of running out of steam. Where is the conflict? Conflict arises if we start to work out the practical implications of Newton's law and test them against what our intuitive understanding leads us to expect or if we try to create a theory of our own—to produce a competing conceptual artifact that is consistent with our intuitive understanding. Modern science educators try to induce such conflicts (cf. Hunt & Minstrell, 1994), and that is laudable. The trouble is that those conflicts can be worked through and resolved and yet implicit understanding is *still* largely untouched. We have resolved some theoretical issues. Our statable knowledge has changed. But we still see the world through pre-Newtonian eyes.

Let me amplify this point by using an example that may apply to you, the reader. The World 3 object in question is the idea of "knowing your way around" in a knowledge domain. David Perkins (1995) has elaborated this idea into what he calls "realm theory." It is one of the central ideas in his revisionist treatment of intelligence. James Greeno (1991) has used this idea to define the elusive concept of number sense. I made extensive use of it in the preceding chapter in developing a conception of understanding. It is not a difficult idea, neither is it controversial. It does not provoke opposition or rejection. So if you have read one or another presentation of the idea I will assume you understand it, according to conventional criteria of understanding. Let us assume, furthermore, that you accept the idea as reasonable and worthwhile. I would nevertheless conjecture that this idea has had no discernible effect on how you normally think about intelligence, understanding, or number sense. I base this speculation on the scarcity of mention of the idea in World Wide Web documents, despite the fact that Perkins and Greeno are widely cited for other ideas and the book in which Perkins presents the idea is itself widely cited.

Why does the "knowing your way around" idea gain so little attention? I suggest it is precisely because it does *not* contradict an existing belief. It offers nothing to get upset about, nothing to marshal arguments for or against. Instead, it offers a different way of thinking about knowledge and mind. Although that is vastly more important than merely offering a different opinion about something, people do not have ready-made ways to deal with it. People know how to argue, criticize, and persuade. That is to say, people know how to deal with statable knowledge. If schooling does nothing else it sharpens those skills. Bringing about changes in statable knowledge may in turn bring about changes in implicit understanding, but these changes are liable to be partial and unsatisfactory (Vosniadou & Brewer, 1987). Instead of regarding this as proof of the strength of naive beliefs, however, we ought to regard it as evidence of the limited overlap between statable and implicit knowledge.

One of the puzzles about misconceptions is why they remained undiscovered for so long. In an essay that might be credited with launching educational inquiry into scientific misconceptions, David Hawkins (1978) remarked, "The partial recognition of these problems is very old, probably as old as formal instruction, but somehow they have not been brought into sharp focus" (Par. 29). Evidently, the kinds of examinations, recitations, and laboratory exercises used in science education enable students to acquire and display statable knowledge without ever revealing the substrate of implicit understanding where misconceptions reside. This does not mean students only learn by rote—Hawkins recognized that. Students may be able to display some competence at all levels of Bloom's (1956) taxonomy, being able to paraphrase what has been taught, apply it to textbook problems, and in some degree evaluate, analyze, and synthesize the material. So what is lacking? Folk epistemology offers no further possibilities, and thus the educational problem not only cannot be solved, it cannot even be formulated.

The problem is how to bring about intended changes in implicit understanding. We know reasonably well how to share or promote all the other kinds of personal knowledge. We share statable knowledge by explanation and argument; episodic knowledge by telling stories; skills by demonstration and coaching; and regulatory knowledge by precept, example, and various subtle and not-so-subtle means of inducing conformity to norms. Impressionistic knowledge may not fare well in schools, but in daily life we know that if we want others to feel the way we do about something (a work of art, for instance) it will not do much good to explain or argue; instead we rely on expressive language and gesture and on directing others' attention to significant features. But how do we change the lens through which people view some aspect of the world? For that is what changing intuitive understanding amounts to, and that is why remedying basic misconceptions is no easy matter. It is getting students to look at motion through a Newtonian rather than an Aristotelian lens, to look at the varieties of life forms through a Darwinian rather than a Lamarkian or a Book of Genesis lens.

One thing that is obvious about intuitive understanding is that it evolves gradually through experience. If only that much were taken into account, the battle with misconceptions would take a turn in education's favor. David Hawkins reminded us that conceptual changes that took centuries for scientists to work their way through cannot be expected to happen with students in a couple of lessons. But it is not simply a matter of repetition, of convincing students and getting them adjusted to a matter of fact. As Hawkins (1978) stated:

> The round Earth-body was not simply a new fact to be stored along with other facts; it was a fact which required a radical reorganization of the whole category structure of geographical and cosmological thinking. If it were taught merely as a fact, without appreciation of the need to help it penetrate into the subsoil of understanding and to rebuild the mind's category structures in the process, it would remain something merely bookish and abstract, to be entertained nervously and then forgotten. Perhaps children of today can grow up without this particular conflict of understanding, one which many of us can remember from our own childhoods. The educational time scale here, that of the transition

from opaque fact to intuitive widespread grasp, has been at least a couple of millennia. We ought to do better. (p. 34)

But how can an idea, a conceptual artifact, "penetrate into the subsoil of understanding"? As I discussed in chapter 3, conceptual artifacts such as Newton's laws may on one hand be regarded as truth claims—statements about how the world really is—and on the other hand as tools—tools whose principal use is in solving problems of understanding. Both are important, but educators tend to put too exclusive an emphasis on the first. The result of treating conceptual artifacts as truth claims is change in students' statable knowledge. This does not mean merely that they learn to parrot textbook statements. It may mean quite significant changes in belief, but these changes are likely to have only limited effect on implicit understanding. Students in an introductory physics class may do plenty of problem solving using Newton's laws, but these are problems of *how fast, how far, what direction*, and so on. As John Sweller (1988) has shown, solving such formulaic problems has little effect on understanding. Sweller suggested replacing them with problems of *figure out whatever you can*. As I argue in chapter 9, it is even more important to replace them with problems of *why*. And these should not be esoteric problems about juggling tennis balls in a plummeting elevator. They should be problems about explaining the phenomena of everyday experience. That is where intuitive understanding holds sway and where new learning must have its effect.

KNOWLEDGE AT THE SOCIOCULTURAL LEVEL

The work of sociocultural theorists has highlighted two kinds of knowledge that belong neither to Popper's World 3 nor to World 2. That is, they are kinds of knowledge that cannot be treated as objects in their own right but that are not attributes of individual minds either. As discussed in chapter 3, these are knowledge constituted in the practices of groups and knowledge embodied in tools. The finely coordinated artistry of an improvisational comedy troupe illustrates the former. The knowledge of photography and physics embodied in an automatic camera illustrates the latter. Both the comedy troupe and the camera are, of course, treatable as objects, but there is knowledge involved that cannot be treated separately from them. "Situated" is perhaps the most widely used term for referring to such knowledge.

A useful way of separating personal knowledge from knowledge embedded in the practices of a group is to ask what happens when the group dissolves. Consider that paradigm of collective knowledge, the tango, as in "It takes two to tango." The fact is that people take lessons to learn ballroom dances such as the tango for the very reason that it is knowledge they can take away with them and that will serve them in new situations. But suppose a couple takes ballroom dancing seriously and starts entering competitions. They will begin to develop skill and artistry as a pair. If they break up, each will carry away some of that skill and artistry, but a distinctive part of it will have been lost and will need to be redeveloped and will not be quite the same with different partners. Thus, we can distinguish a large, basic part of tango knowledge, which is an attribute of individuals even though it is learned in combination with partners, and a smaller but very significant part that is an attribute of a couple and that is unavailable to them as individuals.

Skills are the most obvious kind of knowledge that may be situated at a group level rather than an individual level. What of the remaining five kinds of personal knowledge? Do they have group-level counterparts as well? This is an interesting question that I will not pretend to explore in depth, offering only a few observations which suggest that answers may vary.

Statable knowledge is fundamentally social, for to call knowledge statable presumes it is communicable to others. Most of it originates through discourse, and even when we fabricate it by ourselves, we do so in the imaginary presence of peers (Harré, 1984). Still, statable knowledge is an attribute of individuals. After participating in the same seminar, different people will walk away with different statable knowledge, as may be ascertained by questionnaire or examination. It is, as I said before, the World 2 counterpart of World 3 knowledge. This suggests World 3 knowledge is the group-level counterpart of personal statable knowledge, and this seems to be the common opinion among people who take a sociocultural view. World 3, under this construction, becomes the social world, the world of public discourse. That is quite different from how Popper conceived of it, and I have argued at length for the pragmatic value of Popper's conception of World 3 as a world of abstract knowledge objects that can be dealt with in their own right, apart from the individual or collective minds that relate to them. Supposing we accept Popper's conception, then is there anything comparable to statable knowledge that groups can be said to know but that individuals do not? The closest thing to it is that vague but often-mentioned something called the "state of knowledge" in a field.

In any knowledge-rich field, the "state of knowledge" exceeds what any individual knows. Nevertheless, there are periodic efforts, through annual reviews, handbooks, and the like, to encapsulate the state of knowledge in various fields. Usually these are compilations of efforts by different specialists to summarize the state of knowledge in different sectors, but authors of the separate contributions frequently confess their little subfields are still too vast for them. Thus, the state of knowledge remains elusive. But it is not reducible to the World 3 objects pertinent to the field. It has to do with the status of those objects—which World 3 objects are recognized, which ones are favored, what are perceived to be outstanding problems, where it is perceived progress has been made, and so on. A good state-of-knowledge review will address such issues. The result will be new World 3 objects, debatable propositions concerning the status of the primary objects, the theories and putative facts composing the field. What those secondary propositions are about is this collective, transpersonal knowledge—statable knowledge that is a property of the group rather than of particular individuals, although individuals may know about it. When, for instance, feminist theorists criticize "androcentric" science, they are criticizing this collective knowledge, not the knowledge of particular individuals and usually not any particular World 3 knowledge objects composing the field, either. Their criticisms imply, rightly I think, that statable knowledge at the group level can have its biases, gaps, and unexamined assumptions, just like statable knowledge at the individual level.

Whether it is useful to think of implicit understanding and impressionistic knowledge at a group level I am not sure. Talk about public opinion or a public mood or attitude often seems to imply something that transcends individual beliefs and attitudes, but this may be nothing more than convenient journalistic language, like saying the stockmarket is optimistic or it has adopted a wait-and-see attitude. Naturally, if a certain expectation or attitude is widely held and expressed it will tend to spread, but that does not mean something exists at the group level beyond what exists among individuals. deKleer and Brown (1985) said of physics that although it is expressed formally as what we would call World 3 knowledge, "the laws are all based on the presupposition of a shared unstated commonsense prephysics knowledge" (p. 13). Everyday discourse as well presupposes vast shared implicit understanding, but does this imply some kind of understanding beyond the individual level? I see no compelling reason to suppose so.

Where the idea of suprapersonal understanding and impressionistic knowledge makes most sense is in the realm of ceremony and ritual. A traditional funeral service embodies a constellation of beliefs and feelings that may not correspond to the personal beliefs and feelings of anyone present, yet people may participate wholeheartedly, without hypocrisy, and would take offense at a service that reflected their actual sentiments. There is a related literary genre called "occaral" verse. This is verse written for public occasions such as coronations, graduation ceremonies, and commemorations. It is not intended to express the poet's own sentiments, and the poet is of course not expected to be privy to the actual sentiments of the listeners. Rather, the verse is intended to express the beliefs and sentiments most appropriate to the occasion. If you consider how often in daily life you say things or hear things that are not so much personal expressions as expressions "appropriate to the occasion," you begin to get a sense of a large expanse of implicit and impressionistic knowledge that is part of the culture but that is not attributable to the individuals within it.

Episodic knowledge at the group level consists primarily of episodes that members of the group have experienced in common. These episodes take on a value well beyond that of episodes known only to individuals. An episode can be jointly examined, and individuals can offer their distinctive perspectives on it, thus greatly enriching its potential as a source of ideas, cautions, abstract models, and shared metaphors. First-hand episodic knowledge blends gradually into history and eventually into legend and myth, as old-timers leave and people enter the group who were not around when the episode took place. Myths embody episodic knowledge important to a culture. Knowledge of these objects is personal knowledge, some of it statable, some of it episodic. If there is anything beyond this, it would seem to exist in the relation of myths to the global entities referred to by terms such as "ethos" and "national character." The value of such notions is controversial, and I suspect that most action or situativity theorists would reject them.

With a bit of a stretch, it seems, we can make out kinds of statable, implicit, impressionistic, and episodic knowledge situated at the group level. The case for doing so is not very compelling, however. Most of what needs to be considered beyond the personal level can be handled by positing World 3 knowledge objects and not positing knowledge attributable to a suprapersonal mind or suprapersonal cognitive processes. The same is not true for the remaining two kinds of knowledge, however. There are group-level skills. Recognizing and understanding them is vitally important for the design and training of expert teams, and expert teams are becoming the heroes and geniuses of the knowledge society. There is also regulative knowledge at the group level, however, and this too takes on social importance when what is being regulated is the production of knowledge itself.

An expert team not only develops skills that inhere in the team rather than in the individual members, it also develops ways of managing and regulating itself that are something more than the ways individual members manage and regulate their actions. This is true whether or not there is a designated manager or leader. There are regulative skills that enable the group to adapt to new situations, to maintain performance under stress, and to keep from breaking up when dissensions arise. There are also norms that regulate the collective activity as well as the individual activity of members. When is a job finished? What constitutes a "good enough" result? There are ethics that apply to group as well as individual behavior. Beyond that, there are delicate problems of trade-offs that involve collective knowledge. For instance, how much efficiency or quality may be sacrificed to preserve harmony within the team?

These kinds of regulative knowledge are easiest to discern in small, closely interacting groups, but they may be found as well in larger and looser collectives, such as those of professions and disciplines. The official standards of a profession are World 3 objects and they are meant to regulate individual behavior. But there are unwritten standards that are only to be found implicit in the workings of the discipline or profession as a collective. For instance, in a learned discipline, what constitutes a discovery, a contribution to knowledge? This is something award committees and reviewers of manuscripts and proposals are called on continually to judge, on the assumption their judgments will not be idiosyncratic but will somehow reflect the unwritten (and evolving) standards of the discipline.

Looked at from the outside, the operative standards of a discipline may seem strange and questionable. To make sense of them it must be understood that they do not descend from a disciplinary god but evolve to meet a complex of social requirements. Until very recently my only contact with the world of intelligent tutoring systems had been through reading about some of the more notable ones and being acquainted with the work of some of the leading thinkers and designers. Then I was roped into reviewing proposals for an international conference in this area and for the first time I began to get a glimpse of AI in education as a subculture. Thousands of people make their careers in this area; many are academics, and so publishing and presenting papers at conferences are important. But here problems arise. Intelligent tutoring systems take a long time to build, there is usually little research involved, and the result, even if excellent for its purpose, is not very newsworthy. So how does one fill up a conference program in ways that will demonstrate that AI in education is a discipline and not just a trade? How is a team of developers to produce enough different papers that they can all get on the program and thereby enhance their resumés and perhaps get their travel expenses paid? I doubt if these questions were ever addressed directly by any body, and yet solutions seem to have evolved. From what I have been able to make out (and this is speculation introduced here to illustrate a general point; I would not want to have to defend its validity), a whole substrate of academic writing has evolved in which the game is to translate commonplace ideas into elegant flow diagrams or logical or mathematical formalisms. Thus, an art form has developed that has a superficial relationship to the actual work of the discipline, but that is regulated according to aesthetic norms rather than norms of usefulness and originality of content. The attendant regulative knowledge exists at the group level—it is constituted in the practices of program committees and review panels—and only makes sense when the activity of the discipline is considered in its fullest human sense.[4]

The sociology of science has recently taken an iconoclastic turn in which the regulative norms of scientific communities are seen as not much different from those of most businesses. Truth and objectivity, rather than being regulative ideas that guide research, are a sort of merchandise that scientists package and sell (Latour, 1987). The regulative ideas are those of highly competitive enterprises, armies, sports teams, and the like. Winning and losing are central. This is not the place to evaluate these claims, but it is the place to remark that regulative knowledge at both the group level and the individual level is complex and does not necessarily have a great deal of internal consistency. Central to the practice of all sciences and disciplines are what Dreyfus and Rabinow (1983) called "serious speech acts." These are assertions meant to have significance and validity beyond the immediate situation in which they are made. Failing that, you may have a social club but you do not have a discipline. Accordingly, any discipline develops knowledge concerning what constitutes a serious speech act and how such speech acts are to be judged and responded to. Truth and objectivity are likely to figure prominently as regulative ideas, but if not, there will be other regulative ideas such as moral or political rightness, phenomenological richness, or novelty of insight.

Group-level regulative knowledge is an attribute of long-term social organization. Engestrom (1987) referred to this aspect of social activity as "rules," and it can often be described that way. But we should exercise the same caution in attributing unwritten rules to

---

[4]A somewhat similar story has been told in the domain of cattle breeding. Selecting breeding stock to maximize milk production is straightforward on the female side but problematic on the male side. Nowadays genealogical records make it possible to select bulls from family lines in which the males have good records of siring milk producers. But before genetics became advanced enough to support such strategies, breeders looked for promising physical characteristics in the bulls themselves. Hence developed the esthetics of cattle judging and the breeding of show animals, which became an art form increasingly remote from its original purpose.

groups as we do to individual minds: Unwritten rules are creations of the observer; the actual participants may or may not have rules in mind. In an elementary school classroom, one often sees explicit rules of conduct posted on the walls. In a well-managed classroom observable conduct will show a fair degree of correspondence to these rules, usually as a result of conscious effort by teacher and students. At a deeper level, however, there are norms not represented in posters that are probably not even considered by the teacher and that could not be translated into rules if they were.[5] Yet these are norms at the heart of the educational enterprise. For instance, what constitutes an acceptable level of text comprehension? The norm is obviously different in an elementary school classroom from what it is in a law office, but in each case it is unspecified, though real. There is no limit to how hard one might work to tease out every implication of a text. What constitutes good enough is, accordingly, what will result in favorable response within the particular group.

A philosopher friend of mine used to teach in such a way that it took a whole term to get through a page and a half. "Good enough" comprehension in his class was well beyond the level required in ordinary life. By contrast, I have been in elementary school classrooms where "good enough" comprehension for 10-year-olds meant being able to identify the topics in a text, without necessarily making out anything that was said about them. That level of comprehension would be sufficient to remind a child of personal experiences related to a story and thereby participate in the kinds of discussions that constituted book talk in those classes.

Paul Cobb and his associates (Cobb et al., 1997) have studied the development of what they call "sociomathematical" norms in primary grade classrooms. The classrooms were ones in which much of the work in mathematics was focused on producing, comparing, and judging alternative ways of solving a problem. In this context, sociomathematical norms determined what would be judged as a *different* way of solving a problem and what would be accepted as justification for a method or solution. Neither of these could be formulated as explicit rules, at least not rules children could understand, and yet over the course of a year children's judgments in these matters become stricter and more in line with those of mathematicians. Much of what develops will, we trust, be personal knowledge the children will carry away with them. That, after all, is the point of

---

[5]An interesting perspective on norms of conduct comes from the study of antisocial children, who seem bent on violating them. In *The Aggressive Child* Redl and Wineman (1957) observed that, although these children go out of their way to violate explicit rules, the vast majority of their behaviors conform to implicit social norms. Evidently you have to know a rule in order to disobey it.

teaching mathematics. But an important part of what develops will be regulative knowledge at the group level, which will need to be recreated in the next class the children go to.

WAYS OF KNOWING

In feminist scholarship there is talk about "women's ways of knowing," which are thought to be more subjective and contextual and less analytical than men's ways (Belenky, Clinchy, Goldberger, & Tarule, 1986). Much the same distinction has been made between non-European and European ways of knowing. There is also developing a body of scholarship on "narrative knowing," which may be distinguished from "paradigmatic" or propositional knowledge (Bruner, 1986). Kieran Egan (1997) has elaborated a theory of different forms that understanding takes at different stages of cognitive development. In young children it takes a mythic form, with story characters representing stark contrasts of good and evil, strong and weak. Later it takes a romantic form; tales of adventure are the model within which information is most readily understood. Only in young adulthood, and then not for everyone, does it become possible to understand things in terms of autonomous theories, the principal occupants of Popper's World 3. But throughout life, according to Egan, narrative remains the most natural and accessible form of understanding.

A number of issues get entangled here, ranging from "learning styles," which is a kind of quack pedagogical medicine, to the nature of truth. The central, but at the same time least controversial, issue is qualitative differences in personal knowledge—the claim that the mental states we call knowing are qualitatively or structurally different for different people, varying with gender, ethnicity, and age. From a connectionist point of view, this almost goes without saying. If personal knowledge is a sort of attunement of the brain, then each change in that attunement—each new learning, in other words—is conditioned to some extent by the person's entire past history, which is surely going to reflect age and cultural experience and quite possibly hormonal differences as well. This notion only becomes problematic if you hold to a folk mind-as-container view. For if you imagine knowledge to consist of objects in the mind, then saying there are basic cultural differences implies there are radically different *kinds* of objects in different minds. What could these possibly be? Get rid of mental objects and you get rid of that problem.

The real problem—the one that can lead to departmental coups and political donnybrooks—is not with claims that there are different ways of knowing, it is with claims that out of those different ways of knowing come different kinds of *truth*. Logically, the second claim does not follow from the first; in Popperian terms, the first is an assertion about World 2, the second is an assertion about World 3, and you cannot infer from one world to the other. But what if, according to your kind of *truth*, the second claim does follow? Where can we go from that impasse? It is an impasse that has given rise to all sorts of epistemological vagaries; in an effort to avoid them, let us consider a real case.

One place where the idea of different ways of knowing has received more than academic attention is in environmental policy. There is a movement whose identifying labels are "indigenous knowledge" and "traditional ecological knowledge" (often referred to by acronyms) and whose political program is "co-management" of environments by governments and people indigenous to the environment. The current state of the movement may be tracked by doing a Web search on those terms. The idea is that when plans are being made for protection of an environment or for sustainable use of its resources, people indigenous to that environment ought not only to have a place at the table but their ecological knowledge ought to weigh in with the knowledge of outside experts. This movement has taken hold strongly in the far north. There have been conferences of native peoples from the entire circumpolar region devoted to what might be called native knowledge rights.[6] Traditional environmental knowledge (TEK) became a hot issue throughout Canada, however, when a government-appointed Environmental Assessment Panel declared that TEK should receive "equal consideration with scientific research in assessing the environmental and socio-economic impacts" of a proposed mining development (Howard & Widdowson, 1996, p. 34). But what would "equal consideration" mean?

Howard and Widdowson, whose article in a policy journal touched off the controversy, evidently saw it as meaning that TEK and scientific knowledge were to have equal claims to truth. They objected that TEK's truth claims are untestable:

> There is no mechanism, or will, by which spiritually based knowledge claims can be challenged or verified. In fact, pressure from aboriginal groups and their consultants has made TK a sacred cow for which only uncritical support is appropriate. Traditional knowledge is thus granted a sanctity which could lead to the acceptance of incorrect conclusions. (Howard & Widdowson, 1996, p. 34)

---

[6]In 1996 a seminar was held in Inuvik, Northwest Territories, Canada, on "Documentation and Application of Indigenous Knowledge." The 58 participants included people from Alaska, northern Canada, Greenland, and northern Russia.

The academic response to Howard and Widdowson was to splatter them with pop epistemology—criticizing "the simplistic view that there is such a thing as objective, value-free science" (Berkes & Henley, 1997, p. 30). Although, in response to several criticisms along these lines, Howard and Widdowson (1997) denied that they held such a view, they dug the epistemological hole deeper for themselves by saying, "There are not different ways of knowing. There are different beliefs about the same phenomena" (p. 46).

Clearly, the argument among academicians was destined to go nowhere. But what about the native people whose knowledge was being contested? As I browsed the Web sites devoted to Inuit knowledge exchange I found a refreshing lack of postmodernist and antiracist posturing. Native writers emphasized the compatibility between traditional knowledge, handed down by the elders, and scientific knowledge brought in by outside experts. "The elders are our experts," one said. Both kinds of knowledge are derived from experience and are modified by facts. Put the two together and you should get knowledge that is superior to both. A distinction between World 2 and World 3 is implied here, and it would be helpful to make it explicit. There are differences at the World 2 level—differences in personal knowledge—that go beyond "different beliefs about the same phenomena." There are different ways of seeing the world. But when these different ways of seeing the world give rise to explicit truth claims—to statements of fact or principle, to conceptual artifacts, in other words—it should be possible to compare, combine, or choose between them through a reasonable process of negotiation.

One of the marvels of human history has been the success of trade, despite all the barriers of language, custom, and knowledge that should have made it impossible. Part of that success is no doubt due to the fact that we are all members of the same species and are therefore, in ways we seldom appreciate, much more alike than different. But the other part has to do with the nature of trade. I have yams; you have a chicken. You want yams; I want chicken. There has got to be a way to make a deal. To do that, we will find a way to communicate about yams and chickens. These real objects provide a basis for communication. If, instead, we are meeting to hammer out an environmental policy that matters to both of us, we still need common objects of reference, only now some of these will be abstract rather than concrete. We need conceptual artifacts—concepts, ideas, facts. We may perceive them differently, have different feelings about them, and disagree as to their status, but unless we have some reason to believe we are talking about the same things, our discussion has no chance. The academic arguments about TEK have no chance, because the only objects in common among the disputants are words. With the Inuit there is at least the suggestion that conceptual artifacts of substance can be brought forth as objects of discussion and inquiry.

But traditional knowledge, as described by its native advocates, does not consist of theories or knowledge objects of that sort. The examples offered have to do with skill or know-how. For instance, the elders teach the young how to read many signals—in the look of the sky, the movement of the ice, and the behavior of wildlife—that give them information vital to their survival. This is surely knowledge the visiting scientist does not have. But how is it to be put on the table so as to enter into the formulation of environmental policy? that is not explained, and so it leaves room for what I take to be Howard and Widdowson's real concern: That native participants will use their undeniably superior personal knowledge of the environment to claim authority for statements that do not in fact derive from that knowledge.

This is what seems to be at issue in all the controversies where alternative ways of knowing enter the picture: Some statement is made that would normally be subject to criticisms based on reason and evidence, except that its validity is claimed to rest on the distinctive experience or world view of a certain group and to be immune to criticism by outsiders. This is not much different from claiming revealed truth. I have no intention of tackling the vast societal problems arising from this kind of situation—problems that have often been settled by bloodshed. It should be enough for present purposes simply to recognize that one can appreciate and respect kinds of personal knowledge profoundly different from one's own while insisting that any truth claims, theories, or the like arising from such knowledge are subject to negotiation. Of course, the terms of such negotiation should also be subject to negotiation and so on in what one hopes will not be an infinite regress.

But what is the point of recognizing different ways of knowing if these are not credited with validity in upholding truth claims? The point is much the same as recognizing the value of biological diversity: It is a great resource and it is what makes adaptation possible. Having a lot of often subtle intellectual diversity present in a group that is jointly tackling a problem or a project probably does more than anything else that can be done at a managerial level to ensure a creative outcome. (There is more about this in chap. 7.) To that extent the Canadian Environmental Assessment Panel's controversial recommendation was on the right track and it is what the Inuit writers seemed to be advocating. But putting it as giving equal weight to indigenous knowledge and scientific research is just the wrong way to think of it. That only sets the stage for polarization around non-negotiable truth claims. Evaluating truth claims (or however you want to put it to avoid the term "truth") is always a problem in argument and problem solving. Much has to be taken on authority, yet authority has to be questioned and kept in check. Not to do so is to suppress diversity, not encourage it. When there are power differences, as between imported experts and ordinary village folk, negotiation is notoriously difficult. I am in no way trying to minimize the difficulties. All I am saying is that assigning prior value to World 3 objects on the basis of their source is not a way to overcome the difficulty. It is likely to breed a contempt that carries over into contempt for the people associated with those objects and for the resources of personal knowledge they embody.

Narrative versus paradigmatic knowledge presents a somewhat different problem, which in practice, however, often merges with the kind of problem I have been discussing. Narrative gets identified with women's ways of knowing, and paradigmatic with men's ways. In education, there has been a rapidly growing movement in which narrative is identified as the teacher's natural way of knowing and more generally as the way to advance understanding of teaching, in contrast to the conventional paradigmatic way of knowing represented in educational research journals (Carter, 1993; Clandinin & Connelly, 1996). Activity goes on at different levels, from teachers sharing and discussing their personal narratives to researchers using them as data. Sometimes the discourse surrounding these narratives looks like journalism, sometimes like psychotherapy, sometimes like literary criticism, and sometimes like philosophizing. It also, of course, varies greatly in quality, along almost any dimension you might care to assess. There is also a split, similar to that arising with TEK, between those who see narrative as yielding a fundamentally different kind of "truth" and those who see narrative and paradigmatic knowledge as commensurate and combinable (Bullough & Baughman, 1998).

To me what is most significant about this narrativity movement in education, however, is its divisiveness. It defines a community of practitioners and closely allied education professors who are creating their own domain of inquiry in isolation from the established educational research community with its roots in the behavioral sciences. It is easy to see why teachers find more of value to themselves in the sharing of narratives than they do in reading scientific research reports, but this is symptomatic of something deeply wrong with the way the practitioner and research cultures have evolved in education. Institutionalizing what is taken to be a different kind of knowledge widens the gap between the two cultures—a gap that, I argue in chapter 11, must be closed if education is ever to become a progressive profession.

So it is important to decide whether, in a context like teaching, narrative knowledge represents a distinctive kind of "truth." Narratives are cultural artifacts. They are things out in the world, not things in people's minds. But they are not all the same kind of cultural artifact. Some are tantamount to theories. They are *conceptual* artifacts and can be treated as such. A story about how the dinosaurs became extinct, for instance, can be weighed against an explicit theory (set out in paradigmatic form) and can be judged to be compatible or incompatible and to do a better or a poorer job of accounting for various facts. But then there are fictional narratives, which are also cultural artifacts but not conceptual ones; they do not assert anything to be the case and are not anything like theories. They can be judged as to how realistic or authentic they are, but such judgment is made within the framework of literary criticism, not of theory.

The narratives that figure in the teacher story movement are closer to the literary than the theoretical end of the spectrum. They are not knowledge objects but they may contribute to people's personal knowledge in various ways. Mostly autobiographical accounts of teaching, they can provide other teachers with episodic knowledge that expands the store derived from their own experience and that may be useful in making decisions or understanding events. As literature, they can have an effect on readers' impressionistic knowledge. That is, they can influence how readers feel about things, how they judge them morally or aesthetically. As reflective writing, they can affect readers' intuitive understanding of their students, their situations, and themselves. Also, and not insignificantly, as narrative inquiry becomes institutionalized stories inevitably influence stories. In accordance with the principle that art imitates art, the kinds of stories teachers write are bound to be powerfully influenced by the stories they have read. One of my concerns about the teacher story movement is that a literary genre is emerging that is derived from poor literary models, that leads to stereotypic descriptions and sentiments, and hence to teachers unwittingly falsifying their own experience. The long and the short of it, however, is that the personal knowledge that results from writing, reading, and discussing autobiographical narratives is sure to be highly individual and, by definition, entirely subjective. How its effects combine with other effects, such as those of first-hand experience and the reading of scholarly literature, is unpredictable and probably impossible to evaluate.

A reasonable conclusion, nevertheless, is that teachers writing and reflecting upon personal narratives is a good thing. It may be more valuable to teachers than to most other people because of their isolation from one another behind classroom doors. If it were treated just as a way of enhancing personal knowledge, attention could focus on how to make it serve this purpose better. A problem such as the distorting effects of genre constraints on personal experience would receive due consideration. But none of this implies that narrative is a different kind of knowledge, that it is somehow in competition with knowledge of other kinds and to be judged by a different standard.

Where narrative competes is at the level of representation. If you can represent your theory in multiple ways—as a narrative, as a set of propositions forming an argument, as a diagram, as a computer simulation—there are advantages in using all the ways. They may reveal different implications, different deficiencies. For purposes of communication, you are likely to find that the story reaches more people, that the diagram helps some people and confuses others, and that the argument is best for getting critical response. The differences become more profound when we consider knowledge creation. Stories have the great virtue in constructing explanations of human affairs that they allow motivation and causality to be brought together in a coherent way. Argument forms tend to keep these separate and diagrams tend to end up as boxes connected by arrows every which way—the refuge of the conceptually handicapped— with motives in one box, causal factors in another. Because they favor a one-thing-after-another chain of events, however, stories are not a good way to formulate or understand constraint-based explanations, which are the norm in the physical sciences.

In this way narrative surely does represent a *way* of knowing, or perhaps a family of ways. It is a way in which the human mind, with all its evolved dispositions, capacities, and limitations, can come to grips with problems of understanding and create conceptual artifacts to serve as objects and tools of understanding. If some people are better disposed than others to narrative representation, it is reasonable to say they have a distinctive way of knowing, different from those who favor some other form of representation. Out of these different ways of knowing are likely to come differences in all six kinds of personal knowledge discussed in this chapter. People will see the world differently, will recall different events, will have different feelings and intuitions, will develop different skills and norms of conduct, and will likely end up with different statable beliefs. All of these differences can work to the benefit of collective problem solving and knowledge advancement, unless— and this is a very big "unless"—they become the basis for non-negotiable truth claims.

CONCLUSION

This chapter could have been titled "Ways of Knowing." That is certainly a more graceful expression than "Aspects of Knowledgeability." But as we have seen, "ways of knowing" is a phrase that has collected about it a large bundle of epistemological confusions and loose strings. It illustrates how wrongly things can go when people fail to distinguish World 2 from World 3. As a result, a perfectly noncontroversial statement—that people's personal knowledge is richly varied in ways that reflect the differences in their lives and backgrounds—gets entangled with the notion that there are different kinds of truth. The latter, although controversial, is also a defensible statement, but it draws no backing from the first statement. "Different kinds of truth" is a casual way of saying there are incommensurable theories. "Incommensurability," according to Ronen (1998), "occurs in science where two theories lack a common measure, a standard reference, or an external criterion that could have served as grounds for comparison." (p. 291). It is, thus, a characteristic of conceptual artifacts. It has as much to do with the way theories affect how we perceive the world as it does with the way our perception of the world affects our theories. But in no way does incommensurability imply that the justification for a theory, belief, or policy is unique to the personal knowledge and experience of its authors. Even the stoutest advocates of incommensurability allow that incommensurable theories can be separately described and criticized in a common forum (Feyerabend, 1988). There is, in short, no non-negotiable World 3 knowledge, however inaccessible one person's World 2 might be to others.

Folk psychology and epistemology, which treat knowledge as objects in individual minds and public knowledge as merely the expression of such knowledge, lead to undervaluing both personal and public knowledge. Public knowledge, according to this view, is ultimately just people's opinions. That being the case, why shouldn't my opinion count for as much as yours? It is difficult to argue that in general it should, but equally difficult to argue for a way of deciding when one opinion should count for more. But seeing public knowledge as the externalization of personal knowledge diminishes personal knowledge as well. What is inside the head is assumed to resemble in form if not content what is outside the head: in short, a collection of sentences. That could be taken as a rough characterization of what I called "statable" knowledge. It leaves the other five kinds of knowledge, except for skill, in limbo. They tend either to be ignored or to be romanticized. Either way, they fail to receive the systematic attention required to make them into realistic educational or knowledge management goals.

A workable approach to personal and public knowledge requires recognizing first of all that they are very different. One is not a copy or a manifestation of the other. Popper's distinction between World 2 and World 3 may be too stark a distinction for some purposes, but I have not found anything that works better for dealing with issues of education and knowledge creation. For that epistemology to work well, however, it has to be coupled with a psychology that gets past the folk notion of "things in the mind." A connectionist view of the mind sees learning as the continual tuning of an almost unimaginably vast neural network to the world with which it interacts. It is an embodied mind; in fact, the only reason for talking about minds rather than bodies is to address such phenomena as thoughts, beliefs, plans, intuitions, certainty, and uncertainty—the phenomena of subjective mental life. Out of this interaction with the world come those kinds of attunements that for practical purposes we may distinguish as intuitive understanding, episodic knowledge (memory for events), impressionistic knowledge (feelings that serve as knowledge), self-regulative knowledge, and skills. Something like these kinds of personal knowledge might also be attributed to other intelligent animals. But the human mind has a capability that is evidently unique. It is the ability to create artifacts—objects of deliberate design—which then become part of the world to which personal knowledge becomes attuned. Some of those artifacts—some of the most important in the modern world—are immaterial. They are conceptual artifacts. People can develop intuitive understanding of an idea or theory, which is not the same as intuitive understanding of the things the idea or theory is about. They develop feelings about an idea, which can develop into impressionistic knowledge. They develop skills in use of the idea; they recall episodes involving the idea; they develop norms of conduct related to the idea. And they acquire ability to state some of this knowledge, which therefore enables them to teach, criticize, and argue about the idea. The result is a dynamic process that, viewed from the outside, we call by terms such as "scientific progress" and "the advancement of knowledge." As for what goes on inside, we lack suitable terms. "Intellectual growth," "education," "self-actualization"—these are terms that do not quite make it. In chapter 7, I discuss further what is supposed to happen to the individual in the process of interacting with conceptual artifacts, because it is central to defining the purpose of formal education. As a placeholder, we might call what happens "becoming a fully functioning member of a knowledge society."

6

Learning to Think Differently About Knowledge and Mind

Folk psychology has already been pushed way past its limit.
—E. O. Wilson (1998, p. 202)

The purpose of this chapter is to pull together ideas from the preceding five chapters, in preparation for shifting the focus of discussion in the remainder of the book to education. What I have set out so far is a way of thinking about the mind that is different from the folk way and that I have argued has important advantages for dealing with knowledge. It is not what I would call a theory. Possibly it constitutes some elements of a theory, but that depends on what we intend a theory of mind to be. In any event, the point of my argument has not been to establish matters of truth but rather to argue pragmatically.

To get you to adopt a new way of thinking about knowledge and mind (assuming you are not already there ahead of me), I do not have to convince you of theoretical propositions. In fact, I must try to get you off the theoretical track, because it is a track that can lead to endless quibbling about definitions, demands of "how do you explain such and such," and counter arguments of greater or lesser theoretical weight. Instead, I have to convince you that there is a payoff in making the conceptual shift—that it will help you in your work, for instance—and then I have to help you make the shift. For the shift is not simply a matter of understanding and agreeing with an argument, it is a matter of learning a new way of interpreting and ultimately of perceiving events. In this chapter I take a stab at both, first trying to convince and then doing a walk-through of several cases that show how the alternative way of thinking can work.

HOW FAR CAN FOLK THEORY TAKE US?

Besides providing the commonsense psychology and epistemology to get us through our daily rounds, folk theory also forms the basis of more advanced theories. Until the rise of connectionism, most of cognitive psychology and AI was based on it. And as E. O. Wilson (1998) noted, the social sciences, including economics, generally assume it without question. These more advanced disciplines share the same basic limitations as the naive psychology and epistemology we picked up as children, but this is not always obvious, because of the overlay of sophisticated concepts. Yet the underlying folk theory hampers the social sciences, both in their scientific progress—which was Wilson's concern but not the concern I am pressing here—and in their practical value.

To illustrate the latter point, I examine Nonaka and Takeuchi's (1995) model of knowledge creation. Why pick out this theory among the many epistemological, cognitive, and sociocultural theories that have a more established scholarly reputation? First, because unlike almost all the others its approach is pragmatic. It is intended to help businesses become more successful at making use of the knowledge resources they have and at generating new products and strategies. And unlike most of the business literature, which consists of aphorisms larded with examples, it tries to explain and not merely to instruct. There is another strain of pragmatic theorizing about knowledge that is gaining attention both in the business world and in education. This is a strain that runs from John Dewey on in to contemporary work on situated cognition (Brown, Collins, & Duguid, 1989). However, as we saw in chapter 3, situated cognition represents a rejection of folk epistemology and folk psychology; Nonaka and Takeuchi's model, in contrast, remains solidly rooted in it.[1] Accordingly, their model provides a highly relevant test case for seeing how far folk theory can go in dealing with knowledge creation. It goes pretty far. Among other things, it incorporates ideas of situated cognition to the extent that this is possible within a folk theoretic framework. Finally, it merits critical scrutiny because it has received wide acceptance within one substantial community concerned with knowledge practices; in the field of knowledge management it is practically the only theory going.

Nonaka and Takeuchi's (1995)model of knowledge creation recognizes two kinds of knowledge: tacit and explicit. Although its components are not spelled out, tacit knowledge appears to include five of the six kinds of personal knowledge discussed in chapter 5, the exception being statable knowledge. Explicit knowledge comprises statable knowledge and conceptual artifacts, as is characteristic of folk theory of mind, making no distinction between them. The process of knowledge creation consists of three subprocesses that transform knowledge. These are summarized in the Table 6.1:

TABLE 6.1
Knowledge Creation Processes in Nonaka and Takeuchi's Model

Input	Process	Result
Tacit knowledge	Socialization	Shared tacit knowledge
Tacit knowledge	Externalization	Explicit knowledge
Explicit knowledge	Combination	Synthesized explicit knowledge

Nonaka and Takeuchi were clearly trying to coordinate the two folk conceptions of knowledge—knowledge as things in the mind and knowledge as something out in the world. In keeping with the traditional individualistic view, however, they treated knowledge in the individual mind as primary. Public knowledge is private knowledge brought out into the open—rather like what happens on talk shows. However, Nonaka and Takeuchi recognized that this externalized knowledge can take on properties of its own, much as Popper asserted. So what is missing? We have World 2, represented by tacit knowledge, and World 3, represented by public knowledge. Presumably there is also World 1, the physical world.

[1]This is curious, inasmuch as Nonaka and Takeuchi (1995) maintained that the Japanese have profoundly different conceptions of knowledge and mind from those that characterize the West—more organic, free of the Cartesian dualism, and in fact free of epistemology in the classical sense. But when it comes to theorizing, Nonaka and Takeuchi are right in there with their Western counterparts, positing individual minds that are full of unformulated knowledge and an external world that they must somehow project that knowledge into.

Inasmuch as Nonaka and Takeuchi's is a pragmatic theory, the way to identify what is missing is to see what their theory cannot do or cannot do well. Nonaka and Takeuchi's model falls short on four counts:

1. *Creativity*. Although it holds that new knowledge is always created in individual minds, it does not explain how minds produce original ideas and novel solutions. The book is full of examples of people doing that and suggestions for stimulating mental activity (further developed in von Krogh, Ichijo, & Nonaka, 2000), but the model does not suggest what could be done about a group that is highly productive of unoriginal ideas and ineffective solutions. This is a common failing of the knowledge management genre, but it is worth noting here because of the authors' claim to be uncovering the secrets of knowledge *creation*.

2. *Understanding*. Although the model deals with ways that knowledge gets from person to person, it offers nothing about understanding and depth of understanding.[2] That immediately disqualifies it as a model for education, but it is a serious weakness in a model for knowledge management in business as well. Depth of understanding is a distinguishing characteristic of expertise in knowledge-based fields, and productive creativity presupposes expertise (Bereiter & Scardamalia, 1993). Accordingly, a model that offers nothing about deepening of understanding is severely limited in what it can offer about the creation of knowledge.[3]

3. *Knowledge work*. Although Nonaka and Takeuchi appreciate the importance of knowledge abstracted from practice, their model has little to say about the production, management, improvement, or application of such knowledge—in short, about

---

[2]In a more recent work, von Krogh et al. (2000) adopted a subjectivist view of understanding. Understanding of a concept is achieved when "all the participants in a group truly feel that the expression or concept corresponds with what they know tacitly" (p. 136). Although this corresponds to what I discussed in chapter 5 as "implicit understanding," it does not offer a basis for distinguishing understanding from misunderstanding, much less deep understanding from shallow understanding.

[3]One of the most interesting stories in Nonaka and Takeuchi (1995) would seem to argue against the importance of understanding. It is about the design of a bread-making machine. An engineer apprenticed herself to an expert baker, observed that he twisted the dough in kneading it, and designed this twisting action into the machine with profitable results. Presumably neither she nor the baker *understood* why twisting produced better bread. She simply observed the practice and translated it into another medium. I am inclined to call this an example of dumb luck. In the absence of understanding, there was no reason to believe that twisting the dough was an important part of baking. It just happened that it was. Furthermore, if one understood how twisting made a difference, it might be possible to achieve the effect in ways much more efficient than building a machine to mimic the baker's motion. Centuries of observing birds and trying to mimic them did not produce a flying machine. Success came with growth in understanding of lift.

knowledge work. As interpreted by their model, what all those scholars and scientists who populate the great research universities are busy doing is "combining" pieces of each other's knowledge. Yes, you can interpret it this way, but is it useful to do so? You can also interpret making a shirt as combining pieces of cloth, and although this might provide an interesting slant it does not seem like an interpretation that will carry you very far in trying to improve manufacture. Don't we need a model that treats the production of cognitive artifacts in at least as sophisticated a way as we treat the production of garments?

4. *Collaborative knowledge building.* Although cooperation and teamwork are praised, the idea of cooperating in the creation of knowledge never comes to life in Nonaka and Takeuchi's theorizing. There is a lot about knowledge moving from one mind to another, but the rather straightforward business of a group of people working together to produce a design or plan or to solve a problem seems to become mysterious in their conceptual framework. Because public knowledge in their model is merely an outward extension of personal knowledge, it is hard to deal with the everyday fact of people jointly producing a piece of knowledge that is neither the product of one individual's knowledge nor a combination of several individuals' knowledge. Such knowledge is typically an emergent of discourse and cannot be understood at the level of individual interacting minds. To promote it, you have to know how to promote progressive discourse.

The problem in Nonaka and Takeuchi's model is not so much missing concepts as missing perspectives on those concepts. This comes from flattening everything into the two-dimensional space of folk theory. In this two-dimensional space, where public knowledge is externalized personal knowledge, several very important relational properties are lost. One is the relation of persons to conceptual artifacts: the person's familiarity with, understanding of, and attitude toward a particular theory, technology, problem formulation, or interpretation. Another is the relations of conceptual artifacts to one another and to the tasks or problems to which they may be applied. One theory or design may be destined to win out over others regardless of the vagaries of personal opinion, because it can do things that the others cannot do (Dennett, 1995; Thagard, 1989). Together, these represent the major distinction that both folk and sociocognitive theories have difficulty making: the distinction between the knowledge involved in productive work and knowledge that is the product of that work. Without this distinction, you cannot formulate the essential *educational* challenge that a knowledge-creating organization needs to face: promoting learning that will increase the organization's ability to create knowledge.

AN ALTERNATIVE APPROACH

The failings of folk theory, I have argued, can be traced to its way of treating knowledge. Under the influence of the mind-as-container metaphor, knowledge is treated as consisting of objects contained in individual minds, something like the contents of mental filing cabinets. Although that way of treating knowledge is convenient for many purposes, it severely limits and distorts our dealing with issues of understanding, mastery, and knowledge advancement. To overcome its weaknesses, I have proposed that folk theory of mind needs to undergo two radical changes:

1. The idea of mental content should be reduced to the status of a metaphor, useful for some purposes and not for others, but not to be taken literally. Connectionism provides an alternative metaphor, which enables us to conceive of a mind that can act knowledgeably without containing propositions or other knowledge objects. To gain benefit from the connectionist metaphor, we must find ways to construct mentalistic accounts that do not refer to things residing, being searched for, or undergoing changes in the mind.
2. Abstract knowledge objects, such as theories, numbers, and designs, should be accepted as real things outside the mind—as conceptual artifacts—with which people may develop relationships, much as they do with animate and inanimate material things. Understanding and mastery may then be treated as characteristics of such relationships, and the advancement of knowledge as the creating and improvement of conceptual artifacts.

Let us see how such an altered approach to knowledge and mind can deal with the four points on which I criticized Nonaka and Takeuchi:

1. *An alternative view of creativity.* Folk theory mystifies creativity. This is because ordinary rational thought is believed to proceed in a step-by-step manner, with each step following in some logical (or illogical) way from its predecessor. Creative thinking obviously doesn't work that way. But, according to the connectionist view, ordinary thought doesn't work that way either. Ordinary thought is, in fact, relentlessly creative. Ordinary speech is not anything like an orderly logical process. It is full of invention. Logic comes in after the fact as a way of *justifying* what

we have done or said. Ordinary acts of thought can be justified by logic that is simple enough that we can easily imagine it having been run off in the mind; creative acts cannot. But we can also logically justify the actions of fish and insects, without having to suppose that a reasoning process is actually carried out by the creatures in question. What is remarkable about human cognition, from the connectionist point of view, is not creativity but the ability—achieved with considerable effort and practice and quite fallible for all that—to sometimes control our thinking in such a way that it does proceed in a step-by-step logical manner.

It is not creativity per se that needs explaining and promoting, then; creativity may be taken as a given. It is big-bang type creativity that produces major leaps ahead and sustained creativity, which can be relied on to produce advances year after year and to carry them through until they amount to something. Folk psychology directs all our attention to the first and ignores the second, which in most walks of life is more important. Present a problem to any group of children or to a group of mentally active adults and you will get plenty of ideas. Ideas are a dime a dozen. The children's ideas will mostly be useless because they fail to meet the constraints of the problem. The adults' ideas will mostly be useless because they honor the wrong constraints—constraints arising from convention, habit, and surface appearance rather than constraints of a deeper kind. Useful creativity depends on a deep understanding of the constraints and a fund of relevant impressionistic knowledge (what folk psychology mystifies with the word "intuition") that serves as a basis for recognizing promising ideas. Carrying a promising idea to fruition depends even more on knowledge of many kinds. Accordingly, if an organization wants to increase the creative output of its employees, the starting point ought to be enriching and deepening their knowledge. But this is not a simple matter. The knowledge that makes creative advances possible is knowledge that arises from trying to make such advances.

Thinking of creativity in this way does not lead forthwith to a recipe for promoting it. What it does is naturalize the concept so that it takes its place among other concepts relevant to boosting an individual's or an organization's intellectual capital. In particular, it ties creative capacity to the growth of understanding.

2. *A relational conception of understanding.* Everyone is in favor of understanding, but folk theory diminishes and isolates it, so that in discussions of innovation and intellectual capital (e.g., Nonaka & Takeuchi, 1995; Stewart, 1997) it is barely mentioned. Understanding is reduced to holding true beliefs and being able to ex-

plain, which are anemic virtues compared with having the red-blooded know-how that gets things done and produces innovations. There is a kind of understanding that is more fully appreciated, however. It is the understanding salespeople have of their clients, the understanding craftspeople have of their tools and the materials they work with (cf. Harper, 1987), and the understanding athletes have of their own bodies and what they can do. Understanding of these kinds is not usefully thought of as consisting of things in the mind. It is a sort of intimate familiarity arising from and closely tied to intelligent action. In chapter 4, I tried to show that theoretical understanding is best thought of in the same way. Understanding is the totality of one's knowledge of an object (material or abstract), considered from the standpoint of the ability of that knowledge to support intelligent action. Thus the development of understanding has to be at the heart of any educational effort or effort to enhance the innovative capacity of a person or organization.

3. *Knowledge work as work that creates or adds value to conceptual artifacts.* As I noted in chapter 3, the term "knowledge work" as it is currently used is little more than an honorific. Knowledge work is simply white-collar work that for whatever reason commands a relatively high salary. Until you can conceive of knowledge as real stuff that it is possible to do work on, you cannot pin down what distinguishes knowledge work from lowly paper pushing on one hand and from knowledge-demanding manual occupations like brain surgery and safe cracking on the other. Unless they start licensing knowledge workers, a precise definition is not likely to become a priority. However, if we want to consider educating people to become knowledge workers, or retraining manual workers as knowledge workers, or making the work environment more conducive to knowledge work, it would be helpful to have a clearer idea of what we are talking about. The second of the radical conceptual changes indicated at the beginning of this section leads to a very natural definition of knowledge work. It belongs to the same class as metal work, woodworking, leather work, and personnel work except that the objects worked with are abstract: They are conceptual artifacts. Knowledge workers create, improve, find new uses for, or otherwise add value to conceptual artifacts.

We may now ask what skills and other kinds of knowledge are needed for knowledge work and what kinds of conditions facilitate it. Our very abstract definition of knowledge work ought to suggest that the answers to these questions will depend a great deal on what particular kinds of conceptual artifacts we are talking about. If your job is calculating the heating and air conditioning needs of office towers and mine is allocating the resources of a large social service charity, it is not immediately evident that our skills have anything in common worth mentioning. Or, to put it differently, our knowledge would overlap more with that of *non*knowledge workers in our respective fields—yours with the knowledge of the people who install air ducts, mine with that of the social workers, health care providers, and others who deliver the services I allocate funds for—than it does with each other's.

Are there any special competencies that distinguish knowledge work of all kinds? What about thinking skills and skills in locating and organizing information? To anticipate the conclusions of chapter 10, there is much less to general cognitive skills than folk theory leads one to suppose. Furthermore, although you and I might have certain planning and information-handling skills that go by the same name, we developed those skills through work that got us deeply into the problems, constraints, and know-how of our respective fields. If we exchanged jobs, the amount of intellectual competence that would transfer from one job to the other would be quite limited and would owe more to our genes and to how we have lived our lives than to any identifiable learning experiences. This does not mean that nothing can be done to prepare people for knowledge work, but it means that we must be wary of facile prescriptions. Like any kind of job competence it is mostly acquired on the job; what is done in advance—through schooling and other measures—must be aimed at increasing the likelihood that that learning, which is mostly acquiring job-specific understandings, will actually take place.

4. *Knowledge as a social product* . "In a strict sense," Nonaka and Takeuchi said (1995, p. 59), "knowledge is created only by individuals. An organization cannot create knowledge without individuals." The second statement, which is obviously true, is presented as if it constituted warrant for the first statement, which is a questionable one. The argument does not hold together. If a group of people work together and the product of their collective effort is a dinner or a stone fence, no one would be moved to declare that dinners or stone fences can only be created by individuals. The tacit knowledge and skills of the individuals of course play a vital role in the undertaking, and it is certainly true that neither a dinner nor a stone fence can be created without individuals; but it would be very strange and not very helpful to represent the dinner or the fence as an externalization of things in the individuals' minds. The dinner or the fence is something in its own right, and to explain how it came to be the way it is you would want to con-

sider both individual contributions and the group process. Did too many cooks spoil the soup? Did the fence turn out to be a work of art exceeding the talents and expectations of the workers? Why did Nonaka and Takeuchi treat the matter as so different when the product of the collaborative effort is a piece of knowledge? Why did they treat knowledge as a product of individual minds? Well, because that is where folk theory locates knowledge.

Until there is a way for your coworkers to get inside your brain and fiddle with the synapses, there is never going to be such a thing as the collaborative creation of knowledge, according to folk understanding. But if you can conceive of knowledge as consisting of conceptual artifacts, then you can readily imagine what is in fact an everyday occurrence—a group of people getting together and producing a plan, a theory, a problem formulation, a vision statement, or some other kind of conceptual object. Having established that knowledge can be produced as a social product and that many complex cognitive artifacts can only be produced through collaborative effort, we can then turn our attention to problems of quality. That is what Nonaka and Takeuchi aimed to do, but they were hobbled from the beginning by their belief that everything originates in the individual mind. The mark of a really successful design or problem-solving meeting is that something brilliant comes out of it that cannot be attributed to an individual or to a combination of individual contributions. It is an emergent, which means that if you look at a transcript of the meeting you can see the conceptual object taking shape but you cannot find it in the bits and pieces making up the discourse. There are, of course, instances where the design or solution does come from one person, but then you have a different kind of meeting, one that is devoted to grasping, accepting, and elaborating an idea. The result is still a social product, no matter how much it may bear the stamp of an individual. A "knowing organization" (Choo, 1998)—whether it is a business or a school—needs to find ways to foster individual knowledge creation (I say more about this in chap. 10), but it also needs to find ways to foster the kind of knowledge that emerges from discourse, broadly conceived. Nonaka and Takeuchi, and even more von Krogh et al. (2000), were strong on the importance of discourse and they suggested promising ways of fostering it, but their theory of knowledge continually interfered with their getting at the core issue: How do you foster conversation that creates knowledge rather than conversation that merely shares knowledge?

Nonaka and Takeuchi (1995, p. 61) offer their model as an attempt to convey to Westerners a Japanese view of knowledge. According to them, Westerners put all the emphasis on explicit knowledge and place it in competition with fuzzy tacit knowledge, whereas the Japanese see tacit knowledge as primary and complementary to explicit knowledge. If there ever was validity to that comparison, it is fast vanishing. In *Intellectual Capital*, Stewart (1997) placed enormous emphasis on the tacit knowledge of individuals and groups and cited scores of supportive examples and testimonials, mostly drawn from American business.[4] Nonaka and Takeuchi, I suspect, have been overly influenced by Western philosophers and their concern with the validity of explicit propositions, and have failed to appreciate the extent to which folk epistemology recognizes the virtues of intuition, faith, gut feelings, and knacks. The problem is how to do anything about these—how to promote, guide, and use them effectively. Educators probably recognize them more fully than most people, because of their close engagement with students' thinking and learning, yet they count for next to nothing in educational policy and curriculum planning.

Folk epistemology, I have said, makes tacit knowledge mysterious. Nonaka and his colleagues did not make it any less mysterious; in fact, the subtitle of von Krogh et al. (2000) is "How to Unlock the Mystery of Tacit Knowledge and Release the Power of Innovation." They offered practical advice about how to disseminate tacit knowledge and how to convert between tacit and explicit knowledge, but they did not leave us any wiser about what tacit knowledge is or how to advance it to qualitatively higher levels. The gaping hole in their model is where we would look to find an answer to the main problem facing a knowledge-based organization: How do you develop the tacit knowledge that enables the creation of new explicit knowledge? This is not the same question as how you acquire the tacit knowledge that is converted into explicit knowledge, which is a question Nonaka and Takeuchi addressed. It is a question that only makes sense if you can conceive of conceptual artifacts as real things that people produce, drawing on varieties of tacit knowledge and using other conceptual artifacts in the process.

Of the two radical conceptual changes proposed at the beginning of this section, the shift to treating abstract knowledge objects as real things should not be difficult for people in knowledge-based businesses. They are familiar with the idea of intellectual property, and the idea of conceptual artifacts is only a somewhat broader version of that idea. That idea seems to be much harder for educators to hold onto. It keeps slipping over into learning, to changes taking place in individual minds, because that is what education is mainly about.

---

[4]By the way, Stewart (1977) never cited Nonaka.

The shift to a connectionist view of mind, however, is difficult for everyone. To make it comprehensible and functional takes considerable concentration and practice. In the next section I work through three examples that I hope will be helpful in making sense of the idea of knowledgeability without mental content.

MIND WITHOUT MENTAL CONTENT

Folk theory never tells us what the mind is. That seems to me a sensible evasion and one to be maintained. Mind is just what things come to when they are said to "come to mind." Mental content becomes a mischievous idea when it refers to things that we do not have "in mind" but that are nevertheless assumed to be back in the mind somewhere, ready to be put to use or already covertly at work. Folk theory of mind assumes an infinitude of unattended beliefs that guide action. You are said to believe your coat is on the hook in the closet, through all the hours in which you do not think about your coat at all. The evidence for this is that when you want it that is where you look, and if it should not be there you will say something like, "I was sure this is where I left it." The reason you look for the coat is that you believe it is cold out and that the coat will keep you warm, even though neither of these beliefs actually comes to mind. Behind these are unattended beliefs in object permanence, gravitation, heat transfer (or, erroneously, cold transfer), and everything that one would have to explain to an intelligent being that had no knowledge of this world. Although having a virtually infinite number of beliefs is implausible, it provides the premise for plausible and nontrivial explanations of behavior. Why, when your coat is not on the expected hook, do you look on other hooks and also on the floor but not on the ceiling? Folk theory of mind can not only explain this but can predict it, based on beliefs that are reasonable to attribute to you.

Folk theory undoubtedly took shape to deal with just such mundane and commonsensical behaviors as those described. The same model has then been carried over into education and into the more studied and creative uses of knowledge. Education, in this model, is concerned with adding to and amending the contents of the storehouse of beliefs. Although this suggests a crude, "stuffing the head" conception of education, the model underlies more refined conceptions as well, such as those of constructivism, values education, conceptual change, central conceptual structures, and whole language. Indeed, it is only the most harebrained conceptions of education that disavow an interest in content. Therefore, if mental content is to be eliminated from mentalistic descriptions, or if it is to be reduced to the status of an ungrounded metaphor, there is a serious question as to how education's unavoidable concern with individual knowledge acquisition is to be honored. The rest of this book addresses the challenge implied by that question, the challenge being to improve on, to go beyond what folk theory has to offer education in its concerns with knowledge.

For the present, however, I avoid education and other weighty areas of application and instead deal with cases chosen for their illustrative value. The first case comes from well outside most people's serious concerns. It is dreaming. Dreaming is an unquestionably mental phenomenon, traditionally but, as it appears, wrongly thought of in terms of stored mental content. A contentless approach provides an account of dreaming more closely in accord with current scientific understanding of dreaming. The second case is a trivial example of misperception, which I analyze largely through introspection to show how an adequate account can be developed that restricts the mentalistic part of the account to what is actually experienced. The third case illustrates what is meant by having a relationship to an abstract knowledge object. Again, to avoid weighty issues I have chosen a minor kind of object, the joke, which nevertheless captures the essentials of cognition in relation to conceptual artifacts.

Making Sense of Dreams

Dreams are clearly a part of mental life, and dreams have content. But, with occasional exceptions, the content does not come from outside, via our senses; it comes from within. Dreaming therefore makes a nice first case for trying out the notion that we can account for mental phenomena without positing a storehouse of mental content. Aristotle (in Ackrill, 1987, pp. 214–217) speculated that dreams are a kind of aftereffect of waking experience, much like the visual aftereffects of staring at a bright object. That is an interesting conjecture, for it steers clear of implying the mind is a container of past experiences. But it falls far short of accounting for the rich and novel content of dreams. The mental filing cabinet model does not do much better, however. Dreams are vividly visual, but even if one allows for some powerful mental morphing, it is implausible to imagine them as composites of old film clips.

Modern explanations of dreaming start from electroencephalographic data, which reveal that, during REM (rapid eye movement) sleep, sensory areas of the brain are more active than in the waking state. Evidently there are inhibitory centers in the brain that discourage sensory neurons from firing except in response to incoming stimuli, but during sleep the inhibitory centers shut down and allow the sensory areas—especially the visual—to act at random (Hobson, 1988). What about the meaningful, narrative quality of dreams, then? Why aren't dreams disconnected bits of visualization? The coherence of dreams, according to Hobson, arises from the thinking brain's efforts to make sense of perceptions. The brain, in effect, is making sense out of nonsense. It can't entirely succeed; hence, the occasional bizarre jumps and transformations. But it does remarkably well, considering what it has to work with. Although this may seem a far-fetched theory, there are other evidences of the brain's relentless sense-making. In split-brain patients (people whose right and left cerebral hemispheres have been surgically disconnected) stimuli to the right hemisphere cause the person to act for reasons that the left hemisphere has no knowledge of. Yet when questioned, such people will give confident although wholly fabricated explanations of their behavior (Gazzaniga, 1995; Gazzaniga & LeDoux, 1978). The kind of sense the brain makes of dream sensations will, of course, be influenced by past experiences, by fears and desires—by the same internal conditions that affect waking perception—hence, the relevance of dream experience to our waking preoccupations and recent experiences.

Although this account of dreaming greatly simplifies what recent research is showing to be a very complex and highly variable phenomenon, the main point I want to make from it is not called into question by any findings I am aware of. The idea dream research drives home so dramatically is the human mind's relentless and largely automatic effort to make sense of things—an effort that commonly takes the form of weaving things together into a coherent narrative.

In folk theory, the meaning of events is either obvious (that is, conforming to expectations) or it is problematic, to be worked out through deliberate efforts to explain. Essentially the same view is embodied in information-processing models, such as that of Schank and Abelson (1977), in which normal events are understood in terms of their conformity to stored scripts and explaining is driven by failed expectations. This seems quite valid as far as it goes, and it seems to accord well with the part of sense-making that we are conscious of. Dreaming, however, does not fit these categories. To the extent that the sensory events that occur during REM sleep are random, their meaning cannot be said to be obvious, yet the sense-making that occurs in dreaming is spontaneous, not a matter of effortful seeking of explanations. Just such automatic sense-making goes on throughout our waking hours. The conspicuous difference is that when we are awake sensory events having origins outside the brain predominate, but it is surely not a complete switch-over.

Reading provides the most striking evidence that automatic sense-making during the waking state is not altogether different from what goes on in dreaming. There is abundant evidence that our interpretations of what we read are driven by expectations (Anderson & Pearson, 1984; Rumelhart, 1980). A classic experiment used the following text:

> Rocky slowly got up from the mat, planning his escape. He hesitated a moment and thought. Things were not going well. What bothered him most was being held, especially since the charge against him had been weak. He considered his present situation. The lock that held him was strong but he thought he could break it. He knew, however, that his timing would have to be perfect. Rocky was aware that it was because of his early roughness that he had been penalized so severely—much too severely from his point of view. The situation was becoming frustrating; the pressure had been grinding on him for too long. He was being ridden unmercifully. Rocky was getting angry now. He felt he was ready to make his move. He knew that his success or failure would depend on what he did in the next few seconds. (Anderson, Reynolds, Schallert, & Goetz, 1977, p. 372)

Most people read this as being about a contemplated jailbreak. But when it was presented to members of a wrestling team, most of them read it as being about a wrestler thinking about how to break a hold. Of equal interest, however, is the fact that, whichever interpretation people gave to it, the interpretation seemed obvious. It was not arrived at through a consideration of alternatives or a deliberate effort to resolve ambiguities.

When expectations drive reading beyond a certain point, we get demonstrable misreadings; beyond that, something verging on hallucination. Among students, misreading is so common that teachers at all levels regard it as a significant part of what they must deal with. The misreadings may readily be explained by what the students do not know or by the interpretive frameworks they bring to texts. What is most relevant to the present discussion, however, is the absence of feelings of confusion or incomprehension. Asking students to raise questions about parts of a text that were unclear to them usually produces an uneasy silence. The teacher who fancies a Socratic method must go to considerable lengths to get students to recognize that they have not, in fact, made good sense of what appears on the page.

The more hallucinatory misreadings become evident only when readers can be presumed to have ample background knowledge and skills. My experience in submitting scholarly articles to peer-reviewed journals is that the incidence of glaring misreadings among qualified and supposedly careful peer reviewers is not much different from that to be expected of students in an introductory course. It could be, of course, that the fault is in the manuscript, and that it is my sense-making that is hallucinatory. Evidence that what I describe is not an isolated phenomenon can be found, however, in journals that publish peer commentary along with the "target" article, usually followed by a response from the original author. I have been struck by the extent to which such responses consist of allegations of misreading—particularly complaints that the commentators criticized the article for things that were never said or that were at times the opposite of what was said.

Where reading most closely resembles dreaming, however, is in cases where readers' anxieties are aroused. In recent years I have been involved in several different drawn-out exchanges of correspondence with people who were in high states of anxiety on matters of money, occupational security, or status. These people would respond with alarm or outrage to proposals that were nowhere to be found in what was actually written. All that kept these responses from being utterly fantastic was that they centered on certain keywords that did appear in the texts.

It is not stretching a point terribly far to say that mental life consists of controlled hallucination. Our hard-wired perceptual systems provide the strongest sorts of controls, ensuring that we seldom see things that are not there or grossly distort or misrecognize things that are there. Reflective analysis provides another sort of control. If you ever find yourself uncertain as to whether something really happened or you only dreamed it, you are likely to resort to a consistency check to see whether it fits with other data in which you have more confidence. Finally, social intercourse provides strong and pervasive controls. The surest way to determine whether something really happened or was a dream is to check it with someone else who would know about it if it really happened. The need to coordinate our actions with those of others and to establish shared topics and common ground in conversation means that a great deal (sometimes too much) of what our minds have to make sense of is already highly processed material. But there is still a wild, internally generated flow of data that mixes indiscriminately with sensory inputs, leading at times to imaginative leaps, at other times to craziness, and probably most of the time to mere noise that gets factored out as we make sense of the more interpretable data coming from other sources.

I think I am in accord with a number of recent philosophers of mind when I say that this unremitting sense-making, carried on during our sleeping as well as our waking hours, is really what mind amounts to (Dennett & Kinsbourne, 1992). The mind is not some organ that does the sense-making. That role belongs to the brain. The mind is a product of our sense-making activity. It is what our sense-making postulates when it tries to make sense of itself.

Sense-making, in the view of most people who use that term, is largely a matter of making up stories (Bruner, 1986; Dennett, 1991; Egan, 1986). To say that sense-making is automatic is to say that our making up of stories is, most of the time, involuntary and effortless. (This obviously applies to dreaming, for dreams are almost always stories, however bizarre, and when they are not—when the fevered brain fires away with results that cannot be fitted together into any kind of narrative—we awake tired and vaguely distraught.) A story requires actors and goals and usually a setting of some kind. In our waking as well as our dreaming states, we are usually central figures in our stories. So what kind of story do we create when the story is required to make sense of our sense-making itself? The central figure in the story is, of course, ourself, but it has to be a self that can stand aside from the corporeal body and its sensations and rememberings so as to make sense of them. Hence the mind is this peculiar character that is at once indissociable from the physical being and yet able to view and speculate about it. What about a setting? Descartes posited an internal theater in which percepts and ideas do their turns while the mind observes and makes sense of them. In common usage, the mind is both the theatre and the observer. Cognitive events occur *in* the mind and are at the same time interpreted *by* the mind—a confusing notion that common sense tends simply to gloss over. Philosophers have puzzled over all this at great length. What I am suggesting (and I take this to be in accord with Dennett's 1991 more strongly reasoned proposal) is that we not press too hard for coherence in the consciousness story. The endless story that we construct to make sense of our lives must inevitably include the author as actor, object, observer, and setting, and there is only so much coherence you can expect in a story like that. The important thing, from an educational standpoint, is just to recognize that sense-making happens regardless. It is the starting point of educational processes, not the ending point.

Knowledgeability Without a Mental Filing Cabinet

The following example illustrates automatic sense-making and the role of knowledge in it. I have chosen a mundane example and will interpret it first in the conventional way, in terms of knowledge items in a mental storehouse. Then I show how it can be interpreted without assuming stored mental content. My purpose at this point is not to show that the latter approach works better. For ordinary purposes the conventional approach works fine. My purpose is just to show the difference and to show that the second approach is at least convincing and not so outlandish as might be supposed.

> Looking out the window one wintery day, I saw in a nearby tree a small bird of a peculiar reddish brown color. So unusual was its coloring that I went immediately to an illustrated bird guide to see if I could identify it. Finding no immediate match, I went to an upstairs window from which I could get a better look. From this new vantage point it became immediately obvious that it was not a bird at all but an apple, which had lodged in a branch instead of falling to the ground and had rotted to this reddish brown color.

How could I have been so certain initially that it was a bird, and what made it so immediately obvious, viewing from a different angle, that it was not? After the fact, I can adduce reasons that make my cognitive behavior appear quite rational:

Small solitary colorful objects in the branches of trees are usually birds.

To protect themselves from the cold, small birds will fluff up their feathers and draw in their heads so that they are approximately spherical in shape.

One does not expect to see an apple in a barren tree in the middle of winter.

Viewed from above, a head should have been visible if it were a bird; there being no head, it could be inferred that it was not a bird.

Two quite different psychological accounts can be given of my mistaken recognition of a bird, one supporting the old and one supporting the newer conception of mind. (To simplify, I am leaving out some intermediate kinds of accounts, such as one based on a bird schema). According to the older conception, items of knowledge such as the preceding were actually stored as content in my mind. What I experienced as the direct perception of a bird in a tree was actually the result of a lightning-fast and unconscious reasoning process, more or less similar to my after-the-fact justification.

The other kind of account starts with the premise that our brains are built in such a way that visual stimulation having certain properties of contrast and contour will result in perceiving an object. *Not* to have perceived an object in the tree, to have seen only patterns of light and color, would have required special training of a kind that artists sometimes undergo. There is nothing mental about seeing the patch of reddish brown color as an object. It is not the result of a cognitive process, anymore than it is the result of a cognitive process when my brain sends signals to my heart to beat faster when I am climbing a flight of stairs. It is just how the brain works.

Now, what about seeing the object as a bird? Why not see it as a Christmas tree ornament or a wad of paper or simply as an unidentified reddish brown thing? Here, obviously, effects of past experience are operative and those effects *could* be described in the form of propositions like those listed. But that would lead us back to the first kind of psychological account. Instead, let us suppose that these effects take a form analogous to that of the weights in a connectionist network. That is, they take the form of a large system of relationships among neurons such that perception of the reddish brown object will be, as it were, attuned to the time of year, the features and habits of small birds, and so on. As a result, I do not first perceive an object and then figure out that it must be a bird; I do in fact directly see a bird. Much more than that, actually: I see a bird huddling from the cold on a barren branch. My sympathies are aroused. Also, I am struck by the bird's beauty. And my curiosity is aroused because I do not just see a bird, I see an unknown kind of bird. Mental activity *starts* with this affect-laden awareness of a strange, beautiful bird alone in a bleak northern winter. That is the first mental content to enter the picture. It does not start with a set of rules in the mind that fire off in rapid order to produce this mental state. Discovering my error does not involve undoing a chain of inference that led to a wrong conclusion. Instead, looking at the object from a different direction, I directly see an apple instead of directly seeing a bird. Different visible features cause my neural network to settle on a different perception. When I return to look out the original window, I no longer see a bird, I see an apple that looks somewhat like a bird. None of this is mental either. What is mental is my realization of having made a mistake and being amused by it and starting to think out how I could have made such a mistake.

Regardless of which way it is interpreted, a considerable amount of knowledge would seem to have been involved in the bird–apple episode, albeit knowledge of a commonplace sort: knowledge of what birds are and something about them, that a bird cannot turn into an apple, that apples may be found in trees, that apples turn brown when they rot, and so on. But none of this knowledge was consciously recalled and employed in reasoning. What is this knowledge—and *where* is it—if it is not mental content? The challenge for a new theory of mind is not to answer this question but to find a graceful way of avoiding it. Unfortunately, the available ways are not very graceful, and so to carry on a fluent discussion we are driven to treating knowledge as stuff people have, which suggests it must exist in some form and be somewhere. That is what we did in the preceding chapter. But when we are trying to achieve conceptual clarity, we are better off not talking about knowledge in that way at all and trying to speak instead of *knowledgeability*.

The bird–apple episode, to put it in this other way, reveals some knowledgeability on my part concerning birds and apples. Although propositions such as "Small solitary colorful objects in the branches of trees are usually birds" and "To protect themselves from the cold, small birds will fluff up their feathers and draw in their heads so that they are approximately spherical in shape" never actually entered my mind. I responded and behaved in ways that were consistent with them. Accordingly, a characterization (whether delivered by myself or an observer) of my knowledgeability with respect to birds might well include those two facts. Further justification for doing so might come from my exhibiting other behavior consistent with them and from my answers to questions such as "How could you recognize a bird in a tree?" and "What do small birds do to protect themselves from the cold?" Yet I may never have thought of those facts until asked questions that called for articulating them.

Of course, those facts are just a sample of the bird-related facts with which my behavior is consistent. My behavior is consistent with an infinitude of such facts and principles, this despite my level of ornithological sophistication being, I suspect, below average. Ornithologists and experienced bird watchers will act in ways consistent with strata of facts and principles far beyond those pertinent to my behavior. They can not only identify many more birds, but can identify their nests and eggs. They will notice characteristics of birds and their behavior that I overlook and they will be able to offer explanations beyond anything I would think of.

The common way of wrapping up these contrasts is to say that ornithologists and bird watchers have much more bird knowledge in their heads than I do and that this knowledge enables them to do a variety of things I cannot. Thus, there are two elements in the account, knowledge and abilities, with the first being the cause of the second. If we eliminate the idea of mental content, however, these elements are reduced to one—knowledgeability. A person's knowledgeability can be described in various ways. One way is to describe it in terms of content, as if it were a book. Another way is to describe it in terms of abilities. But these are different descriptions of the same thing, and even in combination these descriptions do not exhaust what might be said in characterizing a person's knowledgeability. The itemization of content will capture the more textbook-like features of a person's knowledgeability but will trail off into metaphor and then inarticulateness just when it is starting to get interesting—that is, when it is starting to touch on the more profound aspects of a person's understanding. A description of abilities will suffer the same fate. There will be some obvious abilities, easy to describe, but when it comes to the subtleties that distinguish one expert from another, description will begin to fail. There is nothing occult about this. Similar difficulties would arise in trying to characterize a painter's or a poet's or a philosopher's *oeuvre* or to describe teaching as it is carried out by a masterful teacher. In all of these there is more than can be captured in a description or in several descriptions done from different vantage points. What we need to be clear about is that the boundaries of the mental include knowledgeability. Items of specific knowledge may enter into our descriptions of knowledgeability, but they are not components of it in anything like the way that pages are components of a book or premises are part of a syllogism. You can to a certain extent describe a pain, and there are situations (such as seeking medical assistance) in which it is desirable to do so, but the description is not a component of the pain. So it is with descriptions of knowledgeability.

Understanding a Joke

Jokes are among the clearest examples of abstract objects. We recognize the same joke even though it is told differently at various times by various people. Jokes have histories. A joke that may have first been recorded during the Crimean War will turn up with suitable updating in subsequent wars. An ethnic joke will be adapted so as to ridicule a different group. When no longer socially acceptable, it will be altered to remove ethnic allusions and dialect, but it will still be recognizable as the same joke. There are of course boundary problems: Are two examples variations on the same joke or different jokes? But these problems are not serious enough to discourage us from such worthy efforts as *telling the same joke that we found so hilarious at last night's party, but modifying it to make it suitable for children.*

Although jokes may be written down and preserved in books, the joke is not any particular literal version. It is the abstract thing that may be variously told, written, sometimes dramatized, sometimes merely referred to as "the one about ...." (Jokes, it should be noted, are not *conceptual artifacts* as we have been using the term. An explanation of a joke would be a conceptual artifact—it could be debated, applied, and so on but, as is well known, the explanation and the joke are two quite different animals.)

Without getting into the fascinating psychology and rhetoric of jokes, we can make do for present purposes with a few commonplace observations:

- To tell a joke well you must understand it.
- Understanding is not purely intellectual. If you do not "see the humor" in a joke you cannot be said to understand it.
- Although liking a joke without understanding it is improbable, you can dislike a joke somewhat independently of understanding it. Distaste for the joke's theme or content may override appreciation of its humor.
- "Seeing the humor" or "getting the point" of a joke is not necessarily accompanied by ability to explain it. People demonstrate their understanding of a joke by laughing in the right way at the right time.
- Explanation is seldom helpful in getting people to see the humor in a joke. Thus, understanding a joke is rather like perception. Either you see it or you don't.
- You can continue to appreciate the humor of a joke even though you have heard it enough times that it no longer makes you laugh; you can delight in telling it or in hearing it well told, and suffer in hearing it badly told.
- Sharing jokes is a common form of social bonding. "Inside" jokes serve to separate insiders from outsiders.

Notice that in all these commonsense observations, the joke is treated as something existing in its own right, to which people have various responses and attitudes. Nothing is implied about content in people's minds. Sharing a joke is like sharing a bottle of wine or enjoying a concert together. It does not depend on two minds having the same content. It depends on two minds (and bodies) being attuned to respond in concordant ways to something in the external world. And yet with jokes—as with wine and music—there is an important intellectual component. To respond in a concordant way, people have to have a fair bit of background knowledge in common. But we could not hope to pin down the essential elements of that knowledge. Let us say, rather, that the shared knowledge is *in* the attunement.

What I have been arguing for, especially in chapter 3, is treating conceptual artifacts of all sorts in the same way we treat jokes, legends, and other kinds of abstract cultural objects—as existing out there in the cultural environment. Our minds do not contain these objects. Our minds have various abilities, attitudes, dispositions, and habits in relation to these objects.

Memory is probably the hardest aspect of cognition to bring under this idea of the contentless mind. Jokes, again, provide a nice test case. Most people, it seems, have trouble remembering jokes, despite a desire to do so. You hear a good joke and try to remember it. You may even think of yourself deliberately putting it into a mental filing cabinet, perhaps even with notes attached as to where you might use the joke or whom you would like to tell it to. But when you go to retrieve it the joke is missing; in fact the whole joke drawer of your mental filing cabinet seems nearly empty. But there may be a few stray items in it, so that if required to tell a joke you can bring forth something, although it may be some childish joke of decades past and quite unsuitable to the occasion.

What does it mean to remember a joke? It does not mean remembering the exact words. But it does not mean just remembering the gist or the punch line, either. You may think you remember a joke and will start telling it, only to find that you have said something that spoils it. Remembering a joke heard only once is more like remembering a route that you have traveled only once before or remembering how to carry out some complicated procedure that you have practiced only once or twice. It is a task of reconstruction and of execution. At your leisure you may be able to mentally reconstruct the joke or the route, but when it comes to actually telling the joke or driving the route, you make mistakes. If you *really* remember a joke, which typically means that you have told it on a number of occasions, then, as with a familiar route or procedure, you can not only reconstruct it easily but you can vary and improvise without losing hold. The ability to reconstruct and execute, therefore, is what your mind has or what your knowledge consists of. This ability depends, of course, on alterations in your brain brought about by previous experience, but we are in no position to say precisely what those alterations are—nor, as educators, should we have to care. As long as the learner's brain is intact, we need hardly concern ourselves at all with what goes on in it. Instead, we can turn our attention to the outer world, to the material and immaterial objects it contains, and to the abilities and dispositions of the learner with respect to those objects.

PUTTING IT TOGETHER

The preceding examples—dreaming and overly imaginative reading, mistaken perception, and the telling and appreciating of jokes—are all intended to show how everyday cognition makes more sense if we abandon the idea of a mind operating on stored mental content and replace it with the idea of a mind continually and automatically responding to the world and making sense of whatever befalls it. I call this the "connectionist view of mind" because connectionist AI currently provides us the only way of imagining how such a mind might work. By itself, the connectionist way of talking about the mind offers advantages that are offset and perhaps exceeded by its disadvantages. One advantage, as I discussed in chapter 2, is that it enables us to talk about feelings and cognition in the same breath. When I saw what I took to be a bird in the apple tree, I had an immediate aesthetic feeling—I saw the bird as peculiarly beautiful—and feelings of sympathy for its solitariness and misery. But thinking it was a bird was not one kind of event, which then gave rise to the feelings. They were all part of one global response, triggered by what I saw, conditioned by all my past experience, and regulated by my whole constitution, which is itself a complex of interacting systems. For decades, educators have been struggling to establish a more holistic view of learning, signaled by expressions such as "teaching the whole child" and "whole language." Folk psychology offers no support for such efforts, and so in this regard the connectionist view of mind should be welcomed.

The other big advantage is that the connectionist view of mind enables us to talk constructively about kinds of learning that elude efforts to treat them as rules or propositions or pictures in the mind: number sense, moral sense, aesthetic sense, a way with words, the effects of immersion in great literature—in short, just about everything that distinguishes a well-educated person from a product of rote learning. The failure of folk psychology to encompass these kinds of learning must take much of the blame for the fact that, against practically everyone's better judgment, we are still stuck with tests that almost exclusively emphasize mastery of facts and rules, which in turn drive curricula with the same emphasis. How much can actually be gained from adopting a connectionist view of learning remains, however, to be demonstrated in later chapters.

These advantages are offset by a lack of explicitness about what a person knows. Folk psychology encourages us to believe that when we say Jack does or doesn't know *x* we are making much the same kind of assertion as when we say that Jack does or doesn't have a Harris tweed coat. Of course, it is much easier to inspect the contents of Jack's closet than to inspect the contents of his mind, but the principle is the same: If we had access, we could supposedly itemize the contents of Jack's knowledge repository just as we could itemize the contents of his wardrobe. Far from being ridiculous, this is an extremely useful notion. I don't see how teachers could ever get along without it. When Jack is in trouble scholastically, a smart thing to do is to inventory his relevant knowledge and when you find something important to be missing, teach it to him. This is the corner-stone of direct instruction (Bereiter, 1968), which I discuss in chapter 8 and which, by the way, all teachers resort to whenever they are prepared to suspend ideology in favor of getting something across. The connectionist way of talking about knowledge and mind does not lend itself to any such direct procedure of identifying what needs to be taught and teaching it.

For that reason, along with other equally down-to-earth reasons, I would never suggest doing away with folk psychology. Like folk physics and folk biology, it serves our daily needs by providing rough-and-ready connections between observation and action. It is just that we should not be limited by it. However, I am not suggesting, either, that the connectionist view of mind should only be activated for special purposes. Quite the contrary—I think it should constitute the fundamental way we think of the mind, even while for practical purposes we treat the mind as a container of rules and beliefs. It is the same as with cosmography. For many practical purposes, such as planning a garden or positioning a patio umbrella, we must think of our patch of earth as stationary and of the sun as passing overhead. Problems would be too difficult for us otherwise. But even while doing so—assuming we have really absorbed the Copernican view of the world—our basic attunement is to a rotating earth and a stationary sun.[5] We do not have to remind ourselves of it when we read about space travel or giant ice balls entering the atmosphere. The Copernican view has become an integral part of *the way we think*. It was not always thus. It is probably not true for most of the world's population, and I suspect that even for educated Westerners the Copernican view was not really incorporated into their world views until the advent of intercontinental air travel.

The connectionist view of mind allows us to address in a straight-forward manner this all-important transition from *knowing-that* to *seeing as*—from knowing that falling bodies accelerate to seeing falling bodies as accelerating, from knowing that genes affect behavior to seeing human behavior as always jointly reflecting inherited dispositions and the effects of experience,[6] from knowing that long

---

[5]The sun also moves, but except for astronomers this fact is of such limited significance that it need not become part of out cosmological attunement, that is our functional image of the cosmos. It is enough that be able to recall the fact on the occasions when it is relevant, whereas we should not have to recall that the earth moves around the sun. That should always be part of what Wittgenstein (1969, par. 211) called the "scaffolding of our thoughts."

[6]Most behavioral scientists these days acknowledge genetic factors in behavior, and yet this knowledge never seems to enter the thought of those who make an issue, for instance, of evidence that violent people tend to have suffered violence at the hands of their parents. Despite *knowing that* genes can affect behavior, they continue to *see* behavior *as* solely the result of past experience.

noun phrases make sentences hard to understand to seeing noun phrases as dissolvable chunks within sentences. To folk psychology and the symbol-processing models based on it, this kind of transition is not just intractable, it is virtually unknowable.

The symbol-processing view serves us best in situations of deliberate, conscious thought—situations in which we have time to reflect on what to do, recall relevant knowledge, and weigh alternatives. When thinking carefully, we try to rationalize or justify each idea as we go along. How the ideas come about is often not of much concern. They may already be laid out for us as choices to be made, and so we are wise to focus on the rationalizing—on the checking for consistency, the scanning for alternatives, the building up of a convincing story about why what we think is right. These are situations, as I have noted before, in which we try to act like symbol-processing computer programs. This kind of thinking is very important, and one of the principal virtues of a good formal education is that it enables us to do a better job of simulating a logic machine. But to base the whole educational program or knowledge management system on such a limited view of cognition is to ignore a very large part of what makes human beings different from logic machines. It is not just that human beings have feelings. If you could program a machine to get angry when it is thwarted and sad when its plans fail, that would not make it into a machine that can create knowledge, fall in love with ideas, develop number sense and historical sense and a literary style that goes with its personality, and become dissatisfied with the shallowness of its understanding. Connectionist simulations cannot do these things, either—at least not yet—but they occupy a design space in which such things are reasonable to contemplate as programming goals. That should be enough to make us question folk theories according to which all the distinctly human aspects of intelligence are mysterious and elusive and the only part that seems comprehensible is the part we share with machines.

SELF-ORGANIZATION AND EMERGENCE

As I noted in chapter 2, connectionism is one part of a much larger research movement aimed at providing scientific explanations of emergent phenomena. *Self-organization* is an idea that ties together many different research programs carried out at various levels of description from the atomic to the cultural. Adopting the way of thinking about knowledge and mind that I have been trying to put across in this chapter amounts essentially to acquiring a mind set that sees learning, thinking, knowing, and the creation of new knowledge as forms of self-organization.

Common sense and whatever biological heritage underlies it have not prepared us for the idea of self-organization. When common sense sees a puzzling phenomenon it looks for a causal agent. When it sees organization it looks for an organizer. This works amazingly well for purposes ranging from the diagnosis of diseases to the creation of governments. But it cannot account for emergence, which E. O. Wilson (1998, p. 86) defined as "the appearance of complex phenomena not predictable from the basic elements and processes alone." Pricing in a free market is perhaps the one example of emergence that is widely recognized. No causal agent or higher authority sets the prices. Prices emerge from the behaviors of buyers and sellers, but you could not predict the price of cucumbers through an analysis of those individual behaviors. A monkey colony exhibits a clearly defined and functional hierarchical structure, but the monkeys did not get together and draw up an organization chart. The complex social organization emerges from the interactions of monkeys, each of which is executing much simpler behaviors of dominance and submission. Human reason tends toward 5-year plans and organization charts. Self-organization tends toward farmers' markets and the informal social networks that exist within and often in spite of bureaucratic structures.

Not surprising, then, that the idea of emergence has been the darling of romantics in their opposition to what they often seen as a campaign by scientists to reduce life's mysteries to chemical reactions. What must be understood about complexity theory, chaos theory, self-organizing systems, and the like is that this is not the romantics starting to win, it is the scientists assaulting yet another bastion. It is not the reinstatement of mystery, it is an important new phase in science's unending program of demystification.

Self-organization and emergence are the rule in nature, and it can hardly be otherwise, unless you introduce the guiding hand of a deity. New structures have to arise from what already exists. The complexity has to result from structures and processes that do not themselves embody that complexity. Understanding self-organization always requires that we consider two levels and try to understand how the lower level phenomena can produce the higher level phenomena. To understand knowledge and mind in this way, we need to consider four different kinds or levels of self-organization:

1. *From neurons to mind.* This is the self-organization that takes place, as Hofstadter (1985) put it, "when thought emerges from billions of in-themselves-meaningless neural firings" (p. 649). It is what connectionists are trying to model. Common sense has to posit a mind that sits like an executive on top of the brain, but then

leaves the executive as something that cannot be explained. Connectionist models try to show how intelligent, knowledgeable behavior could arise from a brain that does not itself contain stored propositions and rules.

2. *From individual behavior to social organization.* How can ants have such complex social behavior, waging military campaigns and the like, and in some species building elaborate dwellings, when no individual ants have anything like the intelligence or knowledge that seems to be exhibited at the group level? Mitchel Resnick (1994) has provided striking computer demonstrations of how self-organization can work at the social level. One of Resnick's programs produces virtual ants, each of which embodies a simple set of rules that cause the ant to scurry about the computer screen, nibbling food that it encounters and laying down a trail of scent. When there are only a few ants, their behavior appears random and disorganized. But once the ant population gets into the hundreds, you start to see systematic ant-like behavior. They follow one another around in a line. They all nibble away at one food object until it is devoured and then spread out until another is discovered. This is a particularly elegant demonstration of behavior that emerges at the group level. Somehow, what accounts for the complex social behavior of ants or people must be embodied in the behavior systems of individuals. There is no collective nervous system. But the individual does not have to embody the complexity and the purposefulness exhibited by the society. It only has to embody capacities and dispositions that, in interaction with others of its kind, produce the systematic social behavior as an emergent. Thus, each ant has the disposition to move toward the scent left by other ants. When there are few ants this has little effect on behavior. But when there are many ants each moving toward the strongest scent and at the same time laying down scent of its own, trails of scent begin to emerge. And, because each ant also has a tendency to move toward food, the trail will tend to lead toward food. Virtual cows would create cattle paths in much the same way, behaving according to different but equally simple rules. In human societies, self-organization is obscured by the involvement of deliberate planning. To see it we have to look in the interstices—at the black markets that emerge, for instance, when governments try to regulate economic activity too closely. Yet we must assume self-organization is at work within deliberate planning and management processes as well. Social systems acquire complexity of their own, beyond that embodied either in the components of the system or in the plans and policies meant to control it.

An important characteristic of self-organization of social behavior is that the low-level components entering into self-organization include not only the individual organisms but also things in their physical environment: the size and location of food objects for the ants, the shape of the terrain for the meandering cows, the hideability and transportability of goods for the black marketeers.[7] From the standpoint of self-organization, therefore, what we have is not organisms behaving in ways that are adapted to the environment. Rather, behavior is an emergent phenomenon of organisms interacting with each other and with the physical environment. Where individual behavior is concerned, this amounts to saying the same thing in different ways, but when we are talking about the emergence of social behavior—of teamwork, of economic transactions, of feuds and warfare, of customs—the self-organization view allows us to make sense of things in ways that the behavioral adaptation view does not.

3. *From adaptation to niche construction.* Organisms change the environment they function in, and such changes influence the behavior that emerges, whether through evolution or through learning or both. As termite behavior evolves in such a way that it produces a massive sort of castle for the termites to live and breed in, this changes the conditions of survival, resulting in the evolution of termite behavior adapted to that kind of termite-made environment. We end up with urban termites. Construction of one's own niche reaches dramatic proportions in human societies, having a profound effect on cultural evolution and ultimately, perhaps, on the coevolution of culture and organism (Laland, Odling-Smee, & Feldman, 1999). Human behavior of nearly every kind is mediated by tools that are themselves human constructions. And these tools are themselves emergents of individual and social behavior. But "niche construction," the term used by Laland et al., is somewhat misleading. Neither we nor any other organisms construct our ecological niche. We construct things that have an impact on our environment, but the results ramify in unpredictable ways, as we are gradually coming to appreciate. What

---

[7]Along Spadina Avenue in Toronto's Chinatown, there are open-air stands facing out on the street in front of nearly every shop. On the street side there are much smaller stands facing inward, mostly selling produce. One day as I was walking up Spadina Avenue, a sudden flurry of activity swept through the street-side vendors. Goods were stuffed into shopping carts, tables were folded, and within a minute the vendors had disappeared into the crowd. I had previously wondered at the small quantities of produce that individual vendors had on display—not enough to make a living from, it seemed. Now the answer was obvious. Unlicenced street vending, which undoubtedly has a complex social structure invisible to the passerby, must accommodate to the physical constraint of involving no more goods than can be removed in a minute.

settles out as our environment is not the pre-existing environment plus what we have constructed in it. It is a new environment that is an emergent result of unimaginably complex interactions that involve our human constructions in nontrivial ways. Unimaginably complex as the interactions may be, environmental scientists are making some headway in making predictions by modeling self-organization in simplified models.

4. *From physical construction to knowledge construction—the emergence of World 3.* Conceptual artifacts—the theories, defined concepts, histories, designs, problem formulations, and so on that make up Popper's (1972) World 3—are themselves emergents. All three of the preceding kinds of self-organization are normally involved. Newton's laws arose from self-organizing processes in his own mind, but they were also a product of a recently emerged international community of scientists whose communication with one another accelerated scientific advancement. Universities provided niches in which theory construction could go on with minimal interference, and towns provided niches within which universities could evolve safely. The emergence of Newton's laws depended on existing conceptual artifacts—the theories of Galileo, for instance, whose work in turn depended on tools, such as the telescope, which emerged from a quite different set of circumstances. Conceptual artifacts in turn become part of the environment. They can serve as tools for the construction of new conceptual artifacts, and so we get the emergence of progressive scientific disciplines. A whole new plane of activity opens up in which self-organization among ideas produces new ideas. The prodigious impact of this fourth level of self-organization can only be appreciated by comparing societies where it has occurred with those where it either has not occurred (the vanishing Stone Age societies) or those where religious strictures or the conditions of survival have held it in check. The other three kinds of self-organization are universal among human beings. The fourth does not seem to be a given of human nature. It has to be recreated in each generation. That—largely unrecognized—is the task of schools in a modern society.

The shift from understanding phenomena in terms of causal chains to understanding them in terms of self-organization is a bigger shift than that from a Ptolmeic to a Copernican view of the solar system but probably no greater than that from a creationist to a Darwinian way of thinking about life forms. There are emotional resistances to all three, because they all involve demoting ourselves. Furthermore, none of them offers a payoff in daily life. Most of our everyday prob-

lems are best handled by looking for causal agents, by assuming a stationary earth and a moving sun, and by regarding species as fixed and
human beings as a special class. Why, then, are most educated people
Copernicans and Darwinians? Because the world makes more sense
that way; there are fewer gaps and inconsistencies; it is easier to relate
one fact to another. Moreover, because that is the way things are
heading. If you have not assimilated the Copernican and Darwinian
models, then each new discovery in astronomy and evolutionary biology leaves you farther behind. For specialists, of course, there are
more pointed reasons. As for self-organization in human knowledge
and cognition, all these reasons apply. Things make more sense.
Self-organization is the way the relevant sciences are heading. And for
specialists in educational design or knowledge management, the old
models are too limited and crude.

RELATED AND OPPOSING VIEWS

Situated Cognition

Researchers and theorists in this tradition have done a great deal to
increase our understanding of the second and third kinds of self-organization described in the preceding section—the emergence of productive social behavior in what are called "communities of practice"
and the essential role of tools in such behavior (Engestrom, 1987;
Wenger, 1995). The first and fourth kinds of self-organization have
been largely ignored, however. Individual cognition has been treated
mainly as the internalization of socially constituted knowledge. This
has had implications for the social organization of instruction but
otherwise has had little to offer for the solution of educational problems. Situativity theorists have also generally been opposed to treating knowledge as detachable from social behavior and from material
tools, and this has meant that they have little to offer regarding the
creation of knowledge. Although it started out with very wide-ranging ambitions, situated cognition seems to have found its applied
niche in management consulting, primarily in helping organizations to foster and take advantage of the implicit knowledge that
grows up among workers (Brown & Duguid, 2000; Wenger, 1995).

Situativity theory is very much in the modern mold of scientific
treatments of emergence, and thus is potentially fully compatible
with the connectionist view of mind and with the idea of cognitive
artifacts. But I think proponents of situated cognition hobble themselves by not making a clear distinction between the situated knowledge inherent in the practices of any productive group and the
*non*situated knowledge which for some groups is the exportable

product of their work and for other groups is the stuff they work with (Bereiter, 1997; compare Engestrom & Cole, 1997). Making this distinction amounts to recognizing World 3. Recognizing World 3 leads naturally to recognizing World 2 as well, the world of personal abilities and dispositions, for it is here that we take account of the abilities and dispositions people have with regard to objects in World 3. Such an enlarged conceptual framework has room in it for the important insights of situativity theory, but it does not force the concept of situated cognition to do more work than it can handle.

Brain Science

With new ways of observing the brain at work, cognitive neuroscience is throwing new light on the nature of learning. Research is not only showing what happens during normal learning, as in becoming a skilled reader, but also what happens when learning goes awry, as in dyslexia (Shaywitz, Pugh, Fulbright, & Gore, 1998). A sizeable literature has developed out of efforts to derive educational prescriptions from brain research (one educational publisher alone offers 36 titles of "materials to apply new knowledge about the brain and learning to the classroom"). I have not actually read any of this material, but from attending conferences where it has been touted and from Internet browsing I have not noticed any ideas that are less than 30 years old. The people I have talked to who have some sophistication in both neuroscience and education are cautiously optimistic that findings of educational significance will start to emerge in a decade or so, but they are not sure what form they will take (see Bruer, 1997). The first contributions are likely to be to the treatment of pathologies of learning. Beyond that—this is happening now—brain research findings will figure in practical matters mainly through lending weight to ideas that are drawn from other sources and that enjoy other kinds of support as well.

The advances in brain science are, nonetheless, impressive; moreover, there are signs of convergence between the behavioral and brain sciences (as shown, for instance, by examining the journal of that name, comparing what was being published in the 1980s with what appeared in the 1990s). Suppose there is a revolution in understanding of mental phenomena, comparable to the 19th-century revolution in the understanding of infectious disease. Will it affect education the way the discovery of bacteria affected medicine? And what will it do to the theoretical premises I have been advancing here? On the practical side, there is reason to keep optimism in restraint, as Bruer (1997) suggested. Medicine is essentially unrestricted in the range of treatments it may undertake (which, incidentally, is why it keeps running into ethical problems). Discoveries in biochemistry may be translated into chemical therapies, advances in cellular genetics may be translated into gene therapies, and so on up through anatomy, psychology, and anthropology. Education, along with other knowledge arts, is much more restricted in what its practitioners can do. Basically, teaching is limited to various forms of communication plus a modest ability to modify the environment within which communication takes place. The separation in levels between brain processes and educational practice may be so great that advances in one can have no direct effect on the other. To assume they should is as unrealistic as expecting that advances in molecular biology should have an effect on the doctor's bedside manner.

But surely scientific advances in understanding learning, memory, thinking, emotion, and the like ought to influence how we *think* about educational issues. No doubt. But, again, the separation in levels argues against high expectations. The question of immediate concern is: What is the likelihood that scientific advances at the level of brain processes will overturn the ideas I have been presenting here? The connectionist view of mind, even in the very general form I have presented, is certainly vulnerable. But what is the likelihood that further research will show folk psychology is right after all? I would say it is about as likely as that further advances in paleontology will vindicate creationism. As for the other main idea, conceptual artifacts, that has nothing to do with natural science at all. It will rise or fall on the basis of its usefulness.

Postmodernism

In academic circles, most of the controversy surrounding knowledge does not have to do with its relation to mind but rather with its social status. I refer especially to what is being called the "science wars," a controversy that pits defenders of mainstream science against various antifoundationalists, postmodernists, sociologists of knowledge, and feminist theorists who are trying to lower scientific knowledge from its privileged status and put it on a par with other belief systems as found in religions, myths, and political ideologies. Although there are very important issues here, some of which I have addressed elsewhere (Bereiter, 1994; Bereiter et al., 1997), they are tangential to theory of mind. Take the issue of how something gets established as a fact. Much of the lighter weight critique of science is devoted to attacking the notion that facts are established on the basis of correspondence with the way things really are. According to what might be called the liberal scientific view (Rauch, 1993), facts are facts by virtue of withstanding empirical tests and cohering with other putative facts. According to what seems to be the modal left-wing view, establishing something as a fact is more in the nature of a political victory, having little or nothing to do with an external nature of things (Collins, 1981). But across the whole spectrum of opinions—which range in both directions beyond those I have indicated—it is accepted that there is a something, the so-called fact, whose origins and status are in question. There must be some sense in which adversaries are talking about the same thing: otherwise there could be no argument. At the least, "fact" has to serve as a "peg" in the sense discussed in the appendix, something to hang assertions on, and that amounts to granting abstract ideas a sort of World 3 status. When that much is granted, opinions may differ wildly and still be consistent with the view of knowledge and mind advanced here.

There is one respect, however, in which the science wars might seem to impinge on the present discussion. I have maintained that one of the inadequacies of folk theory of mind is its inability to deal with advancement of the state of knowledge—with knowledge creation and knowledge improvement, as in the progress of a science. One of the implications of the stronger antifoundationalist positions is that there is no progress in knowledge, only change. Such a position, if you take it seriously, calls into question why anyone would want to pursue science, why governments should be so foolish as to fund research, and so on. But if you are going to go ahead anyway, if only to advance your career, you are going to need tools. One of those tools, I argue, should be a theory of mind suitable to the task of creating new conceptual artifacts. You do not need to be a postmodernist to recognize that some conceptual artifacts are no improvement over their predecessors.

In most segments of society postmodernism is having its main effect on personnel policies, through its campaigns for minority rights, gender equity, and protection from harassment. But in education it is a movement of more far-reaching consequence. At its worst it means censorship and propaganda; at its best it brings a heightened level of sensitivity to all of the human consequences of power differences and prejudice. In either case, however, the result is to seal off certain ideas from critical examination—specifically, any ideas closely associated, positively or negatively, with the identity of a disadvantaged group. Objectionable as it may be on several grounds, this is a constraint that teachers from kindergarten to university are learning to work within. And so the contemporary problem is how to carry on effective education within this constraint. Because folk theory conceives of both the personal development of understanding and the general progress of knowledge as the same kind of event taking place within individual minds, it cannot make much sense out of one proceeding while the other is blocked. With the kind of theory I have been advocating, developing understanding of a knowledge object and improving the knowledge object are different though related activities. In any fundamentalist doctrine—be it religious, political, or of the postmodern breed whose names typically start with "anti"—certain knowledge objects are treated as absolute (absolutely right or absolutely wrong) and unimprovable. If, as it appears, we are in a period in which fundamentalisms of many different kinds are flourishing, we need a theory of mind and knowledge that does not confuse understanding with true belief and that can distinguish advancement of knowledge from individual mental states.

Constructivism

Constructivism has at least three meanings, all of which have some relevance to theories of knowledge and mind. There is a World 1 meaning, a World 2 meaning, and a World 3 meaning. Starting with the World 2 meaning, constructivism as it has come to be known mainly through the works of Jean Piaget asserts that knowledge is acquired by a process of mental construction. Although this was a bold proposition during the reign of behaviorism, it has since lost most of its force. As long as you acknowledge that constructive activity can go on unconsciously and automatically as well as deliberately, it is compatible with every cognitive theory going, including both folk psychology and connectionist models. That is why I have not made an issue of it. In educational practice, Piaget's World 2 meaning has degraded into a World 1 idea. Constructivism has become a synonym for "learning by doing"—in other words, all kinds of hands-on activities and projects. The term has been taken up by reformers who either want more or less of that kind of thing, and so you will see constructivism vigorously advocated and denounced in current phases of the endless debate about pedagogical methods. As I elaborate in later chapters, one of the reasons education needs a new theory of knowledge and mind is to rise above such fruitless controversy. For that to happen, "constructivism" in its degraded World 1 sense is one of the terms that will have to go. That leaves the World 3 meaning, which has two parts. One part is what I have tried to capture in the term "conceptual artifacts." It is the idea that theories and the like are human constructions much like material artifacts. The other and much more controversial part is that the *truth* of propositions is a social construction. The important thing to realize is that the first part does not imply the second part. You can buy the idea of conceptual artifacts and still believe anything you want to about truth. I think this permissiveness is essential if progress in the knowledge arts is not to get hung up on a philosophical controversy that shows no signs of settlement.

CONCLUSION

To common sense, mental content is real. It is something we experience. I am arguing that we should reduce it to a metaphor (a very important and useful metaphor, however). Conversely, ideas, as common sense regards them, are not quite real once they get outside people's heads; they are not things that exist out in the world along with parakeets and pencil sharpeners; at most, they are public manifestations of things people have in their minds. I am arguing that ideas should be treated as real things out in the world—that there are conceptual artifacts, just as there are material artifacts. They deserve the fullest possible recognition because producing, improving, and applying them is one of the most important things human beings do. Especially in a knowledge society. In fact, work with conceptual artifacts is what makes a knowledge society different from an industrial society.

If you happen to be thinking about parakeets and want to call parakeets mental content, there is no problem with that. The problem is with the millions of items that you are not thinking about right now but that are supposedly stored away in your mind. Such a notion not only becomes implausible under examination, it leads to warped and constricted conceptions of learning, knowing, and thinking. The examples I worked through in this chapter—of dreaming and of misrecognition—combined with the discussions of everyday understanding in chapter 4, will I hope go some way toward showing we do not really need a notion of stored mental content to deal sensibly with human knowing.

The alternative to the folk conception of mind as a container of beliefs and other mental objects is the connectionist view of mind as a self-organizing system—a system that does not actually contain mental objects as data but that produces knowledgeable behavior as an emergent. I am pretty sure that this conception of mind is going to win out, that it will continue to develop long after the research program known as connectionism gets assimilated into some more advanced program. It makes better sense of the mind's relation to the brain on one hand and to the physical world on the other hand of the inseparability of thought and feeling. Two of the most serious limitations of folk theory are its inability to make sense of the pursuit of understanding and of knowledge creation. The connectionist view of mind can make sense of these, but only if it is complemented by a conception of ideas as things to which the mind can become attuned and with which it can interact. That is where the notion of conceptual artifacts comes in. There is self-organization at the neural level that produces thought as an emergent. There is self-organization at the level of intellectual artifacts that produces things like sciences and disciplines as emergents. Obviously the two are related, but how? That is a question that is going to require the collaborative efforts of brain scientists, cognitive scientists, and social scientists to answer. In the meantime, however, those of us who are concerned with practical matters like education and knowledge management—with the knowledge arts, to put it more broadly—do not have to soldier on with only a centuries-old folk theory to guide us. The main components of a new theory of knowledge and mind are available, even though the theory proper is not. These components are the connectionist view of mind and the Popperian view of conceptual artifacts. In succeeding chapters I hope to show that these are serviceable even in their pretheoretical state, that they can help us toward a more enlightened approach to education.

Part II

Education
and Knowledge Work

7

Educational Planning:
Reacting to the Future

Richmond, a suburb of Vancouver, British Columbia, is interesting to social scientists as a prototype of the communities that globalization will create as it becomes a human reality. Richmond was a typical large suburb, similar to those found around any North American city. Then suddenly it received a huge influx of what Canadian immigration calls "business-class" immigrants, more generally known to social scientists as "transnational" immigrants. Unlike other opportunity-seeking migrants, these bring substantial wealth with them, they do not sever business connections with their former country, they enter the new society at a high level instead of having to start over on a low rung, and they may well migrate again as other opportunities beckon. These particular transnationals came mainly from Hong Kong, bringing sufficient millions to start new businesses or branches of their Hong Kong businesses. Their children now make up half the population of the local schools, and that is where trouble started.

As Katharyne Mitchell (2001) explained it, the parents were looking for a kind of education that would enable their children to become successful transnationals as well, able to enter any society at a high level. By this standard, they found the education their children were receiving inadequate. Complaints grew, but they changed to calls for positive action when a popular Chinese broadcaster began to publicize an option that is available within the provincial system for educational funding. It is called the "traditional school"—a school that features high standards, emphasis on basic skills and traditional academic subjects, discipline and decorum, hard work, and lots of testing. A poll showed 95% of Asian parents in favor of traditional schools (although efforts to gain school board approval continue to be unsuccessful after 4 years of campaigning).[1]

So here are parents with a strong investment in preparing their children for life in a global, knowledge-based economy, determining that the best way to do this is through a kind of education that is a throwback to olden times. "Back to" movements are of course commonplace, but the Richmond case is interesting because the parents were ones who ought to have had some idea of what transnational excellence really requires, being themselves exemplars of it. Could it be that they made the right choice?[2] That question loses most of its interest if we consider what they had to choose from. They really had only two choices, the same two choices that figure in most of the current school debates. The alternative to the traditional model is what we may call the "standard" model. It is standard not only in the sense that it is the most widely adopted in English-speaking countries, but that it is also the most generally supported by teachers unions and by education officials, except when political pressure forces them to change their spots. Its main outlines are the same as the traditional one. The same subjects form the core of the curriculum, but in the standard model there are more extras and electives, there is less emphasis on performance and more on individual development and self-expression, course content is thinner and geared to the less academically inclined student, and the curriculum features more hands-on and social activities with correspondingly less time given to recitation. In both models, however, seat work occupies much of the time in elementary school and lectures and recitations are a mainstay of secondary education. The models, thus, are not radically different. Depending on your viewpoint, the traditional model is a toughened-up version of the standard one or the standard model is just the traditional model gone flabby. Those viewpoints may be

---

[1]News and archives are currently available on the Web at www.bbr.ca/ParentNetwork.

[2]It is, of course, relevant that in opting for "traditional schools," the Asian parents were opting for something probably closer to what they were familiar with in their country of origin. But, given that many things are different in Canada from how they are in Hong Kong, it remains to explain why the parents were so insistent that the schools should be changed to their liking.

radically different, based on different political and world views. I am not trying to minimize such differences. My point is that the educational approaches associated with them, what pass for right-wing and left-wing or middle-of-the-road pedagogies, do not really offer much choice to people concerned about something like transnational excellence.

EDUCATIONAL PLANNING IN THE FACE OF ECONOMIC UNCERTAINTIES

What would education be like that was well designed to prepare students for the world of the future? To answer that question, we need to look more critically than educational planners usually do at what can be made of current trends and prospects. Like many educationists, I have some aversion to thinking of education in economic terms, but the predicted changes to which education is supposed to have a response are either economic changes, such as globalization and the ascendancy of knowledge-based industries, or they are other kinds of changes with serious economic implications, such as changing demographic profiles of student populations and the workforce.

In 1993 the government of Ontario established a Royal Commission on Learning, with a charge "to set new directions to ensure that Ontario youth are well-prepared for the challenges of the 21st century" (Ontario, Royal Commission on Learning, 1994, p. vii). As to what those challenges might be, however, the Royal Commission reported:

> On the basis of research and policy analysis, we have concluded that predictions about educational ties to the economic future are uncertain at best; it is difficult, if not impossible, to be sure which jobs will be available and which specific skills will be required. (vol. I, p. 27)

Accordingly, they eschewed prediction and based their 167 recommendations largely on what various constituencies spoke up for.

The Royal Commission had good reason to be cautious. Added to the usual uncertainties of economic prediction are two new elements that make education for future employment an especially elusive target:

1. Automation and deskilling. Whatever skills may be required for a job today, we must expect that someone is busy devising a way to reduce those skill requirements if not to eliminate the job

altogether in favor of a machine. Educators tend to regard deskilling as the work of evil forces, especially when applied to their own craft, while at the same time welcoming the deskilling of computer use, for instance, which is a major cause of job downgrading.

2. Globalization and outsourcing. It used to be that unskilled manual work was what got outsourced to poorer nations, thus making a nice argument for persuading kids to stay in school and acquire literate skills. But knowledge work is proving to be eminently outsourceable. We see programming and accounting work being shipped out to India and to states of the former USSR, whereas jobs flipping hamburgers remain at home.

Educational planning does not require certainties. The Royal Commission on Learning, by avoiding prediction, implicitly predicted things will remain the same and accordingly brought forth a bland set of proposals that, except for a nod in the direction of computers, could have been produced any time in the last 50 years. Creative educational planning, like any kind of design, needs to take account of realistic possibilities, however divergent. When there are contradictory scenarios, the task is to invent something that will work in either case. The Royal Commission's mistake, repeated by many other reform-minded bodies, was to listen only to pundits and pressure groups, ignoring designers and problem solvers.

Based on present conditions and plausible eventualities, a number of major design criteria for 21st century education can be set out:

1. Public education must serve the needs of the whole populace, the majority of whom will not be knowledge workers or "symbolic analysts," in Robert Reich's terms (1992). Exactly what they will be doing is not clear. In the worst case, a large proportion of them will be unemployed (Rifkin, 1995). Thus, *education for unemployment*, an idea so horrifying that it is never discussed, ought to figure in educational planning. The proportion of those employed in service occupations is already high and seems likely to grow. This suggests that educational planning must pay attention to the development of social competencies.

2. At the same time, education must produce people who are able to create and exploit the potentialities of new knowledge. Some economists and business analysts assert that such high-level knowledge work will be the main generator of wealth in the future (Drucker, 1993; Romer, 1993). Even if they are only partly right, education has to develop talent for knowledge creation, be-

cause the society that lacks it can expect to end up providing low-priced services to the society that has it.

3. Public education in a democracy must not prejudge who will enter the elite class of high-level knowledge workers and who will not. As nearly as possible, every youngster should have an equal chance, regardless of family background. This means that, despite the widely divergent requirements suggested by points 1 and 2, they must somehow be met within a common educational program.

4. From an economic standpoint, the value of school learning is in what it enables you to learn on the job. This is not a new insight, but it is brought to the forefront by studies of situated action (Wenger, 1995), by studies of expertise (e.g., Lesgold & Lajoie, 1991), and by the rate of technological change. A fuzzy belief in "learning to learn" will not do any longer. Educational planning needs to get serious about the role of knowledge in acquiring knowledge.

5. Although automation, speech recognition, and the like may reduce the amount of reading, writing, and figuring that people have to do, there is no realistic prospect that functional literacy and numeracy will become economically less essential than they are now. The demands of back-to-basics zealots, however misguided they may be in other ways, have to be taken seriously in this respect. In a knowledge-based economy, those who lack competence in the major symbol systems that our civilization has evolved are going to be in bad shape.

6. *Career craft* needs to become an educational objective. We hear much about the pace of change creating a need for lifelong learning, but that truism masks more serious challenges. Aging workers are liable to find themselves out on the street before lifelong learning has a chance to kick in. A career can no longer be based on a particular job or a particular organization. A successful career is likely to thread its way through a number of short-term jobs and service contracts. For it really to be a career—something that has coherence, that adds meaning to your life, and that you can feel is getting someplace—you have to build it yourself. This is something educational planning has not had to think about in the past.

7. Schools need to position themselves with respect to other providers of information and learning opportunities. The effects of new media such as those based on the World Wide Web are difficult to predict, except that we can be sure they will be highly variable, just because of the range of options available. Given greater access to the world of thought, knowledge, and social action,

some young people may become far more sophisticated and responsible than is common today (Tapscott, 1998). Others may merely become increasingly skillful at electronic equivalents of the pinball machine. "Positioning" would include figuring out how to avoid competing head-to-head with things like video games and identifying and concentrating on what schools can do better than other agencies.

8. Learning for the future, whatever form it takes, has to start early. This assertion is not based on critical periods of brain development or anything like that, but simply on the length of learning time required. As Peter Drucker (1994) pointed out, during the Industrial Revolution a relatively brief period of learning was enough for a farm worker to master a semiskilled industrial job. For an industrial worker to master a knowledge industry job, however, is next to impossible. The kind of learning that is required has prerequisites built on prerequisites that reach all the way back into childhood. That is why Drucker saw education as central to a knowledge society.

This may not be an exhaustive list, but it seems fair to claim that it represents a formidable enough set of challenges that, if educational planners could figure out a way to meet them, they could afford to take a breather before going out to look for more challenges. Many of them are already well recognized, however, and so the first job is to evaluate ready-made educational approaches to see what they do and do not have to offer with respect to them.

THE READY-MADE ALTERNATIVES

Although Drucker (1994) did not formulate it as such, his analysis of the role of education in a knowledge society presents a dilemma. Education must become more strongly oriented toward the cognitive demands of adulthood at a time when those demands are becoming increasingly unpredictable. The tables have almost completely turned since the time of Rousseau, whose reflections inform the standard model the Richmond parents were reacting against. Rousseau's most compelling argument for what has since come to be called child-centered education was that the majority of children would never live to see adulthood. Therefore, he argued, education should aim at enriching the present lives of children rather than preparing them for adulthood. Looking back, we could add a further argument to support Rousseau's position: For those children who did survive, their future as adults was pretty much determined by social position, and so education could not have been expected to do much about it anyway. Now, in the developed nations, survival to adulthood is almost certain but what that adulthood will amount to is highly uncertain and education has at least the potential to influence it strongly. Yet Rousseau continues to provide one of the small number of ready-made answers to the question of what kind of education will best prepare for the uncertainties of a rapidly changing, innovation-driven world.

Accepting the idea that preparation must start early does not in any way prejudge what the nature of that preparation should be. The fact that adult knowledge workers need to be literate and to use information technology tells us nothing about when children should be taught to read or how and it is not a compelling reason for use of computers in the schools. During the 1980s, when computer literacy was the rage in North American education, Japan (looked to as the country that had the high-tech future in its grasp) was doing hardly anything with computers in the schools. The Japanese view was that there was plenty of time to acquire computer skills later through a computer science course and on-the-job learning. Instead, they concentrated on things like mathematics, which take many years to learn. In this they were largely right. Learning to use a computer is not much more complicated than learning to drive a car, and we do not send kindergartners to driver training camps. Mathematical competence, on the other hand, does take the average learner a long time. Recognizing this, schools everywhere start mathematics education at an early age and continue it in some more or less coherent way over many years. The heightened need for articulation between school learning and on-the-job learning, however, compels us to ask questions such as "Is the mathematical competence we are developing in schools the right kind?" and "Are we developing mathematical competence rapidly enough and soundly enough?" The second question is the kind back-to-basics advocates are asking. The first is being asked by mathematics associations and, in a more pointed way, by researchers of school-to-work connections (e.g., Lesgold, 1996).

But there is a higher level question that is hardly being asked at all. It has to do with socialization or enculturation and it points to the way in which Japan's early rejection of computers in the schools (since then reversed) was mistaken. To thrive in a modern organization, you need more than the ability to master the software applications used in your work. You need to feel at home in and to know your way around in a world in which computing and network communication are ubiquitous. This is not the matter of a few weeks' training, it is the matter, as Don Tapscott (1998) put it, of "growing up digital." As Tapscott's investigation showed, there are young people who are becoming thoroughly socialized into this world, and they are undoubtedly at a great advantage in terms of future job competence. I shall argue that the kind of socialization Tapscott described still does not go far enough. Students need to be socialized into the world of work with knowledge, and that is an even more radical cultural change than becoming "digital."

To the question of what kind of education best prepares students for the uncertain future, I make out four different kinds of answers, each having some following or installed base. Each has virtues, but even in their best combination they fall short of addressing the higher level need to socialize students into a knowledge society.

1. *Back-to-basics.* Judged according to their timing, back-to-basics movements appear to represent a panic reaction to any sort of menace that shakes confidence in the education system—whether it is a show of strength by a Cold War enemy, a competing economy on the rise, poor averages on achievement tests, or just the uncertainties of future employment. The panicked reaction is to fall back on the few skills that are demonstrably both teachable and critical and to seek assurance that these, at least, are being effectively taught. The effects that this kind of intervention can have on an education system are highly variable, but they are not at issue here. The question is how far the *idea* of going back to basics can carry us, and the answer is not very far. Once people have agreed that students must learn to read, write, and figure, and that schools must take responsibility for making this learning occur, the back-to-basics idea has exhausted itself. That is why, regardless of their pedagogical persuasions, people who care about improving the teaching of any school subject groan when a back-to-basics movement takes over. It means that any new ideas about objectives, content, or process will have to be shelved for the duration. Back-to-basics advocates are not necessarily opposed to new ideas, but they have no basis for evaluating them, apart from proved results on conventional measures. Across the whole spectrum from mathematics to literature, they have nothing to aim for except better mastery of whatever happens to have become established as the conventional content. As far as rallying education to confront the 21st century is concerned, back-to-basics is a bugle that can sound only one note.

2. *Futuristic education.* By this term I refer to a collection of educational ideas that swirl around economic and technological developments and prognostications. Globalization, competiveness,

digitization, the Internet, knowledge-based entrepreneurship, reinventing the corporation—all the same ideas that have inspired a vast futuristic business literature are translated into educational prescriptions. The prescriptions call for less emphasis on instilling knowledge (which is believed to become obsolete within months after being learned), putting the emphasis instead on higher level thinking skills, flexibility, creativity, lifelong love of learning, cooperativeness, and information-finding skills. These objectives are to be achieved by abandoning the content-centered curriculum in favor of an array of projects that engage students with the latest technologies, that involve collaboration in face-to-face and virtual groups, and that draw on widespread human and digitized information sources.[3] For the most part, educational futurism is a mixture of trendiness, bad psychology, and technological impressionability. Its value lies in presenting educators with challenges that need to be taken seriously. It is very likely true that life in a knowledge society requires more high-level thinking, flexibility, creativity, readiness to learn and relearn, cooperation, and skill in the use of knowledge resources. But bad psychology turns these challenges into bad prescriptions. There is an inordinate belief in transfer of learning. Becoming clever at some trivial puzzle is supposed to transfer to creative problem solving in real life; cooperating in mounting a brick wall is supposed to increase one's ability to cooperate in mounting a sales campaign. And there is pervasive failure to recognize the fundamental principle that ability to find or acquire new knowledge depends foremost on what one already knows. That is the foundation of a progressive curriculum, and without it futuristic education merely raises the price of busywork.

3. *Liberal education.* Liberal education still exists conspicuously in some private schools, and remnants—sometimes substantial ones—may be found in public high schools geared to preparation for university. Central to the tradition of liberal education is the *canon*—a designated body of ideas, competencies, and artifacts that together represent the cultural world into which the student is to be introduced (Carus, in press). To forestall one criticism immediately, we should recognize that the canon need not be unchanging or universal. The classical canon changed to incorporate science and more recently literary and historical canons have been changing to represent greater cultural diversity. The canon can be

---

[3]I would not know where to start in documenting this exuberant literature. A World Wide Web search on "school(s)," "computer(s)," and "paradigm shift" turned up 38,750 web pages that contained *all three* of these terms. Adding the word "hype" to the search string reduced this number to 240.

as modern as you please. The International Baccalaureat, which sets examinations aimed at establishing international standards for a liberal secondary school education, includes an examination in computer science that puts most other conceptions of computer literacy to shame. Changes in the canon are always controversial, but that is a strength. It means that liberal education, unlike back-to-basics, contains standards and processes for judging the worth of innovations. "Cultural transmission" is a term often applied to traditional liberal education. The term is accurate, but it invites misunderstanding. "Transmission" suggests students are passive recipients of knowledge, but this has never even in ancient times been the ideal. Active, preferably passionate, engagement with the objects of knowledge has always been prized. The problem, rather, is in the split between established knowledge—the stuff that is being "transmitted"—and the constructive, meaning-making activities of the students. Because of this split, educators have tended to line up on one side of the gap or the other, resulting in ideological warfare. That gap must somehow be closed before liberal education can be more than a partial model of education leading toward competence in knowledge work.

4. *Developmentalism.* This is the term used by J. E. Stone (1996) to characterize approaches that emphasize "(a) the sufficiency of a natural inclination to learning, (b) the dangers of interference with native characteristics and proclivities, and (c) the desirability of learning experiences that emulate those thought to occur naturally." Developmentalism finds its clearest and least controversial expression in the nursery school and kindergarten, but so attractive has it been to educationists that it has gradually worked its way up through the elementary school and into the high school, even being found in some college courses that cater to the academically underprepared. It is the foundation of the standard model that I described earlier, although the standard model shows influences from all the other models. How does developmentalism address the need to prepare students for adult life? The long-standing claim has been that the best preparation for adulthood is a full and happy childhood, proceeding in harmony with the child's own interests (Weber, 1971, p. 170 ff). Although it embodies undeniable wisdom, this has never been an entirely satisfactory argument (Geary, 1995), and it provides little reassurance to people who are anxious about what the future holds. To the more optimistic, however, it means there is no need to modify education according to predicted future needs. Nature has designed us to be creative and adaptable, so all education has to do is nurture and protect those human attributes.

The controversies actually going on about approaches to education are not usually framed according to the four approaches I have represented here. A present-day dispute might pit something called "direct instruction" against something called "constructivism," or it might involve a controversial practice such as phonics or controversial subject matter such as ebonics or evolution. If the issue of preparedness for the future should arise, however, claims and counterclaims will likely fall into the categories described here. That is, the policy in question will be claimed to succeed or fail at teaching basic skills, building foundational knowledge, getting in step with the digital revolution, or promoting optimum personal and social development. Thus, controversies are about which educational approach will do the best job of achieving x, but x itself is seldom brought into question. What I have been trying to get across through this examination of four different xs is that they differ importantly and, moreover, they all fall short.

Forced to choose among the available alternatives, any informed person would opt for liberal education. That is what parents who can afford a private school have been doing for generations. A well-run liberal education program will take care of basic skills, it will be humane and will allow the young plenty of opportunity to enjoy their youth, and it will be attuned to contemporary needs—in addition to cultivating the knowledge that traditionally sets the educated apart from the uneducated. Thus, it offers the best of four worlds to an extent that none of the other four models can do.

This discourse is not about forced choices, however, but about ideas and possibilities. And so what I want to consider here, and in the remainder of this book, is how education could go beyond the ready-made choices. The reason people are bound to the ready-made choices is not merely because policy has to deal with the actual rather than the hypothetical. Debate about basic approaches in education has never been very much constrained by reality. It has been constrained instead by the available concepts, drawn as they are from folk theories of knowledge and mind. These constraints draw discussion away from those realities that folk theory makes it difficult to conceptualize. In this light, we can see the four models as four different lines of retreat from problems too difficult to grasp:

- Back-to-basics retreats from all the intangibles that constitute an educated person and fixates on the few attributes that can be demonstrated, reduced to behavioral objectives.
- Liberal education retreats from the challenge of producing people who can create knowledge, relying instead on building an all-purpose foundation of established knowledge.

- Developmentalism, to put it perhaps too dramatically, retreats from civilization. That is, it retreats from all the ways in which human beings have sought to transcend the limitations of their nature (Bereiter, 1997).
- Futuristic education retreats instead from the need to consider how we actually learn and think. The conceptually most primitive of the four approaches, it deals in surface resemblances: Imagine what the future will look like on the surface; then make education mimic that surface.

It should not be surprising then, that none of these four models addresses future prospects on the basis of a cognitive or sociocultural analysis. Back-to-basics, liberal education, and developmentalism offer solutions to the problem of preparing for the future that are the same today as 80 years ago. Futuristic education, which supposedly rejects past solutions and looks boldly to the future, does not offer anything new either, except a rosy belief in technology. A great deal of the reform currently being pressed forward as innovative or "breaking the mold" represents yet another revival of John Dewey's ideas. I have also seen reform proposals that revive the Human Potential movement of the 1960s and early 1970s, the project method, and the community school concept (I taught in a notable example of the last in the 1950s). Any of these, or some combination of them, *might* be just what we need to educate for the 21st century, but we ought to see some deep analysis and comparison of alternatives to make a case. I have not seen that. Instead, each proposal is put forward as a contrast to the mythical traditional school devoted to drumming dead facts into reluctant minds. By such a contrast they all look good. But if the future really is going to be profoundly different from the past, we ought to have a way to think new thoughts about education. In the remainder of this book I try to make a few steps in that direction.

LEARNING HOW TO LEARN

It has always been true that the workplace value of school learning lies in what it enables you to learn on the job. Recent developments only make this more obvious. As occupations become more numerous and varied, it becomes more evident that school cannot train people for a job. The old clerical skills course, meant to provide girls with an occupation in case they were so unfortunate as to need one, is a museum piece—despite the fact that keyboarding skills are becoming an everyday necessity. And, as the rate of knowledge advancement affects more and more of people's daily lives, it becomes increasingly apparent that purposeful learning has no endpoint.

The traditional school's stock-in-trade, consisting of book learning plus training in the three Rs, makes a clear albeit limited contribution to future learning of diverse kinds. To this extent the back-to-basics reformers are on the right track and the Richmond parents made the right choice in rejecting a system they perceived as failing in this limited role. Advocates of liberal education, however, see it as contributing to future learning in a broader and more powerful way. Mortimer Adler (1984), a leading recent proponent of classics-based liberal education sounded much like today's futurists in saying "the only appropriate 'career education' is *learning how to learn*, so that one can quickly prepare for new jobs and career opportunities as they come along" (p. 157). But what backing is there for his claim that a liberal education produces this remarkable result? Or that any other kind of education does it, for that matter? Perhaps, beyond a few basic skills that are useful everywhere, the benefits of education are all personal and social: It makes you a more complete person and helps you gain entry to the best circles. Those may be all the justification that education needs, but if that is all it warrants the 21st century is no different from any other century as far as education is concerned and there is no educational point to all this millennial fuss.

"Learning how to learn" has become a mantra, uttered as if it means something but in fact conveys no meaning. There is something to it, but there is not sufficient evidence to say how much. Learning to learn has, in fact, only recently developed into an issue that can be researched in an educationally useful way (Bransford & Schwartz, 1999). I give some attention to its theoretical and scientific aspects in the next chapter, but what is called for at this point is simply a touch of realism. Realistically, all we can expect of learning a school subject is that it will help in learning a more advanced level of that subject or its near neighbors. This is by no means a negligible value, but it does deflate the kind of claim that Adler was making and that is echoed by most people who recite the "learning-how-to-learn" mantra. There is no question that learning a foreign language increases your ability to learn foreign languages and that learning history equips you to learn more history, but to claim that either of these helps you to learn a new programming language or a new Internet protocol is a big stretch and claiming it will help you learn how to fix a copying machine or to close deals in the bond market is a leap into fantasyland.

Unfortunately, the same must be said about another Information Age mantra, "lifelong learning." The fact of life that has brought this old slogan to life is, of course, the pace of technological change. We tend nowadays to outlive our skills and to need new ones. But apart from providing ready access to learning opportunities, people have little idea of how to promote the needed learning. The continual chirping about "just-in-time" and "anywhere, any time" learning demonstrates the poverty of educational futurism. There are times when just being able to get hold of the right piece of information when we need it is sufficient, and so we must applaud the search for better search engines. But solving access problems barely scratches the surface of the lifelong learning problem. "Just-in-time" learning may satisfy the engineer who needs to get on top of a new communications protocol. But what about the stock handler, whose $40,000-a-year job has vanished with the closing of the brewery where he worked, and whose only immediate prospects are for jobs that will not pay enough to keep up his mortgage? "Just-in-time" is already long past for him. "Just-in-time" may have been back in high school, when he might have mastered algebra but didn't, or even before that when he might have mastered the fundamental literacies and acquired the understanding-seeking habits of mind that would have put him on a different track of lifelong learning. For everyone does, of course, learn throughout life. It is all a matter of what, how much, and to what purpose.

Discussions of lifelong learning demonstrate the typical naive tendency to make no distinction among things called by the same name. Lifelong learning as a means of personal enrichment has a long history. There has been abundant evidence that a large proportion of mature adults do in fact continue to pursue such learning throughout life (AARP, 2000; Livingstone, 2000, p. 32). A survey conducted for the American Association of Retired People survey concluded, "Adults age 50 and older learn for the simple joy of learning, to enhance their spiritual or personal growth, and to keep up with what is going on in the world." Livingstone's survey of informal adult learning among a cross-section of adult Canadians showed similar engagement in learning for personal enrichment, but it also showed that two thirds of those in the labor force engaged in some kind of job-related informal learning, averaging 6 hours per week. It is important to distinguish the personal enrichment kind of learning from the economically motivated kind, not that the latter is more important but that different criteria apply. The fact that someone is pursuing learning for personal enrichment may be taken as evidence that the learning is serving its purpose, but for economically motived learning we have to ask whether it is successful. Are people actually learning what they need to learn and are they learning it fast enough to keep up with the pace of change? Are they facing new risks and challenges and rebuilding their competence in significant ways, or are they just watching PBS programs on technology? There is little reason to believe that educational agencies need to step in and do anything about the personal enrichment kind of lifelong learning, and there is equally little reason to believe that educational agencies have any idea of how to promote the second and more critical kind.

There are scholars who exhibit fondness for learning to an extreme degree, who always have their noses in an edifying book, yet who break into a cold sweat when told that they will have to put their course announcements on a web page. If it is difficult to learn boring subjects, it is even more difficult to learn frightening ones. Yet if people are really going to thrive in the Knowledge Age, they must be prepared to learn things that are boring, things that are difficult, things that are threatening to the ego, things that require going back and learning kid stuff, and things that they associate with people or positions they don't like. Furthermore, they should be prepared to do more than learn what is immediately relevant. They should be exploring the potentials of new knowledge, seeing what opportunities it may open for them (Bereiter & Scardamalia, 2000).

All things considered, the best preparation schools could provide for future learning is the broadest and deepest possible understanding of the world—of the three worlds, actually, as defined by Popper (1972). The deeper the understanding, the more likely it is to be helpful in understanding the next new thing. And understanding can have motivational benefits as well. We are less likely to be bored or frightened by things if we can make at least some connection between them and our understanding. Although teaching for deep understanding may not seem like an adequate prescription for the uncertainties of our rapidly changing world, it has to be judged against the alternatives. Most of what schools can do in the name of "learning to learn" and "lifelong learning" does not in any way address the problems brought about by rapid change. At best it is aimed at helping kids fare better in school—a worthy objective, but hardly what the futuristists are telling us we need.

UNLEARNING A LIVING

As the futuristic "just-in-time" mentality begins to invade the schools, we see educators being drawn even farther away from the pursuit of understanding. Instead, the typical American mistrust of book learning is amplified by the beliefs, trumpeted by digerati, that stored-up knowledge becomes quickly obsolete and that it constitutes an obstacle that must be overcome in new learning. Both of these beliefs are at least 80% wrong. Unfortunately, the 20% or less that is right is the part we are conscious of. The 80% is mostly unconscious. When new information runs smack against something we thought was true, we may take notice. When rejecting the old hurts, we know it. When an old habit keeps intruding on a new pattern of behavior (when we keep missing the new route home; when we keep calling Elizabeth Lizzy when she has made it clear that she can no longer tolerate that name) we tend to notice that too. We are also very much aware when people around us appear to be stuck in a rut or unable to give up a discredited belief. But we naturally take no notice of the vast amount of knowledge that is as good today as it was yesterday, or of the new learning that just happens, without pain or effort. Paradigm shifts are not a daily occurrence. Once in a lifetime is more like it. And even then, our chances of grasping the new paradigm if we have not grasped the old one are about nil.

When we encounter new information, we have no way of appreciating the wealth of prior learning that makes this new information comprehensible. But we should be aware of the times when new information is incomprehensible because we lack the necessary background knowledge. Such occasions are a daily occurrence for anyone who tries to keep up with what is going on in the world. They ought to make us cautious about disparaging the accumulation of knowledge.

Established habits of thought and action can either support or interfere with acquiring new skills. We sense the interference but are unconscious of the support, even though positive transfer is the rule and negative transfer the exception (Singley & Anderson, 1989). The experienced typist who had to learn word processing was hampered somewhat by the carryover of old typing habits and by thinking of the computer as a kind of typewriter (Carroll & Rosson, 1987). But imagine what it would have been like for Bob Cratchit if computers had suddenly appeared in Scrooge's counting house. He would not have known how to even start thinking about them.

The false dichotomy of new learning and old knowledge is captured in a much-quoted aphorism of Eric Hoffer (1973):

> In a time of drastic change, it is the learners who inherit the future. The learned usually find themselves equipped to live in a world that no longer exists. (Aphorism 32)

Hoffer, who was himself quite learned, should have known better. He was probably carried away by the neat turn of phrase. The truth is that what we already know is always both a help and a hindrance. The good and the bad of prior knowledge arise out of the reciprocal processes that Piaget (1929) called assimilation and accommodation. We are always assimilating new information to existing mental structures and at the same time accommodating existing structures to new information. Without assimilation we couldn't function; without accommodation we couldn't adapt. According to common-sense psychology and the artificial intelligence models based on it, assimilation is the normal thing and accommodation is exceptional. Normally we process new information according to existing rules or schemas. Only when there is trouble do we revise those rules or schemas (Schank, 1982). But according to the connectionist view of mind that I have been advocating, every mental event is a bit of both assimilation and accommodation—which is how Piaget saw it.

When a new situation arises the whole person responds. There is emotion—mild or intense; positive, negative, or more likely mixed. There is interpretation, conditioned by past experience and influenced by what aspects of past experience happen to be most alive at the time. Usually there will be other people responding to the new situation as well, and their responses will affect one another's. Where it happens, the physical surroundings, the other events that command attention—all of these combine to determine whether a person's response to a new situation will be one that, from a distant perspective, we would judge to be satisfactory. Everybody knows this, but its educational import is ignored when people start talking about learning skills, flexibility, and willingness to learn—talking about them as if they were subjects that could be taught in school.

These commonplace observations point to what has come to be called the "situatedness" of cognition and action (Suchman, 1987). Research on situatedness has looked into how people actually cope with the intellectual challenges of work and everyday life—challenges such as learning to use a sophisticated copying machine or doing comparison shopping in the supermarket. The overall effect of this research is to impress us with the resourcefulness of ordinary people and to lower our estimate of the practical value of school learning. For instance, people devise clever and efficient ways of working with quantities and prices that owe little to school mathematics. Although research on situated cognition casts doubt on the practical value of academic learning, it also offers little encouragement to those who would make schooling more practical. Whatever school is, it is one kind of situation. What is learned there will tend to work in that situation but will have doubtful utility in other situations.

So the dilemma intensifies: The learning that is required for competence in the Knowledge Age has to start early, in the elementary school if not before, but what that learning should consist of is rendered obscure both by uncertainties about the future and by increasing awareness of the limited practical value of school learning. In this light, the back-to-basics, liberal education, and developmentalist models of schooling begin to look good. There are a few basic skills that we know can be taught and that are certain to be useful, so schooling should ensure that those are learned. There is a body of knowledge that will not soon go out of date and there are works of literature, art, and music that will not soon cease to be valued. So an education that brings students into intimate association with these ought to be of value in their development as citizens, even if not in any more utilitarian way. And there is surely merit in trying to support healthy physical, social, intellectual, and emotional development. But that leaves us, as I observed before, with no educational wisdom that would distinguish these from earlier times.

SCHOOLING FOR A KNOWLEDGE SOCIETY

There are two recent developments in education that do address preparation for life in a knowledge society in ways that go beyond the traditional answers of back-to-basics, liberal education, and developmentalism and beyond the superficiality of futurism. These developments are

1. A new assault on the problems of teaching for understanding, and
2. The deliberate crafting of school cultures supporting work with knowledge.

Neither teaching for understanding nor the deliberate crafting of school cultures is new, of course. Teaching for understanding has been an objective of education from the time of Socrates. What is new is a heightened awareness of the importance of understanding, mounting evidence of the failure of schooling to produce it, and what look like genuine breakthroughs in ways of teaching for understanding (Bransford, Brown, & Cocking, 1999; Gardner, 1991). There is also a history of school cultures being crafted to support certain systems of values, such as those of the British ruling class, those of participatory democracy, and those of natural human development. What is new is the idea of a culture in which knowledge is central rather than incidental to other values.

The Economic Value of Understanding

Although the value of understanding has long been appreciated, it has been appreciated as a personal good. The pursuit of it, as Socrates taught, makes life worth living. Practical value, however, was thought to reside in skills, rules of thumb, and useful facts. This view survives in the back-to-basics mentality. One of the few arguments you will hear today against teaching for understanding is that, although it is undeniably a good thing, it must yield to the more urgent requirement of teaching skills that will lead to employment. You may lose a job because of inability to subtract 24 from 51, but you will not lose it because of inability to explain why you borrow a 1 from the 5 to do it.

It is difficult, although theoretically possible, to assign a dollar value to understanding. What we can say with some confidence, however, is that the dollar value of learning without understanding is declining. As microchips do more of the arithmetic, what remains for the human operator is to understand the problem and call for the right operations. As speech synthesizers convert printed words to spoken words, what is left is the problem of understanding the message, which depends on understanding the words and having the relevant background understanding. In the limit, it may turn out that the only knowledge-based functions that cannot be automated are those that require deep understanding. This is already becoming apparent, if you regard outsourcing as analogous to automation.

In principle, the dollar value of understanding could be estimated the same way economists estimate the dollar value of a college diploma: compare the earnings of those who have it with the earnings of those who do not, controlling statistically or experimentally for other factors. The problem, of course, is in deciding how to judge whether someone has it, which in turn depends on deciding what *it* is. Suppose, to make it simple, we decide to base our estimate of understanding on only one significant concept—say the Newtonian concept of force—tested by a variety of clever questions and problems and using some reasonable standard such that you do not have to be a physicist to earn a passing score. It is a safe bet that those who pass would on average have higher earnings than those who fail. The difference would probably be significant even after we control for all the obvious correlates, such as years of schooling. But does that mean that studying Newton will raise your income? Not as a rule. The test is just a marker, a diagnostic sign, of something much more general.

We could broaden our scope, testing understanding of a variety of concepts in different areas. This would give us a more precise estimate and ought to result in assigning an even higher dollar value to understanding. The estimated value would probably be higher yet if we were careful to target understanding of those concepts that are central to a discipline, that are the basis for further understanding—Newton's laws in physics, natural selection in biology, supply and demand in economics, the idea of a function in mathematics, and the idea of genre in literature. But we would still be wary of sug-

gesting that the economic value lay in those particular understandings or in any other particular understandings. What we could
reasonably infer, however, is that the *kind of person* who understands
such things has an economic advantage. We could also reasonably
suppose that you cannot be that *kind of person* unless you have pursued and achieved some understanding of the ideas that make further understanding possible.

Thus, there is both a content side and a dispositional side to understanding and both have economic value over and above their value in
constituting a mental life. There are important identifiable things to
be understood. They are conceptual artifacts (see chap. 3), the product of preceding generations' sustained efforts to understand the
world. Then there is being the kind of person who exerts such sustained effort. That is the dispositional side. The content side of understanding is well recognized and all but the most degenerate
schools deal with it in some way. However, they have been obliged to
deal with it on the basis of folk theories of knowledge and mind that,
as we saw in chapter 4, are inadequate.

Schooling As Acculturation

When companies outsource everything they can, what is left? Presumably what is left is the main wealth-producing work of the enterprise. In knowledge-based companies this consists of ill-
structured tasks in knowledge-rich domains. If a job can be well
specified and if the knowledge required to carry it out is of a generic
kind that can be acquired at school or by working anywhere in a particular occupation, the job is susceptible to outsourcing or to being
eliminated through automation. Central to productive thinking in
knowledge-rich domains is deep understanding of the task and of
the resources and conditions relevant to it.

There is a missing link, however, in the argument for teaching for
understanding. It is a link between the understanding that is acquired in school and the highly situated and task-specific kinds of
understanding that knowledge work requires. These are kinds of understanding that can only be acquired on the job. The best that
schooling could hope to do is equip people to acquire such knowledge. This is the consideration that leads people to start beating the
drum for thinking skills. But that does not solve the problem, it only
represents a different (and generally inferior) way of talking about
the same problem. For the thinking skills that make you an expert
have to be learned on the job too, and so we are still faced with the
question of what schooling could do to enhance people's ability to
acquire such skills.

DEFINING A ROLE FOR SCHOOLS

I suggest that one day we will have to revolutionize psychology by looking at the human mind as an organ for interacting with the objects of the third world; for understanding them, contributing to them, participating in them; and for bringing them to bear on the first world.

—Popper, 1972, p. 156

The rise of the Internet makes dramatic a trend that has been going on for well over a century. It is the school's loss of monopoly over knowledge transmission. Of course, schools never did have a monopoly over most kinds of knowledge transmission, and so we need to clarify what that limited monopoly has amounted to. Deferring that question (until chap. 9), however, let us just refer to the school's traditional stock-in-trade by the portmanteau term, "academic knowledge." The growth of public libraries weakened that monopoly, albeit for a small part of the population. Then came radio and television and now the Internet. Modern societies are full of organizations that store, process, and disseminate academic knowledge. Schools ought not to be clinging to the illusion that they are the whole game. They ought to be positioning themselves in such a way as to make use of other societal resources. Like other organizations that are "reinventing" themselves, they ought to identify what they can do uniquely well and concentrate on elevating that function.

The proposal that schools in a knowledge society should focus on what they can do best and what other institutions cannot do better may sound commonsensical, but it is by no means a self-evident precept. As the term *in loco parentis* reminds us, schools have many of the responsibilities of parents, and one would not get away easily with proposing such specialization for parents. There are all kinds of things parents have to do whether they do them particularly well or not, because the welfare of children demands it, and so may it be with schools. But in fact parents who can afford it do "outsource" a lot of their parenting, and in a well-functioning neighborhood or extended family parenting functions may be widely distributed, with different people contributing in ways that particularly suit them. "It takes a whole village to raise a child," according to an overworked proverb. It is this kind of distributed responsibility for bringing up the young that I am thinking about—not nostalgically but in the belief that, with the spread of knowledge work and with the possibilities of decentralization that telecommuting is already demonstrating, a whole new range of opportunities for the distribution of educational responsibilities will emerge (Scardamalia & Bereiter, 1996b). These possibilities have led some enthusiasts to imagine the disappearance of schools, with an Internet-based "global village" taking over the now completely decentralized educational mission. I think this is fantasy, but the reason it gets taken seriously is that we have not identified anything that schools are uniquely suited for other than baby-sitting.

Is there a core function or set of functions that schools could be stripped down to, outsourcing everything else? Back in the 1970s, in *Must We Educate?* (Bereiter, 1974), I argued that the core functions were custodial care and training in basic academic skills. "Education," in its grander sense, was to be left in the hands of parents, to be delegated in whatever ways they saw fit. That was proposed more as a thought experiment than as a feasible design. Evidently, for many educators who tried the thought experiment, the conclusion was that it would result in the end of civilization (Levine & Havighurst, 1971). It now seems, after several decades of tentative experimentation with voucher schemes and other forms of choice, that the result would be the rise of private schools, differing in curriculum and pedagogy, but playing the same many-faceted role that schools do now. Reconceptualizing the role of schools, therefore, does not seem to lie in that direction.

Custodial care remains a core function, which probably ensures that schools for the young will continue to be physical entities and will not dissolve into cyberspace. And providing a safe and healthy living environment is something that a surprising number of schools do surprisingly well, although it is the failures that make news. Beyond that, however, the role of schools is so broad and vague that the idea of narrowing down to a core function and concentrating on performing it well seems preposterous.

Let us therefore look at it the other way. What are functions of the common school that might be "off-loaded" as current jargon puts it? The most obvious is that of information supplier. The traditional expectation has been that the textbook and the teacher between them embody all the knowledge that is to be acquired in a course. That model can only be maintained today by suppressing inquiry. And with schools starting to provide access to the World Wide Web, the practical justifications for the model disappear. It may be argued that schools now have an additional responsibility, in enabling students to deal with the overabundance of information, but that is another matter; it could mean establishing strategic relationships between schools and various information suppliers, but it still means taking schools out of the information-supply business themselves.

Another venerable role of schools ready to fall before advancing technology is that of providing coached practice in cognitive skills. A random visit to a conventional elementary school is unlikely to happen on a lecture in progress or a discussion or any sort of inquiry. More likely, it will find students bent over their tables doing exercises of some kind—arithmetic problems, language skills worksheets, or other varieties of what is aptly called "seat work." Computers are unlikely to take over swimming instruction in the near future because the technology is not up to observing swimmers in the water and evaluating their strokes. Coaching requires monitoring process not just performance—otherwise you have a scorekeeper, not a coach. Classroom teachers are not actually able to provide much cognitive coaching, partly because of the pupil–teacher ratio (most coaching requires individual attention) and partly because teachers are untrained in it. Thus, they tend to be more practice supervisors and scorekeepers than coaches. Most of the skill-development software available to schools does not provide coaching either, but only more refined score keeping. However, the technology for cognitive coaching in mathematics is well advanced and has proven effective (Anderson, Corbett, Koedinger, & Pelletier, 1995). Computer coaching of basic reading processes is on the verge of practicality, now that speech-recognition technology is maturing, and coaching in the technical aspects of writing is also coming closer to practicality. Many educators are categorically opposed to cognitive skill training and would like to see it stricken from the schools. One way or the other, however, coached practice in skills seems a likely candidate for removal from the core functions of school teaching.

If you took away information transfer and skill practice, some schools would find their curriculum quite barren and for many others what remained would not look much like a serious educational program. At the same time, there are schools where such removal would go almost unnoticed. These are schools that practice some version of "open education" or "constructivist learning," in which the students spend almost all their time on projects or in conferences. Such schools, however, are liable to be among those coming under most attack for failure to address the "new economic realities"—that is, the perceived rising standards for employability and wealth creation.

Formal Education as Acculturation to World 3

After schools unburden themselves of information supply and coached practice, what they should be left with is freedom to concentrate on higher objectives. But what ought those objectives be? The futuristic literature, as I indicated, points to higher order thinking skills and traits. Even if one believes in the teachability of these things (but see chap. 10), they cannot realistically be put forth as something schools are ideally positioned to teach. Indeed, schools are uniquely ill-suited for it because of their isolation from real-world problems. Furthermore, thinking skills enthusiasts have almost all come around to thinking that such skills cannot be taught in isolation, through artificial exercises, but must be taught through work that has substance. So the question of what that work of substance should be remains to be answered.

The traditional idea of a liberal education, centering around classics and disciplines, provides a good starting point for considering what schools are actually suited to do. Almost everyone would credit liberal education with some virtues, and it generally requires schooling—that is, some kind of planned and managed program aimed at learning.[4] Accordingly, we may start with liberal education, as traditionally conceived, and ask what is required in addition or how the conduct of liberal education needs to be altered to meet today's challenges.

These matters start to become clearer if we drop the terms "liberal education" and "cultural transmission" and recast the central idea as follows: *The purpose for which formal education is uniquely suited is enculturation into World 3*. Most of the preceding text of this book has been directed toward making this an intelligible statement, and so I cannot be expected to start over and explain it from scratch here, but I will expand briefly on what these 14 words are and are not meant to say.

Note first that the statement refers to *formal* education. This is not a sharply defined category, but in most schools it is not difficult to distinguish the formal part of the school program from the informal. Usually the formal part is marked by some accountability on the part of students for learning and on the part of the teachers for producing that learning. In the informal part of the school program, which typically includes sports, arts, and performing groups, the focus is more on the doing than on the learning. John Dewey (1916) called "the method of keeping a proper balance between the informal and the formal ... one of the weightiest problems with which the philosophy of education has to cope" (p. 9). Central to solving that problem is determining what, if anything, formal education is peculiarly good for. I am suggesting *enculturation into World 3* as an answer.

World 3 is the world of artifacts that may be discussed as knowledge—theories, factual assertions, problem statements, histories, interpretations, and many other products of human thought. World 3

---

[4]There are, of course, examples of self-educated people. Eric Hoffer is a notable modern example; but it could be argued that such people are self-schooled. The autodictat or "self-educated man" most often appears in literature as a somewhat ridiculous figure, however (e.g., Sartre, 1964), characterized by smatterings of largely useless and often distorted knowledge. Snobbery apart, this tells us something important about the value of schools.

is not limited to accepted, verified, or important knowledge objects. It can include discredited theories, crank notions, unsolved problems, and new ideas that may or may not gather a following. In this respect World 3 is more inclusive than the canons of liberal education. This inclusiveness goes a long way toward eliminating the split between established knowledge and students' constructive efforts, because it places the ideas created by students in the same world as the ideas handed down from authoritative sources.

This brings us to *enculturation*.[5] To me, enculturation into World 3 means *joining the ranks of those who are familiar with, understand, create, and work with the conceptual artifacts of their culture*. It is tempting to shorten this statement by saying it means becoming part of the community of knowledge workers, but this implies a level of solidarity and shared identity that does not exist. An analogy would be joining the ranks of those who are familiar with, understand, work with, and make things out of rocks. These ranks would include rock hunters, geologists, quarriers, stonecutters, and masons. Such people do not constitute a single community but rather a set of interacting and partly overlapping communities. However, they share a good deal of knowledge and interest not shared by people outside their ranks; they would have things to talk about, ways of working together, made possible by their shared knowledge and interests. That is what may be expected as well of people who have had a good liberal education, and it is what I am trying to pin down in identifying World 3 as the basis.

Here is another analogy, which offers a different slant on what it means to be enculturated into World 3. In discussing shortcomings of the idea of mental content, I have referred to a kind of knowledge that consists of "knowing one's way around" in some domain. Suppose the domain is a large park, such as Yosemite National Park in California. Those who know their way around in this park do not constitute a coherent community. They do not live in the park, although their paths cross there from time to time. They have different knowledge and interests related to the park. Some are climbers; some are hikers; others are naturalists or artists. But, again, their mutual knowledge—their knowing their way around in the park and all that entails—affords them possibilities of productive interac-

---

[5]Whether to call it "enculturation" or "acculturation" is not entirely clear. As these terms are used by anthropologists, enculturation refers to assimilating the culture one is born into whereas acculturation refers to acquiring a different culture—as an immigrant, for instance. For the child born into a family where ideas are often the subject of dinner table conversation, "enculturation" would seem to be the word, whereas for the child who has never been exposed to intellectual discourse before encountering it at school "acculturation" is more appropriate. Merriam-Webster does not recognize "enculturation" but instead assigns both meanings to "acculturation."

tion not open to the casual visitor. Just so, knowing one's way around in the world of conceptual artifacts affords a wealth of possibilities not open to people who know that world only from a distance, if at all.

Painting with a wide brush, let us say that the World 3 students are to learn their way around in is that of the disciplines represented in a modern university (what those disciplines are, how they are practiced, what they treat as foundational—these of course vary from time to time and place to place and are often in dispute). Most university students, it must be granted, do not learn their way around in that world. They learn their way around in a small part of it. And many do not even do that. They take courses. They learn facts and advance their understanding of some aspect of the real world—its geography, economics, history, or whatever—and acquire some professional competence, but research indicates that many of them never become engaged with the problems of the disciplines they study (Entwistle & Ramsden, 1983). They may hardly make any contact with World 3 at all, their academic efforts being wholly occupied with acquiring learning (World 2) and dealing with the material world (World 1).

There are, however, students who come to university or college already enculturated to World 3 and generally knowing their way around in it, even though they still have a lot to learn. They know something of the classics and of what thinkers of the past were up to. They have a sense of history and a grounding in mathematics and science that extends beyond received knowledge to include some experience of really *doing* history, mathematics, and science. They have not just acquired itemizable knowledge. They have already joined, as novices, *the ranks of those who are familiar with, understand, create, and work with the conceptual artifacts of their culture.*

Regardless of how one might feel about the virtues and limitations of this kind of education, it would have to be acknowledged that enculturation to World 3 is something schools are structurally well suited for and that no other institution could do as well. The detachment of schools from the practical activities of life affords the opportunity for study and reflection. Their social organization affords opportunities for extended discourse, which is the engine of progress in World 3. The essential resources are books and other knowledge media, which schools are in a good position to provide.

Enlarging the Conception of Schooled Knowledge

I am acutely aware of how unfashionable my proposal is. Despite all the talk about a knowledge-based economy and a knowledge society, the idea of schooling being focused on knowledge sounds drab and out of date. Problem-based learning is fashionable, but the problems are never knowledge problems. Project-based learning is fashionable, but the project is never the construction of a knowledge object. A look through the curriculum materials and literature on so-called constructivist approaches to learning suggests it does not even occur to educators that what students set about constructing might be knowledge itself. This, I believe, is a consequence of folk theory of mind. It has no place for knowledge in the World 3 sense. Knowledge is either something in students' heads or it is something lodged in textbooks and multimedia documents, to be reconstructed internally. So one is always dealing with mental states, texts, physical phenomena, or social processes, never with knowledge as such. From this standpoint, a proposal that formal education should consist of enculturation to World 3 can mean little more than that students should acquire a lot of book learning—stored representations of the information contained in books. No wonder, then, that the proposal comes across as unexciting and anachronistic.

Enculturation to World 3 means a great deal more than learning what is in books, however. Enculturation to World 3 encompasses all six of the varieties of knowledgeability discussed in chapter 5:

1. *Statable knowledge.* This kind of knowledge, the "book learning" whose value is so suspect in some educational circles, is of course central to functioning in World 3. It is knowledge whose validity and significance can be critically discussed and that can be improved through such discussion. Enculturation into World 3 means participating in a school culture in which such knowledge is, in fact, continually under negotiation.

2. *Implicit understanding.* Implicit understanding of a conceptual artifact means in effect that it has become part of the way your mind works. You no longer have to remember and apply the idea of natural selection, for instance. It is integral to the way you think about intergenerational change in organisms. Thus, when you read that natural selection takes place among the cells in a cancer, thereby making the cancer as a whole increasingly resistant to chemotherapy, this discomforting fact is instantly comprehensible. Implicit understanding does not negate the importance of statable knowledge, however. Evolutionary theory keeps advancing and what you learned in school about survival of the fittest may no longer be tenable. Important revisions of implicit understanding can descend from changes in statable knowledge.

3. *Episodic knowledge*. Episodic knowledge is the stock of remembered experiences we call on to suggest what to do in the present. School experience is generally not rich in episodes that have practical application in the world at large; that is what the College of Hard Knocks specializes in. But formal education can provide certain kinds of episodic knowledge that are important to the educated person and that are not readily acquired elsewhere. Clear and striking demonstrations of scientific principles are one such kind. Science museums, of course, provide these as well, and with better production values, but those that occur in school have a better chance of occurring at the right time, when students are actively engaged with the underlying questions, so that the episodes become more memorable and interpretable. Not to be discounted is episodic knowledge gained from fiction, biography, and history. Memorable episodes from these sources can function much like personally experienced episodes, especially when it comes to making moral and life-changing decisions. Other important episodic knowledge may concern arguments or discussions, the recall of which helps in the reconstruction of partly forgotten principles and lines of thought.

4. *Impressionistic knowledge*. This is knowledge in the form of hunches and feelings. To the extent that students are engaged in creating or improving conceptual artifacts, they rely, as creative people always must, on impressionistic knowledge that points them in promising directions. The same is true in thinking critically about received ideas. Everything starts vaguely, with an intuition that something is interesting, promising, on the right track, or somehow wrong, and firmer knowledge develops from there. In the conventional view, the acquisition of established knowledge is quite different. It comes to us in the form of clear propositions: Columbus discovered America in 1492, for every action there is an equal and opposite reaction, and so on. The only vagueness arises from the learner's lack of clear understanding. But if the constructivist premise is true (and no one has suggested a way in which it could be false), the initial vague intuition is all there is to start with. Learners have to build conceptual knowledge the same way scientists do, by following promising leads (more about this in the next chapter).

5. *Skills*. As with getting around in a physical environment, getting around in World 3 involves a multitude of skills. There are the cognitive skills involved in reading and research and the social skills involved in argumentation and collaborative problem solving. In a conventional curricular approach, one would try to item-

ize, teach, and test these skills, but that is not the direction implied by the idea of enculturation. Instead, we may assume a whole constellation of skills that develop through working in World 3 and only single out for attention those that prove problematic.
6. *Regulative knowledge.* Included here are all the habits that develop through working in knowledge domains and the norms of conduct and judgment that characterize different disciplines, some of which hold across disciplines. What constitutes an adequate explanation or a proof? What constitutes a novel idea as against a different way of representing an old idea? What is fair use of another person's work and what is plagiarism?

Enculturation, of course, involves more than can be captured in any list of elements. As with enculturation into a profession or a tribe, it involves the whole personality. The preceding list is only meant to convey the range of worthwhile learnings that may occur—all but the first category of which tend to be ignored in the conventional curriculum and to go unrecognized in discussions of educational alternatives. The range of learnings should not be overestimated, however. Even with a very wide-ranging curriculum and careful attention to all the varieties of learning, school learning can still make up only a very small part of the knowledge required to be a fully functioning member of adult society.

To overcome the limitations of school learning, there have been repeated efforts to bring more of the world into the school or to get students out into the world—in short, to make schools less academic. Whatever the merits of these efforts (and they have varied widely), they make it even less clear what schools might be best suited for. It is as if the ideal would be no school at all, just children growing up in society. Schools then become little more than a concession to practical requirements (much as it is with prisons) and the educational challenge is to make the best of an unfortunate necessity.

My proposal, consistent with proposals of Kieran Egan (1997) and Howard Gardner (1999), is the opposite. Instead of trying to make schools less academic, let us look more deeply into what "academic" could mean and see if there is some core virtue that could be more fully realized. This is not to preclude field trips, work-study programs, or any other departure from the walled-in curriculum. It is only to try to pin down kinds of educational activity that schools are uniquely suited for, as distinct from the activities introduced to make up for schools' inadequacies.

That core activity, what I have called "enculturation into World 3," may be put into more familiar terms. The core activity of schooling throughout the elementary and secondary school years should be *to help students build a comprehensive and coherent understanding of the world*. Building such an understanding of the world was Aristotle's project and it remains the project of every thoughtful person growing up. It is a constructive project *par excellence*. Young people must do it for themselves; it cannot be done for them. Schools typically both help and hinder this project. They help by exposing students to the wealth of what is already known. They hinder by interposing all kinds of well-intended but often diversionary "learning activities." How schooling could help more and hinder less is the topic of later chapters. For now the issue is whether this is an adequate conception of the core function of schooling. In particular, is it adequate preparation for life in a knowledge-based economy?

LARGE-D AND SMALL-d DIVERSITY

Any attempt to define a role for schools quickly runs into two clusters of controversial social issues. One cluster of issues has to do with diversity. Another, which I take up in the next section, has to do with equity and elitism, boiling down to the question of whether enculturation into World 3 is being foisted on the masses for the benefit of the minority who will go into professional and managerial occupations.

"Diversity," like "equity," has become a mantra and lost most of its meaning. Whenever a single objective is proposed for all students, alarm bells go off in many educators' minds, warning them that some kind of diversity is in danger. In its naive form, the worry is about schools becoming cookie-cutters that turn out students who are all alike. If there is anything to this fear (and history would suggest there is very little), it ought to be allayed by teaching for understanding. It is ignorance and rote learning that oblige people to act alike; understanding frees people to go their own way.

More sophisticated concerns include the following: that "understanding," as advocated by mainstream psychologists and science educators, is a particular kind of understanding favored by Western science—abstract, rational, contemptuous of traditional and commonsense knowledge; that an exclusively intellectual approach is being advocated, to the exclusion of feelings; and that individual cognitive styles and ways of learning are being swept aside in favor of purely verbal and logico-mathematical skills. All of these warrant extended discussion, but the main point here is that they can be discussed *within* a general commitment to teaching for understanding. It is not predetermined that the kind of understanding to be pursued is that of mainstream science; there is plenty of room for intuition and feeling (see the discussion of impressionistic knowledge in chap. 5). As for individual styles, varieties of intelligence, and the like, we need to be clear whether we are talking about different ways of pursuing understanding or whether we are talking about understanding as an option suitable for certain kinds of students and not others. Only in the latter case is there a critical issue, which I take up in the next section.

That, said, however, I think educators must face up to the fact that teaching for understanding is not culturally neutral. If it is to be undertaken seriously and in the light of a modern conception of understanding, it is strong stuff. It is not about hatching baby chicks or showing off artifacts from your parents' homeland—although such things may go on as part of an inquiry. It is about the relentless effort to improve on existing knowledge. That is not a culturally neutral idea. The advancement of knowledge is a modern notion and it goes against the grain of both premodern and postmodern beliefs. The idea comes easily to today's students, because it is all around them in a culture where progress is the normal expectation. It doesn't have to be taught. The improvability of understanding is implicit in the practice of knowledge building in the same way the improvability of musical performance is implicit in the practice of band rehearsal. But the inevitable result (and by inevitable I mean that it happens whether the teacher presses for it or not) is gravitation toward a kind of mainstream rationality and toward beliefs that stand up under that kind of rational process. The only way to prevent it is by suppressing or subverting inquiry (Bereiter et al., 1997):[6]

> We may freely admit that there are other ways of knowing— through art, myth, and religion—and that these address important human needs, but they cannot possibly address the endless flow of *why* and *how* questions that will occur in any modern elementary school classroom where they are allowed to flourish. There is no alternative biology that explains what bruises are, how you can resemble your aunt more than you do your mother, why mosquitoes do not transmit AIDS, and why your nose runs when you have a cold. (p. 330)

---

[6]A standard complaint about schools is that teachers suppress inquiry by requiring memorization of textbook facts. With the younger generation of teachers, however, one is more likely to find that inquiry is subverted rather than suppressed. It is subverted by a kind of namby-pamby relativism that glorifies personal belief, discounts authority, and throws a cloud of indeterminacy around everything. This approach can be more deleterious than the old one, because it provides an easy way to avoid trying to solve knowledge problems. I fear that may be why it has caught on so well among university undergraduates and education professors.

The likely effect of opening school doors to the pursuit of understanding is a decline in what I call large-D diversity, that is, diversity at the level of culturally distinct bodies of belief and ways of knowing. All schooling—indeed, any kind of inclusive social activity—tends to have this effect, and so it would be astonishing if teaching for understanding were an exception. The positive side is that, with students actively and cooperatively engaged in building an understanding of the world, there is an enlarged possibility for them to work out a relationship to conceptual artifacts that is compatible with their personal and cultural bents. This is one reason why it is useful for educators to think of knowledge as having this artifactual character rather than as things stowed in people's minds. It makes it realistic to consider cultural and personal variations in ways of relating to the same objects. That seems to me a more promising way of dealing with diversity than the romantic way it is generally treated in schools, which has it that every culture houses its own precious store of ideas that are sufficient unto that culture and should in no ways be meddled with. Assimilating the radio into a culture may involve some stresses, but it has been done successfully the world around, without Arabs ceasing to be Arabs or Sumatrans ceasing to be Sumatrans. Why should assimilating a conceptual artifact be that different? Should adopting a biological theory that works better than a traditional one be categorically worse than adopting the snowmobile to replace the dogsled? Perhaps so, but it should be apparent that educators have no more business legislating on these matters than bureaucrats would have deciding that the Inuit must be protected from the snowmobile.

Large-D diversity is diversity defined over very large categories—gender, race (with this variable sometimes reduced to only two categories, people of color and the rest), ethnicity, the five senses (used to categorize people according to their preferred sensory channel for learning), or the multiple intelligences (currently numbering seven or eight). These are important kinds of diversity, and for various reasons they are looming larger and larger in educational policymaking. At the same time, however, their significance in the actual business of the world—their economic significance, broadly defined—is declining. Furthermore, they tend to overshadow what I call small-d diversity, the economic significance of which is beginning to count as never before.

The Declining Importance of Large-D Intellectual Diversity

There was a time when intellectual diversity was treated entirely in terms of differences in IQ or general academic intelligence. Since the early 1970s, however, a virtual holy war has been waged against this practice and the ideas associated with it, so that the very word "intelligence" could not for some years be uttered safely in educational circles. Now, thanks largely to the work of Howard Gardner, the word may be heard again, but almost exclusively in its plural form. Drawing on a wide range of evidence, Gardner (1983) proposed seven distinct kinds of intelligence (recently increased to eight). Gardner pointed out that schools typically concentrate on only two of these—verbal-linguistic and logical-mathematical intelligence—ignoring or relegating to extracurricular activities the exercise of visual-spatial, musical-rhythmic, bodily-kinesthetic, interpersonal, and intrapersonal types of intelligence.

All of these kinds of ability are of obvious value. Each has its geniuses. For each of them there are occupations that depend on that particular ability. And so Gardner's suggestion that schools should broaden the range of abilities they attempt to cultivate appears on its face to be quite reasonable. But are these "intelligences" of equal social value? Assuming that trade-offs would have to be made, is it a good idea for schools to reduce the amount of verbal-linguistic and logical-mathematical activities to make room for the other varieties? In economic terms, at least, there is an unmistakable trend toward increasing importance of verbal-linguistic and logical-mathematical abilities and a corresponding decline in importance of most of the other abilities. The expanding job market is for those who qualify as what former Secretary of Labor Robert Reich (1992, p. 302) called "symbolic analysts." At the same time, technology is reducing the need for various special skills and replacing them by a general ability to work with programmable devices, an ability that is again largely symbolic—verbal-linguistic and logical-mathematical, in Gardner's terms. Of course, interpersonal skills are still important, but probably no more so than at other times in the history of the species, and it would be hard to claim that intrapersonal intelligence (wisdom in the conduct and cognizing of one's own life) counts for more now than it did in times that saw the rise of the great world religions. The "intelligences" whose importance in the working world seems to be declining are those that Gardner labeled visual-spatial, bodily-kinesthetic, and musical-rhythmic.

I first wrote about this in 1969, taking photography as an example: "Whereas the photographer once needed the ability to judge depths and levels of illumination accurately to take a clear picture, he can now be quite deficient in these abilities providing he is intelligent enough to use his equipment properly" (Bereiter, 1969, p. 311). More striking now is the way image-processing software enables anyone who can master its complex functions to create photographic effects that previously took consummate skill in the dark-room—if they could be achieved at all. Of course, to be a great photographer you still need the special kind of visual-spatial intelligence that Alfred Stieglitz had, but Stieglitz also needed a number of other abilities that his present-day counterpart can do without. The limiting factor now amounts to symbolic analysis—how able one is to grasp, hold in mind, and translate into behavior the information contained in a large manual.

The same shift can be observed wherever technology has taken hold, and that includes just about everything from baking bread to flying an airplane. Shoshana Zuboff (1988) has documented the shift in the work of a pulp mill. Whereas earlier the pulp makers took handfuls of pulp coming out of the mill and relied on their feel to adjust the process, today they stand in front of a computer screen and analyze numerical data coming from sensors. There are really two trends, however. One is a general deskilling, which means that tasks that once required special talent and training can now be done by anyone (or no one at all, in the case of automated tasks). The other is an increase in the customizability and flexibility of tools, which puts additional power into the hands of those with the ability to master and use them. And more and more those abilities are intellectual ones. The prime example, as I anticipated in 1969, is the personal computer. Interfaces keep getting simpler to allow more and more people to use computers, and computers are gradually eliminating the peripheral skills needed for competence in a domain. With spelling checkers, for instance, you no longer need to be able to spell to produce socially acceptable writing. At the same time, however, computation is putting increasing power in the hands of those who can comprehend instruction manuals and reason out applications to their purposes. Virtually every high-tech tool reduces the range of skills needed to accomplish tasks and puts more power into the hands of those with the general intellectual abilities that psychometricians identify as *g* or, more notoriously, as IQ.

This is bad news for multiple intelligences advocates, because it suggests schools have been correct in focusing on verbal-linguistic and logical-mathematical abilities and that diversifying to a wider range of intelligences is the right strategy for the wrong century. Of course, there are still going to be artists, musicians, poets, and dancers, whose skills are distinctive and not interchangeable, and practical competence and social skills show no signs of diminishing in importance. But none of that alters the significance of the fact that the bulk of the world's work is coming under the control of people who can read, figure, and reason.

What this analysis suggests to me, however, is not that intellectual diversity is passé but that it needs to be conceived of in much finer terms than the broad categories of Gardner's seven or eight intelligences. Moving from one kind of intelligence to seven or eight may be a refinement, but we are still in the realm of large-D diversity. Perhaps the most serious drawback of education's increasing emphasis on large-D diversity—whether in the form of multiculturalism or of multiple intelligences—is that it takes attention away from a kind of intellectual diversity that actually is rising in importance. This is small-d diversity, to be found within the verbal and logical constellation rather than outside it.

The Value of Small-d Intellectual Diversity

Small-d diversity is perhaps easiest to recognize in the arts. Large-D diversity in the arts comprises differences between cultures, epochs, schools, and movements. It is much of what art history is about. Small-d diversity has to do with differences—mainly individual differences—within these larger categories. One of the great things about art is that even within the most rigidly prescribed forms the hand of the individual artist can be discerned. Were it not thus, art would be pretty boring. For that matter, it is pretty boring for those who cannot discriminate at a small-d level.

Similar diversity can be found in intellectual realms. There is large-D diversity, to be sure. Many people boldly confess to being mathematical morons. Although self-proclaimed deficiencies in general verbal intelligence are much rarer, we probably recognize them among our acquaintances—unless we have been heavily indoctrinated against doing so. But from day to day we are likely to be more struck by subtler differences. Certain differences appear everywhere—the person who is good with details versus the one who has the big picture; the logical reasoner versus the intuitive leaper; the one with lots of knowledge versus the one with lots of questions. But if you press further you will get to finer differences. Observe what happens in a group working on a problem. One person introduces a distinction that changes how others see their task; one puts everything into a useful chart; another brings in an illuminating analogy; one draws people back to an idea that had been passed over. In each case the contribution might have been made by someone else but it is no accident that it comes from whom it does. Each person has a history within which their particular contribution forms part of an intellectual pattern. Thus, there is diversity and it does not take a magnifying glass to see it, but it does have to be viewed close up. It is not discernible from the Olympian heights of theories of intelligence.

The result of this small-d kind of diversity is an increase in collective intelligence. Put together a lot of these subtly different minds and you have a capacity for creativity and problem solving that cloning of the best single mind could not achieve. Although the value of this kind of diversity is probably recognized and appreciated by practically everyone, it is not what diversity has been about in schools and we know very little about how to nurture it. The following are only attempts at reasonable conjecture, with no research and little theory behind them: Not every kind of mentality contributes to the collective intelligence. People who are immune to reason, for instance, may be expected to bring down the intellectual level of every group they join, and when empowered they can become dangerous fanatics. Intellectual diversity of useful kinds develops through people working to solve problems, finding and honing talents and habits that work particularly well for them. Although the solitary genius may not be altogether a myth, people's distinctive intelligences are almost always developed interactively. It is a matter of finding one's niche in an intellectual ecosystem and evolving rapidly in accordance with the potentialities of that niche.

To have a culture that can reliably produce inventions and discoveries, you need not seven but thousands of subtly different varieties of talent encountering different helpful experiences and opportunities. There are going to be many potential Darwins and Edisons who never do anything remarkable because what they learn does not fit their talents or because the opportunities to reveal what they are capable of never arise. George Eliot (1871/1965) wrote about this at a time when merely being born female was sufficient to rule out a vast range of possibilities. Describing St. Theresa as one who overcame this handicap, Eliot went on to say,

> Many Theresas have been born who found for themselves no epic life wherein there was a constant unfolding of far-resonant action; perhaps only a life of mistakes, the offspring of a certain spiritual grandeur ill-matched with the meanness of opportunity; perhaps a tragic failure which found no sacred poet and sank unwept into oblivion. With dim lights and tangled circumstance they tried to shape their thought and deed in noble agreement; but after all, to common eyes their struggles seemed mere inconsistency and formlessness; for these later-born Theresas were helped by no coherent social faith and order which could perform the function of knowledge for the ardently willing soul. (Eliot, 1871/1965, p. 25)

If I understand what Eliot meant by a "coherent social faith and order which could perform the function of knowledge for the ardently willing soul," she was defining what a society must provide if it is to foster the proliferation of genius that everyone is looking for today. We must not rely on the rare match of talent, learning, and opportunity. The diversity of all three must increase if more favorable matches are to occur. But they must increase within a social order that provides developmental pathways leading to these fortunate matches and onward from there to accomplishments. A certain level of chaos may be desirable. George Eliot's 19th-century village England was too organized, especially for women. In some American inner cities there is so much chaos that virtually the only developmental pathways available (apart from athletics and music for the exceptionally talented) are those maintained by organized crime and gangs. Schools, too, can be so highly regimented that they provide only a few developmental pathways or, in the manner of some schools in which project-based learning runs amok, they may be so chaotic as to offer no developmental paths at all. Nothing leads anywhere.

If these conjectures are right, and they are so close to truisms that I do not think they can be altogether wrong, they provide a fairly definite direction for education to take. It is the direction I have already laid out in arguing for education as enculturation into the world of conceptual artifacts. By doing real work in the world of knowledge problems and ideas, students have a chance to develop their individual intellectual strengths. By doing a goodly part of this work collaboratively, they develop strengths that complement and work well with the strengths of others. The aim of intellectual diversity of course requires that the paths of knowledge building not be rigidly limited—certainly not limited to bookish study. There ought to be opportunities and encouragement for the kind of person who thinks best by building things and trying them out—building models, simulations, scenarios, or whatever. What we do not want to see, however, is the literate students reading, acting out, and discussing Shakespeare while the nonreaders build a cardboard model of the Globe Theatre (as I saw happening in a progressive school in London). We want to help students develop their distinctive ways of contributing to knowledge work, not sort themselves at an early age into knowledge workers and nonknowledge workers.

IS WORLD 3 FOR EVERYONE?

In education circles, as elsewhere, there is much talk about the partitioning of the work force into a highly paid minority of knowledge workers and a vast population employed, if at all, in low-level service occupations. What is not talked about is the implication this prospect has for education. Jeremy Rifkin's *The End of Work* (1995) is perhaps the best known of the alarmist works on this topic. The last fourth of Rifkin's book is devoted to healthy ways society could adapt to the decline of jobs, but there is no mention of schools and education.

Although economic predictions are always uncertain, educational policies ought not to be based on only the rosiest of predictions. One part of the schools' job is clear, and that is the only part discussed. It is, for that matter, the only part I have discussed up to this point. The schools must do all they can to ensure that everyone has a chance. To put it negatively, which is perhaps the more accurate way, the people who end up in the ranks of the jobless or the menial must do so through no fault of the education system. That cannot be said today. Indeed, it represents a formidable educational challenge. But is it the whole challenge as far as education and jobs are concerned?

How schools should prepare for the "postmarket era," as Rifkin called it, is a very large problem that needs a great deal of study and experimentation. It is also a problem well beyond the scope of this book, except in one respect: Is the focus on knowledge building that I have been arguing for irrelevant or possibly detrimental to the mass of students who will not end up as knowledge workers? Have I, in fact, been proposing an education geared to (a) training the elite class of knowledge workers and (b) sorting out who will and will not get into that class?

Our schools must produce high-level knowledge workers. Otherwise we will not have the wealth-producing capacity to do anything about burgeoning social problems. Training inevitably leads to sorting, because inevitably some students will demonstrate more promise than others.[7] My argument has been that schools are poorly equipped for the job of producing high-level knowledge workers. The poorer the job they do, the more sorting will be based on what students bring to school with them, and this means the perpetuation of existing inequalities. So, yes, schooling needs to be unabashedly committed to educating what will very likely constitute an elite class. But it does not follow that such education need be irrelevant or detrimental to those who will make up the rest of the population.

There are several grounds for arguing that an education centered on the construction of understanding is the right kind of education for people regardless of whether they end up as high-level knowledge workers or as low-level service providers. Appreciating these grounds requires, however, giving up the stereotype that equates

---

[7]It should be needless to say that eliminating tests or grades will not eliminate meritocracy. However, a well-known political novel, *The Rise of the Meritocracy* (Young, 1961), popularized just that fallacy and it remains firmly intrenched in left-wing educationist thinking.

low occupational status with squalor and inactivity. If, indeed, a declining need for labor in the private and public sectors becomes a fact of life, things will start to happen—are already starting to happen. The question is whether those most affected by the decline will have an active, constructive role in what happens or whether they will be its inert beneficiaries or victims, as the case may be.

1. There will be political activity, which may range from Luddism to adventurous economic schemes to revolution. Unions probably still represent the most effective counterforce to market pressures that eliminate jobs and drive down pay rates (Aronowitz & Cutler, 1977). But union policies have to be sophisticated ones that take account of what Krugman (1999) characterized as the fragility of national economies in the present era. That is, the policies will have to look beyond the survival of the particular company or industry that is the focus of workers' action. The better educated the workers the better the chances of success.
2. Eventually social forms and customs will evolve that make life livable for most people. Something will evolve that constitutes the "normal" and that people may simply grow up in without thinking much about it. But there is bound to be a transitional period—and the urban zones of high unemployment may already be in it—when old forms and customs have broken down and new ones that will make life livable again have not yet taken shape. During that transitional period, which may last a long time if conditions keep changing, people will have to work at making lives for themselves. They must find ways to make life meaningful, when old bases for meaning such as jobs no longer serve that purpose. I referred earlier to the idea of career craft, the creative working out of a career that takes maximum advantage of one's personal assets and that is optimally adapted to some occupational niche. The need for career craft will be even greater for those who must find a niche outside established occupations. Thus, the arguments in an earlier section for education that fosters intellectual diversity are highly applicable to joblessness.
3. Rifkin (1995) argued persuasively for developing what he called the third sector, distinct from the familiar public and private sectors. The third sector is composed of formal and informal nonprofit organizations, sustained by a spirit of voluntarism. According to Rifkin, this sector in the United States is already half the size of the federal government in jobs and income. It offers a way to channel human capital no longer needed in the public and private sectors into the improvement of society. This need not be shovel and broom labor. There are possibilities for all kinds of rewarding

work, but it is work that needs to be motivated by something more than economic interest. Here a serious obstacle looms. Robert B. Putnam (1996), through acknowledging the economic growth of the third sector, has documented a steep decline over the post-World War II decades in "social capital" and civic engagement. Social capital he defined as "features of social life—networks, norms, and trust—that enable participants to act together more effectively to pursue shared objectives" (Par. 2). He showed there has been an intergenerational shift. The voluntary sector is maintained by people whose formative years came before 1970. The younger cohorts are not aging into civic engagement. Thus, the social capital for the kind of cultural transformation that Rifkin urged seems to be running out. According to Putnam's research, education is an important correlate and presumably an important motivator of civic engagement, which is necessary to make the third sector a viable possibility.

4. We must get over the idea that the life of the mind is relevant only to the elite. It has not always been that way. Many people of my parents' generation were intellectuals even though they did manual work and had little formal education. They read books and liked to talk about ideas. It was only with the rapid postwar expansion of the middle class that people with intellectual inclinations could reliably find jobs that were also intellectually engaging. Now that is again ceasing to be the case. Education, accordingly, would do well to reset its values so that having a rich mental life becomes an educational purpose on a par with achieving employability.

In short, there are ample reasons why enculturation into a knowledge-building society is important for all students, not only those who will work with ideas professionally. The reasons all have to do with ensuring full membership in society regardless of occupational status. I must emphasize I am not arguing for an exclusively intellectual education. The prospect of a declining need for labor is grounds for heightening our concern with well-roundedness in education. But the academic curriculum is bound to continue occupying a large part of school time. That is the part that needs to be revolutionized, and it needs to be revolutionized for everyone.

CONCLUSION: WHERE THIS ARGUMENT IS HEADING

Before we can go much further in articulating what enculturation into World 3 would consist of—before I can even make a very persuasive case for the general idea—a number of related ideas have to be developed in greater depth. One of these, an idea that is crucial to advancing educational thought beyond where folk theory of knowledge and mind can take it, is a distinction between *learning* (which is a World 2 phenomenon) and *knowledge building* (which may be thought of as taking place in World 3). The next chapter is devoted to those concepts. Also central to any consideration of the role of formal education is the concept of *subject matter*. Traditionally, subject matter has been the stuff handed down from the academic disciplines to the not overly receptive young. If we are to regard students as active participants in the world of knowledge, the idea of subject matter needs to be not rejected, as some enthusiasts of constructivism would have it, but seriously rethought. That is the focus of chapter 9.

Besides the acquisition of subject matter, enculturation into World 3, as I have already indicated, entails a constellation of skills and dispositions relevant to working with knowledge. There is a strongly held opinion among many people, including not only educators but distinguished scientists and captains of industry, that these are what really count—that teaching students to think is the main task for schools and that subject matter is at best a vehicle for and at worst an impediment to the teaching of thinking. This is an issue that reveals folk psychology at its worst. In chapter 10 I try to retrieve thinking from the dreamland of folk psychology and resituate it in the real world of human activity, where what people know has a powerful influence on how they think.

With that groundwork done, we can then turn to the profession of education itself—not just teaching, but the whole system of governance, administration, research, publishing, and teacher education that combine to constitute the education profession in its full sense. The question I pursue in chapter 11 is whether this unwieldy system, resting on a foundation of solitary teachers practicing a traditional craft, can become a modern profession. Modernization, I argue, will require a radical transformation based on the fusing of what are now two separate cultures, the research culture and the practitioner culture. The final chapter, chapter 12, deals with more immediate issues of reform, where I argue that instructional reform is being impeded and subverted by conceptual limitations that are not the fault of any particular group of players but are common to all the sectors that converge on instructional reform.

Putting Learning
in Its Proper Place

When Marlene Scardamalia and I started using the term "knowledge building" around 1987, we had never encountered it before.[1] A decade later, "knowledge building" was in common use, but like many terms in popular educational discourse, its meaning had become degraded. It became merely a synonym for learning, a term to be used when one wants to add a constructivist flourish to whatever one is saying about that well-worn topic. We saw it as something different, although it took several years to work out the nature of the difference. In fact, the concept is still evolving, as ought to be the case with concepts that are meant to be of service in an advancing field of practice.

The main burden of this chapter is to establish a workable distinction between learning and knowledge building. This is not a hair-splitting distinction. It marks off two importantly different kinds of activities that can go on in schools. Ideally, they should be complementary. But by failing to distinguish between them, educa-

---

[1]Our first public use of the term was in a paper titled "Schools as Knowledge-Building Communities," presented by Scardamalia in 1989 at a workshop on Development and Learning Environments, University of Tel Aviv, Tel Aviv, Israel (Scardamalia & Bereiter, 1989).

tors fail to do full justice to either one and get into needless turmoil through trying to do both in the same way. Or else they make a distinction but make it wrongly, equating "learning" with "rote learning" and "knowledge building" with "meaningingful" or "authentic learning." Both learning and knowledge building ought to be meaningful. Whether knowledge building is "authentic" depends on what is being built.

To head off one potential misunderstanding, we must note at the start that learning accompanies all conscious activity. Therefore, learning necessarily accompanies knowledge building. But this does not make them the same thing. Learning occurs while setting out garbage, too, but we do not conclude from this that learning and setting out garbage are synonymous. The learning that accompanies everything we do does not figure in the distinction I am proposing. Rather, the distinction is between activities carried out *for the purpose* of learning and activities carried out for this other purpose that we call knowledge building.

For those who have tracked the discussion in preceding chapters about World 2 and World 3, there is a quick way to distinguish learning from knowledge building. Learning is activity directed toward World 2. It is doing something to alter the state of your mind to achieve a gain in personal knowledge or competence. Knowledge building is activity directed toward World 3. It is doing something to a conceptual artifact. Popper (1972, pp. 140–141) offered a sample list of actions that a scientist might take toward such abstract objects. It includes thinking of alternatives, thinking of criticisms, proposing experimental tests, deriving one object from another, proposing a problem, proposing a solution, and criticizing the solution. Popper contrasted the kinds of items on this list with psychological states such as knowing, mistakenly believing, or doubting some knowledge object. Those are World 2 phenomena and belong with learning rather than with knowledge building.

If you happened upon a scientist or scholar at work and asked, "What are you doing?" you might expect an answer along the lines of the statements in Popper's list. On occasion, however, you might get a different kind of answer, something like the following:

"I'm trying to learn how to use this new stats program."

"I'm brushing up on my Spanish for a conference in Caracas."

"I'm rereading Dewey."

In these instances, the scientist or scholar has taken time out from normal knowledge-building work to learn something. It may be learning something essential to getting on with the work, such as using a new software application, or learning something incidental, like some useful foreign phrases, or acquiring background knowledge for no very specific purpose.

In the ordinary run of affairs, the distinction between learning activities and knowledge-building activities is not clear-cut. In reading a journal in your field, you may read some articles just for background knowledge—to "keep up with your field." Others you may mine for specific information or ideas to use in the advancement of your work. You may start reading with a learning purpose in mind, then notice something significant that causes you to shift into a knowledge-building mode. This is no cause to reject the distinction. We often have mixed motives, and we often try to make one action serve more than one purpose. This does not detract from but rather adds to the value of distinguishing one purpose from another.

DISTINGUISHING KNOWLEDGE BUILDING FROM LEARNING IN THE CLASSROOM

In the preceding section we distinguished learning from knowledge building in the activities of people whose main work is knowledge building. It becomes trickier but more important to our purposes to distinguish them in the activities of people whose main work is learning—namely, students. When we move into the schooling context, a further distinction becomes relevant: the distinction between being engaged in learning and being engaged in a learning activity.

Consider a fifth-grade class discussing the brain, students having read something about it or seen a video. Certain propositions are advanced by students and contested by others. Occasionally a student raises a question. Sometimes the teacher will answer, but more often will turn it back to the class. The teacher does quite a bit of calling on students who have not contributed: "Mandy, what do you think about that?" "How many of you agree?" The teacher will also ask questions to turn the discussion to neglected points: "Does the brain have anything to do with breathing and heart beats and things like that?" If the point is a minor one, the teacher may accept the first more-or-less adequate answer or may quickly supply an answer if none is forthcoming. On other, more major points, the teacher may solicit a number of opinions and will not leave the point until an acceptable answer has been established and the dissenting opinions have been dealt with.

What is going on here? From the point of view of the teacher, this is what is customarily and appropriately called a "learning activity." Whatever other values might be attributed to it, the success of the discussion will ultimately be judged by its impact on the beliefs and knowledge of individual students. Thus, the locus of the discourse for the teacher is World 2, the contents of individual minds. Among the students, however, there are likely to be a variety of points of view on what is going on. For present purposes let us ignore those students who do not actually participate, who may be daydreaming or dozing, and those who see the activity as an opportunity for clowning around or bullying, and consider only those students who appear to be seriously engaged in the activity. Though outwardly similar, they may have importantly different points of view on the discussion. Research by Evelyn Ng (Ng & Bereiter, 1991)[2] distinguished three kinds of goals that distinguished three different kinds of student orientation:

1. *Task-completion goals.* Students focusing on task completion are engaged in the learning activity at a behavioral level but are not cognitively engaged. They may enjoy the social give-and-take or they may just be trying to do what is expected of them. They are learning, of course (that goes without saying), and, if the activity has been well designed and conducted, they may even be learning what the teacher has intended. But the learning will have been incidental. In Popperian terms, the focus of these students is World 1, the external world of people, things, and actions.

2. *Learning goals.* These goals distinguish students who are purposefully engaged in learning. They have an idea of the educational purpose of the activity and they adopt it. Their interest in learning may only extend to doing well on the next exam or it may have deeper roots; in either case, their focus is on Popper's World 2. They are concerned with the content of the individual mind—specifically, their own. Thus, the goals of these students are complementary to those of the teacher. They are trying to learn what the teacher is trying to teach.

3. *Knowledge-building goals.* These goals distinguish students who are actively engaged with problems beyond the immediate situation. For these students, the teacher-led discussion about the brain is a real discussion, whose purpose (as a fifth-grader is likely to conceive of it) is to arrive at the truth. In other words, this is World 3 discourse dealing with such World 3 objects as theories and explanations, carried out in a mode of critical inquiry. These students also learn, but like students of the first type, their learn-

---

[3]There is also a very large research literature (see Schunk & Zimmerman, 1994, for a compilation) on students' orientations to learning, all of which makes some distinction similar to the one we make between task completion and learning goals, but none of it distinguishes what we call knowledge building goals from learning goals.

ing is incidental—only, in this case, the learning is incidental to knowledge building.

Despite their outward similarities, these students may be said to live in three different worlds as far as the learning activity is concerned. Conveniently, their worlds have names: World 1, World 2, and World 3. Most teachers who conduct discussions of the kind described probably hope to have students engaged with the problem—hence, functioning in World 3. However, because conventional theory of mind does not distinguish between learning and knowledge building, they will not recognize any fundamental difference between the second and third types of students.[3] Because their professional orientation is to World 2, they design and manage activities so that they are most suited to students of the second type. Students of the third type, those with a knowledge-building orientation, are likely to find the teacher's approach somewhat frustrating. There is too much opinion sampling, too much wrapping things up into tidy bundles and moving on to the next topic, too much repetition and not enough working out of implications. To pursue their own World 3 interests, students may carry the discussion on after class, among themselves or with the teacher, and that is when the real discussion will take place—discussion that is less school-like and more like the discussions adults have who are engaged in efforts to advance knowledge.

SHARPENING THE DISTINCTION BETWEEN LEARNING AND KNOWLEDGE BUILDING

At this point I have to start using the word "instruction." It is not the right word, but I do not know of a better one. "Teaching" is a broad term that can refer to everything teachers do in the execution of their jobs, so it includes managing seatwork, maintaining discipline, dealing with individual students' upsets, and so on. As used by me and others of the breed who publish in journals like *Cognition and Instruction*, the term "instruction" picks out that part of teaching that is concerned with the achievement of learning objectives. Unfortunately, "instruction" implies things like lecturing and conducting recitations, whereas I want to use the term in a much less restrictive sense, so that it is possible to compare widely differing approaches.

---

[2]In Ng & Bereiter (1991), three kinds of goal orientations are identified: task goals, instructional goals, and knowledge-building goals. These correspond approximately to the three kinds of students described in the text, except that knowledge building was not so clearly distinguished from learning in the earlier work.

The literature on instructional approaches is full of comparisons, often in tabular form, between the author's favored approach on one side and a caricature of conventional instruction on the other. They commonly go like what I show in Table 8.1. (I have put together bits of several tables so as not to impugn anyone in particular):

Such comparisons are uniformly unenlightening. It is not that they are inaccurate or that the "old" is a harmless straw man. It is just that such comparisons appeal only to those who are already sold on the "new" and for them they obscure differences that matter and bury real problems under a fluff of self-congratulatory clichés.

Knowledge building, of course, belongs on the "new" side of the table, but by no means does everything on the "new" side involve knowledge building. In this section I want to compare two approaches to student inquiry in science that are very close in many respects, which may be said to share a common philosophy, but which nevertheless diverge in ways that help sharpen the distinction between learning and knowledge building. More detailed accounts appear in the same issue of *The Elementary School Journal* (Anderson, Holland, & Palincsar, 1997; Bereiter et al., 1997).

Anderson et al., (1997) analyzed the behavior of a small group of elementary school students over four days during which they worked on the following task. The students had previously observed and taken notes on a laboratory demonstration of what we would recognize as evaporation and condensation: A clear liquid in the bottom part of a glass apparatus was heated, giving off an invisible gas that rose to the top of the apparatus, where it was cooled by ice and condensed back into a clear liquid. The task for the students was to explain the phenomenon and to present their explanation to the class in the form of a poster with drawings and text, accompanied by a demonstration using models of molecules. The

TABLE 8.1

Stereotypic Contrasts Between Old and New Approaches to Education

Old	New
Knowledge transmission	Knowledge construction
Memorization	Reasoning
Teacher directed	Learner centered
Competitive	Collaborative
Tightly scheduled	Opportunistic
Fact centered	Idea centered
Etc.	Etc.

pedagogy here included two elements that are common in science education at all levels:

1. *The demonstration of a puzzling phenomenon.* Real scientific research often starts with puzzling observations. Teachers use such demonstrations to arouse curiosity, to bring forth conjectures, and to stimulate argument and further inquiry (Hunt & Minstrell, 1994).
2. *A material product—what is known in the world of research contracts as a "deliverable."* In school, "deliverables" are likely to be called "projects." Typically they take the form of a report, but in this multimedia age many more dramatic kinds of presentation are often encouraged. The pedagogical assumption behind requiring them is that "products and performances are important sources of evidence about whether students are helping each other to learn, and they play an essential role in building confidence and motivation, especially for students who have traditionally been unsuccessful in school science" (Anderson et al., 1997, p. 379).

The story Anderson et al. told is one of science learning getting overwhelmed by social complexities. The students' concerns are almost wholly with their poster and its presentation, with who gets to perform, with looking good and not making fools of themselves. The teacher gets drawn into these concerns as well. There is the problem of a bright, high-status girl continually upstaging a lower status boy who is actually the one most engaged with scientific issues. The authors' conclusion that if there is to be scientific literacy for everyone, learning will have to be viewed within a sociocultural framework. It would be difficult to dispute that conclusion, but the story can equally well be understood as bringing into question the two pedagogical elements noted earlier:

1. The problem the students were supposed to address did not arise from their own wondering and inquiry but was presented to them. Although the evaporation and condensation demonstration may have aroused some initial interest, the problem of explaining it clearly did not weigh heavily on their minds. When they embarked on the assignment the first thing they did was allocate different tasks to different group members, and the task of producing the explanation fell to the high-status girl. The only discussion occurred when they were practicing their presentation and she coached the boy in presenting his part correctly. It seems

fair to conclude that what was presented as a scientific problem was not really a scientific problem for the students but only part of a task to be accomplished.

2. The task of preparing the deliverables, far from serving as a vehicle for science learning, seems to have obliterated whatever scientific inclinations the students might have had. Although it may have played a role, as claimed, in building confidence and motivation, the confidence and motivation do not appear to have had anything to do with science. Teachers I have talked to report similar problems, but so deeply entrenched is belief in the necessity of a tangible product that it does not occur to most of them to look for alternatives. Anderson et al. (1997) anticipated the objection "that students should be held accountable for helping each other to learn rather than for products and performances" (p. 379), but they said that the two are indissociable. In the next example I try to show this is not true.

The preceding example is an unusually well worked out instance of a common approach to elementary science. Had the authors been less attentive to what actually happened and less candid in reporting it, they might have put this example forth as a model for teachers to follow. The next example, discussed in Bereiter, Scardamalia, Cassells, and Hewitt (1997), is too unusual, to serendipitous to serve as a model for practice. Instead its value is conceptual. It enables us to imagine the possibility of science learning that is not driven by presented problems and by deliverables. It centers around a discussion carried on over a period of 3 months by 17 sixth-grade students, using CSILE, a networked computer environment designed to support knowledge-building discourse (Scardamalia & Bereiter, 1994; Scardamalia, Bereiter, & Lamon, 1994). The discussion in question was initiated by a student, branching off from a discussion that had been initiated by one of their teachers. The subdiscussion, titled "About Growing," consisted of 179 entries.

Initially, the students discussed their personal concerns with growing. For some it was a question of when the adolescent growth spurt would start; for others it was a question of when it would end. The following entries typify the initial phase of the discussion:

Well, as you know, I'm one of the shortest people on this team. I hardly grow any over a year's time .... It actually feels like I'm shrinking. Everyone else is growing ....[4]

---

[4]In all quotations from the student database, punctuation and spelling have been corrected and real names have been replaced with pseudonyms. Otherwise, the quotations are verbatim.

You probably just haven't hit your growth spurt yet. Maybe one day you'll wake up and be taller than everyone else. We all grow at different speeds ….

I know that I am going to be a tall person but in a way I don't want to be a tall person ….

Very soon, however, questions and conjectures of a more scientific sort began to appear:

I wonder why hair and fingernails grow all our lives, but our height doesn't?

Maybe people stop growing when the clock inside their head says they should. Kind of like when you start growing or you have a growth spurt. But, I wonder how doctors or other people that have knowledge about growing know how tall you might be and what age you might stop growing. The doctor has predicted I'll be about 5′4″. He also thinks that my sister is finished growing and he used to think that she was going to be very tall. Do they look for patterns?

Maybe our bodies stop growing because we don't have anything left to grow with. Let's say you order two tons of cement to build a driveway. You can only build a driveway so large until you run out of cement. Maybe our bodies work the same way. We only have so much growth hormone. We just use over the years until we run out ….

The students then began consulting experts and reference sources and feeding their findings into the discussion

To grow in length, a bone adds cells at the end called growth plates. They are made mostly of cartilage cells. I finally found out that the reason you stop growing, and it turned out that my old note, the one that said it might have to do with hormones, was kind of right! It has to do with the reason that the cartilage cells in the bone's growth plates stop responding to your growth hormone.

I found something that really fascinated me. I learned that babies have more bones when they are born than their parents do. That's because their bones haven't really shaped or grown together. When a baby is born it has 270 growth centers. Adults have 206. I also learned that carpals are bones in your wrist and babies don't have a single one when they are born. That makes me wonder though because babies can still grab your hands and they can grip objects. I found a graph in a book that said you have 8 carpals when you are 12. I didn't see any patterns in the graph, so I wondered how many carpals a person that is 40 has ….

As a result of such entries, the scope of the discussion expanded considerably to embrace such issues as the heritability of height, different growth rates of different parts of the body, shrinkage in old age, neural development and growth in knowledge, replacements of skin cells and tree leaves (is there a relation?), and growth patterns in plants and nonhuman species. The issue of hereditary factors particularly interested the students, and so they decided to do a survey, collecting data on the heights of students, their parents, and grandparents (to check also on shrinkage in old age). The survey did not yield conclusive findings. That was hardly to be expected, given that in early adolescence height does not correlate very well with one's own future height, let alone that of relatives. The students did, however, work out the basic idea of correlation.

The inquiry continued up to the end of the school year. As a wrap-up, the teacher asked the students to contribute CSILE entries under the heading, "What We Have Learned." Excerpts from these give a sense not only of what the class accomplished but of how the students felt about it:

> Discussion and learning has changed greatly over the few months. We have had great ideas, some of which have been rather strange …. But, even though these were very strange they were very interesting, and well thought out …. At the start of this note, we talked about what it was like to stop growing. And me being vertically challenged, as I prefer to be called, was asked a lot of questions …. Many adults wrote in, and students asked their parents what they thought. But, as most learning goes, we weren't happy. We wanted to know "why" we stopped growing. This led to many people studying things such as the pituitary glands, and hormones, and learned about all that stuff that we consider rather gross. But we learned a lot, which helped us understand why we stopped growing.

> Many of my theories have changed since I began working on this note …. I thought that you stopped growing. But, as my research continued, I learned that you never stop growing. Your hair, nails, and mind is always growing and expanding. You grow in maturity and of course you grow in weight. I thought that tendons just stretched and I didn't know much about bones and what they are made of.

> I feel that we did a good job making theories but that we needed more time to get new learnings. I would still like to continue my research on this and write in next year with more new learnings. I think that we should learn stuff … over the summer and share it with the others in the fall. We can continue to write letters and make phone calls to experts though. I think that this research has

been fun and we should pick it up next year or start a new one about the brain and its growth.

There are too many differences between this example and the first one to make detailed comparison profitable. The contrasts I want to highlight pertain to the two pedagogical features discussed earlier.

1. Whereas in the first example a problem was presented at the outset that continued to be the only scientific problem to be dealt with, in the second example the problem developed over time, became elaborated and increasingly scientific. A number of scientific subproblems emerged so that by the end a fairly comprehensive effort to understand biological growth was in evidence.

2. Whereas the focus of activity in the first example was on producing a poster and presenting it, there were no deliverables in the second example. The only tangible residue was the trace of the dialogue itself. Of the justifications that Anderson et al. (1997) offered for "products and performances," this computer trace provided one: a source of evidence about children's contributions to the collective effort. As for building confidence and motivation, I think any reader of the complete transcript would agree that such building did occur and in ways relevant to science. Motivation was, in fact, high enough that some students proposed continuing their inquiry over the summer and resuming the discussion in the fall. What kept motivation high, I believe, was the thrill of the chase—the excitement of making progress in pursuit of understanding a compelling phenomenon.

I think it is clear that the second example is one of knowledge building but that the first is not. But if the first had worked better, if the students had been more involved in explaining the demonstrated phenomenon and less in their presentation, would that not have been knowledge building too? To a very limited extent, perhaps. The only knowledge to be constructed was an explanation of the behavior of an outlandish piece of laboratory equipment. Surely, the value in trying to get the students do so is not in the knowledge they construct but in what they are expected to learn in the process of doing so. When the knowledge actually to be constructed is trivial or fantastic, we have the clearest indication we can hope to get that we are dealing with a learning activity that is not a knowledge-building activity.

Nevertheless, when teachers, impressed by examples like the second one, decide that knowledge building is for them, their immediate inclination is to do something like the first example, perhaps augmented by having students state their theories or predictions. Partly it's that they do not trust that students can be sufficiently motivated just by the pursuit of understanding, and so they feel the need for concrete activity that will yield a tangible result. I believe it is also, however, a matter of not yet having a clear distinction between knowledge building and learning, regarding learning as merely an inferior form of knowledge building. Lacking the distinction, they do things that might make sense as part of a learning activity, but they do not go all the way with them, and so they end up with something that is neither good knowledge building nor good learning.

Puzzling and intriguing demonstrations can play a valuable part in teacher-led learning activities. Not long ago I saw a brilliant 20-minute lesson on air pressure put on at a science museum. The presenter went through half a dozen demonstrations with variations, showing things collapsing or exploding, liquid levels rising or falling, and I can't remember what else as air was introduced or removed. She kept firing questions at the audience of drop-in children, getting them intensely involved in predicting and explaining, and I am pretty sure that by the end of it the great majority of them understood that air has weight and that there is no such force as suction.

I think what happens when people try to adopt a constructivist pedagogy without a clear distinction between knowledge building and learning is that they try to take parts of what they recognize as good learning activities and turn them over to the students. Sometimes it works, but in science, especially, the students are in no position to assume responsibility for the stock-in-trade of old-style pedagogy, such as was on display in the science museum session. In the first place, no single demonstration can carry learning very far. There needs to be a series of demonstrations, and they need to be tied together so that they build up a general understanding that extends beyond the particulars. Students cannot be expected to do that. It requires somebody who already understands what the demonstrations are supposed to teach, who can draw out their implications and reveal the conceptual thread that ties them together.

This does not mean that experimental science has to be didactic. Jim Minstrell (Hunt & Minstrell, 1994) has developed an approach to teaching physics that relies heavily on the students' own efforts to explain, to deal with inconsistencies, and to resolve conflicts among their theories. Minstrell starts with a problematic experimental situation, just as in the Anderson et al. example. In the cited account, a unit starts with students being challenged to predict and explain what will happen to the apparent weight of an object on a spring balance when a vacuum is created around it. This is followed by a series of related demonstrations or experiments, which require students to modify and elaborate their explanations. But the demonstrations are chosen by the teacher, who also plays a directive role in the students' deliberations:

The important thing is that the students are encouraged to extract general principles from a variety of specific contexts. They are continually asked, "What can each experiment tell us that might relate to all of the other situations, including the original benchmark problem?" New issues are opened up as well, touching on such concepts as the "stickiness" of water, and the apparent "sucking" by vacuums. In addition to encouraging additional investigation of issues, the teacher can help students note the analogical similarity between what happens to an object submerged in a container of water and what happens to an object submerged in the "ocean of air" around the earth. (Hunt & Minstrell, 1994, p. 60)

Is this knowledge building? I expect that when Minstrell is in charge it is, but that in other hands it might become only a learning activity. It might also fail to materialize as knowledge building if the students proved unable to generate the central ideas themselves and the teacher had to end up providing all the answers. The crucial issue is whether the students are working in World 3. If they are, they are doing knowledge building, regardless of how active a role the teacher plays in their World 3 work. The students in the evaporation–condensation example were not working in World 3, although they were working fairly independently. They were working in World 1. That is how the activity was set up. Its central objects were the physical demonstration, the poster the students were producing, the physical models of molecules that they were to use in their presentation, and of course the students themselves and all the accompanying social considerations. What happened in World 2, their minds, was an incidental result of their work in World 1. World 3, the world of ideas, did not figure in the activity. In the growth example, World 1 was continually referred to, and there was the overt collection of questionnaire information from other people, but the main focus of work was on ideas—on producing and refining explanations and bringing new information into the process. This they did with little adult help, whereas in the Minstrell example the teacher was continually involved, but the focus of the students' work in both cases was on ideas. World 1, in the form of external information sources, entered the picture only insofar as it was relevant to the work with ideas.

THE THREE PILLARS OF CONVENTIONAL PEDAGOGY

Schools are often called on to teach something new: environmental issues, diet, antiracism, drugs, street survival skills, Afro-American history, computer literacy, phonics (what is old sometimes becomes new again), problem solving—the list grows endlessly. Yet schools manage to incorporate this endless stream of new requirements without disintegrating. How do they do it? As I make it out, they do this by relying on a standard set of reductive moves that convert the new challenge into something they already have the tools to handle. These three reductive moves are so heavily relied on that it is not altogether fanciful to call them the pillars of conventional pedagogy. They are:

- reduction to subject matter,
- reduction to activities, and
- reduction to self-expression.

Reduction to subject matter means converting the subject into propositions or procedures that can be directly taught and tested. Reduction to activities is self-explanatory and is far and away the method of choice among modern teachers, just as reduction to subject matter is the old-fashioned choice and the one teachers tend to revert to if they are held accountable for students' learning. Reduction to self-expression is more daring but has long been the ideal in early childhood education. The educational objective is translated into some regulated way of letting students follow their own inclinations—in writing, speaking, making, or doing. It requires structuring the situation, socially or by means of physical arrangements, so that students will spontaneously undertake activities that are expected to produce the desired learning (Weber, 1971, p. 109).

Of course, these three reductive approaches work much of the time. Otherwise schooling in the forms we know it would be a complete failure. But they are also responsible for much of what is useless and silly in formal education. Here are some notable examples:

1. *The reduction of phonics to subject matter.* Phonics is a skill that all normal children acquire in the course of learning to read. It is the ability to "sound out" unfamiliar words according to their spelling, hopefully getting close enough to the actual pronunciation to recognize the word. Its main value, obviously, is in the early stages of learning to read, when children know by sound many words they do not yet know by sight. In the 1930s the teaching of phonics fell out of favor in the United States, but in the 1960s public pressure forced textbook publishers to bring it back. However, it was brought back as a separate body of subject matter. Instead of being taught as a way to identify words, it became a pointless kind of analysis carried out *after* words had been identified (circle the words that contain the "sh" sound, for instance). Instead of being concentrated in the first weeks of learning to read,

it was drawn out over 6 years! As subject matter, as a body of knowledge *about* written language, phonics is ludicrous, and linguists delighted in pointing out how it oversimplifies and distorts the relation between spelling and pronunciation (Smith, 1971). As a *way to help children get started in reading*, the teaching of phonics has demonstrable virtues (Adams, 1990), but that conception of it has been largely lost through reduction to subject matter.

2. *The reduction of science to quiz games.* Since the appearance of Logo in the 1970s and Seymour Papert's *Mindstorms* (1980), educators of a constructivist persuasion have been drawn to the idea that students might get more out of creating computer programs than using them. One direction this idea has taken is to have children design educational computer games. But according to reports from one such project (Kafai, 1996; Yarnall & Kafai, 1996) and what I have seen of another, the results have been of a kind that only a techie could love. Almost exclusively young students create games that quiz one another on isolated facts. Although in principle the software permits them to construct other kinds of games, to do so would far exceed their programming capabilities. Thus, the kind of science teaching that constructivists universally condemn becomes institutionalized in activities intended to promote constructivist learning. This is what happens not infrequently when "project-based learning" takes the form of reduction to activities.

3. *The reduction of literature study to self-expression.* The teaching of literature often succumbs to reduction to subject matter. It is much easier to teach facts about authors, history, and literary features than it is to promote the kind of intense engagement with literary works that educated people recognize as the real point. There has been a strong reaction against this kind of reductionism, however, sparked by Louise Rosenblatt's (1980) influential essay, "What Facts Does This Poem Teach You?" and sustained by a turn in literary theory that emphasizes what readers bring to literary experience (Tomkins, 1980). Questions on the order of "Why did Amy pick the marigolds?" have begun to disappear from textbooks, replaced by questions of "How did it make you feel?" The result, however, has been to replace one kind of reduction with another. Discussions carried out under the aegis of "reader response theory" are no longer about the book but about personal experiences and concerns brought to mind by the book. Among other things, this makes it possible for students to participate without having actually read the work. They need only have picked up a few clues as to what it is about. I have seen animated discussions going on in classes where none of the students could

read well enough to have grasped the content of the book, although they had become adept at spotting keywords and inferring from them the topics of text passages. In these cases the literary work serves the same purpose as the exercises and games that encounter group leaders use to stimulate self-expression. It creates a topical framework within which students can do their own thing.

These are not isolated examples. Reductive pedagogy is the norm—so normal, in fact, that departures from it are likely to be perceived as lapses. The standard reading lesson, as carried out in most North American schools up through the sixth grade, is entirely focused on extracting information from the story or article being read. As observed by Pearson and Gallagher (1983), the standard method is for the teacher to quiz students on text content, continuing to ask the same question until a correct answer has been obtained. If no one answers the question, the teacher does so (or distorts a student's response into the desired answer). This is called teaching reading comprehension. But in fact no teaching of reading comprehension skills is going on (Durkin, 1979). Instead, what we have is reduction to subject matter, the subject matter in this case being whatever the reader selection happens to be about. When the selection is fiction, which it usually is, treating it as subject matter becomes ridiculous. Great attention is lavished on getting every detail of the story right, as if it were something one needed to remember throughout life. Yet if you try to drop this reductive practice in favor of an approach that gets students doing the kinds of things that good readers do in comprehending what they read, there will be complaints that "there's no comprehension."[5] In the traditional teaching of writing, reduction to activities has been the norm. The focus is on producing a good written product rather than on learning to write well. This distinction, I have found, is virtually incomprehensible not only to teachers but to language arts specialists. The result is that any practice that improves the apparent quality of the product—such as assigning a livelier topic—is welcomed, without regard to what effect it may have on learning. Recently there has been a movement away from the standard writing assignment, which sustains this reduction to activity, but the replacement is reduction to self-expression. Students are supposed to find their "voice" and use writing as a medium for rendering their life experi-

---

[5]I write this from the experience of having worked for many years, as an author of Open Court reading programs, to get away from reductive practices and to incorporate what research showed were effective ways to improve reading comprehension abilities. Twenty-five years of well-publicized research on reading comprehension have yet to quiet complaints that any departure from the quiz mode means "there's no comprehension."

ences more meaningful and for expressing their feelings. This is fine as far as it goes, but it reduces writing to only one of its many functions. Reduction to activities is perhaps unavoidable in schools. Teachers have to see to it that some kind of activity is going on all the time, and it cannot always be well calculated to achieve a learning objective. So every teacher relies on a repertoire of activities to fill up a space of time in a way that conforms in a general way to what is supposed to go on in school. I have never seen an exception, even in the most no-nonsense of school programs. In their proper place, activities, subject matter, and self-expression are all legitimate. What has happened, however, is that reductive practices have become elevated to pedagogical virtues. Reduction to activities becomes hands-on or project-based learning. Reduction to subject matter becomes direct instruction or back-to-basics. Reduction to self-expression becomes "reader response theory" and "process writing." As a result, reductive practices are hidden behind respectable principles, and the principles themselves become degraded.

At the extreme of reductionism, educational thought descends into word magic. Word magic endows the names of things with powers of their own. In education, word magic appears as the belief that if you teach people a certain thing, the learning will automatically transfer to everything else called by the same name. In one corporate training program, trainees work in teams to climb a high wall. The express purpose is not, of course, to make them into mountain climbers; the wall climbing is supposed to teach them to work cooperatively on arranging business deals. Any close analysis of the two tasks would show they have almost nothing in common except at the most abstract level. They both involve goals and a need for cooperative effort to achieve the goals. But the kind of cooperation, the obstacles to cooperation, the kind of communication needed for cooperation to occur, the emotions, the motives, the clarity of purpose—all of these differ radically.

If the three reductionist pillars of pedagogy were removed, schooling as we know it—in both its traditional and its "progressive" forms—would crash to the ground. But there are two other pillars that could support a nonreductive pedagogy. These are:

- enlisting students in the pursuit of learning objectives, and
- converting learning objectives into knowledge-building objectives.

The first is the route of intentional learning (Bereiter & Scardamalia, 1989). In terms of the three kinds of goals discussed earlier, it involves shifting students from task-completion goals to learning goals. The second route involves the further shift to knowledge building goals.

These are not alternative routes. Because students engaged in knowledge building are also learning, they can be simultaneously attending to both kinds of goals. In one Ontario classroom students were engaged in a collaborative knowledge-building project concerning pre-Columbian civilizations. Through formulating problems, proposing theories, and revising them in the light of information, the students had compiled a substantial network of notes in a CSILE[6] database. The teacher then inserted into the database a graphic note that itemized the learning objectives that the Ontario Ministry of Education had set out for this unit of subject matter. He had the students link their notes to appropriate objectives and explain how the notes fulfilled the objectives. When this task was completed, the students ended up with notes left over, from which they derived two additional learning objectives they considered relevant to understanding pre-Columbian civilizations. Like most curriculum guidelines, those of the Ministry supplemented the objectives with suggested learning activities for achieving them. Normally—in keeping with the practice of reduction to activities—the students would encounter the activities but would have no contact with the objectives. In this case the activities were bypassed in favor of engaging the students directly with the learning objectives and, more important, with the problems that made the subject worthy of study in the first place.

DIRECT VERSUS INDIRECT LEARNING ACTIVITIES

Teachers must continually choose between teaching something directly or leaving it to be acquired incidentally through indirect learning activities. This ought to be a strategic issue, not an ideological one. Strategically, answers will vary. Ideologically, there is a press to have a uniform answer for all occasions. Either everything must be engineered or everything must be acquired naturally. Combined with a failure to distinguish learning from knowledge building, pedagogical ideologies of all sorts tend toward fanaticism and superstition. The teaching of reading provides the most extreme examples. I have heard someone stand up at a meeting of the Reading Reform Foundation and maintain without challenge that no one could become a good reader unless they were taught phonics (thus branding as illiterate everyone who, like me, was brought up on *Dick and Jane*). A leading advocate of whole language, on the other hand, reportedly called for a stake to be driven through the heart of someone who dared to write a book advocating the teach-

---

[6]CSILE stands for Computer Supported Intentional Learning Environments (Scardamalia & Bereiter, 1994), more recent generations of which are called Knowledge Forum®.

ing of phonics. Fortunately, this level of fanaticism has not taken hold in other areas of education, but there are ideological purists everywhere. I remember the dismay of a group of reformers who were promoting an inquiry approach to mathematics, when they discovered that their prize teacher was starting off each lesson with mental arithmetic drill. My response, however, was "Good for her!" She recognized that there was more than one side to competence in mathematics, and that one side might need one approach and another, another.

When the issue is approached strategically, it seldom turns out that the decision is a simple either-or. Vocabulary acquisition provides a nice illustration. Children of school age learn thousands of new words each year (Anglin, 1993). The most ambitious of vocabulary instruction programs aim to teach only a few hundred. To think of directly teaching thousands of words a year is unrealistic. It would eat up too much instructional time and might prove impossible: The rate of forgetting would probably overtake the rate of learning. But a purely laissez-faire policy is not adequate either. Children differ greatly in vocabulary knowledge, vocabulary figures prominently in achievement and scholastic aptitude tests, and mastering vocabulary is an important part of learning in every academic discipline. "Encourage wide reading," is one answer, but only a partial one. Much surely depends on what and how a child reads. And no amount of normal reading is likely to convey the meaning of *parallelogram*, the literal meaning of *osmosis*, or the difference between *heat* and *temperature*. But understanding parallelograms, osmosis, and the relation between heat and temperature is not simply a matter of vocabulary learning. It is a matter of developing important understandings in mathematics and science. And so vocabulary acquisition becomes a subordinate issue in the larger problem outlined in the preceding chapter—the problem of becoming familiar with the abstract artifacts making up various domains of knowledge. In that context, the question is whether special attention needs to be directed to learning key words, or whether that will come about as a natural consequence of knowledge-building activity in the domain. The answer is to be found in data, not pedagogical philosophy.

THE QUESTION OF "WHAT IS LEARNED?"

With all learning activities, the big question is what is learned. Where direct teaching is concerned, educators are all familiar with the fact that what is supposedly taught is not necessarily learned. That is why a careful teacher will keep checking to see what is getting across and what is being retained, and the teacher will keep reteaching or trying different angles until satisfied the desired learning has taken place. This is the great strength of direct-learning activities and is the reason even teachers ideologically opposed to direct instruction will resort to it when it really counts—for instance, in teaching emergency procedures, computer operations, or classroom routines. But the literature on misconceptions shows how fallible the process is. The instructor teaches Darwin but the students learn Lamark. Case (1985a) has shown that even in arithmetic, that bastion of direct instruction, children will adopt workable procedures that are different from what they have been taught.

When it comes to indirect learning experiences, however, the question of what is learned becomes even less tractable. Word magic and wishful thinking often serve to fill the voids. Hands-on experiences in science and mathematics are supposed to result in deeper understanding, but evidence is lacking and just how the understanding is supposed to come about is seldom explained. In arithmetic, for instance, it is known that children who are directly taught algorithms often learn them as rote procedures and get them wrong, producing senseless answers. A lively industry has grown up around the production of "manipulatives," clever systems of rods, blocks, or other objects, with which it is possible to enact concretely the operations involved in multidigit addition, subtraction, and multiplication. The hope is that working with these palpable things will make the corresponding symbolic operations (such as regrouping or borrowing) more meaningful. The reality, according to studies by Resnick and her colleagues (Resnick & Neches, 1984; Resnick & Omanson, 1987), is that many students can become proficient in both manipulating the concrete objects and performing the symbolic operations yet never see the connection. In science, the gap between what students are supposed to be getting out of hands-on experiences and what they actually get out of them is often even greater (Roth, Anderson, & Smith, 1987).

With the rising concern about standards and accountability, educators given to indirect learning activities have had to become more definite about what students are supposed to learn from such activities. This has forced word magic to a new level. Whatever words may be used to *describe* an activity are translated into *outcomes* of the activity. Thus, an activity in which children team up to make paper airplanes, measure and record how far they fly, and criticize each other's designs may be claimed to teach cooperation, technology, problem solving, force, gravity, measurement, scientific method, subtraction, and critical thinking. "Objectives-Based Education" is a name given to such word play. Although it may also refer to firmer stuff, in its degraded versions "OBE" amounts to a scheme in which the activities *become* the objectives. Fairly expensive software systems are being sold to schools that permit lesson plans and activity descriptions of all kinds to be entered and linked to lists of mandated objectives.

It would be futile, however, to insist that claims about the outcomes of indirect learning activities should be based on evidence. Activities keep being invented and modified at a far greater rate than research could hope to keep up with, and seemingly minor modifications can make a big difference (see, for instance, Scardamalia et al., 1996). Rules of thumb are needed. A rule of thumb implicit in a great deal of computer-based educational fare (and sometimes stated explicitly by software designers) is, "As long as they're having fun, they're learning." Inasmuch as we can be confident that students are also learning when they are not having fun, this is not a very useful rule. It does not help in identifying *what* is likely to be learned.

From the cognitive instructional research of the past quarter century, two rules of thumb can be derived that do generate inferences about *what* will be learned:

1. People learn what they process.
2. The skills most likely to be learned are the minimal ones necessary to accomplish the range of tasks presented.

The first rule marks the great divide between cognitive and behaviorist conceptions of learning. Its point may be illustrated by a little experiment of many years ago, the source of which is lost to me. Someone got the bright idea of teaching children to recognize the names of colors by printing each color name in its appropriate color ("green" was printed in green, "yellow" in yellow, and so on) and then gradually fading the colors away until eventually all the words appeared in black. When this was tried in a first-grade class it worked nicely; the children learned to recognize the color words. When it was tried in a kindergarten class, the children correctly named the words so long as there was the faintest trace of identifying color, but when the final transition was made to black, they called every word "black." Behaviorally, the children were all doing the same thing except at the last step, accurately naming the color words; cognitively they were evidently doing something quite different. The first-graders were processing the spellings or at least the shapes of the words, whereas the kindergartners were processing only their color.

The question of what is actually being processed looms large in any serious consideration of so-called "projects." A favorite in modern classrooms is having students produce multimedia documents on some topic relevant to the curriculum—on an endangered species, say. With the resources available on the Internet and on CD-ROMs and with the use of scanners and multimedia presentation software that permits the incorporation of video, sound, and graphics, students can produce impressive documents. But what do they learn about polar bears from producing a multimedia document on polar bears? It all depends on what information they process in assembling the document. If the only questions they consider are "Is it about polar bears?" and "Does it look nice?" we may infer that not much polar bear knowledge will be acquired. In a later section I argue that knowledge building, as a form of activity, has the advantage over most kinds of project-based activity in that it leads to deeper processing of information.

The second rule of thumb encourages us to think small when making claims about the skills to be acquired from learning activities. If the task is sorting buttons, let us not claim that it is teaching "classification skills"; let us only claim that it is improving children's ability to sort buttons. To do well in the paper airplane activity mentioned earlier, students do not really have to master the scientific method (whatever that is) or become all-around critical thinkers (whatever that means). They have to measure and record distances and work out some way to extract conclusions from variable data. They have to learn what some of the significant variables are in paper airplane performance and use these in evaluating designs. Those may not be trivial attainments, but they are not very far-reaching. Some students will get more out of the activity than that, but others will get less. Those who get more will do so because they have pursued objectives of their own, over and above those implicit in the task (cf. Ng & Bereiter, 1991). Those who get less, even though they appear to perform adequately, will have found some way to get along in the actual situation that circumvents the apparent requirements.

This minimalist view of skill learning does not imply students are shirkers. It simply assumes students will act like other adaptable organisms and will develop ways of accomplishing tasks that reduce time and effort—including cognitive effort. When I first started doing research on writing, I believed, as many teachers do, that the ideal writing assignment was one that posed a problem that made the writers think. What impressed me in the end was writers' ingenuity in evading the need to think—except for people who were serious about writing; with them, it didn't matter how banal the assignment, they would find ways to turn it into a challenge (Scardamalia & Bereiter, 1991). People will go to great lengths to master skills they want to master. They will seek out challenges and they will seek out instruction and guidance. But give them a task that calls for a skill they are not eager to develop and their first recourse will be to find a way to accomplish the task without need for that skill. Thus, natural tendencies are naturally at war with attempts to foster high-level skills through indirect learning activities.[7]

The obvious way out of this dilemma is to enlist the students in the effort to learn. This can have striking results. Valerie Anderson developed a program aimed at involving adolescent poor readers in every aspect of the task of becoming a more capable reader, and it has had the effect of turning discouraged and unmotivated students into alert, critical readers (Anderson & Roit, 1993). Direct learning activities are often criticized for inducing passivity and parrot-like learning, but those are usually secondary consequences of the failure of students to understand or appreciate the value of what they are supposed to be learning.

Not everything can be learned in a direct manner. Sometimes it is because the learners are too young to grasp the purpose. Phonemic awareness—the ability to hear words as combinations of identifiable sounds—has emerged as an important objective for kindergarten and first grade (Adams, 1990), but children of this age could hardly be expected to understand what phonemic awareness lessons are about. Consequently, all the teaching of it is done indirectly, through songs, word play, and exercises. For similar reasons, the most effective approach to teaching number sense to young children is based on games (Griffin et al., 1984).

Sometimes students can understand an objective but cannot see the value in it until after they have attained it. When I was teaching high school English, I presented my students with a list of possible learning objectives and asked them to rank them according to how interested they were in pursuing them. Up at the top of their rankings was learning correct grammatical usage. But 14th out of 14 on nearly every student's list was learning to appreciate good literature. This was a blow to me, because it was near the top of my priorities, but I should not have been surprised. There are adults who feel a need to improve their taste in art, literature, or music, but their need arises out of kinds of social experience unknown to most teenagers. This does not mean it is impossible to develop an appreciation for

---

[7]The principle of "they only learn what the tasks require" applies even when motivation is high. Students who join a chess club may be highly motivated to learn to do well in chess and they may study hard and think hard in pursuit of this objective. But the result will be that they learn skills applicable to chess; they are unlikely to learn much in the way of skills, concepts, or habits that are of use anywhere else. To claim that they will learn reasoning, planning, or pattern-recognition skills is to indulge in the word magic I have been criticizing. They will learn chess reasoning, chess planning, and chess patterns. Beyond that, we should not be venturing claims.

good literature in high school students, only that it must be done indirectly, through activities that have a different purpose in the eyes of the students.

Some kinds of instructional activities, however, only succeed if the students are trying to learn. I mentioned the Omanson and Resnick research on students using "manipulables" intended to promote understanding of elementary arithmetic algorithms. Some students did grasp the relationship between the concrete operations and the algorithms. Interviews revealed they were students who realized there was supposed to be a connection and were actively trying to figure out what it was. Evidently, the relation between the concrete activities and numerical operations only comes across to children who are looking for a relationship (Resnick & Omanson, 1987). It is amazing to what extent Dewey's (1916) aversion to the direct approach[8] has permeated educational thought, to the extent that educators often do not even consider the possibility of letting students in on the secret of what they are supposed to be learning. Partly, though, this is a result of conceptual confusion. When students are eagerly engaged in some intellectual activity, such as a science experiment, this is taken to mean they are eager to learn. But they may not be thinking about learning at all. They may only be thinking about the experiment and its meaning—which is how Dewey would have it. And that may be sufficient, but in some cases it may not. All I am arguing for here is realizing there is a difference.

LEARNING THROUGH KNOWLEDGE BUILDING

Knowledge building, as carried on in the adult world, is not a learning activity. Often it is a form of economic activity, a matter of adding value to knowledge artifacts. Even when it is pursued for its own sake, however, as in pure research and scholarship, it is seldom done for the purpose of learning—that is, for the purpose of mental improvement. It is done to advance knowledge in a more general way. Successful knowledge building may always result in worthwhile learning for the people involved, but that is an incidental outcome, like the gains in physical fitness that may result from manual work.

Knowledge building, as carried on in a school, however, is likely to be viewed and evaluated as a learning activity, whether or not the participants see it that way. According to the distinction developed in a preceding section, knowledge building is an indirect learning activity. It might be interspersed with direct learning activity, with what Hunt and Minstrell (1994, p. 58) called "benchmark instruction,"

---

[8]Dewey (1916) called making learning a "direct and conscious end in itself" one of the "evils in education" (pp. 168–169).

but that is a recognizable departure from the course of knowledge-building work.

Let us revisit the fifth-graders' inquiry into functions of the brain, only this time let us suppose it is conducted as a knowledge-building activity, focused on World 3 rather than on World 2. The students venture tentative theories about how the brain works, and then they seek new information and engage in discussions aimed at improving their theories of brain functioning. Progress is observable. The initial theories tended to be of the homunculus variety: the brain as a little person inside the head who receives information from the senses, thinks about it, then sends instructions to the muscles. Subsequent work does not entirely eliminate the homunculus (psychologists have always found it hard to get rid of), but a number of automatic functions of the brain are identified and there are the beginnings of a conception of an information-processing organ that functions lawfully but without benefit of a wizard behind the curtain.

It is tempting to conclude that these knowledge-building accomplishments represent what was learned, but that will not do. We are talking about a collective accomplishment, and we no more know what each individual has learned in the process than we know what has been learned by each individual member of a team that has built a successful museum exhibit or crossed the ocean on a raft. There should be some relation between the collective advance in knowledge and individual learning, but we cannot infer one from the other. The problem of determining what is learned and the even more taxing problem of predicting what is likely to be learned are the same for knowledge-building as for any other kind of indirect learning activity. Accordingly, the two rules of thumb presented earlier should apply:

1. People learn what they process.
2. The skills most likely to be learned are the minimal ones necessary to accomplish the range of tasks presented.

To see how these rules of thumb apply, let us consider two different knowledge-building activities: planning a trip to Mars and explaining force and motion—what makes things move. The task in each case is to produce a conceptual artifact: a plan, in the first case, and an explanation (or what the students may be encouraged to think of as a theory), in the second case. It will be relevant to issues raised in the next chapter that the first is a sort of pseudoartifact. No one expects the plan to be carried out or to have any use other than as a pedagogical vehicle; thus the value of the activity lies entirely in the learning that results from it. The explanation, by contrast, is a serious knowledge artifact. It constitutes, for the students who create it, genuine World 3 knowledge. It is something they can use in making sense of the world. For present purposes, however, we shall consider both activities only in terms of the learning that results.

Knowledge-building may be considered a variety of problem solving (although not all problem solving is knowledge-building). Planning a trip to Mars is a *design problem*; producing a theory of motion is a *problem of explanation*. Applying the first rule of thumb, we may assume in each case that the knowledge that will be processed is knowledge actually used in solving the problem. Similarly, the second rule implies that the skills acquired or refined will be those actually employed in solving the problem. Design problems and problems of explanation are different enough that we should expect rather different kinds of knowledge to be processed and skills to be exercised.

Planning a trip to Mars and similar many-faceted design problems are popular activities among teachers of a constructivist bent partly because, pursuant to the first rule of thumb, they engage students in processing a great deal of knowledge of different kinds. Planning a trip to Mars calls on knowledge about space, the solar system, gravity, properties of matter, nutrition, physiology, and rocketry. Producing an explanation of motion involves a much more limited range of knowledge but presumably knowledge of greater depth. But what does that mean?

Ever since "learning by doing" became a pedagogical catchword, educators have been promoting the belief that practical problems naturally motivate a drive toward understanding. This is true only in a very limited sense. According to Roger Schank (1982), explanation is "failure driven." When our plans or expectations go amiss, we try to find the reason. This leads to understanding, but within the realm of action in which the failure occurred. By solving fuel-system problems, auto mechanics develop a good practical understanding of carburetion and fuel injection, but how many of them are ever led to inquire into the chemistry of combustion? And, without an understanding of more basic chemistry, how would they understand an explanation if they sought one out? The kinds of failures that lead to theoretical understanding are failures of explanation. And all explanations fail, in that every explanation posits something that itself needs explaining (Miyake, 1986). But pressing on with explanation upon explanation implies a very different kind of purpose from the practical purposes that motivate "learning by doing." There is a gap between theory and practice that interferes with exchange in either direction. Theory does not provide solutions to practical problems, but practical activities do not give rise to theoretical problems, either. Yet both are essential to the advance of knowledge.

Students planning a trip to Mars will likely learn about the use of rocket engines to change the course or speed of a space vehicle. But will they be moved to inquire how a rocket engine can work in outer space where there is no air for the jet gases to push against? That would be a digression from their task. That question might well arise, however, in the course of an inquiry into forces and motion. An initial theory about motion might be that things move because they are pushed or pulled. But examples would arise of things that provide their own motion, such as animals, automobiles, and airplanes. A theory that could account for these cases would be that the motion is caused by pushing against something: The animal's feet push backward against the earth, the canoe paddle pushes backward against the water, and so on. By this reasoning, jet propulsion would be explained by the expanding gases pushing against the surrounding air—a plausible explanation, but one that fails to explain jet propulsion in outer space. To think of this counterexample, however, students would need to be well aware of jet propulsion working in outer space, and a fact like that might only be thoroughly enough absorbed through knowledge-building activities like planning the trip to Mars. Thus, both kinds of activities have their place: the one leading to the processing of a lot of useful world knowledge but skirting basic principles, the other going more deeply into problems of understanding but being hampered by students' limited practical and factual knowledge.

With respect to skills, knowledge-building activities of both kinds encourage high-flown claims: planning skills, reasoning skills, problem solving, creativity, scientific method, and all the higher levels of Bloom's *Taxonomy* (1956). Such claims, as I have been suggesting, are really advertising copy. There might be some truth behind them, but that is more a fancy than a warranted belief. The second rule of thumb enjoins us to keep our expectations closer to what the students actually do in carrying out the activities. On this basis, knowledge-building activities have an outstanding advantage over most other kinds of direct and indirect learning activities that make up formal education. The activities themselves represent worthwhile things to be able to do. Being able to sit down with a group of people and work out a complex design or plan is something real people do in real life. It is not the same as bandying opinions or exchanging anecdotes. It is a demanding sort of discourse, which presents problems in keeping things moving forward without shutting out objections and divergent ideas and in taking account of relevant facts without getting overwhelmed by complications. It seems reasonable to expect that through taking part in the solution of design problems of various kinds throughout their school careers, students would emerge better prepared to take part in similar activity out in the world than if they had not done so. As for the high-sounding general skills, many are involved in the design process, but it is not necessary to claim the skills developed through design work apply outside it. Being able to participate skillfully in design work itself is enough to justify the activity.

The same argument may be made with respect to the second kind of knowledge-building activity, the kind that involves problems of explanation. The overt activities that are carried out will vary. They may consist mainly of discussion, as in the growth discussion described earlier, or the inquiry may involve building or using computer simulations (e.g., Cohen & Scardamalia, 1998; diSessa, 2000) or empirical experiments. These all exercise skills of value in the real world—diSessa (2000) argued persuasively for "computational literacy" as the overriding benefit of his approach—but regardless of the overt activity, the heart of the second kind of knowledge-building activity is participation in theoretical, explanation-seeking inquiry. This may not be a highly marketable skill in its own right, but it is something expected of people in the higher levels of every profession. Furthermore—and this is not a minor consideration in school curricula—it takes on great importance in higher education. High grades and SAT scores may be important for getting into a top-flight university, but being able to participate in intellectual inquiry is essential to doing well there and proceeding into a graduate or professional school. Beyond such practical considerations, there is also the value of explanation-seeking inquiry in any kind of active mental life.

When knowledge-building is considered as a way of learning, attention ought to be paid to all the kinds of personal knowledge discussed in chapter 5. I have been focusing on implicit understanding, because that is the *sine qua non*. If a knowledge-building activity does not deepen understanding—establish a relation to the objects of knowledge that better supports intelligent action—it should be replaced either by another kind of knowledge-building activity or by something quite different. Statable knowledge is what testers will be looking for, however, and that may require a boost from direct instruction. Teachers should have no qualms about that. If the knowledge-building that goes on is relevant to curriculum objectives, direct instruction ought to fit into it quite naturally. If it does not, something is wrong. Knowledge-building should also enhance academic skills. There is evidence that it improves reading comprehension, even though one of the things it typically replaces is reading instruction (Brown & Campione, 1994; Scardamalia et al., 1992). It can also yield gains in such nontraditional skills as graphical literacy

(Scardamalia et al., 1994). It provides a context in which academic skills are not only practiced, but are practiced to a high purpose.

As to the other kinds of personal knowledge, effects of knowledge-building are more conjectural. With difficult ideas, it is often necessary to go through a fairly extensive process of reconstruction in order to recall them well enough to be of use. Episodic memory of previous experiences with the idea are helpful in such a process. What is not very helpful is remembering that your paper airplane flew better than Johnny's while failing to remember what that was supposed to demonstrate. Being able to recall some of the line of thought that led you to an understanding of flight the first time, however, could be very helpful in getting you there again. Thus, knowledge-building ought to lead to the accumulation of episodic knowledge that is useful for later reconstruction, application, or advancement of knowledge.

The impressionistic knowledge acquired through knowledge-building will consist of attitudes and intuitions about what was encountered in the process. This could include, for instance, a sense of what kinds of questions are interesting and promising to pursue and feelings about the power or difficulty of certain ideas. In history and literature it would include a feeling for the events, historical figures, and literary works one studies. There is a legitimate concern that knowledge-building in literature and the arts may interfere with a more direct and intimate experience of the works. The product of knowledge-building is likely to be some kind of interpretation, literal or otherwise. The concern, which has been voiced for centuries, can be expressed in knowledge-building terms as follows: Students, like critics and scholars, are producing derivative artifacts. These are conceptual artifacts, in that they can be used and criticized as knowledge. The concern, therefore, is that these derivative works will be the focus of attention rather than the original works and, moreover, that the analytical and theoretical work that goes into producing them will dull the emotional and aesthetic impact of the original works. Yet research on response to poetry makes two things quite clear. One is that full appreciation of a complex poem depends heavily on knowledge—particularly knowledge of its connections to other literature—and on close reading (Peskin, 1998). The other is that, regardless of what teachers may want them to do, students will form a literal interpretation of a poem before they go on to a more aesthetic response (Church & Bereiter, 1983). I don't know what the proper resolution is, but it surely requires distinguishing the products of knowledge-building from what is learned in the process of knowledge-building.

Finally, there is regulative learning. It is acquiring the discipline that goes with the discipline—for instance, learning how to criticize constructively and how to judge whether one's idea or information is a contribution or whether it is irrelevant or redundant. Transfer of regulative learning from one domain of practice to another is liable to be slight, but even if it only transfers to later study of the same discipline it can be of considerable value as a learning outcome.

KNOWLEDGE-BUILDING AS PRODUCTIVE WORK

If students built the computers they were to use in school, this would have a marked educational advantage compared with doing electronics work of no practical consequence.[9] Part of the advantage would come from what is learned during the building. The students would likely pay closer attention to what they were doing, try harder to detect and solve problems, and thus learn more from it. The other part of the advantage would come from continued learning as they did things with the computers. Because of their knowledge of the computer's innards, they would be able to make more connections between structure and function and would be less bound to rote procedures. Besides that, there would be the enduring satisfaction of having made something they could use.

All these same advantages can be claimed for building knowledge that is subsequently put to use in school activities. I am not speaking metaphorically. As I have been arguing all along, conceptual artifacts should be regarded as real things, albeit immaterial ones. The difference between building a conceptual artifact and building a computer is that with the computer you have the alternative of going out and buying one, whereas with a conceptual artifact there is no alternative to building your own. What that means will warrant closer examination, but let us for the moment take it as a constructivist article of faith.

The comparison to building computers reveals an important difference between the two knowledge-building activities considered previously. Planning a trip to Mars, no matter how engaging and instructive it might be, does not yield a product the students will put to use. Therefore, it lacks something in immediate motivation—the plan doesn't really have to work; it only has to meet with approval—and it does not make for continuing learning. By contrast,

---

[9]The example is somewhat passé. As computers have gotten cheaper and to involve less use of the soldering gun, building one's own computer has become less instructive and less economical. I have not been able to turn up any recent examples of its being done in schools except at the postsecondary level. Students' building their own computers has given way to building their own Web sites, which is not the same kind of activity at all. So let's imagine the year is 1980 and that building a machine with 8 kilobytes of RAM would result in a useful tool.

working on an explanation of force and motion does yield a potentially usable artifact: Call it a theory of motion. If students can see that it is going to be their theory and that they will be using it in subsequent work, there should be motivation to do a good and thoughtful job. And they should learn more in subsequent uses of the theory, having constructed it themselves and being sensitive to its strengths and weaknesses.

Such claims might appear to push the notion of constructivism too far, however. The theory of motion that the students allegedly construct should, if it is to be useful, bear a very close resemblance to Newton's and will in fact owe a great deal to reference book accounts of that theory. So is it really *their* theory? Are their constructive efforts really comparable to those that would go into building a computer? Interestingly, they are. Students would not build a computer from scratch. They would assemble it from available components and according to directions. The result, if successful, would closely resemble something already on the market. Yet they would learn something from building it and would have a sense of ownership. How much learning and how much sense of ownership would at bottom depend on how much problem solving the students had to do in building the computer. This could vary, depending on how the task was structured, but in general the complexity of the assembly and of the testing that has to be carried out ensures that a lot of problem solving would go on, even if there is not the slightest effort to innovate.

The parallels to building a theory of motion are very close. Students do not build the theory from scratch (not even Newton did that), but make use of available resources such as texts, computer simulations, and packaged demonstrations. The learning and sense of ownership that result do not depend on the originality of the theory but on the problem solving and other constructive thought that go into producing the final product. This can vary depending on how the activity is structured. In one approach, where students begin by formulating their own theories and improve them through research, criticism, and comparison with other theories, a great deal of original work goes into the activity (Hewitt & Scardamalia, 1998). But even in the most didactic approach, which starts with a lecture or textbook explanation, students have to do substantial constructive work and problem solving before they can be said to *have* a Newtonian theory of motion. Karl Popper put the point very well:

> What I suggest is that we can grasp a theory only by trying to reinvent it or to reconstruct it, and by trying out, with the help of our imagination, all the consequences of the theory which seem to us to be interesting and important .... One could say that the pro-

cess of understanding and the process of the actual production or discovery of …. [theories, etc.] are very much alike. Both are making and matching processes. (Popper & Eccles, 1977, p. 461)

Of course, didactic teaching often fails to mobilize such constructive effort, but insofar as that is true it fails to do its job and is teaching mere verbalisms.

Should the student be asking, "Have I learned this content? Do I understand this concept?" The first question is generally one the student should ask, as an intentional learner. The second can generally be restated as a World 3 question. Suppose the subject matter is the formula for solving quadratic equations. Instead of asking, "Do I understand this formula?" the student may better ask, "Does this formula make sense?" That then becomes a question to be discussed, explanations or proofs constructed, and so on. In short, restating it as a World 3 issue has more indications for positive action. On the other hand, "Do I remember this formula? Can I apply it?"—these are questions about one's own competence. They are questions to guide learning rather than to guide World 3 discourse.

We need students who are *both* intentional learners and knowledge builders. We need teachers who are good at *both* promoting learning and promoting knowledge-building. The hardest idea I have ever tried to get across to teachers is that there are two jobs here, not one. No amount of enriching learning activities and turning responsibility for them over to the students will ensure knowledge-building. No amount of knowledge-building will produce all the learning that students need to acquire in school.

THE PLACE OF TEACHING

"Teach us science! We want to learn science!"

"What kind?"

"Any kind. We'll stay in at lunch. We'll be your assistants. We want to learn it all!"

> —Fourth-grade children in an inner-city school, after what may have been the first time they ever read and understood a scientific article.

One of the more tedious exhortations to which teachers are subjected (often by other teachers) is to pay more attention to learning and less to teaching. This exhortation is often lightened by the witticism, "I taught it but they didn't learn it." On any reasonable construal of the word "teach," this is nonsense. If they haven't learned it you haven't taught it. But the fact that the witticism always draws an appreciative chuckle, overworked as it is, suggests that it resonates with the experience of teachers.

The three kinds of reduction discussed earlier all tend to separate teaching from learning. Reduction to subject matter converts complex objectives into subject matter to be covered. There is a focus on learning, but it is learning dissociated from the original objectives. When, for instance, the teaching of problem-solving strategies is reduced to subject matter, the learning consists of little more than memorizing a short list of slogans. The trouble in such cases is not that students fail to learn what they are taught but that what they are taught is not what they are intended to learn. Cognitive strategies are ways of managing your mind so as to achieve certain results, and nothing like that is being taught. Really to teach cognitive strategies rather than mere slogans or rituals requires a much more complex and extended kind of teaching (cf. Bereiter & Bird, 1985; Pressley, Goodchild, Fleet, Zajchowski, & Evans, 1989).

Reduction to activities—by far the most common type of reduction in elementary schooling—pushes learning out of the picture. What the teacher does is still, for historical reasons, called teaching, but it might more accurately be called management. It is concerned with keeping the students engaged and seeing that the activities move ahead. The third type, reduction to self-expression, puts the students' interests at the center, leaving the teacher in the role of facilitator and responder. This is often what is meant by focusing on the learning rather than the teaching, although both teaching and learning are rendered ambiguous by this kind of reduction.

Dictionaries offer a range of meanings of the word "teach." One meaning is to give lessons in or hold courses in a subject. By that definition, all these reductive practices count as teaching, and there is merit in calling teachers' attention back to learning. But in the more generic sense of the word, to teach is to cause learning. It is what defines the activity. If they don't learn, you're not a teacher—just as, if they don't laugh, you're not a comedian. Teaching, in this more demanding sense, is inherently problematic. It requires what Newell and Simon (1972) called "means-end analysis," and the end—whether specified in advance or allowed to emerge opportunistically—is learning. There are always things that need monitoring, which may deflect progress toward the hoped-for learning and require strategic teaching moves.

The effect of reductive practices is to remove this problem-solving element, reducing teaching to something that can just be carried out or that presents problems of a more manageable sort. Eliminating problems in favor of routines is normal adaptive behavior. The crucial question always is whether you eliminate peripheral problems in order to devote more mental resources to the central ones or whether you routinize the central problems and thereby become deadwood (Bereiter & Scardamalia, 1993, chap. 4). In all the teachers' meetings I have attended, the most resounding applause is for those whose message is that you don't really have to teach. The message is never put in those bald terms, of course. Most often the message takes the form of an attack on the empty bucket theory of learning, a theory that invites attack because of its complete absence of defenders. Teachers are told that adherence to this discredited theory results in subverting young people's natural readiness to learn, drilling them on meaningless subskills, and boring them with lectures and busywork. But the underlying message, translated into normal English, is that teaching is the enemy of learning. It is in this context that it becomes pernicious to exhort teachers to pay attention to learning rather than teaching. It is shameless exploitation of teachers' uncertainties and disappointments, and yet the audience for it seems inexhaustible.

This probably reads like taking time out for a rant. The reason I think it is important in a chapter on the topic of learning is that this spurious antagonism between teaching and learning has come to be associated with ideas like constructivism and knowledge-building that I have been advocating here. Therefore, it is important to make clear that this isn't so. Sometimes the most important constructivist move you can make, the most vital way of promoting knowledge-building, is to sit students down and teach them something.

The epigraph to this section comes from my own experience. We had a project going in a school where literacy levels were low, much lower than the brightness and eagerness of the children would have led one to expect. The particular kind of reductionism that flourished in this school was reduction to self-expression. This was used to good effect in creating what could properly be called a therapeutic environment for children who lived where murder was a common event. But where reading was concerned it meant chat sessions that required little attention to the book in hand. We were trying to do some science and the teacher brilliantly hit on the topic of sleep, for lack of sleep and troubled sleep were common in the experience of these fourth-graders. So they talked about sleep and raised interesting questions about sleep, but how were they going to learn anything?

The don't-teach philosophy might say that kids talking about sleep, sharing their experiences and feelings, is enough, that that *is* learning. But these kids had developed some real curiosity about the topic. They had begun to ask the question that has motivated much of the research on sleep and dreaming: What is it, anyway? Uninformed discussion cannot get you very far in seeking to answer that question. But what do you do with kids who would be helpless trying to read a children's encyclopedia article? Give a little lecture perhaps or scout up an appropriate video? These might have served the immediate purpose, but we were hoping to make some advance on the more fundamental problem of the children's inability to learn from reading.

Reciprocal teaching (Palincsar & Brown, 1984) is an approach that has been successful in enabling poor readers to learn from reading. The students are taught to ask each other questions answerable from the text, raise points in need of clarification, predict what kind of information is coming next, and sum up what they have learned so far. I have had the hunch that a considerable part of the effectiveness of this approach comes from getting kids to realize that a text can tell them things about the real world that they do not already know.[10] This seems so obvious that it does not occur to educators that it might be anything a person needs to learn. Reciprocal teaching is designed to be carried out in small groups and must be worked up to through coaching. It is not something a teacher can pull out of a hat. I wanted to see whether some of the same effect could be achieved by leading the whole class through reading an informative article, using a rather free translation of the reciprocal teaching procedures. I handed out copies of the simplest article we could find that explained the use of electroencephalographic recordings (EEGs) to study the various phases of sleep. It was, however, a good 4 years beyond the prevalent reading grade level in the class.

My role did not consist of much more than managing the process. I would call on someone to read a few lines, then he or she would call on someone to ask a question, and so on, with plenty of freedom for discussion. The kids read "EEG" as "egg," but I let that pass. Their interest mounted as they began to get on to the idea of electrical events in the brain revealing what the brain was doing during sleep, and before long the formalities of reciprocal teaching gave way to excited discussion of what this all meant. When we got to the end of the article and several children had taken their shots at summing up what they now knew, I raised the question, "How do you know all this?" The question produced a stunned silence. "Do the kids in the next room know this?" I continued. No, they agreed, they probably did not. "Well, then how is it that you know all this and they don't? Did I tell it to you?" Some of them wanted to say yes, but they quickly worked it out that I had not in fact told them anything. Then you could see the light starting to dawn in face after face as they realized that they had learned it themselves by reading. And it was after that, as I was preparing to leave, that they crowded around me and the "Teach us science!" dialogue ensued.

---

[10]Stories, even realistic ones, don't count for this purpose, although they have other estimable values. Indeed, I suspect that an exclusive concentration on fiction in the beginning years of reading instruction contributes to children's seeing reading as having no connection with their efforts to learn their way around in the world.

This was one of the highest points in my life as a teacher, but did I really do any teaching? I had not conveyed information. No knowledge had poured from my head into theirs. I had merely managed an activity, as a result of which the children learned something, but was this any different from the "reduction to activities" that I have been maligning? The crucial difference, in my view, is that I was engaged in a sustained goal-directed effort to achieve a learning objective—in fact, two learning objectives. I wanted the kids to learn something of what scientists know about sleep and I wanted them to learn that they had the capacity to expand their knowledge through reading. It was 40 minutes or so of very hard work during which I was continually problem solving, choosing various strategic moves within the bounds I had set for myself, monitoring progress, and adjusting strategies to move closer to the two goals. Of course, neither goal was fully achieved, nor did I expect that; all I was hoping for was a "glimmer." That seemed enough for 40 minutes' work. So, yes, I would say, that is teaching. Preparing a lecture and rattling it off or showing a videotape would not be teaching. But embedding either of those in a discussion and working at it until there was evidence that learning had been achieved would be teaching. In short, teaching is not defined by the kinds of actions the teacher engages in but by the ends toward which those actions are adaptively employed.

In simple terms, teaching means taking responsibility for someone else's learning and carrying through the actual problem solving required to bring that learning about. Parents accept responsibility for their children's learning, but in sending their children to school they delegate the problem solving to someone else. What is becoming increasingly the practice in schools is that the teachers further delegate the problem solving to specialists. The classroom becomes a center of activities that result in most of the children learning enough to satisfy the parents and other monitors. The children who come up short are then passed on to remedial instructors and therapists, who do the actual problem solving—if it is to be done at all. The unfortunate fact is that many remedial instructors are just as committed to reductive practices as the classroom teachers. Failures may then be passed on to still another specialist, and so on to the extent of the school system's or the parents' resources. This can result in the anomaly I have encountered more than once, where a youngster, by now badly damaged from repeated experiences of failure, ends up with a psychiatrist who becomes the first person in the chain to actually sit down and try to teach the youngster to read.

There is, moreover, something important to be said for teaching even in those cases where reductive practices yield satisfactory learning of the curriculum content. When the educational process is reduced to activities and self-expression or to the teaching of incidental subject matter, the personal rewards of teaching become attenuated. The teacher can take pleasure in the happy buzz of well-occupied students and can share students' pride in jobs well done, but this is pretty thin nourishment to the teacher's ego, especially as the years roll on. When I say that the "EEG" episode was a high point in my life as a teacher, it is clearly because I feel that I made something important happen. Such feelings, whether well-founded or not, make teaching a rewarding experience. I suspect that the absence of such experiences has much to do with the reported decline in morale of school teachers. Such feelings only come from problem solving, from trying to make important things happen and occasionally succeeding. Reductive practices, by eliminating the problem solving, eliminate the experience of having successfully taught.

More important, however, is what teaching episodes mean to the students. As everyone recognizes, successful teaching requires involvement on the part of the learners. This is not easily gained. It is often much easier to get students involved in playing a game, building something, having an argument, doing an experiment, or even just doing pages in a workbook. Students can learn from all of these, and the learning may be of great significance. But the students have no experience of learning. They may experience the excitement of the activity, the joy of winning a game or argument, the satisfaction of having produced something good or of having performed well, but the learning itself is unconscious. The students who crowded around me and begged to be taught science had, I think it is safe to say, experienced something important having happened to themselves and they wanted more of it. I have seen the same thing happen with children as young as 5 or 6. The experience of learning is deeply satisfying, and when it happens for the first time, after years of unconscious learning, the effect can be explosive.

There is much talk these days about how people must become lifelong learners. I am not sure how you produce lifelong learners or even whether that is quite the right objective, but I do think it is clear how not to produce lifelong learners, and that seems to be the way education has been heading. The way not to produce lifelong learners is to divert students from the experience of learning throughout most of their school lives, confining the experience to unpleasant circumstances such as preparing for tests or overcoming a deficit.

Another way not to produce lifelong learners, however, is to make students' experiences of learning always dependent on a teacher. In the example I have been using, it is clear from the students' urgings at the end that they saw the learning they had experienced as dependent on me as teacher. One of my goals had been for them to realize that they could learn by themselves from reading, but they were no doubt correct in believing that what had happened that day could not be repeated without a teacher's help. Being able to proceed independently would lie at the end of a process during which more and more of the direction was turned over to the students. So there is a bit of a dilemma here. If the teacher stays in the background and just oversees indirect learning activities, the students get no experience of learning. If the teacher takes over and teaches, the students experience learning as something that requires a teacher.

I say "a bit of a dilemma," because it is easily resolved by adding a time dimension. In earlier work, Scardamalia and I framed the issue in terms of three kinds of teachers (Bereiter & Scardamalia, 1987a; Scardamalia & Bereiter, 1999). Teacher A reduces teaching to activities, which could be anything from old-style workbook activities to the trendiest of digital-age projects. Teacher B assumes responsibility for students' learning, doing all the problem-solving that that entails. Teacher C does that as well, but with the added objective of continually turning more of the learning process over to the students. Walking into a classroom, you cannot immediately tell these three kinds of teachers apart. One of the things you might see going on these days is the students working in groups to produce videos or multimedia presentations. The teacher is likely to be found going from group to group, checking how things are going and responding to requests. Over the course of a few days, however, differences between Teachers A and B would become evident. Teacher A's focus is entirely on the production process and its products—whether the students are engaged, whether everyone is getting fair treatment, and whether they are turning out good pieces of work. Teacher B, of course, attends to all of this as well, but Teacher B would also be attending to what the students were learning from the experience, and would be taking steps to ensure that the students are processing content and not just dealing with show. To see a difference between Teachers B and C, however, you might need to go back into the history of the media production project. What brought it about in the first place? Was it conceived from the start as a learning activity, or did it emerge from the students' own knowledge-building efforts? In one striking example of a Teacher C classroom, the students had been studying cockroaches and had learned so much from their reading and observation that they wanted to share it with the rest of the school, and production of a video came about to achieve that purpose (Lamon, Caswell, Scardamalia, & Chandra, 1997).

The differences in what might seem to be the same learning activity are thus quite profound. In the Teacher A classroom the students are learning something of media production, but the media production is likely getting in the way of learning anything else. This is much like the evaporation-condensation project reported by Anderson et al. (1997) and discussed earlier—a pure example of Teacher A pedagogy. In the Teacher B classroom, the teacher will be working to ensure that the original educational purposes of the activity are met and that it does not deteriorate into a mere media production exercise. In the Teacher C classroom, the media production is continuous with and a direct outgrowth of the learning that is coming to be embodied in the media production. The greater part of Teacher C's work has already been done before the idea of a media production even comes up, and it remains only to help the students keep sight of their purposes as they carry out the project.

In a typical classroom activity, whatever model of teaching is supposed to be in force, the teacher will manage the intellectually higher level parts of the process, leaving lower level parts to the students. The teacher asks questions, the students answer; the teacher poses problems or issues, the students pursue solutions or offer opinions; the teacher sets out an objective, the students work out ways to achieve it. In taking fourth-graders through reading the article about sleep, I might have seemed to be turning most of the process over to the students, but in fact it was I who decided as they went along whether they were understanding it or whether other questions needed to be raised or other answers or summaries solicited. And if they had become bogged down and were not making progress in understanding the article I would have done more. That is normal Teacher B behavior. Only over a course of weeks might it become evident whether I was helping the students to take over more of these higher level parts of the process, as the Teacher C model stipulates, or whether I was holding on to the reins, perhaps because only in doing so could I continue to see myself as an accomplished teacher.[11]

---

[11]Teachers A, B, and C are abstract models that of course fit real teachers only to a degree—and more on some days than others. The three models correlate with the three levels of goals discussed earlier, but not perfectly. Teacher A's focus is task completion, and any knowledge-building that takes place will likely encounter unwitting interference from the teacher. In Yarnall and Kafai's (1996) study of children designing educational computer games, for instance, the teacher discouraged subject-matter questions because they deviated from the rules of the game-design project. Teacher B's focus is learning goals—that is, goals held by the teacher for what the students are to learn—but this does not preclude knowledge-building as a way of achieving those goals. A climate that genuinely fosters knowledge-building is likely to be found only in a Teacher C classroom, but that does not mean Teacher C will necessarily favor this approach. It is quite within the bounds of the Teacher C model to focus on learning but not knowledge-building, getting students to take the initiative in pursuit of established learning goals and to help other students in the same pursuit. Probably most real-life approximations to Teacher C would see their job that way.

CONCLUSION

I see an important line of pedagogical evolution leading toward knowledge-building. Its early origins were in Dewey, Froebel, and Montessori. It took definite shape in the English infant school movement, with its emphasis on "the child's own question" (Isaacs, 1930; Weber, 1971), and it found a theoretical basis in Piaget's (1929) "constructivism." In the 1950s and 1960s, it began to be modeled on scientific research, and "learning by discovery" and "guided discovery" were born (Shulman & Keislar, 1966). In the 1980s and 1990s, aided by a growing appreciation of the social character of scientific research, the idea of communities of inquiry replaced what had up till then been a strangely individualistic conception of knowledge construction (Brown & Campione, 1990). It received a technological boost and a conceptual setback as computerists took up the cause of "project-based learning."

Throughout this century-long evolution, however, the ideas of knowledge construction and of learning remained not intertwined but hopelessly snarled. This confusion has not diminished but has perhaps reached its ultimate in project-based learning. In its more exalted forms project-based learning amounts to knowledge building:

> Project-based science focuses on student-designed inquiry that is organized by investigations to answer driving questions, includes collaboration among learners and others, the use of new technology, and the creation of authentic artifacts that represent student understanding. (Marx, Blumenfeld, Krajcik, & Soloway, 1997, p. 341)

The last phrase is a killer, however. We have seen how producing "authentic artifacts" can take over as the purpose of the enterprise, leaving the driving questions and the pursuit of understanding out in the cold. This is reduction to activities. Question-driven inquiry, an intellectual pursuit of a high order, becomes reduced to the production of posters, skits, and movies.

So common is this reductionism that I predict "project-based learning" will soon become a term of ridicule, the way "learning by doing" and "basket weaving" did in reaction against the excesses of progressive education. Indeed, what brought about that reaction against progressive education was the same kind of reduction to activities—activities that become silly as soon as they are detached from their original purposes.

To ward off such reductionism, it is essential to distinguish between learning and knowledge-building. Such a distinction enables us to see that the previous description of project-based learning muddles together two purposes that need separate attention. One is the knowledge-building purpose. This is inquiry driven by real, not contrived questions. The intended product of such inquiry is an artifact, all right, but it is a *conceptual* artifact, not a material one like a poster or a movie. Scientists do not set about their inquiries with the objective of producing posters or skits or even books and scholarly articles—or to the extent they do, they should not be serving as examples to the young. Their objective is to produce a piece of knowledge, which is likely first to find embodiment in messages exchanged with peers, before it ever finds its way into a public display. And that is a natural way for things to proceed with students' knowledge-building efforts. The resulting conceptual artifacts will be "authentic" to the extent that they are things the students can actually use—primarily for purposes of understanding real-world phenomena and texts that refer to them. That is why, in the classroom examples I discussed earlier, an explanation of jet propulsion is a more authentic artifact than a plan for a trip to Mars.

The other purpose implicit in the previous description of project-based science is learning. As a result of their question-driven inquiry, the students are supposed to acquire some scientific understanding. That seems to be the intent behind the reference to "artifacts that reflect student understanding." But the appropriate concern here is not with what the class collectively has found out. That concern belongs to knowledge-building. The concern should be with what individual students get out of the effort. A collaboratively produced demonstration is not a very accurate means of assessment for this purpose. It is likely to reflect what the most successful learner understood, or possibly something beyond what any individual has grasped.

The likely result of this muddling of purposes is that knowledge-building gets diminished if not obliterated by the intrusion of activities devised to promote learning, while learning comes to be neglected as a result of its getting confused with collective accomplishments. For the teachers, the only things they can get a firm hold on are the inquiry procedures—the observations, records, discussions, and the like—plus the "authentic artifact," the tangible, visible thing that is produced in the end. Hence, reduction to activities becomes complete.

The best hope I can see for straightening this out is to scrap project-based learning, with its built-in connotations of reduction to activities, and to substitute the idea of knowledge-building. But this is not merely a matter of labels. To grasp the idea of knowledge-building, educators have to understand the following:

- Knowledge-building is not just a process; it is aimed at creating a product.
- That product is some kind of conceptual artifact—for instance, an explanation or a design or a historical account or an interpretation of a literary work.
- A conceptual artifact is not something in the minds of the students.
- It is not something material or visible, either.
- It is nevertheless real and preferably something students can use.

Once these ideas are assimilated, it becomes obvious that what students have learned is a different issue from whether they have created a worthwhile piece of knowledge. The conceptual artifacts students have produced through knowledge-building provide evidence that some learning has occurred, but who has learned what and how well are questions still to be answered—as they are with any other activity carried out for educational purposes.

It is always hard to determine what students are learning and even harder to know what to do in case their learning is inadequate, especially because these judgments must usually be based on grossly inadequate information. But they are what makes teaching teaching. They are what it means to take responsibility for someone else's learning. To avoid them is to become a mere classroom manager. Pretty much everyone recognizes this, but there is a strong temptation to believe that some new technology or some new leap forward in educational thought has rendered those onerous judgments no longer necessary. Constructivism, learning by discovery, learner-centered education, computer-assisted instruction, whole language, hands-on learning, computer conferencing, knowledge-building: Each one comes accompanied by a little demon who whispers in the ear, "You won't have to worry about learning anymore. It will take care of itself. Stop teaching. Just let it happen."

Sometimes, as occurred in the early 1990s in California, the demon's tempting words become official policy, and then you have a disaster. More often, teachers only half believe the message, but going halfway can mean both weaker teaching and missing out on what is most valuable in the new approaches. Instead of such halfway accommodation of inquiry approaches, there ought to be whole-hearted appreciation of both the values and the limitations of three different aspects of knowledge-building:

1. Knowledge-building as productive work. This is the same kind of work in the classroom as it is in the research laboratory. It is working collectively to produce conceptual artifacts that are of

some use. For students, it is mainly a matter of producing conceptual artifacts that help them understand the world.

2. Learning through knowledge-building. This is the learning of scientific, historical, literary, or other kinds of content through knowledge-building—through solving problems of understanding or design in these domains. This is indirect learning, learning that occurs as a by-product of activity carried out for another purpose, and it cannot be taken for granted.

3. Learning to be a knowledge builder. This is the unique added advantage of knowledge-building as an educational approach. It has great potential value for living and working in a knowledge society. But like any other kind of learning, it cannot be taken for granted just because students appear to be engaged in the relevant activity. Teachers have to ascertain whether the learning is actually happening and marshal their best pedagogical resources when it is not.

Finally, it is important to keep in mind that knowledge-building is not supposed to represent everything that is good in education. Putting on a play is not knowledge-building, and yet it is a very good thing for students to do. Building a robot is not knowledge-building, although it may be accompanied by knowledge-building in the form of theories or histories of robotics or attempted solutions to any of the major problems faced in the design of adaptive robots. Community service, sports, art, and music typically do not involve knowledge-building, and it is not necessarily a good idea to supplement them with related knowledge-building activities. There are extremely bright people, geniuses even, who are not knowledge builders. Gifted athletes and performing artists often fall into this category. Inventors, entrepreneurs, and leaders—the Edisons, Carnegies, Gandhis, and Napoleons of the world—create things that embody ideas, sometimes original ideas. But the ideas are incidental to the gadgets, enterprises, causes, or conquests that are the focus of their efforts.

9

Subject Matter That Matters

Only in education, never in the life of farmer, sailor, merchant, physician, or laboratory experimenter, does knowledge mean primarily a store of information aloof from doing.

—Dewey (1916/1944, p. 185)

Education to be living and effective must be directed to informing pupils with those ideas, and to creating for them those capacities which will enable them to appreciate the current thought of their epoch.

—Whitehead (1929, p. 83)

The conventional way of viewing the problem of school subject matter goes like this: There is a huge and growing mountain of things to know. Schools can teach only a small part. Therefore they must select what is most important and what will provide the best foundation for going on and learning more. Everything beyond that is pedagogy—the art of ensuring that students master and retain what has been presented. This is probably still how most of the public thinks about it. However, most of current educational thought reflects an intuition that content and pedagogy are more closely intertwined than this. There is content *in* the pedagogy—the so-called "hidden curriculum," which is conveyed through the manner of teaching. Furthermore, thinking of subject matter as a mountain of things to be learned predisposes toward a certain kind of pedagogy, which most modern educators oppose. Thus, the problem of what to teach has become thoroughly commingled with the problem of how to teach, and there emerges a higher level problem: How to think about what to teach.

That there is a serious problem here becomes evident whenever people start discussing what should be taught in school. Flat assertions of wildly different kinds are made: More content. Less content. Multiple intelligences. Cognitive apprenticeship. Conceptual change. Process not product. Higher order skills. Learner-centered curriculum. Appeals are made to various documents issued by professional associations as if these were the absolute authority on education in the established disciplines, but then these disciplines are accused of artificially partitioning the curriculum. There is no real discussion because there is no paradigm within which it may be conducted (and hence, of course, no possibility of a paradigm shift).

The virtual impossibility of productive discourse is dramatized in an anecdote reported by E. D. Hirsch, Jr. (1996). Pursuant to the ideas set out in his book, *Cultural Literacy*, Hirsch had been editing resource books intended to encapsulate essential knowledge for elementary school children. At a meeting of school administrators, he was asked whether he had enjoyed this task.

> I said, yes indeed, that I had learned a great deal. Next question: What had I learned that was most interesting? I pondered. Well, perhaps, the most exciting thing for me was at last to understand the relations between the earth and the sun during a year's orbit, and why, at the equator, spring and fall are the hottest seasons. Then, from another quarter, a dash of cold water was thrown on this momentary enthusiasm when an educator asked me if I thought that tidbit of information had made me a better person. (p. 55)

It is not recorded what Hirsch replied. But what could one have said that would have even the slightest chance of initiating a worthwhile discussion?

The learning that Hirsch described was much more than a "tidbit of information." It was an understanding that tied together and made sense out of many tidbits of information. It was the very kind of understanding that research reveals is most pathetically lacking in American students. Why could Hirsch's critic not see that? Perhaps if Hirsch had said, "I finally understood the implications of the

Copernican model of the solar system," this would have sounded impressive enough to have averted the criticism. All educators surely recognize that there are big and important principles that are worth learning, but they may not be able to recognize them unless they are so labeled. If Hirsch had reported that he gained in understanding of energy and its importance, this too would probably have been accepted as worthy. *Energy* is a concept that figures prominently in virtually every science curriculum guide. Yet so notable a scientist as Richard Feynman (1997) has declared it unsuitable for elementary education. At the level that children can understand it, he said, *energy* explains nothing.

The suggestion that learning, to be worthwhile, should make one a better person may sound fatuous, and in the reported context it certainly was. But behind it is a legitimate concern that knowledge acquired in school should do something for the learner. If it does not improve character and has no obvious practical application either, however, then what could it do for the learner? Satisfy curiosity, perhaps, but if that is the purpose, it suggests an altogether different approach to content selection from the one Hirsch advocates, which is based on considerations of what members of a society need to possess as shared knowledge.

Early in the 20th century, two important philosophers turned their attention to problems of school subject matter—John Dewey in America and Alfred North Whitehead (although he was later to move to America) in England. Looking at rather different school systems, they saw essentially the same thing: students' heads being crammed with information that was supposed to represent the accumulated riches of a great civilization but that in effect amounted to little more than mental stuffing. Both Dewey and Whitehead held academic subject matter in high regard. The difficulty that both perceived was its remoteness from the lives of students. They did not, as many of their successors have done, recommend replacing it with content more "relevant" to students' interests. Rather, they saw the educational problem as one of making contact. The value of what was being taught had somehow to be realized by students in the here and now. It had to serve some purpose in activities that were already meaningful to them.

That challenge to pedagogy remains largely unmet even to this day. Whitehead's (1929) description of the school curriculum early in the 20th century applies with little modification to what may be observed today:

Algebra, from which nothing follows; Geometry, from which nothing follows; Science, from which nothing follows; History,

from which nothing follows; a Couple of Languages, never mas-
tered; and lastly, most dreary of all, Literature, represented by
plays of Shakespeare, with philological notes and short analyses of
plot and character to be in substance committed to memory. Can
such a list be said to represent Life, as it is known in the midst of the
living of it? The best that can be said of it is, that it is a rapid table of
contents which a deity might run over in his mind while he was
thinking of creating a world, and had not yet determined how to
put it together. (p. 19)

Despite several generations of effort to make school subject matter more meaningful to students, evidence indicates the outcomes
are still deplorable. It is no great exaggeration of the findings from
research on students' misconceptions to say that students understand hardly anything of what they are taught (cf. Gardner, 1991).
Literature teaching has perhaps changed the most since Whitehead
wrote. Shakespeare has largely given way to contemporary writers
whose themes are closer to students' experience; analyses of plot,
character, and language have given way to thematic discussions. Yet
reading assessments in the United States indicate that most students
cannot put together any sort of articulate response to a literary text
(Donahue, Voekl, Campbell, & Mazzeo, 1999).

Although both philosophers concluded that the way to make academic subject matter meaningful was to make it useful (a more radical idea in their day than it seems now), they understood usefulness
somewhat differently. Whitehead, I think, had a broader conception
and one more in tune with modern requirements. Dewey, with his
American pragmatism, saw usefulness in more concrete terms. His
was the conception that prevailed and that became degraded into the
"learning by doing"—which is now part of the mindlessness of
schooling rather than an antidote to it.

Broadly stated, Dewey's position was thoroughly consistent with
Whitehead's, insisting only that there be genuine contact between
students and subject matter. In discussing the value of information
conveyed in school, Dewey (1916) asked:

Does it grow naturally out of some question with which the student is concerned? Does it fit into his more direct acquaintance so
as to increase its efficacy and deepen its meaning? If it meets these
two requirements, it is educative. The amount heard or read is of
no importance—the more the better, *provided* the student has a
need for it and can apply it in some situation of his own. (186)

In moving from these general criteria to the specifics of subject
matter content, however, Dewey made two assumptions that must

have seemed self-evident to him, as they still do to many childhood educators, although both are wrong. The first was that children's knowledge and interests are confined to the concrete and familiar. To appropriate a current term, we may call this the "hands-on" fallacy. Dewey (1916) was quite explicit in endorsing it and in holding that abstraction is bad stuff for the young:

> It is not true that the experience of the young is unorganized—that it consists of isolated scraps. But it is organized in connection with direct practical centers of interest. The child's home is, for example, the organizing center of his geographical knowledge. (p. 183)

> The things we are best acquainted with are the things we put to frequent use—such things as chairs, tables, pen, paper, clothes, food, knives and forks ... the things with which we are not accustomed to deal are strange, foreign, cold, remote, "abstract." (p. 185)

I have encountered teachers, imbued with this Deweyan belief, who could not countenance having children read a story in which a canoe figured without first bringing a real canoe into the classroom and letting the children sit in it and paw it over until they were familiar enough with it to go ahead with the story. Yet these same children would go home, turn on the television, and immerse themselves in worlds of dinosaurs, space travel, fantasy heroes and monsters, princes and princesses. But these exotic interests are only part of the story. As I show later, young students can get interested in such topics as gravity, electricity, evolution, the adaptive mechanisms of animals they have never seen, and the customs of peoples long dead. Dewey remarked at one point on the fact that children outside of school are full of questions yet display no curiosity about the content of school lessons (p. 155). This he attributed to the children's doing things outside school that give rise to questions. But the most profound of children's questions seldom relate to activities of the moment. They relate to the larger issues and forces that shape their world—birth, death, good, evil, power, danger, survival, generosity, adventure (cf. Egan, 1988). Adults, even the most "child-centered," tend to trivialize children's interests, making them out to be more mundane and egocentric than they really are, and thus positing a distance between children's interests and intellectual subject matter that is greater than it needs to be.

The other fallacy that Dewey promoted is one firmly held by today's advocates of problem-centered and project-based learning. It is that practical tasks and problems lead naturally to inquiry into the underlying science. I know of no evidence that this is true, and so I chalk it up to wishful thinking.

If practical problems or projects are significant enough in their own right, there is no need to claim far-fetched cognitive benefits. If students are learning to sail a boat, we do not need to claim that this will arouse their interest in reactive forces. If students are learning to put together their own televised news reports, we may count it as a lucky bonus if their coverage of some event leads them to investigate its historical antecedents. If the students are carrying out a public opinion survey, we need not expect this to fill them with curiosity about the mathematical basis of statistical estimation. In each case the activity can be justified by what is learned up-front. But, as noted in the preceding chapter, schools are sorely limited in the extent of real-world problems and projects they can mount. Few schools can teach sailing or anything else that requires an environment beyond school and neighborhood. And it is very difficult to manage projects such as newscasting or opinion research in such a way that all 20 or 30 students in a class are doing something educationally productive. As a result, school problems and projects tend to be contrived for the purpose of indirect cognitive benefits, and if those should prove illusory the effort will have been wasted. That, I suspect, is why educators cling to the learning-by-doing fallacy despite its incompatibility with reason and evidence. They have to believe in hidden cognitive benefits, because otherwise what students do in school will be seen as contrived and frivolous, a diversion from teaching what students really need to learn.

There is, of course, some truth in both the hands-on and the learning-by-doing fallacies. Not only children but adults are engaged with immediate practical and social matters much of the time and tend to get lost if they stray too far from the concrete and palpable. But we look to formal education to develop precisely that part of human competence, present even in the young, that is able to deal with ideas and other abstract entities. We do learn by doing. The trouble with folk theory of mind is that it does not allow educators to recognize that working with ideas is also learning by doing.

WHAT MAKES KNOWLEDGE USEFUL?

Independently of each other, it seems, Dewey and Whitehead settled on the radical notion that school subject matter should be useful to students in the here and now. If taken seriously, this notion completely undermines the conventional approach to curriculum design. Two criteria guide the conventional approach, both of them vague: the criterion of usefulness in later life and the criterion of adult consensus on what students ought to know. The two tend to merge when it comes to the core academic subjects. Their anticipated usefulness is too diffuse to have a bearing on the selection of specific content and so potential usefulness becomes just one of the issues in discussions of what students ought to know. At the highest levels, where official guidelines are laid down for schools to follow, these discussions tend to be dominated by experts in the academic disciplines, and so what every student ought to know tends to reflect the requirements of the discipline rather than requirements of the world at large, and certainly not the requirements of the students' immediate lives.

To several generations of educators influenced by Dewey, making subject matter useful to students in the here and now has meant trying to twist the traditional school subjects around somehow to make them either practical or significant for the students' personal lives. Practicality has often worked well with older students (witness the technical schools and colleges), but not with the young. At the age when children are supposed to be mastering arithmetic they have little interest in the checkbook balancing, comparison shopping, and home handyperson calculations that represent the everyday uses of arithmetic. In fact, children's practical concerns tend to be of such a highly situated kind that they have little call for formal knowledge of any kind.

In a study concerned with the relations between schooling and work, Alan Lesgold (1996) and his associates interviewed expert machine tool makers. When asked about the relevance of school subjects to their work, they unanimously endorsed trigonometry. Lesgold worked out with them a trigonometric problem representative of those they came across in their jobs but not requiring any machinist's knowledge. When he presented the problem to high school mathematics teachers, they had considerable difficulty with it, although vocational education teachers solved it with ease. Lesgold concluded with the very Deweyan observation that "school subjects have strayed too far from life" (p. 156). He offered sound proposals for bringing school subject matter into closer alignment with needs of the workplace, but—except for students who already have one foot in the workforce—such reforms are not likely to result in subject matter of more immediate use to the learners. They might even have the opposite effect, replacing intrinsically appealing material with material whose value lies in practical applications of no immediate interest to the students. Certainly that has been the case with practical mathematics, a low-road alternative to algebra intended to equip students with mathematical skills useful in everyday adult life but succeeding mainly in setting a standard for dullness.

Whitehead, as I remarked, seemed to have a broader conception of the usefulness of subject matter than Dewey did. "Of course, education should be useful," he wrote (1929, p. 14), "whatever your aim in life. It was useful to Saint Augustine and it was useful to Napoleon. *It is useful, because understanding is useful* [italics added]." Like Dewey, he meant useful in the student's immediate experience: "I would only remark that the understanding which we want is an understanding of an insistent present. The only use of a knowledge of the past is to equip us for the present .... The present contains all that there is." (p. 14). But he did not see usefulness in such pragmatic terms as Dewey (1916) was wont to do:

> By utilising an idea, I mean relating it to that stream, compounded of sense perceptions, feelings, hopes, desire, and of *mental activities adjusting thought to thought*, which forms our life. (p. 15)

The goal was not simply practical efficacy and the enrichment of personal meanings but was, as quoted in the epigraph to this chapter, enabling students "to appreciate the current thought of their epoch" (Whitehead, 1929, p. 83).

Dewey saw the importance of understanding as well and the value of education in enriching meaning, so perhaps the only difference I am talking about is one of focus. The image of the student that comes through from Dewey and that seems to have shaped his educational proposals is that of the energetic 4-H Club member, busy going to meetings, raising a calf, conducting a bake sale, and helping Dad figure out how much seed corn to buy (remember, this was the early 1900s). The image that comes through from Whitehead is that of the forlorn schoolboy, far from home in some moldering academy, boning for exams and wondering what it is all about. Two consequential differences spring to mind. The first is that to produce Dewey's kind of youngster you should not be looking to the schools, you should be looking to 4-H Clubs and the like. Schools will always prove inadequate and fundamentally ill-suited for such a purpose. The second is that, although Whitehead's kind of student may also be absorbed in hobbies and various practical and social pursuits, these take place within an encompassing mental life. The student is not merely trying to solve this or that problem that has arisen out of practical activities but is engaged in a more global effort to make sense of the world. This is an effort in which schooling could be but usually is not profoundly relevant.

As I try to read between the lines of these two estimable philosophers, it seems to me that the most fundamental difference between them lay in Whitehead's greater willingness to regard ideas as real things. Accordingly, an idea could be truly useful without its having to solve some practical or social problem. It could be useful because it helps in understanding some other idea or in resolving an apparent inconsistency or anomaly or because it opens up an exciting new line of thought, leading to the generation of new ideas.

A study reported by Bereiter and Scardamalia (1989) illustrates the use and nonuse of new ideas. We presented what were presumed to be new ideas to elementary school students and asked them to think aloud in response. One was the idea that, contrary to the image projected in television cartoons, commercials, and health lessons, harmful germs are not really trying to be bad: "They just want to live quietly, eat, and make more germs." At the lowest levels of response, children ignored, misunderstood, or contradicted the statement and went on declaiming against microbial aggressors. Then there was an interesting level of response at which children indicated they had grasped the point, but showed no appreciation of its novelty or its incompatibility with their existing conceptions. They might, for instance, merely paraphrase without comment. Such behavior suggests a kind of pathological response to school-based information that Dewey (1916) noted: "All too frequently it forms another strange world which just overlies the world of personal acquaintance" (p. 186). Research on children's scientific conceptions has documented such anomalies. Having been taught in school that the earth is round, whereas they can plainly see that it is flat, some children resolve the discrepancy by concluding there are two earths: the one where they live and the one they hear about at school (Vosniadou & Brewer, 1987, 1992). The children interviewed in our research may similarly have been on the way toward constructing two orders of germs, the hostile kind that make you sick and the indifferent kind existing in the fictitious world of school subject matter.

These reponses indicate a failure or disinclination to think about the relations of ideas to one another, to engage in the "adjusting of thought to thought," as Whitehead put it. But some students did recognize there was something new to think about. "That's not exactly my idea of a germ," one child said. Such students might try to reconcile new ideas and old. For instance, "Well, they don't really know that they're bad, but they're just living their normal way, but everybody else thinks they're bad." And one child started to run with the new idea, expanding on its implications: "I wonder if germs are intelligent. I guess not. Maybe there's a whole new world, like … there is fighting going on between the good and the bad …. It's kind of neat when you think about it, 'cause to think of a whole new world inside your body."

Making sense of the world, increasing coherence, resolving anomalies—these are the most immediate uses of school subject matter. There may also be practical uses, which ought surely to be exploited, but sense-making uses are the bread and olive oil of academic life, whether in the kindergarten or the university. Therefore it is the failure of schools to promote these uses of knowledge that constitutes their most profound failure, a failure that no amount of drill and practice on one hand or practical projects and hands-on activities on the other hand can remedy.

WHAT ARE CONCEPTS FOR?

What is the concept of *gravity* good for—or the concept of *oxygen*, *human rights*, or *triangle*? I am not asking what good does it do students to learn such concepts, although that question follows closely. I am asking what is the good of having such concepts at all? That is a question I have never seen addressed in school textbooks, yet it is surely prior to the question of why students should be expected to learn them. Schoolbooks will say why gravity and oxygen themselves are important, but that is something quite different. The *concept* of oxygen came some years before discovery of the actual substance, and as for gravity, Newton went to his grave dissatisfied because he did not know what it was—and in a concrete sense we still don't know. Theoretical concepts were created to serve certain purposes. It would seem that in at least some cases those purposes ought to be relevant to the students' own purposes. Instead, textbooks present concepts as if they were talking about the natural world. Gravity, capital, metamorphosis, and so on are defined, and explained, illustrated with examples as if they belonged to the same order of things as opposums, thunder storms, and mold. They are treated as constituting how the world is. One no more asks the purpose of the concept of gravity than one asks the purpose of turtles. Children will tell you that the purpose of gravity is to keep us from falling off the earth (one child even brilliantly deduced that the reason there is less gravity on the moon is that there are fewer things there and so less gravity is needed to hold them down). But children are talking about gravity conceived of as perhaps a substance, not gravity the concept. They shouldn't be criticized for this. Nothing they have been taught in school is likely to have suggested anything different.

Gravity, the concept, is something real, too—or so I have been arguing, following Popper. But it is a real artifact. With artifacts, one does ask what they are for. If you have visited collections of gadgetry of the past, such as those found in restored villages, you have probably seen puzzling contraptions that elicit the same question from nearly every spectator: "What's it for?" It is the first thing you ask about a novel artifact, and it is the first thing students ought to be asking about a newly encountered idea. "The vital first step towards understanding a theory," Popper (1972, p. 182) said, "is to understand the problem situation in which it arises." Without that, it is hard to see how academic subject matter could ever be rendered useful.

Oxygen, we know now, is material stuff. You can buy containers of it or purchase whiffs of it in some bars. But before the material stuff was isolated, oxygen existed as a concept, which was invented to account for such puzzling facts as that iron gets heavier when it rusts. Most of the concepts taught in school are of this kind. They were invented in an effort to explain something. Their use lies in making sense of the world.

There is a whole other range of concepts, however, that do not have this problem-solving character. These are everyday concepts like *dog, chair, cloud, man, woman, tree, breathe, run, sleep, green*, and *icicle*. In a practical sense these concepts do simply constitute how the world is. That is, they divide the world up into categories that correspond to how we experience it. Of course, to an extent we experience the world the way we do because of the categories we have learned, but subjectively it all comes to the same thing. An important line of research has produced evidence that these *basic-level* concepts, as they are called, are psychologically quite different from the higher level concepts of the sciences and disciplines.[1] For the most part they are not definable. People learn them by generalizing from instances. And people are astonishingly good at doing it. Very young children will quickly learn to recognize elephants, giraffes, hippos, kangaroos, lions, chimps, and so on from picture books; when they are then taken to a zoo, they will quite amazingly recognize these animals in the flesh, even though all they had previously seen was one cartoonish drawing of each. Basic-level concepts typically have short names and many identifying characteristics, making them easy to learn and hard to confuse with one another. They divide the world up in ways that make a difference in day-to-day living. As I remarked elsewhere (Bereiter, 1992), it makes a difference whether the animal in your garden is a cow or a dog, it makes much less difference what breed of cow or dog it is, and it makes hardly any difference at all that it is a mammal and not a marsupial.

The difference between basic-level concepts and the higher and lower level concepts that are the concern of formal education is essentially the difference between Popper's World 2 and World 3. Basic-level concepts belong to the psychological world. Folk theory would consider them to be things in the mind. They are more accu-

---

[1]See Rosch (1975, 1978) and Smith (1989).

rately thought of as abilities or dispositions. Fairly simple connectionist networks can form basic-level concepts simply by adjusting to covariances in information, without creating anything resembling a mental object (Rumelhart et al., 1986). To say that your concept of *chair* and mine are similar is only to say that our cognitive systems are tuned to respond similarly when it comes to applying the label "chair." We should probably find that the similarity is near perfect as regards objects found in a typical furniture store but that it would falter as we encountered the more fanciful creations found in design galleries. But if you thought something should be called a chair and I did not, we would not find it profitable to argue about the matter. The concept *chair* is not a proper World 3 object. It is not discussible, subject to criticism, and susceptible to improvement the way World 3 objects characteristically are.[2]

Concepts like *gravity*, *genes*, and *contract*, however, are World 3 objects. They have histories. They exist independently of what you or I know or think about them. We can participate in efforts to refine, improve, find new uses for them, or retire them from use. What is most important from an educational standpoint, however, is that students can become knowledgeable aboutthe concepts themselves, not merely about what the concept refers to. In fact, it is a very important consideration that many of the higher-level concepts do not have referents. Students tend to assume that they do, that the concepts refer to objects or substances (Chi, Slotta, & deLeeuw, 1994). But this is further to confuse them with basic-level concepts.

Much of school instruction is of the "all about" variety—all about dinosaurs, Alaska, volcanoes, Harriet Tubman, the Aztecs, fossil fuels, or whatever. There is not much difference between textbook-oriented and activity-oriented classrooms in this regard, except that in the former all the students are likely to be acquiring information about the same things whereas in the latter different students will be collecting information on different topics. Cross-curriculum integration, in the form of "thematic units," is currently hot with progressive educators. This means that a unit on the Aztecs, for instance, will not only occupy social studies but will ring all the other areas of the curriculum as well into amassing information related to the topic. There is also not much change from the primary grades to high school. The most extreme example of an "all about" textbook I have seen was one for high school chemistry, which went on for more than 500 pages of small print describing inorganic substance after inorganic substance according to an unvarying sched-

---

[2]Lexicographers might argue at length about how to define the word "chair," but that only indicates the difficulty of translating habits into rules.

ule. "All about" learning can be fascinating or indifferent or unbearably dull, depending on the appeal of the objects being studied. The chemistry text probably wiped out whatever mild interest a generation of Pittsburgh high school students might have had in the composition of matter. Yet I have seen similar compendia of facts, except that they were about baseball players, which I found pleasantly interesting, and I imagine there are students who would find them equally absorbing. But others would not. Pity the poor elementary school student who happens not to be interested in dinosaurs or space travel!

Whatever its virtues or drawbacks in the school context, "all about" learning is the kind of learning we naturally do with respect to basic-level concepts. The course of learning basic-level concepts typically consists of a brief period of mastering the categorization followed by the life-long accumulation of knowledge associated with the concept. Thus, the young child may go through some months of getting it straight that not every large animal is a horsey and becoming able to distinguish horses from nonhorses in various settings and despite variations in color and stature, whereas the accumulation of knowledge about horses goes on indefinitely. If the child in school undertakes a research project on horses, this will be a natural extension of the knowledge accumulation that has been going on since early childhood. I have elsewhere (Bereiter, 1992) referred to this kind of learning as "referent centered." The only thing that ties it together is the referent, the real-world thing that it is *about*. If the referent is *China*, all kinds of historical, geographical, anthropological, and political information may be processed, which have nothing in common except that they all have to do with China. Whether this constitutes useful knowledge depends entirely on whether it is helpful when one reads about, talks about, or encounters the referent. With basic-level concepts, it is clearly a good thing to have your knowledge associated with the referent. Your knowledge of horses should be available when you encounter a horse—either in discourse or in the flesh. There are not many other occasions when it will come into play. But this is far from the case with your knowledge of gravity. If that knowledge only comes into play when gravity is the topic of discourse, education will have failed.

"Inert knowledge" is the term Whitehead (1929) coined for precisely that kind of failed learning. It is knowledge that students can exhibit when it is specifically called for (on an examination, for instance), but that otherwise plays no role in their lives. Whitehead attributed it to the fragmentation of the curriculum and to the lack of application. I have suggested that at a deeper level inert knowledge arises from treating higher level concepts in the same way as basic-level ones, resulting in referent-centered learning (Bereiter, 1992). The time when we want our knowledge of gravity to come into play is not only when gravity is referred to but, more important, when we encounter a problem that a knowledge of gravity can help us solve. Accordingly, I called gravity a *problem-centered* concept.

The paper in which I introduced the ideas of referent-centered and problem-centered knowledge seems to have been more thoroughly misunderstood by favorably disposed readers than anything else I have written. The difficulty, it appears, arises from confusion with the more familiar idea of "problem-based learning" (Savery & Duffy, 1995). Problem-based learning is actually tangential to the distinction I was trying to make. It refers to a teaching method in which learning arises from work on problems. The learning that occurs could be either referent centered or problem centered, depending on what kind of problem solving goes on. Often the problem posed is an engineering or design problem—for instance, to design a new sports complex. The learning in such cases is likely to be referent centered—knowledge about sports complexes. In other cases the problem may be to explain a perplexing phenomenon or to figure out what is going wrong in a situation. This is often the case with the problems posed in medical education, where problem-based learning originated. Theoretical concepts may well be brought into play to solve such problems, and in this case students should be accumulating what I called problem-centered knowledge. But problem-centered knowledge could also be acquired by listening to a lecture, if the lecturer was successful in getting students to understand the problem situations in which the concepts or principles are relevant.

I am not arguing against referent-centered learning. It is a good idea for students to know something about the various nations, historical figures, plant and animal species, and so on. To the extent that schools pursue this kind of learning, however, they must contend with the perennial problems of too much to learn, too little time, and the lack of use for what is learned. Motivation is consequently a problem for referent-centered learning. If the referent itself is interesting, students will eagerly accumulate knowledge about it. That is why typical school programs devote inordinate attention to dinosaurs and hardly any to soy beans. Making referent-centered learning interesting when the referents themselves are not already interesting to the students has been a continuing problem that teachers and textbooks often treat in a blundering way. Lard the lesson with interesting but tangential stories and students tend to remember the stories and forget the rest (Hidi et al., 1982).

A myth that goes around among futurists is that three fourths of the knowledge acquired in university engineering schools is obsolete within a few years of graduation. The only way this could be true would be if all the learning were referent centered and the referents themselves became obsolete. That has been a long-standing complaint about high school shop courses—that students learn to use obsolete tools to repair obsolete cars, for instance. But no sensible engineering program would be so referent bound. Problem-centered concepts and skills do not go out of date rapidly. Particular problem solutions may go out of date, but the principles behind the solutions do not. Referent-centered knowledge about natural kinds does not go out of date rapidly, either.[3] What is true of dogs today will very likely be true a hundred years from now. It is only high-tech artifacts that become rapidly obsolete. Whatever computer skill you may be acquiring right now, you can be sure clever people are at work figuring out ways to make that skill unnecessary.

With the accelerating growth of knowledge, there are not only more facts but also more concepts than can imaginably be taught. The problem of choosing which concepts are most worthy of being taught is a problem that every good curriculum committee takes very seriously. Solving it typically involves consultation, sometimes wide-ranging consultation with subject-matter experts, curriculum specialists, child developmentalists, teachers, employers, and parents. The result is likely to be a list that is either too long or too short. The consultative process tends inevitably toward a long list. It is much easier to justify the inclusion of a concept than to justify its exclusion. If the list gets ridiculously long, there will be a move to consolidate it. That generally means replacing concepts with categories of concepts, resulting in a short list of broad categories, like the chapter titles in a textbook, and usually just as conventional.

What curriculum planning needs is not a better process but a better criterion for selection. If the criterion is whatever seems important from the point of view of each consultant, then the more consultants you have the longer the list will be. The criterion I suggest is not an easy one to apply, but I think it is the only criterion that can sift out the concepts that are not only important but optimally learnable: *What use can students of the designated age and kind make of this concept in their efforts to understand the world?* It may strike you that this proposal is utterly impractical. On the typical curriculum committee not one person will have a basis for answering the question. I admit it. That's what's wrong with educational thought. That's why we need a new theory of knowledge and mind. That's

---

[3]But referent-centered knowledge about institutions and artifacts does go out of date, of course. I have been told of an impoverished church school where the students were obliged to memorize facts about rice production and railroad lines in China from a textbook that dated from before World War II.

why I am writing a book about knowledge and mind instead of a book about how to reform education.

UNDERSTANDING THE WORLD VERSUS UNDERSTANDING THEORIES ABOUT THE WORLD

One of the most serious objections I encounter to adopting Popper's three worlds metaphor for educational purposes runs as follows: The biggest problem in subject-matter teaching is that teachers are inclined to treat their subject as consisting of a body of knowledge to be transmitted to the students. The World 3 concept reinforces this tendency. It is better, therefore, to focus on the processes of inquiry and meaning making than on knowledge as such.

It could be argued that the cure in this case often turns out worse than the disease (cf. Hirsch, 1996), but more to the point is that the disease has been incorrectly diagnosed. The naive epistemology lying behind knowledge-transmission pedagogy is a two-worlds epistemology. The absence of a clear conception of the third world is what makes it difficult to work out a sensible relationship between already available knowledge and students' own knowledge-building efforts.

In the two-worlds epistemology, subject-matter knowledge is treated as no different from any other worldly knowledge. Suppose your partner asks you where the electric heater is and you say it is in the basement locker. There are two issues in this situation. One is your belief, held with greater or lesser confidence, about the whereabouts of the electric heater. This is a World 2 issue. The other is the actual location of the heater, a World 1 issue. Irrespective of your World 2 state of knowledge, the heater either is or is not in the basement locker. There is no World 3 object involved here. If you say, "My theory is that the heater is in the basement locker," you are not using the word "theory" in a way that distinguishes theories from personal opinions.

For most everyday purposes, two worlds are enough. But see what happens when this naive epistemology is carried over into subject-matter instruction. The teacher states that a meteor hitting the earth caused the extinction of the dinosaurs. The two elements at issue parallel those in the electric heater situation. The World 2 element is the teacher's belief about dinosaur extinction. The World 1 element is what actually happened back in dinosaur times. Again there is no World 3 element involved. This is not to say that the situation is without problems. There may be considerable discussion about the plausibility of the claim that a meteor was responsible for dinosaur extinction, and during this discussion the phrase "meteor theory" may well appear. But unless the teacher makes a point of it, the discussion is not likely to be about the theory. The discussion will be about what *really* happened, just as a household discussion may be about where the heater *really* is.

There is a difference between the household situation and the classroom situation, however, and it has to do with the relative importance of World 2. Where the electric heater is concerned, what people believe or claim to know is quite secondary to the World 1 issue of where the heater actually is. But in schooling, as we have noted, the focus is on World 2. Schooling is not fundamentally concerned with what happened to the dinosaurs, it is concerned with what students believe or know about dinosaurs. Of course, there is a concern that what students learn should be right, and so what actually happened to the dinosaurs is not irrelevant, but that issue has become badly distorted by forcing it into a two-worlds framework.

The pages of science education journals have become full of worrying about how to teach, given the problematic nature of scientific knowledge. Few teachers who read such journals would any longer state baldly that a meteor brought an end to the dinosaurs or even that the earth is a globe. They would hedge their statements somehow or would put it as, "Scientists now think that a meteor was what caused the dinosaurs to become extinct." If they are really *au courant* they will introduce or invite alternative explanations, may even draw in a handy myth, and encourage the students to talk it over and make up their own minds. None of this does much to the underlying epistemology, however. There are still just people's beliefs (World 2), which have some problematic relation to a truth of the matter (World 1). Some bold teachers, influenced by postmodernism, may reject World 1, thus making everything a matter of personal or collective belief, but such advanced notions are unlikely to have any effect on their students. As far as students (and most teachers, we may assume) are concerned, there really were dinosaurs and something really happened to them; that World 1 reality is what they are studying and talking about.

There is nothing particularly wrong with this, and with young children there is probably no alternative to the two-worlds model. Subject-matter learning is then a matter of bringing beliefs into conformity with the way things really are. A lot of good science has been done with just such a model, and a lot of good education as well. The two-worlds model does, however, lend itself to the unfortunate tendencies sophisticated educators worry about. It disposes teachers to think of themselves as intermediaries between a body of truths held by scientists and scholars and the innocent minds of the students. The result too often is slavishness to the printed word, investment of scientists with priestly status, reduction of experiment to demonstration of pre-established truths, and reduction of study to memorization.

As long as the two-world's model remains in force, however, there is no escaping these tendencies. It does no good to harp on the fact that today's truths may become tomorrow's fallacies. Everyone knows that, and it will not trouble the sensible teacher, however much it may preoccupy the educational theorist. The electric heater may not be in the locker after all, but that does not prevent us from declaring it to be there, given that we have no present reason to believe otherwise. Reducing the two worlds to one, by making everything a matter of unfounded opinion, may gratify some philosophical need but all it does educationally is remove any reason to study anything. Shifting the focus of instruction from substance to process can have either of two results. It can simply provide alternative ways to get the truths into students' heads—through discovery learning instead of didactics, for instance. Or it can reduce schooling to edutainment—to activities having some vague relation to a body of subject matter but pursued for their immediate amusement value.

Bringing World 3 into the instructional picture avoids most of the problems and misdirections I have been noting. Now, in addition to the teacher's and students' beliefs about dinosaurs and the actual events of eons ago we have the element of conceptual artifacts—theories—that have been constructed to explain dinosaur extinction. These may now become objects of study. As with other human constructions, such as food processors and fax machines, we may investigate what they do and do not do and how well they do it. In this context, issues of authoritativeness assume a more reasonable place. The fact that most scientists believe a certain theory becomes one among a number of items of information to be taken into account in judging the theory. It may weigh heavily in some cases, where the students have no independent basis for judgment, but in other cases it may be quite incidental to the students' own critical analysis.

Bringing conceptual artifacts into instruction does raise dangers of its own, however. Even postmodernists become uncomfortable with the prospect of students bandying theories about in the absence of experimentation or concern for evidence. And it regularly happens. Discussion focused on ideas can easily degenerate into verbalism and excessive fondness for one's own notions. So, yes, World 1 must also figure in the classroom, and it can do so without our having to settle the timeworn problems of the relation between World 1 and World 3. Students are perfectly capable of recognizing that a theory is in trouble when it implies something contrary to fact. One stark instance occurred when a student offered an account of how monkeys gradually became apes and apes gradually became humans. Another student entered the comment, "According to your theory there shouldn't be monkeys and apes anymore, but monkeys and apes are still alive. If you want proof, go to any zoo."

The problem is in getting students to press far enough in drawing out implications.[4] Failing in that, their theories will never come up against troublesome facts. But to have such implications, theories must go out on an empirical limb. They cannot be mere verbalisms or mere descriptions of what has been observed. I once asked a class of bright seventh-graders how it is that we can see through glass. With one exception, they were all perfectly satisfied with the explanation that we can see through glass because it is transparent. That is verbalism. When, having done some experiments with dry cells and light bulbs, sixth-grade students were challenged to explain how electricity works, few of their theories went beyond stating that the electricity goes out through one wire, does something to make the light bulb light up, and then returns through the other wire. Although one could derive some empirical implications from such an account, as employed by the students it does little more than describe what happened. Including the term "electricity" contributes nothing to the explanation. It is another verbalism, like "transparency."

The conventional antidote to verbalism is hands-on learning—more experimentation, in the electricity case. But a more direct antidote is to ask a deeper question. That was how the teacher Jim Webb (Hakkarainen, 1998) dealt with students' verbalistic explanations of electricity. The next year, instead of simply asking the students to explain how electricity works, Webb instructed them to pay special attention to what goes on inside the wire. In doing so, the students had to deal with the problem of how electricity could get from one place to another through a solid substance. They then started to produce explanations like the following:

> I think that in some materials there might be a certain grain, like the grain in wood, that stops electricity or does not let it go by in it, but this "grain" is only in a few materials so the other materials would conduct electricity. I also think that if materials don't conduct electricity very well then they have a little a bit of this grain in them but not enough to stop electricity totally .... (p. 197)

> I found some information that will probably help you. In order for electricity to flow through a wire, electrons that are loosely bound to atoms are wrenched away (these are called free electrons). This

---

[4]This is not how the problem is commonly seen by science educators. The more common interpretation is that students are unclear about the nature of theory and evidence (Kuhn, 1989). But everyone is unclear about that (Ranney et al., 1996).

is called ionization. If ionization does not occur then electricity cannot flow through the wire. Electrons sometimes collide with other atoms which causes them to slow down or stop. This sometimes appears as heat. Inside the wire the electrons don't move very fast. (p. 252)

The first of these is obviously a conjecture motivated by the observation that wood does not work as a conductor the way metal does. The second is information obviously taken from a book. The first could conceivably lead to empirical testing (there are, for instance, grainy metals); the second could not realistically be expected to do so. But both are significant steps beyond verbalism and mere description. What gives them their added bite is that they are attempts to solve a problem. How electricity works evidently did not strike most students as a problem, anymore than the question of how we see through glass. When there is no problem to solve, that is when verbalism and mere playback of observations take over. How electricity could get through a solid wire was a problem for the sixth-graders. In the seventh-grade class, the one student who was not satisfied with transparency as an explanation recognized a problem there as well. He was so excited he could hardly stay in his seat. "Here I've been looking through glass all my life," he piped, "and I never thought about how the light could get through!" As Popper said, World 3 and World 1 meet each other in World 2, in people's minds. Bringing about that kind of meeting should be the point of subject-matter teaching.

Not just any old problem will produce this meeting of World 3 and World 1, however—not even any old attention-grabbing and intriguing problem. To elaborate this point, I want to go back to the study discussed in chapter 8, in which students had the task of explaining a demonstration of evaporation and condensation. The problem posed to the students was not a general one of explaining how evaporation and condensation work. It was the very specific one of explaining how liquid left one part of an apparatus and reappeared in another without being seen in transit from one place to the other. I expect that almost all teachers would prefer the specific problem to the general one. It is more striking. It arouses curiosity. It poses a much clearer problem of explanation. Furthermore, they may argue, solving the specific problem in detail (recall that the students were required to produce a demonstration using models of molecules) entails explaining evaporation and condensation. And yet the problem was a flop as far as motivating an effort at understanding was concerned.

To scientists, a strange and puzzling phenomenon is often a stimulus for inquiry, but not always. It is a stimulus when they already have an explanation for the general class of phenomena but it doesn't fit the new observations. In other words, what motivates inquiry is a perceived shortcoming in World 3. For the young students observing the migration of liquid in a glass vessel, no prior theory was endangered. For them it was a task of explaining an isolated phenomenon, using whatever knowledge they had available. This can sometimes be engaging, but it is not how World 3 is constructed and transformed. Scientific inquiry is seldom concerned with bizarre phenomena. Most of what appears in supermarket tabloids would not be of much scientific interest even if it were true. It is the problems of explaining the normal that have driven the big scientific advances—the normal motions of the planets, the circulation of the blood, the souring of beer, the spread of disease, the multiplicity of species. It is only as they reveal weaknesses in explanations of the normal that strange phenomena become scientifically interesting—when they result in those collisions of Worlds 1 and 3 in the well-prepared mind.

Students, however, lacking explanations of the normal, are in no position to appreciate the significance of anomalous observations. For them the demonstration of mysteriously migrating liquids is in the same class as card tricks and three-headed calves, only not as amazing. But seeing through glass is not a problem that stimulates inquiry for most of them, either, because it is just the way things are.

Finding the right level of problem is a challenge, for only if it is at the right level is it actually a problem for the students. Explaining condensation and evaporation is too abstract and general to be a problem for school-age students. Explaining the barbell phenomenon is too isolated. Here is a problem in between that I think might work, although I don't know of its having been tried: *Has there always been the same amount of water since the earth began, or is water created and destroyed?* Pursuing an answer to that question will quickly lead into the evaporation-condensation cycle and to the realization that evaporation doesn't destroy water and precipitation doesn't create it. Experiments might then be conducted to determine whether the amount of water does indeed remain constant through such cycles. But then questions would arise about regions we hear of that are getting drier. Are these matched by other regions that are getting wetter? Further probing into chemistry will reveal that there are processes that create water and others that destroy it. But do these take place on a scale that would have much effect on the overall amount of water? I don't know the answers and I would not expect many elementary school teachers to. Yet it is easy to see that the initial problem expands naturally into other interesting problems that build toward a coherent understanding. These subproblems get into geology, geography, climate, and ecology, but so long as they remained tied to the original question, basic scientific knowledge should continue to develop.

Fortunately, students themselves can often generate the problems, and that virtually insures that they will be at the right level.

HOW DO THE HUMANITIES MATTER?

Art and history are the most powerful instruments of our inquiry into human nature. What would we know of man without these two sources of information? We should be dependent on the data of our personal life, which can give us only a subjective view and which at best are but the scattered fragments of the broken mirror of humanity.

—Cassirer (1950, p. 206)

So far my discussion of "subject matter that matters" has dealt almost entirely with science. Note that I have said nothing about the practical and economic value of science. Those values may be why science gets the funding it does and why there is so much emphasis on it in educational policy, but that is not why science will matter to students. Those who adhere to a literal interpretation of Dewey and look for science to emerge from and play a useful role in students' worldly pursuits are going to come up short. My argument has been that scientific ideas matter to students to the extent that they help them solve problems of understanding. That is why, if you want students to take an interest in science, you have got to get them intensely involved in trying to understand the world.

The same argument can apply to getting students to take an interest in the humanities, but with important modifications. For purposes of this discussion let us define the humanities broadly to include literature and the arts, history, and geography and social studies in their cultural rather than theoretical aspects. To the educated adult, these matter in much the same way that science matters. They help in understanding the world—the world of human motives, actions, and values. They may matter in other ways as well, but their contributions to understanding are what mainly justifies their being treated as necessary parts of the curriculum. True, the humanities are treated as poor relations, but they would probably have dropped out of the curriculum altogether if it were not that many influential people experience them as somehow contributing to their own intelligence. The problem is to get students to experience them that way.

If you are pursuing a problem of scientific understanding, getting hold of the right fact or idea can have an immediately illuminating effect. The "aha!" experience convinces you on the spot that this is a valuable piece of knowledge. I have seen this happening with children. To kids who have been wondering about the vagaries of family resemblance—how you can resemble your aunt more than you do your mother, for instance—Mendelian genetics comes as a revelation. Teach it the other way around—present the Mendelian model first and then show how it explains things kids may have observed—and you are likely not to get the same effect. So, problem-driven inquiry becomes the method of choice in teaching science, but it cannot work the same way in the humanities.

If you are puzzling over some current event or some aspect of the human situation, the likelihood that you will hit on an illuminating piece of literature or history is not very high, but if you are 12 years old the likelihood is essentially zero. The reasons boil down to your needing to know a great deal before you know anything of much value. Isolated bits of literature, history, geography, and anthropology have little value. Relatedness brings wisdom. The same is true in science, except that in science there are these big principles (like Newton's laws or the Medelian model) that do the connecting. There is nothing like that in the humanities. You have to learn a great deal of history before you develop enough implicit understanding to draw useful connections between one event and another or between past epochs and our own. The same is true with literature and with knowledge of different peoples and places.

From an instructional standpoint, it is always unfortunate when students have to learn things first before they can appreciate their value. Motivation becomes difficult. Instruction gets caught in a Catch 22, in which students will not learn unless the see the value of what they are being taught and they cannot see its value until they learn. To escape it, teachers find themselves resorting to carrots and sticks, fun and games, and extraneous material to enliven the subject matter. All of these are abundant in the teaching of the humanities, along with generally pathetic efforts to make material relevant to students' present lives. But these all miss the strongest motivational angle of all in teaching the humanities—the fact that they are about humanity.

It is hard to make out why the Boston Tea Party should matter to a Latino student in Houston, Texas. It is foolish even to try. You could, however, try to show why the Boston Tea Party mattered to the people who took part in it. But that is where school history textbooks conspicuously fail (Beck, McKeown, & Gromoll, 1989). Powerful narratives, whether in the form of fiction, history, biography, books

of travel, or some hybrid, create in the reader the experience of significant conditions and events. When in the grip of a story, people
don' t think, "How is this relevant to me and my problems?" They
experience events through the protagonists and do not look for significance outside the world of the story.

This does not mean that good stories are timeless and universal,
although the occasional one is. They must engage our feelings, and
what it takes to do this may vary from age to age and culture to culture.[5] Many historians, following in the tradition of Herder, try to
make the past come alive for their own generation, and this too
means that there may need to be different histories for different
times and different sensibilities (Cassirer, 1950). Thus, there must be
connection to our own concerns, but it is the writer, not ourselves,
who does the connecting. If the novelist, historian, biographer, or
travel writer is successful, we are not even aware of the connections.
We are simply engrossed in the story.

Eventually, of course, we want students to be aware, to read critically, to make their own connections between what they read and
what they are trying to understand. But that is what requires wide
prior knowledge. Stories provide a way around the Catch 22. They
provide a way for students to acquire a great fund of episodic knowledge about human beings and how they feel and act, about the histories and current lives of different peoples, about what it is like to live
in different conditions and with different purposes, without having
first to understand the value of this knowledge. They don't even
need to know they are learning.

No one can come even close to being an educated person without
knowledge acquired in this way. But it is a way of learning that flies in
the face of all the pedagogical conventions. It violates the traditional
conventions because nothing in particular is specified to be learned. It
violates the newer constructivist conventions because it is passive, not
active learning. Progressive educators conveniently ignore this fact,
but our everyday metaphors give it away. A story "grabs you." It
"holds your attention." You are "carried away" by it. Experiencing a
story does not involve critical thinking. (What goes under the label of
critical thinking in reading programs is nothing more than puzzle
solving.) It is not purposeful or problem driven. Although social, it is
not collaborative. And this passivity is if anything even more pronounced when we come to the story via television or cinema.

---

[5]This relativism has been carried to an absurd extreme in the multicultural standards
now imposed on school textbooks. If you are an Asian child it is assumed that you cannot
identify with any character who is not Asian. Unfortunately, there is some truth in this,
because due to other restrictions the characters are likely to be so bloodless and bland that
they have no other basis of appeal.

There should be nothing paradoxical or disturbing in this, if we recognize that different kinds of personal knowledge are at issue. In science, regardless of how it is pursued, the focus is on statable knowledge—especially knowledge of conceptual artifacts. Conceptual artifacts are constructed on purpose; they do not just happen. They are the natural objects of critical thinking. Their construction, criticism, and improvement are best carried out through collaborative work. Therefore, scientific knowledge building properly touches all the constructivist bases. But the main knowledge we get from stories is not statable knowledge. It is impressionistic and episodic. These are kinds of knowledge that arise incidentally from experience. You cannot deliberately acquire such knowledge; you can only deliberately seek out the kinds of experiences that produce it. The expression "soaking up" experience describes the process well.

All of this, I believe, Cassirer (1950) might have agreed with. In fact, I owe much of it to him. But he clearly meant more than the passive absorbtion of stories and impressions when he said "Art and history are the most powerful instruments of our inquiry into human nature" (p. 206). He was talking about purposeful, critical inquiry and was naming art and history as the tools of choice, as against science. Does that mean we are back to "What lesson does this poem teach you?" (Rosenblatt, 1980) No, it means that when we pursue critical inquiry in the humanities we reason from cases rather than from principles, and history and the arts are our main source of cases that go beyond the limits of our personal lives. Young people can carry out critical inquiry into problems of human nature and affairs—I am not suggesting it should be held off till maturity—but they will be mainly limited to their own experience and to what they have absorbed from television and incidental reading. If the television and reading they experience are of low quality,[6] the impressionistic and episodic knowledge acquired may well have negative value as far as understanding the human world is concerned.

There are other reasons for studying the humanities besides acquiring impressionistic and episodic knowledge for use in building knowledge about the human world. If it is construed broadly enough, the word "appreciation" covers many of them. But the providing of tools for understanding the human world is an important educational objective, which results-oriented policymakers ought to be able to recognize. Recognizing that value, however, requires a more complex and differentiated conception of knowledge than folk theory provides. Similarly, teaching in such a way as to allow impressionistic and episodic knowledge to develop unimpeded requires

---

[6]By "low quality" I mean deserving the conventional critical epithets—trashy, maudlin, stereotyped or one-dimensional characters, and so on.

a theory of knowledge and mind that does not fetishize active learning and critical thinking.

In all kinds of inquiry, there needs to be a balance between active pursuit and passive reception. I am always saddened by doctoral students who think that before they sit down and watch the videotapes or whatever they have collected for their research they must have a coding scheme that determines what they will categorize and count. I urge them, "Let the data speak to you," but they don't know what that means. Well, it means, for instance, watch your videotape as if you were watching a movie; allow it to "grab you" and "carry you away"; then, as you begin to sense that something significant is afoot, look for ways to capture it in a discussible and criticizable form. In the humanities, the passive receptive phase is more extended and if you slight it you end up with nothing at all. Schopenhauer (quoted in *The Book of Famous Quotes*, nid.) put it in a rather dated but still compelling way: "A work of art must be treated like a prince. It must speak to you first." In contrast, almost everything that goes on in school—especially everything that goes on in the name of constructivism and critical thinking—is yattering away at the cultural artifact without ever giving it a chance to speak.

WHERE QUANTITY COUNTS

Breadth-versus-depth is an educational issue that will never go away. The long-range hope, of course, is to have students end up with knowledge that is both broad and deep. The controversy is about how best to start. Irrespective of what is the best way to get students to an eventual state of breadth-plus-depth, however, the fact is that for a great many students the first course they take in a subject is the only course they will ever take. Consequently, the breadth-versus-depth issue has a certain finality about it. It is not just a question of strategy.

The whole modern constructivist turn has been toward depth first (Gardner, 1999). Having elementary school students spend half a year studying an exotic species of cockroach is held up as exemplary, on grounds of the depth of learning and the amount of problem-driven inquiry (Lamon et al., 1997). At the opposite extreme is the movement known as Core Knowledge, which itemizes a vast range of things that students at each grade level are to be taught (e.g., *What Your 5th Grader Needs to Know*, Hirsch, 1993). In the meantime, the survey course lives on, because when you get a committee of knowledgeable people together to discuss what ought to be in an introductory course, they will inevitably—and regardless of their pedagogical philosophies—end up with a long list.

Breadth-versus-depth is too big an issue to explore fully here, although it is sorely in need of nonpartisan exploration. Instead, I want to introduce one idea that ought to figure in discussions of the issue but that usually stands no chance because of the way partisan lines are drawn. The idea is this: *There are some domains in which depth is more valuable than breadth, but there are other domains in which how much you know is more important than what in particular you know.*

Much of what bears on this point has already been said in the preceding section. Science provides the clearest case for depth and is invariably the case constructivists base their arguments on. That is because the natural sciences exhibit what E. O. Wilson (1998) called *consilience*—"literally a 'jumping together' of knowledge by the linking of facts and fact-based theory across disciplines to create a common groundwork of explanation" (p. 8). As a result, the pursuit of deeper explanations within any particular problem area will lead to the same conceptual substrate, where the big scientific ideas are. Wilson himself got there by studying ants. Studying Madagascan hissing cockroaches may do just as well for a class of fourth-graders, whereas going hop-skip-and-jump over a number of topics may never bring students into contact with the big ideas at all.

The humanities have their universals too. Wilson (1998, chap. 10) located them in a universal human nature. But however that may be, it is true that deeply understanding one great literary work or one great historical episode is to gain some understanding of all others. But the universality depends on our ability to make connections—connections to other literary experiences, to other moments in history, and to our own life experiences. The connections have not been made for us by a Darwin or an Einstein so that we have only to reconstruct them. The result is that you cannot really understand one great book until you have read many others; you cannot appreciate the significance of a particular history until you know a lot of history.

Here is where quantity counts and qualtity—although not unimportant—takes second place. It does not matter so much what books you have read so long as they have some literary quality. (Don't expect me to say what that means; let it mean whatever you seriously want it to mean.) It does not matter so much what history you have learned so long as it is connectable to other history and to current events in ways that add at least a little to your understanding. What matters is having a lot of hooks to which new information and experiences can be attached.

There is empirical and theoretical support for the claim that quantity counts. Keith Stanovich (1993) has shown that a simple inventory that estimates how many books one has read correlates with a variety of indicators of educational attainment, even after one controls for other variables like IQ. Tom Landauer and his associates (Landauer & Dumais, 1997) have been studying knowledge acquisition using a model, Latent Structure Analysis (LSA), which they have claimed learns word meanings in much the same way humans do, through repeatedly encountering the words in similar meaningful contexts. According to Landauer, when LSA has acquired a vocabulary of 90,000 words it learns new words at four times the speed that it does if it has a vocabulary of only 10,000 words. Both Stanovich's and Landauer's results illustrate the "Matthew effect": the rich getting richer while the poor fall farther behind.

The educational case for quantity was well argued by E. D. Hirsch, Jr. (1987) in *Cultural Literacy*, a book that has drawn hardly anything but abuse from educationists. Hirsch was seen to be arguing for dogmatic prescription of content, superficiality, and rote learning. Hirsch actually advocated none of these, but he brought the criticisms on himself, because where his argument led him was to the creation of long lists of items that students should know a little bit about. Of the three kinds of reductionism I discussed in the previous chapter—reduction to content, reduction to activities, and reduction to self-expression—two are well accepted by contemporary educators and one is scorned. Hirsch chose the one that is scorned—reduction to content.

What would be a nonreductionist approach to teaching for quantity? Assuredly it would not be based on lists. Lists are an accommodation to conventional teaching and testing. If you are running a class in which everyone is supposed to be learning the same things at the same time, you need a list of things to be learned. If you want to test how much students know, using paper-and-pencil tests, you need a list of test items that samples the domain. But modern information media make it unnecessary to march everyone through the same content, if quanitity rather than specific mastery is your objective, and modern analytic tools such as LSA make it possible to assess quantity of knowledge without need to itemize it. Freed from lists, schools could encourage wide reading; viewing of historical and literary films, travelogues, and natural science and public affairs broadcasts; and sharing of interesting information through discussion groups and contributions to collective knowledge bases. This starts to sound suspiciously like having fun, but that is part of the glory of recognizing the educational value of quantity. Getting deeply into a subject is hard work—very satisfying and exciting work, perhaps, but work nonetheless. Lapping up information about interesting and important things is something educated people do for enjoyment. There is no reason to deny students that enjoyment.

Meanwhile, however, curriculum committees produce longer and longer lists, defeating efforts to teach for depth while at the same time reducing breadth to cramming.

PEDANTRY, NEW AND OLD

We are all familiar with the classical manifestations of pedantry— the fussy attention to detail and to unimportant points of form, the emphasis on display of knowledge rather than on use, the avoidance of issues and uncertainties in favor of the cut and dried. The school environment conduces to pedantry. It is an occupational disease. Probably every teacher becomes infected with it and must labor to overcome it. Occasionally, however, pedantry becomes elevated to a virtue. This is never intentional, of course. It occurs when some manifestation of learning becomes the objective of instruction or when reduction to subject matter (as discussed in the preceding chapter) has proceeded so far that it completely supplants the higher level objective that gave rise to it.

Pedantry has been most common in literature and history. The teaching of names, dates, definitions, and lists can altogether take the place of efforts to instill literary or historical understanding. It is easy to see how this happens. If you are preparing a lesson or a text-book section about causes of the French Revolution, it is reasonable and may seem pedagogically desirable to itemize causes in a list. Having produced a list of, say, six items, however, it is but a small step to start thinking of these as *the* causes of the French Revolution and to expect students to demonstrate their understanding by stating these six causes—not five, not seven, and not some other set of six. Thus is pedantry born. It can be found anywhere. I have seen a placard in a home economics classroom that listed 11 steps in the preparation of cinnamon toast. I expect a unit test required listing those 11 steps. That is better than a home economics test item I did actually see: "The _____ flows between the _____ and the _____."

A different kind of pedantry was once common in the teaching of grammar. It is especially interesting because of its similarity to what I shall call the "new pedantry." A legitimate reason for teaching grammar in school is to equip students with a vocabulary for talking about style and usage. If you have ever tried to explain what is wrong with "The generalizability of these laboratory studies are questionable" to a student who has no idea what a simple subject or a prepositional phrase or a modifier or a noun phrase is, you will understand why such vocabulary is important. Diagramming is a way of stripping a sentence down to its core elements ("generalizability," "are," and "questionable") and attaching the other constituents as modifiers. The trouble is that it is really only feasible for certain sentences. It becomes nightmarish if you try to apply it to questions, to quoted dialogue, and to indexicals (expressions that require situated knowledge to be understood, such as saying to a waiter "I'll have the same"). So diagramming evolved into an art form involving rule upon rule, applied to sentences that were contrived to fit the rules. The root reason for teaching grammar, to enable students to discuss style and usage, was lost sight of, and instead grammar teaching came to be based on the belief that just doing it would make you a better writer and speaker. Not surprising, research failed to support this belief, and so diagramming gradually disappeared, taking grammar with it.

The fallacy of traditional grammar instruction is the belief that mastering grammatical terms is prior to using them in discussions of style and usage. Realistically, there isn't any way to learn grammatical terms *except* through using them in discussions of style and usage. But this is a difficult notion to entertain within the framework of folk theory of mind. A similar fallacy has given rise to a new pedantry, which is beginning to be promoted especially in science education, and which I suspect will gain strength just because the fallacy is so firmly grounded in folk theory.

The new pedantry is not concerned with grammatical terms but with epistemological ones such as theory, evidence, hypothesis, knowledge and belief. These are obviously important for critical and knowledge-building discourse, and there is evidence that school-age students are very shaky in the use of them (Kuhn, Amsel, & O'Loughlin, 1988). However, the notion that these could be taught as separate subject matter, in advance of their use in contexts of discourse concerned with real problems of knowledge, is even less realistic than the notion that grammatical terms could be taught that way. Ranney, Schank, Hoadley, and Neff (1996) found that even experts who study reasoning professionally do not agree in their ratings of statements as "hypothesis-like" or "evidence-like." Where evidence leaves off and hypothesis or conjecture begins, what constitutes a theory and what counts as evidence or proof of it—these are not matters to be settled in the abstract. They are deeply embedded in the various disciplines, research programs, and paradigms. Uproot these concepts and they lose their importance, become objects of definitional fussiness and logic chopping—in a word, they become pedantic.

In research on CSILE, we have found that as students become more deeply involved in the pursuit of understanding, their use of epistemological terms increases significantly without any attention being directed toward it (Hewitt, 1996). Of course their use of such terms is not rigorous, but that is not terribly important and is bound to improve if they interact with people who are more sophisticated in their use of the terms.

The new pedantry, like the old, is grounded in the folk mind-as-container metaphor. To learn a new word, according to theories based on this metaphor, is to get the word represented in the mind, along with a definition or rules of use. In the connectionist view of mind, learning a new word is rarely like that. Landauer and Dumais (1997) have modeled vocabulary acquisition using LSA, which belongs to the extended family of what I have been calling connectionist models.[7] Throughout childhood, a child learns thousands of new words each year. Landauer and Dumais not only showed how this is possible, given the child's rate of exposure to words in different contexts, their analysis yielded the surprising result that a fourth of those words are words not actually encountered on the occasion when they are learned. The vast network of connections that represents the child's semantic knowledge is being continually reconfigured as a result of experience and internal processes of constraint satisfaction. A word becomes learned as its associations with other words assume a configuration that is similar to that which exists among the words as they are used in the discourse community.

We cannot define words like "noun" and "verb." The definition you may have learned in school—that a noun is the name of a person, place, or thing—doesn't even work for the word "noun" itself.[8] The definition may help you get started, because it does pick out some words as unequivocally nouns, but you really learn the names for parts of speech by taking part in discussions where parts of speech matter. The concept of *noun* emerges gradually from a sense of the "aboutness" of utterances. You develop a concept of *verb* out of feeling that you are left dangling, not knowing what the point of an utterance is until it appears. Terms like "hypothesis" and "evidence" similarly defy useful definition. A hypothesis, as it figures in knowledge-building discourse, is a conjectural answer to a *why?* question. The first concern is not with whether it is true—that is, whether it is supported by evidence. The first concern is with whether it answers

---

[7]LSA is a kind of factor analysis, but linear connectionist models generally have the same mathematical structure as factor analyses. What makes it connectionist is using it to model constraint-based processes, which is something quite different from the uses to which factor analysis has traditionally been put.

[8]All right, you can say that a noun is a thing, although it enjoys that status only by virtue of accepting "a" or "the" as articles and having a plural form, but what about "nominalization"? "Nominalization" is surely a noun, but it does not refer to a person, place, or thing.

the question. If it does not, then it doesn't matter whether it is true. But whether it answers the question depends on the state of the inquiry at the time the question is asked. You have got to be involved in the inquiry to have a sense of whether something is an explanatory hypothesis or just a stray thought. Having fastened on one or more hypotheses that provide plausible answers to your *why?* question, you ought to have some doubt about what to believe. Evidence is whatever helps to settle the doubt, and this again depends on where you are in gaining an understanding of the matter in question.

There is a time for lessons in the vocabulary of grammar, philosophy of science, and other kinds of meta-disciplines. But that time is when work on style or a scientific problem or some other kind of problem has advanced to the point where uncertainties about terminology arise that are actually critical to further advance of the inquiry. The time is surely not next Tuesday, when we get to that page in the book.

WHY DO WE HAVE TO LEARN THIS?

"Why do we have to learn this?" is a question teenagers begin to ask. When they discover how it annoys and embarrasses their teachers, some of them begin to ask it insistently. Telling them they have to learn Algebra I so they can learn Algebra II only pushes the question up a notch, and so teachers will often resort to feeble claims about the practical or economic value of the knowledge. To forward-looking students, awareness that they need to do well in their courses to get into a good university may provide motivation enough to keep them working, but it is the wrong kind of motivation for the pursuit of knowledge. For students who do not look ahead or who look ahead only to uncertain and low-skilled employment, there is nothing a teacher can say that provides a convincing reason to study.

For several generations of educators, the preferred way of dealing with "Why do we have to learn this?" has been not to answer the question but to try to prevent it from arising. "Intrinsic motivation" is the watchword. If learning activities are sufficiently engaging and sufficiently rewarding in themselves, students should not demand justifications or inducements. Both Whitehead and Dewey were looking for intrinsic motivation. But like all other educational ideas, intrinsic motivation is susceptible to reductionism—the same kinds of reduction I discussed in the last chapter: reduction to subject matter, reduction to activities, and reduction to self-expression. When intrinsic motivation is reduced to subject matter, it means choosing content that is inherently interesting. Roger Schank (1979) has discussed topics that appear to be universally interesting: sex, danger, and so on. And then there are individual interests. Schank & Cleary (1995) suggested that for students who happen to be interested in trucks the whole curriculum could be built around trucks. When intrinsic interest is reduced to activities, it means having students do things that are enjoyable irrespective of what is supposed to be learned. Educational games are an example. Reduction to self-expression means that the motivation comes from self-enlightenment or the solution of personal problems—a sort of psychological version of Dewey's proposal that schooling should be linked to students" real-life needs. There is value in all of this, but it is all peripheral. Motivation may be intrinsic to the learning activities but it is extrinsic as far as knowledge building is concerned.

A kind of motivation that seems to be more central to knowledge acquisition has long been revered under the name "love of learning." In conjunction with "lifelong learning," it has begun to rise in prestige. The Ontario Royal Commission on Learning (1994), whose task was to "set new directions in education to ensure that Ontario youth are well-prepared for the challenges of the 21st century" titled its report *For the Love of Learning.* But love of learning is not an idea that stands up well under critical scrutiny. There is something gratifying about feeling that you are learning something, regardless of what it is. But it is gratification of a lowly sort, on a par with the gratification of finding something to read—anything will do—when you are having to sit and wait somewhere for a long time. Youth "well-prepared for the challenges of the 21st century" ought to care what they are learning and not just learn any old thing for the joy of doing so.

Under labels such as "liberatory education," "women's ways of knowing," and "antiracist mathematics," there is developing a radical critique of what the young are being expected to learn. The premise is that the academic disciplines, having been shaped almost entirely by males of European cultural background, are alienating to students who experience the world differently—alienating at many different levels, from the kind of detached rationality they project down to the sex-and-violence connotations of the names given to objects and processes (Barton, 1997). In an earlier generation—the generation of the 1960s and early 1970s—the complaint against academic subject matter was that it was not "relevant." That was not an arguable criticism, being entirely an expression of feeling. Despite its coming surrounded by postmodernist theorizing, this new complaint is not really contestable either. It is a statement about how academic subjects feel to minority and female students, and so the only contestable point is whether substantial numbers of them actually feel that way or whether certain educators are mistakenly attributing to students their own highly developed sensibilities.[9]

Little evidence is offered. One study of a small but varied sample of African-American male high school students (Price, 1998) showed that, although their attitudes differed in important ways, they were alike in finding nothing of intrinsic value to them in their school subjects. They were especially scornful of history on this account. Yet their complaints seem similar to those of the generation that complained about relevance. In essence, their complaint was *"It's not about me."* As I read the more sophisticated criticisms of the postmodernist educators, I cannot help but feel that at bottom that is their complaint as well.

This is not cause to dismiss the complaint, however. To adolescents and young adults, self-understanding is often an overriding concern. Generations of college students have entered introductory psychology courses with the understandable expectation that they would learn about themselves and have been dismayed to find that the course was more about rats, sense organs, and warring academic camps. In other subjects the expectation may not be as great but the failure to capture student interest is just as pervasive. The unavoidable fact is that a very large portion of academic subject matter is going to have little appeal to students whose principal epistemic concern is themselves. But what is to be done about it? I don't think one answer can fit all subjects. Literature, for instance, has considerable potential for helping students understand themselves; physics has hardly any. Other subjects are distributed in between, but all are problematic.

Let us consider history, which lies somewhere between literature and physics in terms of personal relevance. One can forcefully argue that history *should* speak to us, should help us understand our present situation. If it does not, if students see it as merely a body of knowledge about people and events of no personal relevance, it is the wrong history or it is wrongly taught or the students have not been adequately prepared for it. The first two explanations have received plenty of attention by educators. I would like to urge attention to the third as well. If the only history that has meaning for students is the history of people of the same ethnicity, gender, and social status as themselves, something is clearly lacking in their educational development. That lack will not be remedied by berating them for their

---

[9]Barton (1997) provided an interesting personal account that seems to undermine her arguments for "liberatory education." She evidently had considerable difficulty getting her high school chemistry students to take seriously her efforts to sexualize and politicize the subject, and there are indications that some of her students were learning to think like White male chemists despite her disapproval.

self-centeredness or by force-feeding them historical knowledge. For a high school teacher facing a class of disaffected adolescents, the problem is likely unsolvable. The teacher might scrap the standard curriculum and get students involved in the history of their own kind. But for that to constitute a step in the direction of broader historical literacy, it would have to be followed in later years by a progression from it. Otherwise, it might increase students' resistance to other history. The problem, in short, needs to be addressed at the level of the whole curriculum, from kindergarten on up, rather than at the level of a particular course or grade.

Implicit in the idea of liberal education is the goal of *cosmopolitanism*—initiating the young into a culture that transcends the particularities of their social and ethnic backgrounds. Although fundamentalists on both the extreme right and the extreme left may reject this goal, it is what principally distinguishes education from indoctrination and training. Cosmopolitanism is a gradual process and is, of course, never fully achieved. A crude approximation is embodied in the "expanding environment" or "widening horizons" scheme that has shaped substantial parts of the elementary school curriculum. This is a scheme of starting in the first grade by focusing on families, expanding to the neighborhood in the second grade, and moving concentrically outward until the curriculum embraces the hemisphere and the world in the sixth grade. The high school years are then devoted to more detailed and analytic study of national and world matters (Marker & Mehlinger, 1992, p. 833). Diane Ravitch (1987) has severely criticized this scheme for its banality and shallow content. Although she found that school people believed the scheme to be based on child development research, they could cite no sources and Ravitch could find none. It does, indeed, run contrary to even common knowledge about what interests children. To me it illustrates how *reduction to content* can lose hold not only of educational purposes but of common sense as well. Yet the intent is admirable: to move students gradually from being sheltered homebodies to being citizens of the world.

If large numbers of adolescents are finding no personal relevance in history and literature except when it is, demographically speaking, in their own neighborhood, then this effort to produce citizens of the world has obviously failed very badly. The blame should no doubt be distributed over a number of factors. History's being mostly by and about White males is one factor, but, whether it is a large or small factor, there is very little that can be done about it. Some of the other factors are more susceptible to change. I have already discussed the importance of quantity, the need to establish by hook or crook enough statable and episodic knowledge that students can begin to make connections and develop intuitive understanding. I also touched on the matter of bringing more human character and motivation into historical accounts. A well-told story can engage students' interest even if it is not *about them* in any near sense. This may require fictionalizing historical accounts, however, because available evidence often does not take us inside the minds of the actors.

Kieran Egan's (1997) theory of "forms of understanding," which I discussed briefly in chapter 4, suggests there should be four distinct passes at history, each fostering a different kind of understanding. The first, Mythic pass, would present children with struggles of life against extinction, freedom against oppression, security against danger, "analogous to the struggles and accommodations thay are themselves going through in their early years" (p. 210). In the second, Romantic pass, "we will look for dramatic narratives driven by human emotions and intentions …. An increasingly confident sense of what is possible in human affairs … encouraged by focusing on the extremes of human experience" (p. 210). The third, Philosophical pass, will focus on "content that allows us to construct potent generalizations" (p. 234). Finally, an Ironic pass would bring out the multiple perspectives from which historical events may be interpreted and the shortcomings of "potent generalizations." This is a scheme that could be said to cater to students' interests, but it does not presuppose an interest in the particular subject matter. It is not like teaching Black history to Black students because of their presumed prior interest in it. Egan's theory suggests that, regardless of what history you are teaching, if you want to engage students' efforts at understanding you should adapt the teaching to the form of understanding the students are disposed toward. This does not deny the value of teaching students the history of the people they identify with, but it suggests what parts or aspects of that history ought to be emphasized at different ages if you want to engage understanding. It furthermore suggests, however, that if the teaching is properly adapted to the students' forms of understanding, they will not be constrained by narrow topical interests. Mythic Understanding is concerned with universals of human experience; Romantic Understanding thrives on the exotic; Philosophic Understanding wants principles that explain everything; Ironic Understanding seeks to dispel all forms of narrowness and intolerance. Accordingly, Egan's scheme can be taken as a proposal for how to achieve the liberal goal of cosmopolitanism in a society full of division.[10]

---

[10]This may explain why a good deal of Egan's text goes toward trying to head off the criticisms of illiberal anticosmopolitans, the people who advocate things like "race-based epistemologies" (e.g., Scheurich & Young, 1997).

Egan's proposals could be further strengthened, I believe, by taking into account the distinction I introduced earlier between problem-centered and referent-centered or "all about" learning. Even though the practical value of historical knowledge is supposed to lie in its application to contemporary problems, history teaching is almost always referent centered. It is learning about certain events, people, and periods arranged in chronological order. As with other referent-centered knowledge, motivation to learn depends on the students' interest in the referents. If you are turned off by men in powdered wigs who speak in long sentences, a substantial amount of English and early American history may fail to interest you. The fact that history occurs in chronological order does not mean it has to be taught that way. Instead of plodding through the kings and queens of England and the major events of their reigns, why not a unit on monarchy? Such a unit, if handled in a knowledge-building way, is bound to give rise to significant questions. How did kingship get started? Why has it been so widespread? How do people justify hereditary monarchy? Why do people put up with it? Is monarchy fading away or is it only being replaced by dictatorship? Researching these questions will pull together history from ancient Assyria and Babylon to contemporary Jordan and North Korea. And it will lead naturally into a later unit on revolution, which—unlike an ordinary unit on the American Revolution—would not fasten on a certain sequence of events and set of characters but would investigate questions of causes, motives, strategies, outcomes, and future prospects. Problem-centered learning should not be thought of as limited to Egan's stage of Philosophical Understanding. Monarchy and revolution could be treated as problems of either Romantic or Philosophical Understanding. The difference would be that as matters of Romantic Understanding there would be more emphasis on dramatic aspects and on problems of motives and character, whereas Philosophical Understanding would focus more on generalizations and underlying causes. I would be inclined to do monarchy in the elementary school, where the subject matter is likely to have more appeal and where it will confront the common childhood misconception that all heads of state are benevolent despots who make all the laws. Revolution seems, for obvious reasons, to be a more appropriate problem area for adolescents.

The point of this is to make history learning less dependent on students' being interested in the events and personages and more an indirect consequence of trying to understand how the world works. Many history teachers are trying to break away from the chronological format and engage students in problems. The problems, however, tend to be contrivances to motivate history learning rather than large human problems that history can help to unravel. In one case the problem is to design a Greek temple to serve as setting for a movie, making it as historically accurate as possible (Miller, 1996). In another, the problem is to locate, retrieve, and transport certain delegates to the American Constitutional Convention. Another is to stage a mock trial of various people held to be responsible for starting World War I.[11] These sound like engaging projects that will get students to process a lot of historical information, but insofar as they develop problem-centered knowledge, it is not knowledge related to problems they are ever likely to encounter again. Thus, despite their virtues, they fall under Whitehead's criticism: They don't lead anywhere.

Where Dewey and Whitehead join present-day postmodernists and multiculturalists is in the belief that school subject matter should be experienced by students as advancing their understanding of *their* world. Very likely *their* world does not include the Norman Conquest or the Periodic Table of Elements, and this is true even if we are talking about the world of young White males. So either we must replace the Norman Conquest and the Periodic Table with things they care about, or we must find a way to get them to care about the Norman Conquest and the Periodic Table, or we must design games and other engaging activities that will in effect trick them into processing information about things that policymakers have decided must be in the curriculum. This is not an inviting set of choices, but neither mainstream educators nor advocates of "liberatory education" have offered us any others.

I am trying to suggest there is another way. The three ways previously listed all presuppose referent-centered learning. The fourth way reconstitutes education so that its main focus, in the eyes of the students as well as the eyes of the teacher, is advancing students' understanding of *their* world. But we do not start with the assumption that the world of the young child is the world of the home and the playground. The progression is not from the home out into a wider and wider world. It starts with the whole world and the progression is toward deeper levels of understanding. This will not work if we wait until high school to spring it on students. *Their* world will by that time have shrunk for many of them to the insular confines of teen culture. If we want the teenager's world to include the Norman Conquest and the Periodic Table, they have got to start much earlier trying to understand where languages and customs come from and how they change and how they survive and what the physical world

---

[11]Many projects like these can be found by doing a Web search using the phrases "problem-based learning" and "history teaching."

is made of. As children they will find it gratifying that adults have wondered about the same things they do and they will happily take advantage of what those adults have discovered. As adolescents they may still rebel, but they will not rebel out of ignorance.

IN SEARCH OF THE RIGHT METAPHOR

In Jean-Paul Sartre's (1964) *Nausea*, the protagonist reflects on the difference between a mystery story and ordinary life. In the mystery, every detail is of interest because it may later prove to be a significant clue. Ordinary life offers no such likelihood, and so we ignore everything that does not have immediate significance. He speculates that life would have more meaning if it could be lived like a mystery story. Yet there are people, and not only detectives, whose working lives do have the character of mystery stories. They are researchers. Today's work and observations take on importance to the researcher because of the possibility that they will figure in a solution of the problem that is driving the research. There is no guarantee that this will be the case. In some kinds of research much of the information turns out eventually to be worthless, just like most of the information gathered in a criminal investigation. What sustains effort, however, is the occasional fitting together of pieces, renewing confidence that the search is getting somewhere. Every discipline taught in school potentially has this mystery-story quality. It sustains scholars and scientists through their 60- and 80-hour weeks of effort to advance their disciplines. But how can anything like that be achieved with beginners?

Rather than trying to answer this question directly, let us back off from practicalities and examine the metaphors that may guide or constrain our search for an answer. All metaphors have drawbacks. The building metaphor that I have been pushing—as in "knowledge building"—is appropriately constructivist in connotation, but it suggests a methodical process with a definite point of completion. It has perhaps not carried that suggestion as strongly for Marlene Scardamalia and me as it might for other people. We live in a house that has been under continuous reconstruction and enhancement for a quarter century, the work has been anything but methodical, and there is no end in sight.

A potentially more serious drawback of the knowledge-building metaphor is that it ties in with the foundation metaphor. Educators have been talking about foundations for so long that it no longer seems metaphorical—but that is when metaphors become the most dangerous. All that "foundation" literally means in the context of instruction is something taught initially to facilitate future learning.

This may or may not have anything to do with foundational ideas of the discipline, but the metaphor disposes people to assume it does. The concept of energy figures prominently in elementary science curricula because of its central importance in physics, but, as noted earlier, its value in elementary science is questionable because, as understood at that level, it has no explanatory value. It serves instead as an invitation to verbalism.

But the insidious effect of the foundation metaphor does not stop there. No builder would construct a foundation without having a pretty clear idea of the building to be erected on it; only a subcontractor would do that. Beginning students, having no way to foresee the eventual structure of knowledge, are therefore cast into the role of subcontractors. All the vision is held by the teacher and the student merely executes work orders. "Trust me," the teacher has to say. "The value of what I am teaching you will become clear to you someday." Not a good paradigm for active learning.

The mystery metaphor has not always been a metaphor. If, along with Newton and scientists before him, you believe the visible world is a puzzle with clues set out by God, then science is literally the solving of mysteries. To those of a more naturalistic persuasion, however, mystery solving is a metaphor. It nicely captures the excitement of research and the value of attending to facts whose significance is not immediately apparent. But it has two less fortunate implications. First, it implies there are solutions waiting to be found out. Somebody killed Cock Robin, even if we never find out who. But inquiry in the learned disciplines is not that simple. We may be asking questions to which there are no answers. Second, and much more serious, it implies a world constructed differently from the world we actually occupy. In the world of detective fiction the ratio of significant clues to irrelevant or misleading ones is high enough to keep up the reader's spirits, but in the real world it is vanishingly low. Sartre's protagonist was attracted by the idea of living life like a mystery story, but he recognized it could not actually be done. I take discovery metaphors to be a weaker form of the mystery metaphor, subject to the same criticisms.

We want a metaphor that suggests an endless advance, one that requires effort, which is rewarded by the progress that is made. None of the preceding does this. Here is one that does: "There's a hill beyond the hill beyond the hill beyond the hill ...." As many will recognize, this potentially disheartening thought is actually part of a rousing hiking song. For sufficiently energetic and optimistic young people it evidently serves to put a spring in their step. What is the conceivable appeal of hiking up hill after hill? Surely it is not the pleasure of putting one foot in front of another, even in good company. Each hill represents a new challenge, the attainment of which offers a new vista—a vista that typically includes a yet higher hill. This is a fairly accurate metaphor for the constructive pursuit of knowledge. Each hill is a knowledge problem. Surmounting it allows you to see or understand things you could not before, and this includes being able to see an even more challenging knowledge problem lying ahead. While climbing a hill you do not see the summit, much less the hill beyond, but previous experience and trusted counsel give you confidence that they are there and that they will prove worth the climbing. The hiking metaphor is imperfect, too, of course. The next hill is already there, waiting to be brought into view, whereas the next problem is generated out of the present one. But the hiking metaphor does have a dynamic and forward-looking character the others lack.

How do we apply this open-air metaphor to the confined world of the classroom? To keep the metaphor from becoming entirely fanciful, it helps to regard problems and questions as real things rather than as purely mental states. Climbing a hill and solving a problem may then be seen as similar enough that the analogy is worth pursuing farther. (Hill climbing is, in fact, the name given to a problem solving strategy identified by Newell and Simon, 1972, applicable in situations where you cannot see a path to the goal but you can tell which way is up.) You do not become a hiker in one day. You need to build up not only strength but expectations. Expectations are essential to keep you going, and they serve as guides. You don't know what is coming, but with experience you learn to recognize promising directions. This is impressionistic knowledge—built up through experience, more emotional than rational, but essential in creative work or anything that ventures beyond the familiar.

In developing students as self-motivated, lifelong learners, there is of course the building up of strength—in the form of skills and background knowledge. Schooling is much concerned with that. But there is little attention to building up expectations, the impressionistic knowledge that leads you onward toward the hill beyond the hill that you can see. Impressionistic knowledge isn't recognized as knowledge. It gets folded in with motivation and so teachers concentrate on making learning immediately gratifying or providing extrinsic inducements, neglecting the kinds of experiences that would develop powerful expectations about the longer term rewards of the pursuit of knowledge.

To develop such impressionistic knowledge, it is obvious that students must be engaged in inquiry. Passive uptake of knowledge, as in reading a novel or listening to a lecture, has its value, as I've argued earlier. But, to continue with the hiking analogy, it is like viewing a movie of a hike rather than actually going on it; it can have some instructive and motivational value, but it will not make you into a hiker. An important job for the teacher as a party to student inquiry is to ensure there is plenty of looking back and looking ahead. Students are likely to keep their eyes on what is immediately before them, like novice hikers unsure of their footing. The teacher can help them realize they are making progress: "What do we understand now that we didn't understand last week?" Also remind them of lower hills that have been left behind: "Remember when we thought all we had to explain was how we see things right side up when the lens turns things upside down?" Encourage looking ahead: "Where do you think all this is leading?" And provide hints of future problems: "Right now we're finding out what different parts of the brain do. But what about all those connections between the parts?" Having students work with more experienced students could also help in developing perspective and expectations.

All of these are practices that can already be found, sometimes in the same classroom. The difference would be in pursuing them with a clearer purpose. I am suggesting that the purpose of any inquiry conducted in schools should be not only solving the targeted problem (figuring out what keeps airplanes aloft, understanding why historians generally think the French Revolution was more important than the American Revolution) but also developing in students a sense of where further inquiry might lead, confidence that they can move ahead on their own, and confidence that the knowledge they pursue will prove worth gaining.

CONCLUSION

The traditional view of subject matter, which still holds sway especially in state guidelines and in textbook specifications, starts with an itemization of what is to be learned. The more modern view, associated with labels such as constructivism and conceptual change teaching, looks at subject matter somewhat differently. The focus is on students' ideas and understandings. Students come in with ideas. They leave with ideas. The ideas they leave with ought to be better in some fashion than the ideas they came in with. The two views are not miles apart—they are equally objectionable to postmodernists, who see them both as the powerful dictating what is best for the weak—but if they are pursued deeply enough they lead to quite different educational policies.

To see the difference, however, it is necessary to adopt a three-worlds rather than a two-worlds epistemology. In terms of Popper's three worlds, the traditional view makes education out to be a matter of converting World 3 into World 2. It is taking the knowledge that is out there in the culture and getting it represented in the minds of students. One should not immediately attack this conventional view as being committed to rote learning or to any particular pedagogy. If guided discovery, for instance, is the surest way to get certain parts of World 3 converted into World 2 mental content, then guided discovery it should be. In the view I have been advocating, however, education is entirely a matter of changes in World 2—the students' beliefs, understandings, skills, and so on. World 3 enters the picture in two ways. First, conceptual artifacts, the objects populating World 3, are part of what students' beliefs and understandings are about, part of what they develop skills in working with. An extremely important part, I would add. Second, working in World 3—working to interpret, create, and improve conceptual artifacts—holds promise as perhaps the most powerful way to bring about significant changes in World 2.

In the traditional view, facts, theories, proofs, histories, and so on are the actual stuff of learning. They are *what* students are supposed to learn. Motivation accordingly arises as a problem. "Why do we have to learn this stuff?" the impatient adolescent demands, and after several centuries of trying, pedagogues have not yet come up with satisfying answers. In the view I have been advocating, conceptual artifacts are not things to be learned. What students are about is understanding the world, trying to improve their own theories and beliefs. Conceptual artifacts already available in the culture should help in this effort. Whether a particular artifact is helpful is something for students to investigate, to form considered judgments about. Thus, subject-matter content does not have to be justified to students in advance of their learning. An important part of learning is learning what a conceptual artifact is or is not good for. When education is locked into a two-worlds epistemology, in which concepts are either things in people's minds or distillations of physical reality, there is no way to hold a concept up for examination and ask what it is good for. Accordingly, the question "What's the point of learning this stuff?" is rendered fundamentally unanswerable.

In the absence of theory, educators are apt to demand ideological consistency. In the absence of an epistemology adequate to deal with subject matter, educators will press for conformity to a pedagogical philosophy. The notion that both quantity and quality could be important and that they call for different pedagogies becomes virtually unthinkable. Instead, we have direct instruction pitted against activity methods, as if everything turned on the resolution of this conflict. Meanwhile the overriding questions that Dewey and Whitehead addressed remain neglected: How do we make contact between students' interests and the big ideas that form the intellectual life of a civilization? How do we teach things that lead somewhere? How do we ensure that the quest for understanding maintains a continually growing edge?

Critical Thinking, Creativity, and Other Virtues

Nobody can be a good reasoner unless by constant practice he has realized the importance of getting hold of the big ideas and of hanging on to them like grim death.

—Whitehead (1929, p. 91)

Now that I feel better I ought to think a little more and not to slop about being diffident or charming.

—E. M. Forster (1988, p. 114)

Nobel Laureates, captains of industry, cabinet ministers, school superintendents—any one of them is likely to end a commencement address or a discourse on the current crisis by declaring that schools have got to "teach students to think." The words roll easily off the tongue and the speakers show not the slightest doubt that the words mean something. But do they? Why do we never hear about the need to "teach students to digest"? Like thinking, digestion is a vital natural process, it exhibits large individual differences, and it is influenced by psychological and environmental factors.

I am not going to review actual thinking skills programs here or the research, such as it is, on their effectiveness. The more ambitious programs used in schools are complex. Explicit teaching and practicing of thinking skills may occupy a relatively small part, compared with various entensions and enrichments of regular school subject matter. This makes it difficult to fasten credit or blame on any particular treatment of thinking. Furthermore, the measures used to evaluate thinking usually embody the same assumptions as the program being evaluated. They usually consist of brief, trivial tasks similar to the exercises used in the program, and they offer no evidence that improved scores predict any improvement in real-world performance. But what most dissuades me from a serious consideration of actual thinking skills programs is the collective suspension of critical thought that seems to unite their producers, reviewers, and users. A recent entry into the software market consists of animated stories, each one claimed to teach a specific thinking skill. It has received uniformly enthusiastic reviews and is beginning to be adopted by school systems. The reviewers raise not the slightest question as to whether it actually teaches what is claimed or whether indeed it teaches anything at all that could reasonably be expected to transfer to real life. Teaching thinking is treated as a straightforward matter like teaching furniture refinishing. It does not occur to people to question whether a course that claims to teach it actually does so. Heeding the analogy to teaching digestion, I do not find it obvious that thinking is teachable at all or, indeed, what it would mean to teach thinking.

COMMON APPROACHES TO IMPROVING THINKING

To get down to what it might conceivably mean to teach thinking, we need to clear away layers of rubbish. These are mainly the products of unexamined assumptions—assumptions about modifiability of the brain, about the trainability of mental faculties, about what constitutes a cognitive skill, and about the role of method in thinking.

Improving the Brain

The brain does things that emerge as thinking, just as the liver does things that emerge as bile and urea. How well these organs do their work is influenced by many things, but *how* they do their work is built into their structure. Despite some nonsensical talk by multimedia enthusiasts, there is no more prospect of altering how the brain thinks than of altering how the liver produces bile. At a physiological level, the only prospect is of altering how well, that is, how reliably or efficiently the organ functions. In the case of the brain, this could have to do with the speed at which synaptic connections are formed or dissolved, with levels of neural exitation or inhibition, with spread of activation, and things of that sort. We know such factors can be influenced by fatigue, drugs, and stress, and so it is not out of the question that they could be influenced in more enduring ways by training of certain kinds. But there is no evidence that they can, and if effective brain conditioning were to be discovered, there is hardly any possibility that it would come out of the thinking skills programs educators devise. It is likely to involve training of an intensity and precision far beyond anything schools could manage. In short, brain conditioning is a medical possibility, not an educational one.

Although brain conditioning has been advocated for years with no evidence whatsoever to support it, it has recently received a substantial boost from research on brain development. Blocking or distorting vision in a newborn kitten's eye will permanently affect the development of the visual projection area in the animal's brain (Cynader & Frost, 1999). At the other end of the life cycle, there is some evidence that mental exercises can counteract senile decline in brain functioning (Cotman, 1990). These are probably unrelated phenomena, and the relevance of either one to education is doubtful. The first reflects the fact that the genetic program for development of the brain has not completed its work at birth and that environmental inputs play an important role in fine-tuning the cognitive system to the world it is born into. This means that stimulus deprivation at an early age can have grave anatomical effects, but it is a huge imaginative leap to suppose that similar considerations apply to intellectual development in the school years. Studies of aging indicate that the principle of "use it or lose it" applies to the cognitive system as it does to other systems of the body.

What this research fails to show is that stimulation above some critical minimum can make a difference—in other words, that a normal healthy brain can benefit from additional exercises. The situation is analogous to that with vitamins. There is compelling evidence of the harmful effects of vitamin deficiencies, but showing that there is benefit in augmenting a normal healthy diet with vitamin supplements is a different matter requiring a different kind of evidence. Such evidence, though it is often controversial, has appeared with respect to some vitamins, but it is lacking with respect to brain exercise. Recent brain imaging research has aroused interest in the possibility, but it remains unsubstantiated. I am referring to reports, for instance, that London taxicab drivers show enlargement of the brain area that stores navigational knowledge of the environment. That learning produces changes in the brain is a given, and it is interesting that these changes can sometimes be of a visible magnitude, but it is not clear that these new findings have new practical import. If you were trying to improve the navigational abilities of taxicab drivers, would this evidence make a difference? If it led you to prescribe artificial exercises designed to enlarge the relevant brain area as opposed to engaging the learners in solving navigational problems in the city where they will drive, the best guess on current evidence is that you would be making a mistake. More generally, anything that replaces potentially useful learning with exercises designed to stimulate the brain is, on present evidence, a bad choice. That may change, but of one thing we can remain fairly certain: It is a sorry educational program indeed that has to include thinking exercises just to provide enough mental activity to keep the brain healthy.

Training the Faculties

The next layer has to do with faculties and exercise. From Reid's 24 "powers of the mind" (*Essay on the Intellectual Powers of Man*, 1785, in Lehrer & Beanblossom, 1975) to Gardner's (1983) "7 intelligences," people have been drawn to the belief that the mind consists of trainable faculties. Sorting out educationally relevant truths from the tangle of theories and word magic here is not easy. First, as to faculties: The brain, as we know, is not homogeneous. Localized brain damage can affect some mental abilities and not others. There have been numerous efforts over the years to produce scientifically based categorizations of mental abilities, some based wholly on performance tests, others, like Gardner's, taking account of neurological findings as well. All of them, ultimately, are grounded in observations of how people differ. Before concerning ourselves with the merits of one categorization over another, we need to consider where any such categorization leads us educationally.

Where faculty psychology leads, of course, is back to exercise. There is no other place it can lead. The mental abilities are ones that people already have, so education is not a matter of teaching people to do things they cannot already do. It is a matter of improving some capacity of the brain. Thus, educators who are taken with a scheme of faculties or mental attributes are inevitably led back to trying to improve fundamental brain processes. Having no insight into those processes, however, they can only prescribe exercises in which the overt behavior seems to reflect the underlying faculty. In the 1960s it was exercises to develop the myriad dimensions of Guilford's (1967)

"Structure of Intellect." Now there is a whole catalog of books and videos to provide teachers with ways of developing Gardner's multiple intelligences.

The metaphor underlying the training of mental faculties is the mind as a muscle system. Just as bodybuilders do one exercise for their pecs and another for their abs, mind builders must do different exercises to enhance the 4 or 7 or 27 or J. P. Guilford's record-setting 150 components of intelligence. Not everything that goes on in the name of mental exercise is pure silliness. Sometimes useful things are taught. But to the extent that what is taught can be justified on ordinary curricular grounds, there is no need for a psychological taxonomy to justify them. Gardner (1994, p. 581) referred to "some brilliant, some idiotic" educational approaches conceived in the name of his theory of multiple intelligences. At their best, faculty theories serve a heuristic function, leading educators to think of worthwhile enhancements to the curriculum that might not have occurred to them otherwise. But to the extent that these cannot be justified on their own merits, educators ought to be called to account and not allowed to get away with hand-waving allusions to "inferencing skills," "memory skills," "spatial abilities," "creative thinking," and the like.

Cognitive Skill Training

Let us set the brain aside, then, and turn to skills. Skills improve with practice. (There are some caveats, but we can ignore them here.) So shouldn"t practice in pattern recognition, problem solving, logical inference, and creative thinking improve those skills? Here is where word magic comes to the fore. Suppose I assigned you the task of going through a newspaper and circling every instance in which three consecutive letters occurred in alphabetical order. You would probably find this tedious and intellectually unrewarding. Would it make a difference if I told you the exercise was supposed to improve your pattern recognition ability? Not likely, because the task is too remote from anything you can imagine yourself doing in the way of pattern recognition. Suppose, however, that instead of pages full of letters you were given pages full of numbers and the task was to circle instances in which a pair of numbers was followed by its sum. Now you might begin to give credence to the claim that this exercise developed pattern recognition ability. After all, recognizing pattern in numerical arrangements is something mathematicians do, and the pattern $X, Y, X + Y$, although simple, is a kind of pattern that could be worth noticing, especially by children just getting the hang of functions. And so a thinking skill exercise is born.

All that skills research assures us is that if you work at the letters task you will become increasingly proficient at spotting alphabetical sequences of letters in running text and that if you keep at the numerical task you will become increasingly proficient at spotting sums of adjacent numbers. Skills research gives us no reason for confidence that either task will make you better at anything else. Becoming proficient in the letters task cannot even be expected to make you better at the numbers task or vice versa, except perhaps through developing more efficient ways of scanning lines of print. People have been trained in memorizing strings of digits to the point where they can repeat back strings 10 times as long as the average person can handle, and yet this training does not make them better at other memory tasks (Ericsson & Chase, 1982). This lack of general effects is commonly referred to as failure of *transfer*, but that is a mistaken use of the term. Failures of transfer occur when something has been learned that could help in another situation but does not—for instance, learning a principle or strategy applicable to a new task and failing to apply it (Gick & Holyoak, 1980). In such cases one may profitably inquire whether there is some better way to teach the matter in question so as to increase the likelihood of transfer. In the case of thinking skills training there is no indication that anything of a potentially transferrable nature has been learned.

Thinking Strategy Instruction

The difference between cognitive skills training and thinking strategies instruction is the difference between going to a driving range and hitting hundreds of golf balls and having a coach help you improve your golf stroke. The question, of course, is to what extent thinking is amenable to coaching.

There have been many how-to-think offerings over the years, although you would not know it from examining the catalogs of university libraries. Most of them fall into that category of self-help literature that fills the psychology sections of nonacademic bookstores but seldom receives any critical notice. In recent years, however, a number of books have begun to appear written by research psychologists. These reflect the growing body of research on human problem solving, research that has delved into how people actually go about thinking their way through problems.

The old-fashioned self-help books that I have looked into offer two main approaches to the improvement of thinking: stepwise procedures and slogans. The stepwise procedures are variations on John Dewey's (1933) *How We Think*. They start with recognizing something lacking or amiss, formulating a problem, venturing a hypothesis, reasoning one's way forward from it, testing the result, and going back to the drawing board if the result is unsatisfactory. The slogans could pretty much be reduced to the one used by Norman R. F. Maier (1970) in his pioneering research on problem solving: "Don't be blind!" Maier found that uttering these words at the right time could jar a subject into recognizing, for instance, that a pair of scissors lying on the table could be used as a pendulum bob, thereby solving a perplexing problem.

Both these approaches have serious drawbacks. The trouble with stepwise procedures is that thinking doesn't actually run that way. There is a lot of looping back, starting over, jumping ahead, and so on. Dewey, of course, knew that, and if flow charts had been invented he probably would have used one to depict these properties of thinking. But a list was the best he could do, and so a list is what he passed on to subsequent generations of how-to-think writers. The trouble with "Don't be blind!" and similar exhortations to get out of our cognitive ruts is that we normally do not have a coach standing by to utter the words at the opportune moment. We have to do it ourselves, and doing it opportunely presupposes that we know when we are being blind and that we have at least an inkling of what we are being blind to. Were that the case, we should probably not need coaching.

Modern research on thinking has profited not only from improved ways of representing complex processes but also from the use of thinking aloud as a method of gaining information on what goes on in thinking (Ericsson & Simon, 1980). Most of the research has been inspired by Newell and Simon's (1972) monumental study of problem solving (1972), although an earlier use of thinking aloud by Bloom and Broder (1950) actually pointed more directly to educationally relevant conclusions. Bloom and Broder studied university students who varied in how well they could solve typical textbook problems. Faced with a problem, what the poorest problem solvers appeared to do was nothing. They waited for something to occur to them, and if nothing did they declared themselves unable to solve the problem. Good problem solvers might not always succeed, but they knew how to work at a problem. This difference in sheer amount of manifest mental activity has continued to appear in other studies of thinking, for instance in studies of the thinking that goes on in reading and writing (Bereiter & Scardamalia, 1987; Zbrodoff, 1984). Thinking–aloud studies have also cast useful light on the nature of the mental activity that distinguishes successful thinkers. The following are four contributions this research has made to the search for ways of teaching people to think:

1. Thinking-aloud research has dramatized the discrepancy between what people do while thinking and what they report afterward. Retrospective reports of problem solving, even those of only a few moments delay, tend to be idealizations. Compared with the fragmentary utterances of people instructed to express thoughts as they occur, they are complete, conventionally ordered—and less revealing. Accordingly, we have good reason to be skeptical of approaches to thinking based on introspection or after-the-fact reports. These are likely to be heavily biased by beliefs about how thinking *should* proceed. This is not to imply that thinking aloud opens a "window on the mind," as some enthusiasts have claimed. A lot remains invisible, and what shows is open to various interpretations, but there is no mistaking an authentic thinking-aloud transcript for the contrivances of how-to-think narratives.

2. Thinking aloud research helps in distinguishing strategies thinkers actually use from ones deduced from conventional beliefs. A teacher once told me that she had been looking at the comprehension strategies taught in various reading programs and concluded that imagery must be the most important strategy, because it appeared in every program. I remarked that that was interesting, inasmuch as there is no evidence that good readers actually use such a strategy. The teacher volunteered that she could not recall ever using the strategy herself, but she was not quite ready to turn her back on such an authoritative host. Of course, the textbooks simply reflect conventional pedagogical beliefs (thus, as we see, helping to keep them alive), and one of these is that forming a picture in your mind helps in grasping a narrative or description. People do experience imagery when reading—some much more than others—but this is something that just happens. It is a *result* of or a *part* of comprehension, not something one does as a step on the way toward comprehension. By contrast, thinking-aloud research indicates a number of things that good readers do do when comprehension falters, such as formulating a problem or producing a stripped down version of a lengthy sentence so as to get at the core proposition (Bereiter & Bird, 1985).

3. Although thinking-aloud protocols do not usually reveal anything very startling that people do in thinking, they give us a picture of how people allocate effort to various parts of cognitive tasks. Studies of expert problem solvers in various domains indicate they devote relatively more effort than nonexperts do to understanding the problem and its constraints—to figuring out what makes it a problem and what kind of problem it is—before

laying into its solution (Glaser & Chi, 1988). This seems like something beginners ought to know.

4. Finally, thinking aloud itself affords possibilities of coaching—modeling thinking performance and providing for imitative and supported practice. This is quite different from mental exercise and from having people explain after the fact how they solved a problem. It is much like coaching as it occurs in athletics and performing arts. The coach says, "Do it this way," demonstrates, the learner tries to imitate the demonstration, and the coach provides correction. Until thinking aloud came along, no such coaching was possible in the cognitive realm and this is probably a reason there has been so much quack pedagogy. A correspondence course in acting would probably exhibit similar quackery. Coached thinking may be awkward and unnatural at first, like any other kind of coached performance, but if handled right it can quickly become assimilated into the learner's overall competence. Results have been positive, and transcripts of children using coached strategies ought to allay any fears that such coaching makes children into puppets (e.g., see Bereiter & Bird, 1985; Brown & Palinsar, 1989; Scardamalia, Bereiter, & Steinbach, 1984).

Very little of what I have just outlined has made it into educational practice. The teaching of thinking strategies, although motivated by contemporary research, still relies mostly on stepwise procedures and slogans and could as easily have been designed 50 years ago.

REAL-LIFE THINKING

At this point, having discussed brain conditioning, exercising the faculties, cognitive skill training, and thinking strategy instruction, we have covered the teaching of thinking as it is ordinarily conceived. Yet large areas of importance remain untouched. To name three, we have said nothing about thinking as a social activity, about how thinking relates to knowledge, and about motivation. Ignoring these reduces thinking to a set of parlor tricks, which is what it is in the worst of the thinking programs on the market. Doing justice to these three does not mean merely adding more items to the inventory of approaches to thinking, however. In the foregoing discussion I have tacitly accepted the folk view of thinking as mental operations carried out on stored mental content. It is now time to take a broader view, in which thinking is seen as a primarily social activity (although always with an important private component), carried out in a cultural environment rich with objects (material and abstract) that are the products of previous thinking.

The major difference between real-life thinking and the contrived thinking tasks that occupy much of schooling (as well as much of the experimental research on thinking) is in the role of world knowledge. Contrived problems provide all the information you are supposed to use in solving them. "John had 8 apples. He ate 3 of them. How many apples does he have now?" If you start thinking about the possibility that those 3 apples may still be in John's stomach so that in a sense he still has them you are heading for the wrong answer. Real-life problems are not like that. You are free to bring in any knowledge that will cast light on the problem or suggest ways to solve it. Retrieving relevant knowledge, using analogies, consulting reference sources, or asking others for information—these become crucial parts of real-life problem solving.

People conditioned to the contrived problems of schoolwork can be amazingly obtuse when confronted with problems that look like school problems but in fact require the use of world knowledge. One problem I have used to show this is the problem of how to measure a seventh of a foot using an ordinary foot ruler. Some people do silly things, revealing their inability to manipulate fractions, but those with a firmer hold on arithmetic will divide 12 by 7 and announce that the answer is 1.714 inches. That isn't an adequate answer, of course, because there are no markings corresponding to such a number on an ordinary foot ruler. To solve the problem you need to bring in your knowledge of how foot rulers are ordinarily marked. On this basis, you can then reformulate the problem as one of figuring out how many sixteenths of an inch there are in a seventh of a foot, from which you may work your way to the answer that a seventh of a foot is one inch and somewhere between 11 and 12 sixteenths. When I explain to people why 1.714 is not a good answer, they sometimes object that the problem is unfair. The unfairness is in the real world, which, when it presents you with a problem, does not present you with all the information you need to solve it.

Before tackling the difficult question of what schools can do to improve real-life thinking, let us consider the more limited case in which people already have a job and the goal is to improve the thinking that goes on in their work. Businesses spend substantial amounts of money on this, frequently in the form of workshops advertised as promoting creative thinking. In fact, there is considerable migration between school and business in the kinds of training offered. Sometimes the methods of an industrial training guru are taken up by schools. Sometimes a program created by an educational guru is adopted by industry. In one extreme case, reported to me by an educational guru himself, a high-flying electronics company put their engineers through a program originally designed for backward adolescents. Stepwise procedures and slogans form much of the substance of thinking skills development in industry, because the workshop and short-course formats preclude extensive exercise and because the trainers are ignorant of the actual work that thinking is supposed to enhance.

If we stand back and consider thinking in the context of business enterprise, however, it becomes apparent that the most important aspects are the ones neglected in traditional thinking skills instruction: social process, knowledge, and motivation. The social aspect is coming to be appreciated and is represented in the popular "six hats" approach, which is a way of managing group thinking so as to favor creativity (de Bono, 1985). Often in business the concern is not with the individual thinker but with the overall quality of thought that goes into designs, processes, and decisions. Invariably a number of people are involved, so that it is the success of the whole design or decision process that counts, and it could easily fail even though everyone involved is by ordinary accounts a good thinker. Where individual thinking is an issue, as it is in many service enterprises, we know from studies of expertise that deep knowledge of the task and of the relevant tools is the crucial element in successful problem solving. Accordingly, the first concern ought to be with the kind of thinking that *leads* to deep knowledge rather than with the kind of thinking that *presupposes* such knowledge. To employers it is obvious that ability to think is not enough, there must also be willingness to put forth the effort and to accept the risks that thinking entails. What may not be so obvious is the contribution that effort and risk taking make to developing thinking abilities in the first place.

Thinking As a Social Process

One of the unfortunate consequences of the individualistic focus of folk theory of mind is that far too much emphasis gets placed on isolated bright ideas. Who thought of it first is a recurrent question, for inordinate amounts of credit go to the person who comes up with an idea that initiates some leap forward, be it in science, industry, or almost anything of social significance.[1] Most of the effort to understand creativity has been directed toward explaining how original ideas come about (e.g., Campbell, 1960; Koestler, 1964). Although, in the aggregate, much more creativity may go into bringing an idea to fruition than went into producing it in the first place, it is distrib-

---

[1] E. H. Gombrich (1959) showed, however, that the innovator typically does not get much credit in art. That goes to the artist who adopts the innovation and produces masterpieces. So, my generalization probably only holds for knowledge work, where World 3 objects are the product and their embodiments are not themselves objects of admiration.

uted over a number of people and may not even be recognized as creativity at all, because no individual brilliant contributions can be identified.

It will be surprising if this bias toward individual bright ideas persists in today's knowledge-based businesses. In the glimpses I have had of the workings of such organizations, there is a superabundance of bright ideas. The problem always is to make something of them—ultimately, money. I have known creative programmers and engineers who admit to spending 80% of their time politicking or "evangelizing," as some call it, to marshal support for their notions. Eventual corporate adoption, decision to go ahead with a product, may be their goal, but first they have to enlist the interest of their peers, to get more brains with differing expertise working together to develop the article to the point where it will warrant consideration at an upper management level. Very quickly "my" idea must become "our" project, or it will amount to nothing.

Business contexts also dramatize the importance of sustained mental effort. Except for a few peculiar tasks such as inventing advertising slogans, one-shot creativity is of little value. Seeing a project through to a successful outcome requires not only a series of creative acts but an unrelenting process of productive thinking. Most people cannot sustain that kind of mental effort over long stretches without a good deal of external support—which may be a reason why there are so few solitary geniuses.

Consider the work of a planning committee, which meets for hours at a time over a period of weeks. What we know about the character of human thought tells us that the attention of committee members will fluctuate considerably around the matter at hand, often skipping off to unrelated matters. At any given moment, only some of the individual minds will actually be engaged with the immediate issue, yet the committee's work moves on in a fairly steady fashion, with occasional moments of brilliance. Individuals' thoughts keep being drawn back to the work, whereas if they were by themselves people might well lose hold.

It is perhaps fanciful to say there is a group thinking process that goes on despite the diversions of individual thought, but it is not fanciful to say there is a discourse that proceeds thus. The discourse may proceed in a coherent way despite absences and changes in membership. What people's wandering minds keep being drawn back to is that discourse. If a planning committee is working well, the discourse will be seen to progress. Participants or observers will be able to point out substantive ways in which the discourse has progressed from where it was earlier. If a planning committee is working badly, the discourse will not be seen to progress. It will be seen as stalled, going in circles, or moving along in a way that is not judged to constitute progress.

All of this applies not just to committees but to any sort of collective endeavor that has a cognitive objective—to solve a problem, produce a design, reach a decision, advance a theory, or whatever. There is a discourse that progresses or fails to progress with respect to its objective. What I take to be the essential point of discursive psychology (Harré & Gillett, 1994) is that there is not some underlying group thinking process that is reflected in the discourse; the discourse *is* the group thinking process. Individual thinking figures insofar as the individual contributes to and is in turn influenced by the discourse, but it is the discourse itself that constitutes the collective effort to achieve a cognitive objective. If the discourse succeeds, it does not matter if it is as a result of individual good thinking or a fortunate combination of inputs from people whose individual thinking is unremarkable. If the discourse fails, the effort has failed, and it does not matter how brilliant were the participants and how many bright ideas lay buried in the discourse.

Some credit must be given to this discursive view of thought, no matter how devoted we might be to the idea of individual genius. Having credited it, we must then recognize that ability to participate in and contribute to the success of progressive discourse (see chap. 3) is a vital part of learning to be a thinker in the contemporary world.

Thinking and Expert Knowledge

Another archaic belief fostered by folk theory is a pointless opposition between knowledge, thought of as having a head full of facts, and intelligence, thought of as the ability to do clever things without benefit of knowledge. This has given rise to the myth of the brainy amateur who walks in and solves the problem that has baffled the experts. Detective fiction was founded on this myth, but its influence extends into real life. A common career pattern is one in which a distinguished physicist or biologist or mathematician, passing into old age, decides to take off and solve the problems of some completely different field, such as education or psychology, convinced that his superior thinking abilities and methods ensure success. I do not know of any such efforts that have panned out, and sometimes the results are ludicrous and pathetic.[2]

There are instances in which a naive observer can see something important that the experts overlook. That is one reason shop talk at the dinner table is not an altogether bad practice. But the instances

---

[2]The *Omni Interviews*(Weintraub, 1984) provide several striking examples.

are rare and becoming rarer. Increasingly, you need to know a good deal just in order to understand the problem that is perplexing the expert. Consider computer programming. This is an activity in which getting stuck is common and having a different pair of eyes look at a problem is often helpful. But those eyes have to be connected to a knowledgeable brain. Otherwise, there is not much to offer besides moral support.

In the normal course of events, beginners overlook things, are easily baffled, and make dumb mistakes. As they learn more they act smarter. They become better not only at the routines of their work but also at dealing with novel problems. This is not a matter of developing problem-solving skills in some abstract sense. They are better at solving problems within their area because their past experience helps them avoid bad alternatives and it provides them with pieces that may be assembled into a solution and with memories of related instances (episodic knowledge), which they can mine for ideas and guidance. However, if job experience were all it took to become a good on-the-job thinker, the purveyors of thinking skills training would have long ago gone out of business. At the same time that people are acquiring the knowledge that helps them solve problems, they are acquiring routines that militate against their further growth.

Most of the knowledge that helps in solving problems comes from previous problem-solving efforts, successful and unsuccessful. Harking back to the categorization of knowledge discussed in chapter 5, it is *implicit understanding*. As implicit understanding grows, problems occur less frequently. To the beginning doctor, every new patient brings a new problem. Experienced doctors regularly report that somewhere between 85% and 95% of the cases they see are routine, requiring no problem solving effort. Thus, experience yields diminishing returns. But it can also produce habits that lead to declining expertise. Experienced doctors know ways to treat the remaining 5 to 15 percent of cases in routine ways as well—prescribe broad-spectrum antibiotics, send the patient off for more tests, and so on. These are ways of avoiding problem solving, thus also avoiding learning. Some medical societies screen doctors' files looking for signs of mental withering on the vine, and they find them with enough frequency to be unsettling.

Withering on the vine, becoming deadwood, getting into a rut—there is no shortage of metaphors for this familiar phenomenon. It might seem that it is an inevitable consequence of experience and aging, but it is not. The recognizable experts in any field have both a great deal of knowledge gained through experience and a readiness to tackle problems. We have devoted quite a bit of study to trying to understand this dual character of expertise (Bereiter & Scardamalia,

1993). We have concluded that what keeps experts from succumbing to routine is the same thing that made them experts in the first place. We call it *progressive problem solving*. The key word is "progressive." With experience, more and more of what used to constitute problems becomes reduced to routine tasks. That much is inevitable. It is true for experts and for experienced nonexperts as well. Such routinization or automaticity frees up mental resources (attentional capacity or working memory). Where experts diverge from experienced nonexperts is in what they do with those freed up resources. Experts invest them back into the task, so that problems can now be addressed at higher or more complex levels. In almost all real-world problems there is more that could be taken into account than we have the mental capacity to handle. Thus, we always simplify (Simon, 1957). What the expert does by reinvesting mental resources is to simplify a bit less. Whereas in an earlier career stage the physician may have been able to take account only of the physical symptoms, the expert, who does not require so much mental capacity to deal with the physical symptoms, has capacity to spare to consider the patient's life situation, personality, living habits, and so on. This has three results: It makes the case more complex, more problematic; it generates more knowledge; and it likely results in better treatment. Eventually, this more complex level of problem solving starts to become eased by routines, thus freeing the expert to progress to an even more complex level for addressing problems, and so on.

A nice illustration of this phenomenon comes from research by Patel and Groen (1991) on expertise in medical diagnosis. In one of the cases used in their research, the patient presents confusing symptoms of cardiac problems. Included among various facts in the case description is mention of scratch marks on the arm identified by the patient as cat scratches. These are the key to the case, for once it is hypothesized that they are actually needle tracks resulting from drug abuse, the rest of the facts fall into place. Despite their probably having had more recent exposure to drug abusers, the younger physicians tend to overlook the scratch marks. A likely explanation is that they have such a struggle trying to put together the cardiological data that they are forced to ignore any facts that are not obviously related to cardiac symptoms. The expert cardiologists, however, have learned to recognize many patterns effortlessly. This enables them on one hand to notice discrepancies, facts that don't fit together, and on the other hand to enlarge what Newell and Simon (1972) call the problem space, so as to consider facts and possibilities that may resolve the discrepancies.

Progressive problem solving thus means continually enlarging the problem space as one becomes able to handle more elements. It can be found in all walks of life, but it is a rarity in most. Visit an automobile dealership and you are likely to encounter a salesperson who knows no more about the product than you could learn by reading a brochure, and who takes you through a sales routine enlivened only by his or her zeal to get your signature on a purchase agreement. Such salespeople, in my experience, are usually not even experts at relieving you of your money. They have certain well-practiced tricks that they use, but if those tricks happen not to work, they just want you to go away. Call in a plumber or an electrician, a gardener or a cleaning service, and you may again expect to witness the running off of a well-practiced routine—which may happen to fit your needs, but if it does not you are out of luck. All these specialists have accumulated considerable knowledge, but it is knowledge geared to the avoidance of problems and it is knowledge that has all but ceased to grow. From time to time, however, you may encounter someone in any of these occupations who is immediately distinguished from the rest by (a) seeing more in your problem than you do, (b) relishing the problem, and (c) having an abundance of knowledge to bring to bear on it. That is a progressive problem solver, a genuine expert.

Let us apply this conception of progressive problem solving and expertise to a typical business situation, that of an equipment supplier with a staff of technicians who go out on service calls. The technicians have been put through a course of training to learn about the equipment and about various troubleshooting and repair procedures. However, the employer recognizes that these technicians should also be able to solve novel problems, and therefore considers putting them through a course in problem solving. That is unlikely to have much effect. To judge from research on equipment troubleshooting and repair (Lesgold & Lajoie, 1991), the technicians probably do not lack problem-solving strategies. What they more likely lack is deep understanding of the equipment and how it functions and of the users and their needs and practices. Without that, they do not know enough to get to the source of novel difficulties or to improvise remedies. More formal instruction on the equipment and its uses might help and ought to be investigated because it is the least expensive of appropriate measures. If the service enterprise is large enough, it might be practical to develop a simulation and training system like Sherlock (Katz et al., 1998). Sherlock provides a realistic computer simulation of equipment and instruments and can take learners through a graduated series of problems, in the course of which they develop a rich implicit understanding of equipment, instruments, and job, along with problem-solving strategies finely tuned to the job. Lacking such a system, use might be made of apprenticeship. Send learners out on service calls with experienced technicians who are expert at solving problems and who have been instructed to engage learners in the problem-solving processes as much as possible. Perhaps the most promising approach is arranging informal ways for the techicians to share experiences, so that they amplify their collective knowledge (Wenger, 1995). However the training is handled, it will be important to establish working conditions that encourage continual and progressive problem solving. That means rewarding problem solving, not penalizing technicians for problem solving efforts that fail, and generally trying to support a culture in which progressive problem solving is the name of the game and is what one must do to belong. All of this is a far cry from running employees through a thinking skills workshop. It is what an organization must do if it is serious about improving thinking on the job, whereas the thinking skills training approach seems to me a form of superstitious behavior. Burnt offerings would probably serve equally well.

Motivation, Risk Taking, and Creativity

The preceding discussion may be summarized as follows: To think better you must have deeper understanding; to gain deeper understanding you must solve problems; to solve problems you must put forth effort and take risks. Thus, motivation is at the bottom of anything that can properly be called "learning to think." But it is not just motivation to do well. Motivation to do well can, under many circumstances, defeat efforts to improve thinking. It can produce excessive caution, an inclination to stay safely within the boundaries of one's competence and of one's job (Hirschhorn, 1988).

A connection between creativity and risk taking is widely recognized. On one hand, willingness to take risks may be seen as just one of a constellation of traits that go with being a creative sort of person—other traits being flamboyance and disdain for convention (Barron, 1969). More commonly, though, it is thought of as a kind of releaser, on the premise that we all have the capacity to be creative, but it is held in check by caution. There is no doubt merit in both these views, but they fail to do justice to the role of risk taking in *acquiring* the ability to think creatively. Both, instead, treat creativity as something people have rather than something people achieve.

In practical terms, creative people are successful risk takers. This may not immediately shine forth as an insight, but it covers all cases fairly well. To succeed at low-risk endeavors is not creative because low risk means that a path to success is already known. And if your risky endeavors consistently fail, they will not be credited as creative either. So-called "brilliant failures" in the arts are actually judged to have succeeded in important ways, while falling short of some perhaps impossible goal. "Brilliant failures" may also occur in business and other practical fields and be similarly acknowledged as creative, but, again, they are creative in what they achieve, not in what they fail to achieve.

Defining creativity as successful risk taking is not very helpful in the large grain, but in the small grain it leads to ideas of how to foster creativity. Most of the creativity that is taken seriously in the world falls within the broad category of *design*. It includes not only the design of tangible products but also the design of services, processes, and theories. Design is creative insofar as what emerges from the process is unforeseeable, that is, cannot be deduced from the starting premises. This means that not only is a design project as a whole risky, but every little step along the way is also risky, in that it must be taken without a sure knowledge of what effect it will have on the end result. As David Perkins (1981) explained it, creative work involves the continual adding of constraints on what can come after. Every brush stroke, every word added to a text, every stipulation added to a business agreement constrains the brush strokes, words, or stipulations that may come after. Of course, the glory of design, compared with physical execution, is that the process is reversible. Constraints that prove unfortunate may be removed and different ones tried, but this only means the risks are not grave.

It remains the basic fact of life in all creative work that actions must be taken in the uncertain hope that subsequent developments will prove them right. This has suggested to some theorists that chance and trial and error play a large, perhaps dominant, role in creative work (Campbell, 1960). Nevertheless, there are individuals and groups who dependably produce creative results year after year. Are they just lucky, or do they *know* something that less successful innovators do not?

Creativity research has focused almost exclusively on the innovative aspect and neglected the knowing aspect of creativity. A writer comes up with a story idea; a scientist comes up with a research idea; a management team comes up with a business idea. In each case, much work will have to be done before it becomes demonstrable whether the idea was a good one. The idea may be instantly recognizable as novel or imaginative, but that is close to irrelevant. What matters is *is it promising?* It could be a flawed idea, but is it worth laboring to improve it? Every new idea brings new problems: Will those problems be solvable? Will they prove worth solving? All the way from the level of changes in the direction of life down to the level of the brushstroke, judgments of promisingness steer the creative process. Those judgments are either blind guesses or they are based on knowledge of some kind. In popular parlance, they are based on intuition, but that only means they are not deducible from facts. Hunches, gut feelings, "I just know"—these are the forms in which knowledge of promisingness presents itself. This is *impressionistic knowledge*, which was discussed in chapter 5. There is nothing particularly mysterious about it, I argued. The knowledge is vague and does not lend itself to debate, but it is acquired through experience. We have no trouble accepting this in the case of connoisseurs of fine wines, but ancient biases get in the way of extending the notion to connoisseurs of ideas. The winemaker tastes and examines a new wine and judges whether it is worth laying down to age for some years. This is a judgment of promisingness, just like judging the promisingness of a research idea or a business venture. There are some objective criteria that may be applied, but beyond them judgments must rest on impressionistic knowledge.

With experience, everybody acquires knowledge of promisingness. But if they have always taken cautious steps, they are not going to acquire impressionistic knowledge that will help them in making judgments about more daring steps. In short, you have to take risks to acquire the impressionistic knowledge that enables you to make good risky choices, and without such knowledge you cannot reliably achieve creative results. I am not trying to say that knowledge of promisingness is all there is to creativity, but I am trying to say it is a necessary part, and it may be the only part that education and management can do much about.

Sending people to a creativity workshop might inspire them to start taking greater risks, to start "trusting their intuitions" more. But this would be the *beginning* of the process of acquiring the knowledge that makes creativity possible—making risky choices and learning from their successes and failures. The challenge for managers would be providing a working environment in which such learning could flourish.

THINKING IN SCHOOL

The school's interest in thinking differs in significant ways from that of business. The school's interest is much less specific. Educators must face the problem of what can be done with 10-year-olds that will make them better thinkers at 30, in whatever jobs or roles they find themselves. In doing so, educators must work without benefit of what we have seen to be a crucial factor in thinking on the job: deep knowledge of the job and its particular tools, resources, and constraints. Hence, the school's interest is more general by necessity, but it is also more general by design. Businesses may be concerned only with thinking for the good of the company; schools need to be concerned with thinking for the all-around good of the person and of society. Thus, there is a concern with thinking as an aspect of citizenship and, in the rare and admirable case, thinking as an aspect of personal mental life.

For thinking in school, expectations are high but vague, and they often reflect an unfounded confidence in transfer of training. Blind faith in transfer characterizes not only those who espouse specific training but also those who try to make thinking in school more like thinking in real life. I suspect it is a faith born out of desperation: If thinking in school does not transfer to thinking outside of school, what hope is there? I shall try to offer a moderately encouraging answer to that question.

One approach to thinking has been to turn it into a school subject and allocate slots for it in the curriculum. Although it keeps coming back, this approach never stays in favor for very long. When you concentrate thinking exercises and sloganeering into regular blocks of time, their silliness becomes evident and they are soon displaced by antiviolence education or computer literacy or whatever else is being urged on the always overcrowded curriculum. The currently more favored approach is to incorporate thinking into regular school subjects. This can mean anything from distributing the silliness to taking a thoughtful approach to subject matter, and so it is impossible to say much about this approach except to ask whether there is anything more.

Despite the differences, the points made about thinking on the job apply to thinking in school and serve to point out how much is neglected in typical school approaches. Thinking in school is as much a social process as it is on the job—or, if it is not, we should take a hard look at the social processes of schooling. Certainly understanding plays as big a role in thinking at school as it does on the job, even if it is not so job specific. The same for motivation. Developing these three themes—social process, understanding, and motivation—will, I hope, provide a broader and more useful perspective than is typically suggested by the injunction, "Teach them to think."

Social Process: Classroom Discourse As Thought

When it is applied to the work of a planning committee, the proposition that "the discourse *is* the thinking" makes a fair bit of sense. When applied to classroom talk, however, we immediately sense that something is awry. In the first place one person, the teacher, does most of the talking and controls the rest, and so it might be more fitting to say that the *teacher's* discourse is the thinking. This formula fits not only the traditional recitation format, in which the teacher fires questions at the students, but also the freer sorts of class discussions and such refinements as Socratic teaching. These are mainly variations in the kinds of questions asked. They may give more space to the students' thoughts, but the social process remains one in which the teacher does the initiating and the directing.

It is often alleged that teachers suppress independent and creative thought. In 40 years of working in or dropping in on classrooms, I have never actually witnessed active suppression, although I have heard atrocity stories, some of which may be true. The typical teacher, in my experience, goes out of the way to shower encouragement on any manifestation of original thought. What is stultifying is the over-all form of classroom discourse. Some years ago the institute I belonged to held a retreat to iron out problems and think ahead. A professional "facilitator" was hired to guide us. He began by announcing that he was going to lead us through a process that had been perfected to (he didn't put it quite this way) get old sticks like us out of the mud. For 2 days we responded to prompts while our facilitator danced around and scrawled things on sheets of newsprint. We broke into small groups with specific tasks and then chose one of our number to report back and show off the sheets of newsprint we had filled. None of the problems that had brought us together got solved or even seriously discussed and the future we were to contemplate and perhaps build together never got beyond a splatter of catchwords on the walls. As individuals we were not conspicuously deficient in thinking abilities, but we were trapped into a form of discourse that subordinated everything to the knowledge, skills, and intentions of the person in charge. It was just like being back in school.

Significant efforts are under way to change the nature of school discourse, to make it more of a collective inquiry and less—well, less of whatever you call the anomalous thing that exists now. This is still very much work in progress. Approaches vary and are still experimental; results are poorly documented, consisting mostly of stirring anecdotes. Yet the basic idea is close to axiomatic, and its relevance to teaching students to think is obvious: *If an educational goal is to equip students for thinking in adult life, then discourse in school ought progressively to approximate the discourse adults engage in when they are seriously trying to understand something, to reach a decision, to solve a problem, or to produce a design.*

Depth of Understanding

The person who comes to fix your copying machine may be a moral philosopher or a population geneticist of the first order, but that is not going to help fix your balky machine. To do that—supposing the problem to be one that has defied routine remedies—will require a deep knowledge of copying machines, including the particular model that is giving you trouble. There is no way schools are going to equip graduates with this knowledge or the countless other understandings specific to other jobs, nor should they even try. That, of course, is one reason for the appeal of thinking skills training. But, as we have noted, general thinking skills do not make the expert, either. So what could be taught in school that will increase the likelihood of one's being a resourceful copying machine repair person or specialty baker or trust account manager 20 years later?

In its more general form, that is the question of how to prepare students to thrive in a knowledge-based economy, and it is a question I have been pursuing right along through preceding chapters and will continue to pursue in the following ones. The general answer is that what schooling can best do is ensure that students understand the things that will enable them to understand new things. The only special point to be made here is that this answer also applies to preparing students to be good thinkers when they get out into the world.

Where academic knowledge is likely to have its influence on the thinking of the copy machine repairer is in the shaping of implicit understanding. There is not likely to be much explicit application of school-learned knowledge, despite the fact that copying machines embody sophisticated knowledge of optics, electronics, and chemistry. The working knowledge of the expert copying machine repairer will, however, be consistent with modern scientific knowledge even if it is not informed by advanced levels of it. It will, for instance, regard shadows as the relative absence of light rather than as things having some kind of substance. Of course, you say, but who doesn't know that? First, young children and many primitive peoples do not know that, and so there is something to be learned of a very basic nature that is important in a working knowledge of copying machines. Second, just knowing this as a fact that you can recall when asked is not the same as having developed implicit understanding to the point where you *see* shadows as absences of light. As argued in previous chapters, that is something that comes about through using knowledge to solve problems of understanding, and it is something schools should be working hard to bring about. It is a principal way they can contribute to students' lifelong ability to think productively.

I want to reiterate this point, because it is vitally important and the rhetoric of "teach them to think" tends to obscure it. There is a great deal of reading for the sake of reading, writing for the sake of writing, and lately experimenting for the sake of experimenting and thinking for the sake of thinking that goes on in schools. If all this activity were redirected to reading, writing, experimenting, and thinking for the sake of understanding the world, it would provide the best foundation I can imagine for thinking in later life. One reason it is not done is that educators have no idea how big a job it is to develop understanding to the point where its becomes implicit in the way students perceive and think about the world. Deluded by the filing cabinet model of memory, educators imagine they have done their job if students can recall a principle on demand, say something intelligent about it, and apply it to a problem, whereas that is no more than a good start. The students' view of the world needs to be reshaped around principles so that they no longer have to recall them and deliberately apply them, anymore than they have to recall which way is down to figure out what way objects will fall in their ordinary earthly environment. Only in that way can we have any confidence that a principle learned at school will enhance the problem-solving capabilities of a copying machine repairer, baker, or trust manager 20 years later.

Motivation: Fostering Lifelong Thinking

Programs to teach thinking skills often display the name "critical thinking." On examination it will be found that the word "critical" is merely used to puff up the term "thinking" and carries no additional meaning. A "critical thinking" program is likely to include every sort of thinking, including for instance brainstorming exercises in which students are taught not to be critical. Still, critical thinking in its literal sense has long been valued as a bulwark of democracy: Democracy is at risk if people believe everything their leaders tell them. Pursuant to this Jeffersonian principle, the critical thinking part of "critical thinking" programs is likely to include teaching about different kinds of propaganda, accompanied by exercises that require students to detect fallacies and deceptive rhetoric in arguments of various kinds.

Although there is undoubtedly some value in such teaching, motivational considerations call into question the whole notion of critical thinking skills. People are usually quite adept at finding the flaws in arguments they are opposed to; logic tends to desert us when it comes to recognizing the flaws in arguments we are disposed to believe, especially arguments of our own invention. This has led some philosophers to maintain, quite justly I believe, that critical thinking ought to be treated as a virtue rather than a skill (McPeck, 1984). The problem, as with all virtues, is to practice it in the face of temptations to do otherwise.

It is easy to see why educators prefer to think of critical thinking as a skill rather than a virtue. Schools have been famously unsuccessful at teaching virtues, whereas they have experienced some success in teaching skills. Furthermore, one can reasonably hope that skills, if exercised now and then, will be preserved throughout life, whereas virtue is easily lost. But that way of looking at it simply evades the dispositional issue, which is—in a word—critical. Indeed, if the dispositional problem could be solved, the skill problem—to the extent that there is one—would probably take care of itself. People who have an enduring disposition to think critically about popular, authoritative, or cherished beliefs; who are continually on the lookout for fallacies and tricks; who invest serious effort in finding counterarguments, alternative hypotheses, and interpretations— such people are bound to get better at it and to develop skills far beyond those any instructional program could offer.

Much the same can be said about creative thinking, although with a somewhat different spin. We cannot claim that everybody can rise to creative challenges when they want to. Many try and fail, but that is because we don't call anything a creative challenge unless there is a high probability of failure. What we can claim, however, is that everybody is creative all the time in small, low-risk ways. Virtually every sentence you utter—at least every fairly long one—is a creative construction, one that could not be deduced from initial conditions. The educational task, as with critical thinking, is to foster a lifelong disposition to take up creative challenges. Only by continually venturing beyond the low-risk paths does one accumulate the impressionistic knowledge that enables one to choose promising paths toward creative goals (Bereiter & Scardamalia, 1993, chap. 5). But this knowledge is domain specific. The impressionistic knowledge that enables a creative chef to produce imaginative cuisine does not help in producing imaginative solutions to financial problems. (Consequently the owner-chefs of highly popular restaurants often manage nevertheless to go broke.) Schools can encourage students to take creative risks in the things that are done in school—writing, drawing, explaining, solving mathematics problems, and a few other things. The impressionistic knowledge thus acquired may prove helpful in the further pursuit of those particular activities, but not in the myriad other walks of life where creativity is valued. As for developing some general disposition to take up creative challenges, that smacks of wishful thinking. There may be something to it, but it really is in the same class with expecting schools to foster honesty, truthfulness, industry, and other virtues. Don't bet on it.

An important series of studies on individual differences in thinking has been carried out by Keith Stanovich (1999). Stanovich replicated a number of experiments that have figured in arguments over whether people are inherently rational. These experiments, and many others like them, show that deviations from conventional logic and principles of probability and statistics are common. The results have been variously interpreted. One kind of interpretation is that people do not actually function like logic machines at all but use an assortment of heuristics and shortcuts that approximate logic under favorable conditions but lead to error under conditions that are misleading or abstract. Another kind of interpretation is that people always do function logically but they sometimes interpret situations differently from the way experimenters intended. Stanovich's contribution to this long-running controversy has been to examine individual differences across a variety of tasks. What he found was that few people are consistently illogical but that some people consistently come up with the normatively logical solutions. How do they do this? To simplify a complex and subtle analysis, the answer is that they do it by trying hard to be logical. It is not that they have some logical machinery in their heads that others lack or that they march to a different drummer; it's that they make fuller use of resources that others could use but often don't. At least that is true within the situation of psychological testing. We can't be sure that these star thinkers would continue to shine in real-world situations or that the others would continue to be logical slackers. What Stanovich's results do show, however, is that if you want to improve thinking, the principal challenge is to get people to try harder to think well.

What, then, can schools do? Short of a breakthrough that makes character education into something schools can profitably pursue, I don't see any but weak answers. Maintaining a school environment in which students feel safe in questioning beliefs, changing their minds, demanding evidence, and trying things beyond the comfort zone of their competence is justifiable on other grounds and may possibly help in developing lifelong thinking dispositions. More enduring, I suspect, are social preferences that may develop in school. If you want delinquents to go straight, you need to get them to prefer the company of straight people to that of other delinquents—not always an easy task. Similarly, the best way I can imagine to make students into lifelong thinkers is to get them to prefer the company of people who think, to enjoy the arguing and the analyzing and the playing with ideas that goes on when such people get together. I have been in school classes where that kind of social life was flourishing, and they were not classes where thinking skills were being taught.[3]

---

[3]For some important cautionary notes on this account, however, see Lampert et al. (1996).

BAD THINKING OR BAD READING?

Early in my university teaching career I gave an essay examination, the directions for which read in part, "For each of the following" do such and such, and there followed four topics that were to be treated in the prescribed way. After the exams were graded and handed back, one student came around to inquire why he had received a low grade. "You only answered one of the parts of this question," I said. "You were supposed to answer all four."

"I thought you were only supposed to answer one," he replied.

I pointed out the word "each" and pressed the student to admit that "each" meant "every one." "I can see how you could read it that way," he said, "but I read it as 'pick one.'" The meeting ended on an unsatisfactory note, with me sounding like Humpty Dumpty in *Alice*, turning the issue into one of "which is to be master." It was, in my view, the student who was being Humpty Dumpty, believing that words could mean whatever he chose them to mean, but I could find no way to reach him with rational argument and so ended up settling the matter by decree.

This incident is relevant to the controversy I referred to in the preceding section, about whether people who give seemingly illogical answers to logic problems are really thinking illogically or merely interpreting problems differently from the way the experimenter intended. Was my student being illogical or just a poor reader? Somehow, in this case, there does not seem to be much difference between these two diagnoses. The student was not dyslexic. He could read the words and probably understood what each word meant. And I imagine that most of the time he used the word "each" appropriately. Yet he put the words together so that they meant what he expected or wanted them to mean rather than what I am sure a jury of his peers would have decided they did mean. He was thinking poorly, but his poor thinking showed up in his interpretation of the instructions rather than in his execution of them.

When children are given a mathematics problem that is too complex for them, they frequently solve a simpler problem that uses the same numbers. This, too, looks like a matter of interpreting the problem differently rather than solving it wrongly. But is it not interesting that their interpretation always tends toward a simpler problem, never toward a more complex one? In the logic problem experiments that have been the basis of the controversy over rationality, the same tendency is apparent. No one ever interprets a logic or probability problem to be more complex than was intended. The misunderstandings that plague instruction at all levels are, as I recall them, always matters of reducing the concept to something simpler.

Natural selection becomes purposeful adaptation; acceleration becomes velocity; ratios become differences, knowledge building becomes project-based learning. Verdicts in criminal trials have turned on the failure of jurors to distinguish between "and" and "or" (Lefkowitz, 1997). But *or* is a more difficult concept than *and*. It has more parts; it is harder to infer it from data.

We all have to simplify, as Herbert Simon (1957) explained, because real life is unbounded in its complexity. There is always more that could be taken into account than we have the mental capacity to handle. Every theory, every law, is a simplification. That is how it gains its universality. Simplification, on this view, is a tool of rationality, not a lapse. Logic problems, like textbook problems in general, are different, however. They are carefully constructed to provide you with just the information that is needed to solve them. If you simplify you will get it wrong. Carefully written explanations and instructions are the same. They are crafted so that a normal reader not only can grasp all the elements but needs to do so to comprehend the message. The writer has in a sense simplified the world for you. To simplify it still further is to risk undoing what the writer has done.

One of the most common simplifications is to reduce all relations between two things to either identity or to opposition. The result is either conflation (for instance, treating constructivism and project-based learning as the same thing) or false dichotomy (for instance, as treating teaching phonics and teaching comprehension as opposites). Conflation and false dichotomies account for most of the content of popular educational discourse. For instance, the distinction I have been making between learning and knowledge building (see especially chap. 8) involves a levels distinction: Learning is what goes on at the level of the knower—the individual or group that undergoes a certain kind of change. Knowledge building is what goes on at the level of productive work; it is the creation or modification of an artifact. But people commonly either conflate the two, so that knowledge building is a glorified form of learning, or they dichotomize them: Learning is the bad stuff that goes on in schools and knowledge building is the good stuff. In a classic Piagetian experiment, children are shown a set of wooden beads, most of which are red. Asked whether there are more red beads or more wooden beads, young children typically say there are more red ones. Is this a problem in understanding the rather peculiar question or is it, as Piaget proposed, that they lack the logical equipment necessary to grasp the more complex relationship of red beads being a subclass of wooden beads? Research has not conclusively settled the matter. But when educated adults make similar kinds of errors, it is pretty clear that if they thought more about it they could get it right.[4] It is the *not thinking about it* that is the problem, whether the result is manifested in misunderstanding what was said or in drawing wrong inferences from it.

Thinking-aloud studies of problem solving (Bloom & Broder, 1950) and reading (Scardamalia & Bereiter, 1984) indicate that people vary enormously in the amount of thinking they do while engaged in these activities. At the low end you find people who do not seem to be actively doing anything at all. Things happen in their minds, of course, but they are not *making* anything happen. We all do that when we are in the grip of an absorbing story. We are "carried away" by it. Although the experience may be intense, we are essentially passive. We are not making the experience happen; the author is doing that. But for difficult texts, texts that present new ideas, or texts that for any reason one needs to get *right*, good readers switch into a different mode. Their thinking-aloud protocols reveal they are very much in charge of what is going on. They are carrying on a line of thought in which the text figures as data. This does not mean they are imposing their own meaning on the text willy-nilly. They are treating the data seriously. They are constructing the meaning of the text, to be sure, but what they are doing is something akin to theory building. The meaning they construct is a kind of theory that accounts for the text data.

In chapter 6 I suggested that reading is a form of controlled hallucination. It is very far from an orderly inferential process. Yet if we are reading carefully, we arrive at interpretations that can be justified by rigorous inference from the words of the text along with relevant facts from outside the text. How is this possible? The secret is in the constraints. Some of these come from the words of the text but most of the constraints are internal. According to modern folk psychology, those internal constraints are in the nature of rules. To say that a person is rational or irrational is therefore to say that their in-

---

[4]Here is an example germane to the concepts developed in this book. I published a paper, "Situated Cognition and How to Overcome It" (1997), advancing ideas similar to those in the present chapter 3: All cognition is situated, but human beings have developed a way to overcome its limitations by constructing cognitive artifacts. In a critique, Engestrom and Cole (1997) dismissed this argument by saying "Why is creating and manipulating symbolic representations not a situated action?" (p. 306). Inasmuch as I had acknowledged explicitly that it was, I did not see how this could be turned into an objection. My argument was A (situated cognition) produces B (World 3 knowledge), which is not part of A. I suspect that Engestrom and Cole were used to arguments in which some kind of activity involving abstract knowledge—call it B′—is claimed to deny A. An effective response is to show that A includes B′. Although it is on an abstract plane, what we have here is only one cut above wooden beads versus red beads. A and B in my argument, like wooden beads and red beads, are not comparable categories. Cole and Engstrom reduced them to comparable categories (A vs. B′) and then claimed victory for A because it includes B′.

ternal rules are valid or invalid. According to a connectionist view of mind, however, the constraints are of a different order. To say that people are rational is to say that their internal constraints, the product of neural epigenesis and learning, are attuned in some optimal way to constraints in the environment. Some of the most important of external constraints are those built into the syntax and semantics of language, into genres and other conventions of use. For educated people there is another layer of constraints, those embodied in the learned disciplines. Being a scientific thinker, accordingly, means having a cognitive system attuned to the kinds of constraints honored in scientific disciplines. At a more microscopic level, there are the constraints embodied in a peculiar language game that we call solving logic problems. One could be a rational thinker by most other criteria yet not know how to play that game.[5]

If you could teach people to be better readers or listeners they would be better thinkers. But to become better readers or listeners people have to become better thinkers—more attentive to the constraints embodied in texts and more skillful in constructing interpretations that conform to those constraints. Rather than dismissing this as a chicken-and-egg problem, I think it should be viewed as indicating an opportunity. Beyond the most elementary level, teaching reading is teaching thinking. Unfortunately, in the present lowly state of pedagogical art, the only way most school people know how to teach either one is through practice, and most of the practice is irrelevant or counterproductive. But there are teachable reading comprehension strategies, which have an advantage over most thinking strategies in that they actually work, at least in the short term (Bereiter & Bird, 1985; Pressley, Harris, & Marks, 1992). Students can actually experience the effects of thinking their way through a difficult text and understanding what they did not understand before. Whether in the long term this will make them better readers and thinkers is another matter, but it at least provides a way of introducing intellectually passive students to the *possibility* of actively directing their thought.

Where strategy instruction goes wrong, however, is where the conventional practice approaches also go wrong. The situation provides no reason for students to go to the extra work that careful, thoughtful reading requires. An alternative approach, called "whole language," which emphasizes reading for personal gratification, does not provide such a reason either. Reading, like any other kind of adaptive behavior, is subject to the principle of what

---

[5]Except that learning to play the logic problem game, in its more general form, may be one of the principal things people learn from going to school (Scribner, 1979).

Simon (1957) called "satisficing." Effort and learning taper off at a level that is sufficient to meet needs. In the conventional reading class, this means a level that is sufficient to answer the quiz-type questions that teachers ask. A strategy that meets this demand is what I have called the "minimal comprehension strategy" (Bereiter, 1988). It involves picking out and remembering key words and doing just enough interpretation to link the words together so they can be remembered. Any further interpretation takes place after the question is asked and uses clues from the question to guide inference. Doing too much interpretation in advance of hearing the question can actually get in the way of producing a satisfactory answer. Minimal comprehension also works well for the more informal kinds of book talk that go on in whole language classrooms. It enables students to relate personal experiences to the text, without interpreting the text so narrowly that few personal experiences would apply.

By perpetuating conditions in which a minimal comprehension strategy suffices, schools are in effect teaching students not to think—or at least not to think very much, not to press for anything beyond the merest sketch of text content. The evidences of careless, superficial reading show up at all levels of education and even in professional life. They may not greatly affect day-to-day life, because conversation provides ways to negotiate understanding that do not depend so much on getting it right the first time. I have heard of but not seen a study of e-mail messages that showed that something like a third of them are devoted to clarifying previous messages. More serious is the notorious inability of people to comprehend software manuals, no matter how much effort publishers put into making them comprehensible. But the real importance of bad reading lies in the degraded thinking, the conceptual oversimplification, of which it is one aspect. Minimal comprehension means not only paying limited attention to the words in the message; it means putting little effort into working out the connections between the text and what you already know (Franks, et al., 1982).

There have been many approaches to improving reading abilities. They range from teaching "close reading" and *explication de texte* in literature to study skills courses for students having academic difficulties. One is appropriate when the objective is a refined appreciation of the text itself, another when the objective is mastery of text content for the purpose of meeting academic requirements. None of the approaches gets at reading for the purpose of intelligent action. The nonrecreational reading I do is mainly for the purpose of advancing my own thinking on issues of importance to me. Practically anyone who does knowledge work of any kind or who has an active mental life could say the same thing. Yet that is not the purpose of reading as it is generally promoted in schools.

A knowledge-building approach, such as I sketched in the preceding chapters, has a significant advantage over both skills approaches and whole language approaches: It creates a situation in which there is direct benefit from careful reading. The benefit comes from solving problems of understanding. To improve their theories, students need not only to acquire facts but also to acquire ideas that are beyond those they already entertain. That is where reading comprehension typically fails. Readers can pick up new facts, but they assimilate them to their pre-existing ideas. When that happens in knowledge building, which of course it does, theory improvement fails. But if the students are really committed to advancing their understanding, it only takes one student catching on to the new idea or—failing in that—a hint from the teacher to get things moving. I have seen a whole class happily collecting and sharing information on matter and molecules while remaining content in their belief that molecules get bigger when heated. Then one student enters a note or some comments into the class database indicating her reading that molecules do not get bigger; they just spread farther apart. By the next day everyone has picked up and started using the idea—because they had all read it before, they simply hadn't grasped it or seen how it conflicted with what they already believed. Is this an advance in reading or an advance in thinking? From an educational standpoint it seems to me that there is nothing to gain from trying to make a distinction. Whenever reading is involved in solving problems— whether these are practical problems or problems of understanding—it becomes part of the thinking process and loses its purpose if separated from it.

BEYOND THINKING IN SYMBOLS

At this point I want to redress an imbalance. It has come about through trying to deal with the kinds of thinking that thinkings skills programs deal with, which are quite limited in compass. In so doing I have perhaps referred slightingly to Howard Gardner's (1983) theory of multiple intelligences, although my intent has been only to criticize the faddish school programs that have sprung up around it. The theory itself does an important service in expanding our conception of intelligence—and, by implication, thought—beyond the narrow limits convention has imposed.

Conventionally, thinking is a deliberative process involving symbols. At its fastest, it does not proceed much beyond the rate of speech, and it is often much slower. If you can solve a problem in 5 minutes that takes other people hours to solve, you will be judged very smart and a quick thinker. But if you can solve a problem in a fifth of a second that takes other people minutes to solve, you may not get much credit for intelligence and may not be credited with thinking at all. Yet such fifth-of-a-second problem solving is just what star ball and hockey players do, getting paid millions of dollars a year for it. It remains for the deliberative, symbol-processing sportscaster to take a minute and a half explaining what was so clever about what the player did in a split second. If you are a sports enthusiast, you may doubt that anyone could be so blinkered as to deny that brilliant plays reflect smart thinking, but try it out. You will be shocked. I have had whole graduate classes refusing to grant that executing a risky first-to-third double play instead of a safe second-to-first double play involved thinking. To them it was "just skill": It couldn't be problem solving because it didn't involve steps in thought.

Stepwise thought involving symbols is clearly very important—a major cultural invention, or at least the Greeks thought so (Kitto, 1951)—but it accounts for only a small part of the thinking life, probably even of philosophers. Furthermore, when we are supposedly engaged in such plodding activity the thoughts that move us ahead or lead us astray occur in flashes, occupying no appreciable thinking time; the slow part is interpreting them and working out their implications—just like the star second baseman and the sports analyst, except that we play both parts. Anything that deserves the label, "teaching people to think," amounts to introducing constraints of some kind into a largely uncontrolled and unconscious process. Educators need to be careful. Constraints can be beneficial or they can be detrimental or they can be some of each, in which case further constraints must be added to moderate the first ones. A lot of what passes for teaching thinking, I suspect, is harmless only because it doesn't work. Urging students to visualize as they read is an example. It might be helpful with poor readers because it gets them to pay attention to text content to know what to visualize, but as a regular habit it could interfere with thinking while reading.

Of the seven intelligences that Gardner suggested, two of them—linguistic and logical-mathematical—are the ones normally associated with thinking. They identify the two aptitude subtests of the Scholastic Aptitude Test and they are by far the predominant focus of all kinds of thinking skills programs. The other five may be readily recognized as talents that some people have to much greater degrees than others, but the question to consider here is whether they also constitute forms of thinking. Consider musical intelligence. The conventional view would be that musical creativity involves a combination of musical talent and creative thinking ability, as if what Beethoven and Newton did was much the same process except that one was thinking about musical things and the other about mathematical things. There are no doubt respects in which this is true, but the main part of musical creativity, if you listen to what musicians say, is thinking *in* music, not thinking *about* music. Similarly, Roberto Alomar is not thinking *about* where to throw the ball and how to position himself for the catch to make that throw. He is thinking *in* movements and positionings, directly using what Gardner calls "bodily-kinesthetic" intelligence. Just so, the main part of the thinking of the architect takes place within spatial intelligence, that of the psychotherapist takes place within interpersonal intelligence, and that of the "intrapersonal" expert takes place within the realm of the person's own feelings. Thinking *in* these nonsymbolic realms does not make a great deal of sense if you hold to the container model of mind. For according to that model, you have in your head tokens of those musical tones, movements, spatial relations, or feelings, and the operations you carry out on those tokens are what constitute thinking. Unable to give a plausible account of fifth-of-a-second problem solving like that of the ballplayer or the jazz improviser, this model ignores those and confines thinking to the slower processes that could conceivably work through such manipulation of tokens in the mind. Connectionist models of mind, however, make it quite plausible that there should be musical, spatial, bodily-kinesthetic, and emotional cognition and that the more purposeful and constructive varieties of such cognition have as much claim to be called thinking as do verbal and mathematical cognition.

If we accept this considerably broadened conception of thinking, what does it mean for efforts to teach thinking? I am not here raising the issue of the value of sports, music, interpersonal awareness activities, and other such departures from the bookish curriculum. I have already acknowledged their place in a well-rounded educational program. The question now is whether, over and above classic concerns with well-roundedness, we should be concerned with teaching *thinking* in these various nonsymbolic realms—keeping in mind that such thinking would not consist of sitting around and verbalizing thoughts about these things but really thinking *in* movements, tones, spaces, and feelings. My first reaction is revulsion at the prospect of the offenses against decency and sanity that might be perpetrated in the name of such teaching. But perhaps that just shows that I have become so accustomed to the offenses perpetrated in the cause of symbolic thinking that they no longer affect me so viscerally.

Collecting my wits and trying to look at the matter judiciously, I would suggest the following: Thinking in these nonsymbolic realms is probably a great deal more domain specific than thinking in symbolic realms. That is because the symbolic systems of language and mathematics have evolved so as to apply across diverse situations, to be applicable to a vast and undelimitable range of purposes. But if the motor-kinesthetic thinking you learn to do in playing second base should turn out to be of value in mountain climbing, that is just a lucky accident. There is nothing in the evolution of baseball that should make baseball intelligence useful outside the sport. Musical thinking may have considerable transfer value among different kinds of music, but it is not going to help you climb mountains, ei-ther—whereas thinking in words and numbers may. Spatial think-ing sounds like the most generalizable of the nonsymbolic kinds, given that everything material is spatially situated. It should help you climb a mountain. But the issue is whether thinking abilities de-veloped in one spatial domain, such as baseball, can be expected to transfer to another, such as mountain climbing. Studying student and expert architects, whose business is the design of space, Gobert (1994) found that the experts were decidedly superior in ability to derive three-dimensional information from two-dimensional archi-tectural plans, but that on general measures of spatial abilities the students were superior.

In short, the skepticism I have tried to arouse concerning the teach-ing of general symbolic thinking skills ought to be multiplied several fold when it comes to teaching nonsymbolic ones. This would mean that whatever is taught should be justifiable in its own right and not as a way of improving a system of the brain or developing a thinking skill that is expected to be of service outside its domain. There is now powerful software for visualizing and planning urban landscapes. It is expressly designed to give nonspecialists a way of participating in decisions affecting their visual-spatial environments (Danahy & Hoinkes, 1995). When a version suitable for schools is available, it should make it possible for students to do work that involves them in thinking directly in spaces and vistas rather than only in statements about them. It could be asked whether such software will improve spatial intelligence or whether, on the contrary, it compensates for the lack of it, but I don't think that is the question educators should ask. They should ask how valuable it is for students to gain some knowl-edge of landscape architecture and to develop tastes and convictions in that area. If the answer is positive, then certainly they should aim for a thoughtful and dialogic approach to landscape architecture, as with all other curriculum topics. What multiple intelligences encourages us to keep in mind is that "thoughtful" does not imply only verbal reasoning, that in the case of landscape architecture there should be thinking in spatial visualizations as well, and that the dialogue, accordingly, need not be exclusively verbal: It can include designs, models, and other means by which people try to influence how one another sees things.

ON A MORE POSITIVE NOTE

Up to this point, the message of this chapter could be summarized as "Forget about teaching people to think. Teach people things that are worth learning. Focus on goals and problems that really matter. Create an environment in which quality counts but where people feel safe in taking chances to achieve it. Then the thinking will take care of itself." As a rough guide to educational planning or organizational management, that may be a better guide than most. But thinking is, after all, an important human activity to which wise people, over the centuries, have devoted considerable attention. It would be surprising if nothing had come out of all that effort that was worth passing on to the young.

Among knowledgeable psychologists, perhaps the most optimistic on this account is David Perkins; I recommend his *Outsmarting IQ* (1995) as a source of well-founded thoughts and suggestions about helping people become smarter. Perkins recognized what may be thought of as three layers of intelligence (as distinct from *types* of intelligence, such as Gardner's multiple intelligences). There is a neural layer, which is undoubtedly the source of a good deal of individual variation in thinking ability.[6] As I discussed under "Improving the Brain" and "Training the Faculties," however, there is little prospect except possibly through medicine of improving thinking through efforts directed at this layer. Then there is what Perkins called an "experiential" layer, which encompasses the kinds of knowledgeability discussed in chapter 5 and which Perkins characterized generally as "knowing ones way around" in various domains. Much of my argument in this chapter is to the effect that improvements in thinking depend largely on improvements in this layer. Perkins acknowledged its importance as well, but he added a third layer where he saw the real payoff in efforts to improve thinking. This he called the "reflective" layer, and it consists of thinking about our thinking and about the wisdom of our actions and beliefs.

The idea of a reflective layer has many antecedents, of course, going back to Socrates and the "examined life," said to be the only life

---

[6]In the 1970s it was fashionable to believe that, except for a few obvious genetic defects, there are no heritable influences on thinking ability (df. Kamin, 1974). It would be difficult to find any informed person who now believes this.

worth living. But rarely do we reflect on thought in and of itself. Instead, we reflect on particular ideas, arguments, plans, or on particular observations and what they mean. That is why I have not treated reflection as anything distinct from the pursuit of understanding. However, reflection may involve relating these particulars to abstract categories of thought. This becomes evident in argument when people will characterize something as "circular," "incoherent," "self-evident," "necessary but not sufficient," "a false dichotomy," and any number of other mostly unfavorable but sometimes laudable varieties of thinking. This represents a particularly sophisticated kind of argument, of course. Less learned people will rely on concrete objections, analogies, and counterexamples to serve critical purposes. But certainly the abstract concepts are useful and it may be that some reflective moves are impossible or at least very difficult unless one has the appropriate abstract concepts. For instance, without a well-developed notion of a "category mistake" (Ryle, 1949) it may be impossible to recognize any but the most obvious instances of "comparing apples and oranges."

Concepts of the kind referred to here are the subject of elementary logic courses, especially those that address informal as well as formal reasoning. Whether they *need* to be taught as explicit subject matter, whether that is even a good way to teach them, or whether they are better picked up informally through discussions in which the terms are used—that is an empirical question, to which answers are likely to vary depending on the quality of the formal and informal instruction. But it seems that an educational program ought to insure that one way or other students acquire a vocabulary for talking about thinking. Will this make them better thinkers? Not directly. Its value would lie in enabling them to profit from criticism and guidance and eventually to engage in self-criticism and guidance of their own thought.

I see concepts of thinking playing the same role in learning to think that rhetorical and grammatical concepts play in learning to write. Learning the parts of speech and concepts such as *topic sentence* cannot directly improve your writing. Even a concept like *dangling participle* is unlikely to do that, as witness the number of dangling participles produced by people who know what they are and believe they are bad. But try getting someone who does not know what a dangling participle is to see what is wrong with "Looking at it realistically, your plan is unlikely to succeed." You will find yourself teaching the concept (probably by starting with more obvious examples like, "Vacationing in Yellowstone Park, a bear … "). The most useful piece of stylistic advice I have ever come upon is to avoid long noun clauses and otherwise not to worry much about sentence length. But this advice is useless unless you not only know what a noun clause is but are sufficiently attuned to noun clauses that they so-to-speak stand out in the crowd.

What we are talking about here is not simply learning *about* thinking, but neither is it simply acquiring skills or attitudes toward thinking. It is, like many other important kinds of learning we have considered, learning ones way around in a domain—in this case, the domain we call thinking. It involves mastering the kind of talk that goes on in that domain, which is a very sophisticated kind of talk, using a vocabulary that is difficult to get right. More than that, it means acquiring an implicit understanding of the domain that goes beyond talk. Its character is perceptual. It involves a kind of dual attention: You pay attention to the content of what is said but at the same time you perceive the discourse as made up of quite abstract elements and moves. Folk theory, which has no way of treating this kind of learning, accordingly tends toward one or another of the kinds of reductionism discussed in previous chapters. Reduction to subject matter treats concepts of thinking as material to be learned, like any other sort of bookish subject matter. Reduction to activities engages students in thinking games or exercises that are expected to teach the concepts informally. Reduction to self-expression means the sharing of opinions and feelings, with care not to impose external standards. Any of these may be of some value, but even in combination they do not even begin to confront the challenge of becoming a knowledgeable traveler in the thinking domain.

We ought not to conceive of this thinking domain as a domain distinct from such other domains as history, geology, and needlecraft, however. Perkins's approach of treating it as a layer on top of such domains makes sense here. Learning your way around in any discipline entails learning to think the way people think in that discipline. Historians think differently from physicists, who in turn think differently from biological taxonomists, who seem to think much like descriptive linguists, although one would need to be fairly deeply immersed in these two fields to judge whether the resemblance is more than superficial. The various disciplines, professions, trades, and crafts are communities of practice. Part of belonging to such communities is being able to think along with the other members. One must learn to "speak their language," which always means more than acquiring a certain jargon. It means learning to think in certain ways, to observe certain constraints, to be sensitive to certain patterns, and to guard against certain errors.[7] There are important concepts that are common across

---

[7]The classic work on cognitive and epistemological differences among the disciplines is that of Ernst Cassirer (e.g., 1950).

disciplines: Terms like "circular," "incoherent," "self-evident," "necessary but not sufficient,"and "false dichotomy" may appear in the discourse of any learned discipline, but the implicit understanding required to apply them properly depends on knowledge of the particular discipline. For instance, acquiring rigor in any discipline usually entails considerable narrowing of what one is prepared to accept as "self-evident," but the narrowing is based on the methods and paradigms of the discipline, not on general principles.

Necessarily, this learning to think like a historian, a physicist, a police officer, or a real estate broker comes mainly from participation. But it is not all tacit knowledge. There are things that can be said explicitly about it. See, for instance, Sam Wineburg (1991) on how historians think and Connie Fletcher (1990) on *What Cops Know*. Explicit information about thinking in different fields is especially important in elementary and secondary school, because the teachers are not usually practitioners of the disciplines they teach and so "cognitive apprenticeship" is not readily available as a way of learning to think. However, fiction and biography can convey relevant episodic knowledge, provided they take readers inside characters' minds and are authentic in what they represent. Some of the thinking that goes on in different fields is embodied in the tools that are used. And so learning to use those tools is also a kind of learning to think. I expect you cannot learn to use surveyors' instruments, to read electrocardiograms, to do double-entry bookkeeping, or to use a software developer's toolkit without learning to think a bit like a surveyor, cardiologist, accountant, or programmer.

All of this implies that learning to think is a matter of increasing specialization. That is one part of the story. There is another part of the story, however, which is about things that are learned within particular disciplines that can then be used as tools for thinking outside the discipline. Mathematics provides the best recognized examples. Algebra is a many-purpose tool for problem solving (even though most people do not master it to the point where it becomes useful). The mathematics of probability enables people to deal rationally with a wide variety of problems that are otherwise left to guesswork and superstition. An understanding of statistics is a great aid to critical thinking wherever there are arguments from data (Lehman & Nisbett, 1990). Even when quantitative data are not at issue, it is often useful to have at one's disposal the concepts of covariation (including the understanding that because A and B covary it does not follow that one causes the other) and statistical interaction (the effect of A depending on the status of B).

There are also powerful ideas coming out of the natural and behavioral sciences that can be used to good effect in thinking outside the disciplines in which they arose. Stellan Ohlsson (1993) called them "abstract schemas." Natural selection was his prime example. Once you have caught on to how it works in biological evolution, you can apply it in many different situations where previously you would have assumed there had to be a purposeful agent at work.[8] Some other important abstract models are self-organization, entropy, regression, analogy, deconstruction, gestalt, capital, leverage, and distribution.[9] Abstract models seem generally to be difficult to learn. I think that is because they all involve a change in thinking, the overcoming of some habitual way of construing things. Thus, we could say that acquiring any abstract model is "learning to think." Yet a course in abstract models would probably not be a good idea. Given that they are hard to grasp, they are probably best encountered first in the disciplines where they have received the most attention and done the most work. Extending them beyond those disciplines would seem to be a task that calls for interdisciplinary inquiry rather than for special courses.

Notice how the line between learning to think and learning subject matter has all but vanished. There is an abstract vocabulary that educated people use and that can serve criticism and analysis in all fields. A case can accordingly be made for instruction that focuses specifically on learning to use those terms, but that is about as far as the isolated teaching of thinking could reasonably go. And even that may be superfluous, if all subjects are taught in ways that engage students and teachers in thinking seriously about them.

The separation between thinking and content knowledge is the same separation that we find in Bloom's *Taxonomy* (1956), examined at some length in chapter 4. Grounded in the folk conception of mind as container, it relegates knowledge to the lowly status of stored information that the mind works on through the application of cognitive skills. Thinking skills advocates have been heavy users of Bloom's *Taxonomy* (no surprise there; it justifies their existence). Nevertheless, they have moved toward reducing the separation between thinking and content learning. The overwhelming majority of thinking skills programs and guidelines now call for work on thinking to be integrated into regular school subjects. I advocated

---

[8]The excesses of social Darwinism and more recently of sociobiology only go to show the power of the concept. If a conceptual tool cannot be harmfully misused it probably cannot do much good either.

[9]The "central conceptual structures" studied by Case (Case & Okamoto, 1996) appear to be similar to "abstract models," except they are, as their name implies, central to everyday cognition. Accordingly, they are acquired naturally by children growing up under favorable circumstances, whereas those Ohlsson (1993) talked about are unlikely to be acquired except through study in the learned disciplines. Central conceptual structures include those that embrace the whole numbers, narrative, and causality.

that myself at one time, calling it "infusion" (Bereiter, 1984). I now see it as an effort to patch up an inherently inadequate model of knowledge and mind. The best that can come of "integration" and "infusion" is that you end up with the same educational program you would have produced if you had aimed directly at a knowledge-building approach to "subject matter that matters." But it is an ass-backwards way of getting there. It is like starting with over refined flour and continuing to add nutrients until you have something comparable to whole wheat.

CONCLUSION

My treatment of teaching thinking in this chapter has been heavy on skepticism. I do not apologize for this. I think even a modest dose of skepticism about the teachability of thinking could save organizations many millions of dollars currently spent on quacks. And I think any school program would be improved if it was systematically cleansed of all activities whose purported virtue is the enhancement of thinking abilities, provided the freed-up time was used to pursue worthwhile subjects in greater depth. In fact, however, I have said quite a bit that is positive about the improvability of thinking. It is just that what I have said does not lend itself to a program. It does not fit easily under the head, "teaching people to think." I have stressed the value of knowledge—all six of the kinds of knowledge described in chapter 5, but especially implicit understanding and impressionistic knowledge—as having an active role in productive thought.

Every school subject, if well taught, engages students in serious and sustained thinking—constructing explanations, criticizing, drawing out inferences, finding applications, and so on. There should be no need for the teacher to think of ways to inject more thinking into the curriculum. That would be like trying to inject more aerobic exercise into the lives of Sherpa porters. If the students are not doing enough thinking, something is seriously wrong with the instruction and it is not going to be remedied by inserting thinking activities. Good instruction will also involve talk about the thinking that is going on—again, not to teach thinking but to further learning.

If there is a reason for instruction focused on thinking itself, it is probably to repair the damage caused by poor education. Large numbers of students make it as far as university believing that learning is memorizing (Biggs, 1979; van Rossum & Schenk, 1984). They may have been so overmanaged or so coddled that it never occurs to them in scholastic stituations to think about why they are doing anything or to evaluate the ideas that occasionally pop into their heads. They may have learned that either the answer to a problem comes to you immediately or it is too late. They may not even realize that thinking is something you can *decide* to do, that it doesn't always just happen. They may have developed phobias or become compulsive rule followers or rule violators. They may need to learn procedures that enable a group to do intellectual work without a teacher to lead them. To the extent that thinking skills courses and workshops do any good, I suspect it is through correcting such mislearning and imparting a more hopeful outlook on thinking.

For the general conduct of education, however, a simple rule should suffice: If the only justification for an activity is that it is supposed to encourage or improve thinking, drop it and replace it with an activity that advances students' understanding or that increases their mastery of a useful tool.

Can Education Become
a Modern Profession?

It was not until the end of the 19th century that scientific advances began to catch up with the medical needs of the public. Civil War hospital experiences and the new theories of bacteriology slowly produced fundamental changes in medical practice. Medical training adapted to the growing knowledge base of the profession, and by the end of the century, America was well on its way to having the best medical care in the world.

—Floyd, n.d., par. 7

Schools are being built today that proclaim, by their architecture and facilities, a new era in education. In fact, they look like some of the more trend-setting workplaces in Silicon Valley (which, in turn, are sometimes called "campuses"). Gone are the long corridors with door after door. Instead, there is usually an atrium with greenery, places to sit and talk, sometimes even a sort of café. Branches lead off to rooms arranged in clusters. There are electronic music studios and television production studios, and, of course, computers everywhere. If these are not yet connected by fiber optic cables, the duct-work at least is in place.

The professional staffs in such schools are usually much con-cerned to adopt a pedagogy in keeping with the postindustrial look of the building. Often they have been handpicked with that in mind. But this is where the vision begins to fade. Where is the new peda-gogy to come from? Where are the new discoveries or the new ways of thinking that would open up a new educational vista?

Almost inevitably, the search for a new pedagogy will settle on what has been "new" throughout the past century, the educational approach that first came to prominence under the label "progressive education." It may not be recognized as such, for the labels keep changing; but often they have not changed very much. For instance, Table 11.1 presents some new labels from old sources.

If the ancestry of the current innovations is pointed out, there is a standard response, polished through use by successive generations of reformers: Progressive education, they argue, was ahead of its time and never did take hold widely. Its time has finally come. Al-though the school world at large may still not be ready for it, the people brought together to staff the new 21st-century learning envi-ronment are apt to feel that they, at least, are ready. Well, of course they are. They have no doubt already been practicing project-based, learner-centered, constructivist pedagogy in their former venues. That is how they got selected for the new school. What excites them in their new situation is that they will be able to teach the way they already try to teach, but with less interference and with more sup-port from like-minded colleagues.

TABLE 11.1
New and Old Labels for Similar Educational Ideas

New Label	Old Source
Project based learning	The Project Method (Kilpatrick, 1921)
Learner centered education	The Child-Centered School (Rugg & Shumaker, 1928)
Constructivist learning	Although constructivism is nominally attributed to Piaget, whose ideas began to catch on in North America in the 1960s, the operative meaning of constructivist learning among school people is essentially the same as "learning by doing," which Butts (1947) attributed to the "activities movement" of the 1930s

I do not mean to discount these aspirations. Progressive education, when it works well, can be wonderful to behold. But surely
something is wrong when the best that future-oriented educators
can come up with is an approach that reformers were advocating
back when the horseless carriage was first appearing on the streets.
The horseless carriage has in the meantime evolved from an unreliable, unstable, sputtering contraption, offering questionable advantages over its horse-drawn predecessor, to a smoothly functioning
conveyance that can go 100,000 kilometers before it needs servicing.
Progressive education, by contrast, comes to us with its original deficiencies unremedied and with its advantages over old-fashioned didactic pedagogy still vigorously disputed on the basis of strong
evidence (e.g., see Hirsch, 1996).

The futuristic school I have described represents a very privileged
situation in education. Most of the literature on school change is
concerned with getting schools up to that point—not so much tech-
nologically as socially; getting up to the point where a school staff
has the license and the resources to design its own program. Let us
suppose further that the school board is supportive, that the school
has good connections with a university where education and computer science professors are ready to work with them in a collaborative way, and that the school has been granted at least a temporary
respite from the more onerous kinds of testing and accountability.
This would seem like heaven on earth to most school faculties. There
is a further problem of how the accomplishments of this school are
to be extended to the rest of the system and how they are to survive
once special favors and resources are removed. All kinds of political
and economic issues enter at that point, but I want to focus on the
immediate task, on the effort to produce a superior educational program. It is the crux. If it fails, then all the technology and other resources and the favored status and the teacher empowerment will
have been for naught, and the issues of sustainability and dissemination will be moot: There will be nothing much worth sustaining or
disseminating.

As I have suggested, the school's effort to create a superior new
program is almost sure to fail. I want to get to the bottom of why
such failure is the norm and to explore what could be done about it
and how a better theory of knowledge and mind could help. To get to
the bottom, we need to exclude all those cases that are the perfectly
legitimate concern of those who study the sociology and politics of
school change—the cases where change was imposed from outside
and was defeated by a demoralized but stubborn teaching force, the
cases where change was the pet project of an ambitious school ad-
ministrator anxious to move on in the world before the bubble burst,

the cases where an enthusiastically welcomed innovation collapsed for want of infrastructure and training, the cases where everything seemed to be going along swimmingly until there was a school board election. We need to understand why reform fails at the crux, at the point of deciding what change to make, given even the most propitious conditions for arriving at and carrying out that decision.

This inquiry will take us through the remaining two chapters. The problem, writ large, is education's inability to construct new possibilities and work toward them with sustained creativity. In the contemporary jargon, it is education's inability to function as a knowledge-creating institution. This failure is not to be laid on the teachers, the researchers, the administrators, the politicians, or any other particular group. The failure is systemic. That much is a truism. The nature of this systemic failure, however, is more profound than most analysts imagine. There are, I argue in this chapter, two cultures within the education profession. One is a traditional craft culture and the other is a research culture. There is commerce between them, but each is stultified by the division, a division that does not exist in the more progressive professions. The solution, I suggest, lies in the evolution of a hybrid culture. For such a culture to emerge, the existing craft and research cultures must come together to solve common problems that require the knowledge and talents of both cultures. A problem that seems to have potential for cultural fusion is *teaching for understanding*.

This chapter closes with a discussion of how teacher education, which currently serves to perpetuate and even increase the cultural separation, might be transformed by making teaching for understanding its center. In the final chapter I return to themes introduced earlier. I try to show that both the construction of new educational possibilities and the disciplined creativity required to work toward them are hampered by our folk theories of knowledge and mind. They provide a conceptual framework that is both too narrow for the creation of new educational possibilities and too coarse to make useful distinctions. To get educationists away from their useless battles over methods and so-called philosophies and to get the public away from its fixation on test scores, we need the vision of a new kind of educated person. To work toward such a vision we need to be able to articulate problems and make useful distinctions among proposed solutions. For all of that our conceptual equipment is inadequate.

Throughout these chapters I treat modernization as a desirable objective. I do this in full realization that to many avant-garde educationists, "modern" is not only old hat but evil. "Postmodern" is the thing. "Modern" means greenhouse gases, technical rationality, imperialism, homophobia, and anything else bad you might think of, whereas "postmodern" means the opposite of all these things. Modernity has been mainly analyzed by people who dislike it, and so it is not surprising that they should characterize it by its excesses and lunacies. I'm afraid I tend to do the same when I discuss postmodernism.

The one distinctive characteristic of modernity agreed on by friends and foes alike is *dedication to progress*. Only the most naive and the most sophisticated believe that progress is inevitable, inherent in the nature of things.[1] The normative modern view is that progress is something that can be pursued deliberately, through problem solving and creative effort, with a reasonable likelihood of success. Everyone now expects this, and the postmodernists and others who deny that there is progress are either being disingenuous or are applying extreme criteria. When AIDS appeared as a new, grave, and mysterious disease, a public cry went up for research. It was only the most knowledgeable medical scientists who warned that it might not be possible to find a cure or a vaccine. However they, along with everyone else, assumed that progress of some kind was possible, as indeed it proved to be.

When an educational crisis captures headlines, there is no public cry for research. There is not even a cry for it within the teaching profession. Whether it is declining test scores, evidence of widespread functional illiteracy, or a stunning demonstration of people's scientific ignorance, people assume that the knowledge necessary to deal with it *already exists*. This is the mark of a premodern profession, one that is not systematically generating progress. A modern profession is driven by awareness of what is not known. Each advance in knowledge raises problems that need to be solved to advance further.

The failure of education to modernize has not been for lack of trying. From scientific management in the early part of the 20th century to a web page for every student at the end, school administrators have zealously pursued whatever looked like the coming thing. Every big new idea in the human sciences, and some big ideas from outside, have found their way into educational thought—behaviorism, psychoanalysis, information theory, game theory, hermeneutics, social constructionism, activity theory, symbolic interactionism, semiotics, situated cognition, sociobiology, memetics, and on and on. Sometimes these have been degraded or distorted, but not fatally so, as a rule. Education, as an academic discipline, enjoys a reasonably active and varied intellectual life. The trouble is that for any of this thinking to make its way into practice, it has to be passed through a conceptual ma-

---

[1]Lasch (1991) criticized the naive belief in progress, which he likened to a religion; Dennett (1995) has provided a sophisticated argument to the effect that both biological and cultural evolution progress toward good designs.

chine that coverts it into a product, a procedure, or a slogan. Like the flour mill that removes the bran and the wheat germ, leaving only the starch, this conceptual machine removes all the thought. There have been repeated efforts to put education on a scientific basis by finding ways of translating research and theory into practice, but this too has usually amounted to converting them into products, procedures, or slogans, eliminating core ideas in the process.

FAILURE TO CONNECT RESEARCH AND INVENTION

In late summer nearly every year I get calls from journalists who are preparing feature articles on education to appear at the beginning of the school year. They never ask questions like "What's new?" or "What advances have been made in education in the past year?" Those are the kinds of questions they would ask medical researchers or computer engineers, but it would not occur to them to ask such things of educational researchers. Instead, they ask "What's the evidence that reading is getting worse?" or "I'm doing a story on method A versus method B. Do I have it right that you're in favor of method B?" or "What does research show about whether computers improve learning?" To them education is a field that does not progress. It is a field that has problems and issues but it is not a field in which this year's knowledge is expected to have advanced beyond last year's. There are innovations, and they will do feature articles about those as well, complete with classroom photographs showing students having a swell time learning. But to find out about innovations, the reporters go to the schools. They will only call a university in the vain hope that they will be told of research that shows whether the innovation is good or bad.

For stories on innovations in medical treatment, reporters would not go to the local hospitals (although they might find some there). They would go to the research universities and their teaching hospitals. When educational research was new, when the *Journal of Experimental Education* was founded and there were visions of something comparable to the rise of experimental medicine, many universities and teachers colleges started their own schools. These were intended not only as training grounds for future teachers but as centers of leading-edge experimentation, on the model of teaching hospitals. Now most of those schools have disappeared. With a very few exceptions those that remain have evolved into subsidized private schools that are if anything more conservative and resistant to innovation than the average public school. The story of why educational research failed to realize its dreams has yet to be fully written and I am not going to attempt an off-the-cuff historical analysis. Suffice it to say that the journalists, naive as most of them are about educational matters, accurately sense that the education beat is something quite different from the medicine beat or the science beat or the technology beat. It is more like covering religion—or fashion.

In a magazine circa 1908 there appeared an ad for an automobile—the Reo, I believe it was. Among the claims made for it was that the steering wheel was "where it belongs": in the middle. If automobile design were pursued the same way as educational policy, there would have followed years of research comparing the effects of different locations of the steering wheel. The likely result would be that one location would show up better according to certain criteria and another would show up better according to others. There would be methodological disputes—for instance, between those who place their confidence in quantitative measures and those who prefer more ethnographic approaches to steering wheel research. Eventually, perhaps, the weight of evidence might tip in favor of one location over others, but it would not be compelling enough to convince those strongly inclined toward a different view. To this day there would still be steering wheel on the right advocates, bitterly critical of those advocating steering wheel on the left, and a goodly number resolved that the steering wheel should be in the middle "where it belongs."

The kind of research I am referring to is called "decision-oriented" research, indicating it is supposed to help in deciding what to do. It has an important place in modern life. Should a new drug be approved for use? Should all passengers in an automobile be required to wear seat belts? Where should a toxic waste disposal site be located? These are decisions that one hopes will be aided by solid research, for the alternative is to let prejudice and politics have the field to themselves. New decision-oriented findings on health issues, such as the benefits and risks of hormone replacement therapy, regularly make headlines. But in progressive fields, decision-oriented research goes hand in hand with invention. My doctor tells me that he and his colleagues have started taking a more "aggressive" approach, as he puts it, to high cholesterol levels in people with no evidence of heart disease. One reason is decision-oriented research showing the risks associated with even moderately high levels of serum cholesterol. The other is the appearance of new drugs that are more effective and that have fewer side effects. Belief that the new drugs have these virtues is, of course, also based on decision-oriented research. But decision-oriented research did not produce those improved drugs. That came about through a process of invention, grounded in more basic, explanation-seeking research. Decision-oriented research will not only show which of the new drugs is better under different conditions, however; it will also produce results that spur and guide the next round of invention. Invention, in turn, alters the decision problem, sometimes profoundly. The steering wheel problem was not finally decided by research. Through a series of inventions and design improvements in automobile steering and suspension systems, the problem of where to locate the steering wheel shifted from one of maintaining control over a wobbly set of wheels to one of situating the driver for purposes of vision and convenience—a problem that common sense could solve.

In education, research and invention do not boost each other the way they should. There is invention, of course. Creative teachers keep coming up with novel approaches to teaching problems. But these owe little to research and are seldom the object of research. Educational inventions also come from universities and research centers; these are more likely to draw on and sometimes even be part of more basic behavioral research. But only within the most limited areas do you find what Alfred North Whitehead called "disciplined progress." Invention in education does not have the dependable, cumulative quality that it has in modern professions and modern industries. Most decision-oriented teaching research tests the effects of broadly defined variables, such as phonics versus whole-word methods of teaching reading, the use of questions inserted in texts, types of rewards and feedback, and attributes of teaching performance such as clarity. This kind of research sometimes yields useful findings but, as with the fictitious steering wheel research, they are seldom conclusive enough to resolve a controversy. More important, however, they do not contribute to innovation.[2]

What would automotive engineers have done if research had shown, for instance, that placing the steering wheel in the middle

---

[2]The estrangement of research from invention was dramatized by a research movement that began in the 1960s and that still has adherents. Struck by the failure of decision-oriented research to identify teaching variables that had a strong and consistent effect on learning, Lee J. Cronbach (1975) suggested that the fault might lie in looking for variables that affect all students the same way. Perhaps method A works better for a certain kind of student and method B works better for another. Averaged over all students, the choice of methods will appear to make no difference, but when evaluated in a way that distinguishes the two kinds of students a strong aptitude–treatment interaction or "ATI," as it came to be called, would appear—revealing that method does make a difference, but that the difference depends on the kind of learner. The logic of Cronbach's argument seemed so compelling that it took more than a decade of failure before most educational researchers came to acknowledge that ATIs were no easier to find than variables that affect everyone the same way. More interesting in retrospect, however, is what educational researchers imagined should be the result of finding an ATI. It should be to divide students according to type and use method A for one group and method B for the other. Of course, there would have to be further subdivisions in accordance with other ATIs, so it should not be hard to see that this approach could never work in the real world. Cronbach said as much himself, although his caution seems never to have sunk in to ATI enthusiasts.

worked best for tall people but a steering wheel on the side worked better for short people? Producing different automobiles for tall and short people would not be a likely option, and for more than economic reasons. Once such a process of differentiation started, where would it end? Different braking systems for introverts and extraverts? Right- and left-cranking engines for right- and left-handers? A fledgling industry would never get off the ground that way. Instead, sensible engineers would have investigated what kinds of troubles people had with differently placed steering wheels and would have tried to redesign the car to eliminate those difficulties. Further research might show that in eliminating one difficulty they had created another, but that's the way problem solving often goes. They would then invent a way to eliminate that difficulty, and so on. That is how things are done in any field where there is a good working relation between research and invention.

THE TWO CULTURES IN EDUCATION

Educational research's lack of practical relevance is an old complaint (Kaestle, 1993; Lagemann, 1997). Yet there have been advances in pedagogical science, if I may use that term. Especially in reading and in elementary mathematics, there are methods available that are markedly superior to those available a century ago. Indeed, there is scarcely any academic subject that could not be taught better today than it could have 40 years ago, when I was becoming a school teacher. Researchers complain that these advances are ignored, but that isn't quite the case. The case is worse than that.

Research does have an influence on practice. A small but significant part of the education establishment is dedicated to making that happen.[3] The delay may be 10 years, but the worst part is what happens to it in those 10 years. It undergoes a series of simplifications and corruptions so that by the time it finally reaches the classroom it is no longer an advance in knowledge. It is hardly knowledge at all. New concepts have been translated into familiar ones. New approaches have undergone the kinds of reduction I discussed in chapter 8—reduction to subject matter, to activities, or self-expression. A decade of research on cognitive strategies gets reduced to a wall poster that could just as easily have been produced 50 years earlier on the basis of Dewey's *How We Think* (1933). A theory of multiple intelligences gets reduced to Mickey Mouse activities and the fond belief that everybody is smart in some way. Everything that reaches the schools has gone through several if not many stages of dumbing down.

---

[3]Professional associations, government agencies, curriculum specialists, and teachers' unions all play a part, supplemented now by a number of Web sites of uncertain provenance.

The dumbing down is not calculated, of course. It is symptomatic. Some blame it on the top-down character of a social process that assigns teachers a lowly and dependent status as the recipients of knowledge rather than participants in its creation (Clandinin & Connelly, 1998). Others, less popularly, blame it on the poor preparation of teachers, which leaves them incapable of reading research firsthand. What all may agree is that it results from a largely unsuccessful effort to connect research to the daily concerns of practitioners. But to me all of these are also symptoms of a yet more fundamental failure. It is the failure of education to develop into the kind of profession that continually transforms itself through knowledge creation and invention.

That is why the teachers in the spanking new technology-ridden school are stuck. They have set themselves the task of inventing something—call it a program or an educational approach. They may bring in supervisors, consultants, and university researchers to help them, but their task is one for which the education profession as a whole lacks capacity. It is the task of envisioning a new possibility and working toward it through what Whitehead described as "a process of disciplined attack on one difficulty after another."

The ironic and pathetic situation in which the staff of our self-styled school of the future find themselves amounts to this: Theirs is a preindustrial craft dropped into a postindustrial setting. They really have little choice but to assimilate the new technology as best they can to their traditional practices. For teaching is indeed a traditional craft. It is learned through apprenticeship or, in its absence, emulation and trial and error. Like traditional agriculture, medicine, and metal work, its practices evolve slowly; in a stable world they may become nicely adapted to conditions, but they lack means for rapid change and purposeful innovation.

The traditional craft character of teaching is shown as much by its strengths as by its weaknesses. Any researcher who has tried to actually take over a classroom, as opposed to merely holding forth as a guest of the teacher, quickly appreciates that teachers have an art that they lack. Every skilled teacher has a way of managing a classroom that, under any reasonably favorable conditions, results in a peaceful, orderly, friendly, but down-to-business atmosphere. Skilled teachers are said to have eyes in the backs of their heads. They can attend to individual students in a personable way while simultaneously monitoring and tending to the rest of the class. And most of the time they can do this without undue effort or strain. Beyond this public level of activity, good teachers will have a caring relationship with each student that is mutually rewarding and supportive, yet that is unequivocally a teacher–student relationship rather than a buddy relationship or a parent–child relationship. This is truly impressive art, and the wonder is that it is so widely developed among teachers, given the poor means available for transmission.[4] It is just the kind of art that traditional crafts and professions are good at developing and that traditional mechanisms of apprenticeship are good at transmitting. This does not mean it is a static art. Society changes. In recent times teachers have had to learn to do without corporal punishment and to accommodate to a rising egalitarianism. Such adaptations have not always been easy, but they fall within the range of adaptations that any traditional craft is able to make.

The weaknesses of the traditional craft show up in instruction. ("Instruction," as I have remarked before, is not the right word but no better one is available. What I mean is all the things teachers do, whether of an overtly didactic nature or not, to achieve learning objectives.) Instruction does not progress. Instruction undergoes changes in response to fashion and politics but not as a result of problems having been solved. A 15th-century textbook, marking the dawn of arithmetic instruction, seems quaint to us because of the lack of mathematical notation, but the pedagogy is about the same as that of the currently most popular back-to-basics series (Swetz, 1987).[5] They didn't have a good way of teaching proportionality then, and we still don't.

In modern professions such as dentistry and engineering, progress is taken for granted. But it does not just happen. These professions are organized and conducted in ways that make it happen. They were not always that way. Dentistry and engineering were once slowly evolving traditional crafts, just as education is today. Clearly, scientific knowledge has been essential to their progress, but there is more to it than that. They have not merely been the beneficiaries of scientific advances. These and other modern professions have become knowledge-building communities. Although some members of the communities specialize as creators of new knowledge, the profession as a whole is geared to knowledge advancement, depends on it, and has a part in it. For education to become a modern profession, it must begin to organize itself around the creation of knowledge.

But here we encounter a serious obstacle. Unlike the health and engineering professions, education is a profession in which research

---

[4]Teachers of course vary in their managerial and human relations expertise, and it is relevant to the point I am making that one respect in which many teachers are found wanting is in organizing classroom routines so as to maximize instructional time (Leinhart, Weideman, & Hammond, 1987).

[5]Even the hokey word problem made its appearance in that early Venetian textbook: If the Pope's messenger leaves Rome for Venice at such-and-such time and travels at such-and-such rate, while the Doge's messenger leaves Venice ....

and practice are separate cultures. There is a research culture in which the solutions to educational problems are sought through trying to understand processes, mainly cognitive and social ones. And then there is a culture of educational practice, in which moral precepts and the accumulated lore of the profession dominate discourse. Although there is a good deal of traffic between the two cultures, they differ fundamentally enough that cooperation is difficult and fraught with misunderstandings.

It is no doubt true in other professions as well that the most advanced research is unintelligible to the least sophisticated practitioners. But in medicine, for instance, an unbroken continuity of interest and understanding can be traced from medical researchers to doctors in teaching hospitals to specialists to general practitioners and even to the kind of lay people who read things like the *Berkeley Health Letter* or the medical sections of news magazines. All belong to the same culture, which is a culture of scientific medicine that developed during the 19th century. Even though there are important concepts that people on the less sophisticated end of the continuum may never have heard of or may have grasped in a limited or distorted way, there is nevertheless a shared conceptual framework such that ideas of infection, immunity, risk factors, and the nature of various diseases provide a basis for meaningful cooperation across the spectrum.[6]

Throughout most of the 19th century, however, medicine in North America had a cultural split not unlike that of education in the 20th century. As summarized by Barbara Floyd (n.d.) in her introduction to a University of Toledo exhibition:[7]

> Two parallel threads run through 19th century American medicine: one of evolving medical theory and expanding knowledge that eventually furthered the profession; and the other of the daily practice of medicine in the field. The evolutionary side, or "scientific medicine," was led by the great medical minds such as Benjamin Rush, but was nonetheless ineffective in treating patients. The other side was dominated by quacks who promoted bizarre treatments like water cures and electrical garments which, while also ineffective, were enthusiastically followed. These two paths often crossed one another and mixed theories and tech-

---

[6]The existence of a common medical culture is demonstrated as much by medicine's alleged faults as by its virtues. For instance, the resistance to acupuncture and herbal medicine reflects a shared conviction that treatments should be scientifically explainable. The escalation of extreme measures reflects a shared commitment to forestall death at all costs. The often high-handed treatment of low-status patients reflects the fact that membership in the medical culture is open to only a select portion of the public.

[7]<http://www.cl.utoledo.edu/canaday/quackery/quack1.html>

niques. Scientific medicine took on aspects of quackery to gain patient acceptance, and quackery assumed aspects of scientific
medicine to gain credibility. (par. 2)

The analogy to education in the 20th century is so striking that it is
tempting to expand on it, but that would take us too far afield.[8] The
more important point is this: Pedagogical science at the beginning of
the 20th century was about on a par with medical science at the beginning of the 19th century. Its progress over the ensuing century
was at least comparable to that of medicine in the previous century,
arguably superior in important respects. Yet by the end of the 19th
century medicine had largely resolved its cultural split and was well
on its way to becoming a unified modern profession, whereas education is perhaps more divided than it was at the outset.

The gap between the research and practitioner cultures in education was most impressively brought home to me some years ago
when a teachers' federation in my province commissioned a study of
childhood education. In the archaic way that such things are done in
Canada, the inquiry consisted of a panel of important persons who
set up hearings at which all and sundry were allowed to make presentations. OISE's research director of the time asked me to go
around to the hearings and put in a word for research. I prepared a
mild 5-minute presentation to that end, but I scarcely got through
the first minute of it before the chairman interrupted and obliged me
to spend the rest of my allotted time listening to him heap abuse on
educational research, allowing no time for reply. In truth, however, I
would not have known how to reply.

His complaints were all stated as things that school people had
told him, and they ranged from the unreadability of educational research to its utter irrelevance to practice. Teaching, I was told, is an
art and cannot be reduced to a science. Research says what is true of
the average student, but teachers know there is no such thing. Its
practical implications, when there are any, are things teachers already know. Generations of educational researchers, better prepared
than I, have responded to these criticisms by trying to show that research does in fact have something worthwhile to contribute to educational practice. Their success has not been impressive.

What I now realize is that the importance of these chronic complaints about research does not lie in their substance but in what they
reveal about the estrangement between research and practice in education. I do not mean that the complaints are without substance.
There is plenty of irrelevancy and naivety and occasionally arrogant

---

[8]The parallels emerge strikingly in Rothstein (1985).

scientism to be found in educational research (the estrangement having been bad for research as well as teaching), and there are plenty of problems for which research provides little that is helpful. But in a healthy, modern profession such shortcomings would be seen as shared problems of the profession, not as reasons to dismiss research.[9] There would not be this antagonism, this posturing of "us" against "them." And in a modern profession there should be no issue of science versus art. It should be obvious that the two progress together.

The split between the two cultures is not a simple one of town versus gown. A large part of the faculty in schools of education—especially in those schools of education that carry the main burden of teacher preparation—belong to the craft culture rather than to the research culture. They are former teachers or administrators who obtained graduate degrees studying under people like themselves. In their graduate study they may have acquired advanced ideas that set them apart from their former colleagues (they may have become postmodernists, for instance), but that does not make them members of the research culture. Some of them may seriously take up the role of bridging between the two cultures, a difficult but worthy task. But it does not bring the two cultures together. It does not create the continuity of interest and understanding that binds medical researchers, medical educators, practitioners, and knowledgeable clients together in a progressive endeavor.

Fundamentally, the two-cultures issue is not about human relations. It is about whether people are working in the same or different problem domains. Quite possibly educational researchers and teachers get along better and cooperate better with each other than do medical researchers and practitioners. The issue lies deeper than that. The work of a cancer researcher, experimenting with mouse cells in a laboratory, and the work of the attending physician in a hospital cancer ward have nothing evident in common. The work they do, the tools they do it with, and the people with whom they communicate are all different. To a time traveler from the 17th century, it would indeed be incomprehensible that these two should belong to the same profession. The reason it seems plausible to us is

---

[9]The alleged unreadability of educational research is one of the more telling indicators of the cultural divide. Compared with other social science research, educational research is not particularly jargon laden or inscrutable. The problem is more one of cultural norms. In educational writing, as in all other professional writing, writers must begin by gaining the confidence of the reader. For educational researchers, this is done in the usual academic way—by citing literature and making pronouncements that demonstrate familiarity with the frontier of knowledge on one's topic. In the teacher literature, however, confidence is gained by demonstrating that one is a caring person who speaks from experience, and the typical way of doing this is through a narrative lead. The result is that neither group writes in such a way as to gain the confidence of the other.

that, even with the sketchiest knowledge of cell biology, we can appreciate that what goes on in the cell research laboratory and what goes on in the cancer ward are relevant to the same problem domain. It is not simply that they have the same topic of interest. What is found out in one alters, complicates, or contributes to the solution of problems faced in the other. Educational researchers and practitioners obviously share the same topic of interest. They may share many of the same motives and ideals. But they do not yet share a problem domain. What it will require for them to do so is conceptual change, not just improved quality of social interaction.

WHO NEEDS RESEARCH?

One of the important phases in the evolution of modern medicine was a period that, according to Lewis Thomas (1983), ran from the middle of the 19th century up to the discovery of penicillin in 1928. It was a period when enough was understood about diseases that doctors realized the inadequacy of their treatments—realized, in short, that they did not have the knowledge required to solve most of the problems patients brought to them. Medical practice became conservative, concentrating on the limited number of diseases that were treatable and, for the rest, merely trying to sustain patients while the patients' bodies did the work of fighting disease. But it was also a time when research thrived and many doctors engaged in it, because they realized that was the only way medicine could advance.

Education has not yet entered that phase, although the time is ripe for it. After decades of cognitive learning research, enough is now known about the difficulties of learning various skills and disciplines that the pervasive inadequacy of present means for teaching them is clear. But we don't find teachers saying "I don't know how to teach such and such." They might say "I don't know such and such well enough to teach it," but that is a different matter. The presumption is that if you know something and are a competent teacher, you can teach it. Teaching is where medicine was before the phase I refer to. Medicine was then also a traditional profession.

Traditional professions are marked by a certain complacency, which must not be confused with indifference to results or lack of feeling for the people whose welfare is in their hands. It is a complacency that centers around doing your job well. If you do your job well, according to the standards of your profession, then whatever failures occur are not your fault. At the level of the individual practitioner, that is a sound and virtually essential belief. The best you can do is the best you can do, and you must not lose heart when, having done your best, the patient dies or the student fails to learn. But if that same belief is generalized across the profession as a whole, it is a barrier to progress.

In education, an elaborate conceptual and bureaucratic system has evolved to spare not only the individual teacher but the system as a whole any blame for failure. There is the infamous IQ. It is no longer much used to channel students, but it still serves to maintain professional complacency: As long as the smart kids are succeeding and only dumb kids fail, the education system is free of blame. Society or genetics or the two in combination are at fault. The channeling of students has now been taken over by a much more complex system of categories, mainly constituting what are called "learning disabilities." Students labeled with a learning disability, "limited English proficiency," or some other limiting condition may not be removed physically from the regular classroom, but they cease to count as failures of the classroom process. Often this is literally true; they are excluded from the test score averages by which schools and teachers are judged. Dossiers are compiled for every student and maintained throughout the student's school career, to be mined for explanations in case of failure. Alessi (1988) examined school psychologists' files on 5,000 students diagnosed with one or another learning problem and found not one case in which the problem was attributed to inadequate teaching. From the outside this looks like a cover-up, similar to what might go on in a corrupt police department. But it is better understood as the inevitable tendency of a traditional profession (of which policing happens to be another example) to form a protective belt around the complacency that goes with doing a good job.

This complacency is vulnerable to catastrophic collapse, however. There are signs that this is happening today with teaching. When governments, the press, and parent groups start complaining about low standards and demanding accountability, there is hardly any way for teachers to interpret this except as an accusation that they are not in fact doing a good job. In a traditional profession there is no way to respond to such an accusation. The individual practitioner can say, "I am doing as good a job as my colleagues," but when the whole profession is under attack, there is no standard to fall back on. Then the day-to-day failures and shortfalls that all conscientious teachers are aware of rise up in their minds and make them start thinking that perhaps they are not doing a good job after all, and they start counting the months to early retirement.

Science threatens professional complacency, too, but not in so damaging a way. It does not say to the teacher, "You are not doing a good job." It says, "You do not know enough—nobody knows enough yet—to succeed in the task our profession has taken on."

That realization does not negate professional self-esteem, but it requires it to shift its ground. Professional standards for doing a good job still matter. The issue on which medical malpractice suits are supposed to be decided is whether the physician's performance was up to accepted professional standards.[10] But the standards move with the advancement of knowledge. A physician whose treatment of a patient conformed to the standards of 20 years ago would not only have a poor defense in court but would be in danger of losing his or her license to practice. In a modern profession "doing a good job" is a moving standard that binds practice to scientific progress. Professional pride for a modern teacher would not rest on the stubborn belief that "I am doing a good job regardless of what the critics say." It would rest on the belief that "I am doing my part in a profession that is making progress on formidable and important problems."

In a modernized profession, teachers, being themselves deeply concerned with learning and understanding, would set a more meaningful standard for themselves than tritely "keeping up with the field." The idea of knowledge building, elaborated in chapter 8, applies to teachers' knowledge as well as that of their students. Like their students, teachers should conceive of themselves as part of the culture that is advancing knowledge, not merely onlookers or gleaners. They should not merely be scanning the research literature for ideas and pointers they can use. They should be actively constructing their own theoretical understanding, drawing on and reconstructing the knowledge represented in the literature, and trying to improve and advance it. In short, they should live constructivism, not just preach it and teach according to their understanding of it.

POSSIBILITIES OF A HYBRID CULTURE

Proposals for what to do about the gulf between research and practice take two divergent paths, but along both paths there is insufficient recognition of the extent of the cultural divide. The more frequently traveled path is that of teacher education. William Gardner, who headed a group that produced what was eventually published as the *Knowledge Base for Beginning Teachers* (Reynolds, 1989), summed up the widespread conviction that teacher education needs to be infused with new knowledge. In his preface to the volume

---

[10]The fact that juries in the United States no longer feel restrained by this principle reflects the emergence of a new norm that is tangential to the point I am trying to make. The new norm is based on the premise that somebody is to blame and must make reparations for every misfortune that befalls a person. That norm is applied to teachers as well, and they are justifiably aggrieved by it. It may be only a matter of time before they too have to take out malpractice insurance.

he argued that doing what is normal no longer suffices in teaching, that there is a state of the art and that beginning teachers need to be brought abreast of it:

> This knowledge base has been generated in research, broadly defined to include studies of teaching, group processes, adult learning, and studies of historical change; and in the tested practices of leading professionals, moral propositions, legal precedents, and more. A new and higher norm is now possible for teacher education, one which reflects the best that research and experience can offer. (Gardner, 1989, p. ix)

The objective here is to have teachers assimilate, as part of their professional development, the knowledge generated from research. Even assuming this is done in a thoughtful way, stirring to the imagination, it does not make teachers part of the same culture as researchers. The knowledge is still something produced "out there" in another world. Although assimilating new knowledge might make better teachers, it does not make a progressive profession. Furthermore, this approach fails to reckon with the extent to which teacher education itself is in the hands of people estranged from and distrustful of the research culture.

The other path would have researchers stop pretending to have the answers, listen more to teachers, respect their expertise, and join with them in collaboratively researching questions that really matter to the teachers (Hunt, 1992). At worst, this consists of alienated academics joining with disaffected teachers in an anti-institutional ménage. At best, it results in close and productive working relationships, in which teachers themselves become producers of knowledge (Wells, 1994). Even at best, however, this second approach is a form of surrender as far as the modernization of teaching is concerned. It is a way for researchers to function *within* the traditional craft structure of teaching. They may, in this way, bring new knowledge and ideas into the craft, but we are still looking at an evolutionary process of change to be measured in centuries rather than years.

The first approach may be thought of as an unlikely effort to close the cultural divide by bringing teachers into contact with research. The second approach closes the divide by assimilating research into the traditional craft culture. A modern profession of education would instead constitute a new culture, born out of a fusion of the other two, and exhibiting the hybrid vigor to be expected from such a mating.

This hybrid culture is not pure fantasy. Living examples of it may already be found. Virtually every leading-edge experimental project in teaching involves intense collaboration between researchers and practitioners. In the ones I have had contact with, there is plenty of mutual respect, but there is a good deal more. There is a sense of tackling something big, very challenging but immensely promising. It is a shared sense of mission that brings the two cultures together. Of course there are difficulties, and every successful project seems to require at least one person who puts heroic efforts into human relations. But there is a world of difference between what goes on in these dynamic projects and what goes on in many other professional development efforts, where social relations and personal feelings become so central that it is more like group psychotherapy than professional collaboration. I think it is fair to say that in the successful experimental projects a common culture emerges. Differences in expertise are not minimized; indeed, they are exploited to the fullest. But there is a continuity, such as I described in medicine, a path linking basic research, daily practice, and points in between, with information flowing both ways.

The projects I am referring to are mainly based at a relatively small number of universities with research-oriented education faculties, each project involving a small enough number of practitioners to allow intense collaboration. They cannot serve as a model for educational change because, in the reform jargon, they cannot "scale up." They are bound to remain small and to some extent aberrant. There are much larger projects, designed to scale up to thousands of schools. However worthwhile these efforts may be, they do not solve the two-cultures problem. Some are of the top-down variety, presenting a set of standards and methods the schools implement. Others, which are more concerned with the social dynamics of change than its content, work within the traditional craft framework, facilitating the work of local groups (like the staff of the high-tech school I have been using as an example) to plan their own educational reform. Implicitly, they assume the knowledge necessary for the improvement of practice already exists within practice.

Although the leading-edge projects cannot be expected to expand into large-scale reform movements, they contain the essence of what large-scale reform could aim at. But this essence is poorly understood—by almost everyone, I would say. I earlier described teaching as a traditional craft that changes through an evolutionary process. Bringing science into union with educational practice does not mean replacing bottom-up evolution with top-down design—even if practitioners are made partners in the design process. The introduction of science should instead speed up the evolutionary process, leading it to home in more quickly on good designs.

Here I am drawing on Daniel Dennett's (1995) important work, *Darwin's Dangerous Idea*. Dennett argued that evolution is itself a design process, and is fundamentally the same process as is involved in science and technology, except that in the latter cases ideas— "memes"—are the units rather than genes. Biological evolution cannot look ahead. Science and technology can look ahead a short distance, but most progress has to come about through the same bottom-up processes as biological evolution. I cannot summarize here Dennett's explanation of how evolution converges so readily on designs of elegance and complexity. Suffice it to say, for present purposes, that the necessary conditions are just the familiar Darwinian ones: variation, reproduction, and selection.

Evolution in education is hampered by deficiencies in all three of these conditions. Layers of bureaucracy function to suppress variation. Education in the United States has been perhaps the least constrained in this regard, and despite the continuing efforts of groups internal and external to the education system to stamp out pedagogical diversity, the United States remains education's tropical rain forest. But reproduction of variants is abysmal everywhere. The most brilliant pedagogical idea of all time could arise in one classroom and remain unknown to the teacher next door. If it did become known, however, its brilliance would likely go unrecognized—even by the teacher who hit on it. For in cultural evolution there is more to selection than eliminating the less fit ideas—although that is essential, and education has little capacity for that, either. There is also recognizing good ideas and, if only to a limited horizon, seeing where they could lead and what they could generalize to.

The great and unrecognized role of researchers in the leading-edge projects I have been talking about is to aid in the evolution of ideas, only a few of which come directly from them or from their research. In the first place they create and defend experimental environments within schools where diversity can flourish with less than the usual amount of interference—protected parts of the rain forest, if you will. They act as agents of reproduction, helping to spread ideas both within that environment and to other hospitable environments. But their most distinctive role is in selection. There are many reform projects that serve the first two roles, encouraging variations and facilitating their spread, but they fail in the all-important process of selection. There has got to be a way for good ideas to win out. The use of gross outcome measures, such as standardized achievement test scores, has some value in signaling that a system is doing something wrong or something right, but it is far too crude an instrument for selection at the level of the individual design ideas that must be compounded into a significant new structure. Intelligent selection requires, above all, seeing where a novel idea could lead, and that requires being close to the action, deeply involved in its problems, and at the same time having the large view, the background knowledge, and the leisure to reflect, which are all needed to make something general out of something particular.

I want to elaborate on the idea of "seeing where a novel idea could lead," because to me it is the sine qua non of a progressive discipline, research program, or profession. Decision-oriented research, which has been the norm in education, is necessarily retrospective. It generalizes from what has already happened to predict the results of future choices, assuming the past will repeat itself. This need not be a simplistic assumption. It may be conditional on a number of variables whose effects have been assessed, again with the expectation that those variables will continue to act in the way that they did in the past. It is reasonable to expect such continuity, provided nothing exceptional happens. But one of the exceptional things that can happen is progress. Although method A has typically produced better results than method B, method B may be improvable, may lead somewhere, whereas method A is all it will ever be. Decision-oriented research can say nothing about such possibilities, nor can the many kinds of descriptive and analytic research that are carried out in classrooms. It takes people who are actively engaged in the pursuit of progress. To return to the automobile as an example, early research would have shown the horse to be superior in most respects: faster, stronger, quieter, more dependable. But the automobile was improvable whereas the horse was not. Engineers could see the potential and they devoted great energy to realizing it.

Here is a small example of assisted idea evolution, drawn from work I have been involved with, the design of CSILE (Scardamalia & Bereiter, 1996c). CSILE uses a multimedia database to which all the students in a network have access. Their work on a topic or problem is stored as notes in the database, which other students can view, comment on, add to, or link. A common problem has been that notes proliferate without any organization, with the result that a lot of individually worthwhile findings and ideas appear but integration is lacking. What looks like it is going to be a major advance on this problem appears in the current version of CSILE software, which is called Knowledge Forum®. It is the addition of "views." A "view" is a higher order note that provides a conceptual framework for individual notes, locating them on a map, a picture, a concept net, or whatever. As new notes are generated, students can place these on one or more views and even construct a view of other views. An outside expert can sometimes contribute more to an inquiry by constructing a view of what has been happening than by commenting on individual notes. When a group was working on explaining how airplanes fly, for instance, a university student of fluid dynamics contributed by producing a view that separated explanations based on Bernoulli's principle from ones related to Newton's third law (which the participants were unaware of; van Aalst, 1997).

This idea of a "view"[11] can be traced back about 5 years to an innovation originally created by some schoolchildren. With the equipment in use at that time, disk storage space was a problem. Toward the end of the year the disk was getting dangerously full, and so the teacher instructed students to delete all nonessential graphics notes (graphics being the big hog of disk space). One student had produced a particularly fine picture of a kitchen. Not wishing to delete it, she got together with her friends to devise a way to incorporate it into their current project, which was about fossil fuels. Their solution was to use the picture as an organizer for an inquiry into all the uses of fossil fuels that can be found in a kitchen. Notes were linked to the kitchen scene, and other notes linked to those. You could click on the refrigerator and get a view of the inside of the refrigerator, click on the bowl of jello and get a note explaining how fossil fuels were used in the plastic wrap covering the bowl.

It would seem from this account as if the children did all the inventing and the researchers did nothing but make the invention a feature of their software. But there are at least four additional contributions for which the researchers can claim some credit:

1. Somebody had to notice and appreciate the kids' invention.
2. The kids were only solving an immediate problem; somebody had to recognize that the idea could be applied more widely.
3. There is no indication the kids were thinking about the educational value of the innovation; somebody had to recognize its relevance to knowledge integration.
4. The knowledge integration achieved in the fossil fuels case was of a superficial kind. All that held the various items about uses of fossil fuels together was that they pertained to the same place. Somebody had to see how views could be made to serve more principled kinds of knowledge integration.

In the hybrid culture I have been talking about, teachers would have a part in all four of these contributions, but they would also recognize the value of a division of labor, which has researchers bringing more time and more specialized knowledge to the job of exploiting the potential of idea mutations. When researchers and

---

[11]Other community database systems also have what are called "views," but these are merely different ways of sorting notes—by author, date, and so on. Knowledge Forum® (the second-generation version of CSILE) has this feature too, as part of a "note reader," but that is quite separate from what we call "views."

teachers work together, even under the best conditions of mutual respect and commitment, there is an inevitable division of interests. The teachers, by virtue of their responsibilities, have to be interested in the here-and-now solution of problems and attainment of goals. The researchers are bound to be interested in knowledge of more universal application. Indeed, where this is not so, the supposed researcher is not really a researcher or has stepped out of that role to be of service.[12] This division of interests persists in the hybrid culture, but there is a blending of interests that goes beyond the sort of broadening that one expects to result from any fruitful meeting of minds. There is a shared conviction among the researchers and the teachers that solving the here-and-now problem or achieving the here-and-now goal will result in something of general significance. There is thus a sense of a common mission that is in harmony with and that advances the interests of all the participants. As with medical research, it is recognized that the patient may die but the science advances. That is, the here-and-now effort may not succeed, but what is learned from its failure, coupled with other learning, may advance the field of education. Because of this, the teachers can enjoy a certain objectivity that is denied to those who are isolated in their traditional craft.

There are many worthwhile collaborations between education professors and teachers that do not lead to a progressive hybrid culture. No matter how egalitarian these relationships may be at a personal level, from the standpoint of the work being done it is a relation of servant to master. In the classic case, the professor conducts the research and the teacher enters into it as a subject or as a subordinate collaborator. In the more widely approved contemporary case, the professor assumes the servant role. Sometimes it is an exalted kind of service, that of a guru, or it may be the most mundane of fact-gathering services. But in any case it takes researchers out of their roles as advancers of knowledge, and so the culture of research-based knowledge creation is not brought into the practitioner community, even if some of the creators of knowledge are present in person. They are, we might say, reduced to the status of experts—experts in the limited sense of specialists who are brought in to do a particular job but who are not part of the enterprise within which the job is done.

To generalize, two conditions need to be met before there is much chance at all of a fusing of the research and practitioner cultures:

---

[12]There are educational researchers who disdain universal conclusions, believing them to be an illusion of positivism. But even when the researcher's report is a story, the very publication of that story in a research journal implies that it has general significance, that there is something to be learned from it.

1. There needs to be a shared vision, but it should not be merely a vision of local improvement, nor should it be merely a statement of values or guiding principles. It has to be a vision of possibilities not yet fully discernible. That may sound too airy for some tastes, but I submit that it is the kind of vision that guides every creative enterprise.

2. This vision must create a *need* for research that is keenly felt by the practitioners as well as the researchers. Again, this is something to be found in all progressive enterprises. There is nothing eggheaded about it, nor is it a call for practitioners to bow down before researchers. I am part of a large telelearning research network that includes academics, educators in public and private sectors, and people in various learning media businesses.[13] I have been struck by the fact that it is the business people who keep pressing for research, whereas educators tend to feel that they already have the answers. This has got to change if education is to join the modern world.

TEACHING FOR UNDERSTANDING AS A TEST CASE

To move this discussion to a more concrete level, we need to settle on an example of a sharable vision. There are worthy visions that are already generally shared by researchers and practitioners—most notably social visions, such as equity, and visions of educational process, going by names such as "constructivism." These may unite researchers and practitioners in trying to make something work or in battling a common enemy, but they do not generally create a keenly felt need for research. It is not that research is perceived as irrelevant; sometimes it plays an important role, especially in persuasion. But you do not find practitioners feeling stuck for want of knowledge. You do not find people looking to research to help them separate good from bad, progress from backsliding. People do not look to research to lead them toward a clearer vision.

Teaching for understanding is a sharable vision that can meet the two criteria stated previously. Nearly all practitioners and researchers are in favor of it, although they may differ in how they conceive of it and what priority they would assign to it. But, as I try to show, it represents a vision of possibilities not yet fully discernible and there is a need for research that will be appreciated by everyone who gets seriously into the pursuit of it.

---

[13]This is the Canadian Telelearning Network of Centres of Excellence (URL: www.telelearn.ca).

I intend to dwell on this example through the remainder of this chapter and the next. These chapters will be misread, however, if they are seen as mainly an argument in favor of teaching for understanding. Other writers have argued that well enough already. Rather, I am using teaching for understanding as representive, as a test case. Teaching for understanding is a constitutive problem of education, one that has shaped the profession from the beginning. Yet it is one in which there has been no sustained progress—despite sustained progress in the disciplines that education draws on for its subject matter. We understand the natural world far better than Aristotle did, but it is not clear that we know much more about promoting understanding of it than he did. Teaching for understanding is not the be all and end all of education. None of its advocates, including me, suggests any such thing. But if education cannot make progress in teaching for understanding it is a failed profession; a conceptual framework that cannot usefully illuminate teaching for understanding is a failed conceptual framework. That is the sense in which teaching for understanding is a test case.

The Present State of Teaching for Understanding

Teaching for understanding is given high billing in curriculum guidelines and policy documents, but that does not make it a priority in the actual conduct of schooling.[14] In the elementary school mathematics market research I have seen, understanding did not merely rank low among the priorities teachers identified, it did not even arise with sufficient frequency to make it on to the list!

To me the strongest evidence that understanding doesn't count for much in practice is the lack of response to findings about misconceptions. Starting in the early 1980s, research began to pour out documenting pervasive and deep misconceptions in virtually every school subject, misconceptions that persist despite instruction. The findings stimulated further research into the nature of these misconceptions and, more generally, into the nature of understanding in various disciplines. That research continues to advance and now probably constitutes the largest body of research in cognition and instruction. Findings have percolated down into practitioner journals, so that it is probably safe to assume that at least most curriculum specialists in school systems are aware of them. They have aroused interest and have had some influence, even on textbooks.

---

[14]The 1998 K–8 science curriculum guidelines issued by the Ontario Ministry of Education and Training, for instance, make frequent reference to understanding, but inspection of specific objectives reveals an almost exclusive emphasis on descriptive and taxonomic knowledge with hardly anything that would pose a challenge to understanding.

But if teaching for understanding really were a high priority, these findings should have provoked a crisis. There should have been rending of garments and tearing of hair when teachers learned that their teaching was failing in its main purpose and that the tests they had been using had been keeping this fact hidden. I have not heard of anything remotely like that taking place.

Yet I would not conclude from this that teachers do not really care about understanding. To do so would imply a quite improbable degree of hypocrisy. The teachers I encounter do care about understanding, but the culture they have absorbed from teacher education and from experience provides them little help in getting hold of it. This is where a more powerful theory of knowledge and mind can make a difference. I have argued from the beginning that folk theory lacks what it takes to deal with problems of understanding. This is nowhere more evident than in teachers' efforts to get their heads around teaching for it.

Why Teaching for Understanding Is Elusive

Among practitioners, educational ideas can usually be firmly grasped only when they are translated into things to do. That is generally the case with practical arts, and so it is no particular aspersion on teachers to say this. But teaching for understanding cannot be grasped in that way, and this makes it not quite real as an educational principle. The struggle that many teachers have gone through in achieving a working understanding of knowledge building (as discussed in chap. 8) is largely a struggle to overcome this very natural tendency to proceduralize. From an instructional standpoint, knowledge building is one approach to teaching for understanding. There are others, as discussed in chapter 4, which include Socratic teaching (Collins & Steven, 1983), conceptual change teaching (Anderson & Roth, 1989), and a large variety of inquiry approaches to mathematics and science. These approaches make varying demands on teacher's pedagogical skill and subject-matter expertise, but they are alike in that they cannot be grasped as procedures.

Of course, teaching for understanding involves doing things. What is done can be described at some level of abstraction and examples can be presented. All of the cited instructional innovators have gone to some lengths in trying to show what teachers can do. But examples are only useful to those who understand what they are examples of and procedural principles require a correspondingly principled understanding of objectives and problems. Without these, teaching for understanding gets reduced to the familiar routines of contemporary schooling: "hands-on" learning, "projects," lecture and recitation, "thematic units," and group therapy. Any of these might play a part in teaching for understanding, but when the goal of understanding is not firmly held, the routines become ends in themselves. I have discussed all this before: how the purpose of "hands-on" learning becomes manipulating concrete things; the purpose of "projects" becomes the poster or multimedia document that is the product of the work; the purpose of discussion becomes the airing of experiences, memories, and feelings; and thematic units become so incoherent as to have no discernible purpose at all.

For most educational objectives, reductionism works to an extent and for the most apt students. Understanding is particularly vulnerable, however. Reduction to activities typically means that problems of understanding are not addressed at all. Reduction to subject matter puts all the burden on the teacher's ability to explain—explain in a compelling enough way that understanding follows. Reduction to self-expression may engage students in efforts to understand, but not to understand what is supposedly being taught. Teaching for understanding is not likely to advance in schools until the educational process is reshaped so that problems of understanding become the focus for students and teachers alike. That would be a revolution, a genuine paradigm shift.

In the experimental programs to which I referred earlier, of which our CSILE/Knowledge Building Project is one, teachers and students do become intensely engaged with problems of understanding. When this happens, teachers discover they have a lot to learn from research. Research reveals to them things about students' understanding that they did not realize but that they can often verify from observation. They can observe, for instance, the tendency of students to explain things in terms of substances rather than in terms of processes or relations (Chi et al., 1994). They can see the often ingenious ways in which students reconcile scientific propositions with their pre-existing beliefs (Vosniadou & Brewer, 1987). And, of course, the literature on misconceptions almost always makes them aware that they have misconceptions, too, which they have been unwittingly perpetuating. Once they become engaged in probing and trying to do something about students' understanding, they have things to contribute to research in turn. The kind of dialogue that develops between teachers and researchers begins to have the character of real science: It is concerned with improvement of knowledge rather than final understanding, and there is no end to the possibilities for improvement. Progress is made, but one of its results is that problems keep being redefined at deeper levels. Students become part of the dialogue as well, and valued contributors to it (Scardamalia & Bereiter, 1996b, 1996c), as do any administrators who care to become involved. What is happening can no longer be adequately described as curriculum development, innovative teaching, or teacher development: Education itself, as a process and as a profession, is undergoing transformation into something more characteristic of the Knowledge Age.

EDUCATING TEACHERS FOR UNDERSTANDING

In North America, efforts to modernize teaching have mainly taken the form of moving teacher training out of special colleges and into the universities (although this often meant turning teachers' colleges into universities). The effect on the profession has been mixed. On one hand, the move to universities has fostered educational research that, despite much skepticism from other parts of academia, has demonstrated a capacity for disciplined progress. Experimental education now provides a basis for the improvement of practice that is probably comparable to that provided by experimental medicine a century and a half ago. On the other hand, the move to universities meant that teacher *training* had to become teacher *education*. Nowadays the word "training" cannot be used anywhere near the word "teacher" without giving offense (a sorry indicator of the insecure status of the profession). As how-to-do-it training lost respectability, however, it never became clear what should take its place.

My teacher in the first four grades of elementary school, a product of Union Grove Normal School in Wisconsin, knew how to teach reading. The method she had been trained in was not very good according to present knowledge,[15] but she was highly accomplished in carrying it out and she made it work. Among cohort after cohort of socioeconomically unpromising students, there emerged no nonreaders. My dimmest classmate, whose response to being asked how much a five-pound chicken weighed was "I don't know and I don't care," nevertheless read fluently. Today's teacher education graduates are unlikely to have been trained in any method of teaching reading. They will have learned about and discussed the controversies in reading instruction and, depending on their instructors' ideologies, will have learned which is the right side and which is the evil side or that it doesn't matter. They may have received a smattering of information about what reading research has discovered, but this smattering is

---

[15]For those interested in the interminable controversies about phonics, I make it known that her method did not, as far as I can recall, involve any phonics whatsoever. It was the whole-word method, anchored to the uninspiring Dick and Jane readers. What was special about her method was its emphasis on very rapid oral reading. It was extremely stressful. By the end of second grade, every boy in my class stuttered—from trying to match the pace set by the verbally more fluent girls, I would suppose. But we all learned to read and some of us, at least, learned to like it.

likely to have been connected more to the controversies than to the problem of how to ensure that every child learns to read.

Progress surely does not lie in reverting to the Union Grove Normal School model, however. That model may have been superior for developing certain basic teaching competencies, and so we should not ignore it altogether, but it was not a model for progress. It was a model deeply rooted in the craft tradition. Curiously, many current efforts at improving teacher education involve a return to that craft tradition. In their crudest form, they restore the idea of apprenticeship. Because the faculty members of university education departments can no longer fulfill the role of masters to apprentices, that role is being turned over to schoolteachers, who receive honorific appointments as adjunct professors or whatever and take on the responsibility of transmitting how-to-do-it knowledge to the new generation of teachers. In more sophisticated versions, the return to the craft tradition involves teacher collectives to share knowledge and ideas. Electronic networks are being harnessed for this purpose. Regardless of the medium, however, the presumption is that the knowledge necessary for the improvement of practice already inheres in practice. That is the defining characteristic of a traditional craft. The emergence of a dynamic profession must take place over the dead body of that idea.

University-based schools of education ought to be promising sites for creating the hybrid culture that fuses the existing cultures of research and practice. In such schools the two cultures rub shoulders, sometimes collaborating in the same programs. And there are likely to be examples of hybrid cultures in the university to serve as models—health sciences, for instance, or electrical engineering or agriculture. And there may be other places in the university, such as the business school or the school of social work, where there is a cultural divide similar to that in education, offering the possibility of collaboration on shared problems.

In every school of education worth its salt, there are schemes and programs aimed at closing the gap between research and practice, and there is no shortage of limited successes. But I have never seen or heard of anything that could be called a hybrid culture, a culture in which the student teachers actually experience themselves as part of a profession that is advancing through the continual generation of new knowledge and see a continuity between their interests as teachers and the interests of those who devote their careers to understanding learning, thinking, and knowledge.

Teacher education has a bad reputation based almost entirely, it seems, on the reports of dissatisfied graduates (often spouses of the critics). Those dissatisfactions may be well justified but they are not helpful in identifying what is wrong or what needs to be done. Student teachers that I have encountered tend to be overwhelmed by the multiplicity of responsibilities that teaching entails. They may have chosen teaching with the idea that it consisted of planning and teaching nice lessons or being a friend and mentor to young people. Then they learn that they must also be a social worker, a health officer, a disciplinarian, a psychologist, and a legal custodian; that they must be incessantly concerned with the rights and sensibilities of minorities, the downtrodden, and the impaired; that they must assign grades to students on the basis of evidence that will stand up in court; and that their teaching and the academic achievement of their students must meet the expectations of a society that has little appreciation of what they are trying to do. All that and more dawns on them as they come to see teaching through the eyes of those who do it. No teacher education program could possibly provide them with everything they feel they need. They become impatient of whatever does not translate directly into helping them cope, and that includes practically everything of an academic nature. It certainly includes everything in the nature of theoretical inquiry.

But the helping professions generally impose wide-ranging responsibilities on their practitioners. So does management. Teaching may be extreme in this regard, but it is not unique. The difference is that teaching, at least as it appears to the beginner, lacks a center. It is a conglomeration. To people outside the profession it seems obvious what the center should be—it should be teaching—and they chastize educationists for losing sight of that fact. But, as it is typically presented to those inside the profession, teaching *is* the conglomeration. It is a diffuse responsibility for the present and future well-being of students (not unlike parenthood in this regard). Conservative reform efforts invariably aim to get teaching focused on a more narrowly defined objective, namely, students' academic achievement, usually as measured by standardized tests. They are on the right track to this extent: There does need to be a focus. But if teacher education is to bring about a fusion of the research and practitioner cultures, it needs to be a focus that reveals a continuing need for new knowledge.

Teaching for understanding, as I argued earlier, has this virtue, and so it is worth considering as the focus—not just *a* focus, but as *the* focus around which other aspects of teacher education are arrayed. It has the two properties that I proposed earlier were essential for producing a hybrid culture in education. It represents a vision that points beyond what is presently attainable or fully discernible and it carries with it an obvious need for research. The research culture is already intensely involved in work on the nature of understanding, how it comes about, and how it can go astray—both in general and within particular knowledge domains. If teacher education could take teaching for understanding as its focus there would be an immediate basis for the two cultures' coming together in pursuit of a shared vision.

Many teacher education courses can already be found that deal extensively with problems of understanding. This is especially true of courses in mathematics and science education, but it can be true of almost any education course where the instructor is knowledgeable in cognitive research and has not succumbed to the fashion of turning the course into a course on issues. Making teaching for understanding the core of teacher education would involve several changes in addition to promoting the sorts of attention it already receives in the better sorts of "methods" courses. At the top level, it would mean organizing all aspects of the teacher education program so as to make the ability to teach for understanding definitive of teacher competence. There is much more than that to being a good teacher, but prospective teachers should appreciate that there cannot be less. If they cannot effectively foster understanding, they have no more business in a classroom than dentists have any business going into practice if they cannot drill out a cavity. The criterion for selecting expert teachers as mentors would be not only that they are good at teaching for understanding but that they are actively engaged with problems of understanding. Engagement with such problems ought also to be a criterion for selection of education faculty.

Finally, prospective teachers should not merely study *about* teaching for understanding, they should have intensive *training* in teaching for understanding. The term immediately conjures up images of trainees presenting stilted "model" lessons or lectures. If that sort of thing entered at all, it would be in a minor way. (In these constructivist times it ought to go without saying that teaching for understanding is not some kind of performance, but I am amazed at the extent to which educationists promoting constructivism persist in believing it can be captured by aiming a camcorder at a teacher.) A better idea of what such training might consist of is represented in graduate courses Marlene Scardamalia teaches. To begin with, the graduate students engage in the same inquiries that children are pursuing—trying to understand vision, for instance, or the physics of flight. The adults then start to show the same freshness of thinking, curiosity, and problem-solving zeal that children show. While they are working on understanding phenomena like vision and flight, the education students in Marlene's courses have electronic access to the work of elementary school students trying to understand the same things. These provide the basis for a second level of knowledge building in which the students try to make sense of their own and others' efforts to understand, considering things both from a cognitive-pedagogical standpoint and from a subject-matter standpoint (what it is about vision or flight that is hard to understand). The result is much meatier discussion. Genuine insights emerge. And most important you can see signs among the education students of what is Marlene's main objective, getting them as she puts it "hooked on understanding understanding." As explained in a paper we authored jointly,

> In our experience, the teachers who remain continually fascinated and involved [in knowledge building] are ones who have a dual interest. They are interested in advancing their understanding of history, geology, biology, cultural anthropology, and so forth; and each year they experience some advances themselves as they work with students on problems in those areas. But they are also interested in understanding understanding. The students' efforts (and their own as well) to explain phenomena, to grasp theories, and to overcome naive conceptions, are an endless source of insights into that distinctively human phenomenon, the pursuit of understanding.
>
> An interest in understanding understanding does not seem to be a feature of most people's curiosity. It is an acquired interest, and one that teacher education programs ought to be passionately dedicated to developing. Without it, we find, teachers tend to remain detached from students' knowledge building efforts and to reduce knowledge building activities to merely another set of schoolwork routines. (Scardamalia & Bereiter, 1999, p. 287)

In a preservice program, training would go farther than this. It would engage trainees in doing something about school students' problems of understanding, both at the individual and the group level. But getting future teachers "hooked on understanding understanding" ought to be the first priority. It is the only way I can see to begin making understanding the actual point of teaching. It not only has direct relevance to teaching practice, it introduces them to the idea of a progressive profession in which they have a role in the creation of progress.

The practitioners I referred to earlier, those involved in projects that are trying to advance education's capacity to teach for understanding, are engaged in creating progress in just this way. They have come to recognize teaching for understanding as a constitutive problem, they know that they as well as the researchers have something to contribute in advancing on it, and they draw much of their motivation from feeling that progress is being made. The question now is whether this kind of involvement in the creation of progress can be infused into preservice teacher education, so that it becomes a normal part of socialization into the profession rather than an extraordinary experience. It needs to be salient among the reasons people go into teaching, it should be central among the things they study as teachers in training, and it should be a problem that unites teachers and researchers in an effort to make headway.

This proposal may not sound at all radical to people little in touch with teacher education, and from many people within teacher education it might draw the rejoinder, "We already do that." But because I am using teaching for understanding as a test case to see what it would take to modernize education, it is worth examining just what if anything is radical about this proposal. To do this, we need something for comparison. Fairly representative is the statement of program goals for the undergraduate teacher education program at Wichita State University.[16] It is a bit more detailed than most and it is not as trendy as some, but it indicates the kinds of goals that characterize teacher education generally. The goals are divided into three sets, the last of which, "Manager Goals," need not concern us here. The first, "Professionalism Goals," consists of the following:

The graduate will:
1. Display the behaviors of a reflective professional practitioner who seeks opportunities to grow professionally.
2. Foster collegial relationships with others (e.g., school personnel, parents, and agencies in the larger community) as an advocate for students' learning and well being.
3. Understand and apply legal and ethical concepts related to professional conduct.
4. Compile and maintain important educational information in order to share with the school and community.

Although these are laudable and realistic, they are solidly in the craft tradition, with no indication that the teacher belongs to a larger professional community that includes researchers, philosophers, policymakers, and so on, and no indication that the field progresses in ways that would require a teacher to keep up—much less any suggestion that teachers are expected to contribute to this progress.

The second set, "Instructor Goals," is the one where me might look for something about teaching for understanding:

---

[16]How did I happen to pick Wichita State? Its goal statement at <http://www.twsu.edu/~coewww/undergraduage/goals.htm> was the first one to come up from a Web search using the search string, "teacher education curriculum goals program equity professional philosophy university objectives values."

In planning and implementing instruction, the graduate will:
1. Understand and apply major developmental principles and theories.
2. Assess prior knowledge, skills, attitudes, and beliefs of diverse student populations.
3. Use appropriate instructional techniques for a variety of learning styles, modalities, and intelligences.
4. Use a knowledge of historical, philosophical, social, and cultural factors.
5. Integrate curriculum effectively.
6. Select, use and evaluate a variety of appropriate instructional approaches, formats, materials, and technologies.
7. Assess student progress using formal and informal assessment strategies to ensure (a) the continuous intellectual, emotional, social, and physical development of the learner, and (b) the achievement of specified outcomes.
8. Demonstrate knowledge of the central concepts, tools of inquiry, and structures of the disciplines she or he teaches and makes these aspects of subject matter meaningful to students.

Only the last of these goals could be construed as a call for teaching for understanding, and it is a faint call. These goals all indicate things teachers are supposed to *do* when they teach, but they do not indicate what teachers are supposed to strive for, what they are supposed to bring about. There is no focus, no suggestion of a point to teaching. "Understand and apply major developmental principles and theories"—but to what end? "Assess prior knowledge, skills, attitudes, and beliefs of diverse student populations"—and then do what about them?

If someone at Wichita State had urged that the "Professionalism Goals" should include something about teachers being part of a larger professional community that includes researchers and that the "Instructor Goals" should include teaching for understanding, there would not likely have been much opposition, and so they might well have been included. But it is obvious that their addition would not have signaled any major change. Indeed, they probably would have been accommodated by revisions to the second professionalism goal and the eighth instructor goal of such a minor nature as hardly to be noticed.

A convincing effort to modernize teacher education would not start with goals for teachers. To do that is already to accept the viewpoint of the traditional craft culture. The effort should start at the highest realistic level, which in the case of a college of education would be the mission of the college as a whole. It is at this level that the decision would have to be made whether the faculty was to commit itself to the transformation of education into a modern profession. If so, they would need to consider seriously what their contributions could be, where they saw potential for "disciplined progress," given their resources and limitations and what other institutions were doing.

Not everyone would support such a mission. Some would bridle at the word "modern" and would reject the idea of disciplined progress as positivistic and technocratic. Others would see the idea of a collective mission itself as contrary to academic freedom and the pursuit of scholarly excellence. Others would reject the mission as arrogant and disrespectful of teachers' competence and ways of knowing. Add to these the numbers who would oppose anything that sounds disruptive or taxing, and you have the likelihood that a majority of education faculties would reject the proposal.

Let us suppose, however, that a college of education did accept it and that they chose to focus their efforts on the problems of teaching for understanding in various fields. They would need a plan to organize their efforts, at which point they could profitably begin to think of how to involve student teachers. Student teachers, along with graduate students and affiliated practicing teachers, could be valuable collaborators. Furthermore, getting student teachers deeply involved would be vital for the larger goal of transforming the profession. To achieve such involvement, there would have to be changes in the structure and content of courses and practica, changes in the relations between teacher education and research, changes in the kind of participation expected from associated teachers and schools. The fusing of the research and practioner cultures would have begun.

CONCLUSION

For education to become a modern profession it must be able to generate knowledge—knowledge that sustains progress in the tasks that constitute it as a profession. Educational research has, in the last few decades, begun to acquire that capability, but there is a deep cultural split between it and educational practice. A similar split existed in medicine during the 19th century, but it gradually closed as practitioners became increasingly aware of the nature of unsolved problems, came to see the advancement of science as vital to their practice, and eventually came to see themselves as part of an advancing scientific discipline. Nothing like that has happened yet in education.

The cultural split in education is not one to be closed merely by communication or improved social relations. The recurrent efforts to "translate research into practice" miss the point, as do the complementary efforts to turn teachers into researchers. Although both of these have merit, the point they miss is that teachers experience no urgent need for the kind of knowledge research could provide. In this, education contrasts sharply with modern professions like the health sciences and engineering. But it is not the teachers' fault that they see no need; beating the drum for the importance of research could only be expected to recruit the most impressionable teachers. And it is not the researchers' fault, either—at least not the fault of those who are seriously trying to solve problems of educational practice. The fault seems to lie in the fact that researchers and practitioners work in unconnected problem spaces, even when the problems they are working on have the same name.

The beginnings of a union between the two cultures can be seen in those experimental projects where researchers and practitioners join together in tackling unsolved problems that are of central importance to teaching. Teaching for understanding denotes a range of unsolved problems that are at the very heart of the educational enterprise. Teachers are generally not aware of the unsolved problems, however. When teaching for understanding fails they are apt to attribute it to deficiencies in the students or in themselves rather than to the fact that no one has yet figured out how to produce the kind of understanding that is at issue. Discovering that a problem is unsolved but that there are possibilities of making headway on it is exhilarating and is likely to stimulate the inventive capacities of the teacher as well as putting research in a new light.

If a new hybrid culture is to arise in education, teacher education offers about the only hope for bringing it into being. It cannot be expected to spread from the experimental projects I just referred to, because they are too rare and too talent intensive. Teacher education is typically criticized in ways that imply failure to initiate students into secrets of the traditional craft. In response, teacher education programs have been moving increasingly toward apprenticeship and mentorship by experienced teachers. Commendable as that trend may be in other respects, it works against fusion of the research and practitioner cultures. To achieve such fusion, student teachers must be brought into contact with the growing edge of knowledge in their field and made to feel part of the community that is making it grow. You may recall that I said the same thing about school students in discussing their relation to the subject matter of instruction (chap. 9). Modern teachers need to be simultaneously active in two knowledge-building communities. One is the knowledge-building community they share with their students. Its object is building an understanding of the whole world. The other is a knowledge-building community they share with researchers and other practitioners. Its object is building a working knowledge of teaching and learning. Lying beyond the scope of what I have discussed here, but offering itself as an enticing possibility, is merging those two knowledge- building communities into a larger and more complexly dynamic one (Scardamalia & Bereiter, 1996b).

Why Educational Reform
Needs a New Theory
of Mind

Incogito nullo cupido. (We cannot desire what we do not know.)

—Latin proverb

Nothing is possible, except to extend the area of sanity little by little.

—George Orwell

T he century-long failure of wave after wave of educational reform[1] is now such common knowledge that those of us who persist in trying to design better ways to educate appear to many of our colleagues as if we are engaged in idle academic amusement. Serious reformers are elbow-deep in politics. There is no question that edu-

---

[1]See, for instance, Cuban (1993).

cation is political and that any reform that stands a chance must have a power base. Education also seems to be so constituted that change from either inside or outside the profession is unusually difficult to bring about. But there is a prior question: Is the proposed reform a good idea? Not, is it any good at all, for even the flakiest innovations usually have some good in them. Is it good enough to justify the price—a price that must be measured not only in money but in all the effort and disruption and personal loss that go to make up what Eric Hoffer (1963) aptly called "the ordeal of change"? And is it good enough to meet the need? That is a question of such stupefying complexity that it is almost never raised.

Although the term "reform" is used to cover all kinds of changes, it will help to sharpen our focus if we distinguish reform from transformation. Transformation is what I was talking about in the preceding chapter: transforming education into a modern, progressive profession. Medicine underwent such a transformation in the 19th century. Twentieth-century efforts to provide universal health care and recent efforts to restrain its escalating costs are reforms, having only indirect effects if any on the nature of the medical profession. Reforms can be imposed from outside, and sometimes have to be, whereas transformation can only come from within.

Education has experienced reform but not transformation. Universal access to education is by far the most important reform of recent educational history, and it is well advanced in countries where universal health care is still far off. But teaching is still the same traditional craft it has been for centuries. Indeed, if you look at the Jesuits' *Ratio Studiorum*, which dates from 1599, you may get the impression that the craft has gone downhill since.

Despite the use of phrases like "breaking the mold," practically everything going on in education today has to be counted as reform rather than transformation. Almost all the reforms are aimed at improving the quality of education. The stimulus often comes from unfavorable reports of achievement test results or complaints from employers or parents. But, with one major exception, the reformers' approach to improving educational quality is quite indirect. It may consist of change at an administrative level, such as firing the school superintendent, turning the school over to a private firm, or instituting site-based management. Alternatively, or at the same time, reform may involve try-harder strategies such as accountability schemes or programs like the Georgia HOPE initiative, which rewards good student performance with free college tuition and textbook allowances. Irrespective of the wisdom of particular reform schemes, we must acknowledge that better management and increased motivation could improve the quality of education, but what actually happens at the classroom level is not itself part of the reform agenda.

The one notable exception, of course, is back-to-basics reforms, which frequently specify not only what is to be taught but how (and which may even go on to specify what not to teach and how not to teach). As contrasted with the other reforms, which are administrative, this is *instructional* reform. This is the kind of reform I want to focus on here, because it is primary. The administrative reforms can affect the quality of education only to the extent that they somehow induce instructional reforms, and one of the criticisms of accountability schemes, for instance, is that they induce instructional reforms of a detrimental kind. Many instructional reforms of limited kinds are taking place all the time in education. Most of these originate within the profession and they range from sober curriculum changes to sheer quackery. Back-to-basics movements are often a massive revolt against the cumulative effects of these piecemeal reforms.

The question I now raise is, How successful can instructional reform be without transformation? Surely it can have some success. We are not hopelessly in the dark. But I shall argue two points: First, instructional reforms are not neutral with respect to transforming education. They either nudge it in the direction of modernization—increasing its capacity to solve problems and address new goals—or they further solidify its traditional craft character. "Back to" movements are thus detrimental to the long-range future of education, and this is as true of movements "back to" child-centered education or constructivism as it is of "back-to-basics" movements. Second, reformers are likely to fail in even their immediate objectives if they do not become more deeply engaged with the unsolved problems of pedagogy.

"BEST PRACTICES" ARE NO HELP
IF YOU DON'T UNDERSTAND THEM

The term "best practice" is often heard in educational reform talk these days. It is a conservative approach to improvement. It is about making optimum use of the knowledge already implicit in practice rather than flying off on the wings of some theory or radical notion. I cannot think of any well-supported reform movement that is not grounded in this idea. Sometimes the reform is aimed at a specific "best practice," such as cooperative learning. Other times it is aimed at creating a process, such as a teacher network, devoted to identifying, spreading, and refining best practices. Even the reforms that deal only in accountability and standards must, to make sense, presume that the knowledge of how to meet the standards already exists. Although that is a questionable assumption, it is reasonable to assume that knowledge of how to do better always exists somewhere. But that does not mean that the knowledge of how to use knowledge exists where it is needed.

In the business world, "best practice" is turning into a creative discipline in its own right (O'Dell, Essaides, & Grayson, 1998). A medical center imitates the registration practices of a major hotel chain. An airline speeds up its maintenance procedures by studying the practices of auto racing pit crews. However, such creative copying requires, according to O'Dell (1994):

1. Knowledge of your own process and problems to see the underlying characteristics and spot analogies across other industries.
2. Ability to look for common themes without having them spoon-fed to you.
3. Information about outstanding companies in other industries. This information needs to be organized by process and not only by industry.
4. Language that is common to all. One of the barriers to sharing across industries is finding a common language that describes processes regardless of industry. For example, the medical center had to equate its admissions process with hotel registration to see the analogy and potential transfer.

These are conceptual requirements, and education fails on all of them. Knowledge of processes and problems is so shallow that educators have difficulty seeing useful analogies between one school subject and another or between one kind of student and another, let alone analogies that reach outside the classroom. That has always been one of the frustrations for me in teaching university courses for teachers. Teachers of different subjects and grade levels find little in common except problems of classroom management. The common themes they can recognize are either at a vacuously high level of generality (learner centered versus teacher centered) or they are political. The information flow on which "best practice" depends is, as everyone in education recognizes, terribly deficient. And the common language, once the jargon is translated, is just the language of folk psychology and folk epistemology.

These conceptual deficiencies are all evident at this writing in a growing movement to adopt phonics as a "best practice" in teaching reading. There is, of course, vehement opposition to the claim that teaching phonics is a desirable practice (Goodman, 1998). Tempting as it is to get into that argument here, it would take us away from the point I want to pursue, which is the need for a better conceptual structure for educational reform. We must not ignore, however, the fanaticism that has been so prominent in debates about reading. Fanatics have often been not at the fringes but at the center of reading reform movements. Conceptual equipment is surely in very bad shape when sensible people cannot tell the lunatics from the wise counselors.[2]

Conceptual inadequacies become immediately apparent if we ask what this "best practice" is that is proving so controversial. Calling it "phonics" isn't enough, because when cornered every reading teacher can claim to be teaching phonics already and every publisher can make a similar claim for their reading program. So the legislators and school board officials who are trying to lay down the law add terms like "systematic" or "research-based" or "intensive." But these terms are equally open to everyone's claims. When the David and Lucille Packard Foundation undertook to back a reading improvement effort in Sacramento, California, they went so far as to specify the textbook series that had to be adopted.[3] The outrage that followed on the part of the unchosen was staggering. There were strong suggestions that what the foundation had done was not only unethical but that it marked the beginnings of a police state. But what else was the foundation to do? They had studied the research and had identified what they took to be "best practice."[4] If they tried to mandate it in general terms there was little chance it would happen. Virtually anything could be claimed to fit the mandate. The necessary concepts were missing. Packard had the choice of being too general or being too specific. There should have been a middle range of concepts capable of making significant distinctions among the wide range of approaches that might be called "phonics."

Those middle-level concepts are essential for any worthwhile debate about educational methods. They are the concepts by which a

---

[2]A few examples of lunacy: At a meeting of the Reading Reform Foundation there is no demur when a member proclaims that no one can become a good reader who is not taught phonics. At a scholarly conference, after a presentation of research on the importance of teaching letter–sound correspondences, an official of the International Reading Association declares, "We can't really go along with that; we believe in comprehension." A leader of the whole language movement reportedly expresses in a speech the wish that a stake be driven through the heart of the author of a book presenting reasons why whole language should incorporate teaching of phonemic awareness and phonics (Levine, 1994). More recently, this same leader has been characterizing the move toward phonics as part of a vast right-wing plot.

[3]See the Packard Foundation's 1997 annual report.

[4]I happen to know about this because I am one of the authors of the program Packard chose—SRA/Open Court Reading. But my point here is not that they made the right choice, only that they were pursuing a reasonable and indeed highly ethical course.

putative "best practice" can be characterized with sufficient clarity that people know what they are talking about. Without them you get wars of words, with fanatics leading the charges. In many areas of education the middle-level concepts are altogether absent. It so happens, however, that beginning reading has been the object of sufficiently intense and varied research that a rich fund of concepts does exist (see Adams, 1990; Treiman, 2000). But they are unknown to the multitude of practioners, reformers, and ideologues. As a result, it is fair to say that the participants on both sides of the long-running phonics debate don't know what they are talking about.

Calfee and Drum, in a 1986 review, described what for the previous decade or more had been the standard approach to phonics—what they called the "decoding curriculum, a skill-based, "bottom-up," drill-and-practice program" (p. 812). They characterized it as follows:

> Divide the letter–sound correspondences into specific objectives (e.g., *f, ff, gh,* and *ph* make the sound /*f*/). Teach the child these objectives, often through seatwork. Avoid rules—they are untrustworthy. (p. 812)

When people talk about going "back to phonics," this is what they are talking about going back to. Teachers who remember teaching phonics probably remember something like this. Opponents of phonics object to the pointless drills that occupy hours better devoted to actual reading and writing.

What Calfee and Drum described, however, is something that knowledgeable advocates of phonics find equally appalling. This anomalous practice, aptly labeled by one critic as "Mickey Mouse phonics," was something devised by textbook publishers in the late 1960s and early 1970s as a quick fix in response to public pressure. It was quick and easy because it could simply be added to the existing Dick-and-Jane-type programs without requiring basic revision. It was not based on any research or theory. It was simply a marketing ploy. Yet, because it is what people remember, it is what the contemporary phonics debate is about. In the absence of concepts, people naturally argue about cases, and Mickey Mouse phonics constitutes the known case.

Phonics, to anyone who understands the point of it, is a transitional skill that enables kids to get started reading independently. Everything is focused on that objective. Even on the first day, children are using phonics to derive meaningful words from print, and in a few weeks they are reading interesting stories. Workbook exercises can play only a peripheral role, because the principal task is teaching children to blend letter sounds together well enough to serve in word recognition, and such teaching requires the children to speak and the teacher to listen and respond.[5] Once children are able to read normal texts independently, which may take a few weeks or 18 months at the outside, phonics instruction has served its purpose and can be ended, whereas Mickey Mouse phonics, having no objective, typically drags on for 6 years.

Mainstream publishers naturally hope that the same quick fix can get them through the current surge of public pressure for the teaching of phonics. There is good reason to suppose they will have their wish. The current resurgence is backed by an accumulation of research showing the superiority of sound-it-out type phonics to the Mickey Mouse variety, but it is unlikely to have much effect because *neither the opponents of phonics nor most of its advocates can tell the difference.* If my gloomy prediction is right, Mickey Mouse phonics will return as an add-on. It will be boring and pointless as before and an easy target for its temporarily defeated opponents. A reaction against it will set in. Publishers will remove it, and we will have seen one more swing of the pendulum, with no progress to show for it.

Yet in this case there could be progress instead of pendulum swings. There is no reason why whole language approaches have to be thrown out to bring in phonics. The whole language movement has made some notable contributions, especially in finding ways to involve children seriously in creative writing and in discussing what they have read. Letting children invent their own spellings, the most controversial part of whole language, actually builds on children's efforts to connect sounds and letters. None of this is the least bit incompatible with teaching phonics. And there is no reason why the adoption of phonics has to be a backward swing of the pendulum. A great deal has been learned about what it takes for children to decode print (Treiman, 2000), and this knowledge can lead to improvements in method that may not be obvious to the naive onlooker but that can shorten the time and increase the success rate of beginning reading instruction. But you cannot simply add phonics to whole language. That will give you Mickey Mouse phonics. Whole language teaching at its best creates a literate culture in the classroom—that is, a culture in which reading, discussing, and producing good literature are central to the life of the community. Teaching children how to read is no more out of place in such a culture than teaching them how to use a word processor, but it needs to be done in ways that keep core literary values at the center. That requires sophisticated and creative program design.

---

[5]The responsive listener could in principle be a computer, although at present there is no reading instruction software that provides that. The available software is thus limited to Mickey Mouse phonics.

There is nothing novel about this suggestion. A "balanced approach" is one of the watchwords of the more enlightened reforms (Pressley, 1998). But how do you get people to realize that this does not mean compromise or merely adding A to B? To understand the difference between a phonics-based program that preserves whole language values and something that merely looks like phonics added on to something that merely looks like whole language requires that decision makers and practitioners get into pedagogical analysis to a depth that they do not even know exists. But if they do not do that, the pursuit of "best practice" is a travesty.

WHAT'S THE PROBLEM?

Among educational problems, beginning reading instruction is exceptional in a number of ways. Most notably, its failures are visible (or should I say audible?) and acute, which may explain why it has generated so much emotion on one hand and so much research on the other. But there are many other important educational problems that seldom appear on reform agendas. In fact they receive little attention at all except by the minority of researchers and practitioners who are sensitive to them. The reason is not that people dismiss them as unimportant; it is that the educational failures associated with them are not conspicuous enough to set off alarm bells. As a result, they tend not to be regarded as problems at all but simply as worthy parts of the curriculum. Yet how to teach them is in every case deeply problematic. People serious about teaching them ought to be looking for every piece of knowledge available, yet the reformers' radar seems to sweep past them with hardly a blip on the screen.

Here, mainly by way of review, are some of the instructional problems that remain untouched by reform efforts:

1. Number sense. Widely recognized as the foundation of mathematical competence, it now appears regularly in curriculum standards. But no one ever says what it is, and the curriculum guidelines always reduce it to activities or subject matter that misses the point.
2. Fractions, proportions, ratios, decimals, and percents. These poorly understood terms mark off an area of colossal and sustained failure, unalleviated by the switch from slices of pie to slices of pizza.
3. Scientific misconceptions. Informed educators know about these and can recognize them, but they don't address them as a problem, show little concern about the failure of available remedies, and are distracted by controversy over what to call them.

4. Functional literacy. Study after study shows that large numbers of school graduates cannot cope adequately with real-life reading tasks. The educators' response is to criticize the studies (which is often justified, but diversionary nevertheless) or to adopt reductionist solutions: Introduce realistic reading exercises (reading bus schedules and such) or teach comprehension strategies as subject matter. The notion that *everybody* ought to be reading better than they do cannot really be entertained, because current pedagogy offers no suggestion of how this might be accomplished or even what it would mean.

5. Literature. Although literature teaching has suffered from every kind of reductionism, many teachers have enough personal sense of what the experiencing of literature should be like that they are continually dismayed at their limited success in bringing it about. But there is little they can turn to except tradition and the inspirationalism of language arts journals.

6. World knowledge. This refers to the miscellaneous knowledge of geography, history, and current events that provides a background for further learning and thinking (see chap. 9). Getting students to acquire a lot rather than a little is highly problematic, but the prevailing response is simply to produce lists and expect teachers to teach them.

7. Thinking skills. That the teaching of thinking should be regarded as a straightforward matter—a collection of procedures that can be taught through rules, modeling, and practice—is perhaps the most extreme example of failure to recognize an instructional problem.

Doctors freely admit there are diseases they don't know how to cure, and the public response is not to repudiate doctors but to appropriate money for research. No one ever admits they don't know how to teach fractions, even though generation after generation of students fails to learn them. And so the public response is to blame the teachers, and the response of the teachers is to blame someone else. Ignorance never gets the blame.

Reformers can reply that, although there are of course unsolved problems in education, as in any field, we do know enough to make substantial improvements. Hirsch (1996) has presented this case forcefully, attributing the failure to act on available knowledge to the academic pretensions of education professors. "Research-based" has started to become a watchword of reform-minded politicians and officials (Carnine, 1996). Some parts of the education establishment have reacted hysterically, seeing "research-based" merely as a code word for phonics and rote learning (Taylor, 1998). They are partly right, but not for the reasons their inflamed imaginations suggest. It is true that advocates of research-based methods are in favor of teaching kids phonics and getting them to memorize number facts to a high level of automaticity. These are as close to settled issues as educational research is ever likely to come. The danger is in generalizing from these instances to the full range of instructional issues. That is a mistake that both the advocates and the opponents of "research-based" reform make.

"Of course there are unsolved problems," says the practical reformer. "There always are. But we can't wait around. We have to act on the best knowledge we have." No one can quarrel with that. What I am attacking is the attitude that goes with it. In the last chapter I wrote about the complacency that marks traditional professions, a complacency that rests on "doing a good job." A similar complacency seems to characterize reformers, whether they are fanatics who believe they have the answer or pragmatists who make do with whatever research and common sense suggest. The invariable accompaniments of this attitude are:

1. Absence of need to understand.
2. Reductionism—especially the reduction of everything to subject matter or activities.
3. Absence of forward momentum.

I have remarked on all of these previously. It isn't that people are generally averse to understanding—although the more ideologically zealous may be—it is that practitioners and policymakers never find themselves stuck for lack of understanding. That bespeaks something deeply wrong with the system. Try fixing your automobile or your Internet setup and unless you are a specialist you will almost surely come to a halt where your understanding can carry you no further. But set out to fix education and you will encounter no such roadblock.

Reductionism permeates the education system. I have talked about teachers reducing everything to subject matter, activities, or self-expression. But often the reduction occurs before anything reaches the teacher. The textbooks that come into the teacher's hands have been shaped by a selection process that reduces everything to subject matter. State and local textbook selections are dominated by checklists that specify content, with no regard to whether the textbook affords any promise whatsoever that the students will learn the content. Curriculum guidelines will state airy objectives and then immediately reduce them to activities. The activities may be presented as examples, but inasmuch as there is no basis for generalizing from examples, the suggestions can only be taken as requirements. Get-tough reforms introduce an even more lethal form of reductionism. Education is reduced to training students to perform well on tests.

By lack of forward momentum I do not mean there is never any improvement. A lot of what happens in education can be counted as steps in the right direction. But there is no sense of one step leading to another. Each step has a finality about it, even if it is recognized as only a partial solution to the problem that motivated it. When there is forward momentum in a discipline, profession, or technology, one can look back at the steps that led to the present state and infer a direction for the next step. It affords a kind of running jump into the future, as anyone will recognize who has done a piece of research or development in a progressive field. But in education the best guess is that, whatever the direction of the preceding step, the next step will be in a different direction (frequently the reverse of its predecessor).[6]

Underlying all three of these symptoms is what I take to be the fundamental malady: disengagement from the constitutive problems of instruction. The kinds of instructional problems I reviewed earlier are treated as somebody else's business. This removes the need to understand and it encourages reductionism, a simplistic translation of high-level goals into familiar routines.

HOW FOLK THEORY IMPEDES EDUCATIONAL INNOVATION

Innovation. It is supposed to be the driving force in the new economy. Government agencies are scrambling over one another in their zeal to promote it. There are people who believe that education, like religion, should be shielded from innovation, but let us ignore them in this discussion and concentrate on the more progressive elements, both inside and outside the profession, who regard innovation as at least potentially a good thing.

The first and often decisive barrier to innovation is the response, "We already do that." Those of us involved in educational design encounter it constantly, any time we try to move above the level of specific procedures and offer some principled approach to an educational problem. I used to think this barrier could be overcome by discovering clearer ways of explaining what was new. I have since come to believe

---

[6]In progressive disciplines the next step is not always a running jump from what has gone before. When there is a marked change in direction, this will be called a "paradigm shift." Educationists have taken up this term and applied it so liberally that paradigm shifts are a monthly occurrence. You may infer from this either that education is the most progressive field in the world or that it is not progressive at all.

that the problem lies deeper and cannot be solved on a case-by-case basis. The problem is conceptual, but it is such a massive conceptual problem that it has produced a strong emotional resistance to any departure from familiar categories or habits of thought.

Educational thought, as carried out by practitioners and lay people alike, is in its various aspects moral, subjective, and procedural, but in no significant way theoretical.[7] When a reading pundit declared that teaching phonics is an act of violence against children, he was speaking to the moral aspect of educational thought, which at the elementary level runs heavily toward protecting children from harm. For such a statement to be anything more than sanctimonious claptrap, however, it would be necessary to back it up with a theoretical explanation of the cognitive and emotional effects of phonics instruction. For there is nothing overtly injurious about phonics. Overtly, the behaviors required of children are not unlike those that might be observed in a singing lesson, so if harm is being done it must be at a deeper level. But in the public discourse carried on about educational issues, *there is no deeper level.* That is why a statement like the previous, which I make out to be sheer lunacy, can carry weight in a policy discussion equivalent to that of statements about measured effects on test performance. In phonics debates as elsewhere, however, the most common and destructive response is, "We already do that." It, too, is a claim that needs to be backed up at a theoretical level, for at a procedural level people who make the claim can no doubt show they are doing things that would fall into the category of teaching phonics. The issue is whether they are actually teaching children to recognize unfamiliar words by means of their spellings. Although that may sound like a fairly clear-cut issue, it calls for a level of analysis that is simply absent from practitioner and lay discourse.

I keep coming back to phonics as a case in point because the concepts needed to understand it and to make progress are not very deep. And the conceptual failures are dramatic. Let us turn aside from the lunatics and fanatics and consider what now seems to be the majority, people who have soberly concluded that teaching phonics is a good idea. Suppose you come to them with an innovation that you claim constitutes an advance in the teaching of phonics. How will people judge whether your claim is plausible or even whether what you propose is an innovation at all? At a procedural level, what you propose is not going to look much different. There

---

[7]It is also, of course, political and economic, and these aspects often become salient in judging an innovation, but at this point I am talking about *recognizing* innovations in classroom practice. These must typically be recognized on some other basis first, after which their political and economic implications may come under consideration.

are games and exercises that involve the sounds of words, but those are already commonplace. And you have made some changes in the teacher's patter, but so what? Finally, all people can do is ask for evidence that your supposed innovation produces better results. If so, they may be prepared to adopt it, but with no idea of why or in fact what they are adopting. To give your innovation some identity, you might coin a name for it. Suppose you decide to call it "integrative phonics." That would be a mistake. "Integrative" is a term associated with whole language and project-based learning, the sort of approach that people adopting phonics are eager to reject. That one word, with its train of associations, is liable to obliterate everything you try to say. The power of labels in the marketplace of educational ideas is overwhelming. When there are no concepts, emotive labeling partly fills the void, and it is a tremendous void.

Suppose, however, that you choose a label that catches on. Maybe "coherent phonics" would do the trick. Your window of opportunity for advancing the ideas that this label represents will be too small to put a foot through. As soon as the label catches on, everyone who is trying to make money off phonics will call whatever they are doing "coherent phonics." No one will be able to tell the difference, because they never understood what you were talking about in the first place. The same will be true if, instead of "coherent phonics," you come forth with "coherent number sense," "coherent proportionality," "coherent science," "coherent literacy," "coherent history," "coherent thinking," or just "coherent knowledge." Unless your innovation looks conspicuously different on the surface—unless, for instance, it involves exotic technology—practitioners and decision makers will not be able to recognize what is new about it or to distinguish it from anything else that is being called by the same name.

If we switch from "We already do that" to "Wow! This is what the 21st century is really about!" we view the same dismal scene from the other side. Walk into any well-equipped classroom and you are likely to find students engaged in an activity that has been tediously commonplace for generations—copying information from authoritative sources, organizing it under topical headings, decorating it nicely, and presenting it as a finished "project." The only difference is that now they are copying information from the Internet rather than a book, organizing it by means of a word processor or media authoring application, and decorating it with computer graphics, animations, movies, or whatever the technology allows. This is innovation of a sort, and it may even be beneficial—although it could as easily be the opposite (Moss, 2000). What is discouraging is that only innovations of such instant visibility are recognized. As technology enables ever more spectacular innovations of this superficial kind, it reduces even further the ability of educators to recognize innovations of any deeper sort.

THE CONCEPTS WE NEED
AND WHY WE DON'T HAVE THEM

Philip Agre (1998) has remarked on "the tendency of people who define themselves against something to simply invert whatever it is they oppose, rather than actually having a new idea." (par. 10) That has been the character of much educational reform in the 20th century. Liberal reforms have all been defined in contrast to the stereotype of the teacher at the front of the room lecturing and quizzing. Conservative reforms, reacting against what they perceive to be the abandonment of teaching in the liberal reforms, give us back the teacher as lecturer and quiz master. California has provided the most dramatic example of such unprogressive flip-flops. In the early 1990s they virtually outlawed direct teaching of reading and mathematics; then they did an abrupt switch, producing guidelines that virtually outlawed everything except direct teaching. There were people in California who attempted to use the switch as an opportunity to introduce some new ideas, but they were overwhelmed by the reactionaries who, unable to make discriminations, categorized all new ideas as belonging to the liberal pedagogy they were determined (with fair justification) to overthrow.

Reformers should not be expected to produce new ideas, but they should be able to recognize them and to distinguish them both from the supposed bad ideas they are attempting to eradicate and the supposed good ideas that are simply the reverse of the bad ideas. To do this, they need concepts that allow them to think constructively about issues like the following:

- Why something is worth learning—apart from its conjectured long-term utility in the job market and apart from its traditional backing; why, in other words, a student might feel disposed to learn it.
- What different learning objectives actually mean. What is number sense and what does acquiring it consist of? Similarly for mathematical problem solving ability, understanding a historical period or event, mastering algebra, learning graphical design, understanding Dante, and being able to write a decent paragraph.
- What is teachable and what isn't, why a certain thing is easy or difficult to learn, in what ways the learning of it can go awry.

- What is the normal course of developing competence in particular domains and what are optimal and suboptimal developmental paths; what distinguishes expertise in the domain and what learning leads to it or away from it.

Answering questions like these requires getting deeply into subject matter and into the cognitive developmental and instructional research in the various domains. There are not standard answers that fit all subjects. We cannot expect reformers to have answers or even to be in a position to evaluate them. What they should understand is that these are the issues on which the value of any instructional reform must rest and that knowledge does exist that can be brought to bear on them. They should be aware that knowledge is progressing and that the best reform will not be simply the reverse of the preceding reform. Professional educators ought to know more than that. In their preservice education they ought to have had courses that immersed them in these issues as they arise, not only in the particular subject they are preparing to teach but in all the other major domains of education. Practitioners could then serve as intermediaries between policymakers and researchers.

What we have instead is instructional reform carried out by people who not only know nothing about instruction beyond what common sense and the mass media provide them but do not know that there is anything to know. This ignorance of ignorance is not limited to politicians and representatives of the public. I have run into scientists and psychologists who study the development of scientific understanding but who do not realize there is anything beyond the obvious to be understood about the teaching of science, the same for mathematicians and psychologists of mathematics.

Obviously I have not tried in this book to set out the pedagogical knowledge, the ignorance of which I have been lamenting. That would require a larger book, with multiple authorship, for it would need to delve expertly into the problems of teaching and learning peculiar to different domains, as well as more general insights into these problems. It would be an important book, especially for teacher education. There have been various attempts along these lines, but none, I believe, that has given the task the massive effort it deserves. My chapters 8 and 9 have touched on various aspects of pedagogical knowledge, but my main concern has been with concepts of a more central nature—concepts of knowledge and mind. What I want to do now is show how they are important in the practical work of educational reform.

For perspective, I have adapted a schema used by E. O. Wilson in his book, *Consilience* (1998). Wilson was representing the domains that relate to environmental policy. I am using the same kind of diagram , in Fig. 12.1, to represent the domains that converge on classroom instruction. His diagram had four sections instead of five, but what he said about their intersection conveys the point I want to make about education:

> As we cross the circles inward to the point at which the quadrants meet, we find ourselves in an increasingly unstable and disorienting region. The ring closest to the intersection, where most real-world problems exist, is the one in which fundamental analysis is most needed. Yet virtually no maps exist. Few concepts and words serve to guide us. (Wilson, 1998, p. 10)

An implication of Wilson's schema is that, although concepts may be well developed and well understood within each separate domain, as you move into the region of convergence the problem is not that people have differing concepts but that they share concepts that are poorly developed. In education, I suggest, this "unstable and disorienting region" is occupied by folk theories of knowledge and mind. Although the inadequacies of this folk knowledge may not be evident in the work going on within each of the sectors, it gravely affects the movement of knowledge between sectors. Knowledge moving between sectors must, so to speak, pass through this "unstable and disorienting region," where it becomes degraded. On the surface it typically emerges as mere folk platitudes, such as "Every child is different" or "You can't teach what you don't know." Beneath the surface, however, the degraded knowledge propagates as unarticulated assumptions, and in that form it is really damaging.

In the preceding chapters I have tried to articulate and criticize some of these hidden effects of folk theory. Here I summarize them, with suggestions as to how they impede or subvert instructional reform.

1. Knowledge is narrowly conceived as the contents of a mental filing cabinet. This leads on one hand to devaluing knowledge as an educational objective and on the other hand to hapless efforts to itemize and test it.
2. There is no idea of teachability. Tacitly, it is assumed that if you can measure (or perhaps only name) something, it must be possible to teach it. The result is the imagined teaching of imaginary skills.
3. There is excessive and unfounded belief in transfer of learning. In the extreme, where word magic takes over, it is assumed

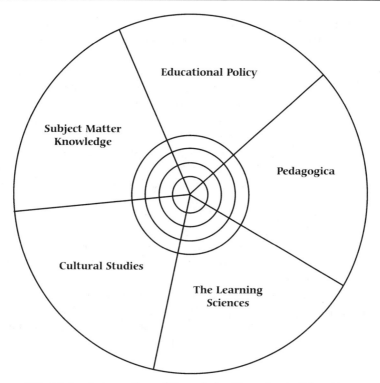

FIG. 12.1.   Intersection of Knowledge Domains in Education.

that what is learned will automatically transfer to everything else that is known by the same name. Word magic and excessive belief in transfer are essential to folk educational thought, because without them it is difficult to justify most school teaching.

4. There is no idea of quantity. The tacit belief, applied to both educational content and procedures, is that if some is good more is better. Quantity as an objective is either scornfully repudiated or is replaced by long lists of items to be learned and tested.

5. There is a shortage of concepts for the analysis of teaching methods. Means are lacking for distinguishing one method from another, and ideological critique takes the place of analysis of means and ends.

6. Reductive practices go unrecognized and are sometimes elevated to pedagogical principles: Reduction to activities becomes "project-based learning," reduction to self-expression

becomes "learner-centered education," and reduction to subject matter becomes "core knowledge" or "building a firm foundation."

7. Science is deeply misunderstood. School science becomes either purposeless activity—the mere exercise of research skills—or the mastery of a body of truths or a branch of social studies. Improvability as a defining characteristic of scientific knowledge does not even enter the educational picture.

8. Understanding, conceived of as a mental state, becomes something that can be pursued only indirectly, whereas the direct pursuit of understanding is characteristic of real scholarship and science.

9. Knowledge creation is reduced to learning and belief. Terms like "knowledge work," "constructivism," and "inquiry" thus lose their meaning. School learning comes to be seen as an impediment to the kinds of productive work that drive a knowledge-based economy.

10. There is no way to formulate a generally acceptable idea of the core job of schooling. With an impoverished conception of knowledge, knowledge development cannot be accepted as the core job. But any other definition is either too global or too narrow.

What I have tried to summarize here are the inadequate concepts that occupy the region where the various sectors bearing on instructional reform come together. These concepts impede the movement of knowledge from one sector to another or degrade it below a useful level. For instance, insightful educators recognize that statable knowledge (the stuff in the mental filing cabinet) and specific skills represent the two visible tips of a very large iceberg, and they are concerned with the whole iceberg. But they have no cogent way to talk about the invisible part. What they say comes out as romantic froth. They spout nonsense about "process versus product," surely one of the most ill-advised rhetorical gambits in the perennial educational debate. They espouse catchwords like "constructivism" and they solemnly aver that children's minds are not empty buckets waiting to be filled. It is no wonder that politicians and business people grow impatient and launch back-to-basics reforms, which are aimed at focusing education on the very limited range of learnings— the two tips of the iceberg—that can be specified in reasonably clear terms and pursued in a no-nonsense manner, and that lend themselves to measurement of results. Other examples could be generated from other segments of Fig. 12.1. Subject matter experts embody vast amounts of the implicit knowledge that constitutes the invisible part of the iceberg, but what comes across from them as educational wisdom tends to be either cut-and-dried content or more romantic froth. Sociocultural researchers are learning a great deal about how knowledge is constituted and communicated in working groups, but when it passes through the inner circle it comes back out as learning by doing, apprenticeship, and informal talk—in other words, what everyone already knows. Learning scientists have produced penetrating critiques of textbooks in every major area of the school curriculum, but what reaches the policymakers cannot be translated into standards that publishers could act on or that could be enforced, so instead the policymakers send out content lists or standards based on conventional tests.

Although some progress can be made by piecemeal attack on the 10 faulty conceptions listed previously, stable improvement is going to be very hard to achieve as long as the underlying folk theory remains unchanged. Throughout I have been arguing for only two basic changes:

1. The idea of mental content should be reduced to the status of a metaphor, useful for some purposes and not for others, but never to be taken literally. To suspend use of the metaphor where it is proving inadequate, we must find ways to construct mentalistic accounts that do not refer to things residing, being searched for, or undergoing changes in the mind.

2. Abstract knowledge objects, such as theories, numbers, and designs, should be accepted as objects in the real world, with which people may develop relationships, much as they do with animate and inanimate material things. Understanding and mastery may then be treated as characteristics of such relationships, and the advancement of knowledge as the creation and improvement of abstract knowledge objects.

Producing these changes remains a tall order. It is not a matter of *convincing* people of propositions like the preceding. People have to *see* learning, teaching, thought, and knowledge in ways that are consistent with these propositions, just as to become a Copernican you have to *see* the terrain outside your window as part of a globe. Furthermore, they have to become proficient at thinking within this altered framework. As I proposed in chapter 3, it amounts to moving out of the two-dimensional world of folk theory and into a three-dimensional world in which there are not only physical reality and mental states but also conceptual artifacts. Compared with folk theory's flatland, this three-dimensional (Popperian) world greatly increases the complexity of relationships one must learn to deal with.

Conceptual change has to start where it can. It is not likely to start among the policymakers, although some of them are business people who have a more modern conception of knowledge than does the typical educator. It is not likely to start among teachers, because by reason of their daily work they are more tightly bound to a things-in-the-head conception of knowledge than most other people. It is not likely to start with subject-matter specialists because folk theory of mind does not normally figure in their work except when they are called on to provide educational counsel. That leaves learning scientists and students of culture, my academic colleagues. Many of them, in different ways, are moving beyond folk theories of knowledge and mind. I am trying to help that process along. But ultimately, taming that "unstable and disorienting" region of concepts where the different kinds of education-related thought meet is going to require cooperative effort.

CRAFTING A VISION

One of the areas in which cooperation is most obviously called for and where conceptualization has been most limiting is in the formulation of goals. A goal is a conceptualized outcome. If it is conceptualized at a high enough level, it becomes a vision or an ideal. If the conceptual framework is strong and complete enough, there will be ways to connect the vision with lower level goals that can actually be achieved. Otherwise, the vision tends to be of only inspirational value and the actual business of reform may not advance toward it at all.

The educational reforms that have stirred the hearts of educators over the past century have been of a liberalizing kind. From a distance they look like the same reform, surfacing under different names: progressive education, child-centered education, learning by discovery, open education, whole language, constructivism, and situated learning. In contrast, the reforms that have gained strong public support have been of a reactionary nature—usually, in fact, reacting against the liberalizing reforms espoused by the educators. This contrast has led many educators to see the conflict as having deep political and philosophical roots—as a conflict in world views, no less. There is just enough truth in this to keep alive in education schools a strain of aggrieved social criticism, culminating in what is called "critical pedagogy."[8]

But it obscures a more mundane yet pregnant truth: The public can never be expected to share the enthusiasm of educators for enlightened methods. The public cares about outcomes. Methods stir up public passion only when they are seen as detrimental to outcomes. The public's position is always going to be reactionary, until educators can offer them new and superior outcomes.

The liberalizing reforms of the past century have not done that. Only when carried to absurd extremes have they produced demonstrably bad results, but evidence of good results has been sparse and unconvincing. The enthusiasm that educators have had for these reforms has not come from evidence that students turn out better. It has come, on the philosophical side, from liberal beliefs about rights, democracy, and humane treatment. On the practical side it has come from demonstrations of process that any open-minded teacher is bound to find impressive. Walk into a well-functioning open classroom and you are going to see students going about their work on their own or in small groups, seemingly interested in what they are doing and not being driven to it by the teacher. The teacher, free of the need to conduct recitations and micromanage schoolwork, has time to work individually with students according to their needs. It's hard to resist. You see students doing what they are supposed to and

---

[8]I find it infortunate that the term "critical pedagogy" has been adopted by people whose critique is mainly of the school as an institution rather than of pedagogical practice. According to Barry Kanpol (1998), "Critical Pedagogy is the challenging of any or all forms of alienation, oppression and subordination—no matter from what identity position one is coming from" (par. 5). Its main concern has been how schools preserve social power differences; there has been hardly any interest in pedagogy except as it pertains to such inequalities and to ways of overcoming them. I would like to think that what I am doing in this book constitutes an effort, however limited, at critical pedagogy in somewhat the way that Philip Agre's *Computation and Human Experience* (1997) constitutes a critical AI—that is, a criticism that tries to clarify the constitutive problems of a practice, identify where it is stuck, and help it get unstuck. Yet there is almost no overlap between the problems I have discussed here and those that occupy the practitioners of "critical pedagogy." To read the literature of critical pedagogy, you would think there are no technical problems in education. That would make education a very strange field indeed. The inspiration for much of contemporary critical pedagogy is the work of Paolo Freire (1970), whose educational efforts with peasants convinced him that the difficulties in teaching them to read were not technical but had to do with their powerlessness. This important idea seems to have been generalized by his followers into a universal diagnosis applicable to all educational problems and a corresponding disdain for any technical analysis. (In medicine, this is known as quackery.) Along with Agre, I believe that a real critical practice needs to get into the technical problems of a field, particularly those that are seeming intractable, and look there for underlying and often unstated beliefs that need to be questioned. It is Freire's method of inquiry, but without Freire's answer being assumed in advance. It is what has led me to identify folk theories of knowledge and mind as the source of much educational stuckness.

teachers doing what they always want to do and not doing what they dislike doing. The amazing thing is that such an attractive reform seems never to have caught on with more than a fourth of the teacher population (Elmore, 1996).

Of course, it has some appeal to parents and to the public at large as well, but not of the same intensity. It does not touch them where they live, the way it does many teachers. And so whenever dissatisfaction arises about results, the public is ready to scuttle liberal reforms and go back to what they imagine to be tried-and-true methods. In this they will be joined by that majority of educators who have either been opposed to the liberal reforms all along or weakly committed, like the public at large. It seems to me that the reformers and those who work at understanding and engineering processes of change have simply failed to face up to this rather straightforward situation. It has nothing intrinsically to do with "resistance to change"; with "ownership," status, or power; with top-down versus grassroots initiative; and with all of those factors that enter the picture once a reform movement is under way. It is simply that no reform is going to gather sufficiently widespread and ardent support unless it can be shown to yield results that people value and value highly.

Vision Versus Test Scores

As soon as you mention results, everyone thinks of test scores. This is not the place to discuss how it came to pass, but I think everyone will agree that the two ideas are welded together in people's minds. Education can make no major advance until that weld is broken, but the tools to break it are not in any reformer's toolkit.

I was once at a meeting where a host of distinguished educators were complaining that politicians and business people, by their insistence on objective test score gains, were making real educational improvement impossible. Among the group, however, was Ralph Tyler, who perhaps more than anyone then living was responsible for the shape that educational testing had taken in America. Tyler at last rose to say that in his experience politicians and business people had no passionate commitment to test scores; it was just that no one offered them anything better. If you can offer them a superior vision, he said, you will find them receptive. Many idealistic reformers would claim that that is exactly what they are trying to do. But what they are offering is a vision of an educational process. I don't think that is what Tyler had in mind. To draw politicians and business people away from their fixation on achievement test gains one must offer them the vision of a superior kind of *outcome*. The failure to do that is, I believe, the most profound failure of professional education in our epoch.

A motivating vision must open people's eyes to educational possibilities beyond those currently imagined. That requires demonstrations. People are properly skeptical of high-sounding educational rhetoric. They need visible evidence of the possible. Moreover, we have already had enough visions of the school as an earthly paradise. The public wants to know what young people will carry with them when they leave that earthly paradise, and the widespread fear is that it will be functional illiteracy, mathematical incompetence, and scientific ignorance. An inspiring vision must not only allay those fears but hold out the promise of higher outcomes worthy of dedication.

Here is where the conceptual difficulties begin. Education is not going to produce some previously unheard of ability or trait of character. The English language contains several thousand words for human attributes, so whatever the educational outcome, it is almost sure to be something that has been recognized for ages and for which there is already a familiar label. But a new vision should give new meaning to that label, introduce a qualitatively higher standard. Let me try to explain that statement with an example from a different field. Art historians talk about the "Greek revolution" (Gombrich, 1960, pp. 99–125). For thousands of years sculptors had represented the human figure facing straight ahead, in a rigid pose, with stylized impersonal features. There were, however, noticeable variations in how lifelike (to modern eyes, at any rate) these stylized figures appear. You could construct a scale of "lifelikeness" and use it to rate these figures, to examine historical trends, regional differences, and the like. But if you then tried to apply that scale to the sculpture of Greece during its Classical and Alexandrian periods, you would find it didn't work. Everything would be piled up at one end of the scale. Yet there was tremendous change over that time as figures became increasingly fluid and natural, eventually acquiring distinctive human expressions. However, you could not capture what happened simply by extending the scale of lifelikeness. Gombrich attributed the visible changes in style to a change in conception of what a statue should be (a change in goals) and a shift from reliance on knowledge to reliance on observation (a shift in method). A *qualitatively* higher standard of lifelikeness would be a standard that was sensitive to the effects of these underlying changes.

A New Standard of Understanding

I believe that something comparable to the "Greek revolution" is beginning to appear in education. It is the emergence of a qualitatively

higher standard of understanding. As an educational goal understanding has been around for thousands of years. Students can be
and often have been rated on it. Using commonly observed variations, you could construct a scale of understanding for any item or
body of subject matter. The scale would range from utter
cluelessness at the low end to, let's say, the most convincing essay
examination papers you could turn up at the high end. What I am
suggesting is that we are beginning to see among students a sort of
understanding for which that kind of scale, even if stretched, will not
work. The old kind of scale, and the conception of understanding
that goes with it, is essentially a scale of conformity to some approved manifestation of understanding—usually a set of propositions. Call this the conformity criterion of understanding. The
conception of understanding I developed in chapter 4 does not exclude this criterion. If you understand something, this ought to be
reflected in congruence between your beliefs and those of acknowledged experts. But a conformity scale would be insufficient. It would
be like a scale for judging sculpture that only took account of conformity to the physical features of the model or person being represented. Greek sculpture would score high on such a scale, compared
with the sculpture of earlier civilizations, but the scale would be insensitive to most of what gives Greek sculpture its quality as art.
Similarly, a conformity scale of understanding would be insensitive
to most of what makes understanding a goal worthy of the fullest
commitment of people's intellectual resources and energy.

To bring this discussion closer to earth, let me introduce a couple
of examples. They are examples drawn from childhood, for it is easier to see what there is to understanding beyond conformity when
one looks at learners who are still a considerable distance away from
expertise. Both examples come from combined grade 5/6 classrooms, but otherwise the conditions are quite distinct: The first
comes from an inner-city classroom in Oakland, California; the second from a middle-class school in a medium-size city in Iowa. The
first comes out of the Fostering Communities of Learners project
(Brown & Campione, 1994); the second out of the CSILE/Knowledge
Building project (Scardamalia et al., 1994).

1. Students who were studying about AIDS came on the reassur-
ing information that AIDS cannot be transmitted by mosquitoes.
This struck them as implausible. If hypodermic needles are a major way the virus is transmitted, why wouldn't mosquitoes,
which in their view are flying needles, also transmit it? They called
a local AIDS hotline to pose the question and were eventually put
in touch with someone who explained to them that mosquitoes

transmit malaria because they become infected with it themselves, whereas the AIDS virus does not infect mosquitoes. Some
students were satisfied with this explanation but others saw that
it did not really answer their question. The hypodermic needle
doesn't get infected either. It transmits the AIDS virus just by the
blood that sticks to it, so why wouldn't the same be true with
mosquitoes? They pursued the question through library research
and asking other informed adults, but as far as I know they never
did get an explanation that satisfied them.

2. Students in the class were divided into teams to study different
biomes—deserts, tropical rain forests, the Arctic tundra. The Arctic
group became interested in the question of why trees don't grow
there. Their initial assumption was simply that trees would freeze,
but then one student questioned this explanation, pointing out that
trees survive in very cold weather. Maybe trees can't freeze. When
they learned about the permafrost, this suggested another explanation: If the earth a foot or two beneath the surface is permanently frozen, roots couldn't penetrate it and so the roots would be
too shallow to hold up a tree. But then the group studying tropical
rain forests reported that trees there had shallow roots. An expert
on the Arctic gave a talk at the school. His explanation for the absence of trees was lack of moisture. This explanation didn't satisfy
them either, because a check with the desert group yielded the information that trees did grow in some very dry places. Finally they
concluded that it must be a combination of factors.

I have intentionally chosen examples in which the quest for understanding did not culminate in anything that would score high on
conformity to established knowledge. Indeed, there was not much
culmination at all. In both cases the question motivating the inquiry
remained unanswered. For that reason, many educators would say
that the value was in the process rather than in the outcome—in
learning to pursue inquiry, to question authority, and so on. But to
treat these cases in that way is to reduce the students' inquiry to
mere exercise. That is the bind that folk theory of mind gets you into.
The value of instructional effort lies either in the resulting mental
content—which can be judged as to its correctness, completeness, or
utility—or in skills and attitudes. That is how it was handled in
Bloom's *Taxonomy* (1956; see chap. 4) and how it continues to be
treated in curriculum guidelines and test standards.

The unique value of the educational experiences represented in
these cases does not lie either in the explicit knowledge acquired (although that may have been considerable) or in the skills and attitudes that were developed (although these are not to be discounted

merely because they would be difficult to assess). Their unique value is in where they lead. The students in the first case had embarked on a path that could lead to a far deeper understanding than most people ever have of the nature of microbial diseases and the complex routes by which they can be communicated. In the second case, we see the beginnings of an understanding of how different environmental characteristics combine to determine whether a particular kind of flora can thrive in a particular environment. In important respects, I would claim, the students' understanding had already progressed beyond that of the average educated adult.

As it happens, I had wondered about mosquitoes and AIDS myself, but it never occurred to me to try to track down an explanation. As for the absence of trees in the Arctic, I had never thought about it. I guess I had implicitly accepted "It's too cold" as an explanation—this despite my having actually been in the Arctic and observed that at the northern limit the conifer forests do not just thin out and then disappear; rather, the trees get smaller until they are the size of Christmas trees—a fact that weighs heavily against the "It's too cold" theory, if I had thought about it. Thus, these examples impress me because the young students were investigating questions that are at my level, so to speak—as distinguished from the schoolbook questions one expects elementary school students to be investigating—and making more progress on them than I ever made or even thought of making.

The higher standard of understanding illustrated in these examples can be formulated like this: *Understanding is to be judged according to its ability to produce further understanding.* This is a qualitatively different standard from the familiar correspondence standards. It represents a dynamic rather than a static conception.[9]

WHAT WOULD IT TAKE TO MAKE TEACHING FOR UNDERSTANDING A REFORM GOAL?

There is a problem in getting *any* objective taken seriously in education. If you argue, as I have done, for the importance of knowledge and depth of understanding, the most common response of critics will not be to disagree but to point out that other things are important too. Then they will give voice to whatever is uppermost in their

---

[9]Dewey (1916) clearly had such a dynamic conception. He defined education as "that reconstruction or reorganization of experience which adds to the meaning of experience, and which increases ability to direct the course of subsequent experience" (p. 76). For him, this idea was part o the larger idea that education is growth. Unfortunately, it was a simplistic version of the larger idea that survived, and the idea that the main value of school learning lies in its enablement of further learning (p. 53) suffered neglect.

minds, be it numerical skills, media literacy, or spirituality. Of course many other things are important and of course everything is related, but the effect of this kind of criticism is to make everything matter less and to avoid any serious criticism of the ideas that were actually set forth. There is a time for talking about education in its fullness but the rest of the time it should be possible to focus on particular problems or objectives while tacitly conceiving of them within a larger picture, which is for the time being not brought into question. Why this should be so much more difficult in education than in most other domains I do not understand.[10] It may have partly to do with the complexity of the enterprise, but it also, I believe, bespeaks the inadequacy of the folk theories of knowledge and mind that frame the discourse.

At this writing, teaching for understanding is not high on reform agendas in North America. Skills are on top. But understanding was up there not long ago and it will be high again. Education focused on skills is inherently mediocre, and its ascendancy usually means public confidence in education has sunk so low that mediocre looks like a step up. Teaching for understanding cannot amount to much as a reform goal, however, if it is just another item on a list of standards. It has to be a goal that alters all the other instructional goals. For that to happen, three things are required:

1. People have to understand what it means.
2. They have to realize why it is important.
3. They have to realize that teaching for understanding embraces a host of unsolved problems.

The last point might seem dispensable or perhaps even countervailing, but I shall argue that, unless the unsolved problems are recognized, teaching for understanding will remain just another slogan to be tossed about during ideological debates, while the pedagogical pendulum continues to swing.

In the previous chapter I discussed why teaching for understanding is an elusive goal for educators. The ordinary reductive moves—reducing goals to activities, subject matter, or self-expression—eliminate the understanding from teaching for understanding. More generally, teaching for understanding is undermined by folk concep-

---

[10]Educational discourse is pervaded by a mistrust of other people's motives, which makes for a paranoia that every once in a while bursts out, as it has among the antiphonics people. The rest of the time it is kept in abeyance by continual manifestations of good intentions. This, however, can lead to hypocrisy, which breeds further suspicion, and so on. Beyond that, however, it further defeats efforts to get on with solving an educational problem.

tions of knowledge. It is thought of as something in the mind, which right away makes it intangible and inaccessible. So we see the goal of understanding replaced by the goal of producing demonstrations of understanding (Bloom, 1956; Perkins, 1992). The criterion becomes correspondence between what the learner demonstrates and what an expert demonstrates. This is reasonable as far as it goes, but it is not a very elevating conception. But how to elevate it? The answer, to liberal-minded educators, is to replace product with process—to espouse "constructivism," "social construction of knowledge," "inquiry," "critical thinking," and other noble processes. That is but another road to reductionism, however, to activities that have lost contact with their goals. And it is also the road to loss of support from a public that wants results, not faddish-sounding processes.

As I argued in chapter 4, the way to make sense of understanding as an educational objective is to conceive of it dynamically and relationally. To understand something is to have an intelligent relationship to it. The main value of scientific and scholarly understanding is that *understanding one thing increases your capacity to understand other things.* That is its practical value, not only for pursuing further education but also for achieving expertise in any knowledge-based occupation.

If this dynamic conception of understanding is accepted, however, it demands that instructional reform be approached at a deeper level than in the past. Evaluation needs to be concerned with the trajectory students are on—where they are going in their efforts to understand the world—rather than only with what they have managed to understand so far. We have to stop thinking of "constructivism" as a pedagogical method of questionable virtue and start thinking of it as something that students should come to adopt as a way of life. We should be concerned about the students who do not adopt it, no matter how good their present performance may be, because they are disqualifying themselves for participation in a knowledge society.

THE MYTH THAT DEFEATS REFORM

To many skeptics, sympathetic as well as unsympathetic, what I have been saying about a higher standard of understanding will sound like just more inflated educational rhetoric. They will want to know what basis there is for believing that the instances I have narrated can be replicated on any considerable scale and that they will have a cumulative effect. Some, less astute, will want to know how "this approach" ensures that graduates will be literate and mathematically competent—not recognizing that at this point I haven't advocated any approach but have only indicated something to work toward. And then there are those, perhaps not great in numbers but enormously influential within educational organizations, who will reject what I have presented because of their gut feeling that it is overly intellectual, scientistic, Eurocentric, and in some undefined way racist and sexist.

Whether these objections have merit and how they might be answered are, of course, important questions. But taken together they suggest a matter of more profound importance. It is the great difficulty—perhaps the impossibility—of having any worthwhile discussion about educational goals. Across ideological boundaries discussion about goals is quickly overwhelmed by animosity. Yet it is only at the political extremes that we find groups advocating goals that others reject. Across a very wide ideological range, everyone wants students to be both proficient in basic skills and able to think. They want students to have factual knowledge as well as understanding. They want economically useful learning and they want moral and cultural values (and there is not much disagreement about what those values should be). The animosity arises because motives are mistrusted and because goals cannot be separated from methods. It does no good for A and B to agree that children need to become fluent readers if A wants to teach phonics and B considers phonics to be a form of violence against children.[11]

But discussion of goals is difficult even among people who agree enough that they should be able to disagree constructively. Such an occasion was a conference on the future of liberal education (Smith, in press). We (I was one of the organizers of the conference) restricted the participants to those who could be expected to agree that a liberal education is a good thing. Within this large category, however, we invited participants with interestingly different viewpoints on the matter—philosophers, economists, and educationists of different persuasions. The result was indeed an interesting conference, but the discussion never got as far as what you could call constructive disagreement. Instead, all the effort went into clearing up misunderstandings, questioning one another's use of terms, denying supposed disagreements, and sometimes denying supposed agreements. Some discussions continued after the conference and a year later were just beginning to bear fruit.

Why is it so difficult? Why is it so much harder for a school system to discuss and arrive at a set of realistic and motivating goals than it is for an information technology (IT) company, for instance? Well, interestingly, IT companies sometimes also lose hold on reality when

---

[11]I'm not being fanciful. This very charge was made by one of the leading spokesmen for whole language in an e-mail discussion group.

they tangle with educational goals. In the middle 1990s, a major IT company announced it was going to shift from marketing educational software to marketing educational "solutions." Having some acquaintance with the educational arm of that company, I wondered where these "solutions" were supposed to come from. Where was the educational problem-solving capacity? The answer it seems, is that there wasn't any. The bold venture quickly faded away. No company would announce they were getting into the genetic engineering business or the machine translation business unless they were sure they had the capacity to do it or knew how to acquire it. The company's marketing people, I suspect, had simply adopted a myth that pervades the whole education system. It is the myth of unlimited problem-solving capacity. Adopt any educational goal and means can be found to achieve it. All it takes is marshalling the resources already available in the system.

To John Dewey (1916) means and ends were inseparable. An aim was the "foreseen end" of an activity (p. 106). He spoke of "having a mind" to do something—a quaint expression that he used to convey a quite modern notion:

> To have a mind to do a thing is to foresee a future possibility; it is to have a plan for its accomplishment; it is to note the means which make the plan capable of execution and the obstructions in the way—or, if it is really a *mind* to do the thing and not a vague aspiration—it is to have a plan which takes account of resources and difficulties. (p. 103)

Yet Dewey seems not to have reckoned with education's incapacity for this kind of foresight and planning. A clue to why he overlooked it comes from his comparison of education to farming:

> The educator, like the farmer, has certain things to do, certain resources with which to do, and certain obstacles with which to contend. The conditions with which the farmer deals, whether as obstacles or resources, have their own structure and operation independently of any purpose of his. Seeds sprout, rain falls, the sun shines, insects devour, blight comes, the seasons change. His aim is simply to utilize these various conditions; to make his activities and energies work together, instead of against one another. It would be absurd if the farmer set up a purpose of farming, without any reference to these conditions of soil, climate, characteristic of plant growth, etc. (pp. 106–107)

Farming, at the time Dewey wrote, was a traditional craft, much as teaching still is. The goals Dewey imagined for the farmer were formed within the scope of that traditional craft and attaining them required no advances in it. They were to plant certain crops that the farmer already knew how to plant, and to cultivate and harvest them, taking into account the variables the farmer already knew how to take into account. That seems to be how he saw teaching as well, and it is how teachers quite reasonably see it on a day-to-day basis. They are to teach certain things they know how to teach, taking into account the variables they already know how to take into account.

Although Dewey (1929) did acknowledge a role for research in shaping educational practice, he seemed to have little sense of large, unsolved problems, of worthy educational goals that we don't know how to achieve and that call for advances in knowledge and invention. Instead, he too seems to have accepted the myth of unlimited problem-solving capacity, so that all that was required for education to advance was clear thinking, resolve, and the abundant resources of experience. In the decades of dispute that Dewey's own ideas helped ignite, all sides have tacitly accepted the myth, as do most reformers of the present day. In the opening chapter of this book I asserted that education is stuck. This myth is what it is stuck on.

Here is the worst of it: The belief that the necessary knowledge is already in hand not only inhibits the search for means, it undermines efforts to construct a new vision. For, as the Latin proverb says, we cannot desire what we do not know. It takes advances in knowledge to create new visions of what is educationally possible.

BEYOND "EXCELLENCE"

When U. S. President George Bush, in 1989, vowed that his nation should be first in the world in science and mathematics achievement by the year 2000, serious educators across the land groaned. It was obvious that it couldn't be done, but that was not the cause for dismay. The dismay was over what would happen to education as a result of pursuing a goal that was not only impossible but retrograde. Instructional researchers in science and mathematics felt at the time that breakthroughs were imminent. The previous decade of research had probably yielded more insight into the difficulties of learning school subject matter and academic skills than all preceding decades together. Instructional experiments were beginning to show promise of student learning of a quality not previously imagined. Now all of that stood to be forgotten in the rush to raise scores on tests—tests that had been created long before any of the knowledge advances that were raising new hopes.

I happened to be in Singapore, meeting with educationists, when word came that Singapore had scored first in the world on the computational part of the Third International Mathematics Study. People were naturally elated, but they scarcely missed a step in their pursuit of what they saw as the next objective, which was to improve mathematical problem solving and invention. Their vision was not borne aloft by romantic fluff but by the economic drive for which that small nation is famous. A front-page newspaper headline appearing in the same week gave the flavor of it:

> **Can Singapore Compete with Bill Gates?**

The article's reasoning was straightforward. Singapore has a population of a few million. Microsoft can select talent from a pool a hundred times larger. How, then, can Singapore hope to compete in an industry based on technically sophisticated inventive and design talent? Answer: Liberalize immigration and do a much better job of developing talent. There was no suggestion that being first in the world in arithmetic skills was even relevant to the problem.

If the current back-to-basics reforms in the United States work, it is just possible that mathematics test scores will in a decade or so be up to where Singapore's were in 1996. But where will Singapore be then—or any of the other high-scoring countries, almost all of which are seriously pursuing higher level goals? I'm not sure. The road to thinking skills and creativity is lined with quacks. Some countries are liable to fall victim to quackery and may even lose ground as a result, but I expect others will not. The Dutch, for instance, not only score well now in mathematics but they seem to have better quack detectors than North Americans do.

International economic competitiveness is not an exalted goal, of course, but it is a notch up from winning a test score race. A still higher notch is that of producing the kinds of citizens who can thrive in and contribute variously to a knowledge society. For strategic purposes it is well to think of these as hierarchically ordered rather than as competing goals. That is, the goal of producing economically competitive talent ought to include the goal of raising conventional achievement test scores. The goal of full citizenship in a knowledge society ought to include development of economically competitive talent. And if a still higher goal is to be proposed, it should include all of those. This is strategically if not logically necessary, because support quickly evaporates when people think they have to give up their sensible goals to adopt your riskier ones. Educational innovators would prefer not to be bothered with goals of a lower order than those they intend to reach, and some of the effort that may have to go into raising conventional tests scores is effort that, in a more ideal world, could better be spent elsewhere. But innovators who want to be taken seriously realize that the admission ticket for being taken seriously is evidence that their innovation satisfies other people's goals as well as the goals they are trying to get people to adopt. Easier said than done? Of course, but no one has suggested that instructional reform is easy.

What are these higher level goals, and how can the sights of educational reform be raised to target them? The metaphor I have just used suggests a major conceptual problem to be overcome. As soon as you move to goals above the level of test scores or specifiable performances, the target-shooting metaphor no longer works. You must conjure up a state of things, a network of conditions that must be met together rather than as separate targets. (This does not mean, of course, that they cannot be reached by stages, only that the stages themselves are complex.) All sorts of organizations must find ways to pursue complex goals. The top-level goal of a for-profit company might take the form of a clear target, such as achieving a certain level of return on investment, but if the company determines that achieving this goal entails providing a superior quality of service, they face a problem not much different from that of a school system that determines its goal is to provide a superior quality of education. Each must craft an image of something beyond what presently exists but that looks achievable. Creativity is required, not only to achieve the goal but to imagine it in a sufficiently realistic way that it can be pursued.

An educational vision, I have been insisting, must offer an image of an outcome, not of a process. It is time now to look more closely at this stricture. When innovators move beyond test scores and other immediate indicators of achievement, they find themselves issuing rather long-term promissory notes for future benefits to the learner and to society. Unless they are among the few who manage to achieve celebrity status, they are likely to find those notes rejected: no credit rating, no collateral. As observed in chapter 7, creditable ideas about what should be done now to prepare students for the uncertain future are in short supply. Back-to-basics, liberal education, and developmentalism offer at most slightly renovated versions of their traditional answers. Futurists generally offer nothing of substance. The people attached to these schools of thought are not fools, they are just faced with a problem that is very difficult.

To keep matters in perspective, it is important to realize that test scores are promissory notes, too, when they are used to judge the worth of an educational program. They require us to believe that if school A's students score higher than those of school B, then school A's graduates will do better in the future than those of School B on worthy criteria of membership in society.[23] These promissory notes have been in circulation long enough that they have come to be accepted as legal tender, but that does not necessarily mean there is anything behind them. There is ample evidence, as one might expect, that reading test scores have wide-ranging predictive value, much like the IQ, with which they are closely associated. But if we move from there to more specialized kinds of achievement, predictive validity trails off. At the extreme, we have no evidence at all that a program that increases scores on thinking skills or creativity tests has any effect on performance in later life.[13]

Futurists stir our imaginations by telling us that the future is going to be qualitatively different from the past. Therefore, the futuristic reasoning goes, education must produce a new kind of educated person. This is an exciting notion, but one that quickly trails off into verbalism and technohype. I would like to see educational reform take on some of this excitement, without the verbalism and hype. We must dismiss suggestions that surfing the Internet or processing hypertext requires a differently functioning brain. Previous discussion has suggested two important constraints that a realistic futurism must honor:

1. New human traits are unlikely to emerge. Whatever may be posited as desirable characteristics for tomorrow's citizen, they are likely to have been recognized as desirable for centuries and already to figure in lists of educational objectives. If that is true, reformers can forget about inventing new objectives and must craft a new vision out of familiar objectives.

2. Whatever new or elevated vision may be pursued, it must be translatable into objectives for the here and now. Achievement test scores will continue to hold sway unless they can be replaced by other immediate indicators of effectiveness.

These constraints may at first seem to rule out everything new and exciting, but as I tried to show earlier, they do allow one possibility. It is the possibility of *qualitatively* higher standards—that is, standards that are not merely an extension of current metrics but that introduce

---

[12]That prediction may be self-fulfilling, of course, if universities and employers believe it and award opportunities on the basis of it. All that does in the present context, however, is add further obstacles to the selling of a new educational vision.

[13]The same, actually, can be said about score increases on any mental test. The fact that reading test scores correlate with future academic performance does not mean that doing something to raise reading test scores will have a corresponding effect on future academic performance. That is a separate empirical issue and one that has hardly been researched at all.

a new and higher realization of things educators have been trying to accomplish right along. The prototype for introduction of a qualitatively higher standard was the so-called "Greek revolution" in sculpture. The educational examples I gave of a qualitatively higher standard of understanding may seem trivial by comparison, but I would not reject the possibility that they mark the beginnings of another Greek revolution. Early Greek sculpture does not look dramatically different from its predecessors, either, except that we can now see where it was starting to head.

Reading reform has of late been almost exclusively concerned with bringing poor readers up to an average level.[14] This is reform aimed at a *quantitatively* higher standard, albeit an extremely important one. But for education as a whole, we should be considering the possibility of a *qualitatively* higher standard of reading. Assuming the world's knowledge keeps increasing not only in quantity but in level of complexity, competent citizens of the future will need to be able to read and understand harder stuff. A competitive edge will be gained by those who can get it right the first time and not require cycles of e-mail messages and phone calls before their initial misreadings are straightened out. (When researchers talk about reading comprehension, they mean comprehending the kinds of discourse that ordinarily come in written form; that these may be received aurally rather than visually is, except for dyslexics, largely irrelevant.)

By a complementary argument, people in a knowledge-based society will have more complex things to communicate and therefore will need a qualitatively higher level of writing or text-composing ability. More communication will be at a distance and so will require more of the literary skill of putting necessary context into the text (Olson, 1996). People whose communication skills depend overly much on pointing will be at a disadvantage.

Qualitatively higher standards of understanding, reading, and writing are so closely tied together that it is hard to imagine getting very far with one without also attending to the others. Reading is the primary means of access to the conceptual tools, facts, and ideas necessary for sophisticated understanding; writing, when carried out in a knowledge-transforming way, is a powerful means of developing understanding (Scardamalia & Bereiter, 1985, 1991).

I am speaking very broadly here. If you look into the cognitive research in any subject area you will see qualitatively higher standards taking shape. Some of the ideas come from studying experts in the

---

[14]*Whose* average is an issue in this context. One highly touted approach, Reading Recovery, is aimed at bringing the poorest readers up to the average of their class. But this typically means bringing them up to the average of a class that is itself markedly below the national average.

disciplines. Others come from studying students who show qualitatively advanced abilities and knowledge. Still others come from educational experiments that yield results beyond the kind anticipated. The last are especially important, because they show that qualitatively higher outcomes can be produced, that they are not just lucky accidents of birth and experience. Taken together, these ideas represent a new kind of educated person. The characteristics of such a person are the same ones that have been honored throughout modern times and many of them go farther back than that. What is new is a quality of understanding; a quality of intellectual skills; and a quality of interest, sensitivity, and appreciation that have heretofore been found only in exceptional people but that may now become expected results of regular education.

This, however, is a promissory note backed by only scattered experiments of limited scope. How could one ever hope to get reformers to honor it? There have to be convincing demonstrations. There have to be evaluations that assure people conventional standards of achievement are not being sacrificed in pursuit of qualitatively different goals. But demonstrations can only be convincing if people understand what you are demonstrating, and that is where the conceptual limitations I have been discussing become crucial. People have to understand knowledge as more than stuff in people's heads. They need a conception of what it is to create and work with knowledge. They need to believe that the hidden iceberg of personal knowledge is as important and much larger than the two peaks of it that show. They need to judge educational reforms according to what they do for the whole iceberg.

STRATEGY: REFORMING THE REFORMERS

Are we not, then, in an impossible bind—where reformers cannot adopt a qualitatively higher goal until they have seen it being achieved and they cannot see it unless they understand it and they cannot understand it unless they see it? Broadly speaking, yes. But there are some breaks in the vicious circle. The breaks are of recent origin. They have come about because of things going on outside education, especially the rise of knowledge-based industries and of occupations devoted to knowledge work, and the spread of ideas such as intellectual property, knowledge management, and knowledge evolution. More and more people are acquiring, through their work, concepts that should help them grasp a new educational vision, if someone can help them make the connection.

At one time our research funding required that we attend a yearly technology fair in Silicon Valley and show off our accomplishments to a flock of engineers. The software we had to demonstrate at that time—CSILE (Scardamalia, Bereiter, McLean, Swallow, & Woodruff, 1989)—was not of a kind to impress techies. It didn't do much. All that made it interesting was what kids did with it. So instead of showing off the technology, we showed videos and transcripts of kids working on problems such as why humans can talk but chimpanzees can't or what happens in an asthma attack. Within minutes the engineers quit acting like engineers and started acting like parents. Their overwhelming reaction was that they wanted this for their own children. They recognized that they had never done anything comparable to that in fifth or sixth grade, and that kids who could do it were at a tremendous advantage over those who were memorizing facts or piddling away the hours on multimedia "projects."

These were not average parents, of course. Two things set them apart. First, they appeared to be little concerned about achievement test scores. If there was a competitive slant to their interest, I would guess it was toward how their children might gain an edge over other high-achieving kids—and we were showing them what that edge could be. Second, they were themselves employed in the creation of knowledge and so were able to recognize it when they saw it and to appreciate its significance. Yet there is no reason to suppose they were especially sophisticated in matters of education. They merely had a better idea of what counts in the modern world.

The lesson I draw from this experience is that if a higher level of reform is to have a chance, it must build a consituency among people like those Silicon Valley engineers—people who are already part of a knowledge-building culture and who have a sense of what it takes to belong. This does not automatically make them favorable to knowledge building in schools. Back-to-basics reformers are often recruited from the same population, and many others are romantic believers in the magic of the Internet and multimedia. All I am saying is that they have many of the conceptual resources needed to understand. They are not stuck in the vicious circle and so they may be educable.

To build a power base among such an elite, however, requires a shifting of priorities. Educational reform, especially in the United States, is overwhelmingly concerned with improving education for the most disadvantaged. This has a great deal of political will behind it. It appeals both to the liberal interest in welfare and equality and to the conservative interest in productivity and self-sufficiency. Although the reasons for this emphasis may be compelling, they introduce a bias into educational policymaking that ultimately works against even the people it is most intended to help.

Educational policymaking typically consists of people with university degrees and secure economic positions deciding what is best for children whose prospects are not of the brightest. In this situation, proposals such as teaching for understanding are unlikely to get far. They will be seen as failing to address the main problems and likely not to work anyway. There will instead be a bias toward quantitative improvement on low-order objectives. This does not mean the policies these people might devise for their own children would be much different or that a more representative group of policymakers would arrive at more enlightened policies. The crack in the vicious circle is very small indeed. All it amounts to this: People are more educable when they are thinking about educating their own children than when they are thinking about educating someone else's. Not because of their emotional involvement; that may work against reason. They are more educable because they can connect their own experience to that of the students who are the targets of their policies. If you can show knowledge workers a much closer connection than they had imagined between things going on in school and what goes on in their professional lives, they may become receptive to a whole new range of possibilities for education. The place to start, I am suggesting, is by getting reformers to want something different for their own children. After that you can try to show them that less advantaged children can have it too.

Sometimes it is possible to merge these two steps into one. In the Jasper Project at Vanderbilt University, they have an ingenious way of presenting their educational approach to business people. "Jaspers" are complex realistic problems conveyed through professionally produced video dramas. Representative Jaspers are one having to do with the logistics of setting up a dunking tank for a school money-raising event and another having to do with the problem of flying a wounded eagle out of a distant field. The central problem may require formulating and solving a score of mathematical subproblems. The Jaspers are aimed at middle school students, who work on them in small groups. The idea is to get students to use mathematics the way it is used in real life, where the needed information is embedded in the environment and in the flow of events rather than being neatly set out as it is in traditional word problems. To give adults a feel for this approach to mathematics learning, the presenters show them a Jasper video and then divide them into small groups and set them to work trying to solve the problem. After the adults have worked at the problem long enough to have run into difficulties, the presenters announce they are bringing in consultants to help out. On signal, a line of sixth-graders, with visible minorities well represented, file into the room, causing an outburst of laughter. The young students fan out to the working groups and proceed to help them move ahead on the problem. It is easy to see why such a demonstration has impact. Here are the kinds of adults who are busy across the land agitating for higher standards in mathematics and a return to the basics, encountering a mathematics problem that is too hard for them now, that would have been unthinkable for them when they were in grade school, and they may well suspect is also beyond the capabilities of their own children. Then suddenly they find themselves being coached by students for whom this kind of problem is familiar fare—students, moreover, who look like the ones they have assumed to be in need of emergency repairs. How can they not believe they have been missing something?

The crucial first step, as illustrated in both the Jasper example and the Silicon Valley technology fair example, is to get influential adults to see themselves, their own work, and their own aspirations and those they have for their children as part of the educational reform picture. This is just a first step, but for it to amount to more than a momentary glimmer, education and knowledge work have to be brought into the same conceptual space, and that is a big order. As it is now, education talk has almost no relation to real-world knowledge talk. Some of the same words are used, but the contexts are perceived so differently that there is little common meaning, as shown in Table 12.1.

The discrepancies obviously are not just semantic. What normally goes on in schools is very different from what goes on in knowledge-based enterprises and no fiddling with the vocabulary is going to bring them any closer. But what I have been arguing in recent chapters is that they could be much closer. Schools could be places where knowledge is a public product and not just something in students' minds; where its production is a collective, collaborative effort and the focus of students' individual efforts is on the success of this joint enterprise; where what is learned is put to use in the further creation of knowledge; and where the problems to be solved are problems in the advancement of knowledge. Much of the more innovative educational research is heading in that direction. But how you talk about things, the concepts you bring to bear, do make a difference. Talk about education tends to sound like the right-hand column no matter who does it. This not only makes it difficult for people outside education to connect it with their own

TABLE 12.1
Same Words, Different Meanings

Word	What It Means in Knowledge-Based Enterprises	What It Means in Schools
Knowledge building	Producing intellectual property	Learning by doing
Achievement	Recognized contributions to the success of the enterprise	Test scores; grades
Understanding	Knowing the nonobvious stuff—the inner workings	Having beliefs that correspond to those of experts; being able to explain
Creativity	Innovative design and strategizing	Uninhibited self-expression
Problem solving	Figuring out ways to achieve goals when off-the-shelf ways won't do	Solving word problems in which all the necessary information is provided
Cooperative work	Collaborative knowledge building	Collaboration on seatwork or in producing reports, displays, presentations, and so on
Science	What you need to know to understand the technology or the causes of many problems	A body of knowledge about physical and biological things; what scientists believe about these things; research methods
Mathematics	Conceptual tools needed in many kinds of technical work	Procedures for solving numerical problems
Research	Finding out things you need to know to solve a problem or produce a result	Exercising research methods; collecting material for a report; pursuing curiosity

work, it impedes the movement of education toward real knowledge building.

Note that I am not saying business people have the answers and educators should learn from them. The business literature on knowledge is just as primitive as the educational literature and equally bound to folk theory. It is just that the nature of their work has led people in knowledge-based enterprises to adopt a more pragmatic approach to knowledge, less encumbered by ritual and fetishism.[15] Conceptual advancement is needed on both fronts. It ought to go on in concert. This book, although tilted heavily toward education, is really about conceptual problems that are common to knowledge businesses and education. Getting people who are already at home in knowledge-producing enterprises to see schools as sharing the same problem space with them would be an enormous step in moving public thinking toward a higher level of educational objectives and this in turn could do much to draw the thinking of educators in that direction as well.

Along with the talk there have to be demonstrations. People have to see instances of real knowledge building going on in schools. In the work that we have been doing on CSILE, we have produced a lot of quantitative evidence of educational gains (Scardamalia et al., 1992) and this has been important for credibility, but by far the most influential results come from simply having young students walk viewers or visitors through the Knowledge Forum® database they and their classmates have constructed, explaining what they have accomplished. One grainy video alone has been worth millions to us in research support. On it, an 11-year-old boy takes you through his investigation of why chimpanzees can't speak. He shows hand-drawn computer graphics comparing the oral cavities and the vocal aparatus of chimps and humans, explaining the critical differences, and then does the same with diagrams of their brains, wrapping up his tour with, "And that's why we can talk and chimpanzees can't." People's jaws drop. They have never seen anything like it. Yet it is obvious that the boy got his information from books, that the neuroscience is simplistic, that the explanation leaves many questions unanswered. And it is also obvious that this is not your average 11-year-old. He is unusually articulate and serious minded. So what is impressive about it as an educational demonstration?

Several qualifications are in order before I try to explain. To be *seriously* impressed—that is, impressed enough to do something—people

---

[15]As for imitating business practices, one hesitates to generalize. There are surely "best practices" here and there that schools could adapt to their needs, but without better conceptual equipment there is no way to recognize them or to do more than imitate surface features.

need to be assured that what they saw on the video was not a one-of-a-kind event. They need to see a whole room full of students doing comparable things. And not everyone is impressed even then, or they are impressed for the wrong reasons. We have had educational technology supervisors who ignore what the students are doing, look at the software, sniff, "It's just a database," or "It's just a bulletin board," and go tell their bosses to forget about it. (This is a version of the "We already do that" syndrome.) And then there are the educators who see it only as a case in support of their pet idea, be it constructivism, project-based learning, or child-centered education. (Yet another version of "We already do that.") That leaves, however, a significant number of people who really seem to get it, and so the question is, what do they get?

A revealing remark came from a visitor who was a highly placed civil servant with the job of promoting knowledge-based industries. After spending an hour in a CSILE classroom, he said, "I think I have seen my first learning organization." We have seen companies where they thought that being a learning organization meant having a company-run school for training employees. If that is what learning organization means, all schools are learning organizations and the visitor's remark was absurd. In business literature, the term is used in different ways by different writers and so its meaning in common usage is far from clear. Business literature relies heavily on examples rather than on definitions, but the examples used to convey the idea of a learning organization range over practically everything that could be considered a smart personnel policy or way of making the most of employee's brain power. What holds the examples together is some vague idea of the pervasiveness and value of knowledge in an organization and the importance of nurturing it. As I argued in chapter 6, I don't think you can get much farther than that unless you trade in folk theory for a better epistemology and theory of mind.

But in the absence of clearer definitions, it helps to have cleaner examples. The CSILE classroom offered one. There wasn't any product or service going out into the world. Yet something was being produced, and about the only thing you could call it was knowledge. What was it made from? Other knowledge—mostly knowledge brought in from the outer world and processed into something of more local value. What was the product good for? For the production of more knowledge. Thus, in the classroom you had a model of a learning organization or, as we would prefer, a knowledge-building organization in relatively pure form, unobscured by the many other functions of a money-making business. I don't suggest that our visitor saw it in just that way. I don't think you can see it that way until you have absorbed the idea of conceptual artifacts. But his experience had sharpened his impressionistic knowledge enough that in some less articulated way he knew what he was looking for and recognized it when he saw it.

There are other approaches to knowledge building in schools that may be as effective or more effective than the CSILE/Knowledge Forum approach in what they are trying to do. Typically, they are less clean as examples because they either look more like conventional schooling—there is a teacher up front leading a discussion, for instance—or there is some tangible project—such as producing a multimedia document—that capture's the observer's attention. But to the extent that schools can provide the public with examples of what it means to produce and work with knowledge, they connect to concerns of the working world at a higher level than before.

Schools presently connect to the concerns of the working world at a very low level. The concerns are over why Johnny can't read or calculate or find Rome on the map. Those are legitimate concerns and they need to be addressed. But if the connection is only at this low level and everything beyond it is hand waving about higher order thinking skills and lifelong love of learning, we can expect a continuation of low-level reforms. To connect at a higher level, people in knowledge-based organizations need to see the work that goes on in schools as similar, at a reasonable level of abstraction, to the work that goes on in their organization. Once they see it that way, they can not only be receptive to a qualitatively higher level of educational goals, they may even begin to understand their own work better. But all of this presupposes a conceptual framework for knowledge building and learning that enables both business people and educators to think more penetratingly and constructively about what they are doing. That is the transformation that will make it possible to reform educational reform.

CONCLUSION

In broadest terms, the problem as I have tried to formulate it in this book is to get educators and others out of the two-dimensional world of folk theory and into a three-dimensional world in which it is possible to do fuller justice to the role of knowledge in a knowledge society. There is no way this can happen overnight. The left–right swings of educational reform and counterreform are likely to continue for years. But if Peter Drucker was right that education will be the most important factor in a nation's prosperity in the 21st century, the future belongs to that society that can fasten onto and achieve qualitatively higher standards. The successful society will steer past back-to-basics movements and the periodic revivals of child-centered education. It will try to steer education to the same place it is trying to steer itself.

The problem is that, in whatever sense a society may be said to know or intend, society does not know where it is trying to steer itself. The envisioned knowledge society that Drucker and many others are now talking about is not a place where any of us have been. We may have experienced intimations of it on a small scale, in our own families or in groups we have worked with, but we have not seen it on an institutional scale. We can make visionary statements, but we cannot say with confidence that any particular reform is a step in their direction.

Schools will continue. Will they continue to be the battleground of old pedagogies or will they become Internet cafes? If those are the only choices, it is a safe bet they will continue to be battlegrounds. There is a third possibility, however, and that is that they become laboratories for testing designs for a knowledge society. Schools have many limitations but for this third possibility many of those limitations are advantages. Schools are places where knowledge creation can go on, but where it does not have to be market driven or competitive. That has been the virtue of research universities, and they continue to demonstrate its value, despite alarming intrusions of the marketplace. But knowledge creation in universities is the work of a minority, and most of it takes place out of eyeshot of the undergraduates, who go about their business much as they did in centuries before the research university was invented. Knowledge creation that goes on *within* the educational process is a different matter, and although it is possible in undergraduate university programs, it is easiest to implement in schools.

Knowledge creation in schools is the creation of knowledge by students for their own use. It is thus like subsistence farming.[16] The school is like an agricultural village. Unlike knowledge-creating companies, its members are not selected because of their skills. They belong because of where they live. Thus, the school is more a miniature society than a miniature enterprise, and accordingly it has the potential to be a model for a knowledge society rather than only a model for knowledge-creating organizations within some perhaps quite different kind of society. If a school is to be a humane and successful knowledge society, everybody in it must have a part and ev-

---

[16]The analogy can be carried further. To the extent that knowledge creatd in schools has value beyond the classroom where it is created, it enters into a barter economy. No one is likely to pay money for it, but it may be exchanged with other classrooms or with other social groups such as museum curators or teacher trainees or more advanced students, who find value in it for their own purposes and who have knowledge of their own to trade (Scardamalia & Bereiter, 1996b).

eryone must find it meaningful and rewarding. A vast range of talents and temperaments must be accommodated. And the knowledge that is produced must be good knowledge. It must be effective in producing more knowledge and it must be worth students' carrying with them when they leave school. Transforming schools in this way presents big and mostly unsolved problems, but they are problems society as a whole must solve if the Knowledge Age is to be a good age for humanity. Schools will have to tackle them too, sooner or later. I am suggesting they do it sooner, thus in certain ways leading social change rather than following in its wake.

For any of this to make sense, however, people have to be able to see knowledge creation by students as genuine productive work, not fundamentally different in kind from the knowledge-creating work that goes on out in the world where people produce knowledge of various kinds for a living. They must not confuse the work of producing knowledge with the learning that inevitably accompanies it or with the media objects and performances that may grow out of it. Such confusion exists to some extent in the world at large, but in education it is endemic. The result is to undermine any effort to make the classroom into a genuine rather than a pretend knowledge-creating community and to give it a role in the functioning of a knowledge society beyond that of merely furnishing students with knowledge and skills that may be of use in the future.

The main point of this closing chapter has been to elaborate on the idea of a qualitatively higher standard of educational outcome. *Quantitatively* higher standards are easy to understand. Simply take the scales by which we currently measure educational results and point somewhere higher up than the current level. *Qualitatively* higher standards require that you imagine a different kind of outcome. You need a different conception of what it means to be a good reader or writer, of what it means to understand a scientific theory, a historical event, or a poem. Folk theory of knowledge and mind fails at this point. Conventional standards are grounded in the folk conception of the mind as a container and in commonsense notions of skill. Raising standards means demanding more items in the mental container and moving the bar a notch higher in tests of skill. A notion like *deeper understanding*, which implies a qualitative shift, becomes either an empty slogan or it gets translated into tests of skill.

Envisioning qualitatively higher standards does not require exceptional imagination. We can point to people who are exemplars of superior kinds of reading and writing ability, of scientific, historical, or literary understanding. What we need are conceptual tools for translating exemplars into goals and goals into pedagogy. The two-dimensional world of folk theory and folk pedagogy does not provide the tools or the space in which to use them. We need, I have argued, a third dimension that allows conceptual artifacts to be distinguished both from the mental states of the people who create or deal with them and from the physical and social world to which these conceptual artifacts relate. Qualitatively higher standards of cognitive skill imply skills in working with conceptual artifacts. Qualitatively higher standards of understanding imply qualitatively different relationships between the knower and conceptual artifacts.

There are plenty of educational problems that can be recognized with our old folk theoretic conceptual equipment, and available knowledge sometimes suggests a solution. But, as we are seeing in the case of reading reform, the equipment is so crude that reformers tend to get it wrong, can't distinguish a solution from a subterfuge, and the counterreformers get it wrong as well. And so we get pendulum swings instead of progress. The society that moves ahead will not be one that fixes the pendulum at one position or another. It will be a society in which there is enough conceptual change that something begins to happen that has not been seen before: the disciplined production of new educational ideas.

Appendix

Conceptual Artifacts: Theoretical Issues

Philosophers have long struggled with the problem of how to characterize a kind of knowledge that is, so to speak, "out there," removed from individual minds and particular contexts. Plato's effort in this vein is the most famous but it is quite tangential to our present concerns. Plato posited a realm of pure ideas separate from human knowledge. Human knowledge represents our imperfect though improvable grasp of those pure ideas. This line of thought was refined by Bolzano (1972) in his conception of "propositions in themselves," a domain that consists not only of all the propositions that have been uttered but of all the propositions, true and false, that might ever be uttered. That idea has been further refined by Erich Reck (in press) into the notion of "conceptual possibilities." Actual human thought, in this view, attends to or develops or comes to believe in certain conceptual possibilities, which then form part of human knowledge. Reck 's formulation comes closer to what I believe we are looking for as a view of knowledge for the Knowledge Age. It is a view of knowledge as the active realization of certain possibilities inherent in the way the world is.

One reason none of these formulations quite does the job, however, is that they were not created with practical purposes in mind. They were created to deal with traditional epistemological issues, in particular, the issue of whether a proposition can be true or false irrespective of what people happen to think. Common sense would say yes, but it has proved difficult to mount a coherent argument to that effect. These postulations of knowledge existing independent of people's minds are all parts of efforts to do so. Interesting as the issue may be, it does not need to be decided for present purposes. We are not trying to establish what knowledge *really* is. Knowledge, like mind, can be pretty much what we choose to make it. We can tolerate some logical incoherence, uncertain boundaries, incompleteness, provided we are able to get on better with our work.

Although Karl Popper, with his idea of World 3, is generally placed by philosophers in a direct line of descent from Plato through Bolzano and Frege, his idea is fundamentally different and different in a way that is crucial for a practical epistemology. World 3 is not a realm of ultimate truths, pure ideas, or hypothetical possibilities. It is a human construction. Popper was a constructivist, through and through, but a constructivist of quite a different stamp from most of the psychologists, social scientists, and educationists who currently go by that name. They are what we might call "World 2 constructivists." They are concerned with things like constructive memory, learning as a process of mental construction, and the social processes by which beliefs become established in a culture.[1]

Popper's World 3 constructivism is about the creation and refinement of World 3 objects—what I have been referring to as *conceptual artifacts*. Whereas "construction" in the World 2 sense is a metaphor, in the World 3 sense it means literally what it says. Whereas the processes of World 2 construction are generally unconscious and in many cases completely inaccessible to awareness, people who are engaged in creating a conceptual artifact—a theory, for instance—generally know that is what they are doing. They see it as real productive work being carried out on something, frequently some other theory or a body of facts, which is also a conceptual artifact.

Ironically, World 3 constructivism is quite compatible, up to a point, with the "strong program" in the sociology of knowledge (Bloor, 1998). Although Popperians and advocates of the strong program occupy opposing camps in the so-called science wars, they

---

[1]There is also a degraded form of constructivism common in education, where it means roughly "hands-on" learning and the avoidance of direct instruction. This we may call "World 1" constructivism.

share the view that knowledge production is a human activity. Among them, Bloor's basic premise should be uncontroversial: that, as a human activity, knowledge production should be open to empirical study the same as any other human activity, and that the study should be carried out as impartially as possible. Where the camps split is on the nature of the products of this activity.[2] To what extent do the products of activity carried out according to the canons of scientific research, for instance, constitute knowledge in some privileged sense, something that should have a special claim on our belief? However, accepting the idea of World 3 or of conceptual artifacts does not carry with it a commitment to any particular answer. Indeed, I have been at pains throughout this book to steer clear of this horrendously difficult question (as have the more sophisticated sociologists of knowledge). Science educators keep getting hung up on it, but for no good reason. Knowledge managers in business are spared the weight of this question, because their ultimate concern is with things that work or make money, not with things that are true. The situation in education is more complicated, but not much.

The simplifying idea, which is also Popperian, is that of knowledge improvement. You cannot know or justly claim that you are getting closer to truth. That would require that you already have an idea of what the truth is. But you can specify ways in which one conceptual artifact is an improvement over its predecessor. You can show how it overcomes faults that were detected in the predecessor, how it accounts for facts that an older theory could not, or merely that it does the same conceptual job more economically or elegantly. Improving a conceptual artifact is thus similar to improving any other sort of artifact. You cannot claim that this year's computer is a step closer to the perfect computer. A mere glance at the history of computing makes clear that what a computer can or should be keeps evolving, so it is nonsense to think of getting closer to a perfect end state. But you can, and computer manufacturers invariably do, list ways in which this year's model is an improvement over last year's. Manufacturers do not mention ways in which this year's model is inferior to last year's, but there often are trade-offs, such that a gain here is offset by a loss there, and the same may be true with conceptual artifacts. But striving for an improved product, while keeping an eye out for potential losses, is the essence of World 3 constructivism. As I tried to show, es-

---

[2]Strictly speaking, the issue is whether matters of truth or factuality should or must enter into an account of scientific activity. Can you, for instance, give an adequate account of the 19th century struggles between evolutionists and creationists without noting the failures on each side to account for certain key facts—failures that were much more devastating to the creationist case? But this issue inevitably devolves into the issue of whether some conceptual artifacts can be judged to be better than others—more successful on grounds more fundamental than their political triumphs.

pecially in chapters 8 and 9, education can be carried out according to this model. By engaging students in creating and progressively improving conceptual artifacts—particularly artifacts that are of value in understanding the world—you can have an intellectually exciting and productive program that avoids entanglement with the hairy issues of truth and authority.

CONCEPTUAL VERSUS NONCONCEPTUAL ARTIFACTS

Conceptual artifacts belong to the large class of artifacts that includes such things as walking sticks, movies, and blimps. What fundamentally sets conceptual artifacts apart, however, is not that they are immaterial. There are other immaterial artifacts, such as musical compositions, which are not conceptual. What sets conceptual artifacts apart is that they can be treated as knowledge. But what does that mean?

Because knowledge can play a variety of roles in human affairs, there is not one universal test for distinguishing conceptual artifacts from nonconceptual ones. Looking at a single case, you may have trouble making a distinction. Does a certain string of words represent a theoretical proposition or a poem or both at once? Looking at an interrelated set of objects, however, you can identify conceptual artifacts by the kinds of logical relations that exist between them. One conceptual artifact may imply or be derivable from another; contradict or constitute an argument in favor of another; be a generalization of or a limiting case of another; justify, elaborate, connect, discriminate, illustrate, pose a problem for, presuppose, apply, or clarify other conceptual objects. Take a set of conceptual artifacts tightly linked in these ways and you have a system—a science or a philosophy or a "state of knowledge"

This systematicity, based on logical relations among elements, is what sets World 3 apart from the larger world of cultural artifacts. Nonconceptual artifacts my relate to each other in many ways but not in the particularly powerful and difficult-to-grasp way of conceptual artifacts. The literary works associated with the Romantic Movement, for instance, have many interrelations that literary scholars can identify. There are common themes and devices; structural similarities may be noted; imitation and influences may be detected. There is a cumulative effect that goes beyond the effect of the individual works. But the relations among the pieces are relations of similarity; there is nothing like the inferential relations that connect conceptual artifacts. One plan can subsume other plans. One definition can be more restrictive than another. One historical account can amplify another. These and many other relations structure a body of knowledge as distinct from a collection of nonconceptual cultural artifact. When I speak in chapter 7 of "enculturation into World 3" I mean not only becoming familiar with the artifacts composing a body of knowledge but also learning the logical relations that make it possible to work systematically with knowledge.

THEORETICAL OBJECTIONS

The most commonest theoretical objections to Popper's World 3 are of the "what if everybody died?" variety, which I hope I disposed of in chapter 3. A more interesting thought experiment along these lines is to imagine what would happen if everybody's working memory capacity—the number of ideas they can hold in mind and coordinate simultaneously—were to decline by half. People would no longer be able to grasp anything very complex. Most scientific ideas, all of mathematics beyond simple arithmetic, and any deep analyses of issues or events would lie beyond their comprehension. This would not be merely a matter of inability to comprehend certain texts. The complex ideas would be incomprehensible no matter how they were presented. But people would still be able to understand reports about these conceptual artifacts, narratives about their invention, and simplifications that gave an inkling of what they were about and what they were good for. There might, indeed, be continual valiant but futile efforts to understand the conceptual artifacts and to learn how to use them. So, would those conceptual artifacts have ceased to exist? You could say so, but for most purposes, it seems this situation is best represented as one in which the conceptual artifacts continue to exist (for the time being, anyway) but are inaccessible, ungraspable. This way of viewing the situation is especially appropriate for education, because what I have described is not some flight of science fictional imagination. It is the actual state of normal 8-year-old children. Major portions of World 3 are inaccessible to them, because—for reasons that have been in dispute—they cannot perform the mental juggling required to achieve an adult level of complexity.[3] However, the situation for the normal educated adult is different only in degree. There are still large tracts of intellectual territory inaccessible to us because we lack the necessary background knowledge and skills or because we have not put forth the necessary effort to master them. But they nevertheless constitute parts of the known world for us, like countries we have never visited. We know

---

[3]Case (1985) developed the theoretical and educational implications of this aspect of cognitive development, with educational implications further developed in Case (1992).

they exist, we know some things about them, and we may pursue understandings that point in their direction. Children, with help from their teachers, could do the same, but this requires treating conceptual artifacts as real things with properties of their own that make them worth knowing about. (This was the subject of chap. 9.)

A more serious theoretical objection to World 3 has its roots in linguistics and semiotics. The objection is that to posit a world of autonomous knowledge objects is to promote what is really only a manner of speaking into an ontological category. In the various registers of scholarly discourse, according to Wells (in press), "event-types that, in everyday speech, are realized in active clauses of doing, feeling and saying, are nominalized as abstract nouns and noun phrases; these abstractions are then treated as •things that can themselves enter into processes and relationships in the construction of descriptive and explanatory tests." The fact that we talk this way—that our language may indeed force us to talk this way— does not mean, however, "that there is a corresponding immaterial object that then exists, independent of the linguistic formulation and argumentation through which it was constructed." I do not see any reason to disagree with Wells on this point. It should be understood, however, that what he has offered is not an argument against treating conceptual artifacts as real things, it is an argument against claiming we are logically compelled to do so. That clears the way for pragmatic arguments about the desirability of doing so, which are the only kind I have used.

An important conceptual distinction has been elaborated by Philip Agre (1997). Agre distinguished between objective concepts and deictic ones. Objective concepts attribute to objects an existence independent of particular situations. They include pretty much everything we refer to using common nouns. So in Agre's terms, I have been arguing that ideas, as conceptual artifacts, should also be treated as objective concepts. Deictic concepts, however, have meanings that are not constant but that vary depending on who is speaking and where and when and to whom. Examples are *the shirt I am wearing, today's weather,* and *the place where we met.* To know what shirt, what weather, or what place, you have to know the context.[4] A deictic concept particularly relevant to the present issue is *the idea we are talking about.* Agre did not argue that objective concepts should

---

[4]Extending the idea, you can say that *shirt* in general is a deictic concept, because you cannot understand what a shirt is apart from the human purposes and human body configurations that make some things shirts and other things nonshirts. That line of reasoning, however, leads to the conclusion that all concepts are deictic, which is not what Agre argued and that, in my view, destroys the point of introducing the idea of deixis in the first place.

be dismissed in favor of deictic ones, but he did claim that deictic concepts are primary. They come first, and objective concepts are derived from them, whereas conventional wisdom would suggest it must be the other way around.

I find Agre's argument especially convincing as it applies to abstract concepts like theories, plans, facts, proofs, and arguments. These probably originate as *what we are talking about* or, in the isolated case, *what I am thinking about*. Their role in conversation is to give it focus and help to move it along. These undefined deictic concepts begin to acquire some ontological status of their own, however, when *what we were talking about yesterday* or *what I was thinking about yesterday* is important enough to be brought up again and pursued further. If this revival of topics goes on, it soon becomes worthwhile to give *what we are talking about* a name—for instance, "your theory." But if "your theory" is going to be discussed in other contexts where you are not present, it will eventually get a name such as "Planck's law" or "quantum theory." It will be described in characteristic ways, will begin to accumulate a body of received opinion, will be discovered to have implications you were unaware of, and so on. Thus, it evolves into an objective concept.

This does not mean objective concepts are superior to their deictic predecessors. The benefits of having something relatively stable to refer to and work on are bought at the price of a certain rigidity and artificiality. For Agre, whose project was to bring computer technology into closer accord with human activity, deictic concepts are the more promising kind. *What we are doing now* is the meeting ground for human and machine intelligence, and so you do not want the machine running according to a lot of fixed concepts built into it, often unwittingly, by engineers far removed from the situation. You want the adaptability that comes from being able to conceptualize interactively and on the fly; the same, of course, is true of human beings. But one of the things human beings do is produce, reconstruct, and refine objective concepts or what I prefer to call conceptual artifacts. That is what education beyond the basic level and the more creative kinds of knowledge work are mainly about. In the discussions through which such activity goes on, deictic concepts will play a large part. But it is important for participants to keep in mind that some of the concepts brought into the discussion have histories outside the discussion and, moreover, that the object of the discussion is to produce ideas that can be carried away from the discussion and used in other contexts.

Perhaps the most serious *practical* alternative to the Popperian three-worlds view is what may be called the Xerox PARC view; two important expressions of it come from people in that institution, although the more recent does not cite the earlier. Rich Gold (1997) criticized what he called the "refinery" model. Raw data get refined into information, which is then refined into knowledge, which may after further work be refined into wisdom sufficient to guide action. Although this model has great appeal to the industrial-age mentality, it is, said Gold, "fundamentally mistaken as to where information sits in the chain." (par. 3)

> Information is not ... part of an evolutionary chain that starts with simple data and ends with complex wisdom. Rather, it is a method of transferring existing knowledge from one person to another (ignoring, for the moment, the pesky problem of machine understanding). For there to be information, there must already be knowledge. Information is the bridge from one person's otherwise closed and inaccessible consciousness to another person's. Information is not slightly more organized data; it is the reification of a gob of human knowledge in a manner that another human can appreciate. (Gold, 1997, par. 6)

In the same vein, Brown and Duguid (2000) elaborated three distinctions between knowledge and information: knowledge usually entails a knower, it is "harder to detach" from persons and situations, and it usually entails a degree of understanding and commitment (people would not normally say they "know" something they do not understand or believe).

According to this view, I would have to revise the argument I gave in chapter 4 for the importance of distinguishing between "the knowledge used in productive work and the knowledge that is the object of such work." I used as an example an opinion research company:

> The work of the opinion research organization ... generates knowledge of two kinds. One kind is knowledge that is inseparable from the work itself, because it is constituted by the evolving skills and practices of the people who compose the organization. The other kind is knowledge that is of no value unless it can be separated from the community that produced it. It is knowledge that the company produces and sells, much as a bootmaker produces and sells boots.

Following Gold, I would have to say that what the company sells is information, not knowledge. Knowledge is what the customer constructs, with help from the information. Thus, knowledge is always a property of knowers; it has no autonomous existence, the way information does.

I will grant that this is a reasonable way to talk about knowledge, and that it is an improvement over the "refinery model" that Gold criticized. Where it fails is in dealing with the all-important phenom-enon of knowledge improvement. Let us suppose that the opinion re-search organization's client is a political party and that they are looking for an answer to the question, "Why did our candidate lose the election?" Let us suppose that, in addition to reporting factual in-formation, the opinion research organization also provides a tenta-tive answer to the question. The political party staff would treat this as information: "Those opinion research people think we lost be-cause ... " However, they could also treat it as a theory, to be com-pared with other theories that have been going around. Drawing on other information, they might be able to improve the theory. If they wanted to be scientific about it, they could come up with tests: If this theory is right, then such and such ought to be the case. They could then engage the opinion research organization in testing whether such and such was indeed the case, the new information could lead to further theory changes, and so on. You could still say, with Gold, that what passes back and forth among people is information, not knowledge, but it is information used to develop and improve a the-ory, and the theory surely is not mere information and neither is it the beliefs held by individual people. It is a third kind of thing, which I am calling a conceptual artifact.

BOUNDARY PROBLEMS

There are problems with conceptual artifacts. When are we talking about the same idea? When has a theory changed so much that it is no longer the same theory? If you are the kind of person who takes definitions and categories very seriously, these are likely to be vexing questions. But we should not be looking to epistemology for an-swers. Such problems are part of the work of any discipline, not something outside it. Drawing distinctions, showing that two hy-potheses, problems, or proofs are really the same or that one is a spe-cial case of the other—these are part of the creative work of scientists and scholars, along with producing new conceptual artifacts or re-vising old ones.

Popper (1972) spelled out some of the things that a scientist, *S*, might do with respect to a knowledge object, *p*:

S tries to understand *p*.

S tries to think of alternatives to *p*.

S tries to think of criticisms of *p*.

S proposes an experimental test for *p*.

S tries to axiomatize *p*.

S tries to derive *p* from *q*.

S tries to show that *p* is not derivable from *q*.

S proposes a new problem x arising out of *p*.

S proposes a new solution of the problem x arising out of *p*.

S criticizes his latest solution of the problem x. (pp. 140–141)

These are clearly actions, and they fall well within the normal scope of scientific activity, yet they are not actions carried out on the physical world (Popper's World 1). They are mental actions, but they are clearly actions carried out *on* or *with respect* to *something*. Furthermore, they are all carried out with respect to the *same* "something," and so to make sense of the scientists' actions and to see how they fit together, it is important that this "something" have enough of a fixed identity that we can talk about different things being done to it, with cumulative results. This does not mean we have to be able to say precisely what *p* is and where *p* leaves off and non-*p* begins. It just means that we have to identify something as the object that ties together a variety of actions. In the famous story of the blind men and the elephant (where, feeling different parts of the elephant, one blind man concludes that it is a tree, another that it is a snake, and so on) there is the possibility that through discussion the blind men could work out a coherent description of the animal. But this possibility depends on their being aware that they are all talking about the same entity. Failing in that, they would have no reason to try to reconcile their descriptions.

To deal with constancy and shift in conceptual artifacts, Landman (1986) has proposed the concept of "peg." *Electron* is a peg to which we attach information, just as a clothes hook is a peg to which we attach clothes. You can add more information or you can take some away and replace it with other information, so that eventually what is hanging on the peg is entirely different from what was there originally, but the peg is continuous over time.

"Peg" is a makeshift notion, to be sure, but it deals with what is really just a practical problem. When long time periods are involved or large conceptual distances, as between theoretical scientists and schoolchildren, we need to consider seriously what we have to gain by treating these disparate groups as talking about the same thing. If we are writing history, changes in meaning are part of the story and we must guard against producing a history that has today's theoretical pegs existing long in the past, with people in earlier times hanging quaint notions on them (Danziger, 1990). Similarly, if we are writing child development, we need to consider that concepts to which children attach labels such as "heat," "energy," and "gravity" may be in entirely different ontological categories from the concepts scientists associate with those labels (Chi et al., 1994). If, however, we contemplate having children and scientists enter into discourse together, then it would be good to work out some realistic sense in which they might see themselves as talking about the same conceptual artifacts. This would mean agreeing on some pegs on which both groups could hang their ideas. These do not have to be rigorously defined; they just have to serve their purpose of enabling people to share ideas and to preserve some continuity as their ideas progress over an extended conversation.

POTENTIAL MISUSES

Ideas can be misused, and so a legitimate objection to the idea of conceptual artifacts may be that, although harmless when properly used, it is liable to be used to bad effect. Gordon Wells (in press) has raised two objections of this pragmatic sort: first, that treating knowledge as consisting of autonomous objects "misrepresents the way in which knowledge is constructed and used"; second, that "knowledge, by being reified, becomes a commodity to be transmitted to students and its possession subsequently assessed and quantified." The upshot is that strategically "there is more to be lost than gained by using Popper's three world model ... "

Against these pragmatic objections it is not enough to show that, on the contrary, the three-worlds model sets the stage for unrestricted investigation of how knowledge is constructed, of the role of discourse and of the effects of various psychological and sociological factors on its development, and that it makes clear the artifactual character of textbook knowledge, its fallibility and improvability. Such virtues will be lost on educators who are liable to equate World 2 with students' naive beliefs and World 3 with the body of truths that are supposed to replace them. And people do tend to assimilate new ideas to their existing categories.

If we are going to be pragmatic about it, however, we have to consider alternatives on the same basis. The alternative that is probably favored by most advanced thinkers these days is one that treats knowledge as inseparable from the contexts of discourse and action in which it is constituted. As Wells (in press) put it,

> Knowledge does not have an existence apart from the situated acts of knowing in which it is constructed, reconstructed and used. Theories and explanations only exist in the particular occasioned use of the semiotic representations of various kinds in which they are realized (or the reconstruction of these representations from memory) by specific individuals who are engaged in some activity in which these semiotic artifacts play a central role in the knowing of those involved.

With variations, that is the alternative favored by all the critics I cited in chapter 3—Smith, Bernstein, Wells—and behind them the growing number of people who adopt labels like "semiotics," "socio-cultural," "situated cognition," and "action theory." But this conception lends itself to misuse as well. At best it is hard to get hold of and to do much with. At worst, it becomes degraded into the anything-goes relativism of Stanfield (1985) and even such suicidal concoctions as "race-based epistemologies" (Scheurich & Young, 1997).

The one idea I have been advocating that seems to be at least potentially acceptable to a wide range of critics is the idea of regarding theories and the like as tools. Wells explicitly recognizes conceptual artifacts in this sense, though adding the qualification that "these do not themselves constitute knowledge; they only play a role as tools that have a potential for facilitating problem solving and further knowledge building ...." The tool idea is not hard to grasp and it would seem to be safe from the worst excesses of relativism. No one would claim that every tool is as good as every other. The value of a tool is relative, but always relative to some purpose. So far so good. It may well be that pushing the notion of conceptual artifacts as tools is the entering wedge for breaking through folk theory's barriers to understanding knowledge. But it seems important to press on from there to a recognition that conceptual artifacts are not just tools. Some of them make assertions about the world that we may want to judge as true or false. Some of them function like recipes, which is not quite the same as fuctioning as a tool. Even as tools, they may themselves be objects of inquiry. We can investigate how they work, what their limitations are, and how they might be improved. Conceptual artifacts relate to one another in ways that physical tools cannot; one of them may imply or be implied by others. This creates the possibility of assembling them into larger and more integrated structures—which suggests treating them more as building materials than as tools.

There is no use looking for an idiot-proof way of treating knowledge. Into the foreseeable future, most people are going to continue thinking of knowledge as stuff variously contained in people's minds and in books and of education as a business of getting it moved from one container to another. There is no official theory to that effect and no group committed to upholding it. It is just a matter of the way we were born and bred. For that reason, however, I do not believe that it is a bad mark against any theory of knowledge that it can be distorted so as to support this unenlightened view. The unenlighted don't need any such support. Some advanced ideas can do harm. I suspect that relativism generally has had a bad effect on education because, regardless of the merits of its more sophisticated versions, in practice it has discouraged the serious pursuit of understanding. What would be the effect of trying to put into practice the ideas developed in this book? If its only effect is to provide spurious theoretical support for an educational approach that people were going to follow anyway, that is the same as having no effect at all. If, however, it can get educators to start treating knowledge as something that can in fact be treated in different ways for different purposes, it may have opened a door through which education could conceivably enter the Knowledge Age.

TOOLS AND OTHER ARTIFACTS

The Russian activity theorists have made tool use a fundamental characteristic of human action. Animals and human infants act directly on objects in their environments. Mature human action, however, is always, as the activity theorists say, *mediated* by something external to both the actor and the object. The mediator may be a physical tool such as a hammer or shovel or it may be a nonphysical aid such as language or mathematics. Research by Vygotsky and Luria, from which activity theory grew, focused on young children learning to use language to regulate their own actions. There is also social mediation, as when parents help children with their homework. On this view, cognition, like every other form of human action, encompasses external mediation and therefore cannot be adequately characterized by internal mental operations performed on mental content.

On one construal, conceptual artifacts would count among the tools that mediate human action. On another construal, which seems to be the more accepted one among Western thinkers who have taken up activity theory, there are no abstract tools such as Popper proposes. Tools are either material things, such as books and instruments, or they are practices, such as writing and mathematical notation. A good reason for preferring the first construal is that it allows for treating the same object—a theory or an algorithm, say—as a tool in one situation and as an object of inquiry or improvement in another.

One way or the other, a broadened conception of tools is useful for thinking about human intelligence. I have never understood why activity theorists are so vociferous about it, however, as if in proclaiming the ubiquity of tools in human activity they have cleared away a dense cloud. It seems to me that, like many another contribution to human thought, this one merely highlights something we already know and makes it more available for use but does not produce any rumblings of a paradigm shift.[5]

In advancing the idea of *distributed intelligence*, however, Roy Pea (1993) has carried activity theory a step or two beyond where common sense easily follows. "When I say that intelligence is distributed," Pea explained (p. 50), "I mean that the resources that shape and enable activity are distributed in configuration across people, environments, and situations." Distributed characteristics of any kind are a bewilderment to common sense, but distributed *intelligence* adds a further twist. In Pea's usage, this means that tools as well as people embody intelligence—and he is not referring particularly to so-called intelligent machines. His examples are "jogger pulse meters, automatic street locators, currency exchange calculators, world-time clocks, and weight-loss calculators" (p. 53). Of such devices, Pea (1993) said:

> These tools literally carry intelligence *in* them, in that they represent some individual's or some community's decision that the means thus offered should be reified, made stable, as a quasi-permanent form, for use by others. In terms of cultural history, these tools and the practices of the user community that accompany them are major carriers of patterns of previous reasoning .... They may now be used by a new generation with little or no awareness of the struggle that went into defining them and to adapting their characteristics to the tasks for which they were created. (p. 53)

Pea's position is to be contrasted with the more ordinary view, which sees tools as parts of the real world that may be treated intelligently or not, according to one's lights, the same as anything else. People who will use wood chisels as screwdrivers (and according to my experience the majority of human beings fall into this class) are behaving in a way that they may consider intelligent, inasmuch as they are exploiting affordances of the tool, but that anyone who owns a prized set of wood chisels will consider to fall below the normal range for human intelligence. A lot of intelligence goes into the design and manufacture of a good wood chisel, that we may agree. The chisel constitutes a partial solution to problems of removing precisely delimited portions of a substance (wood) that is nonhomogeneous in a particularly refractory way. (Wood seems to have a mind of its own, as woodworkers sometimes remark.) As Pea would have it, the intelligence that went into the design of the wood chisel is

---

[5]By this I mean, following Thagard (1992), that the tools idea does not call for any drastic restructuring of the tree of concepts that we apply to human knowledge and intelligence.

now embodied in the tool itself and thus becomes a part of the intelligence that goes into solving the problems attendant on, for instance, cutting a mortise. You could cut a mortise (a squarish hole, for those unfamiliar with the term) using a sharp pocket knife, but that would take more intelligence on the part of the actor, to compensate for less of the relevant intelligence being embodied in the tool.

If our concern is with what it takes to produce a particular intended result (as in cutting a neat mortise or reducing the federal deficit), Pea's idea of distributed intelligence provides a nice basis for considering the full range of possible contributors. If, for instance, the goal is to produce a sharp photograph of a spouting whale and tourist A has a state-of-the-art automatic camera whereas tourist B has a cheap camera with a few manual controls, we can set out necessary and sufficient conditions in ways that will assign most of the conditions to the camera in the case of tourist A and most of them to the person in the case of tourist B, although the total set of conditions is the same.

Notice, however, that in adopting this viewpoint, we are setting ourselves apart from the activity and are asking how a certain task may be accomplished, given certain tourists and certain cameras. From this standpoint, the human actor is also a tool. This is the standpoint of the manager, who decides whether a job should be done by a person or by a machine or by a low-paid worker and an expensive machine or by a higher paid worker and a not-so-expensive machine. The decision may or may not involve humane considerations. That is not the point here. The point is that to view intelligence as distributed across people and artifacts is to view the people as artifacts. Such a viewpoint may be appropriate, may even be essential, where the design and management of work are concerned, but it is not the viewpoint of the worker or actor. Neither, I must emphasize, is it the viewpoint of the educator—unless, of course, the purpose of education is to produce human tools, as cynics of a Marxist persuasion like to allege.

Educators need a viewpoint on action that enables them to focus on what is learnable (by individuals or a collective) that will contribute to success. Intelligence comes into the picture in two forms. One is intelligence involved in the learning itself. This is how intelligence is usually considered in education—as a prerequisite to learning. The other is intelligence as the objective. This is the intelligence at issue here. We are interested in people's learning things that will contribute to intelligent action. In this regard, it seems to me that the commonsense approach is preferable to Pea's admittedly very appealing approach. We should attend to what it takes to use tools intelligently. Any intelligence that we attribute to the tool itself becomes simply part of what must be taken into account in using it intelligently. This commonsense approach is the one Pea (1993) himself reverted to when he addressed educational implications:

> We should reorient the educational emphasis from individual, tool-free cognition to facilitating individuals' responsive and novel uses of resources for creative and intelligent activity alone and in collaboration. Such an education would encourage and refine the natural tendency for people to continually re-create their own world as a scaffold for their activities. (p. 81)

There is, however, a more radical version of the idea of artifacts invested with intelligence. It comes from the Russian philosopher, Ilyenkov (Bakhurst, 1991), and it has something important and in a way disturbing to offer our conception of what it means to relate intelligently to things in the world. Underlying the whole treatment of tools and mediated action that we have been considering is the idea of artifacts—human creations that become part of the environment, part of the situation to which situated activity is attuned. Ilyenkov went further, however, and argued in effect that to human beings *everything* is an artifact. Everything is invested with meaning, purpose, roles, affordances and resistances to our activity. We have no cognizance of things in the world except as they enter into our activity, and as we incorporate them, they become in a sense our own creation. We did not, of course, make the stars, but, depending on our knowledge and our purposes, we may know them as guides to navigation or as scenic backdrop to a nightscape. Indeed, it is only through their incorporation into human practice that things in the world can become objects of thought (Bakhurst, 1991, p. 201).

This sounds like idealism, but Ilyenkov was trying to find a place for ideas within the world of Marxist materialism, and so his idealism has a practical edge to it: To the person with a job to do or a problem to solve, everything becomes a tool. All of our past history of productive effort, all of our internalization of cultural practice—all of our practical intelligence, if you will—finds expression in the tool-like characteristics with which we invest the objects about us. This is the basis of human beings' boundless capacity to create technology. Everything, from a practical standpoint, already is technology; we just keep improving it.

Although there is a strong family resemblance between Pea's view and Ilyenkov's, Ilyenkov's is broader. The *artifactualization of the natural world*, as I shall call it,[6] is an all-encompassing cultural phenomenon. We not only invest objects with the properties of tools, we invest them with aesthetic and moral properties as well. A tree is a radically different kind of artifact for the lumber baron, the romantic poet, and the ecowarrior (treating these as stereotypes). The first invests the tree with instrumental properties, the second with aesthetic properties and the third with moral properties. Education's aim would be to see that all of these are developed and harmonized. A too exclusive emphasis of tool-like properties leads toward dehumanization and alienation. If everything is a tool, then our fellow human beings are tools. When you are tying a bow in a tightly drawn ribbon, there is no better tool than somebody else's finger. But carry the tool use of human beings much farther than that and you are into exploitation, manipulation, "objectification" in its most negative sense, and ultimately slavery. But a too exclusive emphasis of aesthetic properties can also be inhumane, and impractical to boot. And people who fasten on moral or political aspects to the exclusion of everything else tend to become fanatics and beyond reason.

Regarding everything as an artifact, we can nevertheless see artifacts as arranged on a continuum. At one end are things that we artifactualize but have no control over: stars, weather phenomena, and so on. Then there are natural things that we do not create but that we can arrange or modify to serve our purposes: Trees can be planted to serve as windbreaks or providers of shade, for instance; animals can be trained to do work. Then come all the material artifacts that people produce, and finally abstract artifacts—pure knowledge objects. There are not many distinct gaps in this continuum, and technology is busy filling those in.

THE AUTONOMY OF CONCEPTUAL ARTIFACTS

There are many different kinds of abstract artifacts and nothing to stop people from creating more. Any nonmaterial creation will count: a song, a crossword puzzle, a paradox, a travelogue, a predic-

---

[6]Ilyenkov's terms, as translated by Bakhurst (1991), include "idealization" and "spiritual culture"—terms that require considerable explanation to separate Ilyenkov's meaning from conventional meanings. To avoid such excursions, I have substituted terms that are already part of the present discussion. This means leaving out much of what is most distinctive in Ilenkov's ideas and no doubt distorting what remains, but I am not trying to give an exposition or critique (see Bakhurst for that) and have only taken pains to avoid making Ilyenkov out to say what I want him to say. In particular, I am not trying to make Ilyenkov into an advocate for Popper's World 3, although some of his quoted utterances might be construed that way.

tion, a historical account, an aphorism, a number system, a movie critique, a statute (but not a statue). All share three fundamental characteristics: discussibility, modifiability, and autonomy. Only the last is controversial, and to Popper (1972) it was the key:

> The idea of autonomy is central to my theory of the third world: although the third world is a human product, a human creation, it creates in its turn, as do other animal products, its own domain of autonomy. (p. 118)

His prime example of autonomy is natural numbers: an ages-old human creation, yet mathematicians are continuing to find out new things about them and they keep impinging on our lives in new ways. Similar autonomy is exhibited by material products of human enterprise, such as aspirin.

The autonomy of physical things has given philosophers trouble: the idea that things exist and have properties independent of our cognition. Understandably, then, the notion that mental constructions could enjoy similar autonomy has proved a great deal harder to swallow. Keeping in mind that our project here extends only to trying to produce a more *useful* theory of knowledge and mind, however, we can be pragmatic about such metaphysical issues. I do not see how discourse above the "Me Tarzan, you Jane" level is possible without treating ideas as things. Everybody does it. Radical behaviorists, while using laborious circumlocutions to avoid mentalistic language, never hesitated to treat theories, hypotheses, arguments, and the like as real things. Situated cognition theorists do it, even in the process of arguing against doing so. Jean Lave (1988), for instance, criticizes "the view that culture is the evolutionary accumulation of knowledge" (p. 91). This *view*, she said, has *prevailed* through most of the last century. But a *problem* has *emerged* from this *view*. After considering two possible ways of dealing with the problem, she asserted that neither one "appears to offer a *solution*." The italics, of course, are all mine and are meant to draw attention to Lave's treating a *view* as a thing having identifiable properties and implications.

Certain kinds of intellectual products are treated as real, autonomous objects, without any hesitation or thought to alternatives. A sonata is an example. A sonata is not regarded as something in the composer's mind—at least, not once it has been composed. But it is not the notes on paper, either. The notation is fallible. An editor may revise it to eliminate errors or to make it easier for a performer to follow. A sonata is not any particular performance or a totality of performances. It is the abstract thing that those are performances of.

When people discuss a sonata they are discussing the abstract object, although what they have to say about it will undoubtedly be influenced by the performances they have heard. It takes some rather fancy theorizing to raise any serious doubt about treating musical compositions as autonomous objects. This is because they do not *refer* to anything. It is when conceptual artifacts refer to things outside World 3 that troubles begin to arise. Those are the troubles that the discipline of epistemology has assumed the burden of dealing with.

With a two-worlds epistemology, the troubles have to do with warrant for belief: What grounds have we to be sure of anything? With a three-worlds epistemology the problems become clearer though perhaps still unsolvable: What is the relation between the conceptual artifacts we create and a putative real world? Although I have no wish to discount the significance and interestingness of the problems surrounding this question, I have tried as best I could to show that a useful epistemology can be adopted without having to solve them.

References

AARP. (2000, September/October). The why and how of adult learning. *TechKnowLogia, 2*(5), 30–32.

Ackrill, J. L. (Ed.). (1987). *A new Aristotle reader.* Princeton, NJ: Princeton University Press.

Adams, M. J. (1990). *Beginning to read: Thinking and learning about print.* Cambridge, MA: MIT Press.

Adler, M. J. (1984). *The Paideia program: An educational syllabus. Essays by the Paideia Group.* New York: Macmillan

Agre, P. E. (1997). *Computation and human experience.* Cambridge, UK: Cambridge University Press.

Agre, P. (1998, Nov.15). [RRE] *notes and recommendations* Retrieved July 14, 2001, from http:/commons.somewhere.com/rre/1998/RRE.notes.andrecommenda1.html

Alessi, G. (1988). Diagnosis diagnosed: A systemic reaction. *Professional School Psychology, 3*(2), 145–151.

Alexander, P. A., Schallert, D. L., & Hare, V. C. (1991). Coming to terms: How researchers in learning and literacy talk about knowledge. *Review of Educational Research, 61,* 315–343.

American Association for the Advancement of Science. (1967). *Science: A process approach* (1st ed.)Washington, DC: American Association for the Advancement of Science, Commission on Science Education. Distributed by Xerox Corporation.

Anderson, C. W., & Roth, K. J. (1989). Teaching for meaningful and self-regulated learning of science. In J. Brophy (Ed.), *Advances in research on teaching* (pp. 265–309). Greenwich, CT: JAI Press, Inc.

Anderson, C. W., Holland, J. D., & Palincsar, A. S. (1997). Canonical and sociocultural approaches to research and reform in science education: The story of Juan and his group. *Elementary School Journal, 97,* 359–383.

Anderson, J. R. (1983). *The architecture of cognition.* Cambridge, MA: Harvard University Press.

Anderson, J. R. (1987). Skill acquisition: Compilation of weak-method problem solutions. *Psychological Review, 94,* 192–210.

Anderson, J. R. (1993). *Rules of the mind.* Hillsdale, NJ: Lawrence Erlbaum Associates.

Anderson, J. R., Corbett, A. T., Koedinger, K. R., & Pelletier, R. (1995). Cognitive tutors: Lessons learned. *The Journal of the Learning Sciences, 4*(2), 167–207.

Anderson, R. C., Hiebert, E. H., Scott, J. A., & Wilkinson, I. A. G. (1985). *Becoming a nation of readers: The report of the Commission on Reading.* Pittsburgh, PA: National Academy of Education.

Anderson, R. C., & Pearson, P. D. (1984). A schema-theoretic view of basic processes in reading comprehension. In P. D. Pearson (Ed.), *Handbook of reading research* (pp. 255–292). New York: Longman.

Anderson, R. C., Reynolds, R. E., Schallert, D. L., & Goetz, E. T. (1977). Frameworks for comprehending discourse. *American Educational Research Journal, 14,* 367–381.

Anderson, V., & Roit, M. (1993). Planning and implementing collaborative strategy instruction for delayed readers in grades 6–10. *Elementary School Journal, 94*(2), 121–137.

Anglin, J. M. (1993). Vocabulary development: A morphological analysis. *Monographs of the Society for Research in Child Development, 58*(10), Serial No. 238.

Aronowitz, S., & Cutler, J. (Eds.). (1997). *Post-work: The wages of cybernation.* New York: Routledge.

Astington, J. R. (1993). *The child's discovery of the mind.* Cambridge, MA: Harvard University Press.

Attewell, P. (1990). What is skill? *Work and Occupations, 17,* 422–448.

Bakhurst, D. (1991). *Consciousness and revolution in Soviet philosophy: From the Bolsheviks to Evald Ilyenkov.* New York: Cambridge University Press.

Barkow, J. H., Cosmides, L., & Tooby, J. (1992). *The adapted mind: Evolutionary psychology and the generation of culture.* Oxford: Oxford University Press.

Barron, F. (1969). *Creative person and creative process.* New York: Holt, Rinehart & Winston.

Barton, A. C. (1997). Liberatory science education: Weaving connections between feminist theory and science education. *Curriculum Inquiry, 27*(2), 141–163.

Beck, I. L., McKeown, M. G., & Gromoll, E. W. (1989). Learning from social studies texts. *Cognition and Instruction, 6*(2), 99–158.

Belenky, M. F., Clinchy, B. M., Goldberger, N. R., & Tarule, J. M. (1986). *Women's ways of knowing.* New York: Basic Books.

Bereiter, C. (1968). A nonpsychological approach to early compensatory education. In M. Deutsch, I. Katz, & A. R. Jensen (Eds.), *Social class, race and psychological development* (pp. 337–346). New York: Holt, Rinehart & Winston.

Bereiter, C. (1969). The future of individual differences. *Harvard Educational Review, 39,* 310–318.

Bereiter, C. (1974). *Must we educate?* Englewood Cliffs, NJ: Prentice-Hall.

Bereiter, C. (1984). How to keep thinking skills from going the way of all frills. *Educational Leadership, 42*(1), 75–77.

Bereiter, C. (1985). Toward a solution of the learning paradox. *Review of Educational Research, 55,* 201–226.

Bereiter, C. (1988). A cognitive adaptational interpretation of reading disability. In C. Hedley (Ed.), *Reading and the special learner* (pp. 21–34). Norwood, NJ: Ablex.

Bereiter, C. (1991a). Commentary on "Special topic: Confronting the learning paradox." *Human Development, 34,* 294–298.

Bereiter, C. (1991b). Implications of connectionism for thinking about rules. *Educational Researcher, 20,* 10–16.

Bereiter, C. (1992). Referent-centered and problem-centered knowledge: Elements of an educational epistemology. *Interchange, 23*(4), 337–361

Bereiter, C. (1994). Implications of postmodernism for science, or, Science as progressive discourse. *Educational Psychologist, 29*(1), 3–12.

Bereiter, C. (1995). A dispositional view of transfer. In A. McKeough, J. Lupart, & A. Marini (Eds.), *Teaching for transfer: Fostering generalization in learning* (pp. 21–34). Hillsdale, NJ: Lawrence Erlbaum Associates.

Bereiter, C. (1997). Situated cognition and how to overcome it. In D. Kirshner & J. A. Whitson (Eds.), *Situated cognition: Social, semiotic, and psychological perspectives* (pp. 281–300). Mahwah, NJ: Lawrence Erlbaum Associates.

Bereiter, C., & Bird, M. (1985). Use of thinking aloud in identification and teaching of reading comprehension strategies. *Cognition and Instruction, 2,* 131–156.

Bereiter, C., & Scardamalia, M. (1987a). An attainable version of high literacy: Approaches to teaching higher-order skills in reading and writing. *Curriculum Inquiry, 17*(1), 9–30.

Bereiter, C., & Scardamalia, M. (1987b). *The psychology of written composition.* Hillsdale, NJ: Lawrence Erlbaum Associates.

Bereiter, C., & Scardamalia, M. (1989). Intentional learning as a goal of instruction. In L. B. Resnick (Ed.), *Knowing, learning, and instruction: Essays in honor of Robert Glaser* (pp. 361–392). Hillsdale, NJ: Lawrence Erlbaum Associates.

Bereiter, C., & Scardamalia, M. (1992). Cognition and curriculum. In P. W. Jackson (Ed.), *Handbook of research on curriculum* (pp. 517–542). New York: Macmillan.

Bereiter, C., & Scardamalia, M. (1993). *Surpassing ourselves: An inquiry into the nature and implications of expertise.* La Salle, IL: Open Court.

Bereiter, C., & Scardamalia, M. (1996). Rethinking learning. In D. Olson & N. Torrance (Eds.), *Handbook of education and human development: New models of learning, teaching and schooling* (pp. 485–513). Cambridge, MA: Basil Blackwell.

Bereiter, C., & Scardamalia, M. (2000). Process and product in problem-based (PBL) research. In D. H. Evensen & C. E. Hmelo (Eds.), *Problem-based Learning: A research perspective on learning interactions* (pp. 185–195). Mahwah, NJ: Lawrence Erlbaum Associates.

Bereiter, C., Scardamalia, M., Cassells, C., & Hewitt, J. (1997). Postmodernism, knowledge building, and elementary science. *Elementary School Journal, 97,* 329–340.

Berkes, F., & Henley, H. (1997, March). Co-management and traditional knowledge: Threat or opportunity? *Policy Options, 18*(2), 29–31.

Bernstein, B. (1996). *Pedagogy, symbolic control and identity.* London: Taylor & Francis.

Bettelheim, B., & Zelan, K. (1982). *On learning to read: The child's fascination with meaning.* New York: Knopf

Biggs, J. B. (1979). Individual differences in study processes and the quality of learning outcomes. *Higher Education, 8,* 381–394.

Bloom, B. S. (Ed.). (1956). *Taxonomy of educational objectives: Handbook 1. Cognitive domain.* New York: McKay.

Bloom, B. S. (1969). Letter to the editor. *Harvard Educational Review, 39,* 419–421.

Bloom, B. S., & Broder, L. J. (1950). *Problem-solving processes of college students.* Chicago: The University of Chicago Press.

Bloor, D. (1998). The strong program in the sociology of science. In R. Klee (Ed.), *Scientific inquiry: Readings in the philosophy of science* (pp. 241–250). New York: Oxford University Press.

Bolzano, B. (1972). *Theory of science: Attempt at a detailed and in the main novel exposition of logic with constant attention to earlier authors [Wissenschaftslehre]* (R. George, Trans.). Berkeley, CA: University of California Press.

Book of Famous Quotes., The (n.d.) Retrieved July 14, 2001, from http://www.bsu.edu/classes/misner/133/quotes.htm.

Boom, J. (1991). Collective development and the learning paradox. *Human Development, 34,* 273–287.

Bransford, J. D., Brown, A. L., & Cocking, R. R. (Eds.). (1999). *How people learn: Brain, mind, experience, and school.* Washington, DC: National Academies Press.

Bransford, J., & Schwartz, D. (1999). Rethinking transfer: A simple proposal with multiple implications. *Review of Research in Education, 25.*

Bronowski, J., & Mazlish, B. (1960). *The western intellectual tradition.* New York: Harper.

Brown, A. L., & Campione, J. C. (1990). Communities of learning and thinking, or A context by any other name. *Contributions to Human Development, 21,* 108–126.

Brown, A. L., & Campione, J. C. (1994). Guided discovery in a community of learners. In K. McGilley (Ed.), *Classroom lessons: Integrating cognitive theory and classroom practice* (pp. 229–270). Cambridge, MA: MIT Press.

Brown, A. L., & Palincsar, A. S. (1989). Guided, cooperative learning and individual knowledge acquisition. In L. B. Resnick (Ed.), *Knowing, learning, and instruction: Essays in honor of Robert Glaser* (pp. 393–451). Hillsdale, NJ: Lawrence Erlbaum Associates.

Brown, J. S., Collins, A., & Duguid, P. (1989). Situated cognition and the culture of learning. *Educational Researcher, 18,* 32–42.

Brown, J. S., & Duguid, P. (2000). *The social life of information*. Cambridge, MA: Harvard Business School Press.

Brownell, W. A. (Ed.). (1946) *Forty-fifth Yearbook of the National Society for the Study of Education, Part I*. Chicago: National Society for the Study of Education.

Brownell, W. A., & Sims, V. M. (1946). The nature of understanding. In W. A. Brownell (Ed.), *The measurement of understanding*, Forty-fifth yearbook of the National Society for the Study of Education, Part I (pp. 27–43). Chicago: National Society for the Study of Education.

Bruer, J. T. (1997). Education and the brain: A bridge too soon. *Educational Researcher, 26*(8), 4–16.

Bruner, J. (1986). *Actual minds, possible worlds*. Cambridge, MA: Harvard University Press.

Bruner, J. S. (1990). *Acts of meaning*. Cambridge, MA: Harvard University Press.

Bullough, R. V., Jr., & Baughman, K. (1998). Thinking about "Thinking about 'Narrative Reasoning'": A rejoinder to Annie Davies. *Curriclum Inquiry, 28*(485–490).

Bunge, M. A. (1977–1979). *Ontology: Treatise on basic philosophy*. Boston: Reidel.

Butts, R. F. (1947). *A cultural history of education*. New York: McGraw-Hill.

Calfee, R., & Drum, P. (1986). Research on teaching reading. In M. C. Wittrock (Ed.), Handbook of research on teaching (3rd ed., pp. 229–270). New York: Macmillan.

Campbell, D. T. (1960). Blind variation and selective retention in creative thought as in other knowledge processes. *Psychological Review, 67*, 380–400.

Carnine, D. (1996). *Diverse learners and prevailing, emerging, and research-based educational approaches and their tools*. Eugene, OR: National Center to Improve the Tools of Educators, University of Oregon.

Carroll, J. M., & Rosson, M. B. (1987). Paradox of the active user. In J. M. Carroll (Ed.), *Interfacing thought: Cognitive aspects of human–computer interaction* (pp. 80–111). Cambridge, MA: MIT Press.

Carter, K. (1993). The place of story in the study of teaching and teacher education. *Educational Researcher, 22*(1), 5–18.

Carus, A. (in press). Moral expertise. In B. Smith (Ed.), *Liberal education in a knowledge society*. Chicago: Open Court.

Case, R. (1985a). A developmentally based approach to the problem of instructional design. In S. F. Chipman, J. W. Segal, & R. Glaser (Eds.), *Thinking and learning skills: Vol. 2. Research and open questions* (pp. 545–562). Hillsdale, NJ: Lawrence Erlbaum Associates.

Case, R. (1985b). *Intellectual development: Birth to adulthood*. Orlando, FL: Academic Press.

Case, R. (Ed.). (1992). *The mind's staircase: Stages in the development of human intelligence*. Hillsdale, NJ: Lawrence Erlbaum Associates.

Case, R., & Okamoto, Y. (1996). The role of central conceptual structures in the development of children's thought. *Monographs of the Society for Research in Child Development, 61*(2), Serial No. 246.

Cassirer, E. (1944). *An essay on man*. New Haven, CT: Yale University Press.

Cassirer, E. (1950). *The problem of knowledge: Philosophy, science, and history since Hegel*. New Haven, CT: Yale University Press.

Chi, M. T. H., Feltovich, P. J., & Glaser, R. (1981). Categorization and representation of physics problems by experts and novices. *Cognitive Science, 5,* 121–152.

Chi, M. T. H., Slotta, J. D., & deLeeuw, N. (1994). From things to processes: A theory of conceptual change for learning science concepts. *Learning and Instruction, 4,* 27–43.

Chomsky, N. (1975). *Reflections on language*. New York: Pantheon Books.

Choo, C. W. (1998). *The knowing organization: How organizations use information to construct meaning, create knowledge, and make decisions*. New York: Oxford University Press.

Church, E., & Bereiter, C. (1983). Reading for style. *Language Arts, 60,* 470–476.

Church, J. (1961). *Language and the discovery of reality*. New York: Random House.

Clancey, W. J. (1987). *Knowledge-based tutoring: The GUIDON program*. Cambridge, MA: MIT Press.

Clancey, W. J. (1991). Situated cognition: Stepping out of representational Flatland. *AI Communications, 4*(2/3), 109–112.

Clandinin, D. J., & Connelly, F. M. (1996). Teachers' professional knowledge landscapes: Teacher stories—stories of teachers—school stories—stories of schools. *Educational Researcher, 25*(3), 24–30.

Clandinin, D. J., & Connelly, F. M. (1998). Stories to live by: Narrative understandings of school reform. *Curriculum Inquiry, 28,* 149–164.

Clement, J. (1982). Students' preconceptions in introductory mechanics. *American Journal of Physics, 50,* 66–71.

Cobb, P., Gravmeijer, K., Yackel, E., McClain, K., & Whitenack, J. (1997). Mathematizing and symbolizing: The emergence of chains of significance in one first-grade classroom. In D. Kirshner & J. A. Whitson (Eds.), *Situated cognition: Social, semiotic, and psychological perspectives* (pp. 151–233). Mahwah, NJ: Lawrence Erlbaum Associates.

Cohen, A., & Scardamalia, M. (1998). Discourse about ideas: Monitoring and regulation in face-to-face and computer-mediated environments. *Interactive Learning Environments, 6,* 93–113.

Cohen, D. K., McLaughlin, M. W., & Talbert, J. E. (Eds.). (1993). *Teaching for understanding*. San Francisco: Jossey-Bass.

Collins, A., & Stevens, A. L. (1982). Goals and strategies of inquiry teachers. In R. Glaser (Ed.), *Advances in instructional psychology* (pp. 65–119). Hillsdale, NJ: Lawrence Erlbaum Associates.

Collins, A., & Stevens, A. L. (1983). A cognitive theory of inquiry teaching. In C. M. Reigeluth (Ed.), *Instructional-design theories and models: An overview of their current status* (pp. 247–278). Hillsdale, NJ: Lawrence Erlbaum Associates.

Collins, H. M. (1981). Stages in the empirical programme of relativism. *Social studies of science, 11,* 3–10.

Cosmides, L., & Tooby, J. (1999). *Evolutionary psychology: A primer.* Retrieved July 14, 2001, from http://www.psych.ucsb.edu/research/cep/primer.html.

Cotman, C. (1990). Synaptic plasticity, neurotrophic factors and transplantation in the aged brain. In E. Schneider & J. Rowe (Eds.), *Handbook of the biology of aging* (3rd ed., pp. 255–274). New York: Academic Press.

Cronbach, L. J. (1975). Beyond the two disciplines of scientific psychology. *American Psychologist, 30,* 116–127.

Cuban, L. (1993, October). The lure of curricular reform and its pitiful history. *Phi Delta Kappan, 75,* 182–185.

Cynader, M., & Frost, B. (1999). Mechanisms of brain development: Sculpting by the physical and social environment. In D. Keating & C. Hertzman (Eds.), *Developmental health and the wealth of nations: Social, biological and educational dynamics* (pp. 153–184). New York: Guilford Press.

Danahy, J. W., & Hoinkes, R. (1995). Polytrim: Collaborative setting for environmental design. In M. Tam & R. Teh (Eds.), *CAAD Futures '95: The global design studio.* Singapore: Centre for Advanced Studies in Architecture, National University of Singapore. Available: <http://www.clr.toronto.edu:1080/PAPERS/CAAD95/caadf.jd8.html>.

Danziger, K. (1990). Generative metaphor and the history of psychological discourse. In D. A. Leary (Ed.), *Metaphors in the history of psychology* (pp. 331–356). Cambridge, UK: Cambridge University Press.

Davydov, V. V., & Radzikhovskii, L. A. (1985). Vygotsky's theory and the activity-oriented approach in psychology. In J. V. Wertsch (Ed.), *Culture, communication, and cognition: Vygotskian perspectives* (pp. 35–65). Cambridge, UK: Cambridge University Press.

Dawkins, R. (1976). *The selfish gene.* Oxford, UK: Oxford University Press.

deBono, E. (1985). *Six thinking hats.* Boston: Little, Brown & Company.

deKleer, J., & Brown, J. S. (1985). A qualitative physics based on confluences. In D. G. Bobrow (Ed.), *Qualitative reasoning about physical systems* (pp. 7–84). Cambridge, MA: MIT Press.

Dennett, D. C. (1991). *Consciousness explained.* Boston: Little, Brown & Company.

Dennett, D. C. (1995). *Darwin's dangerous idea: Evolution and the meanings of life.* New York: Simon & Schuster.

Dennett, D. C., & Kinsbourne, M. (1992). Time and the observer: The where and when of consciousness in the brain. *Behavioral and Brain Sciences, 15*(2), 183–247.

Dewey, J. (1916). *Democracy and education.* New York: Macmillan.

Dewey, J. (1929). *The sources of a science of education.* New York: Liverright.

Dewey, J. (1933). *How we think.* New York: Heath.

diSessa, A. A. (2000). *Changing mind: Computers, learning, and literacy.* Cambridge, MA: MIT Press.

Donahue, P. L., Voekl, K. E., Campbell, J. R., & Mazzeo, J. (1999). *NAEP 1998 Reading Report Card for the nation and the states.* U.S. Office of Education, National Center for Educational Statistics. Washington, DC.

Dreyfus, H. L. (1988). The Socratic and Platonic basis of cognitivism. *AI and Society, 2,* 99–112.

Dreyfus, H. L., & Rabinow, P. (1983). *Michel Foucault: Beyond structuralism and hermeneutics* (2nd ed.). Chicago: University of Chicago Press.

Drucker, P. (1993). *Post-capitalist society.* New York: HarperBusiness.

Drucker, P. F. (1994, November). The age of social transformation. *Atlantic Monthly*, pp. 53–80.

Dunbar, K. (1995). How scientists really reason: Scientific reasoning in real-world laboratories. In R. J. Sternberg & J. Davidson (Eds.), *Mechanisms of insight* (pp. 365–395). Cambridge, MA: MIT Press.

Durkin, D. (1979). What classroom observations reveal about reading comprehension instruction. *Reading Research Quarterly, 14*, 481–533.

Egan, K. (1979). *Educational development.* New York: Oxford University Press.

Egan, K. (1988). *Primary understanding: Education in early childhood.* New York: Routledge.

Egan, K. (1989). *Teaching as story telling: An alternative approach to teaching and curriculum in the elementary school.* Chicago: University of Chicago Press.

Egan, K. (1997). *The educated mind.* Chicago: University of Chicago Press.

Eliot, G. (1871/1965). *Middlemarch.* New York: Norton.

Elmore, R. F. (1996). Getting to scale with good educational practice. *Harvard Educational Review, 66*, 1–26.

Engestrom, Y. (1987). *Learning by expanding: An activity-theoretical approach to developmental research.* Helsinki, Finland: Orienta-Konsultit Oy.

Engestrom, Y., & Cole, M. (1997). Situated cognition in search of an agenda. In D. Kirshner & J. A. Whitson (Eds.), *Situated cognition: Social, semiotic, and psychological perspectives* (pp. 301-309). Mahwah, NJ: Lawrence Erlbaum Associates.

Entwistle, N. J., & Ramsden, P. (1983). *Understanding student learning.* New York: Nichols.

Ericsson, K. A., & Chase, W. G. (1982). Exceptional memory. *American Scientist, 70*, 607–615.

Ericsson, K. A., & Simon, H. A. (1980). Verbal reports as data. *Psychological Review, 87*, 215–251.

Feyerabend, P. (1988). *Against method,* Rrev. ed. London: Verso.

Feynman, R., Hutchings, E. (Eds.)., & Leighton, R. (1997). *Surely you're joking, Mr. Feyman! Adventures of a curious character.* New York: W. W. Norton.

Fletcher, C. (1990). *What cops know.* New York: Pocket Books.

Floyd, B. (1995). *From quackery to bacteriology: The emergence of modern medicine in 19th century America.* Available at http://www.cl.utoledo.edu/canaday/quackery/quack1.html

Fodor, J. A. (1975). *The language of thought.* New York: Crowell.

Fodor, J. A. (1980). Fixation of belief and concept acquisition. In M. Piattelli-Palmerini (Ed.), *Language and learning: The debate between Jean Piaget and Noam Chomsky* (pp. 142–149). Cambridge, MA: Harvard University Press.

Fodor, J. A. (1985). Fodor's guide to mental representation: The intelligent auntie's vade-mecum. *Mind, 94*, 76–100.

Forster, E. M. (1988). *Commonplace book.* Aldershot, UK: Wildwood House.

Franks, J. J., Vye, N. J., Auble, P. M., Mezynski, K. J., Perfetto, G. A., Bransford, J. D., Stein, B. S., & Littlefield, J. (1982). Learning from explicit vs. implicit text. *Journal of Experimental Psychology: General, 111*, 414–422.

Freire, P. (1970). *Pedagogy of the oppressed*. New York: Seabury.

Gagné, R. M. (1977). *The conditions of learning* (3rd ed.). New York: Holt, Rinehart & Winston.

Galway, W. T. (1974). *The inner game of tennis*. New York: Random House.

Gardner, H. (1983). *Frames of mind: The theory of multiple intelligences*. New York: Basic Books.

Gardner, H. (1991). *The unschooled mind: How children think and how schools should teach*. New York: Basic Books.

Gardner, H. (1993). *Multiple intelligences*. New York : Basic Books.

Gardner, H. (1994). Intelligences in theory and practice: A response to Elliot W. Eisner, Robert J. Sternberg, & Henry M. Levin. *Teacher's College Record, 95,* 576–583.

Gardner, H. (1999). *The disciplined mind: What all students should understand*. New York: Simon & Schuster.

Gardner, W. E. (1989). Preface. In M. C. Reynolds (Ed.), *Knowledge base for the beginning teacher* (pp. ix–xii). New York: Pergamon Press.

Gazzaniga, M. S. (1995). Principles of human brain organization derived from split-brain studies. *Neuron, 14,* 217–218.

Gazzaniga, M. S., & LeDoux, J. E. (1978). *The integrated mind*. New York: Plenum Press.

Geary, D. C. (1995). Reflections of evolution and culture in children's cognition: Implications for mathematical development and instruction. *American Psychologist, 50*(1), 24–27.

Gelman, R. S., & Gallistel, C. R. (1978). *The child's understanding of number*. Cambridge, MA: Harvard University Press.

Ghent, P. (1989). *Expert learning in music*. Unpublished master's thesis, University of Toronto.

Gick, M. L., & Holyoak, K. J. (1980). Analogical problem solving. *Cognitive Psychology, 12,* 306–355.

Gilbert, M. A. (1997). *Coalescent argumentation*. Mahwah, NJ: Lawrence Erlbaum Associates.

Glaser, R. (1984). Education and thinking: The role of knowledge. *American Psychologist, 39,* 93–104.

Glaser, R., & Chi, M. T. H. (1988). Overview. In M. T. H. Chi, R. Glaser, & M. Farr (Eds.), *The nature of expertise* (pp. xv–xxvii). Hillsdale, NJ: Lawrence Erlbaum Associates.

Gobert, J. (1994). *Expertise in the comprehension of architectural plans: Contribution of representation and domain knowledge*. Unpublished doctoral dissertation, University of Toronto.

Gold, R. (1997). *No information without representation*. Retrieved July 14, 2001, from http://www.parxxerox.com/red/members/richgold/inform/information6.html.

Gombrich, E. H. (1959). *Art and illusion: A study in the psychology of pictorial representation*. London: Phaidon Press.

Gombrich, E. H. (1960). *The story of art*. London: Phaidon Press.

Goodman, K. (Ed.). (1998). *In defense of good teaching: What teachers need to know about the "Reading Wars"* Yourk, ME: Stenhouse.

Gopnik, A. (1993). How we know our minds: The illusion of first-person knowledge of intentionality. *Behavioral and Brain Sciences, 16*, 1–14.

Greeno, J. G. (1991). Number sense as situated knowing in a conceptual domain. *Journal for Research in Mathematics Education, 22*, 170–218.

Griffin, S. A., Case, R., & Siegler, R. S. (1994). Rightstart: Providing the central conceptual prerequisites for first formal learning of arithmetic to students at risk for school failure. In K. McGilly (Ed.), *Classroom lessons: Integrating cognitive theory and classroom practice* (pp. 25–49). Cambridge, MA: MIT Press.

Guilford, J. P. (1967). *The nature of human intelligence.* New York: McGraw-Hill.

Hakkarainen, K. P. J. (1998). *Epistemology of inquiry and computer-supported collaborative learning: An epistemological analysis of knowledge-seeking inquiry in the Computer-Supported Intentional Learning Environment (CSILE).* Unpublished PhD dissertation, University of Toronto.

Hanna, P. R., Hanna, J. S., Hodges, R. E., & Rudorf, E. H. (1966). Phoneme-grapheme correspondences as cues to spelling improvement. In Washington, DC: Government Printing Office, United States Office of Education. (ERIC Document Reproduction Service No. ED003321)

Harper, D. (1987). *Working knowledge: Skill and community in a small shop.* Chicago: University of Chicago Press.

Harré, R. (1984). *Personal being: A theory for individual psychology.* Cambridge, MA: Harvard University Press.

Harré, R., & Gillett, G. (1994). *The discursive mind.* Thousand Oaks, CA: Sage.

Harris, J. R. (1998). *The nurture assumption: Why children turn out the way they do.* New York: Free Press.

Hawkins, D. (1978). Critical barriers to science learning. *Outlook, 29*, 3–23.

Hebb, D. O., & Thompson, W. R. (1954). The social significance of animal studies. In G. Lindzey (Ed.), *Handbook of social psychology: Vol. 1. Theory and method* (pp. 532–561). Reading, MA: Addison-Wesley.

Hewitt, J. (1996) *Progress toward a knowledge-building community.* Unpublished doctoral dissertation, University of Toronto.

Hewitt, J., & Scardamalia, M. (1998). Design principles for distributed knowledge building processes. *Educational Psychology Review, 10*(1), 75–96.

Hidi, S., Baird, W., & Hildyard, A. (1982). That's important but is it interesting? Two factors in text processing. In A. Flammer & W. Kintsch (Eds.), *Discourse processing* (pp. 63–75). Amsterdam: North-Holland.

Hirsch, E. D., Jr. (1987). *Cultural literacy: What every American needs to know.* Boston, MA: Houghton Mifflin

Hirsch, E. D., Jr. (Ed.). (1993). *What your 5th grader needs to know (Core Knowledge series).* New York: Doubleday.

Hirsch, E. D., Jr. (1996). *The schools we need and why we don't have them.* New York: Doubleday.

Hirschfeld, N. A., & Gelman, S. A. (Eds.). (1994). *Mapping the mind: Domain specificity in cognition and culture.* New York: Cambridge University Press.

Hirschhorn, L. (1988). *The workplace within: Psychodynamics of organizational life.* Cambridge, MA: MIT Press.

Hobson, J. A. (1988). *The dreaming brain.* New York: Basic Books.

Hoffer, E. (1963). *The ordeal of change.* New York: Harper and Row.

Hoffer, E. (1973). *Reflections on the human condition.* New York: Harper & Row.

Hofstadter, D. R. (1985). *Metamagical themas: Questing for the essence of mind and pattern.* New York: Basic Books.

Howard, A., & Widdowson, F. (1996, November). Traditional knowledge threatens environmental assessment. *Policy Options, 18*(3), 34–36.

Howard, A., & Widdowson, F. (1997). Revisiting traditional knowledge. *Policy Options* (April, 1997), 46–48.

Hunt, D. E. (1992). *The renewal of personal energy.* Toronto: OISE Press.

Hunt, E., & Minstrell, J. (1994). A cognitive approach to the teaching of physics. In K. McGilley (Ed.), *Classroom lessons: Integrating cognitive theory and classroom practice.* (pp. 51–74). Cambridge, MA: MIT Press.

Isaacs, N. (1965). *Piaget: Some answers to teachers' questions.* London: National Froebel Foundation.

Isaacs, S. (1930). *Intellectual growth in young children.* London: Routledge.

Jaynes, J. (1976). *The origin of consciousness in the breakdown of the bicameral mind.* Boston: Houghton Mifflin.

Jaynes, J. (1986). How old is consciousness? In R. M. Caplan (Ed.), *Exploring the concept of mind* (pp. 51–72). Iowa City, IA: University of Iowa Press.

Kaestle, C. (1993). The awful reputation of education research. *Educational Researcher, 22*(1), 23–31.

Kafai, Y. B. (1996). Software by kids for kids. *Communications of the ACM, 39*(4), 38–39.

Kaiser, M. K., Proffitt, D. R., & McCloskey, M. (1985). The development of beliefs about falling objects. *Perception & Psychophysics, 38*, 533–539.

Kamin, L. (1974). *The science and politics of IQ.* Hillsdale, NJ: Lawrence Erlbaum Associates.

Kanpol, B. (1998). Critical pedagogy for beginning teacher: The movement from despair to hope [paragraphs]. *Journal of Critical Pedagogy* [Online serial], *2*(1). Available: http://www.wmc.edu/pub/jcp/issueII-1/kanpol.html.

Karmiloff-Smith, A. (1992). *Beyond modularity: A developmental perspective on cognitive science.* Cambridge, MA: MIT Press.

Katz, S., Lesgold, A., Hughes, E., Peters, D., Eggan, G., Gordon, M., & Greenberg, L. (1998). Sherlock II: An intelligent tutoring system built upon the LRDC tutor framework. In C. P. Bloom & R. B. Loftin (Eds.), *Facilitating the development and use of interactive learning environments* (pp. 227–258). Mahwah, NJ: Lawrence Erlbaum Associates.

Kauffman, S. (1993). *The origins of order: Self-organization and selection in evolution.* New York: Oxford University Press.

Keil, F. C., & Silberstein, C. S. (1996). Schooling and the acquisition of theoretical knowledge. In D. R. Olson & N. Torrance (Eds.), *Handbook of education and human development: New models of learning, teaching and schooling* (pp. 621–645). Cambridge, MA: Basil Blackwell.

Keynes, J. M. (1956). Newton, the man. In J. R. Newman (Ed.), *The world of mathematics* (pp. 277–285). New York: Simon & Schuster.

Kilpatrick, W. H. (1921). *The project method*. New York. *Teachers College Press*.

Kintsch, W. (1998). *Comprehension: A paradigm for cognition*. New York: Cambridge University Press.

Kitto, H. D. F. (1951). *The Greeks*. Baltimore, MD: Penguin Books.

Koestler, A. (1964). *The act of creation*. New York: Dell.

Krugmann, P. R. (1999). *The return of depression economics*. New York: W. W. Norton.

Kuhn, D. (1989). Children and adults as intuitive scientists. *Psychological Review, 96*, 674–689.

Kuhn, D. (1993). Science as argument: Implications for teaching and learning scientific thinking. *Science Education, 77*, 319–337.

Kuhn, D., Amsel, E., & O'Loughlin, M. (1988). *The development of scientific thinking skills*. San Diego, CA: Academic Press.

Kuhn, T. (1970). *The structure of scientific revolutions*. Chicago: University of Chicago Press.

Lagemann, E. C. (1997). Contested terrain: A history of education research in the United States, 1890–1990. *Educational Researcher, 26*(9), 5–17.

Lakoff, G. (1987). *Women, fire, and dangerous things: What categories reveal about the mind*. Chicago, IL: University of Chicago Press.

Lakoff, G. & Johnson, M., (1980). *Metaphors we live by*. Chicago: University of Chicago Press.

Laland, K. N., Odling-Smee, J., & Feldman, M. W. (1999). Niche construction, biological evolution and cultural change. *Behavioral and Brain Sciences, 23*(1), 131–146.

Lamon, M., Caswell, B., Scardamalia, M., & Chandra, N. (1997, August). *Technologies of use and social interaction in classroom knowledge building communities*. Paper presented at the Meeting of the European Association for Research in Learning and Instruction, Athens, Greece.

Lampert, M. (1988). Connecting mathematical teaching and learning. In E. Fennema, T. P. Carpenter, & S. J. Lamon (Eds.), *Integrating research on teaching and learning mathematics: Papers from the first Wisconsin Symposium for Research on Teaching and Learning Mathematics* (pp. 132–165). Madison, WI: University of Wisconsin, Wisconsin Center for Education Research.

Lampert, M. (1990). When the problem is not the question and the solution is not the answer: Mathematical knowing and teaching. *American Educational Research Journal, 27*(1), 29–64.

Lampert, M., Rittenhouse, P., & Crumbaugh, C. (1996). Agreeing to disagree: Developing sociable mathematical discourse. In D. Olson &. N. Torrance (Eds.), *Handbook of education and human development: New models of learning, teaching and schooling* (pp. 731–764). Cambridge, MA: Basil Blackwell.

Landauer, T. K., & Dumais, S. T. (1997). A solution to Plato's problem: The Latent Semantic Analysis theory of the acquisition, induction, and representation of knowledge. *Psychological Review, 25*, 211–240.

Landman, F. (1986). Pegs and alecs. In J. Y. Halpern (Ed.), *Theoretical aspects of reasoning about knowledge: Proceedings of the 1986 conference* (pp. 45–61). Los Altos, CA: Morgan Kaufman.

Lasch, C. (1991). *The true and only heaven: Progress and its critics*. New York: Norton.

Latour, B. (1987). *Science in action*. Milton Keynes, UK: Open University Press.

Latour, B., & Woolgar, S. (1979). *Laboratory l Life: The social construction of scientific facts*. Beverly Hills, CA: Sage.

Lave, J. (1988). *Cognition in practice: Mind, mathematics, and culture in everyday life*. Cambridge,UK: Cambridge University Press.

Lave, J., & Wenger, E. (1991). *Situated learning: Legitimate peripheral participation*. Cambridge, UK: Cambridge University Press.

Lefkowitz, B. (1997). *Our guys: The Glen Ridge rape and the secret life of the perfect suburb*. Berekeley, CA: University of California Press.

Lehman, D., & Nisbett, R. (1990). A longitudinal study of the effects of undergraduate training on reasoning. *Developmental Psychology, 26*(6), 952–960.

Lehrer, K., & Beanblossom, R. E. (Eds.). (1975). *Thomas Reid's Inquiry and Essays*. Indianapolis, IN: Bobbs-Merrill.

Leinhardt, G., Weidman, C., & Hammond, K. M. (1987). Introduction and integration of classroom routines by expert teachers. *Curriculum Inquiry, 17*, 135–176.

Lesgold, A. (1996). Quality control for educating a smart workforce. In L. B. Resnick & J. Wirt (Eds.), *Linking school and work: Roles for standards and assessment* (pp. 147–191). San Francisco: Josey-Bass.

Lesgold, A. M., & Lajoie, S. (1991). Complex problem solving in electronics. In R. J. Sternberg & P. A. Frensch (Eds.), *Complex problem solving: Principles and mechanisms* (pp. 287–316). Hillsdale, NJ: Lawrence Erlbaum Associates.

Levine, A. (1994, December). The great debate revisited. *Atlantic Monthly, 274*, 38–44.

Levine, D. U., & Havighurst, D. U. (Eds.). (1971). *Farewell to schools???* Belmont, CA: Wadsworth.

Livingstone, D. W. (2000). Exploring the icebergs of adult learning: Findings of the First Canadian Survey of Informal Learning Practices. *Canadian Journal for the Study of Adult Education, 13*(2), 49–72.

Loving, C. C. (1997). From the summit of truth to its slippery slopes: Science education's journey through positivist-postmodern territory. *American Educational Research Journal, 34*(3), 421–452.

Lundberg, I., Frost, J., & Petersen, O. (1988). Effects of an extensive program for stimulating phonological awareness in preschool children. *Reading Research Quarterly, 23*, 263–284.

Maier, N. R. F. (1970). *Problem solving and creativity in individuals and groups*. Belmont, CA: Brooks/Cole.

Manis, F., Seidenberg, M. S., Doi, L., McBride-Chang, C., & Petersen, A. (1996). On the basis for two subtypes of developmental dyslexia. *Cognition, 58*, 157–195.

Marker, G., & Mehlinger, H. (1992). Social studies. In P. W. Jackson (Ed.), *Handbook of research on curriculum* (pp. 830–851). New York: Macmillan.

Marx, R. W., Blumenfeld, P. C., Krajcik, J. S., & Soloway, E. (1997). Enacting project-based science. *Elementary School Journal, 97*, 341–358.

McClelland, J. L., & Rumelhart, D. E. (1988). *Explorations in parallel distributed processing: A handbook of models, programs, and exercises.* Cambridge, MA: MIT Press.

McClelland, J. L., Rumelhart, D. E., & the PDP Research Group (Eds.). (1986). *Parallel distributed processing: Explorations in the microstructure of cognition: Vol. 2. Psychological and biological models.* Cambridge, MA: MIT/ Bradford.

McCloskey, M., Caramazza, A., & Green, B. F. (1980). Curvilinear motion in the absence of external forces: Naive beliefs about the motion of objects. *Science, 210,* 1139–1141.

McPeck, J. E. (1984). Stalking beasts, but swatting flies: The teaching of critical thinking. *Canadian Journal of Education, 9,* 28–44.

Miller, G. A. (1956). The magical number seven, plus or minus two: Some limits on our capacity for processing information. *Psychological Review, 63,* 81–97.

Miller, M. P. (1996, Spring). Introducing art history through problem-based learning. *About Teaching: A Newsletter of the Center for Teaching Effectiveness* No. 50, Retrieved July 14, 2001: http://www.udel.edu/pbl.cte/ spr96-arth.html.

Minstrell, J. (1989). Teaching science for understanding. In L. Resnick & L. Klopfer (Eds.), *Toward the thinking curriculum: Current cognitive research* (pp. 129–149). Alexandria, VA: Association for Supervision and Curriculum Development.

Mitchell, K. (2001). Education for democratic citizenship: Transnationalism, multiculturalism, and the limits of liberalism. *Harvard Educational Review, 71*(1), 51–78.

Miyake, N. (1986). Constructive interaction and the iterative process of understanding. *Cognitive Science, 10,* 151–177.

Molenaar, P. C. M. (1986). On the impossibility of acquiring more powerful structures: A neglected alternative. *Human Development, 29,* 245–251.

Moss, D. M. (2000). Bringing together technology and students: Examining the use of technology in a project-based class. *Journal of Educational Computing Research, 22*(2), 155–169.

Murray, B. A. (1998). Gaining alphabetic insight: Is phoneme manipulation skill or phoneme identity knowledge causal? *Journal of Educational Psychology, 90*(3), 461–475.

Newell, A., & Simon, H. A. (1972). *Human problem solving.* Englewood Cliffs, NJ: Prentice-Hall.

Ng, E., & Bereiter, C. (1991). Three levels of goal orientation in learning. *The Journal of the Learning Sciences, 1*(3,4), 243–271.

Nickerson, R. S. (1985). Understanding understanding. *American Journal of Education, 93,* 201–239.

Nonaka, I. (1991). The knowledge-creating company. *Harvard Business Review, 69*(6), 96-104.

Nonaka, I., & Takeuchi, H. (1995). *The knowledge creating company.* New York: Oxford University Press.

Novak, J. D., & Gowin, D. B. (1984). *Learning how to learn.* Cambridge, UK: Cambridge University Press.

O'Dell, C. (1994, April). Out-of-the-box benchmarking. [32 paragraphs]. *Continuous Journey*, <http://www.apqc.org/free/articles/story03.htm>.

O'Dell, C. S., Essaides, N., & Grayson, C. J., Jr. (1998). *If only we knew what we know: The transfer of internal knowledge and best practice*. New York: Simon & Schuster.

Oatley, K. (1992). *Best laid schemes: The psychology of emotions*. Cambridge, UK: Cambridge University Press.

Oatley, K., & Johnson-Laird, P. N. (1987). Towards a cognitive theory of emotions. *Cognition and Emotion, 1*, 29–50.

Ohlsson, S. (1993). Abstract schemas. *Educational Psychologist, 28*(1), 51–61.

Olson, D. R. (1996). *The world on paper: The conceptual and cognitive implications of writing and reading*. New York: Cambridge University Press.

Olson, D. R., & Bruner, J. S., (1996). Folk psychology and folk pedagogy. In D. O. Torrance & N. Torrance (Eds.), *Handbook of education and human development: New models of learning, teaching and schooling* (pp. 485–513). Cambridge, MA: Basil Blackwell.

Ontario, Royal Commission on Learning. (1994). *For the love of learning: Report of the Royal Commission on Learning*. Toronto, Canada: Publications Ontario.

Palincsar, A. S., & Brown, A. L. (1984). Reciprocal teaching of comprehension-fostering and comprehension-monitoring activities. *Cognition and Instruction, 1*, 117–175.

Papert, S. (1980). *Mindstorms: Children, computers, and powerful ideas*. New York: Basic Books.

Patel, V. L., & Groen, G. J. (1991). The general and specific nature of medical expertise: A critical look. In K. A. Ericsson & J. Smith (Eds.), *Toward a general theory of expertise: Prospects and limits* (pp. 93–125). Cambridge, UK: Cambridge University Press.

Pea, R. D. (1993). Practices of distributed intelligence and designs for education. In G. Salomon (Ed.). *Distributed cognitions*. (pp. 47–87). New York: Cambridge University Press.

Pearson, P. D., & Gallagher, M. C. (1983). The instruction of reading comprehension. *Contemporary Educational Psychology, 8*, 317–344.

Perfetti, C. A., & Roth, S. (1981). Some of the interactive processes in reading and their role in reading skill. In A. M. Lesgold & C. Perfetti (Eds.), *Interactive processes in reading* (pp. 269–297). Hillsdale, NJ: Lawrence Erlbaum Associates.

Perkins, D. N. (1981). *The mind's best work*. Cambridge, MA: Harvard University Press.

Perkins, D. (1992). *Smart schools: From training memories to educating minds*. New York: Free Press.

Perkins, D. (1995). *Outsmarting IQ: The emerging science of learnable intelligence*. New York: Free Press.

Perkins, D., & Blythe, T. (1994). Putting understanding up front. *Educational Leadership*, 4–7. <http://www.ascd.org/pubs/el/nov96/overview.html>

Peskin, J. (1998). Constructing meaning when reading poetry: An expert-novice study. *Cognition and Instruction, 16*(3), 235–263.

Piaget, J. (1929). *The child's conception of the world*. New York: Harcourt, Brace.

Plimpton, G. (Ed.). (1992). *The Paris Review interviews, ninth series*. New York: Penguin.

Polanyi, M. (1964). *Personal knowledge: Towards a post-critical philosophy*. New York: Harper & Row.

Popper, K. R. (1972). *Objective knowledge: An evolutionary approach*. Oxford, UK: Clarendon Press.

Popper, K. R., & Eccles, J. C. (1977). *The self and its brain*. Berlin, Germany: Springer-Verlag.

Premack, D., & Premack, J. (1996). Why animals lack pedagogy and some cultures have more of it than others. In D. O. Torrance & N. Torrance (Eds.), *Handbook of education and human development: New models of learning, teaching and schooling* (pp. 302–323). Cambridge, MA: Basil Blackwell.

Pressley, M. (1998). *Reading instruction that works: The case for balanced teaching*. New York: Guilford Press.

Pressley, M., Goodchild, F., Fleet, J., Zajchowski, R., & Evans, E. D. (1989). The challenges of classroom strategy instruction. *Elementary School Journal, 89*(3), 301–342.

Pressley, M., Harris, K. R., & Marks, M. B. (1992). But good strategy instructors are constructivists!! *Educational Psychology Review, 4,* 1–32.

Price, J. N. (1998). Accommodation and critique in the school lives of six young African-American men. *Curriculum Inquiry, 28*(4), 443–471.

Putnam, H. (1986). How old is the mind? In R. M. Caplan (Ed.), *Exploring the concept of mind* (pp. 31–50). Iowa City, IA: University of Iowa Press.

Putnam, R. D. (1996). The strange disappearance of civic America [_ paragraphs]. *The American Prospect*, [Online serial] ___ Available: [http://www.prospect.org/print/v7/24/putnam-r.html].

Quartz, S. R. (1993). Neural networks, nativism, and the plausibility of constructivism. *Cognition, 48,* 223–242.

Ranney, M., Schank, P., Hoadley, C., & Neff, J. (1996). "I know one when I see one": How (much) do hypotheses differ from evidence? In R. Fidel, B. H. Kwasnik, C. Beghtol, & P. Smith (Eds.), *Advances in classification research, Vol 5 (ASIS Monograph Series)* (pp. 141–158). Medford, NJ: Learned Information.

Rauch, J. (1993). *Kindly inquisitors*. Chicago: University of Chicago Press.

Ravitch, D. (1987). Tot sociology: Or what happened to history in the grade schools. *The American Scholar, 56*(3), 343–354.

Reck, E. H. (in press). Education, knowledge, and the world of objective ideas: Some philosophical remarks. In B. Smith (Ed.), *[Future of liberal education]*. Chicago: Open Court.

Redl, F., & Wineman, D. (1957). *The aggressive child*. Glencoe, IL: Free Press.

Reich, R. (1992). *The work of nations: Preparing ourselves for 21st century capitalism*. New York: Random House.

Reif, F., & Heller, J. I. (1982). Knowledge structure and problem solving in physics. *Educational Psychologist, 17,* 102–127.

Reigeluth, C. (Ed.). (1983). *Instructional design theories and models: An overview of their current status*. Hillsdale, NJ: Lawrence Erlbaum Associates.

Resnick, L. B. (1987). The development of mathematical intuition. In M. Perlmutter (Ed.), *Minnesota symposium on child psychology* (pp. 159-194). Hillsdale, NJ: Lawrence Erlbaum Associates.

Resnick, L. B., & Neches, R. (1984). Factors affecting individual differences in learning ability. In R. J. Sternberg (Ed.), *Advances in the psychology of human intelligence* (pp. 275–323). Hillsdale, NJ: Lawrence Erlbaum Associates.

Resnick, L. B., & Omanson, S. F. (1987). Learning to understand arithmetic. In R. Glaser (Ed.), *Advances in instructional psychology* (pp. 41–95). Hillsdale, NJ: Lawrence Erlbaum Associates.

Resnick, M. (1994). *Turtles, termites, and traffic jams: Explorations in massively parallel microworlds*. Cambridge, MA: MIT Press.

Reynolds, M. C. (Ed.). (1989). *Knowledge base for the beginning teacher*. New York: Pergamon Press.

Rifkin, J. (1995). The end of work: The decline of the global labor force and the dawn of the post-market era. New York: G. P. Putnam.

Rogoff, B., & Lave, J. (Eds.). (1984). *Everyday cognition: Its development in social context*. Cambridge, MA: Harvard University Press.

Romer, P. (1993). *Two strategies for economic development: Using ideas and producing ideas* (No. EC-R72). Toronto, Canada: Canadian Institute for Advanced Research.

Romer, P. (1994, July-August). Beyond classical and Keynesian macroeconomic policy. *Policy Options*, 15–21.

Ronen, R. (1998). Incommensurability and representation. *Applied Semiotics, (5)*, 291–302. Available: http://www.epas.utoronto.ca/french/as-sa/ASSA-No5/RR1.html.

Rorty, R. (1991). *Objectivity, relativism, and truth: Philosophical papers, Vol. 1*. Cambridge, UK: Cambridge University Press.

Rosch, E. (1975). Cognitive representations of semantic categories. *Journal of Experimental Psychology: General, 104*, 192–233.

Rosch, E. (1978). Principles of categorization. In E. Rosch & B. B. Lloyds (Eds.), *Cognition and categorization* (pp. 27–48). Hillsdale, NJ: Lawrence Erlbaum Associates.

Rosenblatt, L. (1978). *The reader, the text, the poem: The transactional theory of the literary work*. Carbondale, IL: Southern Illinois University Press.

Rosenblatt, L. (1980). What facts does this poem teach you? *Language Arts, 57*, 386–394.

Rosenbloom, P., & Newell, A. (1987). Learning by chunking: A production system model of practice. In D. Klahr, P. Langley, & R. Neches (Eds.), *Production system models of learning and development* (pp. 221–286). Cambridge, MA: MIT Press.

Roth, K. J. (1992). Science education: It's not enough to "do" or "relate." In M. Pearsall (Ed.), *Relevant research: Vol II* (pp. 151–164). Washington, DC: National Science Teachers Association.

Roth, K. J., Anderson, C. W., & Smith, E. (1987). Curriculum materials, teacher talk and student learning: Case studies in fifth grade science teaching. *Journal of Curriculum Studies, 19*, 527–548.

Rothstein, W. G. (1985). *American physicians in the 19th century*. Baltimore: Johns Hopkins University Press.

Rugg, H., & Shumaker, A. (1928). *The child-centered school: An appraisal of the new education.* New York: World Book.

Rumelhart, D. E. (1980). Schemata: The building blocks of cognition. In R. J. Spiro, B. C. Bruce, & W. F. Brewer (Eds.), *Theoretical issues in reading comprehension* (pp. 33–58). Hillsdale, NJ: Lawrence Erlbaum Associates.

Rumelhart, D. E. (1989). The architecture of mind: A connectionist approach. In M. I. Posner (Ed.), *Foundations of cognitive science* (pp. 133–159). Cambridge, MA: MIT Press.

Rumelhart, D. E., McClelland, J. L., & the PDP Research Group. (1986). *Parallel distributed processing: Explorations in the microstructure of cognition: Vol. 1. Foundations.* Cambridge, MA: MIT Press.

Rumelhart, D. E., Smolensky, P., McClelland, J. L., & Hinton, G. E. (1986). Schemata and sequential thought processes in PDP models. In J. L. McClelland, D. E. Rumelhart, & the PDP Research Group (Eds.), *Parallel distributed processing: Explorations in the microstructure of cognition: Vol. 2. Psychological and biological models* (pp. 7–57). Cambridge, MA: MIT Press.

Ryle, G. (1949). *The concept of mind.* London: Hutchinson.

Sartre, J. P. (1964). *Nausea.* New York: New Directions.

Savery, J. R., & Duffy, T. M. (1995, September-October). Problem-based learning: An instructional model and its constructivist framework. *Educational Technology, 35,* 31–38.

Saxe, G. B. (1991). *Culture and cognitive development: Studies in mathematical understanding.* Hillsdale, NJ: Lawrence Erlbaum Associates.

Scardamalia, M., & Bereiter, C. (1984). Development of strategies in text processing. In H. Mandl, N. L. Stein, & T. Trabasso (Eds.), *Learning and comprehension of text* (pp. 379–406). Hillsdale, NJ: Lawrence Erlbaum Associates.

Scardamalia, M., & Bereiter, C. (1985). Development of dialectical processes in composition. In D. R. Olson, N. Torrance, & A. Hildyard (Eds.), *Literacy, language, and learning: The nature and consequences of reading and writing* (pp. 307–329). Cambridge, UK: Cambridge University Press.

Scardamalia, M., & Bereiter, C. (1989, October). *Schools as knowledge-building communities.* Invited presentation at the workshop on Development and Learning Environments, University of Te Aviv, Israel.

Scardamalia, M., & Bereiter, C. (1991). Literate expertise. In K. A. Ericsson & J. Smith (Eds.), *Toward a general theory of expertise: Prospects and limits* (pp. 172–194). Cambridge, UK: Cambridge University Press.

Scardamalia, M., & Bereiter, C. (1994). Computer support for knowledge-building communities. *The Journal of the Learning Sciences, 3*(3), 265–283.

Scardamalia, M., & Bereiter, C. (1996a). Adaptation and understanding: A case for new cultures of schooling. In S. Vosniadou, E. DeCorte, R. Glaser, & H. Mandl (Eds.), *International perspectives on the design of technology-supported learning environments* (pp. 149–163). Mahwah, NJ: Lawrence Erlbaum Associates.

Scardamalia, M., & Bereiter, C. (1996b). Engaging students in a knowledge society. *Educational Leadership, 54*(3), 6–10.

Scardamalia, M., & Bereiter, C. (1996c). Student communities for the advancement of knowledge. *Communications of the ACM, 39*(4), 36–37.

Scardamalia, M., & Bereiter, C. (1999). Schools as knowledge building organizations. In D. Keating & C. Hertzman (Eds.), *Today's children, tomorrow's society: The developmental health and wealth of nations* (pp. 274–289). New York: Guilford.

Scardamalia, M., Bereiter, C., Brett, C., Burtis, P. J., Calhoun, C., & Smith Lea, N. (1992). Educational applications of a networked communal database. *Interactive Learning Environments, 2*(1), 45–71.

Scardamalia, M., Bereiter, C., Hewitt, J., & Webb, J. (1996). Constructive learning from texts in biology. In K. M. Fischer & M. Kirby (Eds.), *Relations and biology learning: The acquisition and use of knowledge structures in biology* (pp. 44–64). Berlin, Germany: Springer-Verlag.

Scardamalia, M., Bereiter, C., & Lamon, M. (1994). The CSILE project: Trying to bring the classroom into World 3. In K. McGilley (Ed.), *Classroom lessons: Integrating cognitive theory and classroom practice* (pp. 201–228). Cambridge, MA: MIT Press.

Scardamalia, M., Bereiter, C., McLean, R. S., Swallow, J., & Woodruff, E. (1989). Computer-supported intentional learning environments. *Journal of Educational Computing Research, 5*, 51–68.

Scardamalia, M., Bereiter, C., & Steinbach, R. (1984). Teachability of reflective processes in written composition. *Cognitive Science, 8*, 173–190.

Schacter, D. L. (1989). Memory. In M. I. Posner (Ed.), *Foundations of cognitive science*. Cambridge, MA: MIT Press.

Schank, P., Ranney, M., & Hoadley, C. (1995). Convince Me [Computer program and manual]. In J. R. Jungck, N. Peterson, & J. N. Calley (Eds.), *The BioQUEST library*. College Park, MD: Academic Software Development Group, University of Maryland.

Schank, R. C. (1979). Interestingness: Controlling inferences. *Artificial Intelligence, 12*, 273–297.

Schank, R. C. (1982). *Dynamic memory: A theory of reminding and learning in computers and people*. New York: Cambridge University Press.

Schank, R. C., & Abelson, R. P. (1977). *Scripts, plans, goals, and understanding*. Hillsdale, NJ: Lawrence Erlbaum Associates.

Schank, R. C., & Cleary, C. (1995). *Engines for education*. Hillsdale, NJ: Lawrence Erlbaum Associates.

Schank, R. C., Collins, G. C., & Hunter, L. E. (1986). Transcending inductive category formation in learning. *Behavioral and Brain Sciences, 9*, 639–686.

Sheurich, J. J., & Young, M. D. (1997). Coloring epistemologies: Are our research epistemologies racially biased? *Educational Researcher, 26*(4), 4–16.

Schunk, D. H., & Zimmerman, B. J. (Eds.). (1994). *Self-regulation of learning and performance: Issues and educational applications*. Hillsdale, NJ: Lawrence Erlbaum Associates.

Scribner, S. (1979). Modes of thinking and modes of speaking: Culture and logic reconsidered. In R. O. Freedle (Ed.), *New directions in discourse processing* (pp. 223–243). Norwood, NJ: Ablex.

Scribner, S. (1984). Studying working intelligence. In B. Rogoff & J. Lave (Eds.), *Everyday cognition: Its development in social context* (pp. 9–40). Cambridge, MA: Harvard University Press.

Shaywitz, S. E., Shaywitz, B. A., Pugh, K. R., Fulbright, R. K., & Gore, J. C. (1998). Functional disruption in the organization of the brain for reading in dyslexia. *Proceedings of the National Academy of Science, 95*, 2636–2641.

Shulman, L. S., & Keislar, E. R. (Eds.). (1966). *Learning by discovery: A critical appraisal.*

Simon, H. A. (1957). *Models of man: Social and rational: Mathematical essays.* New York: Wiley.

Simon, H. A., & Simon, D. P. (1973). Alternative uses of phonemic information in spelling. *Review of Educational Research, 43*, 115–137.

Singley, M. K., & Anderson, J. R. (1989). *The transfer of cognitive skill.* Cambridge, MA: Harvard University Press.

Smith, B. (Ed.). (in press). *[Future of liberal education].* Chicago: Open Court.

Smith, D. E. (1990). *The conceptual practices of power: A feminist sociology of knowledge.* Toronto, Canada: University of Toronto Press.

Smith, E. E. (1989). Concepts and induction. In M. I. Posner (Ed.), *Foundations of cognitive science* (pp. 501–526). Cambridge, MA: MIT Press.

Smith, F. (1971). *Understanding reading: A psycholinguistic analysis of reading and learning to read.* New York: Holt, Rinehart & Winston.

Smolensky, P. (1988). On the proper treatment of connectionism. *Behavioral and Brain Sciences, 11*, 1–74.

Spelke, E. S. (1982). Perceptual knowledge of objects in infancy. In J. Mehler, E. C. T. Walker, & M. Garrett (Eds.), *Perspectives in mental representation: Experimental and theoretical studies of cognitive processes and capacities* (pp. 409–430). Hillsdale, NJ: Lawrence Erlbaum Associates.

Spiro, R. J., Feltovich, P. L., Jacobson, M. J., & Coulson, R. L. (1991). Cognitive flexibility, constructivism, and hypertext: Random access instruction for advanced knowledge acquisition in ill-structured domains. *Educational Technology, 31*(5), 24–33.

Stanfield, J. H. (1985). The ethnocentric basis of social science knowledge production. *Review of Research in Education, 12*, 387–415.

Stanovich, K. (1993). Does Reading Make You Smarter? Literacy and the Development of Verbal Intelligence. In H. Reese (Ed.), *In Advances in Child Development and Behavior* (pp. 133–180). San Diego, CA: Academic Press.

Stanovich, K. E. (1999). *Who is rational? Studies of individual differences in reasoning.* Mahwah, NJ: Lawrence Erlbaum Associates.

Stanovich, K. E., & Cunningham, A. E. (1991). Reading as constrained reasoning. In R. J. Sternberg & P. A. Frensch (Eds.), *Complex problem solving: Principles and mechanisms* (pp. 3–60). Hillsdale, NJ: Lawrence Erlbaum Associates.

Stewart, T. A. (1997). *Intellectual capital: The new wealth of nations.* New York: Doubleday.

Stone, J. E. (April 26, 1996). Developmentalism: An obscure but pervasive restriction on educational improvement, *Education Policy Analysis Archives, 4*(8), Available at: http://epaa.asu.edu/epaa/v4n8.html.

Suchman, L. A. (1987). *Plans and situated actions: The problem of human-machine communication*. Cambridge, UK: Cambridge University Press.

Svyantek, D. J., & Brown, L. L. (2000). A complex-systems approach to organizations. *Current Directions in Psychological Science, 9*(2), 40–45.

Swanson, H. L. (1990). Influence of metacognition and aptitude on problem solving. *Journal of Educational Psychology, 82*, 306–314.

Sweller, J. (1988). Cognitive load during problem solving: Effects on learning. *Cognitive Science, 12*, 257–285.

Swetz, F. J. (1987). *Capitalism and arithmetic: The New Math of the 15th century*. La Salle, IL: Open Court.

Tait, W. W. (1986). Truth and proof: The Platonism of mathematics. *Synthese, 69*, 341–370.

Tapscott, D. (1998). Growing up digital: The rise of the net generation. New York: McGraw-Hill.

Taylor, D. (1998). *Beginning to read and the spin doctors of science*. Champaign, IL: National Council of Teachers of English.

Taylor K. (1989) Narrow content functionalism and the wind-body problem. *Nous, 23*, 355–72

Thagard, P. (1989). Explanatory coherence. *Behavioral and Brain Sciences, 12*, 435–502.

Thagard, P. (1992). *Conceptual revolutions*. Princeton, NJ: Princeton University Press.

Thelen, E., & Smith, L. B. (1994). *A dynamic systems approach to the development of cognition and action*. Cambridge, MA: MIT Press.

Thomas, L. (1983). *The youngest science: Notes of a medicine-watcher*. New York: Viking.

Thorndike, E. L. (1949). *Selected writings from a connectionist's psychology*. New York: Appleton-Century-Crofts.

Tompkins, J. (Ed.). (1980). *Reader-response criticism: From formalism to post-structuralism*. Baltimore: Johns Hopkins University Press

Treiman, R. (2000). The foundations of literacy. *Current Directions in Psychological Science, 9*(3), 89–92.

van Aalst, J. C. W. (1997, November). *The study of flight: Exploring interactivity between communities of learners using WebCSILE*. Poster session presented at the second annual meeting and conference of Telelearining NCE, Toronto, Canada.

van Rossum, E. J., & Schenk, S. M. (1984). The relationship between learning conception, study strategy and learning outcome. *British Journal of Educational Psychology, 54*, 73–83.

von Krogh, G., Ichijo, K., & Nonaka, I. (2000). *Enabling knowledge creation*. New York: Oxford University Press.

Vosniadou, S., & Brewer, W. F. (1987). Theories of knowledge restructuring in development. *Review of Educational Research, 57*, 51–67.

Vosniadou, S., & Brewer, W. F. (1992). Mental models of the earth: A study of conceptual change in childhood. *Cognitive Psychology, 24*(4), 535–585.

Wandersee, J., Mintzes, J., & Novak, J. (1994). Research on alternative conceptions in science. In D. Gabel (Ed.), *Handbook of research on science teaching and learning* (pp. 177–210). New York: Macmillan.

Wason, P. C. (1980). Specific thoughts on the writing process. In L. W. Gregg & E. R. Steinberg (Eds.), *Cognitive processes in writing* (pp. 129–137). Hillsdale, NJ: Lawrence Erlbaum Associates.

Weber, L. (1971). *The English infant school and informal education*. Englewood Cliffs, NJ: Prentice-Hall.

Weintraub, P. (1984). *The Omni interviews*. New York: Ticknor & Fields.

Wells, G. (1994). *Changing schools from within: creating communities of inquiry*. Toronto: OISE Press.

Wells, G. (in press). Dialogue about knowledge building. In B. Smith (Ed.), *[Future of liberal education]*. Chicago: Open Court.

Wenger, E. (1995). *Communities of practice: Learning, meanings, and identity*. New York: Cambridge University Press.

White, L. A. (1956). The locus of mathematical reality: An anthropological footnote. In J. R. Newman (Ed.), *The world of mathematics* (pp. 2348–2364). New York: Simon & Schuster.

Whitehead, A. N. (1925/1948). *Science and the modern world* (Mentor ed.). New York: New American Library.

Whitehead, A. N. (1929). *The aims of education*. New York: Macmillan.

Wilson, E. O. (1996). *In search of nature*. Washington, DC: Island Press.

Wilson, E. O. (1998). *Consilience: The unity of knowledge*. New York: Knopf.

Wittgenstein, L. (1969). *On certainty*. New York: Harper Torchbooks.

Wineburg, S. S. (1991). Historical problem solving: A study of the cognitive processes used in the evaluation of documentary and pictorial evidence. *Journal of Educational Psychology, 83*, 73–87.

Wittgenstein, L. (1969). *On certainty*. New York: Harper Torchbooks.

Wittgenstein, L. (1980). *Remarks on the philosophy of psychology, Vol. 1* (G. E. M. Anscombe, Trans.). Chicago: University of Chicago Press.

Woodruff, E., & Meyer, K. (1997). Explanations from intra- and inter-group discourse: Students building knowledge in the science classroom. *Research in Science Education, 27*(1), 25–39.

Yarnall, L., & Kafai, Y. (1996, April). *Issues in project-based science activities: Children's constructions of ocean software games*. Paper presented at the annual meeting of the American Educational Research Association, New York.

Young, M. (1961). *The rise of the meritocracy, 1870–2033*. Baltimore: Penguin.

Zbrodoff, N. J. (1984) *Writing stories under time and length constraints*. Unpublished doctoral dissertation, University of Toronto.

Zuboff, S. (1988). *In the age of the smart machine: The future of work and power*. New York: Basic Books.

Author Index

Y

Z

Subject Index

A

Abstract cultural artifact, 75 (fig), 76, 115–117, 179, 195
Abstract schema, 379
Accountability/standards, 4, 126, 421–422
Acculturation, 3, 232, 235–238
Acquired instinct, 134
Active learner, 70
Activities, reduction to, 267, 268, 270, 286, 293, 294, 328, 377, 390, 408
Activities movement, 383 (tab)
Activity theory, 58, 477
"All about" instruction, 308–309
"All about" learning, *see* Referent-centered learning
Antifoundationalism, 77
Antiracist mathematics, 329
Aptitude-treatment interaction (ATI), 389 fn. 2
Aquinas, Thomas, 23
Argumentation, 88–89
Aristotle, 186, 406
Arithmetic, 61, *see also* Mathematics
Artifact, definition of, 64–65
Artifactualization, of natural world, 480–481
Artificial intelligence, ix, 5, 27–28, 229
Assertive conceptual artifact, 76–78
Assessment, and behaviorism, 11

Assimilation, and accommodation, 228–229
Associationism, 48
ATI, *see* Aptitude-treatment interaction
Attention deficit, 49–50
Authentic conceptual artifact, 293, 294
Automatic sense-making
  in dreams, 186–187, 189–190
  during reading, 188–189
  role of knowledge in, 190–194
Automotive research, 388, 389–390, 402
Autonomous theory, 165

B

Background knowledge, 134
Back-to-basics, 3, 4, 214, 217, 219, 220, 223, 224, 225, 229, 230, 392, 450, 461
Becoming a Nation of Readers (Anderson et al.), 151
Behaviorism, ix, x, 9, 10–11, 10 fn. 2, 18, 53
Beliefs, in artificial intelligence, 27–28
Benchmark instruction, 277–278
Best practice, 421–426, 453 fn. 15
Bodily-kinesthetic intelligence, 373
Brain
  as different from mind, 19
  improving thinking, 342–344
  as supporting knowledgeable action, 33–34